WIDER WORLD

SECOND EDITION

3

Teacher's Book

CONTENTS

Welcome to *Wider World Second Edition*	2
Course Components	3–6
Key Concepts	7–11
A Unit of the Student's Book	12–15
Student's Book Contents	16–17
Student's Book with answer key	18–155
Teaching notes	156–231
Need support? worksheets	232–240
Need support? worksheets answer key	241
Student's Book audioscripts & videoscripts	242–255
Workbook audioscripts	256–262
Workbook answer key	263–271

Welcome to Wider World Second Edition

Wider World is a portal to a wider world of English language knowledge and resources specially designed for teenage learners. It enables teenage students to develop the ability to communicate well in English and boosts their confidence so that they can participate as educated citizens in the global community of the 21st century with all its unique challenges and opportunities.

Wider World Second Edition is the direct result of extensive research among teachers using the first edition. It builds on the highly successful and trusted methodology of the series but has been brought up to date with fresh content and a new modern look and feel. There are also a lot of new features and brand new digital tools and resources in response to teachers' feedback and new expectations in a post-pandemic world.

The new edition prepares teenagers for their future lives and careers both as language learners and citizens of the world through the focused Life Skills programme, *Set for Life*. Printable *Set for Life* 'bookmarks' provide tips on how to successfully apply the skills in real life, and serve as a quick reference to key language areas introduced in the lessons.

New *BBC Culture* videos showcase a huge diversity of life and culture, expose learners to authentic English, inspire them to develop their language skills, build communicative competence and arouse curiosity in the world outside the classroom. New and expanded project work provides motivating contexts for engaging teamwork and collaboration.

Comprehensive teacher support materials with numerous resources and new digital tools make *Wider World Second Edition* intuitive to teach in class and online, with minimal preparation. It enables you to adapt your teaching to the needs of individual students, whatever their ability, so that every student can achieve their highest potential.

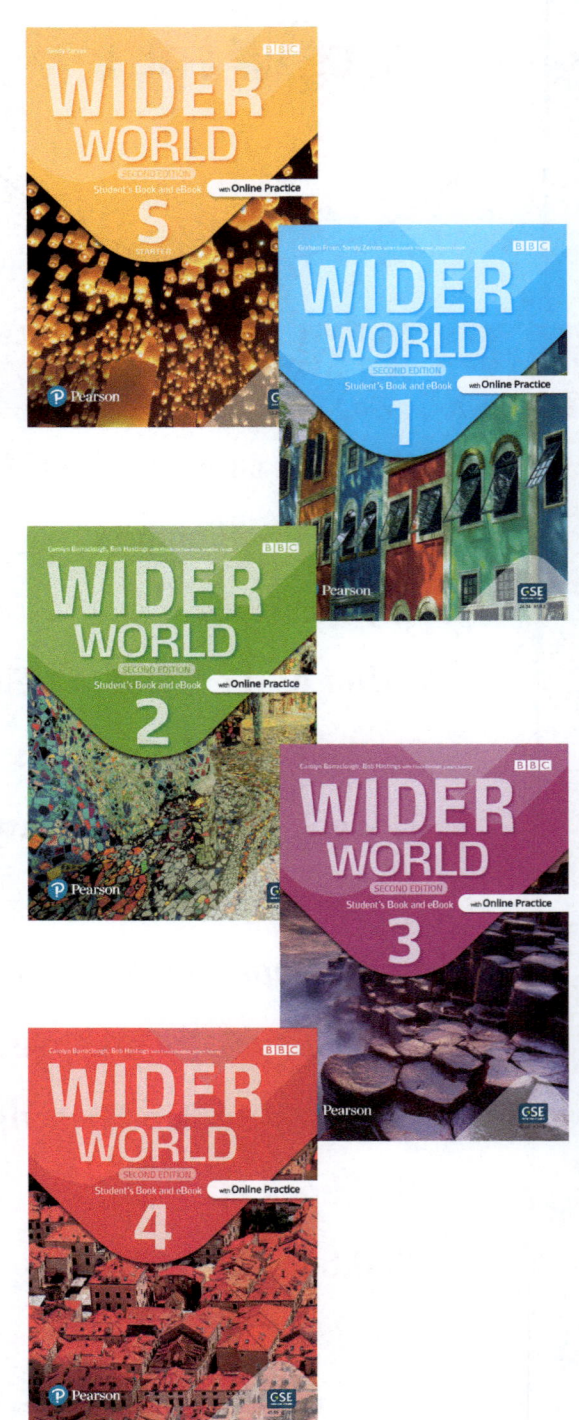

Course Components

For Students

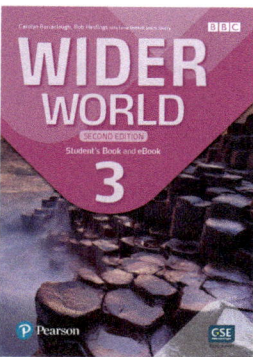

STUDENT'S BOOK

- Access code for Student's eBook, Online Practice and Tests (depending on the version)
- Course map showing how to use the Student components
- Ten units per level: nine core units and one revision unit. Each unit includes a wordlist with exercises to activate key vocabulary and a *Revision* section.
- Grammar and Speaking videos
- Cumulative *Progress Checks* for units 1–3, 1–6 and 1–9
- *BBC Culture* lessons based on BBC video documentaries and project work
- *Set for Life* lessons focusing on developing future skills
- *Grammar Time:* grammar reference and practice activities for every Grammar lesson
- Four CLIL lessons
- Audio and video available online

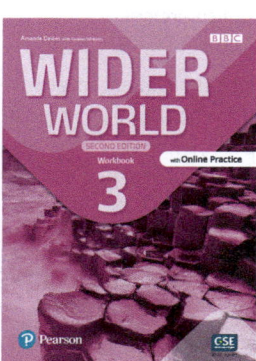

WORKBOOK

- Access code for audio, Online Practice and tests (depending on the version)
- Additional grammar, vocabulary and skills practice to supplement the material in the Student's Book
- *My Language Files* for storing key vocabulary from each unit
- *Self-Check* section at the end of each unit
- *Reading Time* sections to encourage reading for pleasure
- *Exam Time* sections for exam preparation
- Audio available online

STUDENT'S eBOOK

- Full Student's Book in digital format with embedded audio, video and interactive activities
- Tools for managing and assigning self-study and practice activities for students, with automatic marking to save time
- Personal gradebook for students to review their performance

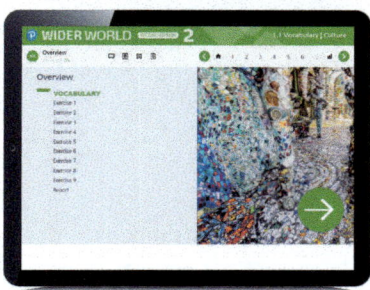

ONLINE PRACTICE

- Digital version of the Workbook activities and Extra Practice Activities with automatic marking to be used for self-study or teacher-assigned work
- Fully accessible on computer, tablet or mobile

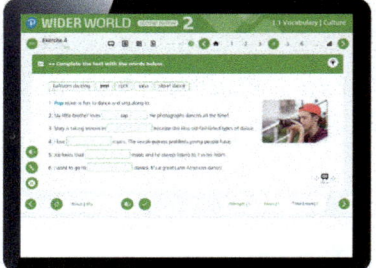

- Extra Practice Activities to provide additional vocabulary practice as well as remediation activities for grammar. Students can view and monitor their results in the gradebook. (For more details please see Online Practice in For Teachers on page 4.)

3

Course Components

For Teachers

TEACHER'S BOOK

- Student's Book pages with overwritten answers and a list of teacher and student resources available for each lesson
- Detailed teaching notes with useful tips on areas such as mixed-ability classes and Assessment for Learning
- Background notes, extra activities, additional tasks for fast finishers and students who need support
- Photocopiable *Need support?* worksheet for each unit with simplified versions of more difficult tasks
- Student Book and Workbook audioscripts and videoscripts, Workbook answer key
- Access code to Teacher's Portal with a wealth of tools and resources to make teaching more effective in class and online. (For more details please see page 5.)

PRESENTATION TOOL

- Digital versions of Student's Book and Workbook
- Interactive activities for display in class and online
- Teaching notes for each lesson and individual exercises
- Embedded audio and video
- Built-in virtual classroom and whiteboard functionalities: integrated video conferencing with breakout rooms, interactive whiteboard, chat, question posting, discussions, live task assignment and real-time view of student performance

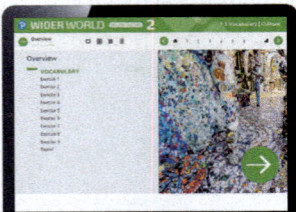

ONLINE PRACTICE

- Fully interactive digital version of the Workbook and Extra Practice Activities with instant feedback and automatic gradebook
- Activities can be assigned at the touch of a button for homework or in class.

EXTRA PRACTICE ACTIVITIES

- Extra activities based on BBC Vox Pops, with embedded video
- Extra activities based on video presentations from Grammar and Speaking lessons
- Additional grammar and vocabulary activities
- Remediation activities for grammar
- *Self-Check* activities for each unit
- Use of English activities
- Vocabulary Memory Games

TEST GENERATOR

- Adaptable tests from the Assessment package to tailor to students' needs
- Tests to assign online with automatic marking

GRADEBOOK

- Overview of individual student and class results for assigned activities from the Student's eBook, Online Practice and Test Generator

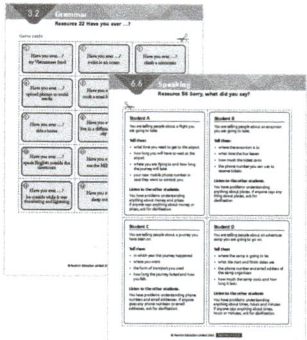

PHOTOCOPIABLE RESOURCES

- Ninety photocopiable worksheets with full teaching notes and answer key including:
  - one worksheet for every lesson plus two additional vocabulary and grammar revision worksheets for each unit
  - *Set for Life* worksheets to supplement the lessons in the Student's Book
  - Project worksheets with step-by-step support for digital projects in *BBC Culture* lessons
- Assessment for Learning response cards designed to support feedback
- *Need support?* worksheets for each unit with simplified versions of selected tasks from the Student's Book
- *Set for life* 'bookmarks' with tips and key language from *Set for Life* lessons

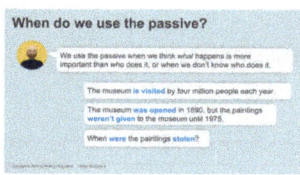

GRAMMAR PRESENTATIONS

- Interactive grammar presentation with practice exercises for each Grammar lesson

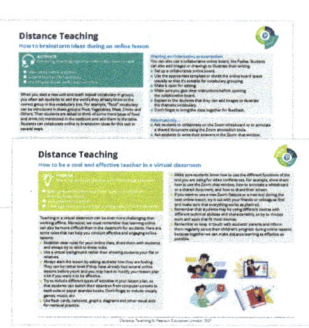

ONLINE CLASSROOM

- Online video tutorials and materials on the *ESAP* (*Engage, Study, Activate, Practise*) framework – an online teaching methodology to help teach effective and engaging online lessons
- A set of guides on distance teaching with ideas and tips for each stage of the lesson to help implement the *ESAP* approach successfully in everyday teaching

ASSESSMENT PACKAGE

- A range of language, skills and exam tests for use throughout the course
- All core tests in A/B versions to prevent copying: ready-to-print PDFs and editable Word documents, which can be administered online via the Test Generator
- Tests versioned for dyslexic students

EXAMS

- Exam correlation tables showing detailed alignment between Pearson English International Certificate, Cambridge English exams and each level of *Wider World Second Edition*
- Cambridge Exam Practice for A2 Key and B1 Preliminary for Schools

TEACHING WITH *WIDER WORLD SECOND EDITION* VIDEOS

- Series of short instructional videos to familiarise teachers with key aspects of the course

GSE MAPPING BOOKLETS

- Alignment of each level of *Wider World Second Edition* with The Global Scale of English (GSE) and the Common European Framework of Reference (CEFR)

OTHER USEFUL RESOURCES

- Teacher's Book in PDF format
- Class, Workbook and Test audio with scripts
- All in-course video with scripts
- Student's Book and Workbook
- Wordlists with audio
- Syllabus of future skills taught across levels

Course Components

Wider World Second Edition Videos

There are three types of video in *Wider World Second Edition 1–4*. Additionally, *Get Grammar!* animations are available with Starter level. All videos can be accessed from the Resources area on the Teacher's Portal. They are also embedded in the Student's eBook.

GRAMMAR AND SPEAKING VIDEOS

An entertaining drama about a group of teenagers, their families and friends
The videos present the key language for one of the two Grammar lessons and all the Speaking lessons in an engaging and relatable way. Real-life dialogues provide natural and memorable models. New language is backed by visual clues and presented in context to help students acquire new language.

The episodes also have an additional focus on future skills and are accompanied by a *Set for Life* task to show students how learning specific skills can be useful for their lives outside the classroom.

All the video episodes are also available in audio-only format.

BBC VOX POPS

Short clips of people filmed by the BBC on the streets of London answering questions about their lives and opinions
Students are exposed to authentic, spontaneous speech uttered by speakers of English from around the world. The purpose of the videos is to provide short manageable chunks of language in real contexts to help students develop compensation strategies for understanding, and to improve their listening skills.

BBC CULTURE VIDEOS

A series of inspiring culture videos produced in co-operation with the BBC
The videos recycle the topic and language from the preceding units. They are aimed to spark students' imagination and curiosity about the wider world so that they are enthused to continue their English learning independently.

GET GRAMMAR! ANIMATIONS

Funny animated clips about the adventures of Hammy, a cute Hamster and his friends
The videos present the key grammar structures taught in each Grammar lesson of Starter level. The animations enable teachers to explain new grammar structures in an entertaining and meaningful way. The videos can be used multiple times as an effective presentation tool or for quick revision of grammar structures.

Key Concepts

The Global Scale of English

The Global Scale of English (GSE) is a numerical scale which measures English language proficiency. It is also a framework of learning objectives which describe what a learner can do at each level of proficiency on the scale for each of the four skills: listening, reading, speaking and writing. The Global Scale of English enables teachers and students to answer the following questions accurately:
- How good is my English?
- What progress have I made towards my learning goal?
- What do I need to do next to improve?

The Global Scale of English is fully aligned to the Common European Framework of Reference for Languages (CEFR), but the numerical scale enables proficiency to be measured more accurately, more regularly and within a CEFR level. This keeps learners motivated as they see regular evidence of progress.

The Global Scale of English helps you to find the right course materials for the exact level and learning goals of your students. The chart on the back of your coursebook shows the range of objectives that are covered within the content. Knowing this range helps you select course materials with the right level of support and challenge for your students to help them make progress.

Wider World Second Edition has been created using the GSE Learning Objectives for Young Learners and Adult Learners. These have been used to ensure that the content and activities are at the correct level and have informed the lesson goals given at the start of each unit.

GSE TEACHER'S RESOURCES

You can find a full list of all the GSE Learning Objectives covered in this coursebook in the Global Scale of English Teacher Booklet, available on the Teacher's Portal. For more information about how the GSE can support your planning and teaching, your assessment of your learners, and the selection or creation of additional materials to supplement your core programme, please go to www.pearsonenglish.com/gse.

For easy access to all the GSE Learning Objectives, GSE Grammar, GSE Vocabulary and the GSE Text Analyzer (to estimate the GSE level of a written text), use the GSE Teacher Toolkit – freely available online at www.english.com/gse/teacher-toolkit/user/lo.

GSE	10	20	30	40	50	60	70	80	90
CEFR		<A1	A1	A2	A2+	B1	B1+	B2	B2+	C1	C2

Exams

Wider World Second Edition provides many opportunities for students to get acquainted with the format of international exams with special focus on the Pearson English International Certificate and Cambridge Exams.

The Pearson English International Certificate (formerly known as PTE General) gives learners official certification of their English language skills at any level. Awarded by Edexcel, the International Certificate is recognized by universities in many countries around the world.

Exam preparation is seamlessly integrated in the Student's Book and Workbook and clearly signposted for the teacher in the Teacher's Book. Detailed information about exam tasks covered in each level can be found in the Exam Alignment Tables available on the Teacher's Portal.

The table below shows the correlation between the language level of each part of *Wider World Second Edition* and the requirements for Pearson English International Certificate and Cambridge Exams.

	GSE	CEFR	Pearson English International Certificate	Cambridge
Starter	10–35	> A1/A1		
Level 1	24–34	A1/A2	Levels A1/1	A2 Key for Schools
Level 2	32–42	A2/A2+	Level 1	A2 Key for Schools
Level 3	40–50	A2+/B1	Level 1/2	A2 Key for Schools, B1 Preliminary for Schools
Level 4	45–55	B1+	Level 2	B1 Preliminary for Schools

STUDENT'S BOOK

Exam-style reading and listening comprehension tasks are integrated in skills lessons in every unit and there is a strong focus in the Speaking lessons on teaching the necessary skills for the international exams. Cumulative *Progress Check* sections include Use of English tasks as well as speaking, listening and reading tasks in an exam-like format.

WORKBOOK

Exam Time sections in the Workbook provide exam practice in a format which mirrors the real tests. Exam Tips familiarise students with typical exam task types and help them overcome common exam difficulties.

TEACHER'S BOOK

All exam tasks in the Student's Book are clearly signposted in the Teacher's Book. The notes explain which exam (and which exam paper) a given task comes from. Teaching notes also include additional tips and exam strategies.

> **EXAM**
> **Exercise 2**
> **International Certificate Level 2**, Reading, Section 6, (open-ended question)

Key Concepts

Measuring Progress

Students' progress can be measured through a variety of methods: student self-assessment, peer assessment, observation, class participation, written work, homework tasks, and both in-course and summative assessment. *Wider World Second Edition* provides you with a full range of tools to help measure the progress of your students.

STUDENT'S BOOK

Each lesson in *Wider World Second Edition* has a learning objective which is available for you to explore with your students at the start and end of each lesson. It is important to check how confident students feel before moving on to the next unit. The *Revision* sections help check how well students have mastered the language from the unit. The *Progress Check* sections allow students to consolidate their knowledge from the previous units in a summative way. They systematically cover all language learned through Use of English, listening, reading, writing and speaking activities.

WORKBOOK

In the Workbook there is a *Self-Check* section at the end of each lesson which covers key grammar and vocabulary from the unit. After completing the tasks, students can assess their score to check how comfortable they feel.

GRADEBOOK

You can assign activities from the interactive Student's Book and Workbook and students' results will report to the gradebook so that you can monitor their progress.

TEACHER'S BOOK

For each lesson, we highlight in the teaching notes which learning objectives the students will cover. Each lesson starts with an activity to identify the lesson goals and helps students understand what they will have learned by the end of the lesson. Students can review the lesson aims and assess their achievement at the end.

The **Assessment package** for each level includes five categories of tests:
1. **Placement Test** to assess students' language level at the beginning of the course and choose the right course level
2. **Vocabulary and Grammar Checks** to test key points from individual Grammar and Vocabulary lessons
3. **Unit Tests** focusing on vocabulary, grammar, functions, listening and reading as well as separate **Unit Writing Tests**
4. **Progress Tests** including **Progress Writing** and **Speaking Tests** every three units to assess students' progress
5. **Exam Practice Test** with **Exam Speaking** and **Exam Writing** tests which can be administered at the end of the school year to see how well students are prepared to take external exams

 Benchmark

Benchmark tests are a perfect companion to any English teaching programme. They are independently-verified proficiency tests designed to measure progress in detail and offer targeted direction for both students and teachers. Depending on their age and performance, students can take either English Benchmark Young Learners or Benchmark Test.

English Benchmark Young Learners is a motivating English test for 6-14 year old learners delivered on a tablet. Testing speaking, listening, reading and writing, it measures English proficiency through a fun, game-like test. English Benchmark gives you recommendations for what to teach next, based on students' scores.

The **Benchmark Test** has been designed for older teenagers. This straightforward yet powerful tool makes it easy to measure real progress, fast. And with just a few basic requirements, the test can even be taken from home. Use the Benchmark Test alongside *Wider World Second Edition* to smooth and accelerate the journey to fluency. Benchmark tests are clearly signposted in the Teacher's Book.

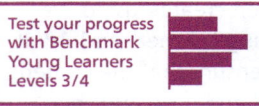 

We recommend taking two tests per year to check or monitor students' progress and inform teaching plans. The table below shows how *Wider World Second Edition* is aligned to Benchmark levels:

Starter	Benchmark YL Level 1
Level 1	Benchmark YL Level 2
Level 2	Benchmark YL Levels 3/4 Benchmark Test A
Level 3	Benchmark YL Levels 4/5 Benchmark Test A/B1
Level 4	Benchmark YL Levels 5/6 Benchmark Test B1

For more information about Benchmark tests and delivery, please go to Pearson English Assessment Portal at www.pearson.com/english/assessment.html.

ACCURATE   AI-BACKED   USE WITH ANY COURSE   COMPLETE ASSESSMENT

Assessment for Learning (AfL)

Most teachers are familiar with assessment of learning, i.e., assessments/tests that take place at the end of a unit of study, which are used to report achievement. Assessment for Learning (AfL) complements and supports this type of assessment, but differs in two key ways:
- AfL takes place at *all* stages of the learning process. Teachers continuously monitor and assess students' needs and progress during lessons, give feedback and support where necessary, and modify future teaching and activities based on their observations.
- AfL means students take responsibility for learning and take an active role. They become more independent, and more able and confident to continue learning beyond the classroom. Because AfL focuses on the process of learning, and emphasises progress and achievement rather than failure, it increases student motivation and maximises attainment. It is now established as one of the most powerful ways of improving learning and raising standards.

ASSESSMENT FOR LEARNING IN THE CLASSROOM

AfL can take different forms, but fundamentally it consists of anything you do to help students focus on and answer these three questions:
1 *What am I going to learn?*
2 *Can I do what is expected of me?*
3 *How can I improve?*

These three questions underlie the Assessment for Learning strategies that are incorporated in *Wider World Second Edition*. The table below lists the most common strategies included in the teaching notes for each lesson, together with examples of recommended classroom techniques.

AfL strategies	Examples of recommended classroom techniques
Set and review lesson goals At the start, share lesson aims and write them on the board so you and your students can refer to them at different stages of the lesson. (1 *What am I going to learn?*) At the end, ask students to re-read the aims and reflect on the extent to which they have achieved them. (2 *Can I do what is expected of me?*)	**Setting lesson goals:** Write the aim on the board and read it out. Ask questions to check understanding. **Reflection:** At the end of the lesson students re-read the lesson aim and write a number from 1–5 to say how confident they feel (1 – it's easy to 5 – it's difficult), together with a reason why. Read and if necessary, review or offer individual support. **Self-assessment:** Students reflect on the lesson and their learning. Give them questions to answer in their notebooks.
Monitor students' learning and give constructive feedback Throughout the lesson, observe how students participate, monitor progress and assess their work. Give all students the opportunity to respond to questions. Give regular constructive feedback to individual students: praise and show them what they can improve and how. (3 *How can I get better?*)	**Yes/No, Traffic Light, and Emoji response cards:** Students choose and hold up a card to show how well they understand, e.g., a language item. Look at the responses and if necessary, re-teach, review or offer individual support. **Popsicle Stick technique:** Students write their names on popsicle sticks and put them in a cup. A student picks a stick. The student whose name is on the stick answers the question. **Basketball technique:** A student gives the answer, then throws a ball to another student to give his/her answer and so on. The teacher only gives feedback after all the students involved have spoken.
Peer Learning Use pair work and group work to encourage peer learning and collaboration. Encourage learners to assess each other's ideas and work.	**Peer teaching:** Students raise their hands if they have a question. Other students answer. Only provide support when needed. **Think-Pair-Share:** Students think of the answer to a question alone. Then they discuss in pairs. Finally, they discuss their ideas in groups, or as a class.
Independent Learning Promote independent learning by giving students responsibility and choices.	**Spider diagram:** Students create a spider diagram with the words in Vocabulary box A. Then they add any other words they know. **Visual dictionary:** Students create a visual dictionary with the new vocabulary. They can draw pictures or find images. Give them the option of creating the visual dictionary in their notebooks or on a laptop, tablet or smartphone.

Wider World Second Edition offers you the support you need to incorporate Assessment for Learning in your everyday teaching:
- Teaching notes offer quick and easy-to-use AfL techniques for all key lesson stages (clearly signposted with symbols).
- Photocopiable Assessment for Learning response cards are available on the Portal.
- *Self-Check* pages in the Workbook help students monitor where they are in their learning and become more independent learners.

Key Concepts

Inclusive Classroom

Wider World Second Edition recognizes the need for all students to reach their potential and encourages teachers to adopt inclusive practices in the classroom by offering strategies and tailored materials.

An inclusive classroom is a learning environment that is flexible enough to respond to the needs of students with learning differences as well as those who are exceptionally gifted. In an inclusive classroom, all students are engaged in learning and making progress and students' individual differences are recognized. Inclusivity also means respecting people from *all* backgrounds and cultures.

There are numerous benefits of creating an inclusive learning environment. Above all, it promotes a growth mindset in the classroom and gives students a chance to learn values such as respect and tolerance as well as realise that learning is about focusing on their own progress, rather than comparing themselves with others.

MIXED-ABILITY CLASSES

Mixed ability refers to the differences that exist in a group of learners in terms of each student's competencies, strengths, difficulties, learning preferences and abilities. *Wider World Second Edition* recognizes that all classrooms are mixed-ability, and offers strategies and support for teaching more and less confident students. More confident students may be simply more confident, or they may have high language proficiency levels, strong literacy, or be quicker to understand and apply new information. Less confident students, on the other hand, may be less confident, or they may have difficulties with some areas e.g., grammatical accuracy or reading.

Wider World Second Edition incorporates two key strategies to help all students achieve the learning objectives according to their readiness level and preferred ways of learning:

- **Differentiation** means students can work on and learn what they are ready for. This may involve adapting the process of teaching (e.g., staging the presentation of new material more and breaking down complex tasks into smaller steps); differentiating learning outcomes for students, (e.g., asking students to provide yes/no answers instead of open answers or produce a shorter written answer) or adapting tasks for different learners in class.
- **Peer collaboration** (pairwork, group work) is a useful way of involving all students in a mixed-ability group. It draws on students' different strengths and knowledge and encourages them to share and learn from each other. Depending on the activity, students can work in the same ability pairs or you can decide to pair less and more confident students.

SPECIAL EDUCATIONAL NEEDS AND NEURODIVERSITY

Special Educational Needs (SEN) is a term used to refer to students who face learning challenges due to physical, behavioural, cognitive or literacy differences.
Examples of SEN include:
- Autism spectrum disorder
- Attention Deficit (Hyperactivity) Disorder (ADHD/ADD)
- Dyslexia
- Anxiety disorder.

The term neurodiversity can be a more positive way of describing SEN as it focuses on the strengths of these students, while acknowledging and embracing their differences.

Wider World Second Edition recognizes that many students will have special needs of some kind at some time during their school life, and teachers need support in order to understand these challenges and make changes in the way they teach in order to help remove barriers to learning. While SEN students will have difficulties which affect learning, they also have some key strengths which you can capitalise on to avoid stigmatising, and promote self-esteem. For example, dyslexic learners have strong visual memories; students with ADHD tend to have boundless energy, which can be effectively channelled during project work, role plays and action games. Learners on the autistic spectrum often have an excellent memory for rules and facts, which can make grammar appealing. They can also develop a keen interest in a particular topic, which can be exploited during vocabulary building or project work.

Wider World Second Edition offers strategies and materials to cater for mixed ability and neurodiversity in the classroom. These include:

Teacher's Book
- There are teaching notes and detailed suggestions as well as ideas for differentiated tasks for less and more confident students under *Need support?* and *Finished early?* These also include tips for exploiting pair and group work in mixed-ability classes.
- There are *Need support?* worksheets with four activities for each unit with simplified versions of more difficult tasks in the Student's Book.

Workbook
- The exercises progress from less to more difficult to allow teachers to allocate suitably graded material to less and more confident students.
- *My Language File* page is a useful tool to help students build their own bilingual dictionary as well as memorise and revise new words.

On the Portal
- There are additional remediation tasks for each Grammar lesson to provide extra practice.
- There are tests versioned for dyslexic students.
- There are additional supplementary resources for students with special needs.

Future Skills

Soft skills (also referred to as '21st century skills' or 'transferable skills') are becoming increasingly important in a rapidly changing and uncertain future. Modern learners need to develop not just English language skills, grammar and vocabulary, but also skills which will help them become fully rounded citizens of the global community.
Wider World Second Edition is aligned to the *Pearson Personal & Social Capabilities (PSC)* framework. Based on extensive research with employers, educators and learners, *PSC* identifies six categories of skills which are critical for lifelong learning and success at work:
- Critical Thinking and Creativity
- Communication
- Collaboration
- Self-management
- Leadership
- Social responsibility.

Wider World Second Edition has been designed to place a special emphasis on helping students develop future skills:
- **A dedicated life skills syllabus for each level**
  The *Set for Life* programme has been integrated into all five levels of the course and the syllabus has been adjusted to students' cognitive abilities.
- *Set for Life* **lessons**
  In every level there are four *Set for Life* sections which introduce future skills in real-life contexts. Students learn about how to apply a given skill through a sequence of practical tasks. They are provided with useful tips and key language pulled together in the 'bookmark' section for quick reference. The lessons can be supplemented with photocopiable worksheets which explore the topic of the lesson in more detail.
- *Set for Life* **tasks**
  In every unit there is a *Set for Life* task integrated into the video story. These short tasks are guided and help students focus on one specific skill.
  For more information about personal and social capabilities and employability please go to www.pearson.com/en-us/efficacy/skills-for-today.html.

Visible Thinking

The ability to think critically, i.e., question, explore, challenge and solve, is arguably one of the most important skills students will need for their future lives. However, a key question is how teachers can gain insight into students' thinking processes and help them to become better thinkers. This question underpins the research on the Visible Thinking Routine (VTR) undertaken at Harvard University by Project Zero, an educational research group.
Thinking routines are simple exercises designed to help students understand how they think and learn by making their ideas and thinking 'visible'.
They usually comprise a few steps which scaffold and guide students' thinking, and are designed to be frequently repeated so that students develop thinking habits typical of critical thinkers.

VTR examples in *Wider World Second Edition*:
- *See*, *Think*, *Wonder* (What do you see? What do you think about that? What does it make you wonder?) This VTR aims to develop learning through careful observation and interpretation of images, topics and objects.
- *Why do you say that?* (What do you know/see that makes you say that?) This VTR promotes evidence-based reasoning and critical thinking, to help students support opinions with evidence.

Thinking routines provide you with an effective tool for promoting the development of a thinking culture in the classroom, where students are encouraged to go beyond passively learning and remembering facts to actively questioning and taking multiple perspectives. Key factors to consider in order to use VTRs effectively are:
- Students need sufficient time to think in depth before verbalising and discussing their ideas.
- Teachers should serve as role models and participate in the thinking process too.
- The focus should be on the process, or interactions, rather than the outcome.

In *Wider World Second Edition*, a range of visible thinking routines are incorporated into all the *BBC Culture* lessons across all levels. These VTR-based activities are designed to awaken curiosity about cultural and social issues and help students develop a deeper understanding of the topics. Each level features visual thinking routines appropriate to students' cognitive development and language level. For example, Level 1 features simple, guided routines such as *Think See Wonder, Why do you say that?* and *Think Pair Share*. In Levels 3 and 4 students move on to more complex, open routines such as *Connect, Exchange, Challenge; Your viewpoint, The writer's viewpoint, What do you think now?*

A Unit of the Student's Book

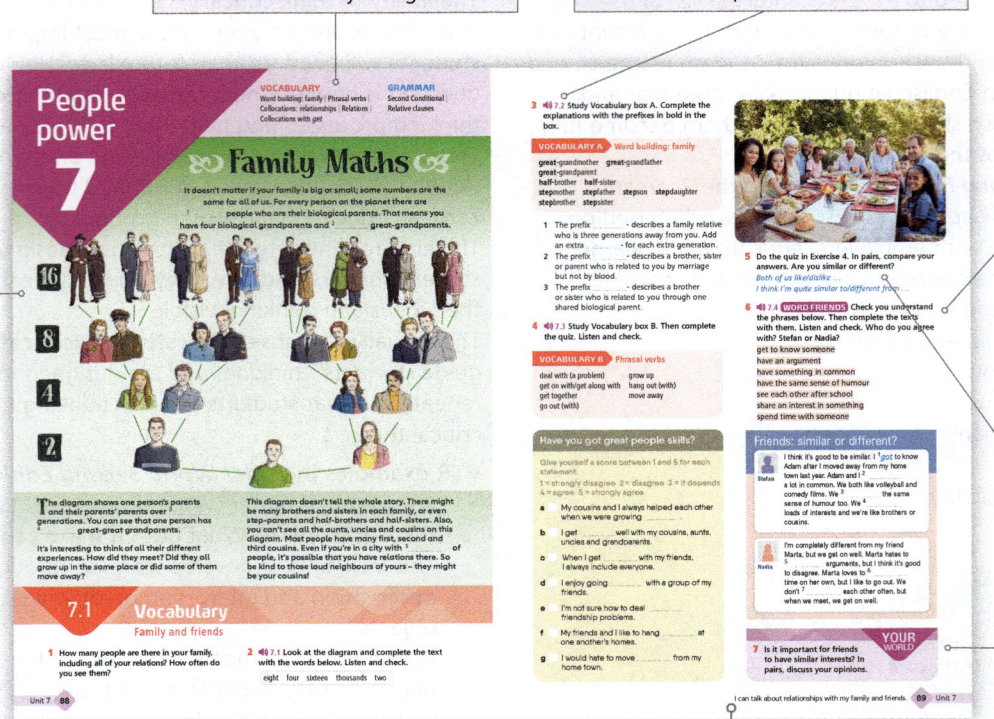

- Clear summary of unit contents in terms of vocabulary and grammar
- All lexical items recorded for students to listen and repeat
- Special focus on teaching collocations and vocabulary chunks
- Vocabulary presented in real-life contexts with engaging visuals
- Integrated skills practice to help students consolidate new vocabulary
- Personalized speaking practice to help students achieve the learning objectives
- Learning objective (can-do statement) for every lesson based on the Global Scale of English
- Grammar presented through videos
- Recorded versions of all reading texts 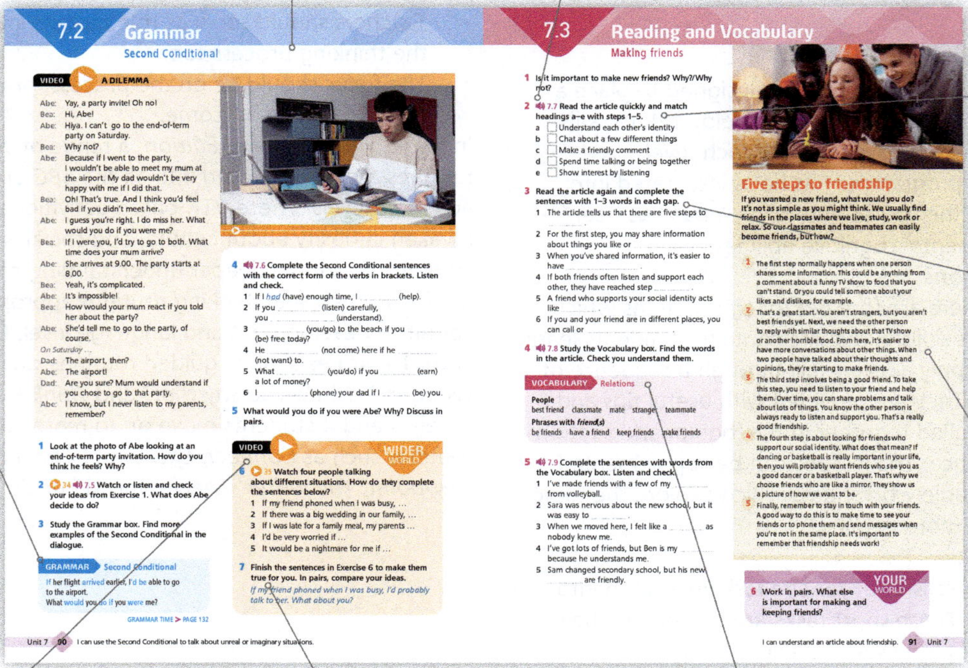
- Comprehension tasks in exam-like format to prepare students for exams
- Grammar tables to highlight target structures
- Step-by-step reading practice to develop students' reading skills
- Manageable texts about contemporary issues to engage students' attention
- BBC Vox Pop videos to expose students to real-life examples of language from the lessons
- Final productive task to encourage students to use the grammar in a personalized context
- Vocabulary sets contextualized in the reading text and recorded

12

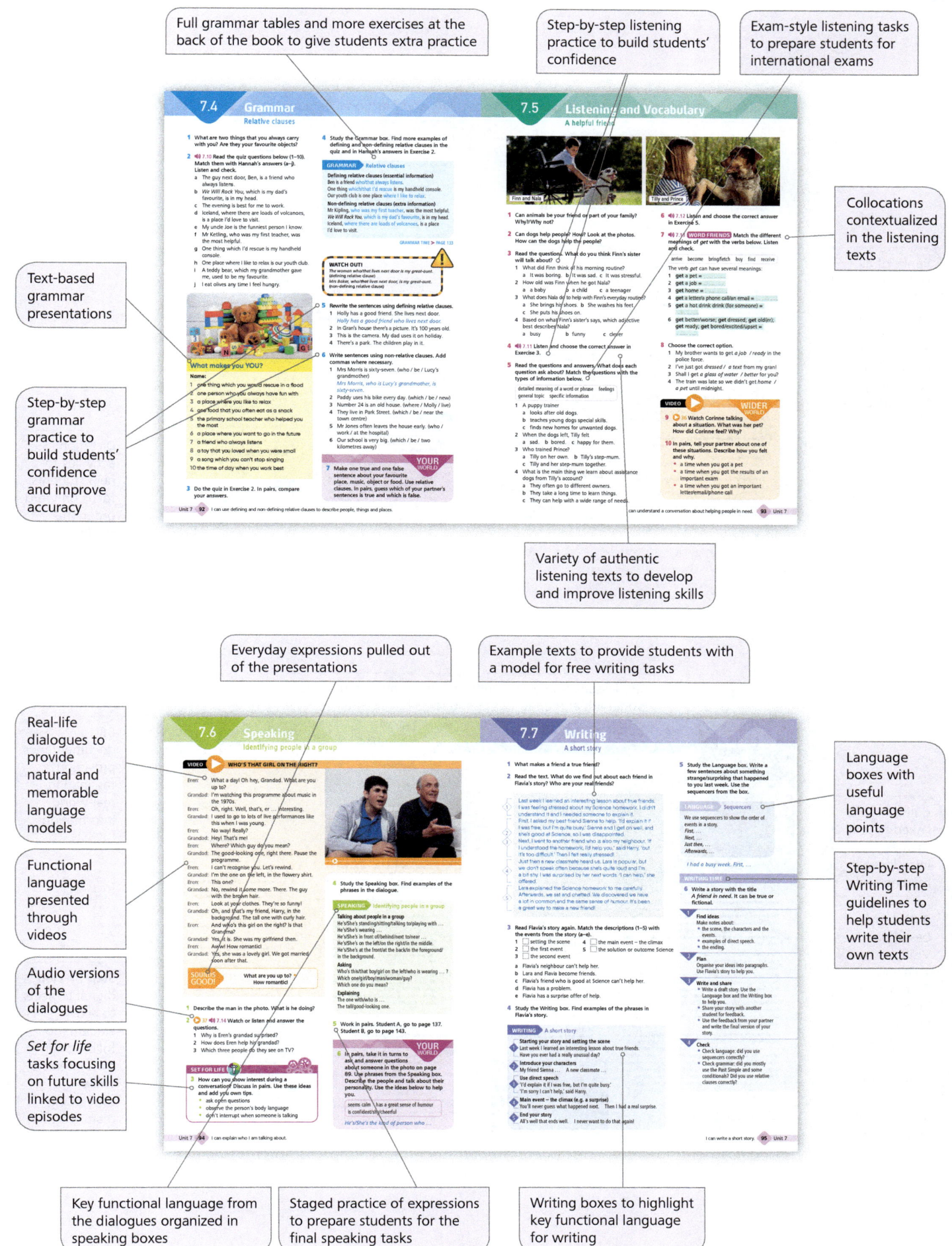

A Unit of the Student's Book

Effective and engaging revision of grammar, vocabulary and functional language from the units

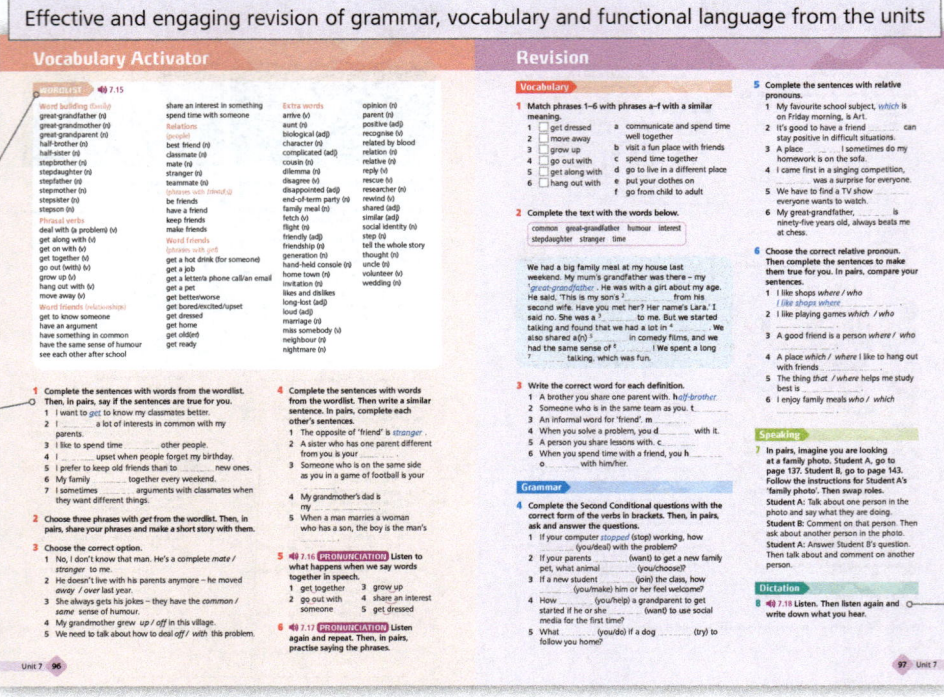

Banks of all vocabulary sets followed by engaging practice activities to consolidate vocabulary from the units

Dictation activities to help students focus on word order and spelling

BBC lessons (every two units) providing opportunities to work with authentic videos and real-life content

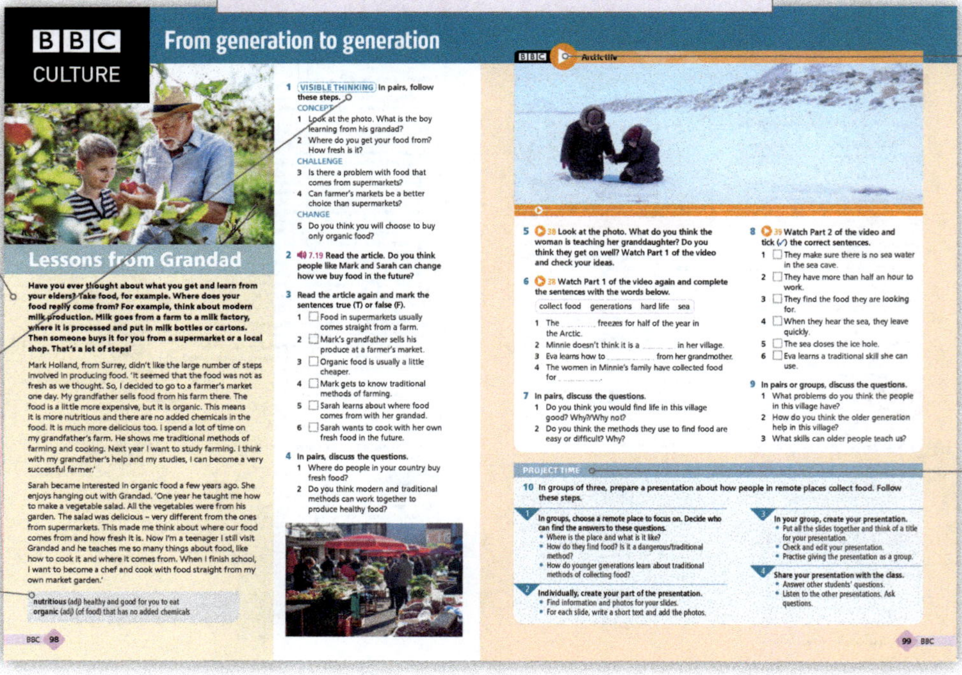

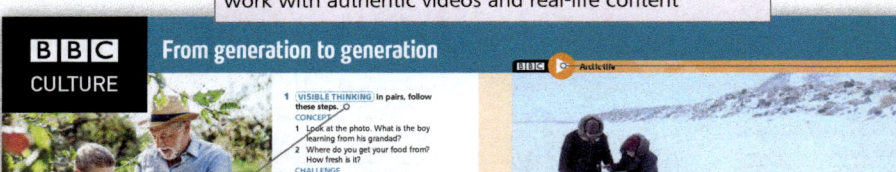

Culture topics linked to unit themes introduced in reading texts

Activities based on Visible Thinking Routines to help students understand the topics

Glossary of the most difficult words in the texts

BBC documentaries providing fascinating real-world information

Step-by-step digital projects to allow students to follow their own interests while developing team work and ICT skills

Thought-provoking and authentic contexts which reflect situations and problems from students' lives

Set for Life lessons (every two units) to equip students with future skills they need to enjoy their social lives, and succeed in their studies and career

Useful tips to help students remember key takeaways

Practical tasks to help students develop specific skills

Useful phrases linked to specific life skills

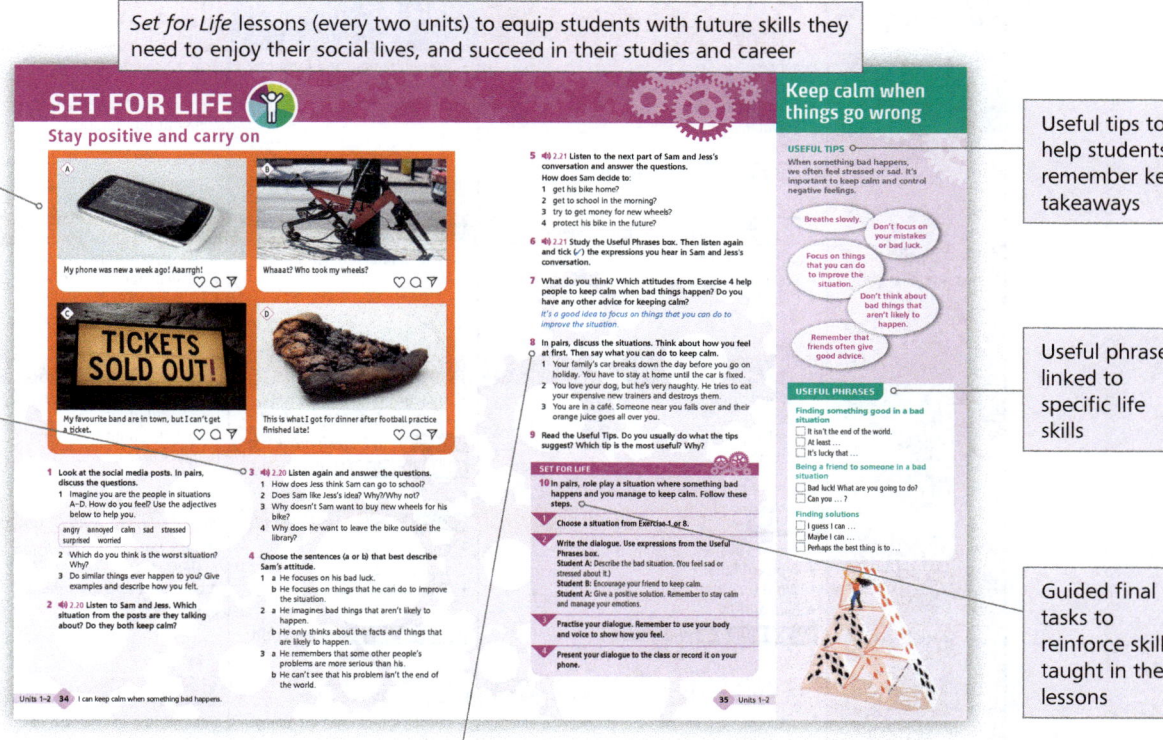

Guided final tasks to reinforce skills taught in the lessons

Activities which encourage working collaboratively (pairwork and group work)

Cumulative revision of grammar, vocabulary and skills

Use of English tasks to revise vocabulary and grammar in context

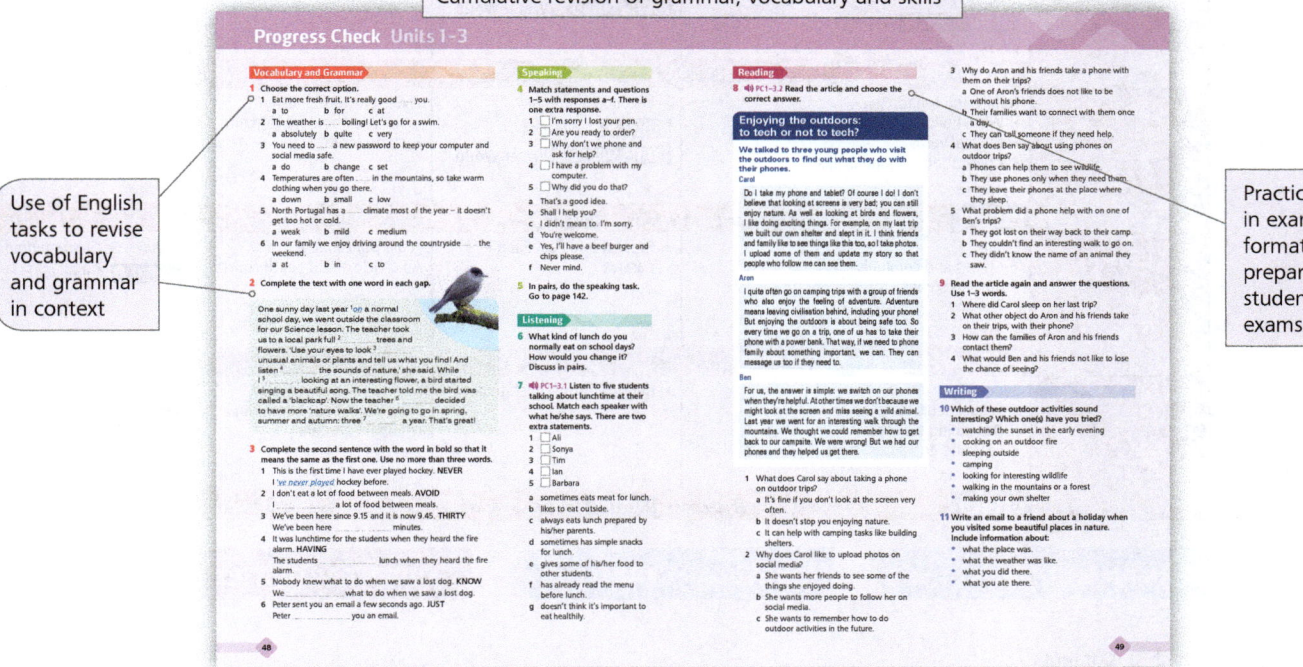

Practice tasks in exam-style format to prepare students for exams

At the back of the book: Grammar Time with reference and practice, CLIL lessons, Irregular verbs

15

Contents

Unit		Vocabulary	Grammar	Reading and Vocabulary	Grammar
Welcome to New Park 0		**0.1 Introducing Abe** — Activities and interests | Home and furniture | There is/are with some/any | Possessive adjectives and possessive 's — pp. 6–7		**0.2 Introducing Bea** — Present Simple with adverbs of frequency | Jobs | Everyday activities — p. 8	
Tech check 1		Lifestyle: • Technology • Using technology • Social media • Time BBC VIDEO Wider World pp. 12–13	• Present Simple and Present Continuous, state verbs BBC VIDEO Wider World p. 14	Science competitions and projects Short texts about Science competitions and projectss p. 15	Verb + -ing, verb + to-infinitive VIDEO The video call p. 16
		BBC CULTURE Screenagers	VIDEO Disconnecting	Visual Thinking: What makes you say that?	
Wild and beautiful 2		Weather and climate: • Weather • Climate pp. 24–25	• Past Simple: regular and irregular verbs p. 26	A dangerously hot place An article about Death Valley, USA p. 27	• Past Continuous and Past Simple VIDEO A crazy day BBC VIDEO Wider World p. 28
		SET FOR LIFE Self-Management	Keep calm when things go wrong	Keep calm and carry on pp. 34–35	
Tasty treats 3		Food and drink: • Food • Cooking • Flavours pp. 36–37	• Present Perfect with ever, never, just, already and yet VIDEO An English breakfast BBC VIDEO Wider World p. 38	Five superfoods – they're tasty and healthy! An article about the health benefits of five foods p. 39	• Present Perfect with for and since • Present Perfect and Past Simple p. 40
		BBC CULTURE Fantastic food	VIDEO Indian food, Liverpool style	Visual Thinking: Think, Puzzle, Explore	
Entertain us! 4		Film and TV: • Types of film • Word building • Film and TV BBC VIDEO Wider World pp. 50–51	• Comparatives and superlatives • Too/(not) enough, (not) as … as BBC VIDEO Wider World p. 52	What's the best way to listen to music? A blog post about listening to music p. 53	• Quantifiers: some, any, much, many, (a) few, (a) little, a lot of, lots of VIDEO The short video challenge p. 54
		SET FOR LIFE Leadership	Lead a team	Lead the team! pp. 60–61	
To the limit 5		Sport: • Sports equipment • Sporting events • Sports collocations pp. 62–63	• Future forms: will, be going to, Present Continuous, Present Simple VIDEO The fitness class p. 64	Competitive sport or just a hobby? An article about different attitudes to sport BBC VIDEO Wider World p. 65	• First conditional with if and unless BBC VIDEO Wider World p. 66
		BBC CULTURE Sporting tradition	VIDEO The Highlands Games	Visual Thinking: Connect, Extend, Challenge	
Explore more 6		Holidays and travel: • Types of holidays • Holiday equipment • Holiday accommodations BBC VIDEO Wider World pp. 74–75	• Modal verbs: must, have to, ought to, should VIDEO A weekend break BBC VIDEO Wider World p. 76	Getting around Venice An article about transport in Venice, Italy p. 77	• Modal verbs: must, could, may/might, can't (speculation) p. 78
		SET FOR LIFE Social responsibility	Be an eco-friendly traveller	Eco-friendly travel pp. 84–85	
People power 7		Family and friends: • Word building: family • Phrasal verbs • Collocations: relationships pp. 88–89	• Second conditional VIDEO A dilemma BBC VIDEO Wider World p. 90	Five steps to friendship An article about making and keeping friends p. 91	• Relative clauses p. 92
		BBC CULTURE From generation to generation	VIDEO Arctic life	Visual Thinking: Concept, Challenge, Change	
Just justice 8		Crime: • Crimes and criminals • Solving crimes • The law pp. 100–101	• Present and Past Simple passive p. 102	A fair punishment An article about youth courts p. 103	• Have/Get something done VIDEO A new look p. 104
		SET FOR LIFE Critical thinking	Make a decision	You decide! pp. 110–111	
Lessons in life 9		Education: • School subjects • Describing students • Learning and assessment pp. 112–113	• Reported speech: statements p. 114	How to train your brain! An article about becoming a confident student p. 115	• Word order in questions VIDEO An interview p. 116
		BBC CULTURE Different forms of education	VIDEO Learning goals	Visual Thinking: Your viewpoint, the writer's viewpoint, what do you think now?	

GRAMMAR TIME pp. 126–136   **IRREGULAR VERBS** p. 136   **STUDENT ACTIVITIES** pp. 137, 142–143

2 Contents

0.3 Introducing Eren Clothes and accessories | Present Continuous p. 9	**0.4 Introducing Carla** Countries and languages | *Was/Were* | *There was/There were* | Past Simple: regular verbs p. 10	**0.5 Revision** p. 11		
Listening and Vocabulary	**Speaking**	**Writing**	**Revision**	**Progress Check**
A radio programme about using technology p. 17	VIDEO ▶ *Let's give it a try* Problem-solving p. 18	A description of your daily routine and online hobbies • Connectors p. 19	Vocabulary Activator p. 20 Revision p. 21	**1–3** pp. 48–49 • Vocabulary and Grammar: multiple choice, open cloze, transformations • Speaking: role play • Listening: matching • Reading: multiple choice, open questions • Writing: an opinion essay
Project: a digital presentation about an app pp. 22–23				
A conversation about an adventure camp p. 29	VIDEO ▶ *I can explain* Criticising and explaining BBC VIDEO ▶ Wider World p. 30	An article describing your local area and climate • Indefinite pronouns p. 31	Vocabulary Activator p. 32 Revision p. 33	
An advert for a cake competition BBC VIDEO ▶ Wider World p. 41	VIDEO ▶ *Are you ready to order?* Ordering food p. 42	An email to a friend • Giving instructions p. 43	Vocabulary Activator p. 44 Revision p. 45	
Project: an international menu for charity pp. 46–47				**1–6** pp. 86–87
An interview about a festival p. 55	VIDEO ▶ *I'd rather not dance* Talking about preferences p. 56	A review on a blog • Adverbs p. 57	Vocabulary Activator p. 58 Revision p. 59	• Vocabulary and Grammar: multiple choice, transformations, word formation • Speaking: role play • Listening: gap-fill • Reading: matching • Writing: a review of a film or documentary
A conversation about a sports award p. 67	VIDEO ▶ *What are you up to today?* Talking about plans p. 68	Short messages • Prepositions + *-ing* form p. 69	Vocabulary Activator p. 70 Revision p. 71	
Project: a video podcast about a traditional sport pp. 72–73				
An interview about holidays for visually impaired people p. 79	VIDEO ▶ *Can you say that again?* Understanding a conversation p. 80	An email about travel arrangements • Future time clauses p. 81	Vocabulary Activator p. 82 Revision p. 83	
Two monologues about assistance dogs BBC VIDEO ▶ Wider World p. 93	VIDEO ▶ *Who's this girl on the right?* Identifying people in a group p. 94	A short story • Sequencers p. 95	Vocabulary Activator p. 96 Revision p. 97	**1–9** pp. 124–125 • Vocabulary and Grammar: word formation, open cloze, multiple-choice cloze • Speaking: role play • Listening: multiple choice • Reading: gapped text • Writing: an opinion essay
Project: a presentation about how people in remote places collect food pp. 98–99				
A podcast about a burglary BBC VIDEO ▶ Wider World p. 105	VIDEO ▶ *Is something wrong?* Keeping a conversation going p. 106	An opinion essay • Connectors of purpose and result p. 107	Vocabulary Activator p. 108 Revision p. 109	
Conversations between teachers and students BBC VIDEO ▶ Wider World p. 117	VIDEO ▶ *What a coincidence!* Exchanging information p. 118	A formal letter asking for information • Talking about learning goals p. 119	Vocabulary Activator p. 120 Revision p. 121	
Project: a website for a new school pp. 122–123				

CLIL   **SCIENCE** p. 138   **MUSIC** p. 139   **GEOGRAPHY** p. 140   **SCIENCE** p. 141

Contents **3**

Welcome to New Park

0

VOCABULARY
Activities and interests | Home and furniture | Jobs | Everyday activities | Clothes and accessories | Countries and languages

GRAMMAR
There is/are with *some/any* | Possessive adjectives and possessive *'s* | Present Simple with adverbs of frequency | Present Continuous | *Was/were, there was/were* | Past Simple: regular verbs

This is Abe. His name's Abel Kerr, but his friends and family call him Abe. He's fifteen and he's from the USA. But now his new home is in the UK. His dad's name is Will and he is British. He's a scientist and he's got a new job in London. Abe's mum is American. She's a dentist. She hasn't got a job in the UK, so she's staying in the USA at the moment.

Abe's new house in the UK is nice, but it's a bit small. There are three bedrooms and there's a small garden too.

Abe's favourite hobby is photography. He's got a blog with lots of his photos. He likes reading, watching movies and making videos too.

He hasn't got any brothers or sisters, but he's got a British cousin. Her name's Bea. Bea's mum is Abe's aunt. She's his dad's sister. They all get on very well.

Exercise 1
1 Abel Kerr, but his friends and family call him Abe
2 the USA
3 in the UK/in England/in London
4 photography

Exercise 2
1 His mum is a dentist. His dad is a scientist.
2 His dad has got a job in the UK.
5 Abe's got a cousin called Bea. He hasn't got any brothers or sisters.

Exercise 3
2 I'm from the USA.
3 It's nice, but it's a bit small. There are three bedrooms and a small garden.
4 No, I haven't.

Exercise 5
Possible answers: playing football, playing the guitar, swimming, watching TV

0.1   Introducing Abe

Activities and interests | Home and furniture | *There is/are* with *some/any* | Possessive adjectives and possessive *'s*

1 ▶ 1 🔊 0.1 Watch or listen and answer the questions.
1 What's the boy's name?
2 Where is he from?
3 Where is his new home?
4 What's his favourite hobby?

2 In pairs, read the text about Abe again and mark the sentences T (true) or F (false). Correct the false sentences.
1 [F] Abe's dad is a dentist.
2 [F] Abe's mum has got a job in the UK.
3 [T] Abe's new home isn't very big.
4 [T] Abe's interested in films.
5 [F] Abe's got a sister called Bea.
6 [T] Abe's dad and Bea's mum are brother and sister.

3 Write Abe's answers to the questions.
1 What's your name? *My name's Abe.*
2 Where are you from?
3 What's your house like?
4 Have you got any brothers or sisters?

4 In pairs, ask and answer the questions in Exercise 3 about you.

5 🔊 0.2 **I KNOW!** Study Vocabulary box A. In pairs, add as many words as you can to the box.

VOCABULARY A   Activities and interests
going to the cinema   listening to music
playing computer games   reading books   taking photos

6 Study the Speaking box. In pairs, talk about what you and the people in your family like/don't like.
I love reading comic books, but my sister doesn't like reading.

SPEAKING   Likes and dislikes
I like/love …   He likes/loves …
I don't like …   She doesn't like …
I don't mind …   He doesn't mind …
I can't stand …   She can't stand …

Unit 0   6

For the teacher	On the Portal
• Teaching notes, page 156	• Vocabulary Memory Game

For the student	On the Portal
• Workbook, page 2	• Workbook: Lesson 0.1

7 🔊 0.3 **I KNOW!** Study Vocabulary box B. In pairs, add as many words as you can to the box.

VOCABULARY B	Home and furniture
bath bathroom bed bedroom ceiling cupboard dining room floor garage garden kitchen mirror roof shower wall window	

Exercise 7
Possible answers: carpet, chair, desk, sofa, table, wardrobe

8 Find the words from Vocabulary box B in the messages.

Abe

Your photo of your house in the USA on your blog is amazing. How many rooms are there? *Bea*

There are four [bedrooms] and three [bathrooms]. There's a big [dining room], but we usually eat in the [kitchen]. *Abe*

What's your [bedroom] like? *Bea*

It's nice. I like bright, comfortable rooms. *Abe*

Yes, me too! *Bea*

I've got my own [bathroom]. *Abe*

Really? That's fantastic! I can't stand waiting to use the [bathroom] in my house. Is there a [bath] in your [bathroom]? *Bea*

No, there isn't, but there's a [shower]. I don't mind having a [bath], but I prefer [showers]. *Abe*

Yes, me too! *Bea*

There are trees outside my [bedroom] [window] so my room never gets hot in the summer. *Abe*

That's cool! Do you like your new house in the UK? *Bea*

Yeah, it's nice but … *Abe*

But what? *Bea*

There isn't a wood nearby and I love walking or cycling there. *Abe*

Yes, me too. *Bea*

9 Study Grammar box A. Look at the dialogue and the photo in Exercise 8 and complete the sentences below with *there is/are* or *there isn't/aren't*.

GRAMMAR A	*There is/are* with *some/any*	
	Singular	Plural
+	There's a bed.	There are some books.
−	There isn't a desk.	There aren't any mirrors.
?	Is there a table?	Are there any chairs?

1 *There are* four bedrooms.
2 *There is* a big dining room.
3 *There isn't* a bath in Abe's bathroom.
4 *There are* some trees next to the house.
5 *There aren't* any chairs in front of the house.

10 In pairs, make more sentences about Abe's house in the USA using *there is/are* and the prepositions below.

between in near next to on opposite under

11 Study Grammar box B. Complete the sentences below with possessive adjectives or the possessive *'s*.

GRAMMAR B	Possessive adjectives and possessive *'s*
's = singular	Bea's mother is my dad's sister.
s' = plural	My friends' homes are near my house.
Possessive adjectives	my/your/his/her/its/our/their bedroom

1 A: Whose photo is it?
   B: It's Abe*'s* photo.
2 A: Is Abe Bea*'s* brother?
   B: No, he's *her* cousin.
3 A: Is that Abe*'s* room?
   B: No. It's *his* dad *'s* room.
4 A: Is that *your* house?
   B: No, it's not mine. It's my friend*'s* house.

Exercise 10
Possible answers:
There are some flowers in the garden.
There are big windows in the house.
There is a garage under the roof.
There is a bed in the bedroom.
There is a pillow/cushion on the bed.
There is a wood near the house.
There is a tree opposite the house.
There is a garden next to the house.

YOUR WORLD

12 Write sentences about your home. Use *there is/are* and the prepositions in Exercise 10.

7 Unit 0

0.2 Introducing Bea

Present Simple with adverbs of frequency | Jobs | Everyday activities

Exercise 1
1 Barker
2 Drama teacher, scientist, journalist
3 breakfast
4 the park

Exercise 3
2 She likes gardening.
3 No, I don't. I usually get up late.
4 I spend a lot of time with my cousin and my friends.
5 I chat to/with her every day.
6 I do sport, I walk in the park with my mum, and I write a nature blog.

Exercise 5
2 are often
3 never gets up
4 Do you live
5 doesn't see
6 always writes

Exercise 6
Possible answers: doctor, journalist, shop assistant, teacher

Exercise 8
Phrases in the text: Bea always gets up early; she usually gets up late and has a big breakfast
More everyday activities: clean your teeth, get ready (for school), go to bed, go to sleep, make breakfast/lunch/dinner, prepare your bag, wake up, watch TV

This is Bea. Her name's Bea Barker and she's fifteen. Penny is her mum. She's a Drama teacher and <u>she works</u> in a college. Bea's mum is funny and kind, and <u>she likes</u> gardening.

On school days <u>Bea</u> always <u>gets up</u> early. She doesn't usually <u>eat</u> much for breakfast, but at weekends <u>she</u> usually <u>gets up</u> late and <u>has</u> a big breakfast.

<u>She spends</u> a lot of time with her friends: cousin Abe, Carla and Eren.

Carla is Bea's best friend. <u>Bea</u> never <u>feels</u> sad when <u>she talks</u> to Carla. <u>She chats</u> to her almost every day.

In her free time <u>Bea does</u> sport. <u>She enjoys</u> walking in the park with her mum and <u>she writes</u> a nature blog. <u>She wants</u> to be a scientist or a journalist.

1 ▶ 2 🔊 0.4 Watch or listen and find these things in the text.
1 a surname 2 three jobs 3 a meal
4 a place you can go to in your free time

2 Study the Grammar box. Find examples of the Present Simple in the text.

GRAMMAR	Present Simple with adverbs of frequency
+	**–**
I live in a small town. She works in a school.	I don't live in a big city. She doesn't teach Maths.
?	
Do you read a lot? Does she get up early?	Yes, I do./No, I don't. Yes, she does./No, she doesn't.

Always, usually, often, sometimes and *never* go before most verbs but after the verb *to be*.
I usually get up early. I'm never late for school.

3 Choose the correct option. Then write Bea's answers to the questions.
1 What do /(does) your mum do?
   She's a Drama teacher – she works in a college.
2 How do /(does) your mum spend her free time?
3 (Do)/ Does you get up early at weekends?
4 Who (do)/ does you like spending time with?
5 How often (do)/ does you chat with your best friend?
6 What (do)/ does you do in your free time?

4 In pairs, ask and answer the questions in Exercise 3.

5 Complete the sentences with the Present Simple form of the verbs in brackets.
1 We *don't go* (not go) to school on Saturdays.
2 Bea and Carla _____ (often/be) together.
3 Bea's mum _____ (never/get up) after 8 a.m.
4 _____ (you/live) in a big house?
5 Bea _____ (not see) Eren every day.
6 Bea _____ (always/write) her blog in her room.

6 🔊 0.5 Study the Vocabulary box. In pairs, add as many words as you can to the box.

VOCABULARY	Jobs
chef   farmer   hairdresser   mechanic   nurse   scientist

7 In pairs, describe a job from the Vocabulary box. Your partner has to guess what job it is.
A: *This person works in a hospital with doctors.*
B: *A nurse.*

8 🔊 0.6 **WORD FRIENDS** Find examples of the phrases below in the text in Exercise 1. Can you add more everyday activities?

chat to/meet/see/spend time with friends   do homework
get dressed   get home   get up early/late   go out
go to school   have a shower   have breakfast/lunch/dinner

9 In pairs, describe a school day. Use the phrases in Exercise 8 to help you.
I always wake up at six o'clock.

YOUR WORLD

10 In pairs, describe the people in your house. What do they do? What's their routine?

Unit 0   8

For the teacher
• Teaching notes, page 156

For the student
• Workbook, page 3

On the Portal
• Workbook: Lesson 0.2

20

0.3 Introducing Eren
Clothes and accessories | Present Continuous

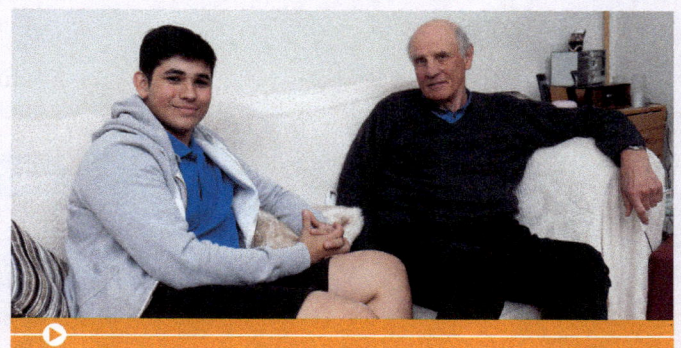

This is Eren King. He lives near his new best friend, Abe. And this is Eren's grandad, Frank. He's staying with Eren and his family at the moment. They get on really well. Eren loves his other grandparents too, but they live in Turkey, so he doesn't see them often.

Eren's grandad has got a great sense of style! They're both wearing similar colours today. Grandad's wearing his favourite bright shirt and grey jumper. Eren's wearing his favourite hoodie and his dad's watch. At the moment, Grandad's feeling relaxed because he's watching TV.

Tennis is one of Eren's favourite sports. He is planning to enter a tennis competition soon, so he's practising nearly every day at the moment. He's a bit nervous about it. He really wants to win!

1 Look at the photo. Do you think these two people get on well? Why?/Why not?

2 ▶ 3 ◀) 0.7 Watch or listen and mark the sentences T (true) or F (false).
1 [F] The man in the photo is Eren's father.
2 [T] Both people in the photo are wearing their favourite clothes.
3 [F] The watch belongs to Eren.
4 [T] Eren doesn't live in Turkey.
5 [F] Eren is planning to play more online games.
6 [T] Eren often plays tennis.

3 ◀) 0.8 Study the Vocabulary box. Which clothes and accessories from the box can you see in the photo?

> **VOCABULARY** Clothes and accessories
>
> baseball cap   earrings   hoodie   jacket   jumper   school uniform   watch

4 **I KNOW!** In pairs, add as many words as you can to the Vocabulary box.

5 Study the Grammar box. Find examples of the Present Continuous in the text.

> **GRAMMAR** Present Continuous
>
> **+**
> I'm wearing a watch.
> He's watching TV.
> They're staying with us.
>
> **–**
> I'm not wearing a cap.
> He isn't watching a film.
> They aren't staying in the UK.
>
> **?**
> Are you feeling relaxed?
> Is she wearing a skirt?
>
> Yes, I am./No, I'm not.
> Yes, she is./No, she isn't.

6 Order the words to make questions. Then answer the questions about you.
1 you / are / sleeping / ?
2 are / wearing / trainers / you / ?
3 the students / are / working hard / ?
4 sending / text messages / your friend / is / ?

7 Study the Speaking box. In pairs, add as many words to describe feelings as you can to the box.

> **SPEAKING** Talking about feelings
>
> How do you feel?
> I'm annoyed/bored/excited/frightened/nervous/relaxed/tired.

8 ◀) 0.9 Listen to a dialogue and answer the questions.
1 How does Max feel about the tennis match?
2 What is Max's problem?

9 In pairs, talk about how you feel before an exam/on your birthday/on holiday/after a party.  YOUR WORLD

Exercise 4
Possible answers: boots, coat, dress, jeans, shirt, shoes, shorts, sweater, top, tracksuit, trainers, trousers, T-shirt

Exercise 6
1 Are you sleeping? Yes, I am./No, I'm not.
2 Are you wearing trainers? Yes, I am./No, I'm not.
3 Are the students working hard? Yes, they are./No, they aren't.
4 Is your friend sending text messages? Yes, he/she is./No, he/she isn't.

Exercise 7
Possible answers: embarrassed, happy, interested, surprised, worried

Exercise 8
◀) audioscript page 242
1 He's excited about the match.
2 He wants to go to the party, but he doesn't want to feel tired for his match.

9 | Unit 0

For the teacher
- Teaching notes, page 157
- Audioscript, page 242

On the Portal
- Vocabulary Memory Game

For the student
- Workbook, page 4

On the Portal
- Workbook: Lesson 0.3

0.4 Introducing Carla

Countries and languages | *Was/were* | *There was/were* | Past Simple: regular verbs

Exercise 1
Countries: China, France, Germany, Italy, Poland, Spain, Turkey
Languages: Chinese, French, German, Italian, Polish, Spanish, Turkish

Exercise 2
Possible answers: Brazil, Japan, Mexico, Sweden, the USA

Exercise 5
Possible answers:
She can speak Spanish well.
She's having Portuguese lessons.
She's into keeping fit.
She enjoys singing.
She loves acting.
She wants to be an actor.

Exercise 7
🔊 audioscript page 242
1 She visited Poland.
2 She stayed with her cousin.
3 They walked (along the beach) (every day).
4 She learned (some) German.

This is Carla Silva. She's Bea's best friend.

Carla's dad's from [Brazil] and her mum's half Spanish. Carla was born in [the UK], so she speaks English most of the time. And she talks a lot, by the way! She speaks Spanish well and last summer she visited her mum's family in [Spain]. Carla can understand Portuguese, but she doesn't speak it very well, so she's having lessons. Carla is really into keeping fit. At the moment she's doing an online fitness class with Bea. She was surprised the first time she did a fitness class because she didn't think online lessons were hard work. Luckily, the classes are great fun.

Carla loves trying new things. She likes singing, so she tried singing lessons, but the lessons weren't easy and they didn't help her! She loves acting and she wants to be an actor.

1 🔊 0.10 Copy the Vocabulary box. Add the words below to the correct groups in the box. Listen and check.

China	Chinese	France	French	German
Germany	Italian	Italy	Poland	Polish
Spain	Spanish	Turkey	Turkish	

VOCABULARY Countries and languages

Countries	Languages
Brazil/Portugal	Portuguese

2 **I KNOW!** In pairs, name as many countries as you can.

3 ▶ 4 🔊 0.11 Watch or listen. Find three countries and three languages in the text.

4 What languages do you and your family speak? Tell the class.
My dad speaks Spanish and a little French.

5 Read the text again, then cover it. Write three things about Carla.

6 Study Grammar box A. Complete the sentences below with *was/were* or *wasn't/weren't*.

GRAMMAR A *Was/were, there was/were*

+	–
She was on holiday.	She wasn't on holiday.
We were on holiday.	We weren't on holiday.
There was a party.	There wasn't a party.
There were lots of people.	There weren't lots of people.

?	
Was it fun?	Yes, it was./No, it wasn't.
Were they at home?	Yes, they were./No, they weren't.
Was there a party?	Yes, there was./No, there wasn't.
Were there many people?	Yes, there were./No, there weren't.

1 The weather *was* terrible when we ___were___ in Spain.
2 A: ___Were___ you at the cinema last night?
   B: No, I ___wasn't___.
3 The film festival ___was___ fun and there ___were___ lots of films to watch. It was great!
4 ___Were___ your parents angry when you ___were___ late home?
5 A: ___Was___ the English test difficult?
   B: Yes, it ___was___. There ___were___ lots of difficult exercises.

7 🔊 0.12 Study Grammar box B. Listen and answer the questions.

GRAMMAR B Past Simple: regular verbs

+	–
She lived in Rio.	They didn't invite him.

?	
Did they like the film?	Yes, they did./No, they didn't.

1 Which country did the girl visit last year?
2 Who did she stay with?
3 What did they do on the beach?
3 What language did the girl learn?

YOUR WORLD

8 In pairs, tell your partner about three or four things that were true for you last year but are not true now.

For the teacher
• Teaching notes, page 157
• Audioscript, page 242

For the student
• Workbook, page 5

On the Portal
• Workbook: Lesson 0.4

0.5 Revision

1. In pairs, describe the photo. Make as many sentences as you can. How do you think the friends are feeling?

2. 🔊 0.13 Listen and mark the sentences T (true) or F (false).
   1. [T] The friends are sitting in the garden because the weather is nice.
   2. [F] New Park has lots of things for young people to do.
   3. [T] Bea is planning to visit her family in Bath.
   4. [F] Eren's got a Maths test that he isn't happy about.

3. Complete the quiz questions with one word in each gap.

4. In groups, do the quiz in Exercise 3. Use the texts in Lessons 1–4 to help you. How much can you remember?

5. **YOUR WORLD** In pairs, write two similar quiz questions about you. Give the questions to your teacher and have a class quiz with two teams.

The big character QUIZ

1. Where **do** Abe, Bea, Eren and Carla live?
2. Who **is** staying with Eren?
3. Where **does** Carla's dad come from?
4. **Is** Abe's dad British?
5. What **is** Bea's mum's name?
6. **Who** lived in America last year?
7. **What** is Eren's favourite sport?
8. **Was** Carla born in the UK?
9. Who **does** Bea chat to almost every day?
10. **Where** did Carla travel to last year?
11. **Does** Bea write a sports blog?
12. **Did** Abe's mum stay in the USA?

Exercise 2
🔊 audioscript page 242

Exercise 4
1. in New Park
2. his grandad, Frank
3. Brazil
4. Yes, he is.
5. Penny
6. Abe
7. tennis
8. Yes, she was.
9. Carla
10. Spain
11. No, she doesn't. She writes a nature blog.
12. Yes, she did.

For the teacher
- Teaching notes, page 157
- Audioscript, page 242

For the student
- Workbook, page 5

On the Portal
- Workbook: Lesson 0.5

Tech check 1

VOCABULARY
Technology | Using technology | Social media | Opposites | Time

GRAMMAR
Present Simple and Present Continuous, state verbs | Verb + -ing, verb + to-infinitive

Grace's tech blog

Everyday essentials?

One of the most important gadgets in our house is the remote control. It's old technology, but in our family everybody wants to choose the channel.

In the shower I listen to music on a waterproof speaker. This is a great gadget, but I want a waterproof bathroom TV so I can watch music videos, too! But is that essential? No.

Then there's the problem of passwords. I have so many, I sometimes forget them. It's a nightmare! So I use a password app to help me remember them all. That's pretty important.

My personal favourites at the moment are my new wireless earbuds. I posted a review and uploaded some pictures of them on my blog, so have a look! I listen to music all the time, so this is the tech I can't live without!

My final choice is for my family. We all love our new smart speaker. Mum uses the voice assistant to ask for food recipes and I enjoy asking it to play music. Luckily, it is connected to the wi-fi router, so we don't have to use our data because my little sister can't stop talking to it. Unfortunately, her favourite command is 'Tell me a joke!'

Do you agree with my choices? Let me know your tech essentials.

1.1 Vocabulary
Lifestyle

Exercise 1
(wireless) ear buds, smart speaker, remote control

1 Look at the photos. What do you think is happening in each one? Find three items of technology in the photos.

2 Read the article. Do you agree with Grace's choices?

Unit 1   12

For the teacher
- Teaching notes, page 158
- Audioscript, page 242
- Videoscript, page 242

On the Portal
- Vocabulary Memory Game
- Photocopiable activity: *Social media word friends*
- Test: Vocabulary Check 1

For the student
- Workbook, pages 6–7

On the Portal
- Workbook: Lesson 1.1
- Extra Practice Activities: Vocabulary, BBC Vox Pop

3 🔊 1.1 Study the Vocabulary box and check you understand the words. Which is your number one essential item?

> **VOCABULARY** ▶ Technology
>
> charging cable   password app   power bank
> remote control   smart speaker   wi-fi router
> wireless earbuds

4 **I KNOW!** In pairs, add as many words as you can to the Vocabulary box.

5 🔊 1.2 Listen and guess the objects. Listen again and check.

6 In pairs, think of two gadgets or items of technology for each adjective. Which object would be the best present for you? Why?

> awesome   essential   old-fashioned   terrible   useful

I'd like to have a smart speaker because it's really useful, so my family would like it too.

7 🔊 1.3 **WORD FRIENDS** Match phrases 1–6 with icons A–F. Listen and check.

1. D connect to the wi-fi router
2. C search for information online
3. B send/share a link
4. E set a new password
5. A take a screenshot
6. F upload pictures

8 🔊 1.4 Listen to five people talking. Write down the phrases from Exercise 7 you hear.

9 🔊 1.5 **WORD FRIENDS** Check you understand the phrases below. Then choose the correct option in sentences 1–7 below. Listen and check. In pairs, say if the sentences are true for you.

> add someone to a group
> chat with friends
> connect with someone on social media
> delete a post/photo
> follow someone on social media
> message someone
> post on social media
> take a selfie
> update your story

1. I *follow* / set my favourite singers and groups on social media.
2. When I have some great news, I search / *update* my story.
3. I spend a lot of time *chatting* / uploading with friends on social media.
4. I can update / *add* people to groups on my social media.
5. I don't often connect / *delete* posts.
6. My brother *posts* / chats things on social media nearly every day!
7. I probably *take* / message a selfie every week.

10 Complete the text with one word in each gap.

> According to a recent study, over eighty percent of teenagers say that social ¹*media* has a positive effect on their lives. It's a great way to ² *chat/connect* with friends, catch up with people's news or connect ³ *with* someone. And it's also incredibly easy. When we search for information ⁴ *online*, we don't often use PCs or laptops any more. Instead, over ninety percent of us use our smartphones to get on the internet. Many people spend three hours a day this way. Think about that next time you want to ⁵ *update* your story. In your life, you might spend about five years online!

VIDEO **WIDER WORLD**

11 ▶ 5 Watch three people talking about technology. What gadgets do they mention?

12 Who in your family uses technology the most? What do they use it for?

My brother uses it the most. He's got a really good smartphone. He uses it for shopping online, watching films and studying.

Exercise 4
Possible answers: digital camera, earphones, games console, phone charger, printer

Exercise 5
🔊 audioscript page 242
1 remote control
2 charging cable
3 password
4 wi-fi router
5 power bank
6 (wireless) earbuds

Exercise 6
Possible answers:
A remote control and a wi-fi router are useful.
A smartphone and a laptop are essential.
A smart speaker and earbuds are awesome!
A TV and a remote control are old-fashioned, but we need them.

Exercise 8
🔊 audioscript page 242
1 connect to the wi-fi router
2 send you a link
3 take a screenshot
4 share a link
5 set a new password

Exercise 11
▶ videoscript page 242
1 computer, iPad, phone
2 computer, tablet, smartphone
3 design programs

I can talk about everyday technology.   13 Unit 1

Exercise 1
The text is about a band (Way In).

Exercise 2
Examples of Present Simple: underlined in red
Examples of Present Continuous: underlined in green
Examples of state verbs: underlined in blue

Exercise 4
1 Does Evy normally write the band's blog? (No, she doesn't. Ziggy does.)
2 Do the band members usually travel on Saturday afternoons? (Yes, they do.)
3 Is the band playing a lot of concerts these days? (Yes, it is./Yes, they are.)
4 Are the skateboarders performing in a competition today? (No, they aren't.)
5 Is Sara wearing a helmet in the photo? (Yes, she is.)
6 Does Sara know lots of awesome tricks? (Yes, she does.)

Exercise 6
▶ videoscript page 242

Holly: yoga, spinning, circuits, step classes (classes at a health club), water skiing
Chee: jogging, strolling, badminton, bouldering, rock climbing, skydiving
Reema: baking, singing
Akshay: baking, eating
Mary: self-defence
Annette: volleyball

1.2 Grammar
Present Simple and Present Continuous, state verbs

Filming in A Skate Park

I'm Evy, Way In's lead singer.
People often ask us questions about our lives:

'Do you write the band's blog?'
I don't normally write it. Ziggy does. But he's busy, so I'm doing it today.

'What do you normally do on Saturdays?'
On Saturday afternoons we often travel from one city to the next. Then, in the evening, we usually play live in concert. We're playing a lot of concerts these days! It's good to be popular!

'What are you doing today?'
We're not playing music and I'm not singing. We're filming our new music video in a skate park. The skateboarders are doing some amazing things. One girl, Sara, knows lots of awesome tricks! I love her style!

1 🔊 1.6 In pairs, look at the photo and the title of the text. What do you think the text is about? Read it and check your guesses.

2 Study the Grammar box. Find examples of the Present Simple, Present Continuous and state verbs in the text.

GRAMMAR | Present Simple and Present Continuous, state verbs

Present Simple
They usually travel on a tour bus.
She doesn't write the blog every day.
Do they speak English? Yes, they do.

Present Continuous
He's travelling a lot these days.
They aren't recording a song at the moment.
Is he skateboarding now? No, he isn't.

State verbs
Some verbs don't normally have a continuous form:
love, like, hate, know, think, see, feel, understand, want, need

GRAMMAR TIME > PAGE 126

3 🔊 1.7 Choose the correct option. Listen and check.
1 Ziggy and Evy sit / are sitting on a bench at the skate park at the moment.
2 Evy usually sings / is singing in concerts on Saturday evenings.
3 The band members don't often visit / aren't often visiting skate parks.
4 The skateboarders do / are doing some fantastic skateboard tricks now.
5 Sara always wears / is always wearing her lucky helmet.
6 Several people film / are filming the skateboarders.

4 Make questions about the text. Use the Present Simple or Present Continuous. Then ask and answer the questions in pairs.
1 Evy / normally / write / the band's blog / ?
2 the band members / usually / travel / on Saturday afternoons / ?
3 the band / play / a lot of concerts / these days / ?
4 the skateboarders / perform / in a competition / today / ?
5 Sara / wear / a helmet in the photo / ?
6 Sara / know / lots of awesome tricks / ?

5 Complete the text with the Present Simple or Present Continuous forms of the verbs in brackets.

My name's Sara. I ¹*love* (love) skateboarding – I'm a real fan. I ² *practise* (practise) at a local park every weekend. I ³ *don't often do* (not often/do) competitions because I'm from a small town. I'm very excited today because I ⁴ *am performing* (perform) in a music video for *Way In*. At the moment we're ⁵ *getting* (get) ready. Lots of people ⁶ *are coming* (come) into the park now. My mum and dad ⁷ *are sitting* (sit) near the front because they ⁸ *want* (want) to take photos and upload them for their friends!

VIDEO ▶ WIDER WORLD

6 ▶ 6 Watch six people talking about the sports and hobbies they enjoy. Write down as many sports/hobbies as you can.

7 In pairs, talk about your favourite sports and hobbies.

Unit 1 | 14 | I can use different tenses to talk about the present.

For the teacher
• Teaching notes, page 159
• Need support? worksheet, page 232
• Videoscript, page 242

On the Portal
• Grammar presentation
• Photocopiable activity: Find someone who …
• Test: Grammar Check 1

For the student
• Workbook, page 8
• Grammar Time, Student's Book, page 126

On the Portal
• Workbook: Lesson 1.2
• Extra Practice Activities: Grammar, BBC Vox Pop

1.3 Reading and Vocabulary
Science competitions and projects

A

Help the world, win a prize and have fun!

Our Science and Technology Group (STG) is hoping to win this year's National Science Competition and we need your help.

This is a competition for young people aged 11–16. It takes place every year. The participants look for tech answers to important problems. The winners can get a prize of up to £25,000 for their school or youth group.

Here are some ideas we are thinking about:
- an easy-to-use remote control for older people
- using technology to help an animal in danger
- a robot dolphin that cleans plastic from the sea

If you like Science and Technology, come and join us, and help us win the prize.

Kieran Malone, STG

B

Hi Angie,

I've got an idea for our end-of-term Science project. I'd like to help animals that are in danger – all sorts of animals, not just cute ones. I found some <u>cool</u> activity sheets online. They don't seem <u>complicated</u>. One of them shows how to make bat boxes – <u>safe</u> homes for bats. Yes, bats! They look a bit <u>strange</u>, but they're really <u>interesting</u> animals. I know we're studying for our final exams right now, but I'm really excited about the Science project. So, come on! Let's make a bat box!

Lorraine

C

Hi Lorraine,

That's a <u>fun</u> idea, and it's <u>original</u>, too. You're so <u>clever</u> (but you know that, don't you?)! My grandfather makes bird boxes, so he could help us make an <u>excellent</u> bat box. And we could put a small waterproof camera in the box to film the bats! What do you think?

Angie

---

1 In groups, discuss the questions.
1. Do you ever do Science projects at your school? What are they like?
2. Would you like to take part in a national Science competition? Why?/Why not?

2 🔊 1.8 Read the texts quickly. Who is writing about:
1. a Science competition? *Kieran*
2. a school Science project? *Lorraine and Angie*

3 Read the texts and answer the questions.
1. What group is Kieran part of?
2. What does the group want to participate in this year?
3. How old are participants in the competition?
4. What is the maximum prize in the competition?
   B and C
5. What animals does Lorraine want to help?
6. What are Lorraine and Angie studying for at the moment?
7. Who is Angie thinking of asking for help?
8. What does Angie suggest putting in the box?

4 🔊 1.9 Complete the Vocabulary box. Find the opposites of the adjectives below in the texts.

VOCABULARY	Opposites
boring	– <u>cool</u>, ¹<u>interesting</u> ²<u>original</u>, ³<u>fun</u>
dangerous	– ⁴<u>safe</u>
easy	– ⁵<u>complicated</u>
normal	– ⁶<u>strange</u>
stupid	– ⁷<u>clever</u>
terrible	– ⁸<u>excellent</u>

5 In groups, think of examples of these things.
- a strange animal
- an interesting book
- a fun game
- an original idea
- a complicated game
- a safe place
- an excellent TV show
- a clever person

6 Complete the entry form for a Science project. Include a short description of the project. Then, in pairs, talk about your project idea.

YOUR WORLD

Science project – Entry form
Name: _____   School: _____
Age: _____   Project: _____

EXAM

Exercise 3
International Certificate Level 1/2, Reading, Section 6, (open-ended question)

Exercise 3
1. Science and Technology Group/SGT
2. National Science Competition
3. 11–16
4. £25,000
5. bats/animals that are in danger
6. their final exams
7. her grandfather
8. a (waterproof) camera

I can understand a message and an email about Science competitions and projects.   15 Unit 1

For the teacher
- Teaching notes, page 160
- *Need support?* worksheet, page 232

On the Portal
- Vocabulary Memory Game
- Photocopiable activity: *Match and create*
- Test: Vocabulary Check 1

For the student
- Workbook, page 9

On the Portal
- Workbook: Lesson 1.3
- Extra Practice Activities: Vocabulary

1.4 Grammar

Verb + -ing, verb + to-infinitive

VIDEO ▶ THE VIDEO CALL

Bea: Hello, Abe. Is now a good time to talk?
Abe: It's fine, but I need to pack while I'm talking. We need to go to the airport soon.
Bea: OK, sooo I just waaanted to cheeeck …
Abe: Bea, I can't see you. And there's something wrong with your sound.
Bea: Hang on. Is that better?
Abe: Yes, that's better. I can see and hear you now.
Bea: Great! That beach background looks amazing!
Abe: Good! My room's a mess at the moment. Look. Do you prefer seeing the beach?
Bea: No, I don't mind seeing your room. Did you remember to … ?
Abe: What's that noise?
Bea: It's Mum. Can you stop vacuuming? Mum? I'm trying to talk to Abe! Sorry about that, Abe.
Abe: No worries. I'm really looking forward to seeing you in person.
Bea: Me too. And don't forget to bring me that basketball shirt.
Abe: Of course. Look, I'm packing it now.
Bea: Fantastic! Thanks, Abe. See you in the UK soon. Safe journey!

Exercise 2
Possible answers: Bea wants Abe to remember to bring her a basketball shirt. There are problems with the video call: the sound doesn't work well, and her mum is making too much noise.

Exercise 3
Examples of verb + -ing: underlined in red
Examples of verb + to-infinitive: underlined in blue

1 Look at the photo. What do you think Abe is doing? Why?

2 7 🔊 1.10 Watch or listen. What does Bea want Abe to do? What problems does she have?

3 Study the Grammar box. Find more examples of verbs followed by -ing or to-infinitive in the dialogue.

GRAMMAR Verb + -ing, verb + to-infinitive

Verb + -ing
After: avoid, can't stand, enjoy, finish, look forward to, (not) mind, miss, practise, stop; after prepositions
I don't mind seeing your room.
She is tired after driving the whole night.

Verb + to-infinitive
After: agree, allow, ask, choose, decide, forget, hope, learn, need, offer, plan, remember, try, want, would like/love
I'm trying to talk to Abe.

Verb + -ing or to-infinitive
After: like, love, hate, prefer, start
Do you prefer seeing/to see the beach?

GRAMMAR TIME ▶ PAGE 126

4 Choose the correct option. In which sentence are both options correct?
1 Are you planning *getting* / *to get* a new smartphone soon?
2 I love my Science project and would like *being* / *to be* a scientist.
3 I like *thinking* / *to think* of new passwords. I can be creative!
4 We're planning *watching* / *to watch* a sci-fi film tonight.
5 We're packing to go on holiday. We enjoy *going* / *to go* to new places.
6 Freddie misses *seeing* / *to see* his friends from his old school.

5 Complete the text with the correct form of the verbs below.

chat check look see share use

Top tips for video calls

Most people love [1] *chatting* to family and friends via video calls, but what about online lessons? You want to make a good impression, so don't forget [2] *to check* the microphone before you join a new video call. Have the camera at eye level and learn to [3] *to look* straight at it some of the time.

Maybe you don't mind [4] *seeing* untidy rooms, but it's a good idea to check that the room behind you is tidy. Finally, if you enjoy [5] *using* different backgrounds, make sure you choose them carefully. That's especially important if you plan [6] *to share* your screen during the call.

YOUR WORLD

6 In pairs, write some tips on how to use a gadget.

Unit 1 16 I can use verbs followed by the -ing form and/or the to-infinitive.

For the teacher
- Teaching notes, page 161

On the Portal
- Grammar presentation
- Photocopiable activity: *I'm the same as you!*
- Test: Grammar Check 1

For the student
- Workbook, page 10
- Grammar Time, Student's Book, page 126

On the Portal
- Workbook: Lesson 1.4
- Extra Practice Activities: New Park video, Grammar

1.5 Listening and Vocabulary
Are you technology crazy?

Do you need a digital detox?

1. **When do you first check your phone?**
   a in the evening
   b probably at lunchtime
   c the minute I wake up
2. **When is it too late to message somebody?**
   a after 10 p.m. on a weekday
   b at midnight
   c It's never too late.
3. **What do you do when you have a free moment?**
   a I listen to music.
   b I read a book.
   c I go online.
4. **How often do you check your messages?**
   a Once a day. I don't get many.
   b At school. I check them at break time.
   c I check them all the time.

1 Do you think you spend too much time looking at screens?

2 Do the quiz and compare your results. Then go to page 142 to read what your answers say about you.

3 🔊 1.11 Study the Vocabulary box and complete the gaps with words from the quiz. Listen and check.

> **VOCABULARY** Time
>
> second, ¹*minute*, hour
> 6 a.m., ²*10/ten p.m.*
> in the morning/afternoon/³*evening*
> on a school day/⁴*a weekday* /Sunday(s)
> at the weekend/⁵*midnight* /mealtimes/lunchtime/
> ⁶*break time*
> ⁷*once* /twice/three times a day/week/
> month/year

4 Ask and answer the questions in pairs. Compare your ideas with the class.
1. What's your favourite mealtime? Why?
   I love lunchtime because I eat with my friends.
2. What time do you go to bed at the weekend?
3. How many seconds are there in five minutes?
4. What time do you get up on a school day?
5. What do you normally do at break time?
6. What do you do 'the minute' you wake up?

5 🔊 1.12 Listen to the first part of a radio programme. What is the programme about? Choose the correct answer.
a the number of families that use phones or tablets in their free time
(b) how much time families spend on their phones or tablets

6 🔊 1.13 Listen to the second part of the programme. Match the people to the way they use the technology.
1. *e* Lara
2. *c* Mum
3. *d* Dad
4. *a* Lara's brother
5. *b* Everyone

a looks at funny video clips and laughs.
b often shares photos.
c reads the news on a tablet.
d downloads and uses running apps.
e uses the phone alarm and checks messages.

Exercise 5
🔊 audioscript page 242

EXAM
Exercise 6
🔊 audioscript page 243
A2 Key for Schools, Listening, Part 5, (matching)

YOUR WORLD

7 How important is technology in your life? What technology do you use and what do you like doing with it? Write five sentences.
Technology is important. It's useful because I can go online, do my homework and chat with friends. In my free time I use technology to listen to music, …

I can understand a radio programme about using technology.

For the teacher
- Teaching notes, page 162
- *Need support?* worksheet, page 232
- Audioscript, pages 242–243

On the Portal
- Photocopiable activity: *What do you do?*

For the student
- Workbook, page 11

On the Portal
- Workbook: Lesson 1.5
- Extra Practice Activities: Vocabulary

1.6 Speaking
Problem-solving

VIDEO ▶ **LET'S GIVE IT A TRY**

Bea: What's that?
Abe: It's the router! Great, let's install it! Um, where do you think you plug it in?
Bea: By the front door! The same place as in my house. There!
Abe: Right, it should be working now. We could upload that new video on my vlog to see if the router works. Come on!

A few minutes later

Abe: The internet is working, but it's so slow. Look, the page is still loading!
Bea: Maybe the signal's too weak? I know there are apps … to test the wi-fi. Why don't we download one?
Abe: Yes, let's give it a try.
Bea: Hmm, the signal's really weak in here!
Abe: Yeah, there's no way I can play video games here. Shall we check the other rooms?
Bea: Yes, what about the kitchen?
Abe: That's a good idea.
Bea: The signal's a bit better here. Look, it's getting stronger!
Abe: What about here?
Bea: Not out there! You can't play video games outside!
Abe: But it's not raining … today!

SOUNDS GOOD! • Come on! • Not out there!

Exercise 3
🔊 audioscript page 243

Possible answers:
1 Why don't you charge it?
2 Let's look for it.
3 What about downloading another one?
4 We could look online for an English version.

1 ▶ 8 🔊 1.14 Look at the photo. What are Abe and Bea doing? Watch or listen and check.
They are installing the new router.

2 Study the Speaking box. Find examples of the phrases in the dialogue.

SPEAKING — Problem-solving

Describing the problem
The internet is working, but it's slow.
Where do you think you plug it in?
The signal's really weak in here!

Suggesting solutions
We could upload the video to see if the router works.
Let's install it!   What about looking online?
Why don't we download one?
Shall we check the other rooms?

Accepting or rejecting solutions
(That's a) good/great idea.
Yes, let's give it a try.
You can't play video games outside!

3 🔊 1.15 Listen to four problems and suggest solutions. Use the Speaking box to help you.

SET FOR LIFE
4 What do you usually do when you have a problem with technology?
• Ask your friends for help.
• Search online for solutions.
• Ask an IT specialist for help.

5 In pairs, go to page 142 and follow the instructions.

YOUR WORLD
6 In pairs, think of some problems you can have with technology and suggest solutions.

A: Sometimes it's complicated to download a new app.
B: Yes, I know what you mean, but you can usually find help online.

Unit 1 | 18 | I can describe a problem, suggest solutions and respond to suggestions.

For the teacher
• Teaching notes, page 163
• Audioscript, page 243

On the Portal
• Photocopiable activity: *Help! What should I do?*

For the student
• Workbook, page 12

On the Portal
• Workbook: Lesson 1.6
• Extra Practice Activities: New Park video

1.7 Writing

A description of your daily routine and online hobbies

Post

What are your daily routine and online hobbies?

1 In real life I live in a big flat near the centre of Manchester. In my everyday life I go to Belton School on weekdays. I sometimes go for a run before school. I **also** often play football at the weekend. After school I always do my homework, of course, **and** then I usually go on my laptop.

2 My favourite online hobby is building a virtual world. After school and at the weekend I usually spend a few hours in my online world. It has lots of great places, **but** my favourite is a theme park I'm building on an island. It's very different from Manchester! There are loads of amazing rides. As well as a beautiful beach, there are also lots of trees. I design new rides for about an hour a day. At the moment I'm testing the rides to make sure they work.

3 I enjoy my online hobbies. However, I also really like chatting to friends at school about my theme park plans **because** they have good ideas for new rides. I often take screenshots of my virtual world and I enjoy sharing them on social media **too**. Although it's not a real place, my virtual world is very relaxing, so I look forward to spending time there!

Zak Murphy

1 Read the article quickly. What is Zak writing about?
He's writing about his daily routine and online hobbies.

2 Read the article. Which of the things below does Zak write about in paragraph 1? Which are in paragraphs 2 and 3?
- a [1] daily routines
- b [3] friends
- c [2] an online place
- d [2] hobbies
- e [3] summary

3 Study the Writing box and look at the article again. Complete the sentences to make them true for you.

> **WRITING** — A description of your daily routine and online hobbies
>
> **1** Describe daily routines (real world examples)
> In the morning/Before school ¹_____ .
> In the afternoon/On weekdays ²_____ .
> I usually/often/sometimes/never ³_____ .
>
> **2** Describe online hobbies (virtual world examples)
> My favourite hobby is ⁴_____ .
> After school ⁵_____ .
> At the weekend ⁶_____ .
>
> **3** End your article: show contrast and sum up
> I enjoy my online lifestyle. However, I also really like chatting to friends online.
> Although it's not a real place, my virtual world is very relaxing.
> I look forward to spending time there.

4 Study the Language box. Write the connectors in bold from the article in the correct group.

> **LANGUAGE** — **Connectors**
>
> **Adding similar information**: as well (as), ¹ *also* , ² *and* , ³ *too*
> **Showing contrast**: however, although, ⁴ *but*
> **Giving reasons**: so, ⁵ *because*

5 Write some true sentences about you. Use connectors from the Language box.

WRITING TIME

6 Write an article for your school website describing your daily routine and online hobbies.

1 **Find ideas**
Make notes about:
- your daily routine and habits.
- your online hobbies.
- how you can combine your daily routine with your online hobbies.

2 **Plan**
Organise your ideas into three paragraphs. Use Zak's article to help you.

3 **Write and share**
- Write a draft article. Use the Language box and the Writing box to help you.
- Share your article with another student for feedback.
- Use the feedback from your partner and write the final version of your article.

4 **Check**
- Check language: did you use connectors correctly?
- Check grammar: did you mostly use the Present Simple and adverbs of frequency?

I can write a description of my daily routine and online hobbies.

For the teacher
- Teaching notes, page 164
- *Need support?* worksheet, page 232

On the Portal
- Photocopiable activity: *Correct connectors*

For the student
- Workbook, page 13

On the Portal
- Workbook: Lesson 1.7

Vocabulary Activator

WORDLIST 🔊 1.16

Technology
charging cable (n)
password app (n)
power bank (n)
remote control (n)
smart speaker (n)
wi-fi router (n)
wireless earbuds (n)

Word friends
(using technology)
connect to the wi-fi router
search for information online
send a link
set a new password
share a link
take a screenshot
upload pictures

Word friends
(social media)
add someone to a group
chat with friends
connect with someone on social media
delete a photo
delete a post
follow someone on social media
message someone
post on social media
take a selfie
update your story

Time
6 a.m./6 p.m.
at lunchtime
at mealtimes
at the weekend
hour (n)
in the afternoon
in the evening
in the morning
minute (n)
on a schoolday/Sunday(s)
once/twice/three times a day/week/month/year
second (n)

Opposites
boring – cool, fun, interesting, original
dangerous – safe
easy – complicated
normal – strange
stupid – clever
terrible – excellent

Extra words
awesome (adj)
background (n)
blog (n)
catch up with (v)
channel (n)
charge (v)
choice (n)
choose (v)
command (v)
competition (n)
effect (n)
essential (adj)
gadget (n)
helpful (adj)
icon (n)
impression (n)
install (v)
live in concert
look for (v)
luckily (adv)
microphone (n)
participant (n)
perform (v)
plug in (v)
popular (adj)
practise (v)
pretty (= quite) (adv)
recipe (n)
record a song
robot (n)
Science project (n)
set up (v)
signal (n)
sound (n)
study (n)
style (n)
switch on/off (v)
take place
tech answer (n)
tell a joke
trick (n)
video call (n)
virtual world (n)
vlog (n)
voice assistant (n)
youth group (n)

Exercise 2
Sample answers:
My wireless earbuds are important to me because I can chat to my friends when I go running. I would like wireless earbuds so that I can chat to my friends when I go running.

Exercise 4
1 at the weekend, in the afternoon, in the evening, in the morning
2 on a school day, once/twice a day/week, etc.
3 chat with friends, search for information, follow someone
4 smart speaker, wireless earbuds

Exercise 5
Oo: background, earbuds, laptop, password, smartphone
oO: connect, upload, online

---

1 Complete the sentences with words from the wordlist.
1 I use the <u>remote control</u> to turn on the TV.
2 I can never think of a good password, so I downloaded a useful <u>password app</u>.
3 I took a <u>screenshot</u> of the picture on that webpage with my smartphone.
4 You should <u>set</u> a new password if you want to keep your information safe.
5 Please send me the <u>link</u> to that useful website – I want to check it out.

2 Tick (✓) the correct column for each gadget. Then, in pairs, say which items are important to you and why.

Gadget	I have this.	I would like one or a new one.
wireless earbuds		
power bank		
smart speaker		
wi-fi router		

3 Complete the phrases with words from the wordlist. Then, in pairs, say which things you do.
1 <u>search</u> for information <u>online</u> to help with homework projects
2 <u>chat/connect</u> with family or friends abroad
3 <u>post</u> comments with my opinions on blogs
4 <u>take</u> selfies and upload them on social media
5 <u>follow</u> famous people on social media

4 Use words from the wordlist to find these things.
1 four time phrases that use *the*
2 two time phrases that use *a*
3 two things you can do with and without a computer or phone
4 two objects which can help you to listen to music

5 🔊 1.17 **PRONUNCIATION** Listen to the words below and write them in the correct column according to the word stress.

> background connect earbuds laptop online password smartphone upload

1 Oo	2 oO
background	

6 🔊 1.18 **PRONUNCIATION** Listen, check and repeat.

For the teacher
• Audioscript, page 243

On the Portal
• Photocopiable activities: Find the words, How about you?
• Tests: Unit 1 Test, Unit 1 Writing Test

For the student
• Workbook, pages 14–15

On the Portal
• Workbook: Self-check
• Wordlist
• Extra Practice Activities: Self-check

Revision

Vocabulary

1 Choose the correct option.
1. I get up early *at* / **on** a schoolday.
2. Remember to take the **charging** / *loading* cable for your phone when you go on holiday.
3. Do you *update* / **follow** any famous people on social media?
4. If there's no electricity, *an energy* / **a power** bank can charge your phone.
5. I usually eat a sandwich *in* / **at** lunchtime in school.

2 Write the correct word for each definition.
1. Something you plug into your mobile phone to charge it. _charging cable_
2. You do this to a photo when you remove it from your smartphone. _delete_
3. You do this to pictures when you move them from your phone to your computer or the internet. _upload_
4. Times when you eat breakfast, lunch or dinner. _mealtimes_
5. Put a message on the internet. _post (on social media)_

3 Complete the conversation with the words below.

   add   chat   message   search   ~~send~~   update

A: Hi, Greg. Can you ¹_send_ me today's Maths homework? I don't have it.
B: Sure. The teacher also says we can use a Maths app to do our homework. Maybe we can ²_search_ online for a free app?
A: Well, the app only helps a bit. Maybe we need to ³_message_ Jackie for help. She's good at Maths.
B: That's a good idea. I ⁴_chat_ with her on social media sometimes, but not about homework.
A: She has a group where students help each other with homework. Do you want me to ⁵_add_ you to it?
B: Yes, please. I'll check her homepage now. Maybe she's there because she likes to ⁶_update_ her story in the evening.

Grammar

4 Choose the correct option. Then, in pairs, say which sentences true for you.
1. *I'm usually walking* / **I usually walk** to school.
2. *I'm feeling* / **I feel** happy when I can stay in bed on Saturday morning.
3. **I'm studying** / *I study* a lot at the moment.
4. My best friend **needs** / *is needing* a new phone now.
5. *I learn* / **I'm learning** how to play a new computer game. It's hard!

5 Complete the dialogues with the Present Simple or Present Continuous form of the verbs in brackets.

A
A: What music ¹_does Uncle Ted like_ (Uncle Ted/like)? It's his birthday next week and I ²_don't know_ (not know) what he ³_wants_ (want).
B: He ⁴_listens_ (listen) to a lot of music. Maybe some wireless earbuds?

B
A: You ⁵_aren't doing_ (not do) much right now. Can you help Grandma with her mobile?
B: What ⁶_is she trying_ (she/try) to do?
A: Use social media, but she ⁷_doesn't know_ (not know) how to update her story. She ⁸_wants_ (want) to post a selfie.

6 Complete the technology tips with the correct form of the verbs in brackets. Then, in pairs, put the tips in order from most to least important.

Technology tips

1. Don't agree _to share_ (share) a link without knowing it's safe.
2. Avoid _spending_ (spend) too much time looking at screens.
3. Stop _working_ (work) on your laptop and have a screen break when your eyes feel dry and tired.
4. Practise _using_ (use) a new app before you really need it.
5. Remember _to save_ (save) a document when you finish _working_ (work) on it.

Speaking

7 In pairs, follow the instructions to role play a dialogue about a problem with technology. Then swap roles.
- Student A: ask Student B what the problem is.
- Student B: describe the problem.
- Student A: suggest a solution to Student B's problem.
- Student B: reject the solution.
- Student A: suggest a different solution.
- Student B: accept Student A's new solution and thank him/her.

Dictation

8 🔊 1.19 Listen. Then listen again and write down what you hear.

Exercise 7
Sample answer:
A I can't find my mobile phone anywhere.
B Shall I call you with my phone? We can try to hear it.
A I'm not sure that's a good idea.
B Why not?
A I think I switched it off.
B What about looking in the last place you had it?
A That's a good idea. Thanks!

EXAM

Exercise 8

🔊 audioscript page 243

International Certificate Level 1/2, Listening and Writing, Section 2, (dictation)

BBC CULTURE — Screenagers

UK/USA: how do teenagers use their mobile phones?

Most British teenagers own a mobile phone. These 'screenagers' spend a large part of their day online, looking at screens. They can connect when and where they like with their smartphones and tablets. Apparently, UK teenagers avoid using smartphones to call their friends. Instead, they prefer to watch video clips, play games, share photos and stories, and send instant messages. As for social media, teens like keeping in touch via the latest apps and videos. They leave older websites and apps to their mums and dads! The same applies to teenagers in the USA.

Teenagers may be connected all the time, but there is one place where most UK teenagers can't use their digital devices: school! In the UK there is no law about phone use in schools, but teachers can ban devices from students if necessary. However, not all teachers agree and some even try to use smartphones in class.

A recent British report said that banning smartphones from schools will give students more time for their education. It said that smartphones are a distraction, make students less productive and are bad for learning.

However, in the US it's a different story. Recently, some schools across the US decided to allow students to use smartphones at school. They said that smartphones can be an excellent resource in the classroom. We carry a lot of information in our pockets and this information can be really useful. In these schools, smartphones can definitely make you smarter!

distraction (n) something that stops you thinking clearly
ban (v) not allow something

Exercise 1
Possible answer: people looking at their mobile phones

Exercise 3
1 They avoid using their phones to call friends. They prefer to watch video clips, play games, and share photos and stories. They use the latest apps and videos.
2 They can ban devices from students.
3 No, they don't. (Some even try to use them in class.)
4 Because they can be a useful tool that has access to a lot of information.

---

1 Look at the photo. What can you see?

2 🔊 1.20 **VISIBLE THINKING** In pairs, follow these steps.
   WHAT MAKES YOU SAY THAT?
   1 Study the discussion questions and give your opinion.
      a Are smartphones a necessary part of our lives?
      b Do you think teenagers use smartphones too much?
   2 Read the article and discuss the questions.
      a Do you think it is a good idea to use phones in class? Why?/Why not?
      b Can smartphones make you smarter? How?

3 Read the article again and answer the questions.
   1 How are teenagers in the UK similar to teenagers in the USA?
   2 How can teachers stop students using mobile phones in the classroom?
   3 Do all teachers in the UK stop students from using their smartphones in class?
   4 Why do some teachers in the US want students to use smartphones in class?

4 In pairs discuss the questions.
   1 Are you a 'screenager'? Do you find it hard not to use your phone?
   2 How do you think mobile phones change how people communicate with each other?

For the teacher
- Teaching notes, page 165
- Videoscript, page 243

On the Portal
- Photocopiable activity: Project worksheet: a digital presentation

BBC Disconnecting

5 In pairs, look at the photos. What information do you think they show about phones?

6 ▶ 9 Watch the video. What information are scientists trying to find?
   if smartphones are a serious problem

7 ▶ 9 Watch the video again and choose the correct option.
   1 The professor secretly sends text messages so she can *contact* / *see the stress levels in* people.
   2 Matt and Natalie take a break from *work* / *digital devices*.
   3 Natalie *wanted* / *didn't want* her phone back so soon.
   4 After the break, Matt and Natalie used their phones *as usual* / *less*.

8 In pairs, discuss the questions.
   1 Do you think using technology is a bad habit? Why?/Why not?
   2 Do you think we should take more breaks from technology?

Exercise 6
▶ videoscript page 243

PROJECT TIME

9 In groups of three, prepare a digital presentation about an app. Follow these steps.

1 In groups, choose a learning app. Decide who can find the answers to these questions.
- What can the app help you to do?
- How can you download and use it?
- What are the advantages and disadvantages of using it?

2 Individually, create your part of the presentation.
- Research the information online.
- Create a slide or a few slides to present your information.
- Remember to say where you found the information.

3 In your group, create your presentation.
- Put the slides in order and give each slide a title.
- Write a short summary of your research.
- Check and edit your presentation.
- Practise giving the presentation as a group.

4 Share your presentation with the class.
- Answer other students' questions.
- Listen to the other presentations. Ask questions.

23 BBC

Wild and beautiful
2

VOCABULARY
Word building: weather | Weather and climate | Adverbs of degree | Camping | In the wild

GRAMMAR
Past Simple: regular and irregular verbs | Past Continuous and Past Simple

Rising water

Lorenzo Quinn's sculpture in Venice, Italy, makes us think about the problem of rising sea levels. This isn't because of rain but because of climate change. Rising temperatures have caused ice in the Arctic and Antarctic to melt faster. As a result, more water is entering the oceans. Other cities located near the sea are also affected by global warming. Jakarta in Indonesia and New Orleans in the USA are sinking about five centimetres a year, so they may be under water by 2100. In cities like these, strong winds from storms and hurricanes make flooding worse. Trees can help us to fight climate change. They not only help clean the air, but they also keep places cool during times of drought. When there is heavy rain, tree roots can keep soil in place so that it isn't washed away in floods. For these reasons, we should plant lots of trees each year.

Exercise 1
Possible answers:
Venice is by the sea. There are no cars there, but there are special boats (gondolas). Sometimes seawater covers the streets in the city.

Exercise 2
1 the problem of rising sea levels
2 because of climate change
3 They are sinking about five centimetres a year.
4 They help us fight climate change, keep places cool and keep soil in place so that it isn't washed away during floods.

2.1 Vocabulary
Weather and climate

1 Look at the photo of the sculpture in Venice above. What do you know about Venice, Italy? What do you think is happening to the water there?

2 In pairs, read the article above. Answer the questions.
1 What does the sculpture represent?
2 Why are sea levels higher?
3 What problem do Jakarta and New Orleans share?
4 What are the benefits of planting trees?

Unit 2   24

For the teacher
- Teaching notes, page 166
- Audioscript, page 243

On the Portal
- Vocabulary Memory Game
- Photocopiable activity: *What's the weather like in … ?*
- Test: Vocabulary Check 2

For the student
- Workbook, pages 16–17

On the Portal
- Workbook: Lesson 2.1
- Extra Practice Activities: Vocabulary

3 🔊 **2.1** Study Vocabulary box A and complete the table with the correct nouns. Listen and check.

VOCABULARY A — Word building: weather

Noun	Adjective
cloud	cloudy
fog	foggy
ice	icy
rain	rainy
snow	snowy
storm	stormy
sun	sunny
wind	windy

WATCH OUT!
To describe the weather, we use *it's* + adjective.
It's rainy/foggy/windy.
Rain and *snow* can be verbs too.
It's raining/snowing. It rains/snows here every day.

4 In pairs, describe the weather for two days this week.

On Monday it was cold and rainy. Yesterday it was cloudy and warm.

5 🔊 **2.2** Study Vocabulary box B and complete the sentences below. Listen and check.

VOCABULARY B — Weather

breeze   drought   flood   gale   hurricane   lightning
shower   sunshine   thunder

1 When the wind isn't very strong, it's a *breeze*.
2 You always hear thunder after you see the *lightning*.
3 When water from a river covers the roads, there's a *flood*.
4 It's a bright, warm day with no clouds. There's lots of *sunshine*.
5 There isn't much rain, just a little bit of a *shower*.
6 The wind is really strong. It might be a *gale* or a *hurricane*.

6 🔊 **2.3** **WORD FRIENDS** Complete the phrases with the words below. Check you understand all the phrases. Listen and check.

bad   climate   cold   dry   ~~low~~   rising

1 The weather forecast for today is for:
 a heavy rain/snow.
 b strong winds.
 c high/*low* temperatures.
2 It will be:
 a ten degrees Celsius (10°C).
 b minus five degrees.
 c wet/*dry*.
 d cool/warm.
 e boiling hot.
 f freezing *cold*.
3 The temperature is *rising*/falling.
4 The weather is good/*bad*/fine.
5 This area has a hot/mild/cold *climate*.

7 In pairs, ask and answer questions about the weather.
1 Do you know what the temperature is today?
2 What's the weather like?
3 What's the forecast for this evening/tomorrow/next week?

8 🔊 **2.4** Listen to three weather forecasts. Which city is the warmest at the moment?

Krakow    Barcelona  ✓   Istanbul

9 🔊 **2.4** Listen again to the weather forecasts and complete the gaps. Then, in pairs, compare your answers.
1 Krakow: *cold*, *−2°*, *ice*
2 Barcelona: *sunny*, *warm*, *19°*, *rain*
3 Istanbul: *cloudy*, *fog*, *7°*, *cool*

10 **YOUR WORLD** In pairs, talk about the climate in your country. What kind of weather do you like?

Exercise 6
🔊 audioscript page 243

Exercise 8
🔊 audioscript page 243

I can talk about the weather and climate.   **25**   Unit 2

2.2 Grammar

Past Simple: regular and irregular verbs

Exercise 2
colour: pinkish orange **place:** high mountains by the lake **frequency:** place with the most lightning bolts per square kilometre

Exercise 3
Regular: underlined in red
Irregular: underlined in blue
Because we don't see the past form of the verb – we see its base form.

Exercise 4
2 The lightning scared the sailors in 1595.
3 The storms helped many sailors to find their way.
4 The lightning appeared in the same place again and again.

Exercise 5
2 didn't feel
3 didn't think/ weren't
4 didn't take place

Exercise 7
2 What did Professor Mendes study?
3 When did Marianna go to Lake Maracaibo?
4 How many storms did she see?
5 Where did she put the photos?

Exercise 8
🔊 audioscript page 243

1 Marianna met a scientist/ Professor Mendes.
2 He studied storms.
3 She went there two weeks ago.
4 She saw three storms.
5 She put them on their website.

1 Do you enjoy storms? Why?/Why not?

2 🔊 2.5 Read the article. Find three unusual facts about the colour, place and number of lightning strikes it describes.

3 Study the Grammar box. Find the Past Simple forms of the verbs below in the article. Which are regular? Which are irregular? Why is this hard to decide with negatives and questions?

| create | feel | happen | know | look | mean | move |
| save | see | spot | stay | take | use | want |

GRAMMAR Past Simple: regular and irregular verbs

Regular verbs
It looked pinkish orange.
The storms didn't move.
When did that happen?

Irregular verbs
We saw an unusual storm.
I didn't know what to do.
Did you take any photos? Yes, I did./No, I didn't.

We use the Past Simple with past time expressions,
e.g. yesterday, last week/year; two hours/days/weeks/years ago, in April, in 1595.

GRAMMAR TIME > PAGE 127

4 Rewrite the sentences in the positive form.
  1 The Catatumbo storms didn't happen in Venezuela.
    The Catatumbo storms happened in Venezuela.
  2 The lightning didn't scare the sailors in 1595.
  3 The storms didn't help many sailors to find their way.
  4 The lightning didn't appear in the same place again and again.

5 Rewrite the sentences in the negative form.
  1 The sailors saw green lightning.
    The sailors didn't see green lightning.
  2 The sailors felt excited about the storm.
  3 Sailors thought the Catatumbo storms were normal.
  4 The storms took place over the sea.

6 Complete the sentences with past time expressions to make them true for you.
  1 I saw snow _____ .
  2 We had really bad weather _____ .
  3 We loved the warm weather on our holiday _____ .
  4 I went out in the rain _____ .

Venezuela's special storm

You might find storms fascinating or frightening. But can they be positive? If you live in Venezuela, your answer may be yes!

In 1595 a storm in Venezuela saved the country. How did that happen? Foreign sailors wanted to attack, but they saw strange lightning. It looked pinkish orange, so they didn't know what it was. They felt scared. In the bright light of the storm, soldiers on land spotted the ships.

This took place over Lake Maracaibo on the Catatumbo River. It is an area famous for its special storms. Long ago sailors used storms in the same way as lighthouses: to help them find their way. The geography of the high mountains by the lake created unusual but perfect storm conditions. It meant that the storms didn't move – they stayed in the same place.

Nowadays the Catatumbo Lightning holds a Guinness World Record as the place with the most lightning bolts per square kilometre.

7 Make questions in the Past Simple.
  1 who / Mariana / meet / ?
    Who did Mariana meet?
  2 what / Professor Mendes / study / ?
  3 when / Mariana / go / to Lake Maracaibo / ?
  4 how many storms / she / see / ?
  5 where / she / put / the photos / ?

8 🔊 2.6 For each question in Exercise 7, write the beginning of the answer, with the main verb. Then listen to the interview and complete the answers.
  1 *Mariana met …*

YOUR WORLD

9 In pairs, ask and answer the questions about the last storm you saw.
  1 Where were you?
  2 Did you hear thunder and see lightning?
  3 How did you feel?

Unit 2 26 I can use the Past Simple to talk about past events.

For the teacher
- Teaching notes, page 167
- *Need support?* worksheet, page 233
- Audioscript, page 243

On the Portal
- Grammar presentation
- Photocopiable activity: *When did it happen?*
- Test: Grammar Check 2

For the student
- Workbook, page 18
- Grammar Time, Student's Book, page 127

On the Portal
- Workbook: Lesson 2.2
- Extra Practice Activities: Grammar

2.3 Reading and Vocabulary
Life in a hot place

1 What do you do when it's very hot outside? Add your own ideas.

go outside   have a cold drink   stay inside   wear cool clothes

2 Look at the photo and read the article. What does Miguel like about the place where he lives?

3 Study the two sentences in red in the article. Which one is a fact and which one is an opinion? Find more facts and opinions in the article.

4 🔊 2.7 Read the whole article again and choose the correct answer.
1 Miguel says that the temperature
   a is the same in Beatty and Death Valley.
   b makes you feel tired.
   c is normal for the time of year.
2 The volcano crater was
   a quite cold.
   b really unusual.
   c not very big.
3 One night in the desert Miguel
   a felt worried about something.
   b slept in the open air.
   c saw something special in the sky.
4 According to Miguel, sand dunes
   a look like mountains.
   b can make noises.
   c can be used for sport.
5 Which of the following is an opinion, not a fact?
   a In March or April it's cooler than in summer.
   b Sand can make a noise.
   c The trip was totally awesome.

5 🔊 2.8 Study the Vocabulary box. Find the highlighted phrases in the article and complete the box with the correct adverbs. Listen and check.

VOCABULARY — Adverbs of degree

Adverb + strong adjective	Adverb + regular adjective
¹*absolutely* boiling	⁴*really* boring
²*completely* different	⁵*very* strange
³*totally* awesome	⁶*quite* worried

AMAZING WORLD
On this blog we publish articles about the most amazing places on our planet.

This week's article is by Miguel Garcia.
Miguel is from Beatty, USA, a town next to Death Valley National Park, which has record-breaking high temperatures.

A dangerously hot place

What are summer temperatures like where you live? It's August, so it's forty degrees Celsius in Beatty town and forty-five degrees Celsius in Death Valley, which is absolutely boiling. When you wake up in the morning, your eyes feel dry and you don't want to move because it is hot.

Some people think it's really boring in Death Valley, but I really love outdoor adventures in the desert. We usually go on a camping trip in March or April, when it's cooler than in summer. This year we visited a huge volcano crater, about a kilometre wide. It was amazing, completely different from any other place! They filmed some famous science fiction movies there because it looks like another planet.

The night sky is so clear in the desert that you can see thousands of stars. I wanted to sleep outside, but Dad was quite worried about scorpions, so I couldn't do that. I took some great photos of the Milky Way above us, though.

Did you know that sand can make a noise? On the final day of our trip we visited sand dunes at Mesquite and heard the sound of wind blowing the sand. It was very strange. We also tried sandboarding down the dunes. It's like snowboarding down a mountain, but on the sand. It was my favourite activity on a totally awesome trip.

6 Choose the correct option.
1 Wow! The sand dunes are **absolutely** / very amazing!
2 Your photos are totally / **quite** good.
3 Walking in the heat without a drink is **completely** / very ridiculous!
4 The stars in the desert sky look **really** / totally nice.

7 Make sentences about the things below. Use adverbs of degree and adjectives from Exercises 5 and 6.
1 the place where you live
2 an interesting place to visit near you
3 things you do in summer
4 something you did last weekend

YOUR WORLD
8 Write a blog post about something you did or saw recently that is typical of life in your area.

It was really hot yesterday. My sister and I went to the beach and bought ice cream. …

Exercise 2
Possible answers:
He loves outdoor adventures in the desert. He likes going on camping trips. He enjoys watching stars in the night sky, which is very clear in the desert. He loves sandboarding on the sand.

Exercise 3
The first sentence is a fact. The second one is an opinion.
Other facts – possible answers:
It's August, so it's 40°C in Beatty town and 45°C in Death Valley …
The night sky is so clear in the desert …
… sand can make a noise …
Other opinions – possible answers:
… I really love outdoor adventures in the desert.
It was amazing, completely different from any other place!
It was very strange.
It was my favourite activity on a totally awesome trip.

EXAM
Exercise 4
A2 Key for Schools, Reading and Writing, Part 3, (3-option multiple choice)

I can understand an article about life in a hot place.   27   Unit 2

For the teacher
- Teaching notes, page 168
- Need support? worksheet, page 233

On the Portal
- Photocopiable activity: Very good, absolutely awesome
- Test: Vocabulary Check 2

For the student
- Workbook, page 19

On the Portal
- Workbook: Lesson 2.3
- Extra Practice Activities: Vocabulary

2.4 Grammar
Past Continuous and Past Simple

VIDEO ▶ A CRAZY DAY

Dad: What's that noise? Abe, is that you?
Abe: It's blowing a gale out there. We had a bit of an adventure.
Dad: Really? Here, have a towel. Now go upstairs and put on some dry clothes.
Abe: But Dad, not now! I've taken a super cool photo for my blog. I just need to download and check it. And then post it.
Dad: OK, fine, but put this hoodie on then. I'll make you a nice warm drink. So, tell me about it …
Abe: I was walking in the park with Bea when we met Eren and Carla. They were playing with a frisbee, so I decided to take some photos. The sun was shining and we were having a great time, so we weren't thinking about the weather. Then I noticed some dark storm clouds were getting closer. Eren was throwing the frisbee when suddenly, lightning hit a tree near us, and I took a photo at the same time!
Dad: Here's your hot chocolate. Great photo!
Abe: Thanks, Dad. It started raining hard then, and the wind got stronger too. We realised we weren't safe, so we all ran home.
Dad: Thank goodness you're home. Are your friends OK?
Abe: They're all fine. Yeah, that was completely crazy! Right, time to upload my work.

Exercise 2
Examples of Past Continuous: underlined in red
Examples of Past Simple: underlined in green

Exercise 5
▶ videoscript page 244

Exercise 5
Neal: family – his dad
Cecile: weather – awful, rained (every day)
Affie: transport – flight (airport)
James: family – parents; transport – ferry/ship

1 ▶ 10 ◀)) 2.9 Look at the photo. What do you think happened to Abe? Watch or listen and check. *He got caught in a storm.*

2 Find examples of the Past Continuous and the Past Simple in the dialogue.

GRAMMAR — Past Continuous and Past Simple

Past Continuous
It was raining.
We weren't thinking about the weather.
Were you running? Yes, I was./No, I wasn't.

Past Continuous and Past Simple
Abe downloaded his photo while his dad was making a warm drink.
He was throwing the frisbee when lightning hit a tree.

GRAMMAR TIME > PAGE 127

3 Choose the correct option.
1 We drank / **were drinking** hot chocolate when we **heard** / were hearing the thunder.
2 The rain **started** / was starting while we sat / **were sitting** on the beach.
3 George was travelling on the bus while / **when** he found a phone.
4 I **took** / was taking a lot of photos while I walked / **was walking** in the desert.
5 We were putting up the tent **when** / while the wind got stronger.
6 Daisy **fell** / was falling on the ice while she skated / **was skating** with friends.

4 Complete the extract from an email with the Past Simple or Past Continuous form of the verbs in brackets.

Hi Sara,
How was your History trip? When I was studying History, we ¹*went* (go) on a trip to France. It was spring, but it was freezing cold. One day, the weather suddenly ²*changed* (change) while we ³*were walking* (walk) in the hills. We soon ⁴___*got*___ (get) lost in the fog! Our teachers had to phone for help. While we ⁵*were waiting* (wait), I ⁶___*heard*___ (hear) a strange noise. It was …

VIDEO ▶ WIDER WORLD

5 ▶ 11 Watch four people talking about holidays. Make notes about weather, family and transport.

6 In pairs, talk about funny things that happened on a school trip or holiday. Use the Past Simple and Past Continuous.

Unit 2 **28** I can use the Past Continuous and the Past Simple to talk about past events.

For the teacher
- Teaching notes, page 169
- Videoscript, page 244

On the Portal
- Grammar presentation
- Photocopiable activity: *What were they doing?*
- Test: Grammar Check 2

For the student
- Workbook, page 20
- Grammar Time, Student's Book, page 127

On the Portal
- Workbook: Lesson 2.4
- Extra Practice Activities: New Park video, Grammar, BBC Vox Pop

2.5 Listening and Vocabulary
In the wild

1 Look at the photos. Do you enjoy being outdoors? Why?/Why not? Compare your ideas with the class.

2 🔊 2.10 Listen to an advert for an activity camp and mark the sentences T (true) or F (false).
1. _T_ The camp is a summer camp.
2. _F_ The camp is for families.
3. _T_ The campsites are in different locations.

3 🔊 2.11 **WORD FRIENDS** Complete the phrases with the verbs below. Listen and check.

~~discover~~ listen look make (x2) sleep watch

1. _discover_ unusual plants
2. _sleep_ outside
3. _make_ a shelter
4. _listen_ to the wildlife
5. _watch_ the stars
6. _look_ for wild animals
7. _make_ a fire

4 🔊 2.12 Listen to Poppy talking about Wild Adventure camp and complete her diary with activities from Exercise 3.

Monday: ¹_make a shelter_
Tuesday: ²_make a fire_
Wednesday: ³_look for wild animals_
Thursday: ⁴_watch the stars_
Friday: ⁵_discover unusual plants_

5 🔊 2.12 Listen again and answer the questions.
1. Why didn't Poppy sleep outside in the end?
2. Why didn't she listen to the wildlife?
3. Why weren't there any spiders in the camp?
4. What did Poppy see in the cave?

6 🔊 2.13 Study the Vocabulary box. Write the words from the box in the correct group below. Listen and check.

VOCABULARY ▶ In the wild

bat bear cave leaf path sky spider star
sunset waterfall wildlife

1. Elements of landscape: _cave_ , _leaf_ , _path_ , _sky_ , _star_ , _sunset_ , _waterfall_ , _wildlife_
2. Wild animals: _bat_ , _bear_ , _spider_

7 **I KNOW!** In groups, add more words to each group in Exercise 6. Each word scores a point. Which group wins?

8 Choose the correct option.
1. My favourite season is autumn, when the stars / **leaves** fall off the trees.
2. We walked into the **cave** / waterfall where it was cold and dark.
3. In the distance there was something big and brown. A **bear** / spider was standing and looking at us.
4. At the end of the day, there's an amazing path / **sunset** over the lake.
5. The sun was shining and the **sky** / star was blue – a perfect day to go out on the boat.

9 Choose the correct option to make the sentence true for you. Then write a short paragraph. **YOUR WORLD**
I'd love / I'd hate to go to an adventure camp because …

Exercise 2
🔊 audioscript page 244

EXAM
Exercise 4
🔊 audioscript page 244
International Certificate Level 1/2, Listening, Section 3, (note completion)
A2 Key for Schools, Listening, Part 2, (gap fill)

Exercise 5
1. (Because) it was cold at night (so they slept in tents).
2. (Because) she slept (so) well and didn't hear a thing.
3. (Because) it was too cold for them.
4. (She saw) (hundreds of) bats.

I can understand a conversation about outdoor activities. 29 Unit 2

For the teacher
- Teaching notes, page 170
- *Need support?* worksheet, page 233
- Audioscript, page 244

On the Portal
- Vocabulary Memory Game
- Photocopiable activity: *Categorise and draw*

For the student
- Workbook, page 21

On the Portal
- Workbook: Lesson 2.5
- Extra Practice Activities: Vocabulary

2.6 Speaking
Criticising and explaining

VIDEO ▶ **I CAN EXPLAIN**

Abe: Bea? What are you doing?
Bea: Abe, hi! I'm trying to help Mum with the garden. Can you give me a hand?
Abe: Yeah, no problem. I know you know about gardening, but I don't.
Bea: Don't worry. It's easy. You can take the weeds out of this flower bed. Is that OK?
Abe: Sure.
Bea: You put the weeds in here … See? And these are Mum's favourite flowers, OK? So, be careful. Right, I have to cut the grass.
Abe: Weeds bad, flowers good. Flowers, weeds. Got it.
Later …
Bea: What's going on?
Mum: What's going on? My poor flowers!
Bea: What? I didn't realise … Mum, I can explain.
Mum: Honestly! Why did you do that?
Abe: Aunt Penny? It's my fault. I didn't mean to pick your flowers. I was helping Bea and I thought they were weeds.
Mum: I see. Abe, were you really trying to help?

SOUNDS GOOD! Can you give me a hand? • No problem. • Got it.

Exercise 1
Possible answers: They might enjoy being in the garden. Perhaps they are helping one of the parents. Maybe they are earning some pocket money.

Exercise 2
Possible answer: Abe didn't listen carefully enough, and Bea's instructions weren't clear enough.

Exercise 7
▶ videoscript page 244

1 ▶12 🔊 2.14 Look at the photo and think of reasons why Bea and Abe are working in the garden. Do you think they are enjoying it? Watch or listen and check.

2 Why do you think Abe did the wrong thing?

SET FOR LIFE
3 In groups, discuss the questions.
 1 Why is it important to give clear instructions?
 2 Why is it important to look and listen carefully?

4 Study the Speaking box. Find examples of the phrases in the dialogue.

SPEAKING Criticising and explaining

Criticising
What's going on?
Why did you do that?

Explaining and apologising
I can explain. I'm so sorry. I thought …
I didn't mean to … I didn't realise …

Accepting explanations and apologies
I see. That's all right. Never mind.

5 🔊 2.15 Complete the dialogues with phrases from the Speaking box. Listen and check.
 1 A: Hey, why did you take my seat?
   B: Oh. I *didn't realise* you were sitting there.
 2 A: What's *going on* ? This is my phone!
   B: Oh, sorry!
   A: Never *mind* . It does look like yours!
 3 A: Oh dear! I just shouted at my friends.
   B: *Why did you do* that?
   A: I was angry. I *didn't mean* to hurt their feelings.

6 In pairs, turn to page 142 and follow the role play instructions.

VIDEO ▶ **WIDER WORLD**

7 ▶13 Watch four people talking about problems. Number the problems below in the order the people mention them.
 a [2] climbing a ladder
 b [3] late for work
 c [4] not being serious
 d [1] no money

8 In pairs, tell your partner about a time when you had a problem.

Unit 2 **30** I can criticise and explain when things go wrong.

For the teacher
- Teaching notes, page 171
- Videoscript, page 244

On the Portal
- Photocopiable activity: *I didn't mean to …*

For the student
- Workbook, page 22

On the Portal
- Workbook: Lesson 2.6
- Extra Practice Activities: New Park video, BBC Vox Pop

2.7 Writing

An article describing your local area and climate

ARTICLES WANTED Write about your local area and climate. Email your article to us – we'll put the best ones in our magazine.

Is Lima a good place to visit?

1 <u>Everybody</u> knows Peru has lots of mountains, but Lima, where I live, is on the coast. On many days of the year it's very cloudy here, but it doesn't often rain. Sometimes I think it's very cloudy here, but the climate is just right. For example, it's usually between 15 and 25°C, so it's never boiling hot or freezing cold. Don't come here between June and September, though, as many days are very foggy.

2 In Lima you can find great food and music <u>everywhere</u>. There are lots of activities such as adventure sports too. Last year while my little cousin Jorge was staying with us, we went to the beach at Barraca. My cousin looked up and saw a 'big bird'. At first he was quite worried and then he realised that <u>somebody</u> was paragliding. It looked amazing!

3 If you want to visit <u>somewhere</u> outside Lima, the Palomino Islands are about forty-five minutes away by boat. We took my cousin there in November. The sun was shining and the sea was warm. While we were travelling, some big sea lions swam past! To sum it up, you can have a totally fantastic experience here. There isn't <u>anywhere</u> better!

1 Is your local area a good place to visit? Why?/Why not?

2 Read the advert and article. Would you like to visit Lima? Why?/Why not?

3 Read the article again. Which of these things does it mention and in which paragraph?
  a [2] food and music   d [ ] population
  b [1] location   e [1] weather and climate
  c [3] another place nearby f [2] activities

4 Study the Writing box. Make similar true sentences about the area where you live.

WRITING — An article describing your local area and climate

1 **Describe the area, weather and climate**
  Lima, where I live, is on the coast.
  It doesn't often rain.
  The climate is just right.

2 **Describe typical activities and places**
  You can find great food and music everywhere.
3 There are lots of activities …
  The Palomino Islands are about forty-five minutes away …

Give examples
For example, …   One/An example is …   … , like …
… such as …

5 Study the Language box. Find five indefinite pronouns in the article. Then use indefinite pronouns to write some true sentences about your local area.

LANGUAGE — Indefinite pronouns

People	Things	Places
somebody/-one	something	somewhere
everybody/-one	everything	everywhere
anybody/-one	anything	anywhere

WRITING TIME

6 Write an article for the advert in Exercise 2.

1 **Find ideas**
Make notes about:
• some facts about the weather, climate and things to do where you live.
• a trip you went on. Think about the situation and what you did.

2 **Plan**
Organise your ideas into three paragraphs. Use the article about Lima to help you.

3 **Write and share**
• Write a draft article. Use the Language box and the Writing box to help you.
• Share your article with another student for feedback.
• Use the feedback from your partner and write the final version of your article.

4 **Check**
• Check language: did you use indefinite pronouns correctly?
• Check grammar: did you use the Past Simple and Past Continuous to illustrate your points?

I can write an article about my local area and climate. 31

For the teacher
• Teaching notes, page 172
• *Need support?* worksheet, page 233

On the Portal
• Photocopiable activity: *Tell me anything*

For the student
• Workbook, page 23

On the Portal
• Workbook: Lesson 2.7

Vocabulary Activator

WORDLIST 🔊 2.16

Word building (weather)
cloud (n)
cloudy (adj)
fog (n)
foggy (adj)
ice (n)
icy (adj)
rain (n)
rainy (adj)
snow (n)
snowy (adj)
storm (n)
stormy (adj)
sun (n)
sunny (adj)
wind (n)
windy (adj)

Weather
breeze (n)
drought (n)
flood (n)
gale (n)
hurricane (n)
lightning (n)
shower (n)
sunshine (n)
thunder (n)

Word friends (weather and climate)
boiling hot
degrees Celsius
freezing cold
heavy rain
heavy snow
high/low temperature
hot/mild/cold climate
minus five degrees
strong wind
the temperature is rising/falling
the weather is bad/cool/dry/fine/good/warm/wet

Adverbs of degree
absolutely (boiling) (adv)
completely (different) (adv)
quite (worried) (adv)
really (strange) (adv)
totally (awesome) (adv)
very (boring) (adv)

Word friends (camping)
discover unusual plants
listen to the wildlife
look for wild animals
make a fire
make a shelter
sleep outside
watch the stars

In the wild
bat (n)
bear (n)
cave (n)
leaf (n)
path (n)
sky (n)
spider (n)
star (n)
sunset (n)
waterfall (n)
wildlife (n)

Extra words
adventure (n)
Antarctic (n)
Arctic (n)
bright (adj)
camping trip (n)
conditions (n)
degree (n)
desert (n)
find your way
foreign (adj)
freezing (adj)
grow (v)
huge (adj)
lake (n)
land (n)
lighthouse (n)
local (adj)
melt (v)
Milky Way (n)
mountain (n)
ocean (n)
perfect (adj)
planet (n)
record-breaking (adj)
root (n)
sand dune (n)
scared (adj)
scorpion (n)
sea level (n)
sink (v)
sleep in the open air
soil (n)
special (adj)
treetop (n)
volcano (n)
wash away (v)
weather forecast (n)

Exercise 1
1 boiling/freezing; high/low; hot/cold; bad/good; cool/warm; dry/wet (sunny/rainy is also correct)
2 drought, flood
3 bat, bear, spider
4 cloud, lightning, star (sunshine and sunset are also correct)

Exercise 3
1 The others refer to water/bad weather.
2 The others are moving air.
3 You can see or feel the others./The others are all adjectives.
4 The others are things you can see outside.

Exercise 6
1 perfect
2 amazing, completely
3 absolutely
4 totally

---

1 Use the words from the wordlist to find these things.
  1 six pairs of opposite adjectives
  2 two weather words that refer to too much or too little water
  3 three animals
  4 three things you can see in the sky

2 Match words 1–8 with words a–h to make phrases. In pairs, use the wordlist to check your answers. Then make true sentences using four of the phrases.
  1 *g* low   a a shelter
  2 *f* absolutely   b the stars
  3 *a* make   c Celsius
  4 *b* watch   d weather
  5 *h* sleep   e snow
  6 *e* heavy   f boiling
  7 *c* degrees   g temperature
  8 *d* warm   h outside

3 Choose the odd one out.
  1 rainy   snowy   (sunny)   icy
  2 breeze (rain) wind   gale
  3 cloudy (thunder) rainy foggy
  4 cave (temperature) waterfall leaf

4 Complete the sentences about the weather with words from the wordlist. Then, in pairs, talk about the type of weather you prefer and the type of weather you don't like.
  1 The roads are *icy* today, so please drive carefully.
  2 It's freezing *cold* today, so wear your warmest clothes.
  3 The weather forecast said it will be thirty *degrees* Celsius today. That's hot!
  4 I can hear *thunder*. Can you see any lightning?
  5 The river is *rising* quickly because of all the rain. I hope there won't be a flood.

5 In pairs, make true sentences using strong adjectives and adverbs of degree from the wordlist.
The weather today is absolutely amazing!

6 🔊 2.17 **PRONUNCIATION** Listen to the words below and write them in the correct column according to the word stress.

absolutely   amazing   completely   perfect   totally

1 Oo	2 oOo	3 ooOo	4 Ooo

7 🔊 2.18 **PRONUNCIATION** Listen, check your answers to Exercise 6 and repeat.

Unit 2 **32**

For the teacher
• Audioscript, page 244

On the Portal
• Photocopiable activities: N in everything, Create a story
• Tests: Unit 2 Test, Unit 2 Writing Test

For the student
• Workbook, pages 24–25

On the Portal
• Workbook: Self-check
• Wordlist
• Extra Practice Activities: Self-check

Revision

Vocabulary

1 Choose the word that does NOT go with the noun in bold.
1 dry / cloudy / ~~sunshine~~ / rainy **WEATHER**
2 high / low / rising / ~~fine~~ **TEMPERATURE**
3 absolutely / totally / ~~very~~ / completely **AWESOME**
4 ~~falling~~ / mild / hot / cold **CLIMATE**
5 listen to / discover / ~~sleep~~ / look for **WILDLIFE**

2 In pairs, use phrases from Exercise 1 to say what you like and don't like. Remember: you can make negative sentences too.

3 Complete the words in the email.

Dear students,
This year's Science project is a camping trip. Here are some of the things we want to do:
- look for ¹wi_ld_ animals and birds
- ²di_scover_ unusual plants
- walk an amazing ³pa_th_ around the lake and through the forest
- make a ⁴sh_elter_ that can keep you dry from falling rain
- listen to the sounds of birds and other ⁵wi_ldlife_
- ⁶sl_eep_ outside and watch the ⁷st_ars_

Pack clothes for ⁸ra_iny_, windy and even ⁹st_ormy_ weather. Bring enough clothes to put on dry ones if you get completely wet.
Thank you,
Your Science teachers

4 Complete the definitions with the correct word. Then write two more definitions.
1 _Foggy_ weather is when it is difficult to see because clouds are close to the ground.
2 _Icy_ conditions happen when temperatures below 0°C change water.
3 _Wild_ plants and animals don't live with people.
4 A _leaf_ is the green part of a plant that uses sunshine.

Grammar

5 Choose the correct option.
1 A: I *hear* / ~~heard~~ a bat flying in my room last night.
   B: How did you ~~know~~ / *knew* it was a bat?
2 A: I didn't ~~see~~ / *saw* you at school yesterday.
   B: That's because I *go* / ~~went~~ to the doctor.
3 A: Which places did your parents ~~visit~~ / *visited* in Scotland last summer?
   B: Mostly lakes and mountains. They *stay* / ~~stayed~~ away from the cities.
4 A: Why did Dr Sanchez ~~take~~ / *took* photographs of the volcano?
   B: He *want* / ~~wanted~~ to show them to some colleagues.

6 Make questions in the Past Simple. Then ask and answer the questions in pairs.
1 you / go / for a walk / yesterday / ?
2 you / have / dinner with your grandparents / at the weekend / ?
3 you / sing / songs on your birthday / ?
4 where / you / go / on holiday / last year / ?
5 who / you / chat to / on social media / last night / ?

7 Complete the sentences with the Past Simple or Past Continuous form of the verbs in brackets.
1 My mum _saw_ (see) a bright star when she _____ (watch) the night sky a short time ago.
2 We _____ (walk) home on rainy weather yesterday when we _____ (hear) thunder.
3 While I _____ (do) my homework, my cat _____ (jump) onto my desk.
4 Dad _____ (find) a scorpion in his shoe once when he _____ (camp) in the desert.
5 I _____ (leave) home with an umbrella this morning because it _____ (rain).

Speaking

8 In pairs, turn to page 142 and follow the instructions to role play a dialogue.

Dictation

9 🔊 2.19 Listen. Then listen again and write down what you hear.

Exercise 6
1 Did you go for a walk yesterday?
2 Did you have dinner with your grandparents at the weekend?
3 Did you sing songs on your birthday?
4 Where did you go on holiday last year?
5 Who did you chat to on social media last night?

Exercise 7
1 was watching
2 were walking; heard
3 was doing; jumped
4 found; was camping
5 left; was raining

Exercise 8
Sample answer:
A I'm sorry, I don't want to go on the camping trip.
B That's OK, but why don't you want to go?
A The weather forecast is bad. I don't like heavy rain and I don't want to get wet and sleep outside.
B I see. That's alright. You're right about the weather. Maybe we can go camping in the summer.

EXAM
Exercise 9
🔊 audioscript page 244

International Certificate Level 1/2, Listening and Writing, Section 2, (dictation)

Unit 2

SET FOR LIFE

Stay positive and carry on

A My phone was new a week ago! Aaarrgh!

B Whaaat? Who took my wheels?

C My favourite band are in town, but I can't get a ticket.

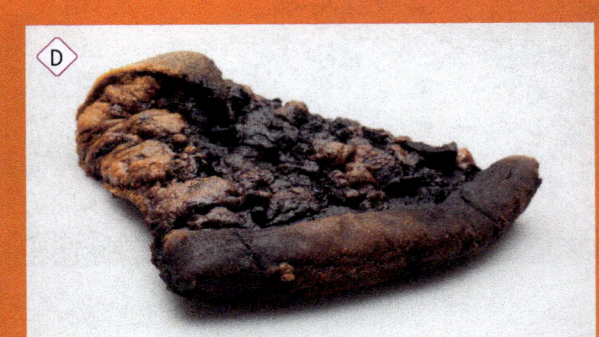

D This is what I got for dinner after football practice finished late!

Exercise 1
Sample answers (photo A):
1 I feel really stressed and sad. My new phone was really expensive, and I loved it. And now it doesn't work!
2 I think situation A is the worst because it's the most expensive problem.

Exercise 2
🔊 audioscript page 244

Exercise 3
1 by bus
2 No, because it's slow.
3 Because he doesn't want to pay for them, and he thinks that someone might take them too.
4 Because he doesn't want it now.

1 Look at the social media posts. In pairs, discuss the questions.
   1 Imagine you are the people in situations A–D. How do you feel? Use the adjectives below to help you.

   angry   annoyed   calm   sad   stressed
   surprised   worried

   2 Which do you think is the worst situation? Why?
   3 Do similar things ever happen to you? Give examples and describe how you felt.

2 🔊 2.20 Listen to Sam and Jess. Which situation from the posts are they talking about? Do they both keep calm?
   The bike (situation B). No, Sam doesn't keep calm.

3 🔊 2.20 Listen again and answer the questions.
   1 How does Jess think Sam can go to school?
   2 Does Sam like Jess's idea? Why?/Why not?
   3 Why doesn't Sam want to buy new wheels for his bike?
   4 Why does he want to leave the bike outside the library?

4 Choose the sentences (a or b) that best describe Sam's attitude.
   1 (a) He focuses on his bad luck.
      b He focuses on things that he can do to improve the situation.
   2 (a) He imagines bad things that aren't likely to happen.
      b He only thinks about the facts and things that are likely to happen.
   3 a He remembers that some other people's problems are more serious than his.
      (b) He can't see that his problem isn't the end of the world.

Units 1–2   **34**   I can keep calm when something bad happens.

For the teacher
- Teaching notes, page 173
- Audioscript, pages 244–245

On the Portal
- Photocopiable activity: *Keep calm and carry on*

46

Keep calm when things go wrong

5 🔊 **2.21** Listen to the next part of Sam and Jess's conversation and answer the questions.
How does Sam decide to:
1 get his bike home?
2 get to school in the morning?
3 try to get money for new wheels?
4 protect his bike in the future?

6 🔊 **2.21** Study the Useful Phrases box. Then listen again and tick (✓) the expressions you hear in Sam and Jess's conversation.

7 What do you think? Which attitudes from Exercise 4 help people to keep calm when bad things happen? Do you have any other advice for keeping calm?
It's a good idea to focus on things that you can do to improve the situation.

8 In pairs, discuss the situations. Think about how you feel at first. Then say what you can do to keep calm.
1 Your family's car breaks down the day before you go on holiday. You have to stay at home until the car is fixed.
2 You love your dog, but he's very naughty. He tries to eat your expensive new trainers and destroys them.
3 You are in a café. Someone near you falls over and their orange juice goes all over you.

9 Read the Useful Tips. Do you usually do what the tips suggest? Which tip is the most useful? Why?

SET FOR LIFE

10 In pairs, role play a situation where something bad happens and you manage to keep calm. Follow these steps.

1 Choose a situation from Exercise 1 or 8.

2 Write the dialogue. Use expressions from the Useful Phrases box.
Student A: Describe the bad situation. (You feel sad or stressed about it.)
Student B: Encourage your friend to keep calm.
Student A: Give a positive solution. Remember to stay calm and manage your emotions.

3 Practise your dialogue. Remember to use your body and voice to show how you feel.

4 Present your dialogue to the class or record it on your phone.

35 Units 1–2

USEFUL TIPS
When something bad happens, we often feel stressed or sad. It's important to keep calm and control negative feelings.

- Breathe slowly.
- Don't focus on your mistakes or bad luck.
- Focus on things that you can do to improve the situation.
- Don't think about bad things that aren't likely to happen.
- Remember that friends often give good advice.

USEFUL PHRASES

Finding something good in a bad situation
☐ It isn't the end of the world.
✓ At least …
✓ It's lucky that …

Being a friend to someone in a bad situation
✓ Bad luck! What are you going to do?
✓ Can you … ?

Finding solutions
✓ I guess I can …
✓ Maybe I can …
✓ Perhaps the best thing is to …

Exercise 5
🔊 audioscript page 245
1 He can carry it.
2 on the bus
3 Maybe he can do jobs for his mum.
4 He can lock the wheels to the rest of the bike.

Exercise 8
Sample answer (situation 1): At first, I feel really sad. I was very excited about the holiday, and now we can't go on the right day. It isn't fair! But then I think, 'It isn't the end of the world.' We can have a shorter holiday, and some people don't have holidays at all. I try to think of nice activities to do at home with my family while we wait for the car.

Tasty treats

3

VOCABULARY
Food | Cooking | Flavours | Word building: food | Collocations about food | Describing food

GRAMMAR
Present Perfect with *ever*, *never*, *just*, *already* and *yet* | Present Perfect with *for* and *since* | Present Perfect and Past Simple

KNOW YOUR FOOD
Do you know these fascinating facts about everyday food?

1. **B** You can eat them raw, cooked or in a hot, spicy sauce. In Africa, farmers use them to keep elephants away: they don't like the smell.

2. **D** It's delicious boiled, roasted or in soup. It has beautiful flowers and you can eat its leaves. It looks like a potato, but it's different.

3. **A** You can eat this small green or black fruit raw. Its oil is a basic ingredient in Mediterranean cooking. In Spain, they put it on toast instead of butter.

4. **F** It's green on the outside, red on the inside, its seeds are black and it's good in salads. It's ninety-two percent water, so it makes delicious juice.

5. **E** It comes in all shapes and sizes and we can eat this for breakfast, lunch and dinner. It's usually baked, but we can fry it too and it's great with butter on it!

6. **C** This is made from milk and you can buy it in lots of different flavours. When it's frozen, it can make a fantastic dessert, especially when you add some nuts and fresh fruit.

3.1 Vocabulary
Food and drink

1 Look at photos A–F. Do you know any of these foods? Which did you eat yesterday?

2 🔊 3.1 Read the clues in the quiz and match them with photos A–F. Listen and check.

Unit 3 36

For the teacher
- Teaching notes, page 174
- *Need support?* worksheet, page 234
- Audioscript, page 245

On the Portal
- Vocabulary Memory Game
- Photocopiable activity: *Food choices*
- **Test:** Vocabulary Check 3

For the student
- Workbook, pages 26–27

On the Portal
- **Workbook:** Lesson 3.1
- **Extra Practice Activities:** Vocabulary

3 🔊 **3.2** Study Vocabulary box A and write the words in the correct group below. One word does not belong to any of the groups.

VOCABULARY A ▶ **Food**

chillies garlic green pepper mushroom nuts oil olives
onion peach pear pepper pineapple sausage seeds
sweet potato tuna vinegar

Vegetables	potato	chillies, garlic, green pepper, onion, sweet potato
Fruit	apple	olives, peach, pear, pineapple
Meat/Fish	chicken	sausage, tuna
Condiments	salt	oil, pepper, vinegar
Snacks	nuts	nuts, seeds
Cereals	bread	
Dairy products:	milk	

4 **I KNOW!** In groups, add more words to each group in Exercise 3. How many can you add in one minute? Compare your ideas with the class.

5 Circle the odd one out. Use the groups in Exercise 3 to help you. Explain your answers.
1 beef lamb sausage (tuna)
   Tuna is a fish, the other three are kinds of meat.
2 chillies garlic (nuts) onion
3 butter cream (noodles) yoghurt
4 (mushroom) peach pear pineapple
5 burger curry (salad) soup
6 bread rolls flour (honey) toast
7 (ice cream) oil pepper vinegar

6 🔊 **3.3** Complete the text with the words below. Listen and check. What are your favourite three extra toppings on pizza? Discuss in pairs.

mushrooms olives onions peppers pineapple ~~sausage~~ tuna

FAVOURITE PIZZA TOPPINGS: CLASS SURVEY

Most pizzas have mozzarella cheese and tomato, but what are our school's top ten extra pizza toppings? Well, in our survey, it's clear that we like meat because number one is ¹*sausage*, number four is beef and number five is chicken. Number two isn't a meat, but it isn't a fruit or a vegetable, either. It's ² *mushrooms* – in thin slices, of course. Number three is a very useful vegetable that we use in lots of recipes: ³ *onions* . Number six is extra cheese, number seven is green ⁴ *peppers* . Number eight is ⁵ *olives* but black ones, not green. Number nine is a fish: it's ⁶ *tuna* . And finally, number ten is surprising because it's a fruit: ⁷*pineapple* ! Yes, I know. I think it's strange too.

7 🔊 **3.4** Study Vocabulary box B.
In pairs, ask and answer the questions below.

VOCABULARY B ▶ **Cooking**

boiled cooked flavour fresh fried frozen
ingredients raw recipe roasted sauce

1 Do you prefer boiled potatoes or fried potatoes? Raw carrots or cooked carrots? Fresh fruit or frozen yoghurt?
2 How often do you eat roast chicken? How often do you have hot, spicy sauces?
3 Who does the cooking in your house? Do they prefer easy recipes or difficult ones with lots of ingredients?

8 🔊 **3.5** Study Vocabulary box C. In pairs, add more words to the box. Then say which flavours of ice cream you love/can't stand.

I love vanilla ice cream, but I can't stand chocolate ice cream.

VOCABULARY C ▶ **Flavours**

chocolate coconut coffee mango
melon mint strawberry vanilla

⚠️ **WATCH OUT!**
We can use flavours as nouns or as adjectives. When we use them as adjectives, they always appear in singular form.
I like **strawberries**. (noun)
I like **strawberry** ice cream. (adjective)

9 🔊 **3.6** Which ice cream flavours do these people mention? Which ones are unusual? Which one is fake?

YOUR WORLD

10 Which of the foods in the lesson do you love eating at these meals or as a snack? Which meal is your favourite? Say why.
• breakfast • lunch • dinner

I love eating toast with olive oil for breakfast. It's my favourite meal.

Exercise 3
Mushroom doesn't belong to any of the groups.

Exercise 4
Possible answers:
Vegetables: beans, carrots, peas **Fruit:** apple, banana, strawberries **Meat/Fish:** beef, chicken **Condiments:** salt, sauce **Snacks:** biscuits, crisps

Exercise 5
2 Nuts are a snack, the other three are vegetables.
3 Noodles are a cereal, the other three are dairy products.
4 A mushroom is neither a fruit nor a vegetable, the others are fruits.
5 A salad is a cold meal, the others are hot meals.
6 Honey is sweet, the other three are (made with) cereals.
7 Ice cream is a sweet thing and a dairy product, the other three are condiments.

Exercise 9
🔊 audioscript page 245

strawberry, vanilla
unusual flavours: honey and mango, pear and blue cheese, pepper, chocolate and chilli
fake flavour: salt and vinegar

I can talk about food and drink.

3.2 Grammar

Present Perfect with *ever*, *never*, *just*, *already* and *yet*

Exercise 2
1 baked beans on toast, a fried egg and tea
2 He thinks it's unusual and thinks she's eating a lot.
3 Students' own answers

Exercise 4
1 Abe's just eaten breakfast.
2 Bea hasn't had her fried egg yet.
3 Bea's already eaten a plate of beans.
4 Bea's never tried brown sauce with crisps.
5 Brown sauce is the worst thing (that) Abe has ever tasted.
6 Have you ever tasted strong tea?
7 Have you had your breakfast yet?

Exercise 5
1 haven't decided where to go yet
2 Have you tried that new Japanese restaurant yet?
3 've already been
4 Have you ever eaten
5 I've never tried
6 I've just booked

Exercise 6
videoscript page 245

Holly: likes the sushi restaurant; has been a few times; went 3 weeks ago; tried sashimi and soft shell crab
Corrine: Vietnamese café in London; goes once a month; has tried Bánh mì (baguettes filled with meat and vegetables)
Akshay: likes Thai food in Thailand and classic British food in Britain, e.g. bangers and mash, shepherd's pie, fish and chips (He's tried Japanese food but not Australian or African.)
Reema: likes fish and chips

VIDEO — AN ENGLISH BREAKFAST

Abe: Good morning. Oh! Am I early?
Bea: No. Sorry, I've just got up. I haven't finished eating yet. Are you hungry?
Abe: No, I've already eaten. What's that?
Bea: Baked beans on toast.
Abe: I've never heard of anyone eating beans for breakfast. It looks kind of strange.
Bea: Have you ever tried it?
Abe: No, I haven't.
Bea: It's really good. Try some.
Abe: I've just eaten. Have you finished yet?
Bea: No. I haven't eaten my fried egg yet.
Abe: You've already eaten a plate of beans!
Bea: So? I love big breakfasts on Saturdays.
Abe: What's that?
Bea: It's brown sauce. It's great with chips.
Abe: With potato chips?
Bea: They're not chips, they're crisps. Chips are hot. I've never tried brown sauce with crisps … Mmm, it's good. Try some.
Abe: Ah! That's the worst thing I've ever tasted! Ah! What's that?
Bea: Have you never tasted tea before?
Abe: I've never had tea like that. It's so strong!
Bea: I'll be ready in five minutes.

1 What is a full English breakfast? What is the typical breakfast in your country?

2 ▶ 14 🔊 3.7 Watch or listen and answer the questions.
1 What does Bea have for breakfast?
2 What does Abe think of her breakfast?
3 What do you think of it?

3 Study the Grammar box. Find more examples of the Present Perfect with *ever*, *never*, *just*, *already* and *yet* in the dialogue.

GRAMMAR — **Present Perfect with *ever*, *never*, *just*, *already* and *yet***

Have you ever tried beans on toast?
I've never heard of anyone eating beans for breakfast.
Bea's just got up.
I've already eaten.
She hasn't woken up yet.
Have you finished yet? Yes, I have./No, I haven't.

GRAMMAR TIME ▶ PAGE 128

4 Make sentences in the Present Perfect.
1 Abe / just / eat / breakfast
2 Bea / not have / her fried egg / yet
3 Bea / already / eat / a plate of beans
4 Bea / never / try / brown sauce with crisps
5 brown sauce / the worst thing / Abe / ever / taste
6 you / ever / taste / strong tea / ?
7 you / have / your breakfast / yet / ?

5 🔊 3.8 Complete the dialogue with the words in brackets. Use the Present Perfect form of the verbs. Listen and check.

Joe: I want to go out for my birthday on Friday, but I ¹_____ (not decide/where to go/yet).
Kim: ²_____ (you/try/that new Japanese restaurant/yet)?
Joe: No, I haven't. Have you?
Kim: Yes, I ³_____ (already/be) there twice. The noodles are great! ⁴_____ (you/ever/eat) sushi?
Joe: No, ⁵_____ (I/never/try) Japanese food.
Kim: You should. It's brilliant.
Joe: OK, that's it. ⁶_____ (I/just/book) a table for four for next Friday night.

VIDEO — WIDER WORLD

6 ▶ 15 Watch four people talking about their favourite food and places to eat. Make notes about these things for each speaker.
• place
• when or how often they go/went there
• food they like/have tried

7 In pairs, ask and answer questions about places to eat where you live.
Have you ever eaten at Big Burger Bar?

I can use the Present Perfect to talk about experiences.

For the teacher
• Teaching notes, page 175
• Videoscript, page 245

On the Portal
• Grammar presentation
• Photocopiable activity: *Have you ever … ?*
• Test: Grammar Check 3

For the student
• Workbook, page 28
• Grammar Time, Student's Book, page 128

On the Portal
• Workbook: Lesson 3.2
• Extra Practice Activities: Grammar, New Park video, BBC Vox Pop

3.3 Reading and Vocabulary
Super healthy foods

1 Look at the foods in the photos. Which foods do you like the most/least?

2 🔊 3.9 Read the article quickly and choose the correct answer.
The article looks at five foods and describes how
a much they cost. (b) healthy they are.
c to cook them.

3 Read the article again and complete the sentences with 1–3 words from the article.
1 Your memory can improve if you eat _chocolate regularly_.
2 Dark chocolate is better for you than _chocolate cake_.
3 Salmon can stop you having _(serious) health problems_.
4 Pickles are good in burgers or on their own as a _(crunchy) snack_.
5 You should eat pickles if you are _shy and/or nervous_.
6 Eating raw pumpkin seeds is _healthier (for you)_.
7 You can add garlic to all sorts of _recipes_.

4 🔊 3.10 Complete the Vocabulary box with adjectives from the article. Listen and check.

VOCABULARY — Word building: food

Noun	Adjective	Noun	Adjective
butter	buttery	health	5 healthy
cream	1 creamy	juice	6 juicy
crisp	2 crispy	salt	7 salty
crunch	3 crunchy	spice	8 spicy
fat	4 fatty	taste	9 tasty

5 In pairs, ask and answer about foods using adjectives from Exercise 4.
A: Are raw carrots crunchy or juicy?
B: They're crunchy. Are peanuts creamy or salty?

6 🔊 3.11 **WORD FRIENDS** Complete the sentences with the phrases below. Listen and check. In pairs, say if the sentences are true for you.

| add to | ~~full of~~ | go well with | good/healthy for |
| protect from | | | |

1 I love sweet things that are _full of_ sugar.
2 I think pickles _____ cheese.
3 I _____ too much salt _____ my food.
4 I never eat anything that isn't _____ me.
5 I try to eat foods that can _____ me _____ illnesses.

Five superfoods – they're tasty and healthy!

Eating chocolate regularly seems to improve your ability to multitask, to understand abstract ideas and to remember things like phone numbers. It's good for your skin and keeps your heart healthy, too! But it must be dark chocolate with 75–80 percent cocoa, not chocolate cake full of sugar!

Fresh or frozen, raw or cooked, salmon is a juicy fish with a rich, buttery flavour. It's also full of Omega-3 fatty acids. Studies have shown that Omega-3 can protect you from serious health problems such as heart disease, dementia and some kinds of cancer. It's also good for your eyesight and your hair. Salmon is the medicine your body needs.

We often eat pickles in a burger or sandwich. But have you ever thought of eating pickles as a crunchy snack instead of crisps or peanuts? You should because they're very good for you. Pickles also have a positive effect on the brain: they help shy and nervous people feel more relaxed.

If you've never tried pumpkin seeds, you should. These tasty little treats give you energy, make you feel happy and help you sleep better. Their slightly salty flavour goes well with all sorts of dishes, but it's healthier for you to eat them raw. Add them to salads, breakfast cereal or fruit and vegetable smoothies. Or just eat them as a healthy snack.

It's a medicine that keeps the common cold away, strengthens your bones and protects your heart. It can help you run faster and live longer. Its strong taste is great in recipes from spicy curries to creamy sauces. I fry it in olive oil until it's crispy and add it to salads. Have you guessed what it is yet? It's garlic!

> **EXAM**
> Exercise 3
> International Certificate Level 1/2, Reading, Section 7, (note completion)

YOUR WORLD

7 Make a list of the healthy and unhealthy food and drink you often consume. Then, in groups, compare your lists and say if you eat or drink too much/many or not enough of these things.
Healthy: carrots …   Unhealthy: crisps, …
I eat a lot of biscuits.
I don't eat any fresh fruit.

> **Exercise 6**
> 2 go well with
> 3 add; to
> 4 good/healthy for
> 5 protect; from

I can understand an article about superfoods.

3.4 Grammar

Present Perfect with *for* and *since* | Present Perfect and Past Simple

1 What's your favourite flavour for a fruit juice or smoothie?

2 🔊 3.12 Read the blog post. In pairs, answer the questions.
   1 What surprises Ashley about Rio?
   2 How many types of fruit are there in Brazil?
   3 What drink did Ashley try?

3 Study the Grammar box. Which set of words and phrases, a or b, do we use with *for*? Which do we use with *since*?
   a two o'clock, yesterday, Monday, last weekend, 1958
   b five minutes, a few hours, a long time, two weeks, three years

> **Exercise 2**
> 1 that there are so many fruit bars/that there is so much fruit
> 2 300/three hundred
> 3 cashew apple juice

> **Exercise 3**
> a since
> b for

> **Exercise 4**
> Examples of Present Perfect: underlined in red
> Examples of Past Simple: underlined in green

GRAMMAR — Present Perfect with *for* and *since* | Present Perfect and Past Simple

Present Perfect with *for* and *since*
I've lived in Rio **for** many years. (a period of time)
They've had this bar **since** 1970. (a point in time)

Present Perfect and Past Simple
We've **been to** São Paulo.
We **went** to São Paulo in 2012.
Have you ever **drunk** a mango smoothie?
Did you **like** it?

GRAMMAR TIME > PAGE 128

4 Find more examples of the Present Perfect and Past Simple in the blog post.

5 Make sentences in the Present Perfect. Use *for* or *since*.
   1 I / not have / a chocolate bar / a month
   2 my family / own / this café / 2010
   3 we / not eat / any food / breakfast time
   4 this cookery programme / be / on TV / a few months
   5 you / see / the cookery teacher / last lesson / ?
   6 they / be / at the juice bar / half an hour

6 🔊 3.13 Complete the dialogue with one word in each gap. Listen and check.
   Mia: ¹*Have* you had any fruit juice yet today?
   Leo: No, I ² *haven't* had any yet, but I'd like some now.
   Mia: ³ *Have* you ever tried sugar apple juice?
   Leo: Yes, I ⁴ *tried* some yesterday. Sugar apples look like pears! They're very good for you.
   Mia: ⁵ *Did* you like it?
   Leo: Yes, I ⁶ *did*. Why don't you try some?
   Mia: Yeah. I'd love to try it. Where ⁷ *did* you buy it?
   Leo: At the juice bar on the beach.

> **Exercise 5**
> 1 I haven't had a chocolate bar for a month.
> 2 My family has/have owned this café since 2010.
> 3 We haven't eaten any food since breakfast time.
> 4 This cookery programme has been on TV for a few months.
> 5 Have you seen the cookery teacher since the last lesson?
> 6 They've been at the juice bar for half an hour.

The best drink ever!

We've been in Rio since yesterday afternoon. I'm so excited! My parents are from Brazil, but we haven't visited the country many times – the plane tickets are very expensive. Anyway, I'm in Rio now and I love it here, especially the juice bars. They're on every street corner. I've never seen so much fruit!
The owner of one juice bar, Rodrigo, has lived in Rio for many years. His father opened Rio's first juice bar in 1958. Many other bars have opened since then. I found out that there are 300 different types of fruit in Brazil! Some of them are very unusual. Have you heard of cashew apple? It looks like a red apple, but the cashew nut grows at the top of the fruit. It makes delicious juice. I've just had some!

Ashley

YOUR WORLD

7 Write questions in the Present Perfect and Past Simple. Then ask and answer the questions in pairs.
   • Start with a general question with *ever* (Present Perfect).
     Have you ever eaten … ?
   • Then ask about details (Past Simple).
     When did you try it? Did you like it? What was it like?

Unit 3 — 40 — I can use the Present Perfect and the Past Simple to talk about experiences.

For the teacher
- Teaching notes, page 177
- *Need support?* worksheet, page 234

On the Portal
- Grammar presentation
- Photocopiable activity: *She's lived here all her life*
- Test: Grammar Check 3

For the student
- Workbook, page 30
- Grammar Time, Student's Book, page 128

On the Portal
- Workbook: Lesson 3.4
- Extra Practice Activities: Grammar

3.5 Listening and Vocabulary
A dream cake

1 Is it important to have a special cake on your birthday? Compare your ideas with the class.

2 🔊 3.14 Study the Vocabulary box. Can you add more words?

VOCABULARY › Describing food

bitter delicious dry hard hot rich sour spicy sweet

3 🔊 3.15 Complete the sentences with words from the Vocabulary box. Listen and check.
1 I like chilli popcorn because it's so sour / [hot].
2 This cupcake isn't bitter / [sweet] enough. Put some jam on it.
3 I love this fruit juice – it's really dry / [delicious].
4 There's a lot of butter and cream in this cake, so it's very [rich] / spicy.
5 This milk has been in the sun too long – it tastes fresh / [sour].
6 This bread is old – it's too [hard] / hot to eat.

4 🔊 3.16 Listen to Gianni talking about a very special cake and mark the sentences T (true) or F (false).
1 [T] Gianni saw the cake in New York.
2 [F] The cake took a week to make. *four days*
3 [T] The baker didn't make the cake in his shop.
4 [F] The cake weighed around seventy kilos. *about 700 kg*
5 [F] Gianni didn't like the cake at all. *It was really tasty and sweet.*

Win your dream cake from Zany Cake Bakery!

Send us a photo or drawing of your ideal cake! We will make the best cake and send it to you.

- Email address: ¹orders@ *amazingcakes* .com
- Usual cost: ²€ *50*
- Choose a flavour: chocolate, ³ *coffee* or vanilla?
- Don't forget: tell us your ⁴ *birthday* !
- Closing date of competition: Friday
  ⁵ *31st/31* January
- Other prizes for five runners-up: twelve
  ⁶ *cupcakes*

5 Read the advert. In pairs, decide what kind of information is missing from each gap: a word or a number?
words: 1, 3, 4, 6; numbers: 2, 5

6 🔊 3.17 Listen to information about how to enter the competition. Complete the text in Exercise 5.

VIDEO ▶ **WIDER WORLD**

7 ▶ 16 Watch four people talking about the best cake they have ever had. What flavour was each cake?

8 In pairs, describe the best cake you have ever had.
The best cake I've ever had was a chocolate cake I had for my last birthday.

Exercise 2
Possible answers: cold, fresh, horrible, salty, tasty

Exercise 4
🔊 audioscript page 245

EXAM
Exercise 6
🔊 audioscript page 245
International Certificate Level 1/2, Listening, Section 3, (note completion)
B1 Preliminary for Schools, Listening, Part 3, (gap fill)

Exercise 7
▶ videoscript page 245
Nympha: strawberries and cream
Miguel: chocolate and cream
Jamie: chocolate and raspberry jam
Liam: chocolate

I can understand people describing food. | 41 | Unit 3

For the teacher
- Teaching notes, page 178
- Audioscript, page 245
- Videoscript, page 245

On the Portal
- Vocabulary Memory Game
- Photocopiable activity: Food adjectives

For the student
- Workbook, page 31

On the Portal
- Workbook: Lesson 3.5
- Extra Practice Activities: Vocabulary, BBC Vox Pop

53

3.6 Speaking
Ordering food

VIDEO ▶ **ARE YOU READY TO ORDER?**

Abe: Hi, guys. <u>Take a seat and I'll get you the menu. Here you are. Can I get you something</u> to drink?
Bea: <u>I'll have</u> a large smoothie, please.
Mum: <u>Just water for me, please.</u>
Bea: Wow! That's a big smoothie!
Abe: It's good for you! <u>Are you ready to order?</u>
Mum: <u>Could we share</u> a starter? Nachos?
Abe: Sure thing. And <u>for your main course?</u>
Bea: <u>I'd like</u> a burger, please.
Mum: Sorry, I'm a vegetarian. <u>Have you got any</u> vegetable dishes?
Abe: Hold on! There's salad and pumpkin pie.
Mum: Pumpkin pie? That's a dessert, isn't it?
Abe: Yeah, it is ... You can have more nachos if you prefer.
Mum: No, it's OK. <u>I'll have</u> salad and <u>a slice of</u> pumpkin pie. <u>Can I have</u> some cream with that?
Abe: Sure. Would you like fries with your meal?
Bea: Yes, please.
Mum: <u>Not for me, thanks.</u>

Later ...
Abe: <u>Would you like anything else?</u>
Mum: You must be joking!

SOUNDS GOOD! Sure thing. • Hold on! • You must be joking!

Exercise 1
Possible answers:
hamburgers, cheeseburgers, hot dogs, fries, nachos, apple pie, peanut butter, popcorn, fried chicken, chocolate chip cookies, deep dish pizza, turkey dinner

Exercise 2
Bea orders a large smoothie. Mum just has water. They share nachos for their starter. Bea has a burger with fries for her main course and Mum has salad and pumpkin pie with cream.

1 In pairs, list at least three typical American foods. Say which one you like the most. Then compare with the rest of the class.
pumpkin pie, ...

2 ▶ 17 🔊 3.18 Watch or listen. What do Bea and Penny order?

3 Study the Speaking box. Find the phrases which are in the dialogue.

SPEAKING Ordering food

Customer
I'll have/I'd like a slice of ...
Excuse me, can/could I/we have/share ... ?
Just ... for me, please.
Have you got any ... ?
Not for me, thanks.

Waiter
Take a seat and I'll get you the menu.
What would you like to drink?
Are you ready to order?
Would you like anything else/to eat?
Can I get you something?
For the/your starter/main course/dessert?
Here you are.

4 Match questions 1–5 with answers a–e. Use the Speaking box to help you.
1 [c] Are you ready to order?
2 [e] Could we share a dessert?
3 [a] Have you got any fresh fruit?
4 [b] What can I get you to drink?
5 [d] Would you like chips with that?

a Yes, we have pineapple or melon.
b A fresh orange juice, please.
c Yes, can I have a chicken curry?
d No, not for me, thanks.
e Yes, of course we can.

SET FOR LIFE

5 In groups of four, discuss how you could work together to do different tasks for an event. Use these ideas to help you.
• choose a leader
• make a list of tasks
• share the tasks

I'd like to organise a group to tidy up.
If you buy the snacks, I'll organise the music.

YOUR WORLD

6 In pairs or small groups, order food from the menu on page 142. Use the Speaking box to help you.

Unit 3 42 I can order food in a café or restaurant.

For the teacher
• Teaching notes, page 179
• *Need support?* worksheet, page 234

On the Portal
• Photocopiable activity: *What's in it?*

For the student
• Workbook, page 32

On the Portal
• Workbook: Lesson 3.6
• Extra Practice Activities: New Park video

54

3.7 Writing
An email to a friend

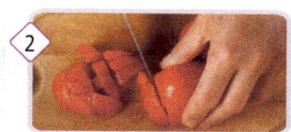

1 Work in pairs. What food do you usually have at a party with friends?

2 Match the verbs below with photos 1–4.

chop [2]   mix [3]   pour [4]   slice [1]

3 Read Elsie's email. Does it mention any of your ideas from Exercise 1?
Answers will depend on students' answers to Exercise 1.

Subject: Party time!

Hi Shannon,

1 Thanks for getting in touch.

2 It was great to hear about your school trip. The photos were awesome.

3 Liam and I have just finished our exams and we've decided to have a party tomorrow at his house to celebrate! He's bought lots of yummy food, including sausages and cheese. I'm thinking about making my famous chicken salad. Here's the recipe for you – it's really easy. First, boil some eggs and slice them. Then, chop a few tomatoes into small pieces. Next, add some roast chicken. After that, mix everything together. Finally, pour some olive oil on it. I can't tell you how good it is!

4 Anyway, I was wondering if you'd like to come. We're asking everybody to bring some fruit or some juice because we want to make lots of different flavoured smoothies.

5 Let me know if you can make it.

Elsie

---

4 Read the email again. Number the things below in the order Elsie does them in her email.

a [2] She talks about what's happening in her life now.
b [3] She invites her friend and asks her friend to do something.
c [1] She thanks her friend and comments on her friend's news.
d [4] She asks her friend to reply to the invitation.

5 Study the Language box. Find sentences with sequencers in the recipe in Elsie's email.

> **LANGUAGE** Giving instructions
>
> *First, then, next, after that* and *finally* are sequencers. We use them to explain the order in which we do things. We often use them with imperatives in recipes.

6 Study the Writing box. Find examples of the phrases in Elsie's email.

> **WRITING** An email to a friend
>
> 1 **Start your email**
> How are things?
> Great to hear from you./Thanks for getting in touch.
>
> 2 **Respond to news**
> It was great to hear about your school trip.
> I can't wait to hear more about it.
>
> 3 **Give your news**
> We have just finished our exams.
> We've decided to have a party.
> I'm making a cake for the party.
>
> 4 **Explain why you're writing**
> Anyway/By the way, I was wondering if you'd like to come.
> I'm writing to ask if you'd like to come to the party.
>
> 5 **End your email**
> Let me know if you can make it.
> See you soon./Bye for now.

WRITING TIME

7 Write an email inviting a friend to a party. Include a recipe for some food for the party.

1 **Find ideas**
- Where and when are you having the party?
- What are you celebrating?
- What food are you planning to make?

2 **Plan**
Organise your ideas into paragraphs. Use Elsie's email to help you.

3 **Write and share**
- Write a draft email. Use the Language box and the Writing box to help you.
- Share your email with another student for feedback.
- Use the feedback from your partner and write the final version of your email.

4 **Check**
- Check language: did you use sequencers and imperatives for your recipe?
- Check grammar: did you use the Present Perfect correctly?

I can write an email to a friend.   43   Unit 3

For the teacher
- Teaching notes, page 180

On the Portal
- Photocopiable activity: *Hi!*

For the student
- Workbook, page 33

On the Portal
- Workbook: Lesson 3.7

Vocabulary Activator

WORDLIST 🔊 3.19

Food
chillies (n)
garlic (n)
green pepper (n)
mushroom (n)
nuts (n)
oil (n)
olives (n)
onion (n)
peach (n)
pear (n)
pepper (n)
pineapple (n)
sausage (n)
seeds (n)
sweet potato (n)
tuna (n)
vinegar (n)

Cooking
boiled (adj)
cooked (adj)
flavour (n)
fresh (adj)
fried (adj)
frozen (adj)
ingredients (n)
raw (adj)
recipe (n)
roasted (adj)
sauce (n)

Flavours
chocolate (adj)
coconut (adj)
coffee (adj)
mango (adj)
melon (adj)
mint (adj)
strawberry (adj)
vanilla (adj)

Word building
(food)
butter – buttery
cream – creamy
crisp – crispy
crunch – crunchy
fat – fatty
health – healthy
juice – juicy
salt – salty
spice – spicy
taste – tasty

Word friends
(collocations about food)
add to (v)
full of (adj)
go well with
good/healthy for (adj)
protect from (v)

Describing food
bitter (adj)
delicious (adj)
dry (adj)
hard (adj)
hot (adj)
rich (adj)
sour (adj)
spicy (adj)
sweet (adj)

Extra words
bakery (n)
beef (n)
body (n)
bone (n)
carrot (n)
cereal (n)
chips (n)
chop (v)
cool (adj)
curry (n)
dairy (n)
dessert (n)
eyesight (n)
flour (n)
heart (n)
honey (n)
leaf/leaves (n)
meal (n)
meat (n)
medicine (n)
menu (n)
mix (v)
peanuts (n)
pickles (n)
pie (n)
plate (n)
pour (v)
salad (n)
salmon (n)
serious (adj)
skin (n)
slice (v, n)
smell (n)
snack (n)
strange (adj)
surprising (adj)
survey (n)
taste (v)
toast (n)
topping (n)
treats (n)
vegetarian (n)

Exercise 1
1 green pepper, nuts, olives, peach, pear, pineapple
2 garlic, onion, sweet potato
3 mushroom
4 oil, pepper, sauce, vinegar

Exercise 5
1 olives, sausage
2 mushrooms, onions
3 bakery, tasty
4 raw, salty

1 Use the wordlist to find these things.
  1 six foods which grow on plants above ground
  2 three foods which grow under the ground in the soil
  3 one food which grows on the ground
  4 four things you can add at the table to make food tastier

2 Complete the menu for Tom's birthday meal with words from the wordlist. Then, in pairs, describe your ideal birthday meal.

- Pizza with a mushroom and pineapple topping
- Tomato, green ¹_pepper_ and lettuce ²_salad_ with vinegar and olive ³_oil_
- Dessert: ice cream (choose from five different ⁴_flavours_: vanilla, milk or dark ⁵_chocolate_, strawberry, mango)

3 In pairs, decide if the things below are healthy or unhealthy. Write them in two lists.

chillies chocolate mushrooms nuts oil pear pineapple sausage sweet potato tuna

4 Read the information in the quiz and identify the food. Then, in pairs, write three clues about other foods from the wordlist. Give your clues to another pair.

What is it?   **THE FOOD QUIZ**
1 • It is white outside and inside.
  • It grows under the ground.
  • We use it to make food taste better. _garlic_
2 • It is red and yellow, or orange outside, and yellow inside.
  • It is soft, sweet, round and juicy.
  • It has a big seed or 'stone' inside _peach_

5 🔊 3.20 **PRONUNCIATION** Listen to how we pronounce the underlined vowel in the words in the table. Write the words below in the correct column.

b<u>a</u>kery   m<u>u</u>shrooms   <u>o</u>lives   <u>o</u>nions
r<u>a</u>w   s<u>a</u>lty   s<u>au</u>sage   t<u>a</u>sty

1 h<u>o</u>t /ɒ/	2 n<u>u</u>ts /ʌ/	3 fl<u>a</u>vour /eɪ/	4 s<u>au</u>ce /ɔː/

6 🔊 3.21 **PRONUNCIATION** Listen, check and repeat.

Unit 3 44

For the teacher
• Audioscript, page 246

On the Portal
• Tests: Unit 3 Test, Unit 3 Writing Test

For the student
• Workbook, pages 34–35

On the Portal
• Workbook: Self-check
• Wordlist
• Extra Practice Activities: Self-check

Revision

Vocabulary

1 Choose the correct option.
1. What's your favourite ice cream *recipe* / *flavour*? Mine is *melon* / *olive*.
2. For lunch, I had a *boiled* / *roasted* egg on toast and a *vinegar* / *peach*.
3. *Chillies* / *Seeds* and green *pears* / *peppers* are vegetables.
4. I can't eat this cereal! It's too *hard* / *fresh* and the milk tastes *delicious* / *sour*.

2 Complete the advice with the words below.

add   frozen   ~~full~~   good   healthy
protect   raw   well

Eat right!

Fruit and vegetables are ¹*full* of good things like vitamins A, C and E.

Fresh vegetables taste better than ² *frozen* ones and are better for you.

Fruit and vegetables make your body strong and help to ³ *protect* you from illness.

Olives go ⁴ *well* with lettuce and other salad vegetables, and they are ⁵ *healthy* as well as tasty.

You can also ⁶ *add* some sunflower seeds to your salad. They're really good for you!

Carrots are better for you ⁷ *raw* than cooked.

Don't put too much sugar on your breakfast cereal – it isn't ⁸ *good* for you.

3 Complete the definitions with the correct words.
1. The different things you add when you are cooking are the i*ngredients*.
2. The instructions you follow when you are cooking are the r*ecipe*.
3. S*picy* food like chillies has a hot taste.
4. 'S*our*' is the opposite of 'sweet'; it's the taste you get from lemons, for example.
5. 'D*elicious*' means 'very tasty', 'great to eat'.

Grammar

4 Complete the dialogues with the words below.

already   ever   ~~just~~   never   yet

1. A: Oh dear! I've *just* broken a glass!
   B: Never mind.
2. A: Have you done your homework *yet*?
   B: I've *already* done Maths. I'm having a break now, before I do the rest.
3. A: Have you *ever* been to Australia?
   B: No. I've *never* been outside Europe, actually, but I want to travel more in the future.

5 Complete the sentences with the Present Perfect form of the verbs in brackets and *for* or *since*.
1. I *have known* (know) my best friend _____ six years.
2. I _____ (not eat) anything _____ nine o'clock. I'm hungry!
3. The English teacher _____ (not give) us any homework _____ a few days.
4. The weather _____ (be) great here _____ last Friday.
5. I _____ (be) at this school _____ four years.
6. I _____ (have) my phone _____ March.

6 Rewrite the sentences in Exercise 5 to make them true for you.

7 In pairs, match words from A with words from B to make questions beginning *Have you ever … ?* Write one more question of your own. Then ask and answer the questions.

A   cook   drink   eat   read   visit

B   a cookbook   a meal   mint tea   Italy   sweet potato

Have you ever cooked a meal for your family?

Speaking

8 In pairs, follow the instructions to role play a dialogue at a restaurant. Then swap roles.
- Waiter (Student A): Show the customer a seat and give him/her a menu.
- Customer (Student B): Thank the waiter. Go to page 142, look at the menu and order.
- Waiter: Take the customer's order and ask if he/she would like something else/a drink.
- Customer: Finish your order and thank the waiter.

Dictation

9 🔊 3.22 Listen. Then listen again and write down what you hear.

Exercise 5
1. for
2. haven't eaten; since
3. hasn't given; for
4. has been; since
5. have been; for
6. have had; since

Exercise 7
Have you ever drunk mint tea?
Have you ever eaten sweet potato?
Have you ever read a cookbook?
Have you ever visited Italy?

Exercise 8
Sample answer:
Waiter: Take a seat and I'll get you the menu.
Customer: Thank you.
Waiter: Are you ready to order?
Customer: Yes, I'll have a tuna sandwich, please.
Waiter: Would you like anything else?
Customer: Just a salad, please.
Waiter: What would you like to drink?
Customer: Orange juice, please.
Waiter: Here you are.

EXAM

Exercise 9
🔊 audioscript page 246

International Certificate Level 1/2, Listening and Writing, Section 2, (dictation)

BBC CULTURE

Fantastic food

POPULAR FOOD IN THE UK

Most people think that food in Britain is all about fish and chips or afternoon tea, but that's not the whole story. There are so many different cultures in the UK that you have a huge choice of flavours and cuisines to choose from.

1 Indian food has been the country's favourite for years. Almost every town has at least one Indian restaurant. A very popular dish is chicken tikka masala, a spicy curry usually served with rice or Indian bread called naan. It's delicious!

2 American food is everywhere. There's not only McDonald's now, but new gourmet burger restaurants like Five Guys. American food is popular because the recipes are very familiar to British people – hot dogs, pepperoni pizza, nachos and BBQ ribs are all big favourites.

3 People have a passion for fresh and healthy food these days, and that's why Japanese food is popular. It's also easy to eat as a takeaway meal. Young people now prefer to eat sushi at lunchtime to the traditional British sandwich, although some still have problems with using chopsticks!

Do you want to try more international food? Then check out the amazing Za Za Bazaar in Bristol! It opened in 2011 and quickly became one of the most popular places to eat in the city. It's also the biggest restaurant in the UK; they can serve over 1,000 people and have food from everywhere – Vietnam, Italy, China, Thailand, as well as Britain's three favourites, of course!

cuisine (n) style of cooking
gourmet (adj) (of food) high-quality

1 🔊 3.23 **VISIBLE THINKING** In pairs, follow these steps.
THINK
1 Look at the photo. What can you see? Where do you think you would see this?
2 What do people like eating in your country? What are your favourite dishes?
PUZZLE
3 Why do you think people enjoy eating food from other countries?
4 What do you think is the most popular international food?
EXPLORE
5 Read the article and find out more about international food in Britain. Answer the questions in the PUZZLE section.

2 Read the article again. What are these foods? Write *A* for American, *J* for Japanese or *I* for Indian.
1 curry __I__
2 BBQ ribs __A__
3 sushi __J__
4 naan __I__

3 In pairs, discuss the questions.
1 Pizza is an Italian food and nachos are Mexican. Why do you think American food includes pepperoni pizza and nachos?
2 What international food do you like? Is it easy to prepare?
3 What three national dishes from your country would you suggest to a British friend to try? Why?

BBC 46

For the teacher
- Teaching notes, page 181
- Videoscript, page 246

On the Portal
- Photocopiable activity: Project worksheet: a digital poster

BBC ▶ Indian food, Liverpool style

4 Look at the photo. What are the women doing?

5 ▶ **18** Watch Part 1 of the video and answer the questions.
1. Who are Anjum and Lynn?
2. What are they doing?
3. What three traditional dishes does Lynn learn how to cook?

6 In pairs, discuss the questions.
1. Do you go to food markets? Why?/Why not?
2. Would you buy food that you have never tasted before for charity? Why?/Why not?

7 ▶ **19** Watch Part 2 of the video. Does Anjum like Lynn's cooking? *yes*

8 ▶ **19** Watch the video again and tick (✓) the correct sentences.
1. ☐ Lynn always makes mistakes when cooking.
2. ✓ Lynn's daughter helps her.
3. ✓ Lynn also cooks at the market.
4. ☐ Everyone at the market buys food right from the start.
5. ✓ The food is a little spicy but delicious.

9 In pairs, discuss the questions.
1. Does cooking make people happy in your country?
2. Is it a good idea to cook food for charity?
3. What food would you like to learn to cook?

PROJECT TIME

10 In groups of three, prepare a digital poster of a menu for International Day Celebration at school. Follow these steps.

1 In groups, choose the country whose food will be in your menu. Decide who in your group can find information about the dishes in the menu: a starter, a main dish and a dessert. Find answers to these questions.
- Is the dish served cold or hot?
- Is it spicy, bitter or sweet?
- What ingredients does your dish contain?

2 Individually, prepare your part of the menu for the poster.
- Find information and write your text.
- Find photos to illustrate the information.

3 In your group, create your poster. You can use an online poster maker.
- Import everyone's text and photos.
- Decide on a layout.
- Think of a title for the poster.
- Check and edit the poster.

4 Share your poster with the class.
- Answer other students' questions.
- Look at other posters. Ask questions.

Exercise 4
They are cooking. The woman on the left is chopping something. The woman on the right is frying something.

Exercise 5
▶ videoscript page 246

1. Anjum is a food writer and chef. She travels to different cities in the UK to find Indian food and she teaches Indian cooking. Lynn works in a hospital. She is learning to cook Indian food.
2. Anjum is teaching Lynn how to cook Indian food to sell at a farmer's market for charity.
3. coconut chicken with ginger; salmon wraps with curry leaves; rice noodles

Exercise 7
▶ videoscript page 246

Progress Check Units 1–3

Vocabulary and Grammar

1 Choose the correct option.
1. Eat more fresh fruit. It's really good ____ you.
   a to **b for** c at
2. The weather is ____ boiling! Let's go for a swim.
   a absolutely b quite c very
3. You need to ____ a new password to keep your computer and social media safe.
   a do b change **c set**
4. Temperatures are often ____ in the mountains, so take warm clothing when you go there.
   a down b small **c low**
5. North Portugal has a ____ climate most of the year – it doesn't get too hot or cold.
   a weak **b mild** c medium
6. In our family we enjoy driving around the countryside ____ the weekend.
   a at b in c to

2 Complete the text with one word in each gap.

One sunny day last year ¹ *on* a normal school day, we went outside the classroom for our Science lesson. The teacher took us to a local park full ² *of* trees and flowers. 'Use your eyes to look ³ *for* unusual animals or plants and tell us what you find! And listen ⁴ *to* the sounds of nature,' she said. While I ⁵ *was* looking at an interesting flower, a bird started singing a beautiful song. The teacher told me the bird was called a 'blackcap'. Now the teacher ⁶ *has* decided to have more 'nature walks'. We're going to go in spring, summer and autumn: three ⁷ *times* a year. That's great!

3 Complete the second sentence with the word in bold so that it means the same as the first one. Use no more than three words.
1. This is the first time I have ever played hockey. **NEVER**
   I *'ve never played* hockey before.
2. I don't eat a lot of food between meals. **AVOID**
   I *avoid eating* a lot of food between meals.
3. We've been here since 9.15 and it is now 9.45. **THIRTY**
   We've been here *for thirty* minutes.
4. It was lunchtime for the students when they heard the fire alarm. **HAVING**
   The students *were having* lunch when they heard the fire alarm.
5. Nobody knew what to do when we saw a lost dog. **KNOW**
   We *didn't know* what to do when we saw a lost dog.
6. Peter sent you an email a few seconds ago. **JUST**
   Peter *has just sent* you an email.

EXAM
Exercise 5
International Certificate Level 1/2, Speaking, Section 13, (role play)

EXAM
Exercise 7
🔊 audioscript page 246
A2 Key for Schools, Listening, Part 5, (matching)

Speaking

4 Match statements and questions 1–5 with responses a–f. There is one extra response.
1. *f* I'm sorry I lost your pen.
2. *e* Are you ready to order?
3. *a* Why don't we phone and ask for help?
4. *b* I have a problem with my computer.
5. *c* Why did you do that?

a That's a good idea.
b Shall I help you?
c I didn't mean to. I'm sorry.
d You're welcome.
e Yes, I'll have a beef burger and chips please.
f Never mind.

5 In pairs, do the speaking task. Go to page 142.

Listening

6 What kind of lunch do you normally eat on school days? How would you change it? Discuss in pairs.

7 🔊 PC1–3.1 Listen to five students talking about lunchtime at their school. Match each speaker with what he/she says. There are two extra statements.
1. *f* Ali
2. *b* Sonya
3. *a* Tim
4. *e* Ian
5. *d* Barbara

a sometimes eats meat for lunch.
b likes to eat outside.
c always eats lunch prepared by his/her parents.
d sometimes has simple snacks for lunch.
e gives some of his/her food to other students.
f has already read the menu before lunch.
g doesn't think it's important to eat healthily.

48

Reading

8 🔊 PC1–3.2 Read the article and choose the correct answer.

Enjoying the outdoors: to tech or not to tech?

We talked to three young people who visit the outdoors to find out what they do with their phones.

Carol

Do I take my phone and tablet? Of course I do! I don't believe that looking at screens is very bad; you can still enjoy nature. As well as looking at birds and flowers, I like doing exciting things. For example, on my last trip we built our own shelter and slept in it. I think friends and family like to see things like this too, so I take photos. I upload some of them and update my story so that people who follow me can see them.

Aron

I quite often go on camping trips with a group of friends who also enjoy the feeling of adventure. Adventure means leaving civilisation behind, including your phone! But enjoying the outdoors is about being safe too. So every time we go on a trip, one of us has to take their phone with a power bank. That way, if we need to phone family about something important, we can. They can message us too if they need to.

Ben

For us, the answer is simple: we switch on our phones when they're helpful. At other times we don't because we might look at the screen and miss seeing a wild animal. Last year we went for an interesting walk through the mountains. We thought we could remember how to get back to our campsite. We were wrong! But we had our phones and they helped us get there.

1 What does Carol say about taking a phone on outdoor trips?
   a It's fine if you don't look at the screen very often.
   (b) It doesn't stop you enjoying nature.
   c It can help with camping tasks like building shelters.
2 Why does Carol like to upload photos on social media?
   (a) She wants her friends to see some of the things she enjoyed doing.
   b She wants more people to follow her on social media.
   c She wants to remember how to do outdoor activities in the future.
3 Why do Aron and his friends take a phone with them on their trips?
   a One of Aron's friends does not like to be without his phone.
   b Their families want to connect with them once a day.
   (c) They can call someone if they need help.
4 What does Ben say about using phones on outdoor trips?
   a Phones can help them to see wildlife.
   (b) They use phones only when they need them.
   c They leave their phones at the place where they sleep.
5 What problem did a phone help with on one of Ben's trips?
   (a) They got lost on their way back to their camp.
   b They couldn't find an interesting walk to go on.
   c They didn't know the name of an animal they saw.

9 Read the article again and answer the questions. Use 1–3 words.
1 Where did Carol sleep on her last trip?
2 What other object do Aron and his friends take on their trips, with their phone?
3 How can the families of Aron and his friends contact them?
4 What would Ben and his friends not like to lose the chance of seeing?

Writing

10 Which of these outdoor activities sound interesting? Which one(s) have you tried?
- watching the sunset in the early evening
- cooking on an outdoor fire
- sleeping outside
- camping
- looking for interesting wildlife
- walking in the mountains or a forest
- making your own shelter

11 Write an email to a friend about a holiday when you visited some beautiful places in nature. Include information about:
- what the place was.
- what the weather was like.
- what you did there.
- what you ate there.

EXAM

Exercise 8
A2 Key for Schools, Reading and Writing, Part 3, (multiple choice)

EXAM

Exercise 9
International Certificate Level 1/2, Reading, Section 6, (open-ended question)

Exercise 9
1 in a/her own shelter
2 a power bank
3 message them/ by messaging/ (by) sending messages
4 a wild animal

Entertain us!

4

VOCABULARY
Types of film | Word building: entertainment | Film and TV | Collocations: music | Compound nouns

GRAMMAR
Comparatives and superlatives, too/(not) enough, (not) as … as | Quantifiers

The *Raj Mandir* cinema, Jaipur, India

MMB MYRA'S MOVIE BLOG

Did you know India is the world's biggest film producer? Read on to find out more.

Indian directors make almost 2,000 films a year – about four times more than the USA. Bollywood, based in Mumbai, is the home of Hindi cinema, but Indians make films in over twenty languages for people that speak them in other regions of the country. Sometimes they make one film in several languages – the same dialogues and locations but different performers.

Indian audiences want entertainment so they love masala films, which are often musicals with spectacular dance scenes. Masala films mix different types, e.g. thriller and romance. A good example is the romantic comedy drama *Monsoon Wedding*, winner of the Golden Lion at the Venice Film Festival.

Indians produce cartoons too. Check out the 3-D animated film *Delhi Safari*! It's fun!

But the biggest hit in Indian film history is a biographical sports drama called *Dangal*. It won several awards including best actor for Aamir Khan and best director for Nitesh Tiwari.

Akshay Kumar, star of over 100 films, including the science fiction action film *2.0*, is one of the world's top five best-paid actors.

Have you seen any Indian films? Leave your comments below.

4.1 Vocabulary
Film and TV

1 What do you know about Bollywood films?

2 Read the blog post and check your ideas. Then, in pairs, answer the questions.
1. What language are Bollywood films made in? *Hindi*
2. How many films do Indian directors make each year? *almost 2,000*
3. What did *Monsoon Wedding* win? *the Golden Lion award at the Venice Film Festival*
4. What type of film is *Dangal*? *a biographical sports drama*

Unit 4 50

For the teacher
- Teaching notes, page 182
- Audioscript, page 246
- Videoscript, page 246

On the Portal
- Vocabulary Memory Game
- Photocopiable activity: *That's entertainment*
- Test: Vocabulary Check 4

For the student
- Workbook, pages 38–39

On the Portal
- Workbook: Lesson 4.1
- Extra Practice Activities: Vocabulary, BBC Vox Pop

3 🔊 **4.1** Study Vocabulary box A and say which words are not mentioned in the blog.

action, documentary

VOCABULARY A — Types of film

action   cartoon   comedy   documentary   drama
musical   romance   science fiction   thriller

4 What other types of films can you add to Vocabulary box A?

5 🔊 **4.2** Listen and identify the film types.
1 musical
2 action
3 cartoon
4 science fiction
5 romance
6 documentary

6 🔊 **4.3** Study Vocabulary box B. Then complete the review below with the correct form of words from the box. The first letter of each word is given. Listen and check.

VOCABULARY B — Word building: entertainment

Verb	Noun	Person
act	acting	actor
entertain	entertainment	entertainer
perform	performance	performer
produce	production	producer
review	review	reviewer

Tanhaji: The Unsung Warrior

★★★★★

An Indian version of *Braveheart*

Ajay Devgn

Based on the true story of a seventeenth-century soldier, *Tanhaji* is an exciting action film that is one of Indian cinema's most successful ¹p*roductions*. ²R*eviews* of this film agree that Om Raut knows how to tell a historical story and ³e*ntertain* an audience at the same time. He gets his actors to ⁴p*erform* at their very best. Although the ⁵a*cting* in general is fantastic, I must mention an absolutely wonderful ⁶p*erformance* by lead ⁷a*ctor* Ajay Devgn. The ⁸p*roducers* and everyone else involved in this film should be proud. It's great ⁹e*ntertainment*.

7 🔊 **4.4** Study Vocabulary box C. Choose the correct option to complete the text below. Listen and check.

VOCABULARY C — Film and TV

audience   channel   character   episode   hit   series
special effects   TV show   viewer

How TV has changed

In the UK, ¹ **viewers** / characters are watching less TV a day than ten years ago, but does this mean they are not watching TV at all? While many Brits still like to watch traditional TV ²episodes / **channels**, the younger ³ **audience** / viewer prefers to watch on-demand TV like Netflix or Amazon. The ⁴ **hit** / series show Cobra Kai for example, became one of the most watched ⁵ **series** / episode on Netflix. The first ⁶TV show / **episode** of the comedy drama, which has no ⁷hits / **special effects** but some great action scenes, was watched by over 48 million households. Not only are people finding different places to watch their favourite ⁸ **TV shows** / special effects, but many are watching on different screens too – laptops, tablets and smartphones.

8 In pairs, ask and answer the questions.
1 What kind of TV shows do you prefer?
2 Which TV channels have the best shows?
3 Who is your favourite character from a TV series?
4 What happened in the last episode of your favourite series?
5 Would you like to go on a TV show? Why?/Why not?

VIDEO — WIDER WORLD

9 ▶ **20** Watch two people talking about TV series they like. Write down what kind of series it is and why the speakers like it.

10 In pairs, talk about your favourite film or TV series. Use these phrases to help you.
- My favourite film/show is … It's a comedy.
- What's it about? It's about a group of friends.
- Who's in it? … is/are the main actor(s).
- What's it like? It's dramatic/exciting/funny/scary/strange.

My favourite TV series is Anne With an E. It's about a teenage girl with no parents. It's dramatic and exciting and sometimes it's quite funny.

Exercise 4
Possible answers: animated, horror, musical, western

Exercise 5
🔊 audioscript page 246

Exercise 9
▶ videoscript page 246
1 Jaycee's favourite British TV series is *Not Going Out*. It's a sitcom about housemates doing normal things.
2 Jay's favourite series is *Wolf Hall*. It's a historical drama about Henry VIII. He likes it because he's studied British history of that period.

I can talk about films and television.   51   Unit 4

4.2 Grammar
Comparatives and superlatives, too/(not) enough, (not) as … as

1 Do you prefer watching films at home or at the cinema? Why?

2 🔊 4.5 Read the article quickly and choose the correct option.
1 Adam, Jessica and Alice watched a film in *3-D* / **4-D**.
2 They watched the film *at home* / **at the cinema**.

4-D experience

Your seat moves, you feel water on your face and you can smell something. It's the latest 4-D cinema experience. The screens are bigger and the seats are in the most comfortable position for your eyes and neck. But is it fun? 'It's more exciting than 3-D,' said fifteen-year-old Adam, 'because it's brighter and louder.' His friend Jessica agrees. 'The most exciting scene was in the car. I felt like I was driving, but my car wasn't fast enough.' For others, the experience isn't as good as 3-D and you can feel sick.

'The moving seats were worse than the sound!' said Alice. 'I was too uncomfortable.' Some special effects are also scarier in 4-D. Of course, the tickets are also more expensive, but it seems some people are happy to pay for 'the best feeling in the world'!

Exercise 3
Examples of comparatives: underlined in red
Examples of superlatives: underlined in green

Exercise 4
2 cheaper; more relaxing
3 funniest
4 more interesting
5 most expensive
6 worst

Exercise 6
▶ videoscript page 247

Sophie: theatre is better – more of an experience; comedies are better – they allow you to relax
Jacqui: theatre is better – it's live
Jonathan: theatre is better – closer experience with actors
Ellie: theatre is better – you're more involved, you get the real feel from it
Celia: documentaries are better – you learn things and they can be funny
Jaycee: books are better – they allow you to imagine things as you read

3 Study the Grammar box. Find more examples of comparatives and superlatives in the text.

GRAMMAR Comparatives and superlatives, too/(not) enough, (not) as … as

Comparatives
The screens are bigger.   It's more exciting than 3-D.

Superlatives
It's the latest 4-D experience.
The most exciting scene was in the car.
It's the best feeling in the world.

too/(not) enough
I was too uncomfortable.   My car wasn't fast enough.

(not) as … as
The experience isn't as good as 3-D.

GRAMMAR TIME ▶ PAGE 129

4 Complete the sentences with the correct form of the words in brackets.
1 They filmed the *best* (good) Doctor Who episodes in Wales.
2 It's _____ (cheap) to watch films at home than at the cinema and it's _____ (relaxing).
3 Top Gear is the _____ (funny) show on TV.
4 The book is often _____ (interesting) than the film.
5 The _____ (expensive) cinema ticket I bought cost £20.
6 It can be noisy in the cinema. The _____ (bad) thing is when people keep talking.

5 Complete the second sentence so that it means the same as the first one.
1 The adults aren't as good as the children in that film.
   The children are *better than* the adults in that film.
2 Our town isn't big enough for a theatre.
   Our town is *too small* for a theatre.
3 The film is funnier than the book.
   The book isn't *as funny as* the film.
4 The main character in the film is too boring.
   The main character in the film isn't *interesting enough*.
5 The French thriller isn't as scary as the Danish thriller.
   The Danish thriller is *scarier than* the French thriller.

VIDEO ▶ WIDER WORLD

6 ▶ 21 Watch six people talking about entertainment. Make notes about each person's opinion.

7 What's your opinion? Write two sentences for each comparison. Use the adjectives in brackets or your own ideas.
1 the theatre/the cinema (cheap/exciting)
2 comedies/documentaries (funny/interesting)
3 books/films (good/relaxing)

The cinema is cheaper than the theatre.
The theatre isn't as exciting as the cinema.

Unit 4 52 I can use the comparative and superlative of adjectives to describe things.

For the teacher
- Teaching notes, page 183
- *Need support?* worksheet, page 235
- Videoscript, page 247

On the Portal
- Grammar presentation
- Photocopiable activity: *Black Widow is better than Spider-man*
- Test: Grammar Check 4

For the student
- Workbook, page 40
- Grammar Time, Student's Book, page 129

On the Portal
- Workbook: Lesson 4.2
- Extra Practice Activities: Grammar, BBC Vox Pop

4.3 Reading and Vocabulary
How do you listen to music?

1 How do you get and listen to music? In pairs, make a list.

2 Read the post on a music blog. Which ideas from Exercise 1 does it mention?

What's the best way to listen to music?

The way we listen to music has changed since the days of CDs. Downloading playlists and streaming lip-synch music videos have ¹_____ very popular ways to enjoy your favourite music, but there are lots of other options too. I asked friends from my music college for their opinions.

Damon
Damon, a guitarist, doesn't like streaming music playlists or watching ²_____. Instead, he prefers going to live performances. 'Live performances are more exciting than videos and they're very important for musicians. We can ³_____ our music with the audience and see their reaction.'

André
André is a singer and he thinks online streaming services are fantastic. 'I'd rather ⁴_____ to music on my headphones and sing along to the songs. It's a fun way to practise!' He also says that musicians can find a new audience through the playlists on streaming services. That's a big help when you're starting in the music business.

Carmela
Finally, I find someone who agrees with me that music videos are the best. Carmela is a singer and guitarist, and she explains her reasons. 'I've learned a lot of great lyrics from lip-synching to music videos because you can often see them on your screen.' She says, 'I write my own song lyrics and streaming music videos is a good ⁵_____ to study other people's lyrics and learn what works. Most of all, I love making music videos and livestreaming my own songs.'

After I've spoken to everyone, I feel lucky that we have so many different ways to enjoy music. Are music videos the best? Send me your comments.

Next week: What's the best way to get a part in a musical?

3 ◀)) 4.6 Choose the correct answer to complete the blog post. Listen and check.
1 a grown   (b) become   c happened
2 (a) music videos b songs   c radios
3 a make   (b) share   c take
4 a sound   b hear   (c) listen
5 a idea   b time   (c) way

4 Read the blog post again and write D (Damon), A (André) or C (Carmela).
1 [A] Who thinks you reach different people on streaming services?
2 [C] Who has similar views to the blogger?
3 [C] Who plays and instrument and also sings?
4 [D] Who likes going to concerts?
5 [C] Who makes his/her own music?

5 ◀)) 4.7 **WORD FRIENDS** Complete the sentences with the correct form of the verbs from the phrases below. Listen and check.

> download a playlist   go to a live performance
> lip-synch to music videos   livestream an event
> record a track   sing along to songs   stream music
> write lyrics

1 When there's nobody else around, my mum _____ along to songs.
2 The organisers of the popular annual event are _____ it on the internet too.
3 I love music videos, but I also enjoy _____ to live performances.
4 We've booked a studio so we can _____ some new tracks.
5 Yesterday evening I _____ a new playlist.
6 She's always written poems and she sometimes _____ lyrics for singers.
7 I love that app that you can use to _____ to your favourite music videos.
8 I often stream lots of different kinds of _____ that I wouldn't usually listen to.

YOUR WORLD
6 In pairs, tell your partner about some music you listened to this week. What was it? How did you listen to it? Did you like it?

Exercise 2
Answers depend on students' answers to Exercise 1. The ideas mentioned in the text are: downloading music, streaming music, watching music videos, buying vinyls

EXAM

Exercise 3
A2 Key for Schools, Reading and Writing, Part 4, (3-option multiple-choice gap fill)

Exercise 5
1 sings
2 livestreaming
3 going
4 record
5 downloaded
6 writes
7 lip-synch
8 music

I can understand a post on a music blog.   53   Unit 4

For the teacher
- Teaching notes, page 184
- *Need support?* worksheet, page 235

On the Portal
- Photocopiable activity: *She's a star*
- Test: Vocabulary Check 4

For the student
- Workbook, page 41

On the Portal
- Workbook: Lesson 4.3
- Extra Practice Activities: Vocabulary

65

4.4 Grammar

Quantifiers: *some, any, much, many, (a) few, (a) little, a lot of, lots of*

VIDEO ▶ THE SHORT VIDEO CHALLENGE

Abe: Look, I've got more information about the video challenge. First, it can't be more than three minutes long. Second, there aren't many actors.
Eren: How many actors are there?
Abe: Three. And there are some things we need to include: a song, a postcard and an interview. What do you think, Bea?
Bea: I've got lots of ideas, but I like this one the best: this girl wants to be a star. She's got a lot of style, but she hasn't got any talent. She can't act or sing or …
Abe: Great idea!
Carla: I love it! There are very few people who sing as badly as I do. But I haven't got any clothes for this part. How much money have we got? Can we get a nice dress, for example?
Abe: We haven't got any money, so we can't buy any costumes.
Carla: Oh, and I only have a little make-up. Can I buy some more?
All: No!!!

TAKE 3 VIDEO CHALLENGE

Rules:
1. No more than 3 actors,
2. No more than 3 minutes long,
3. You must include 3 things:
 • a song,
 • a postcard,
 • an interview.

Exercise 2
1 It can't be more than three minutes long. There are only three actors. You must include three things: a song, a postcard and an interview.
2 a girl who wants to be a star but has no talent
3 Abe thinks it's a good idea. Carla loves the idea and wants to play the part.
4 Students' own answers

1 Read the poster. What is it about?
It is about a video challenge.

2 ▶ 22 ◀)) 4.8 Watch or listen and answer the questions.
1 What are the rules for the film challenge?
2 What kind of person is the character in Bea's idea for the video challenge?
3 What do Abe and Carla think of Bea's idea?
4 Would you like to make a short video? Why?/Why not?

3 Study the Grammar box. Find the sentences in the dialogue. Who says each sentence?

GRAMMAR Quantifiers

Countable nouns	Uncountable nouns
I've got a lot of/lots of ideas. How many actors are there? There aren't many actors.	She's got a lot of/lots of style. How much money have we got? We haven't got much money.
There are some things we need to include. I haven't got any clothes. Have you got any ideas?	I've got some information. She hasn't got any make-up. Have you got any make-up?
I've written down a few things. There are very few people.	I only have a little make-up. We've got very little time.

GRAMMAR TIME ▶ PAGE 129

4 ◀)) 4.9 Read about making a film. Choose the correct option. Listen and check.

You don't need ¹(much)/ few money to make a short film. In fact, you probably have ² any /(some) of the things you need at home! With your smartphone and a ³ few /(little) imagination you can create a short film in a ⁴ little /(few) hours. Ask your friends to be stars – there aren't ⁵ little /(many) people who haven't got ⁶(any) / many acting talent. Finally, think about how ⁷(many) / much things around your house you can use – costumes, make-up … and get filming!

5 Complete the sentences with one word in each gap.
1 How *much* time do you think it takes to make a short video?
2 Have you got *any/many* funny videos on your phone?
3 How *many* films have you seen in the last month?
4 I don't spend *much* time on my phone. Do you?
5 There are only a *few* actors I really like. What about you? Who are they?
6 There's *some* music from films or TV series that everyone knows. Do you agree? Can you think of *any* examples?

YOUR WORLD

6 In pairs, ask and answer the questions in Exercise 5.

Unit 4 54 I can talk about quantities.

For the teacher
• Teaching notes, page 185

On the Portal
• Grammar presentation
• Photocopiable activity: *Similarities and differences*
• Test: Grammar Check 4

For the student
• Workbook, page 42
• Grammar Time, Student's Book, page 129

On the Portal
• Workbook: Lesson 4.4
• Extra Practice Activities: Grammar, New Park video

4.5 Listening and Vocabulary
The June Festival

1 What's your favourite festival?

2 🔊 4.10 Listen to the first part of an interview with Bruno. Where are his parents from?
 a the USA
 b Portugal
 c Brazil

3 🔊 4.11 Listen to the second part of the interview and choose the correct answer.
 1 Why is the festival special for Bruno?
   a He doesn't have to go to school.
   b He enjoys the winter in Brazil.
   c He likes being with his family.
 2 How are the costumes different now?
   a Girls often wear the same type of clothes as boys.
   b Many boys don't wear checked shirts any more.
   c They don't paint their faces now.
 3 What happens in one funny race?
   a People in the race get a secret message.
   b Runners hold a spoon with an egg in it.
   c The winner gets some fish.
 4 What does the music celebrate?
   a old and young people
   b country life
   c carnival tradition
 5 What is Bruno's favourite food at the festival?
   a corn cake
   b popcorn
   c corn pudding

4 🔊 4.12 Study the Vocabulary box. Make compound nouns from the words below. Listen and check.

cake clothes dance dress hat holiday music party

VOCABULARY — Compound nouns

Noun	+	noun
family		holiday, party
summer		party clothes, dress, hat, holiday
country		clothes, dance, music
straw		hat
party		clothes, dress, hat, music
carnival		clothes, dance, dress, music
square		cake, dance

5 Write a few sentences to describe a festival or an event. Use the compound nouns from Exercise 4.
Last summer we had a big family party.

6 **YOUR WORLD** In pairs, discuss what makes a good festival for you. How important are the things below? Compare your ideas with the class.

☐ carnival music   ☐ cheap tickets
☐ friendly people ☐ fun games
☐ good entertainment
☐ sunny weather   ☐ tasty food

✗ not important   ✓✓ important
✓ quite important   ✓✓✓ very important

We think fun games are very important for all the family.
We don't think sunny weather is important.

Exercise 2
🔊 audioscript page 247

EXAM
Exercise 3
🔊 audioscript page 247
B1 Preliminary for Schools, Listening, Part 4, (3-option multiple choice)

4.6 Speaking
Talking about preferences

VIDEO ▶ **I'D RATHER NOT DANCE**

Abe: And … action!
Carla: Hello, I'm Gloria and I want to be a star!
Bea: Sit down, Gloria. You're in the right place.
Eren: I'm Van Dixon, agent to the stars. The most successful agent in the UK. Now, do you want to be a theatre actor?
Carla: No, <u>I'd rather not perform</u> on the stage.
Eren: <u>Would you rather work</u> in film or TV?
Carla: No, I'm too shy to be an actor. <u>I'd rather work</u> in the music business.
Eren: Fantastic! What instrument do you play?
Carla: Well, I played the triangle in the school orchestra.
Eren: Hmm, there aren't many big stars who play the triangle. Can you sing? Why don't you sing this song for me?
Carla: <u>I'd prefer to sing</u> a different song if that's all right.
Eren: <u>Which song would you prefer to sing</u>?
Carla: *All By Myself*. It suits my voice much better.
Eren: OK, please sing the song.
Carla: 'All by myself in the morning … '
Eren: I don't think singing is your special talent. Wouldn't you rather do something else? Perhaps dancing?
Carla: <u>I'd rather not dance</u>, but I can show you a trick.
Eren: Sure. Show me a trick that's better than your singing and you can have the job!
Carla: Great! Well, I can read your mind. I know the next word you're going to say. Do you know what word is on this card?
Eren: No, I don't know. Ha ha, well done!
Abe: Cut!

SOUNDS GOOD! You're in the right place. • I can read your mind.

Exercise 2
Possible answers:
Carla's character likes expensive, elegant clothes and jewellery. Eren's character is the 'boss'.

Exercise 3
Carla's character, Gloria, is clear she wants to be a star, but she isn't clear about how that can happen. Eren's character asks her useful questions to help her. By giving clear answers to the questions, they work out what 'Gloria' is good at.

Exercise 5
Carla's reasons: She's too shy to be an actor. *All By Myself* suits her voice much better.

Exercise 6
2 What would you prefer to watch?
3 What would you rather be?
4 Where would you prefer to go after school?
5 What would you rather learn?

1 What do you like doing with your friends? Choose two of the things below and say which one is better.

doing dance classes   eating out   listening to music
performing on stage together   playing games

I think eating out is better than doing dance classes.

2 ▶ 23 🔊 4.13 Look at the photo. What can you guess about Eren and Carla's characters? Watch or listen and check.

3 Is Carla's character clear about her career plans? How does Eren's character help her?

SET FOR LIFE

4 Have you thought about your future career? Discuss in pairs. Think about:
• your dreams
• your skills, interests and hobbies
• how you can learn about your strong and weak points

5 Study the Speaking box. Find examples of the phrases in the dialogue. What reasons does Carla give for her preferences?

SPEAKING Talking about preferences

Asking about preferences
(What) would you rather + verb?
(What) would you prefer to + verb?

Expressing preferences
I'd rather (not) + verb   I'd prefer (not) to + verb

Giving reasons
It sounds funny/great/boring.
It looks good.   It's healthier.

YOUR WORLD

6 Make questions from the prompts below. Then, in pairs, ask and answer the questions.
1 you / rather / do / tonight / ? (stay in/go out)
A: *What would you rather do tonight?*
B: *I'd rather stay in.*
2 you / prefer / watch / ? (a film/a sports programme)
3 you / rather / be / ? (an actor/a director)
4 you prefer / go / after school / ? (home/to a festival)
5 you rather / learn / ? (singing/a musical instrument)

Unit 4   56   I can talk about preferences.

For the teacher
• Teaching notes, page 187

On the Portal
• Photocopiable activity:
I'd rather not

For the student
• Workbook, page 44

On the Portal
• Workbook: Lesson 4.6
• Extra Practice Activities: New Park video

68

4.7 Writing
A review on a blog

TRENT'S THEATRE BLOG

MY LATEST REVIEW

BACK TO THE FUTURE THE MUSICAL
the Manchester Opera House

1. I've just seen a wonderful new musical that took me back to the past. It's *Back to the Future*.

2. The musical is based on the well-known 1985 Hollywood movie. It tells the story of a teenager (Marty McFly) who travels back in time to the 1950s with a crazy scientist, Doc Brown. In order to save his life, he has to work fast to make his parents fall in love before he can go back to the future.

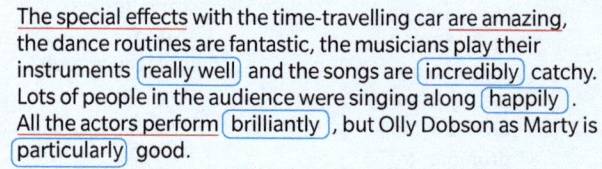

3. The special effects with the time-travelling car are amazing, the dance routines are fantastic, the musicians play their instruments [really well] and the songs are [incredibly] catchy. Lots of people in the audience were singing along [happily]. All the actors perform [brilliantly], but Olly Dobson as Marty is [particularly] good.

4. I love the film, but the musical is even better. Time flies in *Back to the Future* – it's over before you know it. Go and see it; it's the best show in town.

5. What's the best play you've seen recently? Write about it below.

1 Have you ever seen a play or musical at the theatre? What was it like?

2 Read the review quickly and answer the questions.
1. What is the play about?
2. Does the reviewer tell us the whole story?
3. How good are the performers?

3 Study the Writing box. Find examples of the phrases in the review.

WRITING › A review on a blog

1 Start your review
- Today I'm going to tell you about … You must see …
- I've just seen a wonderful new musical.
- It's the latest new film/play/book …

2 Describe the story
- The play is based on a movie/book …
- It tells the story of a teenager who …
- The story is about a girl who …

3 Describe the performance
- The special effects are amazing.
- All the actors perform brilliantly.
- A few people were crying quietly.

4 End your review
- I really love the film, but the musical is even better.
- I highly recommend this show.
- It's the best show in town.

5 End your blog post
- What's the best play you've seen recently? Write about it below.

---

4 Which other phrases from the review could you add to part 3 of the Writing box?

5 Study the Language box. Find examples of adverbs in the review. Then use adverbs to talk or write about films or live performances you have seen.

LANGUAGE › Adverbs

Adverbs come **after** a verb or subject
All the actors performed brilliantly.

or **before** an adjective or adverb.
She sang really well.

WRITING TIME

6 Write an online review of a film or a live performance.

1 Find ideas
Make notes for a review.
- Where and when did you see it?
- What was it about?
- What's your opinion about the performance/performers?

2 Plan
Organise your ideas into paragraphs. Use the review in Exercise 2 to help you.

3 Write and share
- Write a draft review. Use the Language box and the Writing box to help you.
- Share your review with another student for feedback.
- Use the feedback from your partner and write the final version of your review.

4 Check
- Check language: don't forget to use adjectives and adverbs.
- Check grammar: did you use comparatives, superlatives and quantifiers correctly?

I can write a review on a blog.

Exercise 2
1 It's about a teenager who travels back in time to the 1950s to make his parents fall in love in order to save his life.
2 No, we only get the most important details.
3 The dancers (dance routines) are fantastic. The musicians play really well. The actors perform brilliantly, especially Olly Dobson in the main role.

Exercise 4
The dance routines are fantastic.

The musicians play their instruments really well.

The songs are incredibly catchy.

Lots of people in the audience were singing along happily.

Olly Dobson as Marty is particularly good.

For the teacher
- Teaching notes, page 188
- *Need support?* worksheet, page 235

On the Portal
- Photocopiable activity: *A spectacular film*

For the student
- Workbook, page 45

On the Portal
- Workbook: Lesson 4.7

Vocabulary Activator

WORDLIST 🔊 4.14

Types of film
- action (n)
- cartoon (n)
- comedy (n)
- documentary (n)
- drama (n)
- musical (n)
- romance (n)
- science fiction (n)
- thriller (n)

Word building (entertainment)
- act (v)
- acting (n)
- actor (n)
- entertain (v)
- entertainer (n)
- entertainment (n)
- perform (v)
- performance (n)
- performer (n)
- produce (v)
- producer (n)
- production (n)
- review (v, n)
- reviewer (n)

Film and TV
- audience (n)
- channel (n)
- character (n)
- episode (n)
- hit (n)
- series (n)
- special effects (n)
- TV show (n)
- viewer (n)

Word friends (music)
- download a playlist
- go to a live performance
- lip-synch to music videos
- livestream an event
- record a track
- sing along to songs
- stream music
- write lyrics

Compound nouns
- carnival dress (n)
- country music (n)
- family holiday (n)
- family party (n)
- party dress (n)
- square dance (n)
- straw hat (n)
- summer holiday (n)

Extra words
- 4-D experience (n)
- album (n)
- animated film (n)
- based on (adj)
- biographical (adj)
- carnival (n)
- celebrate (v)
- challenge (n)
- check out (v)
- collect (v)
- costume (n)
- dialogue (n)
- dramatic (adj)
- drummer (n)
- exciting (adj)
- fantastic (adj)
- film festival (n)
- get a part
- guitarist (n)
- headphones (n)
- interview (n)
- location (n)
- main character (n)
- make-up (n)
- musician (n)
- old-fashioned (adj)
- personal (adj)
- programme (n)
- proud (adj)
- radio station (n)
- reaction (n)
- record player (n)
- romantic comedy (n)
- scary (adj)
- scene (n)
- seat (n)
- spectacular (adj)
- stage (n)
- star (n)
- style (n)
- successful (adj)
- talent (n)
- theatre (n)
- voice (n)
- wonderful (adj)

Exercise 1
1. entertainer, performer, producer, reviewer, character, viewer
2. act, entertain, perform, produce, review
3. cartoon, comedy

Exercise 5
1. The others relate to TV.
2. The others relate to music.
3. The others refer to people.
4. The others are types of film.

Exercise 6
1. audience, character, comedy, theatre
2. performance, producer, production, reviewer

---

1 Use the wordlist to find these things.
1. six words for people that end in -er
2. five verbs about things you do when you work in film
3. two types of film that can make you laugh

2 Choose the correct option. Then tick (✓) the sentences that are true for you. In pairs, compare your answers.
1. ☐ I like going to live performers / *performances*.
2. ☐ I read *reviews* / reviewers of films.
3. ☐ I watch a lot of special effects / *series*.
4. ☐ I sing along at / *to* songs.
5. ☐ I'd like to take part in a TV channel / *show*.

3 In what type of film might you hear each of these lines?

I love you. I've always loved you. Marry me!	Put your hands up and lie face down!
1 *romance/drama*	2 *action/thriller*

This is a rare animal that you can only see in this part of Africa.	There is life here, but not the kind we know on Earth.
3 *documentary*	4 *science fiction*

4 In pairs, talk about the types of film you prefer.

5 Choose the odd one out.
1. episode   viewer   channel   *audience*
2. voice   lyrics   *actor*   song
3. musician   producer   *thriller*   entertainer
4. musical   drama   romance   *viewer*

6 🔊 4.15 **PRONUNCIATION** Listen to the words below and write them in the correct column according to the word stress.

~~audience~~ character comedy performance producer production reviewer theatre

1 Ooo	2 oOo
audience	

7 🔊 4.16 **PRONUNCIATION** Listen to the first word from Exercise 6 again. The underlined sound is a weak sound (/ə/). Listen to the rest of the words again and underline all the weak /ə/ sounds.

audi<u>e</u>nce

audi<u>e</u>nce, char<u>a</u>cter, com<u>e</u>dy, perform<u>a</u>nce, pr<u>o</u>ducer, pr<u>o</u>duction, review<u>e</u>r, theatre

---

For the teacher
- Audioscript, page 247

On the Portal
- Photocopiable activities: What's the word?, Make a sentence
- Tests: Unit 4 Test, Unit 4 Writing Test

For the student
- Workbook, pages 46–47

On the Portal
- Workbook: Self-check
- Wordlist
- Extra Practice Activities: Self-check

Revision

Vocabulary

1 Complete the sentences with words formed from the words in brackets.

WHAT MAKES A GOOD FILM?

1. ☐ The director knows how to get the best *performance* (perform) from the film stars.
2. ☐ The *acting* (act) is good.
3. ☐ The *actors* (act) are famous.
4. ☐ The *producer* (produce) spends a lot of money on the film.
5. ☐ The film gets good *reviews* (review) from most *reviewers* (review).

2 Put the sentences in exercise 1 in order of importance for you (1 = most important). Then, in pairs, compare your answers.

3 Complete the compound nouns in the sentences with the words below.

| country | dress | family | holiday | ~~party~~ |
| square | straw | | | |

1. We need to help Gina choose a *party* dress for her 18th birthday party.
2. The summer *holiday* begins in a few weeks when the spring school term ends.
3. We have a *family* party every Saturday when I see my grandparents, uncles and aunts.
4. In a *square* dance, dancing partners stand on four sides looking to the middle.
5. The carnival *dress* that people are wearing often tells you about what they are celebrating.
6. I like *country* music: I like the sound of banjos and guitars.
7. Wear a *straw* hat because it will keep your head cool and go with your clothes!

4 Write the correct word for each definition.

1. A type of film that has a lot of songs in it. *musical*
2. A selection of songs for a particular purpose, or that you most enjoy listening to. *playlist*
3. The people who watch or listen to a film, play, concert, etc. *audience*
4. You change this on your TV to watch a different programme. *channel*
5. Play video or sound on your computer directly from the internet. *livestream*

Grammar

5 Complete the sentences with one word in each gap. Then, in pairs, say if you agree or disagree.

1. Some films just aren't funny *enough* to be called comedies – they should be called something else.
2. Musicals are better *than* science fiction films.
3. Animated films are *the* best kind of film.
4. The seats in the back of the cinema aren't *as* good as the ones at the front.
5. One-hour TV documentaries are *too* long for me to watch – I get bored at the end.
6. Action films are *more* exciting than comedies.

6 Complete the sentences to show your opinion. Use the superlative form of the adjectives in brackets.

1. *Salads are the healthiest* (healthy) kind of food.
2. _____ (good) kind of TV show.
3. _____ (easy) musical instrument to learn.
4. Documentaries about _____ (interesting) ones.
5. _____ (difficult) job in film-making.

> **Exercise 6**
> 2 … are the best
> 3 … is the easiest
> 4 … are the most interesting
> 5 … is the most difficult

7 Complete the dialogue with the words below.

| any | few | little | lot | ~~lots~~ | many | much (x2) | some |

Jo: Come on! Let's go and see this film tonight. It had ¹*lots* of good reviews.
Ian: When does it start? We need a ²*little* time to get ready.
Jo: 8 p.m. We've got a ³*lot* of time. How ⁴*many* tickets do we need?
Ian: Four. Can you get them at the front?
Jo: No, there aren't ⁵*any* seats left at the front.
Ian: How ⁶*much* money do we need, with drinks and maybe a ⁷*few* snacks?
Jo: Not ⁸*much*. I think ten pounds each should be enough for everything.
Ian: Hmm… I'll need to ask my mum for ⁹*some* money, then. I've only got six pounds!

> **Exercise 8**
> Sample answer:
> A What would you prefer to watch: the action film or the science fiction film?
> B I'd rather watch the science fiction film.
> A Why?
> B It sounds more interesting and I like the actors.

Speaking

8 In pairs, follow the instructions to role play a dialogue. Then swap roles.
You want to watch a film together. Decide what to watch.
- Student A: Ask Student B about his/her preference.
- Student B: Express your preference.
- Student A: Ask why.
- Student B: Give reasons for your preference.

Dictation

9 🔊 4.17 Listen. Then listen again and write down what you hear.

> **EXAM**
> **Exercise 9**
> 🔊 audioscript page 247
> **International Certificate Level 1/2**, Listening and Writing, Section 2, (dictation)

SET FOR LIFE

Team up!

Exercise 2
Possible answer:
They have to organise a charity event on the school field or in the school hall, find some volunteers and think about the jobs that they want them to do.

Exercise 4
🔊 audioscript page 247

Cake sale
Advantages: People like baking cakes and eating them; easy to organise
Disadvantages: A lot of people don't want to eat too much sugar.
Video games competition
Advantages: fun
Disadvantages: People don't pay to watch events like that.
Fashion show
Disadvantages: difficult to organise

Exercise 5
🔊 audioscript page 247

Exercise 6
Tessie never loses things, so the money will be safe with her. David plays in a band, so he probably knows lots of musicians. Connor is creative and Stanley is good at art. Ed is strong and Lucy is probably strong too because she plays rugby.

SCHOOL CHARITY EVENT

We need volunteers!

Do you want to help us to raise money for charity?

- We're planning this year's school charity event and we need your help.
- If you're interested, please write and tell us about your personality, skills and interests.

Layla, Connor, Tessie and Ed
Charity Team Leaders

✉️
Dear Charity Team Leaders,
Well done for your posters. I hope you've got lots of volunteers now.
How is your other planning going? Have you chosen the type of event yet? Remember, you can hold it either on the sports field or in the school hall. And you'll need to start thinking about the jobs that you want your volunteers to do. You are leading the team!
Please let me know your plans.
Yours,
Mr Hussein
Head Teacher

charity video games competition

charity concert    charity cake sale

charity fashion show

1 Work in pairs. Have you ever been to the types of event in the photos? Would you like to go to one? Why?/Why not?

2 Read the advert and email. What does the charity team have to do?

3 In pairs, answer the questions about the events in the photos.
  1 How can these events raise money for charity?
  2 What are the advantages and disadvantages of each type of event?

4 🔊 4.18 Listen to the first part of the charity team meeting. Which event do they choose? Do they mention any of your ideas from Exercise 3? *They choose a music concert.*

5 🔊 4.19 Listen to another part of the meeting. Answer the questions with the names below.

   Connor and Stanley   David   Ed and Lucy   Tessie

  1 Who will print and sell the tickets? *Tessie*
  2 Who will invite the bands? *David*
  3 Who will design tickets and prepare the sports field? *Connor and Stanley*
  4 Who will move the tables and equipment? *Ed and Lucy*

6 Why do they think these are the right people for the jobs?

Units 3–4 **60** I can lead a team of people.

For the teacher
- Teaching notes, page 189
- Audioscript, page 247

On the Portal
- Photocopiable activity: *Team up!*

Lead a team

7 🔊 4.19 Study the Useful Phrases box. Listen again and tick (✓) the expressions you hear in the second part of the meeting.

8 You are organising a charity fashion show. In pairs, discuss which job is the most suitable for each volunteer.

I think that's a good job for … because …

JOBS LIST

Before the event
1. encourage local shops to lend clothes for the show
2. advertise the event
3. design and sell tickets
4. move furniture to prepare the hall

During the event
5. announce each clothes design to the audience
6. help the models change clothes and do hair and make-up – at least two people

After the event

LIST OF VOLUNTEERS

Mia: 'I'm confident, polite and organised. I want to have my own business one day.'

Adi: 'I'm very friendly and confident. I love to make people laugh. I'm good at Maths.'

Alfie: 'I'm very kind and helpful. I'm good at swimming and I love video games.'

Sairi: 'I'm friendly and I'm good at making people feel more confident. I'm good at doing make-up, and arts and crafts too.'

Rachel: 'I'm creative and good with technology, but I'm quite shy. I can design websites.'

Will: 'I write a blog about everything from fashion to food. I like to be a leader, but I can be a bit bossy sometimes!'

9 Read the Useful Tips. In pairs, discuss the questions.
1. Do you think it's easy to be a good leader? Why?/Why not?
2. Would you like to be the leader of a team or group? Why?/Why not?
3. Why do you think it is a good idea to vote on decisions?

SET FOR LIFE

10 In small groups, plan a charity event. Follow these steps.

1. Vote on which charity event to organise and who or what to raise money for.
2. Decide on a jobs list with tasks to do before, during and after the event.
3. Match volunteers with the tasks. Remember to consider their skills, strengths and interests.
4. Present your plan for the charity event to the class.

61 Units 3–4

USEFUL TIPS

When you are leading a team of people, it's important to think carefully about how you work together.

- Vote to make team decisions.
- Remember that you can't do everything yourself.
- Spread the jobs fairly between the people in the team.
- Explain clearly what you want people to do.
- Encourage people and thank them for their ideas.

USEFUL PHRASES

Choosing an event
☐ I love the idea of a …
☐ … is probably (not) the best way to make a lot of money for charity.
☐ Let's vote. Who votes for a … ?

Giving the right job to the right person
✓ People who … are usually good at …-ing.
✓ I think creative/shy/funny people enjoy that kind of job.
✓ We need creative/strong/confident people to …
✓ Can … print … ?
✓ Who can we ask to … ?
☐ Let's ask … to …

Exercise 8
Possible answers:
1. I think that's a good job for Mia because she's confident and polite. She's interested in business, too, so she will like meeting the owners of local shops. Or maybe Will can do it because he's interested in fashion. Then Mia can do job 3.
2. Rachel can do that. She's creative, so she can design adverts, and good with technology, so she can put the adverts on the internet. She can design a website for our event too.
3. That's a good job for Mia because she's confident, polite and organised. It might also suit Sairi because she's good at arts, and she's friendly and good with people. Adi can help to sell tickets, too, because he's good at Maths.
4. Alfie is probably strong because he's good at swimming. He's kind and helpful too.
5. That's a good job for Adi because he's confident and he likes to make people laugh.
6. That's a good job for Sairi because she's good at doing make-up. And she can make the models feel more confident for the show.

73

To the limit

5

VOCABULARY
Sports equipment | Sporting events | Sports collocations | Fitness and training | Word building: sport

GRAMMAR
Future forms: *will*, *be going to*, Present Continuous and Present Simple | First Conditional with *if* and *unless*

Four amazing sporting records

1 Surfing
Standing on a surfboard is difficult enough normally, but in 2013 American Bernie Boehm surfed for thirty-three seconds while spinning a basketball on one finger!

2 Athletics
In 2008 German Christopher Irmscher ran 100 metres along a running track and jumped over ten hurdles. It took him 14.82 seconds. That's not fast. That's because he was wearing flippers on his feet instead of trainers, and a mask and snorkel on his head! How strange!

3 Cycling
In 2013 another German, Jens Stotzner went cycling … underwater! He rode his bike around the bottom of a swimming pool seventy-eight times – a distance of 6.708 kilometres! I wonder if he was wearing a helmet!

4 Ice hockey
In 2008, the Slovakian women's ice hockey team beat Bulgaria. They won the match very easily, scoring a goal every forty-four seconds! On the electronic scoreboard, the final score was 82–0!

Exercise 1
Possible answers:
Indoor sports: judo, weight training, yoga
Outdoor sports: cycling, jogging, roller skating, tennis, walking
Team sports: baseball, basketball, hockey, rugby, volleyball
Individual sports: surfing, swimming
Water sports: kite surfing, sailing, windsurfing
Winter sports: skating, skiing, snowboarding

Exercise 2
Photo A: helmet, skis
Photo B: flippers, mask, snorkel
Photo C: rackets, net

5.1 Vocabulary
Sport

1 **I KNOW!** Add as many sports as you can to these groups.
1 indoor sports: *table tennis, …*
2 outdoor sports: *running, …*
3 team sports: *football, …*
4 individual sports: *jogging, …*
5 water sports: *swimming, …*
6 winter sports: *skiing, …*

2 🔊 5.1 Study Vocabulary box A. Which of the things in the box can you see in photos A–C?

VOCABULARY A — **Sports equipment**

basketball   bat   flippers   football kit   helmet
life jacket   mask   mat   net   racket   skateboard
skates   skis   snorkel   snowboard   surfboard

Unit 5   62

For the teacher
- Teaching notes, page 190
- Audioscript, page 248

On the Portal
- Vocabulary Memory Game
- **Photocopiable activity:** *Sports*
- **Test:** Vocabulary Check 5

For the student
- Workbook, pages 48–49

On the Portal
- Workbook: Lesson 5.1
- Extra Practice Activities: Vocabulary

3 Answer the quiz questions with words from Vocabulary box A. What sports do you do? What equipment do you use? In pairs, compare your answers and discuss the questions.

Test your sports knowledge

1. What do you hit a baseball or a cricket ball with? *bat*
2. What do you wear on your head to protect you when you go cycling? *helmet*
3. What do you wear when you go kayaking or sailing to keep you safe? *life jacket*
4. What equipment do you need to do snorkeling? *flippers, mask, snorkel*
5. What can you put on the floor to make yoga exercises more comfortable? *mat*
6. What two things do you need to play badminton or tennis? *net, racket*
7. What can you use to ride the waves on the sea? *surfboard*

4 Read the article quickly. Find all the items of sports equipment it mentions. *surfboard, basketball, flippers, trainers, mask, snorkel, bike, helmet, scoreboard*

5 Read the article again and answer the questions. In pairs, compare your answers.
1. Which record do you think is the most amazing?
2. Which is your favourite? Why?
3. What other sporting records do you know?

6 🔊 5.2 Listen to a radio interview. According to Sandi, which two sports are NOT Olympic sports? *(roller) skating and yoga*

7 🔊 5.3 Study Vocabulary box B. Complete the blog post below with words from the box in the correct form. Listen and check.

VOCABULARY B | **Sporting events**

changing room court fan opponent pitch
scoreboard stadium tournament track

8 🔊 5.4 **WORD FRIENDS** Complete the phrases with the words below. Listen and check.

beat goal medal record take part
take up team ~~volunteer~~

1. *volunteer* at a sports event/club
2. *take part* in a race/competition
3. *take up* a sport
4. win a *medal*/game/match
5. break/hold a *record*
6. score a *goal*
7. support a *team*
8. *beat* a team/an opponent

YOUR WORLD

9 In pairs, ask and answer the questions.
1. Do you prefer team sports or individual sports? Why?
2. What is your favourite sporting event to watch on TV?
3. What sport would you like to take up in the future?

Exercise 6
🔊 audioscript page 248

My greatest sporting success

My greatest sporting success didn't take place on a running ¹*track* in a big ²*stadium*. It was on the tennis ³*court* behind my school last June. It was the first game in a tennis ⁴*tournament*. I didn't feel nervous as I took my kit out of my bag in the ⁵*changing* rooms. Nobody expected me to win, not even me. (I'm not very good at tennis.) But that day I played brilliantly. My racket felt like part of my arm. Almost every ball I hit went flying over the net. My ⁶*opponent* didn't know what to do. I won the match easily. The final score was 6–1, 6–2. I've never played so well since then!

I can talk about sports equipment and sporting events. 63 Unit 5

5.2 Grammar

Future forms: *will, be going to*, Present Continuous, Present Simple

VIDEO ▶ THE FITNESS CLASS

Bea: You're wet.
Abe: It's raining. I'm doing the 5K Fun Run next month, so I need to train or I won't be able to finish. But they say it's going to rain all week.
Bea: Are you really going to run five kilometres? It's hard. Carla's coming round to do our fitness class. It starts in ten minutes. Do you want to do it with us?
Abe: Fitness class? Will that help me run 5K?
Bea: Yes, it will. Come on, you'll enjoy it!
Abe: OK, I'll do it.
Later …
Bea: Right, this is going to be fun. First, skipping.
Abe: I can't do it!
Bea: I'll show you.
Carla: Maybe you'll do better with this.
Abe: I'll fall off.
Carla: No, you won't. Oh!
Bea: OK, I'm sure you'll manage this.
Abe: This is tough. This is going to kill me!
Bea: Abe! What are you doing?
Abe: I'm going home. And you know what? I'm never going to complain about running in the rain again!

1 In groups, ask and answer the questions.
  1 What do you do to keep fit?
  2 Is it better to go to a gym to keep fit or to exercise at home? Why?

2 ▶ 24 🔊 5.5 Watch or listen and answer the questions.
  1 Why is Abe unhappy?
  2 What's Bea's suggestion?
  3 How easy does Abe find the class?

Exercise 2
1 Because he needs to train for a fun run, and he doesn't like running in the rain.
2 Abe should take part in the fitness class that Bea does with Carla.
3 He finds it very hard.

3 Study the Grammar box. Find all the examples of future forms in the dialogue.

> **GRAMMAR** Future forms
>
> **Predictions or decisions made at the moment of speaking**
> I'll do it!
> I won't be able to finish.
> Will that help me run 5K? Yes, it will.
>
> **Plans and predictions based on things we know now**
> It's going to rain all week.
> Are you really going to run five kilometres?
>
> **Arrangements**
> I'm doing the 5K Fun Run next month.
>
> **Timetables**
> It starts in ten minutes.

GRAMMAR TIME > PAGE 130

4 Complete the sentences with the correct form of the verbs in brackets. Use the future form in bold.
  1 Over 200 people *are going to take* (take) part in the 5K charity run. **be going to**
  2 The run *starts* (start) at 10 a.m. tomorrow. **Present Simple**
  3 I'm sure I *won't win* (not win) the race. **will**
  4 What *are we going to do* (we/do) after the run? **be going to**
  5 We *'re having* (have) a picnic in the park. **Present Continuous**
  6 I *'ll bring* (bring) some crisps and juice. **will**

5 🔊 5.6 Choose the best option. Listen and check.
A: What ¹*are you doing* / do you do tomorrow morning?
B: I don't know. ²I / *I'll* probably just stay in. Why?
A: I've decided ³I'll / *I'm going to* get fit this summer, so ⁴I'll take / *I'm taking* part in a new fitness class in the park. It's ⁵being / *going to be* great. Why don't you come?
B: What time ⁶*does it* / is it going to start?
A: ⁷It's starting / *It starts* at 8 o'clock, but ⁸I'll / *I'm going to* try to get there ten minutes early.
B: OK, ⁹*I'll try* / I'm trying it.
A: Great! ¹⁰I / *I'll* see you there!

YOUR WORLD

6 Complete the sentences to make them true for you.
  1 I think I'll … this evening.
  2 When I'm fifty, I won't …
  3 Next weekend I'm going to …
  4 My best friend is never going to …
  5 My football team is playing …
  6 This year the school holidays begin …

I can talk about plans, predictions, arrangements and timetables.

For the teacher
• Teaching notes, page 191

On the Portal
• Grammar presentation
• Photocopiable activity: *Future chat*
• Test: Grammar Check 5

For the student
• Workbook, page 50
• Grammar Time, Student's Book, page 130

On the Portal
• Workbook: Lesson 5.2
• Extra Practice Activities: Grammar, New Park video

5.3 Reading and Vocabulary
Sports and hobbies

Competitive sport or just a hobby?

We talked to three teenagers about how they train and how seriously they take their sports.

Carrie, 14 – rhythmic gymnastics

I go to the gym twice a week. My <u>coach</u> says it's really important to <u>warm up</u>, so we do lots of <u>exercises</u> before the class: we <u>stretch</u> and jump and jog. Then we <u>practise</u> the different techniques. I prefer working with the ribbon. Afterwards, we <u>warm down</u> to some relaxing music. I love rhythmic gymnastics, but I don't think I'll ever take part in any serious competitions. I just do it for fun and to keep fit. But I'm going to volunteer at the next big competition.

Ryan, 16 – ice hockey

You have to be fit to play ice hockey, so I <u>work out</u> at a local gym most days to build up <u>strength</u> in my legs and body. Being fit and strong helps you keep your <u>balance</u> when you're on the ice. I watch a lot of games on my computer to learn new <u>skills</u> and I <u>practise</u> with my team at the ice rink three times a week. My dad's our <u>coach</u>. He's a volunteer, not a professional, but he's really good. I'm never going to take up ice hockey professionally, but it's a great hobby.

Suzy, 15 – triathlon

In a youth triathlon competition, you have to swim 750 metres, cycle 20 kilometres and run 5 kilometres. So, you have to train very seriously. I'm going to follow a new <u>training programme</u> from next week. My mum's a doctor. She says that at my age, you shouldn't train more than twenty hours a week, so I'm going to swim two kilometres three times a week, go running on Tuesdays, Thursdays and Saturdays, and cycle every Sunday for three hours. That's eighteen hours. Maybe one day I'll be good enough to compete in the Olympics. I hope so!

1 In which sports do athletes train the hardest, in your opinion?

2 🔊 5.7 Work in pairs. Look at the photos and read the article quickly. Have you tried any of these sports? If not, which would you like to try?

3 Read the article again, and write C (Carrie), R (Ryan) or S (Suzy).
1. [R] Who follows his/her sport online to get better?
2. [C] Who mentions a favourite piece of equipment?
3. [R] Who trains with a family member?
4. [S] Who would like to get involved in competitive sport?
5. [C] Who mentions how training starts and finishes?
6. [S] Whose coach warns younger people not to train too much?

4 🔊 5.8 Study the Vocabulary box and find the words in the article. Then complete the sentences below with the correct form of words from the box. Listen and check.

VOCABULARY Fitness and training

balance   coach   exercise   practise   skill
strength   stretch   training programme
warm up/down   work out

1. I find it easy to learn new _skills_.
2. I'm good at keeping my _balance_.
3. I get bored if I have to _practise_ a sport a lot.
4. I've never had a personal fitness _coach_ or followed a _training programme_.
5. I think it's important to _warm_ up before you jog or do _exercises_.
6. I think I'll start going to a gym so I can _work_ out and build up my _strength_.

5 In pairs, say if the sentences in Exercise 5 are true for you.

VIDEO **WIDER WORLD**

6 ▶ 25 Watch four people talking about volunteering at a sports event. What reason(s) does each speaker give for wanting to be a volunteer?

7 In pairs, say what sports event you would like to volunteer at and why.

I would like to volunteer at a rhythmic gymnastics event because I love watching it and I'd like to get free tickets.

EXAM

Exercise 3
A2 Key for Schools, Reading and Writing, Part 2, (matching)

Exercise 6

▶ videoscript page 248

Josie: to help others get inside, to get insight into something you wouldn't see as a customer, to be part of a large-scale sports event
Athena: it's good for her CV, to meet some new people with similar interests
Monica: it's important and fun
Sunita: has never done it before, thinks she'll enjoy it

I can understand an article about fitness and training.

For the teacher
- Teaching notes, page 192
- *Need support?* worksheet, page 236
- Videoscript, page 248

On the Portal
- Vocabulary Memory Game
- Photocopiable activity: *Running up that hill*
- **Test:** Vocabulary Check 5

For the student
- Workbook, page 51

On the Portal
- Workbook: Lesson 5.3
- Extra Practice Activities: Vocabulary, BBC Vox Pop

5.4 Grammar
First Conditional with *if* and *unless*

SLACKLINING CLUB

Have you ever thought of slacklining? If you like gymnastics, you'll love this modern sport! The only equipment you need is a simple rope, or 'line', about five centimetres wide. You start with a very low line, about fifty centimetres above the ground. If you fall, you won't hurt yourself and if you improve, you will soon try some new tricks. You can do slacklining anywhere, but you need a tree or something strong to fix each end of the line.

Are you a climber, a surfer or a skateboarder? Slacklining can help your balance. Also, if you don't enjoy team sports, this will be a good choice for you. So, if you want to try something different, come along.

Our club is free!

Will you be a champion slackliner? You won't know unless you try!

WHERE? Baxter's Park   **WHEN?** Saturdays, 10 a.m.

Exercise 1
Possible answer: She's balancing, walking and jumping on a rope.

Exercise 2
It's like a rope, and it's above the ground. You walk on/along it, so you can practise balancing.

Exercise 6
▶ videoscript page 248

1 … I will probably go there.
2 … I will probably go with them to a park to throw a Frisbee or something.
3 … I will buy a meal for my family./… I will look at flights and see where I can book a flight to./… I will maybe travel in Africa.

---

1 Look at the photo in the advert. What is the girl doing? Use the words below to help you. Do you think you can do this activity? Why?/ Why not?

> balance   fall   jump   rope   walk

2 🔊 5.9 Read the advert. What is a slackline?

3 Study the Grammar box. Find more examples of the First Conditional in the advert.

> **GRAMMAR** — **First Conditional with *if* and *unless***
>
> You **won't know** if you **don't try**!
> You **won't know** unless you **try**!
>
> Time clauses with *when* follow a similar pattern.
> **When** I**'m** back home, I**'ll watch** some slacklining videos.

GRAMMAR TIME ▶ PAGE 130

4 Match the sentence halves.
1 [c] If you do slacklining,
2 [a] You won't do any special tricks
3 [d] I won't go to the slacklining club
4 [b] You'll see people slacklining

a unless you're very good.
b if you go to the park on Saturday.
c you will improve your balance.
d unless a friend comes too.

5 🔊 5.10 Read the information and complete the sentences below with the correct form of the verbs in brackets. Listen and check.

> **Goodbye to the sports centre!**
> The old Riverside Sports Centre is closing next week. The new sports centre, with a large pool, tennis courts and a modern gym, won't be ready until next year.

1 If they _close_ (close) the sports centre, we _won't be_ (not be) able to play handball for ages.
2 I _won't stop_ (not stop) playing badminton if they _close_ (close) it.
3 We _won't have_ (not have) karate lessons unless the teacher _finds_ (find) a new classroom.
4 I _'ll go_ (go) swimming every week if they _build_ (build) a pool at the new centre.
5 If there _are_ (be) tennis courts, I _'ll take up_ (take up) tennis.
6 We _'ll join_ (join) the new gym if it _isn't_ (not be) too expensive.

VIDEO ▶ **WIDER WORLD**

6 ▶ 26 Watch four people talking about different situations. How do they complete the sentences below?
1 If there's a new sports centre in town, …
2 If my friends are free this evening, …
3 If I get some money for my birthday, …

7 Finish the sentences in Exercise 6 to make them true for you. In pairs, discuss your ideas.

Unit 5   66   I can use the First Conditional to talk about possible situations in the future.

For the teacher
- Teaching notes, page 193
- Need support? worksheet, page 236
- Videoscript, page 248

On the Portal
- Grammar presentation
- Photocopiable activity: What if … ?
- Test: Grammar Check 5

For the student
- Workbook, page 52
- Grammar Time, Student's Book, page 130

On the Portal
- Workbook: Lesson 5.4
- Extra Practice Activities: Grammar, BBC Vox Pop

5.5 Listening and Vocabulary
A fascinating footballer

1 Who is your favourite sportsperson? Why?

2 Read the fact file and mark the sentences T (true) or F (false).
1. [T] The Sports Personality Award is over sixty years old.
2. [T] You must be British to win the award.
3. [F] Nobody has won the award more than once.

FACT BOX

The BBC Sports Personality of the Year Award

Every December since 1954 the British public have chosen their sports personality of the year. He or she is the sportsperson that has achieved the most in that year. The winner must be British or live and play sport in the UK. Tennis player Andy Murray is the only person who has won the award three times.

3 What do you think sportspeople have to do to get a nomination for Sports Personality of the Year Award?

4 🔊 5.11 You will hear two friends talking about the Sports Personality of the Year Award. Listen and choose the correct answer for each question.
1. Callum thinks Marcus Rashford is
   a the best sportsperson in the UK.
   b the best English football player.
   c not as good as another player.
2. When Marcus Rashford plays for Manchester United, he wears the number
   a seven.   **b** ten.   c eleven.
3. Megan thinks the winner of the BBC award should be
   a the best athlete.   b the top goalscorer.
   c the best person.
4. How many free meals did Marcus Rashford's charity pay for?
   a 20 million   **b** 3 million   c 400,000
5. Marcus Rashford
   a can understand sign language.
   b studies at university.
   c writes for a magazine.

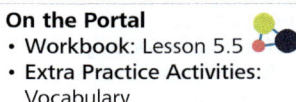

5 🔊 5.12 Study the Vocabulary box. Then look at the sentences below and decide if each underlined word is a verb, a noun for an action or a noun for a person.

VOCABULARY — Word building: sport

Verb	Noun (action)	Noun (person)
attack	attack	attacker
support	support	supporter
score	score	scorer
defend	defence	defender
manage	management	manager
train	training	trainer
coach	coaching	coach
practise	practice	–

1. He <u>scored</u> two goals in his first match.
2. The <u>supporters</u> want their team to <u>attack</u> more.
3. There's no football <u>practice</u> today because of the snow.
4. Our new <u>coach</u> makes us <u>train</u> very hard.
5. They lost 5-0 so their <u>manager</u> wasn't happy with the <u>defence</u>.

6 Complete the table.

Verb	Noun (action)	Noun (person)
kick	¹ kick	–
play	–	² player
present	–	³ presenter
race	⁴ race	–
win	⁵ win	⁶ winner

7 🔊 5.13 Complete the text with the correct form of words from Exercises 5 and 6. The first letter of each word is given. Listen and check.

5–0! That's a great ¹w<u>in</u>, isn't it? I'm not surprised our ²s<u>upporters</u> are singing. I'm delighted with the ³p<u>layers</u>. I always tell them that ⁴p<u>ractice</u> makes perfect and I've got to say they've been great in ⁵t<u>raining</u> all week. Our ⁶d<u>efenders</u> didn't have much to do today because our ⁷a<u>ttackers</u> were so good. They ⁸s<u>cored</u> some great goals. I'm so lucky to be their ⁹m<u>anager</u>!

Exercise 5
1 verb
2 noun (person); verb
3 noun (action)
4 noun (person); verb
5 noun (person); noun (action)

EXAM
Exercise 4
🔊 audioscript page 248

A2 Key for Schools, Listening, Part 3, (3-option multiple choice)

YOUR WORLD

8 Imagine you are going to vote for a Sports Personality of the Year. In groups of four, decide on three people. Share your ideas with the class, defending your choices. Then vote to decide.

I can understand a conversation about sports personalities.

5.6 Speaking
Talking about plans

VIDEO ▶ WHAT ARE YOU UP TO TODAY?

Eren: Guys, what are you doing next Saturday?
Abe: Nothing special. I don't have any plans.
Eren: Have you got any plans, Bea?
Bea: I don't think so.
Eren: What about you, Carla? What are your plans?
Carla: I don't know yet. Why?
Eren: I'm playing an important tennis match at 3 p.m. If you guys don't come, I won't have any fans. Can you make it?
All: Sure!/Yeah!/ Maybe.

Later …

Carla: I'm sorry, Eren, but I won't be able to come on Saturday. We're visiting my grandma …
Bea: Look, I'm so sorry. I'm going to help a friend paint her room on Saturday. And then we're going to the cinema.
Abe: Hey, Eren. What are you up to today?
Eren: I'm training for the tennis match.
Abe: Oh yeah, about that … I won't be able to make it. I'm going to a soccer match with my dad.

On Saturday …

Eren: What are you guys doing here?
Abe: We changed our plans!

SOUNDS GOOD!
• Nothing special.
• Can you make it?

1 In pairs, describe the photo. Why do you think the kids are at the tennis court? How does Eren feel?

2 ▶ 27 🔊 5.14 Watch or listen and check your answers to Exercise 1. Then match the people (1–4) with the plans they had (a–d).
1 [d] Abe   2 [a] Bea   3 [c] Carla   4 [b] Eren
a hang out with a friend
b play a sports match
c spend time with his/her family
d watch a sport event

SET FOR LIFE

3 In pairs, talk about a time in your life when you changed your plans for someone or when they changed their plans for you. Then decide on good reasons for changing your plans.

4 Study the Speaking box and read the dialogue again. Who says each sentence in the box?

SPEAKING   Talking about plans

Asking
What are you up to today/at the weekend? *Abe*
Have you got any plans for this evening/tomorrow? *Eren*
What are you doing on Sunday/next Saturday? *Eren*

Answering and following up
I'm/We're visiting my grandma/going to the cinema. *Carla, Bea*
First I'm going to a soccer match … *Abe*
I'm going to help …   *Bea*
Then …   After that …   Later … *Bea*
I don't have any plans.   I don't know yet. *Abe, Carla*
What about you?   And you?   What are your plans? *Eren*

5 🔊 5.15 Put the dialogue in the correct order. Use the Speaking box to help you. Listen and check.
a [7] Sam: Yes, that's a great idea.
b [1] Sam: What are you up to this weekend?
c [4] Tara: Sunday? Well, I'm definitely going to have a lie-in. Then I'll probably do some homework. Have you got any plans?
d [2] Tara: Well, first I'm visiting my aunt on Saturday morning. Then we're going to an ice hockey match. It starts at 3 p.m.
e [3] Sam: Sounds good. What are you doing on Sunday?
f [6] Tara: Do you want to go cycling?
g [5] Sam: I don't know yet. Nothing special.

YOUR WORLD

6 In pairs, ask and answer questions about your plans for the weekend. Use these ideas to help you.
• sports and activities   • shopping
• family and friends   • relaxation
• homework   • entertainment
• trips   • special events

7 Tell the class about your partner's plans.

Unit 5 **68** I can ask and talk about plans.

For the teacher
• Teaching notes, page 195
• *Need support?* worksheet, page 236

On the Portal
• Photocopiable activity: *Tell me your plans*

For the student
• Workbook, page 54

On the Portal
• Workbook: Lesson 5.6
• Extra Practice Activities: New Park video

80

5.7 Writing
Short messages

1 How do you and your friends usually send messages to each other? How long does it usually take you to reply?

2 Read the messages. What event did Dev, Alison, Callum and Mo take part in? Who won?
parkrun. Callum won the race.

3 Read the messages again and answer the questions.
1 What does Dev thank the volunteers for? Why does he congratulate them? What request does he make?
2 What does Alison thank her friends for? What request does she make?
3 Why does Mo congratulate his friend? What request does he make?

4 Study the Writing box. Find examples of the phrases in the messages in Exercise 2.

WRITING — Short messages: thanking, congratulating and making requests

1 **Greeting**
Hi …   Hi there …   Hiya …   Hey …

2 **Thank someone**
Thanks (so much) for your help/note/message/present …
Just a quick note to thank you for …

3 **Congratulate someone**
Congratulations on making/doing/organising …
Well done on winning/helping to …

4 **Make a request**
Could you (please) … ?   Would you mind … ?
If it's OK with you, I'll … ?
Would it be possible to … ?   Let me know if that's OK.

5 **End your message**
Bye,   Cheers,   All the best,   Best wishes,
See you later,

5 Study the Language box. Find similar sentences in the messages in Exercise 2. Then, in pairs, finish the sentences using your own ideas.

LANGUAGE — Prepositions + -ing form

Thanks **for** help**ing** me.
I felt nervous **before** start**ing** the race.
I was tired **after** runn**ing** so far.
I'm looking forward **to** see**ing** you again.
I'd like to congratulate you **on** winn**ing** the race.

Hi everyone,
Just a quick note to thank you all for volunteering at the parkrun on Saturday. And congratulations on making it such a success! Did anyone take photos of the event? If so, could you please send them to me so I can post them on the parkrun blog?
Best wishes,
Dev

← Alison

Hey guys,
Thanks for your help during the parkrun. I was ready to stop after running up that first hill, but then you stayed with me and encouraged me. Thanks so much! I'm already looking forward to taking part in next month's race. Would it be possible to train together this weekend? Let me know if that's OK.
Cheers,
Alison

Hi Callum,
Well done on winning the race! You're a fantastic runner! By the way, I forgot my trainers in your dad's car. 😳 If it's OK with you, I'll pick them up before going to school on Monday. Would you mind cleaning them for me? (Just joking!)
See you later,
Mo

WRITING TIME

6 You participated in a sports event. Write three short messages to people involved in the event.

1 **Find ideas**
Make notes for your messages.
• Who do you want to write to?
• What do you want to thank them for, or to congratulate them on?
• What would you like them to do for you?

2 **Plan**
Organise your ideas into three short messages. Use the messages in Exercise 2 to help you.

3 **Write and share**
• Write your draft messages. Use the Language box and the Writing box to help you.
• Share your messages with another student for feedback.
• Use the feedback from your partner and write the final version of your messages.

4 **Check**
• Check language: did you use the *-ing* form after prepositions?
• Check grammar: did you use future forms correctly?

Exercise 3
1 Dev thanks everyone for volunteering at the parkrun. He congratulates them for making the event a success. He asks them to send some photos of the event if they have any.
2 Alison thanks her friends for helping her finish the parkrun. She asks them if they can train together.
3 Mo congratulates his friend on winning the race. He asks him if he can pick them up at his friend's house and if his friend could clean his trainers (but that's a joke).

I can write a short message to thank, congratulate and make a request.

For the teacher
• Teaching notes, page 196

On the Portal
• Photocopiable activity: *Would you mind … ?*

For the student
• Workbook, page 55

On the Portal
• Workbook: Lesson 5.7

Vocabulary Activator

WORDLIST 🔊 5.16

Sports equipment
basketball (n)
bat (n)
flippers (n)
football kit (n)
helmet (n)
life jacket (n)
mask (n)
mat (n)
net (n)
racket (n)
skateboard (n)
skates (n)
skis (n)
snorkel (n)
snowboard (n)
surfboard (n)

Sporting events
changing room (n)
court (n)
fan (n)
opponent (n)
pitch (n)
scoreboard (n)
stadium (n)
tournament (n)
track (n)

Word friends (sports)
beat a team
beat an opponent
break a record
hold a record
score a goal
support a team
take part in a competition
take part in a race
take up a sport
volunteer at a club
volunteer at a sports event
win a game
win a match
win a medal

Fitness and training
balance (n)
coach (n)
exercise (n)
practise (v)
skill (n)
strength (n)
stretch (v)
training programme (n)
warm down (v)
warm up (v)
work out (v)

Word building (sport)
attack (v, n)
attacker (n)
coach (v, n)
coaching (n)
defence (n)
defend (v)
defender (n)
manage (v)
management (n)
manager (n)
practice (n)
practise (v)
score (v, n)
scorer (n)
support (v, n)
supporter (n)
train (v)
trainer (n)
training (n)

Extra words
award (n)
badminton (n)
baseball (n)
champion (n)
charity (n)
compete (v)
competition (n)
competitive (adj)
Congratulations!
cricket (n)
encourage (v)
event (n)
fitness (n)
follow (v)
ice hockey (n)
kayaking (n)
keep fit
professional (n)
race (n)
rink (n)
rope (n)
rugby (n)
sailing (n)
skipping (n)
spin (v)
sports personality (n)
sports centre (n)
success (n)
trick (n)
yoga (n)

Exercise 1
1 flippers, skates, skis
2 flippers, life jacket, mask, snorkel, surfboard
3 net, racket
4 skateboard, snowboard, surfboard
5 court, pitch, stadium, track

Exercise 2
1 The others are equipment.
2 The others are places.
3 The others are people.
4 The others are training exercises.
5 The others are things you can wear/equipment.

1 Use the words from the wordlist to find these things.
1 three things you can wear on your feet
2 five pieces of equipment for water sports
3 two things you need to play tennis
4 three kinds of board you use for sports
5 four places where you can do sport

2 Choose the odd one out.
1 flippers   [coach]   mat   mask
2 track   pitch   [fan]   court
3 fan   opponent   [exercise]   coach
4 stretch   [volunteer]   work out   warm up
5 mask   [skill]   helmet   kit

3 Answer the questions with words from the wordlist.
1 What do you hit the ball with in tennis? *racket*
2 What can help you breathe if you are swimming underwater? *snorkel*
3 Where can you put on your sport clothes before you play a sport? *changing room*
4 What object shows how many points the players or teams have? *scoreboard*
5 What can you lie on to make some sport activities more comfortable? *mat*

4 Complete the questions with words from the wordlist in the correct form. Then, in pairs, ask and answer the questions.
1 Which football team do you *support* ?
2 Have you ever taken *part* in a race?
3 Have you ever *won* a medal?
4 Would you like to volunteer at a sports *event* ?
5 Which sport would you like to *take* up?

5 Write the correct word for each definition.
1 The person you play against in a game. o*pponent*
2 You wear this to stay safe in water sports. l*ife jacket*
3 A competition with planned games to find a winner. t*ournament*
4 To win against a player or team. b*eat*

6 🔊 5.17 **PRONUNCIATION** Listen to how we pronounce the underlined sound in each group of words. Write the words below in the correct group.

c<u>oa</u>ch   c<u>o</u>urt   opp<u>o</u>nent   r<u>a</u>cket   sk<u>a</u>tes
snowb<u>oa</u>rd   st<u>a</u>dium   tr<u>a</u>ck

1 /əʊ/: g<u>oa</u>l, pr<u>o</u>gramme, *coach*, *opponent*
2 /eɪ/: t<u>a</u>ke up, tr<u>ai</u>n, *skates*, *stadium*
3 /ɔː/: sp<u>o</u>rt, sc<u>o</u>re, *court*, *snowboard*
4 /æ/: f<u>a</u>n, m<u>a</u>tch *racket*, *track*

Unit 5   70

For the teacher
• Audioscript, page 249

On the Portal
• Photocopiable activities: *Collect the words, The party*
• Tests: Unit 5 Test, Unit 5 Writing Test

For the student
• Workbook, pages 56–57

On the Portal
• Workbook: Self-check
• Wordlist
• Extra Activities: Self-check

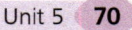

Revision

Vocabulary

1 Choose the correct option. Then, in pairs, say which sentences are true for you.
1. I like to wear a football net / **kit** with my favourite team's colours.
2. My school has a full-sized football **pitch** / mat.
3. We won / **beat** the other school 1–0 at football and I scored the goal.
4. After training hard I always **warm down** / work out for a few minutes to help feel relaxed.
5. I'm good at sports where I have to stay on my feet and not fall because I have good skill / **balance**.

2 Complete the text with the words below. There are two extra words.

> attack hold manage score ~~support~~
> take part take up train volunteer

I'm football crazy and I ¹*support* a famous team. They ² *take part* in both national and international competitions. They ³ *hold* the record in one of those competitions for winning the most times. My friend Josh thinks I should ⁴ *take up* football as well as just watching it. I think it's a good idea. I haven't played in a team before, but when I play with friends, I always ⁵ *score* the most goals. Josh says that if I ⁶ *train* hard, I'll be a great player one day. As well as playing, I'm also going to ⁷ *volunteer* at my school football club – I'd like to help in any way I can.

3 Complete the second sentence so that it means the same as the first one. Use the correct form of the underlined word.
1. I've <u>supported</u> this football club since I was a child.
   I've been a *supporter* of this football club since I was a child.
2. We need to <u>defend</u> better – we're losing!
   We need a better *defence* – we're losing!
3. You need a lot of <u>practice</u> to be good at karate.
   You need to *practise* a lot to be good at karate.
4. Who <u>manages</u> the team?
   Who is responsible for the team's *management*?
5. You can play many sports if you're <u>strong</u>.
   There are many sports where *strength* helps you play well.

Grammar

4 Complete the dialogues with the correct form of *will* or *be going to* and the verbs in brackets.
1. A: Who do you think *will win* (win) the world cup this summer?
   B: I'm not sure yet, but I _____ (read) about the teams in my football magazine.
2. A: Hi, Sally. Change of plan: we _____ (not practise) outdoors today. It's too cold.
   B: Oh. So where _____ (we/practise)?
   A: In the school sports hall. I haven't told Sharon yet.
   B: No problem. I _____ (tell) her.
3. A: Why are you carrying a football?
   B: I _____ (play) football in the park with some friends. Do you want to play?
   A: Sure! I _____ (be) there there in a minute.

5 Make a plan for next week. Use the ideas below or your own ideas.

> compete in a school quiz   go to the gym
> meet friends after school   train with my team
> watch a match on TV

1. Monday: *I'm competing in a school quiz.*
2. Tuesday: _____
3. Wednesday: _____
4. Thursday: _____
5. Friday: _____

6 Choose the correct option.
1. What time will we meet / **are we meeting** tomorrow?
2. I'm sure we'll win our next basketball game, if / **unless** we do something silly!
3. **We'll have** / We have a chance to try snowboarding if we go to Austria this winter.
4. Welcome to our club! Training **starts** / is going to start at 7 p.m. every Tuesday evening.
5. Please give me a call when **you get** / you'll get home from the match.

Speaking

7 In pairs, talk about your plans for this evening, tomorrow and next Saturday. Student A, go to page 137. Student B, go to page 143. Follow the instructions.

Dictation

8 🔊 5.18 Listen. Then listen again and write down what you hear.

Exercise 4
1. 'm going to read
2. aren't going to practise; are we going to practise; 'll tell
3. 'm going to play; 'll be

Exercise 7
Sample answer:
A What are your plans (for)/are you up to/are you doing this evening?
B I'm cooking dinner. And after that, I'm working out at the gym. What about you? What are your plans?
A Well, I'm working on my History project. And then I'm watching TV.

EXAM
Exercise 8
🔊 audioscript page 249

International Certificate Level 2, Listening and Writing, Section 2, (dictation)

71 Unit 5

BBC CULTURE
Sporting tradition
AUSSIE RULES

If you think the most popular sport in Australia is rugby or cricket, think again. It's a sport that you have probably never heard of, called Australian Rules Football. Commonly known as 'Aussie Rules', big matches attract huge crowds, especially in the large stadiums of Sydney or Melbourne.

So what is Aussie Rules? Well, it's very different from the football that you and I know. Two teams of eighteen players take part in each match, and the field is oval-shaped. Though called football, it is more similar to rugby. For example, the ball is oval and you score points by kicking it between two goalposts, just like in rugby. However, players can be anywhere on the field and they can use any part of their bodies to move the ball. Running with the ball is fine, but you have to bounce it or touch it on the ground at the same time. Throwing the ball is not allowed. Aussie Rules includes a lot of physical contact and can be dangerous. Players can tackle each other with their hands or even their whole body!

The sport was invented in the 1850s in Melbourne, but amazingly, a national competition didn't take place until the 1980s. It is equally popular among men and women, and children learn to play it at school. Because it is purely Australian, it is rich in cultural history and references. Australians are very proud to have a sport that they can call their own. It is only really played in Australia, but it has fans worldwide. Who knows? Perhaps one day it will become very popular in the UK too!

bounce (v) (of a ball) hit the ground then go back up
league (n) a group of sports teams or players who compete against each other
tackle (v) try to take the ball from another player

Exercise 1
4 a Because it is purely Australian, it is rich in cultural history and references. They are very proud to have a sport that they can call their own.

1 🔊 5.19 **VISIBLE THINKING** In pairs, follow these steps.
CONNECT
1 Look at the photo. Would you like to play Aussie Rules football? Do you think this sport is dangerous? Why?/Why not?
EXTEND
2 What is the national sport of your country?
3 Why is it important in your country?
CHALLENGE
4 Read the article and answer the questions.
  a In what ways is Aussie Rules culturally important for Australians?
  b Do you think many sports have this cultural role? Why?/Why not?

2 Read the article again and mark the sentences T (true) or F (false).
1 [F] Aussie Rules is played only in Sydney and Melbourne.
2 [T] Aussie Rules and football are two different sports.
3 [F] You can bounce, touch and throw the ball.
4 [T] Players use their bodies to stop another player.
5 [T] It plays a big role in Australian culture and history.
6 [T] People all over the world enjoy Aussie Rules.

3 In pairs, discuss the questions.
1 What are the most popular sports in your country?
2 Are they traditional or international sports?

BBC 72

For the teacher
- Teaching notes, page 197
- Videooscript, page 249

On the Portal
- Photocopiable activity: Project worksheet: a video podcast

BBC ▶ The Highland Games

4 Look at the photo. Where are the girls? What do you think they are doing and why?

5 ▶ 28 Watch Part 1 of the video. Put the activities below in the order you see them (1–4).

- [3] playing bagpipes
- [4] running a race
- [1] throwing wood
- [2] traditional dancing

6 ▶ 28 Watch the video again and complete the sentences with the words below.

disappeared   families   strength   tradition

1 The Highland Games are a very old _tradition_.
2 They aim to bring together Scotland's historical _families_.
3 They include symbols of a culture that almost _disappeared_.
4 They are a meeting place of _strength_, speed and celebration.

7 ▶ 29 Watch Part 2 of the video. Which is the most important sport?
tossing the caber

8 ▶ 29 Watch the video again and choose the correct option.
1 The Games usually include athletics and *sometimes* / **always** heavy events.
2 The wooden pole used in the caber toss event weighs *fifteen* / **fifty-five** kilos.
3 There are more Highland Games celebrated *in* / **outside** Scotland.
4 The Games are about competing and making time for old *events* / **friends**.

9 In pairs, discuss the questions.
1 Would you like to go to the Highland Games? Why?/Why not?
2 Which traditional sport would you like to try? Why?

Exercise 4
Scotland; Scottish dancing as part of the Highland Games

Exercise 5
▶ videoscript page 249

Exercise 7
▶ videoscript page 249

PROJECT TIME

10 In groups of three, prepare a video podcast about a traditional sport. Follow these steps.

1 In groups, choose a traditional sport. Decide who can find the answers to these questions.
- When did it start? Why is it culturally important? Who plays and watches it?
- Is it a dangerous sport? What equipment do you need?
- What are the rules of the sport?

2 Individually, create your part of the video podcast.
- Find the information and write the script for your section.
- Find photos, music or videos for each piece of information.

3 In your group, create your video podcast. You can use a video app.
- Review your research and decide what to include.
- Decide the order, who will say what and when.
- Record the script and add photos or videos.
- Make and edit your video podcast.

4 Show your video podcast to the class.
- Answer other students' questions.
- Watch the other video podcasts. Ask questions.

Explore more 6

VOCABULARY
Types of holidays | Going on holiday | Holiday equipment and accommodation | Traffic and transport | Travel: confusing words

GRAMMAR
Modal verbs: *must, have to, ought to, should* | Modal verbs: *must, could, may/might, can't*

6.1 Vocabulary
Holidays and travel

TRENT'S TOP TRAVEL TIPS

How to have a great holiday without spending too much

1. On a typical family camping trip, you <u>go by car</u> and <u>stay on campsites</u>. It's not expensive and sleeping in a tent can be a lot of fun – if you get on well with your family and it doesn't rain too much.

2. Activity camps are fun and everything is included, so you know how much you're going to spend before you go. It's the same with ocean cruises, but it costs a lot more to <u>go on a cruise</u>!

3. For a family, there's nothing better than a relaxing beach holiday in the sun. Is it expensive? It depends where and when you go. It can be cheaper to <u>get on a plane</u> and <u>go abroad</u> than to <u>travel by train</u> in your own country. Crazy, right?

4. Why not <u>have a short city break</u> instead of a long holiday? You'll spend less money, especially if you <u>rent a holiday flat</u> and <u>eat in</u> instead of <u>booking a hotel</u> room and <u>eating out</u> all the time. Go with friends and you'll save even more.

5. Sightseeing holidays needn't be expensive. A backpacking holiday where you <u>travel around Europe by rail</u> and stay in youth hostels can be surprisingly cheap.

For the teacher
- Teaching notes, page 198
- Audioscript, page 249
- Videoscript, page 249

On the Portal
- Vocabulary Memory Game
- Photocopiable activity: *Words and definitions*
- Test: Vocabulary Check 6

For the student
- Workbook, pages 58–59

On the Portal
- Workbook: Lesson 6.1
- Extra Practice Activities: Vocabulary, BBC Vox Pop

Unit 6 74

86

1 🔊 **6.1** Study Vocabulary box A. Which of the types of holidays can you see in the photos?

VOCABULARY A — Types of holidays
activity camp   backpacking holiday   beach holiday
camping trip   city break   ocean cruise   sightseeing holiday

2 Read the blog post. What is your favourite type of holiday. Discuss in pairs.

3 🔊 **6.2** **WORD FRIENDS** Find the phrases below in the blog post. Then choose the correct option in sentences 1–7 below. Listen and check.

book a hotel
eat in/out
get on/off a bus/coach/plane/train
go abroad
go/travel around Europe/the world
go/travel by car/road; train/rail; plane/air; boat/sea
go on a cruise
have a city break
rent a holiday flat/a car/a bicycle
stay on a campsite

1 I've (booked) / gone on a hotel for next weekend.
2 I'd love to go (around) / by the world one day.
3 Last year we went (on) / around a trip to France.
4 It's cheaper to eat / (travel) by coach.
5 Are you old enough to go / (rent) a motorbike?
6 We're going to rent / (stay) in a youth hostel.
7 Don't (get) / have off the bus until it stops.

WATCH OUT!
We say **by** sea/road/rail/air and **by** boat/car/bus/train/plane but **on** foot.

4 🔊 **6.3** Study Vocabulary box B. In pairs, take turns to describe a word from the box for your partner to guess.

A: This has your personal information and a photograph, and you need it when you go abroad.
B: Is it a passport?

VOCABULARY B — Holiday equipment
[2] guidebook   [2] map   [2] passport
[1] rucksack/backpack   [4] sleeping bag   [2] suitcase
[3] sun cream   [2] sunglasses   [3] swimsuit   [4] tent
[4] torch

5 🔊 **6.4** Listen and match the words in Vocabulary box B with dialogues 1-4.

6 🔊 **6.5** Study Vocabulary box C. Complete the messages below with words from the box in the correct form. Listen and check.

VOCABULARY C — Holiday accommodation
check in/out   double room   facilities   floor   guest
pool   reception   reservation   single room   view

Where did you stay on your last holiday? What was it like?

Bskybloo 11.24
The campsite has fantastic sports ¹_facilities_: two tennis courts, a football pitch and a large outdoor ²_pool_.

DcCd 11.06
When we tried to ³_check in_ at the hotel, the guy at the ⁴_reception_ said there was a problem with our ⁵_reservation_. They had too many ⁶_guests_, so we shared a tiny ⁷_single room_.

emmmeee 11.01
The flat's lovely. It's on the top ⁸_floor_, with a brilliant ⁹_view_ of the city. We slept in a large ¹⁰_double room_ with a big bed. At the end of our stay, we didn't want to ¹¹_check out_.

VIDEO — WIDER WORLD

7 ▶ **30** Watch four people talking about what to take on holidays 1–3. What things do they mention?
1 a backpacking holiday with friends
2 a city break in Ireland
3 a cruise around the Mediterranean

8 In pairs, talk about the last time you travelled. Use these questions to help you.
1 Where did you go?
2 What did you take with you?
3 How did you get there?
4 Where did you stay?
5 What facilities were there?

I went to Austria with the school. We went by coach and we stayed in a big hotel. We had a view of the mountains, but we didn't have a pool.

Exercise 1
Possible answers: activity camp, backpacking holiday, beach holiday, camping trip, sightseeing holiday

Exercise 5
🔊 audioscript page 249

Exercise 7
▶ videoscript page 249

1 **Harry:** a backpack, strong walking boots or shoes, a tent
Cecile: sunglasses, an umbrella, suntan lotion, anti-mosquito products
Jan: medicine, a sleeping bag
2 **Cecile:** a camera, good shoes, an umbrella
3 **Harry:** sun cream, a large brimmed hat
Jan: a bikini, a good book, something to write, sun cream, your camera
Cecile: sunglasses, bikinis
Tasha: your passport, visas, cheques

I can talk about holidays and travel.

6.2 Grammar

Modal verbs: *must, have to, ought to, should*

VIDEO — A WEEKEND BREAK

Bea: I'm so excited about this boat trip.
Abe: Do we have to sleep on the boat?
Bea: Yes. Oh! That reminds me – we have to get something from upstairs.
A few minutes later …
Abe: What's in this box?
Bea: Wait and see … We should take sleeping bags. It can get cold at night. And you ought to take these to help you swim. Seriously, you shouldn't forget your swimsuit, but you must have a shower after swimming in the canal. The water can be dirty.
Abe: Do we have to wear life jackets?
Bea: No, if you're fourteen or older, you don't have to wear a life jacket, but you must be careful. And you mustn't do anything silly.
Abe: Is there anything else I ought to know?
Bea: You should bring a torch and mosquito spray.
Abe: Seriously? Mosquitoes?
Bea: We have to clean the boat three times a day. And there must always be one person awake at night so we'll have to take turns. Two hours each.
Abe: Please tell me we don't have to do that. Oh, you're joking!

Exercise 6

▶ videoscript page 249

1 Jamie: … remember to bring your swimsuit.
Liam: … jump in the water and look at the fish.

2 Jamie: don't have to see them very much (if I'm clever about it)
Liam: don't have to worry about showing up at work on time

3 Jamie: have to be good at activities
Liam: have to make sure you enjoy the outdoors

1 Look at the photo. What kind of trip do you think Abe is getting ready for?

2 ▶ 31 ◀) 6.6 Watch or listen and check your ideas from Exercise 1. What things does Abe need for the trip? *Abe needs a sleeping bag, a swimsuit, a torch and a mosquito spray.*

3 Study the Grammar box. Find more examples of these modal verbs in the dialogue.

GRAMMAR — Modal verbs: *must, have to, ought to, should*

Obligation and prohibition
You **must** be careful.
Do we **have to** sleep on the boat?
You **mustn't** do anything silly.

Advice
You **ought to** take these to help you swim.
You **shouldn't** forget your swimsuit.

Lack of obligation
You **don't have to** wear a life jacket.

GRAMMAR TIME ▶ PAGE 131

4 Choose the correct option.

How to rent a canal boat

¹*Do you have to* / *Ought you* have a licence to drive a canal boat? You ²*mustn't* / *don't have to* have a licence for small groups, but you ³*must* / *should* have one if there are more than twelve passengers. You ⁴*don't have to* / *ought to* take care when getting on or off. You ⁵*should* / *shouldn't* keep the boat neat and tidy. You ⁶*should* / *shouldn't* run or play silly games on board. You ⁷*mustn't* / *ought to* forget to take a torch. It can be very dark at night.

5 ◀) 6.7 Complete the advert with the words below. Listen and check.

| don't have to | have to | must | mustn't | ~~ought~~ | should |

Are you looking for adventure this summer? Then you ¹*ought* to try our sailing holiday in the Mediterranean. You ²*don't have to* bring any special equipment because we provide everything. You ³*must* be between thirteen and seventeen years old and have your parents' permission. All you ⁴*have to* bring are suitable clothes for a week of sailing and, of course, you ⁵*mustn't* forget your swimsuit! You ⁶*should* bring something warm too. It can get cold at night on board!

VIDEO — WIDER WORLD

6 ▶ 32 Watch two people completing sentences 1–3. What do they say?
1 When you're on a beach holiday, you should …
2 When I am on holiday with my family, I …
3 On an activity camp, you …

7 Finish the sentences in Exercise 6 to make them true for you. In pairs, compare your ideas.

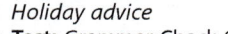

Unit 6   76   I can talk about obligation, prohibition and advice.

6.3 Reading and Vocabulary

Getting around Venice

1 Look at the photo and title of the text. What can you see in the photo? What do you know about Venice? Would you like to go there? Why?/Why not?

2 🔊 6.8 Read the text quickly. What kind of text is it?
- a a leaflet for a water bus company
- b an advert for a travel agent
- **c an article in a travel guide**

3 Read the text again. Answer the questions.
1. Why can't water buses take you to some places?
2. What kind of trips are gondolas best for?
3. What transport can you take to cross the Grand Canal if there's no bridge?
4. What two problems might you have if you rent a boat?
5. Why should you take a map when getting around Venice on foot?

4 🔊 6.9 Study the Vocabulary box. Find the words in the text. Then complete the sentences below with words from the box in the correct form.

VOCABULARY Traffic and transport

pedestrian   route   return ticket   single ticket
traffic jam   travel card

1. I've got a _travel card_ so I don't have to worry about buying a _single ticket_ every time I travel.
2. It's not easy to walk around my home town. In fact, it's quite dangerous for _pedestrians_.
3. My house is on the bus _route_, so it's really easy to get into the city centre quickly.
4. When I'm in a _traffic jam_ and can't move on, I close my eyes and listen to music.

5 In pairs, change the sentences in Exercise 4 so they are true for you.

I haven't got a travel card, so I just buy a single or return ticket when I take the bus.

6 In pairs, think about a city you visited and ask and answer the questions.
1. How did you get around the city?
2. Did you need a travel card or did you buy single tickets?
3. What was the city like for pedestrians and cyclists?
4. Was there a lot of traffic?

Getting around Venice

118 islands, 400 bridges, 177 canals … and no cars. It's the perfect place for <u>pedestrians</u>, and Europe's largest car-free city. But how do people get around Venice?

By boat, obviously. You can catch water buses called vaporetti at bus stops all around the city. They're fast and convenient. But they're not cheap. A <u>single ticket</u> costs €7.50 and a one-day <u>travel card</u>, which lets you get on and off as often as you like, is €20 for tourists. Another problem is that the water buses are too wide to take you everywhere. So, to get to some places, you have to take a water taxi.

Venice is famous for its gondolas, but gondolas aren't taxis. They won't go everywhere; they follow fixed <u>routes</u>. A gondola trip is like a sightseeing tour – it's not for getting from A to B.

To get a cheap ride, take a traghetto. These are special boats that cross the Grand Canal in places without bridges. It takes no more than a minute or two, but you can't complain. It only costs €2!

Jet skis, kayaks and other small boats are banned from the canals. However, you can rent a motor boat – you don't even need a licence. But you shouldn't be surprised if you get stuck in traffic. With all the water buses, gondolas, rowing boats and speedboats, there are lots of <u>traffic jams</u>. You ought to drive carefully. There are accidents on canals just as there are on roads.

Venice isn't very big, so the best and safest way to get around the city isn't on the water, but on foot. Walk through the narrow streets and discover beautiful canals and bridges. But don't forget to take a map. Venice is a lovely place, but it's easy to get lost there.

EXAM

Exercise 3
International Certificate Level 2, Reading, Section 6, (open-ended question)

Exercise 3
1. They're too wide to take you everywhere.
2. Gondolas are best for sightseeing trips.
3. a traghetto
4. You might get stuck in a traffic jam or you might have an accident.
5. It's easy to get lost.

YOUR WORLD

7 How do you and the people in your family get around when you are in a big city? Discuss in pairs.

We usually buy travel cards and use public transport. It's quick, and easy to get around on the tram or bus and it's fun too.

I can understand an article about traffic and transport.   77   Unit 6

For the teacher
- Teaching notes, page 200
- *Need support?* worksheet, page 237

On the Portal
- Vocabulary Memory Game
- Photocopiable activity: Draw *it!*
- Test: Vocabulary Check 6

For the student
- Workbook, page 61

On the Portal
- Workbook: Lesson 6.3
- Extra Practice Activities: Vocabulary

6.4 Grammar

Modal verbs: *must, could, may/might, can't* (speculation)

In the wild

Hi guys,
Welcome to my camping blog – the best place for all the latest camping news. This month I've discovered these amazing tree tents. It might be difficult to find them in the shops at the moment, but I think they're going to be popular. They're warm, comfortable and great fun. I slept in one last weekend in the middle of a forest and it was awesome! Have a look and let me know what you think.

Jo123 6.30 p.m.
They don't look very big. It can't be easy to stand up in them if you're tall.

TimABC 8.00 p.m.
They're cool! But they must be expensive because I haven't seen many of them.

TentFan 7.10 p.m.
It might be fun to sleep up in the air, but it must be difficult to go to the loo in the middle of the night!

Camper 8.30 p.m.
They may look cool, but I think they could be really uncomfortable because they move around with the wind.

---

1 Look at the photo in the blog post. Is this a fun place to sleep? Why?/Why not?

2 🔊 6.10 Read the blog post and comments. What are the advantages and disadvantages of tree tents?

3 Study the Grammar box. Find more examples of modal verbs for speculation in the blog post and comments.

> **GRAMMAR**
> **Modal verbs:** *must, could, may/might, can't*
>
> **Speculation**
> It must be cold outside. People are in jackets.
> It may/might/could be difficult to travel with the suitcase because it's very big.
> That can't be our tent. It's the wrong colour.
>
> GRAMMAR TIME > PAGE 132

4 Choose the correct option.

A: That's a strange tent. It looks like a balloon.
B: Oh, that ¹**must** / can't be the new tree tent. I've seen them on the internet.
A: I'd love to get one. Are they expensive?
B: They ²**can't** / could be expensive because my uncle's got one and he hasn't got much money.
A: Is there a campsite near here?
B: I'm not sure. There ³**might** / must be one near the lake. I've seen people there in summer. Why?
A: I'd love to try a tree tent. Can we ask your uncle if we can borrow it?
B: OK but today ⁴**could** / can't be a bad time. He's going on holiday with it!

Exercise 2
Advantages: warm, comfortable and (great) fun
Disadvantages: not very big, not easy to stand up in them if you're tall, difficult to get out at night, expensive, uncomfortable because they move around with the wind

5 Complete the second sentence with a modal verb for speculation. Sometimes more than one answer is possible.

1 I'm sure this is Ellie's tent. That's her rucksack.
   This _must_ be Ellie's tent. That's her rucksack.
2 They're very quiet. Perhaps they're sleeping.
   They're very quiet. They _may/might/could_ be sleeping.
3 I'm sure this isn't the same campsite.
   This _can't_ be the same campsite.
4 Dad thinks this is your ticket, but your ticket is in your hand.
   This _can't_ be your ticket because your ticket is in your hand.
5 I'm sure the map is on the table. I put it there.
   The map _must_ be on the table. I put it there.
6 Here's a guidebook but perhaps it's the wrong one.
   Here's a guidebook but it _may/might/could_ be the wrong one.

YOUR WORLD

6 What do you think of these ideas for unusual holiday accommodation? In pairs, share your ideas using modal verbs for speculation.
- a tree house in a forest
- a canal boat in Holland
- an ice hotel in Sweden
- a castle on an island

It could be noisy in a tree house in a forest because of all the animals.

I can speculate about the present.

For the teacher
- Teaching notes, page 201
- *Need support?* worksheet, page 237

On the Portal
- Grammar presentation
- Photocopiable activity: He must be …
- Test: Grammar Check 6

For the student
- Workbook, page 62
- Grammar Time, Student's Book, page 132

On the Portal
- Workbook: Lesson 6.4
- Extra Practice Activities: Grammar

6.5 Listening and Vocabulary
Jess lives the dream!

1 In pairs, describe the photo. What do you think is happening?

They're on a boat.
It might be a sailing holiday.

2 🔊 6.11 Listen to the first part of an interview. What does Mike do?

3 🔊 6.12 Listen to the second part of the interview and mark the sentences T (true) or F (false).
1 [F] Mike was working in South America when he met a girl who couldn't see.
2 [T] The girl was on holiday with her family.
3 [T] Special bikes are popular with kids who don't usually cycle.
4 [F] Mike thinks the journey is less important than the holiday.
5 [T] Hotel staff don't always realise how difficult it is for blind guests.
6 [F] The winter holidays are the most popular.

4 🔊 6.12 Listen again and write down the following. Then compare your answers in groups of three.
1 four activities mentioned in the interview
2 three kinds of holidays
3 three problems that blind people might have

5 🔊 6.13 Listen and compete the information form about Jess with one or two words in each gap.

Activity camp information form
Name: ¹ *Jess*
Age: ² *16*
Where from: ³ *New Zealand*
Disability: Jess is ⁴ *blind*
Likes: ⁵ *adventure*
Recent holidays: went to a ⁶ *sailing holiday* last year
Activity camp achievement: climbed a ⁷ *(sailing) mast*

6 In pairs, discuss why this sort of holiday is important for people like Jess. Compare your ideas with the class.

It's an adventure.
It might help them to meet people.

7 🔊 6.14 Study the Vocabulary box and check you understand the words. Then choose the correct option in the sentences below. Listen and check.

VOCABULARY — Travel: confusing words

excursion   journey   travel (n)   travel (v)   trip   voyage

1 It was a three-hour car *journey* / excursion to the beach.
2 The trip / *voyage* across the Atlantic took two months and the cabins were comfortable.
3 Air *travel* / journey is very expensive at the moment.
4 The school is organising a two-day travel / *trip* to London.
5 Let's get tickets for the afternoon journey / *excursion* to the castle.
6 I'd love to *travel* / trip to the North Pole one day.

8 Imagine your school has invited some students from another country. In pairs, discuss the best trips and excursions in your area. Compare your ideas with the class.

They could go on an excursion to the water park.
They could visit the capital city but it's a long journey.

YOUR WORLD

Exercise 2
🔊 audioscript page 250

He organises holidays for blind teenagers/ teenagers who need help because they can't see.

Exercise 3
🔊 audioscript page 250

Exercise 4
Activities: climbing (a (high) mountain)/ mountain climbing, sailing, hiking, cycling
Holidays: city breaks, beach holidays, activity camps
Problems: can't read a menu, eating can be frustrating, can't read the number on their key or the door to their room

EXAM

Exercise 5
🔊 audioscript page 250

International Certificate Level 2, Listening, Section 3, (note completion)
B1 Preliminary for Schools, Listening, Part 3, (gap fill)

I can understand a radio interview about travelling.

For the teacher
- Teaching notes, page 202
- *Need support?* worksheet, page 237
- Audioscript, page 250

On the Portal
- Photocopiable activity: *Complete the gaps*

For the student
- Workbook, page 63

On the Portal
- Workbook: Lesson 6.5
- Extra Practice Activities: Vocabulary

6.6 Speaking
Understanding a conversation

VIDEO ▶ CAN YOU SAY THAT AGAIN?

Bea: Hi, Carla. You know I'm staying in London with my gran? Well, there's an exhibition on Hyperloop at the Transport Museum and …
Carla: Sorry, I didn't catch that. Hyper what?
Bea: Hyperloop! It's like a train but cooler. I just wanted to ask if you'd like to come and see it tomorrow.
Carla: That might be fun. Yeah!

The next day …

Carla: Hi, I'm at the station. How do I get there? Should I take a bus?
Bea: No, you shouldn't take a bus. The tube's better.
Carla: Sorry, what was that?
Bea: I was just saying you can take the underground. It's the Piccadilly line.
Carla: Can you say that again? I didn't get the last part.
Bea: I said you have to take the Piccadilly line.
Carla: Sorry, but could you speak more loudly? It's really noisy here. I can't hear a thing.
Bea: Take the Piccadilly line to Covent Garden. It's the third stop. You can walk from there.
Carla: OK, thanks. See you soon.

Later …

Bea: You made it!
Carla: Thanks to your directions. Sorry, I couldn't hear you before.
Bea: Oh, never mind. You're here now. Let's go!

SOUNDS GOOD! I can't hear a thing. • You made it! • Never mind.

1 Have you ever had problems finding your way around a city? What did you do? Discuss in pairs.

2 ▶ 33 🔊 6.15 Watch or listen and answer the questions.
1 Why does Bea call Carla at the start of the dialogue?
2 Why does Carla find it hard to understand Bea?
3 How does Carla get from the station to the museum?

3 Did Bea's instructions help Carla find the way? Why/why not? Discuss in pairs.

SET FOR LIFE

4 What can you do to make sure you understand the information someone is giving you? Discuss in pairs. Use the ideas below to help you.
- listen carefully
- ask for clarification if you don't understand
- ask for more information
- repeat the information with your own words

5 Study the Speaking box. Find examples of the phrases in the dialogue.

SPEAKING Understanding a conversation

Asking for clarification
Sorry, I didn't catch that. What was that?
Can you say that again?
Sorry, I didn't get the first/last part.
Could you speak more loudly/more slowly?

Clarifying
What I said/asked was …   I said (that) …
I was just saying …   I just wanted to ask (you) if/about …

6 Complete the dialogue with phrases from the Speaking box. Sometimes more than one answer is possible. In pairs, practise the dialogue.

A: We're going to Italy on holiday this summer.
B: Sorry, ¹ *I didn't catch that* .
A: What ² *I said was* we're going to Italy this summer. I just ³ *wanted to ask you* if you wanted to go with us.
B: Great, thanks! I'll have to get a passport.
A: ⁴ *Sorry, can you say that again* ?
B: I was ⁵ *just saying that* I need to get a passport.
A: Could ⁶ *you speak more loudly* ? I couldn't hear you.
B: ⁷ *I said* I need a passport.

7 In pairs, go to page 137 and role play the situations. **YOUR WORLD**

Exercise 2
1 to invite her to go to an exhibition with her
2 First, because someone is vacuuming in Carla's house and then because of street noises.
3 She takes the underground (the Piccadilly line, three stops) to Covent Garden and then she walks from there.

Unit 6 80 I can clarify what I have said and ask for clarification.

For the teacher
- Teaching notes, page 203

On the Portal
- Photocopiable activity: *Sorry, what did you say?*

For the student
- Workbook, page 64

On the Portal
- Workbook: Lesson 6.6
- Extra Practice Activities: New Park video

6.7 Writing
An email about travel arrangements

1 If you could travel by train across Europe, where would you like to go?

2 Read the emails and answer the questions.
1. What does Jill need to buy before the trip? *a rucksack*
2. Who else is going on the trip? *Jo and Jo's mum*
3. Which places might they visit? *Geneva, Turin, Lyon*

Hi Jo,

I'm so looking forward to our rail trip across Europe. Let me know what the plan is. I'll write more later.

Bye for now,
Jill

PS I must buy a rucksack for the trip!

Hey Jill,

1. I just wanted to check the plan with you.
2. We're meeting at the station at 8 p.m. Mum and I have got the tickets, so I'll give you your ticket when you arrive. We'll have something to eat at the station before we catch the train.
3. We still need to decide on the route. I don't think we should stop in Geneva overnight. It might be better to spend a day in Geneva and do a walking tour of the city. Then we could travel overnight to Turin. Or we could catch a train to Lyon. We should decide before we leave. Let me know what you think.
4. Let's talk later.
5. Love,
Jo

---

3 Study the Writing box. Find examples of the phrases in Jo's email.

WRITING — An email about travel arrangements

1 Say why you are writing
Here's a quick note to tell you about the plan.
I just wanted to check the plan with you.

2 Explaining arrangements
We're meeting at the station at 8 p.m.
Jane's mum will drive us to terminal 1.

3 Make suggestions about the route
I don't think we should stop in Geneva overnight.
It might be better to spend a day in Geneva.
We could catch a train to Lyon.

4 Before you finish
Let's talk later.
Let me know what you think.

5 Ending your email
Bye for now,
Love,
See you soon,
Speak soon,

4 Study the Language box. Find three sentences with future time clauses in Jo's email.

LANGUAGE — Future time clauses

We use the Present Simple in future time clauses with *when*, *after*, *before*, *until* and *as soon as*.

We'll decide our route **before** we **leave**.

When the time clause comes first, we use a comma.

As soon as they arrive, I'll call you.

5 Write sentences about yourself. Use future time clauses with *when*, *after*, *before*, *until* and *as soon as*.

WRITING TIME

6 You are going on a trip with a friend. Write an email about the travel arrangements.

1 Find ideas
Make notes about:
- the type of trip and means of transport.
- the time and place to meet.
- what to take with you.
- the route to take.

2 Plan
Organise your ideas into paragraphs. Use Jo's email to help you.

3 Write and share
- Write your draft email. Use the Language box and the Writing box to help you.
- Share your email with another student for feedback.
- Use the feedback from your partner and write the final version of your email.

4 Check
- Check language: did you use future time clauses correctly?
- Check grammar: did you use modal verbs correctly?

I can write an email about travel arrangements.

For the teacher
- Teaching notes, page 204
- *Need support?* worksheet, page 237

On the Portal
- Photocopiable activity: *Remember your passport!*

For the student
- Workbook, page 65

On the Portal
- Workbook: Lesson 6.7

Vocabulary Activator

WORDLIST 6.16

Types of holidays
activity camp (n)
backpacking holiday (n)
beach holiday (n)
camping trip (n)
city break (n)
ocean cruise (n)
sightseeing holiday (n)

Word friends (going on holiday)
book a hotel
eat in/out (v)
get on/off a bus
get on/off a coach
get on/off a plane
get on/off a train
go abroad
go/travel around Europe
go/travel around the world
go/travel by boat/sea
go/travel by car/road
go/travel by plane/air
go/travel by train/rail
go on a cruise
have a city break
rent a holiday flat
rent a bicycle

rent a car
stay on a campsite
stay in a hostel

Holiday equipment
guidebook (n)
map (n)
passport (n)
rucksack/backpack (n)
sleeping bag (n)
suitcase (n)
sun cream (n)
sunglasses (n)
swimsuit (n)
tent (n)
torch (n)

Holiday accommodation
check in/out (v)
double room (n)
facilities (n)
floor (n)
guest (n)
pool (n)
reception (n)
reservation (n)
single room (n)
view (n)

Traffic and transport
pedestrian (n)
return ticket (n)
route (n)
single ticket (n)
traffic jam (n)
travel card (n)

Travel: confusing words
excursion (n)
journey (n)
travel (v, n)
trip (n)
voyage (n)

Extra words
abroad (adv)
airport (n)
banned (adj)
bridge (n)
brilliant (adj)
bring (v)
campsite (n)
canal (n)
complain (v)
convenient (adj)
country (n)
dark (adj)

dirty (adj)
get stuck
gondola (n)
island (n)
jet ski (n)
lovely (adj)
Mediterranean (n)
mosquito spray (n)
narrow (adj)
on board
on foot
permission (n)
provide (v)
rail trip (n)
reserve (v)
resident (n)
ride (n)
rowing boat (n)
sailing holiday (n)
station (n)
stay (n)
suitable (adj)
super-friendly (adj)
take turns
tour (n)
travel agent (n)
youth hostel (n)

Exercise 1
1 sun cream, sunglasses, swimsuit
2 sleeping bag, tent, torch, (also possible: map, rucksack/backpack)
3 learn a language, plan a trip

Exercise 3
2 guidebook
3 map
4 traffic jam
5 travel card
6 double room

---

1 Use the words from the wordlist to find these things.
  1 three things you can pack for a beach holiday
  2 three things you can pack for a camping holiday
  3 two things you can do to prepare for a holiday before you go

2 Read what the people say and recommend a type of holiday for each one. In pairs, recommend a holiday for each other.

Louise, 21
I want to visit interesting places and take photos of them.
1 _sightseeing holiday_

Derek, 47
We have one day and night to eat in a nice restaurant and visit museums.
2 _city break_

Peter, 15
I want to hear the sounds of nature as I fall asleep.
3 _camping trip_

Helen, 66
We want to just look at the sea and have everything we need close by.
4 _ocean cruise_

Julia, 13
My friends don't want to be bored! We need things to do.
5 _activity camp_

Tim, 23
I love to lie on the sand and enjoy the sun.
6 _beach holiday_

3 Answer the quiz questions with words from the wordlist. Then write one more question. In pairs, answer each other's questions.

TRAVEL QUIZ
1 What kind of ticket do you need if you plan to come back the same way? _return ticket_
2 What kind of book can tell you about interesting places to visit?
3 What will help you find walking routes and not get lost?
4 What's it called when a lot of cars are moving slowly?
5 What can you get to save money if you plan to use local transport a lot?
6 What kind of hotel room is for two people?

4 6.17 **PRONUNCIATION** Listen to the chant and underline two stressed syllables in each line.
I <u>packed</u> my <u>suit</u>case
And <u>made</u> my reser<u>va</u>tion.
Then I <u>trav</u>elled to the <u>air</u>port
But I for<u>got</u> my <u>pass</u>port.

5 **PRONUNCIATION** Practise saying the chant in Exercise 4 in a rhythmic way. Stress the correct syllables.

For the teacher
• Audioscript, page 250

On the Portal
• Tests: Unit 6 Test, Unit 6 Writing Test

For the student
• Workbook, pages 66–67

On the Portal
• Workbook: Self-check
• Wordlist
• Extra Practice Activities: Self-check

Revision

Vocabulary

1 Choose the correct option.
1. We checked *in* / **out of** our hotel at noon and arrived back home at 6 p.m.
2. In our family, we go **on** / *to* holiday every year.
3. We want to include *a voyage* / **an excursion** to a castle on one day of our holiday.
4. Cars can't enter this area. It's for *residents* / **pedestrians**.
5. They won't let you get on the plane without your **passport** / *guidebook*.
6. Let's all take a **trip** / *travel* to Africa next year!

2 Complete the advert with the words below.

> ~~facilities~~ guest pool reception
> reservation shower single view

Stay at our backpacking hostel!

If you want great accommodation at the right price, our backpacking hostel is for you! We have all the ¹*facilities* of a hotel, for people who need to save money. Every ² _single_ and double room has its own ³ _shower_ and a fantastic ⁴ _view_ : the sea on one side and the mountains on the other. The beach is near the hotel, but we also have a small ⁵ _pool_ . You can make a ⁶ _reservation_ online or simply arrive and ask for a room at ⁷*reception* . We do our best to help each ⁸ _guest_ to enjoy their stay.

3 Complete the email with the words below. There is one extra word.

> break floor guidebook passport
> pool sightseeing ~~traffic~~

Hi Jan,

We've arrived at the hotel safely, but a bit late because there was a ¹*traffic* jam! But we're relaxing now. Ella and I are in our room, and Mum and Dad are swimming in the ² _pool_ . We're on the highest ³ _floor_ and we have a great view of the city. It looks beautiful, so I'm happy we're taking a city ⁴ _break_ here before we visit the rest of the country. It's a ⁵ _sightseeing_ holiday, so we have our cameras ready to take photos of the interesting places. We also have an excellent ⁶ _guidebook_ with all the information we need.

I'll write again soon. Bye for now!
Gordon

Grammar

4 Choose the correct option to complete the information about visiting a new country.
1. You **should** / *must* talk to local people to learn something interesting about the culture.
2. You **must** / *should* show your passport when you enter the country.
3. You **don't have to** / *mustn't* learn the language because a lot of people speak English.
4. You **ought** / *should* to be polite and show respect for their way of life.
5. You **ought to** / *must* learn something about the country first, to make your trip more interesting.
6. You *don't have to* / **mustn't** take photos of people without their permission.

5 Make questions you can ask about visiting wild areas like mountains or jungle. Then, in pairs, choose a wild area and discuss the questions.
1. should / check / the weather before we go / ?
2. should / tell / someone where we plan to go / ?
3. have / get / permission to visit / ?
4. might / see / any wild animals / ?
5. should / take / our own food and water / ?
6. what clothes / should / wear / ?

6 Complete the dialogue with *must*, *might* or *can't*.

A: Look at this poster of a river. There's information and prices, so it ¹*must* be an advert for a river trip. Do you like the idea?
B: I thought rivers were kind of boring, but it ² _might_ be interesting if there's an organised trip.
A: It says, 'You need a camera,' so there ³ _must_ be some cool things to see.
B: Yes, but what? There ⁴ _can't_ be any museums or historical buildings. There aren't any cities.
A: No, but the boat ⁵ _might_ go near some places with wild animals to see. I hope so.
B: Why? Are you interested in going?
A: Well it ⁶ _can't_ hurt to find out more! I'm going to phone them.

Speaking

7 In pairs, turn to page 137 and follow the instructions to role play a dialogue. Then swap roles and role play a different situation where you ask for and give clarification.

Dictation

8 🔊 6.18 Listen. Then listen again and write down what you hear.

Exercise 5
1. Should we check the weather before we go?
2. Should we tell someone where we plan to go?
3. Do we have to get permission to visit?
4. Might we see any wild animals?
5. Should we take our own food and water?
6. What clothes should we wear?

Exercise 7
Sample answer:
A Do you like the Mediterranean?
B Sorry, can you say that again? I didn't get the last part.
A What I said was: do you like the Mediterranean?
B Thank you. I understand. Yes, I do.

EXAM

Exercise 8
🔊 audioscript page 250

International Certificate Level 2, Listening and Writing, Section 2, (dictation)

83 Unit 6

SET FOR LIFE

Eco-friendly travel

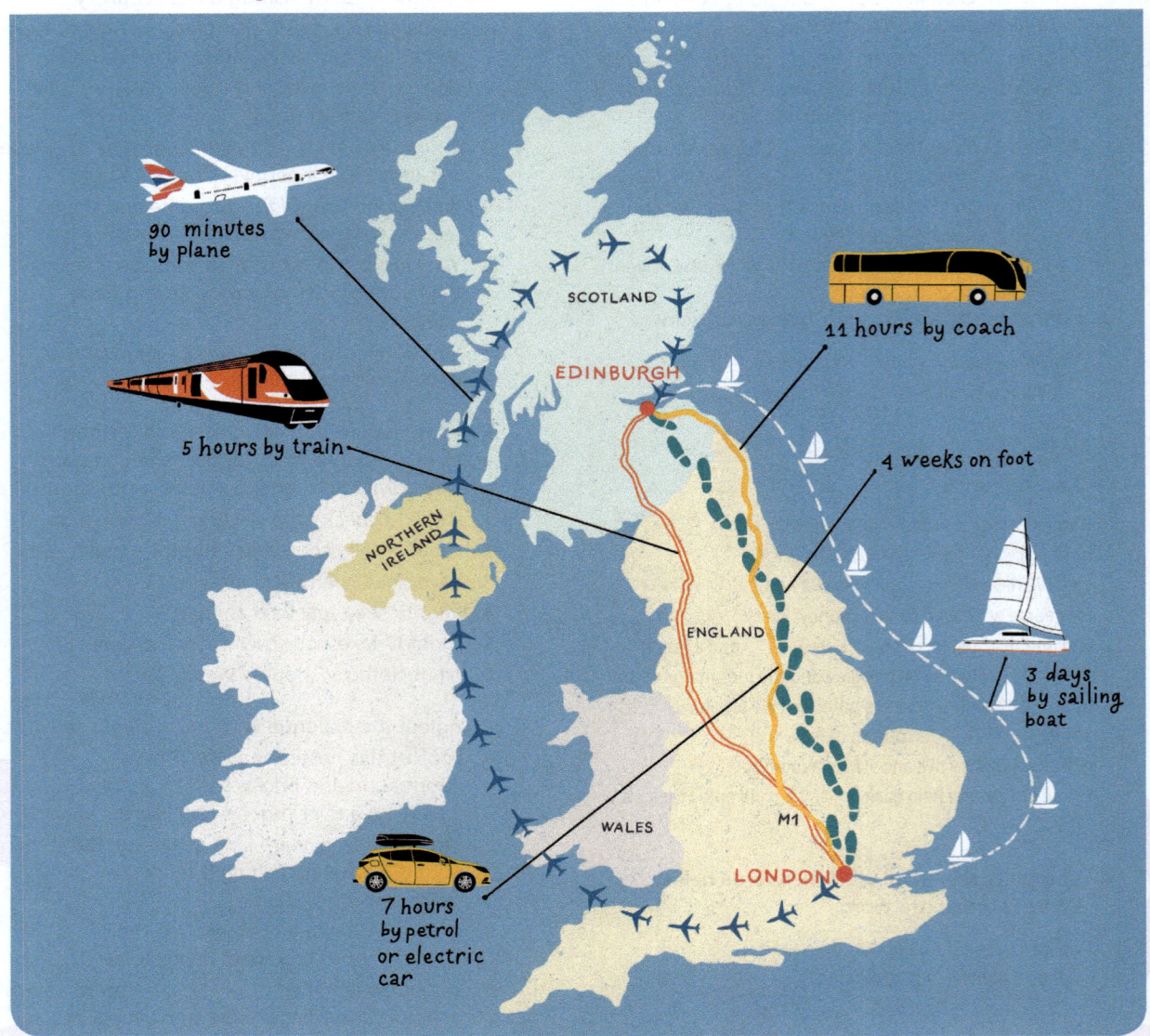

- 90 minutes by plane
- 5 hours by train
- 11 hours by coach
- 4 weeks on foot
- 3 days by sailing boat
- 7 hours by petrol or electric car

Exercise 2

audioscript page 250

Train and bike, because they're better for the environment than the other choices. They're eco-friendly.

1 In pairs, look at the map. How would you prefer to travel from London in England to Edinburgh in Scotland? Why?

I'd prefer to travel by … because it's the … -est way to get there.

2 🔊 6.19 Listen to a dialogue. Which two types of transport is Charlie using for his holiday? Why?

3 In pairs, do the quiz. Use types of transport from the map to help you.

The eco-friendly transport QUIZ

1 What has the advantages of a petrol car, but produces much less air pollution? *electric car*
2 Which types of public transport aren't as fast as flying, but produce less greenhouse gas? *coach, train*
3 By which type of transport can a three-hour journey produce as much greenhouse gas as someone in Uganda produces in a whole year? *plane*
4 Which types of transport don't produce any greenhouse gas? *walking, (bike), (skateboard), sailing boat*

Units 5–6 **84** I can plan an eco-friendly holiday.

For the teacher
- Teaching notes, page 205
- Audioscript, page 250

On the Portal
- Photocopiable activity: *Eco-friendly travel*

4 🔊 **6.19** Listen to the dialogue from Exercise 2 again and check your answers to Exercise 3.

5 In pairs, imagine you are going on a weekend trip together. Choose a destination and discuss which means of transport you can use to get there. (Think about the cost, ecology and time). Use expressions from the Useful phrases box.

A: *Why don't we go by train? It's an eco-friendly choice.*
B: *True, but it'll be slow. It takes only two hours by car.*

6 Do the questionnaire. In pairs, compare your answers.

What are your travel habits?

1 How do you usually get to school?
 a on foot or by bike   **b** by public transport
 c by car

2 How far do you travel by car in a typical week?
 a less than 5 km   **b** 5–20 km
 c more than 20 km

3 If you go away from home for a holiday, how do you usually travel there?
 a by train or coach   **b** by car
 c by plane

4 How do you usually travel when you are at your holiday destination?
 a on foot or by bike   **b** by public transport
 c by car

7 Read the Useful Tips. In pairs, discuss how you can become more eco-friendly travellers.

SET FOR LIFE

8 In small groups, plan an eco-friendly holiday. Follow these steps.

1 Decide where you are going to go.

2 Plan how to travel to your holiday destination. Use expressions from the Useful Phrases box.

3 Plan how to travel around when you are at your destination.

4 Present your plan for the eco-friendly holiday to the class.

85 Units 5–6

Be an eco-friendly traveller

USEFUL TIPS
When you choose transport, it's important to make eco-friendly choices when you can. Transport can have a big effect on the environment.

- Avoid vehicles with engines. Use vehicles without engines and travel on foot.
- Avoid planes and petrol cars. Share transport, or use coaches, trains and electric cars.
- Avoid longer journeys.

USEFUL PHRASES

Why don't we … ?
Maybe we could …
… is an eco-friendly choice.
… is better for the environment than …
… (don't) produce a lot of greenhouse gas.
It'll be fun/interesting/cheaper.
It'll be slow/boring/more expensive.

Progress Check Units 1–6

Vocabulary and Grammar

1 Choose the correct answer.

1 We have a ___ time before the other players get here; let's practise!
   a some   **b little**   c few
2 I've only watched two ___, but this looks like a very interesting series.
   a episodes   b channels   c productions
3 We don't ___ take food on the trip because the teachers are going to give us a packed lunch.
   a must   b ought to   **c have to**
4 The runners are on the ___ in their starting positions. The race will start any moment.
   a court   b race   **c track**
5 Please check in at the hotel ___ and you will get a key card to your room.
   a reception   b facilities   c reservation
6 Horse-riding is ___ than swimming.
   a the most exciting
   b most exciting
   c more exciting

2 Complete the second sentence with the word in bold so that it means the same as the first one. Use no more than four words.

1 In my opinion, an ocean cruise is better than a beach holiday for relaxing. **GOOD**
   In my opinion, a beach holiday isn't _as good as_ an ocean cruise for relaxing.
2 I don't know what Rome is like because I haven't seen it yet. **BEEN**
   I don't know what Rome is like because I've _never been_ there.
3 I'm sure Jeff is already in the swimming pool – his bike is next to the building. **BE**
   Jeff _must be_ in the swimming pool already – his bike is next to the building.
4 Is learning Spanish part of your travel plans to Argentina? **GOING**
   Are _you going to learn_ Spanish when you travel to Argentina?
5 Try to hit the ball hard when you train for tennis. **PRACTISE**
   You should _practise hitting_ the ball hard when you train for tennis.
6 We have many different kinds of sports on our camp. **LOTS**
   There _are lots of_ different kinds of sports on our camp.

3 Complete the text with the correct form of the words in brackets.

A lot of ¹_reviewers_ (REVIEW) these days are writing about *On the Pitch*, Giles Holmes' new film about a young footballer. For this film, Holmes found that he needed people with ²_acting_ (ACT) and football skills. He used real ³_actors_ (ACT) for most of the players on the pitch. They played all the ⁴_defenders_ (DEFEND). However, he decided to get a real footballer to play an ⁵_attacker_ (ATTACK). She gave a good ⁶_performance_ (PERFORM) both on and off the pitch. This film is a great ⁷_production_ (PRODUCT) and everyone should go and see it!

Speaking

4 Complete the dialogue with the words below. There is one extra word.

> meeting   plans   prefer   rather   sounds   ~~up~~   yet

A: Hi! What are you ¹_up_ to on Saturday?
B: I don't know ²_yet_. What are you going to do?
A: I'm ³_meeting_ a few friends in the afternoon. Do you want to join us?
B: Thanks. Maybe I will. What are your ⁴_plans_?
A: Maybe we'll watch a film or check out the new shopping centre. Which do you think is better?
B: I'd ⁵_rather_ watch a film. There's a really good new science fiction film at the cinema.
A: That ⁶_sounds_ good! I'll ask the others.

5 In pairs, follow the instructions to role play two dialogues.

1 Plan a fun afternoon.
Student A
- Ask Student B what his/her plans are for Saturday afternoon.
- Suggest doing something together and ask what he/she prefers to do: visit the park or the shops? walk or cycle? something else?

Student B
- Respond to what Student A says. Decide together what you're going to do.

2 Plan another fun afternoon.
Student B
- Ask Student A what his/her plans are for this afternoon.
- Suggest doing something together and ask what he/she prefers to do: café or cinema? pizza or ice cream? something else?

Student A
- Respond to what Student A says. Decide together what you're going to do.

EXAM
Exercise 5
International Certificate Level 2, Speaking, Section 13, (role play)

Listening

6 🔊 **PC1–6.1** Listen to part of a podcast and complete the sentences. Use 1–3 words in each gap.
1. Melanie trains _three times/days_ a week and at weekends.
2. She has to do _schoolwork_ as well as play tennis.
3. Tomorrow she has a meeting with _her coach_.
4. She's going to try to improve her tennis skills by finding out and practising _the worst_ parts of her game.
5. She says that if players fall over during a game, they usually _lose the point_.
6. Melanie took up playing tennis when she saw _a sport(s) video_ on a bus journey.
7. She admires Serena Williams because she always tries _to be better_.

7 🔊 **PC1–6.2** Listen. Then listen again and write down what you hear.

Reading

8 🔊 **PC1–6.3** Read the article quickly. In pairs, say which album you would like to listen to.

9 Read the article and answer the questions.
Which album (A–C):
1. is a recording of a live music event? _A_
2. has songs about real people? _C_
3. has a song which is the best song because of a musical instrument? _B_
4. was made by two people working together? _B_
5. was recorded partly outdoors? _C_
6. used technology later to improve the sound? _A_
7. has music for TV programmes? _B_

Writing

10 Think about a film or a documentary where people live in or travel to another place. Answer the questions. Then, in pairs, take turns to tell your partner about the film/documentary. Would they like to see it?
1. What was it about?
2. What places did you see in it?
3. What was one thing you learned about the place(s)?
4. What two things did you like about the film/documentary? (e.g. photography, music, presenter/actor)

11 Write a review of the film or documentary about a place (100–150 words). In your review:
- say the name and at least one more fact about the film/documentary.
- describe the story and say why the place is important.
- say why you liked/didn't like the film/documentary.

> **EXAM**
> **Exercise 6**
> 🔊 audioscript page 250
> **International Certificate Level 2**, Listening, Section 3, (note completion)

> **EXAM**
> **Exercise 7**
> 🔊 audioscript page 250
> **International Certificate Level 2**, Listening and Writing, Section 2, (dictation)

> **EXAM**
> **Exercise 9**
> **A2 Key for Schools**, Reading and Writing, Part 2, (matching)

Top albums this year

Which albums have we all enjoyed this year? There have already been a few really good ones and here are three of them.

A *Stage Style* – Banana Bread
It isn't often that a recording of a concert performance makes it to a short list of the best albums of the year. But *Stage Style* certainly does. The album has many Banana Bread favourites, but also a few surprises we've never heard, including the wonderful *Know Me Better*. Why is the sound so clean? It's because further production after the concert used computers to take out the audience noise.

B *The Dried and the Roasted* – The Fine Fellows
If you're a fan of the soap *Pretty Players*, then you probably enjoy the great music at the start of each episode. This album has it, but there are a lot of other great tracks too. The Fellows – duo Sally Oddy and Mark Freeman – recorded some songs for the screen and others not. But the best song, *Darkness Calls*, appeared in the film of the same name. Why is it the best? It's the drum parts which create the excitement the director really wanted in that key scene. No spoilers!

C *Painted Creatures* – Lisa Scott
Some people want to be successful in the music business and others just want to tell their own story! The lyrics on *Painted Creatures* are so interesting that you want to stop lip-synching and just read and think about them.
If you do that, you'll learn a lot about Lisa and those closest to her. Another thing that makes this album special is the way the sounds of weather and wildlife are mixed in! 'We took the microphones into the open air for those tracks,' Lisa explains in a recent music documentary.

People power 7

VOCABULARY
Word building: family | Phrasal verbs | Collocations: relationships | Relations | Collocations with *get*

GRAMMAR
Second Conditional | Relative clauses

Family Maths

It doesn't matter if your family is big or small; some numbers are the same for all of us. For every person on the planet there are ¹ _two_ people who are their biological parents. That means you have four biological grandparents and ² _eight_ great-grandparents.

The diagram shows one person's parents and their parents' parents over ³ _four_ generations. You can see that one person has ⁴ _sixteen_ great-great grandparents.

It's interesting to think of all their different experiences. How did they meet? Did they all grow up in the same place or did some of them move away?

This diagram doesn't tell the whole story. There might be many brothers and sisters in each family, or even step-parents and half-brothers and half-sisters. Also, you can't see all the aunts, uncles and cousins on this diagram. Most people have many first, second and third cousins. Even if you're in a city with ⁵ _thousands_ of people, it's possible that you have relations there. So be kind to those loud neighbours of yours – they might be your cousins!

7.1 Vocabulary
Family and friends

1 How many people are there in your family, including all of your relations? How often do you see them?

2 🔊 7.1 Look at the diagram and complete the text with the words below. Listen and check.

> eight   four   sixteen   thousands   two

Unit 7 88

For the teacher
- Teaching notes, page 206

On the Portal
- Vocabulary Memory Game
- Photocopiable activity: *Complete and answer*
- **Test:** Vocabulary Check 7

For the student
- Workbook, pages 70–71

On the Portal
- Workbook: Lesson 7.1
- Extra Practice Activities: Vocabulary

100

3 🔊 **7.2** Study Vocabulary box A. Complete the explanations with the prefixes in bold in the box.

> **VOCABULARY A** — Word building: family
>
> **great**-grandmother   **great**-grandfather
> **great**-grandparent
> **half**-brother   **half**-sister
> **step**mother   **step**father   **step**son   **step**daughter
> **step**brother   **step**sister

1 The prefix _great-_ describes a family relative who is three generations away from you. Add an extra _great-_ for each extra generation.
2 The prefix _step-_ describes a brother, sister or parent who is related to you by marriage but not by blood.
3 The prefix _half-_ describes a brother or sister who is related to you through one shared biological parent.

4 🔊 **7.3** Study Vocabulary box B. Then complete the quiz. Listen and check.

> **VOCABULARY B** — Phrasal verbs
>
> deal with (a problem)   grow up
> get on with/get along with   hang out (with)
> get together   move away
> go out (with)

Have you got great people skills?

Give yourself a score between 1 and 5 for each statement.

1 = strongly disagree 2 = disagree 3 = it depends
4 = agree 5 = strongly agree

a ☐ My cousins and I always helped each other when we were growing _up_.
b ☐ I get _on/along_ well with my cousins, aunts, uncles and grandparents.
c ☐ When I get _together_ with my friends, I always include everyone.
d ☐ I enjoy going _out_ with a group of my friends.
e ☐ I'm not sure how to deal _with_ friendship problems.
f ☐ My friends and I like to hang _out_ at one another's homes.
g ☐ I would hate to move _away_ from my home town.

5 Do the quiz in Exercise 4. In pairs, compare your answers. Are you similar or different?
Both of us like/dislike …
I think I'm quite similar to/different from …

6 🔊 **7.4** **WORD FRIENDS** Check you understand the phrases below. Then complete the texts with them. Listen and check. Who do you agree with? Stefan or Nadia?

get to know someone
have an argument
have something in common
have the same sense of humour
see each other after school
share an interest in something
spend time with someone

Friends: similar or different?

Stefan: I think it's good to be similar. I ¹_got_ to know Adam after I moved away from my home town last year. Adam and I ² _have_ a lot in common. We both like volleyball and comedy films. We ³ _have_ the same sense of humour too. We ⁴ _share_ loads of interests and we're like brothers or cousins.

Nadia: I'm completely different from my friend Marta, but we get on well. Marta hates to ⁵ _have_ arguments, but I think it's good to disagree. Marta loves to ⁶ _spend_ time on her own, but I like to go out. We don't ⁷ _see_ each other often, but when we meet, we get on well.

YOUR WORLD

7 Is it important for friends to have similar interests? In pairs, discuss your opinions.

I can talk about relationships with my family and friends.

7.2 Grammar
Second Conditional

Exercise 2
Abe feels sad because he wants to go to the end-of-term party but if he does, he won't be able to meet his mum at the airport. He decides to go to the airport and meet his mum.

Exercise 6
▶ videoscript page 251

1
Rebecca: I would ignore them.
Jamie: I would send him to voice mail.
Liam: I would drop everything to help them.

2
Jamie: I would try to find a very attractive date to go with me.
Craig: I would try to avoid it.
Rebecca: I'd be happy to go.
Liam: I would invite all my friends and go and have a great time.

3
Jamie: would start without me
Craig: would kill me
Rebecca: would probably kill me too
Liam: would understand if I made something up

4
Jamie: I lost my keys.
Liam: I didn't hear from my girlfriend late at night.

5
Jamie: I did not get into drama school.
Craig: I had no money.
Rebecca: I had no friends.
Liam: I had to stay in one place for the rest of my life.

VIDEO ▶ A DILEMMA

Abe: Yay, a party invite! Oh no!
Bea: Hi, Abe!
Abe: Hiya. I can't go to the end-of-term party on Saturday.
Bea: Why not?
Abe: Because <u>if I went to the party, I wouldn't be able to meet my mum at the airport. My dad wouldn't be very happy with me if I did that.</u>
Bea: Oh! That's true. And I think <u>you'd feel bad if you didn't meet her.</u>
Abe: I guess you're right. I do miss her. What would you do if you were me?
Bea: <u>If I were you, I'd try to go to both.</u> What time does your mum arrive?
Abe: She arrives at 9.00. The party starts at 8.00.
Bea: Yeah, it's complicated.
Abe: It's impossible!
Bea: <u>How would your mum react if you told her about the party?</u>
Abe: She'd tell me to go to the party, of course.

On Saturday …
Dad: The airport, then?
Abe: The airport!
Dad: Are you sure? <u>Mum would understand if you chose to go to that party.</u>
Abe: I know, but I never listen to my parents, remember?

1 Look at the photo of Abe looking at an end-of-term party invitation. How do you think he feels? Why?

2 ▶ 34 🔊 7.5 Watch or listen and check your ideas from Exercise 1. What does Abe decide to do?

3 Study the Grammar box. Find more examples of the Second Conditional in the dialogue.

GRAMMAR ▶ Second Conditional
If her flight **arrived** earlier, **I'd be** able to go to the airport.
What **would** you **do if** you **were** me?

GRAMMAR TIME > PAGE 132

4 🔊 7.6 Complete the Second Conditional sentences with the correct form of the verbs in brackets. Listen and check.
1 If I *had* (have) enough time, I *would help* (help).
2 If you *listened* (listen) carefully, you *would understand* (understand).
3 *Would you go* (you/go) to the beach if you *were* (be) free today?
4 He *wouldn't come* (not come) here if he *didn't want* (not want) to.
5 What *would you do* (you/do) if you *earned* (earn) a lot of money?
6 I *would phone* (phone) your dad if I *were* (be) you.

5 What would you do if you were Abe? Why? Discuss in pairs.

VIDEO ▶ WIDER WORLD

6 ▶ 35 Watch four people talking about different situations. How do they complete the sentences below?
1 If my friend phoned when I was busy, …
2 If there was a big wedding in our family, …
3 If I was late for a family meal, my parents …
4 I'd be very worried if …
5 It would be a nightmare for me if …

7 Finish the sentences in Exercise 6 to make them true for you. In pairs, compare your ideas.
If my friend phoned when I was busy, I'd probably talk to her. What about you?

Unit 7 **90** I can use the Second Conditional to talk about unreal or imaginary situations.

For the teacher
- Teaching notes, page 207
- *Need support?* worksheet, page 238
- Videoscript, page 251

On the Portal
- Grammar presentation
- Photocopiable activity: *Tell your group why*
- Test: Grammar Check 7

For the student
- Workbook, page 72
- Grammar Time, Student's Book, page 132

On the Portal
- Workbook: Lesson 7.2
- Extra Practice Activities: Grammar, New Park video, BBC Vox Pop

7.3 Reading and Vocabulary
Making friends

1 Is it important to make new friends? Why?/Why not?

2 🔊 7.7 Read the article quickly and match headings a–e with steps 1–5.
a [4] Understand each other's identity
b [2] Chat about a few different things
c [1] Make a friendly comment
d [5] Spend time talking or being together
e [3] Show interest by listening

3 Read the article again and complete the sentences with 1–3 words in each gap.
1 The article tells us that there are five steps to _friendship_.
2 For the first step, you may share information about things you like or _dislike/can't stand_.
3 When you've shared information, it's easier to have _(more) conversations_.
4 If both friends often listen and support each other, they have reached step _three_.
5 A friend who supports your social identity acts like _a mirror_.
6 If you and your friend are in different places, you can call or _send messages/texts_.

4 🔊 7.8 Study the Vocabulary box. Find the words in the article. Check you understand them.

VOCABULARY | Relations
People
best friend   classmate   mate   stranger   teammate
Phrases with *friend(s)*
be friends   have a friend   keep friends   make friends

5 🔊 7.9 Complete the sentences with words from the Vocabulary box. Listen and check.
1 I've made friends with a few of my _____ from volleyball.
2 Sara was nervous about the new school, but it was easy to _____ .
3 When we moved here, I felt like a _____ as nobody knew me.
4 I've got lots of friends, but Ben is my _____ because he understands me.
5 Sam changed secondary school, but his new _____ are friendly.

Five steps to friendship

If you wanted a new friend, what would you do? It's not as simple as you might think. We usually find friends in the places where we live, study, work or relax. So our <u>classmates</u> and <u>teammates</u> can easily become friends, but how?

1 The first step normally happens when one person shares some information. This could be anything from a comment about a funny TV show to food that you can't stand. Or you could tell someone about your likes and dislikes, for example.

2 That's a great start. You aren't <u>strangers</u>, but you aren't <u>best friends</u> yet. Next, we need the other person to reply with similar thoughts about that TV show or another horrible food. From here, it's easier to have more conversations about other things. When two people have talked about their thoughts and opinions, they're starting to <u>make friends</u>.

3 The third step involves being a good friend. To take this step, you need to listen to your friend and help them. Over time, you can share problems and talk about lots of things. You know the other person is always ready to listen and support you. That's a really good friendship.

4 The fourth step is about looking for friends who support our social identity. What does that mean? If dancing or basketball is really important in your life, then you will probably want friends who see you as a good dancer or a basketball player. That's why we choose friends who are like a mirror. They show us a picture of how we want to be.

5 Finally, remember to stay in touch with your friends. A good way to do this is to make time to see your friends or to phone them and send messages when you're not in the same place. It's important to remember that friendship needs work!

6 Work in pairs. What else is important for making and keeping friends?

I can understand an article about friendship.

> **EXAM**
> **Exercise 3**
> International Certificate Level 2, Reading, Section 7, (note completion)

> **Exercise 5**
> 1 teammates
> 2 make friends
> 3 stranger
> 4 best friend
> 5 classmates

7.4 Grammar
Relative clauses

Exercise 2
🔊 audioscript page 251

Exercise 4
Defining relative clauses:
All the sentences 1–10 contain defining relative clauses.
Also, sentences e, g and h contain defining relative clauses.
Non-defining relative clauses:
Sentences b, d, f, i and j contain non-defining relative clauses.

Exercise 5
2 In Gran's house there's a picture which/that is 100 years old.
3 This is the camera which/that my dad uses on holiday.
4 There's a park where the children play.

Exercise 6
2 Paddy uses his bike, which is new, every day.
3 Number 24, where Molly lives, is an old house.
4 They live in Park Street, which is near the town centre.
5 Mr Jones, who works at the hospital, often leaves the house early.
6 Our school, which is two kilometres away, is very big.

1 What are two things that you always carry with you? Are they your favourite objects?

2 🔊 7.10 Read the quiz questions below (1–10). Match them with Hannah's answers (a–j). Listen and check.
 a The guy next door, Ben, is a friend who always listens.
 b *We Will Rock You*, which is my dad's favourite, is in my head.
 c The evening is best for me to work.
 d Iceland, where there are loads of volcanoes, is a place I'd love to visit.
 e My uncle Joe is the funniest person I know.
 f Mr Ketling, who was my first teacher, was the most helpful.
 g One thing which I'd rescue is my handheld console.
 h One place where I like to relax is our youth club.
 i A teddy bear, which my grandmother gave me, used to be my favourite.
 j I eat olives any time I feel hungry.

What makes you YOU?

Name:
1 one thing which you would rescue in a flood *g*
2 one person who you always have fun with *e*
3 a place where you like to relax *h*
4 one food that you often eat as a snack *j*
5 the primary school teacher who helped you the most *f*
6 a place where you want to go in the future *d*
7 a friend who always listens *a*
8 a toy that you loved when you were small *i*
9 a song which you can't stop singing *b*
10 the time of day when you work best *c*

3 Do the quiz in Exercise 2. In pairs, compare your answers.

4 Study the Grammar box. Find more examples of defining and non-defining relative clauses in the quiz and in Hannah's answers in Exercise 2.

GRANMAR Relative clauses

Defining relative clauses (essential information)
Ben is a friend **who/that always listens**.
One thing **which/that I'd rescue** is my handheld console.
Our youth club is one place **where I like to relax**.

Non-defining relative clauses (extra information)
Mr Kipling, **who was my first teacher**, was the most helpful.
We Will Rock You, **which is my dad's favourite**, is in my head.
Iceland, **where there are loads of volcanoes**, is a place I'd love to visit.

GRAMMAR TIME > PAGE 133

WATCH OUT!
The woman who/that lives next door is my great-aunt. (defining relative clause)
Mrs Baker, who/~~that~~ lives next door, is my great-aunt. (non-defining relative clause)

5 Rewrite the sentences using defining relative clauses.
 1 Holly has a good friend. She lives next door.
   Holly has a good friend who lives next door.
 2 In Gran's house there's a picture. It's 100 years old.
 3 This is the camera. My dad uses it on holiday.
 4 There's a park. The children play in it.

6 Write sentences using non-relative clauses. Add commas where necessary.
 1 Mrs Morris is sixty-seven. (who / be / Lucy's grandmother)
   Mrs Morris, who is Lucy's grandmother, is sixty-seven.
 2 Paddy uses his bike every day. (which / be / new)
 3 Number 24 is an old house. (where / Molly / live)
 4 They live in Park Street. (which / be / near the town centre)
 5 Mr Jones often leaves the house early. (who / work / at the hospital)
 6 Our school is very big. (which / be / two kilometres away)

YOUR WORLD
7 Make one true and one false sentence about your favourite place, music, object or food. Use relative clauses. In pairs, guess which of your partner's sentences is true and which is false.

Unit 7 92 I can use defining and non-defining relative clauses to describe people, things and places.

For the teacher
- Teaching notes, page 209
- *Need support?* worksheet, page 238

On the Portal
- Grammar presentation
- Photocopiable activity: *The student who …*
- Test: Grammar Check 7

For the student
- Workbook, page 74
- Grammar Time, Student's Book, page 133

On the Portal
- Workbook: Lesson 7.4
- Extra Practice Activities: Grammar

7.5 Listening and Vocabulary
A helpful friend

Finn and Nala

Tilly and Prince

1 Can animals be your friend or part of your family? Why?/Why not?

2 Can dogs help people? How? Look at the photos. How can the dogs help the people?

3 Read the questions. What do you think Finn's sister will talk about?
1. What did Finn think of his morning routine?
   a It was boring. b It was sad. **c** It was stressful.
2. How old was Finn when he got Nala?
   a a baby   **b** a child   c a teenager
3. What does Nala do to help with Finn's everyday routine?
   a She brings his shoes. b She washes his feet.
   c She puts his shoes on.
4. Based on what Finn's sister's says, which adjective best describes Nala?
   a busy   b funny   **c** clever

4 🔊 7.11 Listen and choose the correct answer in Exercise 3.

5 Read the questions and answers. What does each question ask about? Match the questions with the types of information below.

> detailed meaning of a word or phrase   feelings
> general topic   specific information

1. A puppy trainer *detailed meaning of a word or phrase*
   a looks after old dogs.
   b teaches young dogs special skills.
   c finds new homes for unwanted dogs.
2. When the dogs left, Tilly felt *feelings*
   a sad.   b bored.   c happy for them.
3. Who trained Prince? *specific information*
   a Tilly on her own.   b Tilly's step-mum.
   c Tilly and her step-mum together.
4. What is the main thing we learn about assistance dogs from Tilly's account? *general topic*
   a They often go to different owners.
   b They take a long time to learn things.
   c They can help with a wide range of needs.

6 🔊 7.12 Listen and choose the correct answer in Exercise 5.

7 🔊 7.13 **WORD FRIENDS** Match the different meanings of *get* with the verbs below. Listen and check.

> arrive   become   bring/fetch   buy   find   receive

The verb *get* can have several meanings:
1. get a pet = *buy*
2. get a job = *find*
3. get home = *arrive*
4. get a letter/a phone call/an email = *receive*
5. get a hot drink drink (for someone) = *bring/fetch*
6. get better/worse; get dressed; get old(er); get ready; get bored/excited/upset = *become*

8 Choose the correct option.
1. My brother wants to get *a job* / ready in the police force.
2. I've just got dressed / *a text* from my gran!
3. Shall I get *a glass of water* / better for you?
4. The train was late so we didn't get *home* / a pet until midnight.

VIDEO ▶ **WIDER WORLD**

9 ▶ 36 Watch Corinne talking about a situation. What was her pet? How did Corinne feel? Why?

10 In pairs, tell your partner about one of these situations. Describe how you felt and why.
- a time when you got a pet
- a time when you got the results of an important exam
- a time when you got an important letter/email/phone call

I can understand a conversation about helping people in need.   93   Unit 7

Exercise 3
Possible answers:
- Finn's daily routine
- when Finn got Nala
- how Nala helps with Finn's daily routine
- Nala's personality

EXAM
Exercise 4
🔊 audioscript page 251
B1 Preliminary for Schools, Listening, Part 4, (3-option multiple choice)

EXAM
Exercise 6
B1 Preliminary for Schools, Listening, Part 4, (3-option multiple choice)

Exercise 9
▶ videoscript page 251
Corinne got a dog. She was upset/crying because a car hit it.

For the teacher
- Teaching notes, page 210
- *Need support?* worksheet, page 238
- Audioscript, page 251
- Videoscript, page 251

On the Portal
- Photocopiable activity: *Get*

For the student
- Workbook, page 75

On the Portal
- Workbook: Lesson 7.5
- Extra Practice Activities: Vocabulary, BBC Vox Pop

7.6 Speaking
Identifying people in a group

VIDEO ▶ **WHO'S THAT GIRL ON THE RIGHT?**

Eren: What a day! Oh hey, Grandad. What are you up to?
Grandad: I'm watching this programme about music in the 1970s.
Eren: Oh, right. Well, that's, er … interesting.
Grandad: I used to go to lots of live performances like this when I was young.
Eren: No way! Really?
Grandad: Hey! That's me!
Eren: Where? <u>Which guy do you mean?</u>
Grandad: <u>The good-looking one,</u> right there. Pause the programme.
Eren: I can't recognise you. Let's rewind.
Grandad: I'm the one <u>on the left,</u> in the flowery shirt.
Eren: This one?
Grandad: No, rewind it some more. There. <u>The guy with</u> the brown hair.
Eren: Look at your clothes. They're so funny!
Grandad: Oh, and that's my friend, Harry, <u>in the background</u>. <u>The tall one with</u> curly hair.
Eren: And <u>who's this girl on the right?</u> Is that Grandma?
Grandad: Yes, it is. She was my girlfriend then.
Eren: Aww! How romantic!
Grandad: Yes, she was a lovely girl. We got married soon after that.

SOUNDS GOOD!
• What are you up to?
• How romantic!

Exercise 1
Possible answer:
He's watching something. He's making a gesture with his hand.

Exercise 2
1 Because he sees himself in the programme.
3 He uses the TV remote to rewind the programme.
4 Grandad (when he was young), his friend Harry and Grandad's girlfriend/ Eren's grandma

1 Describe the man in the photo. What is he doing?

2 ▶ 37 🔊 7.14 Watch or listen and answer the questions.
1 Why is Eren's grandad surprised?
2 How does Eren help his grandad?
3 Which three people do they see on TV?

SET FOR LIFE
3 How can you show interest during a conversation? Discuss in pairs. Use these ideas and add you own tips.
• ask open questions
• observe the person's body language
• don't interrupt when someone is talking

4 Study the Speaking box. Find examples of the phrases in the dialogue.

SPEAKING Identifying people in a group

Talking about people in a group
He's/She's standing/sitting/talking to/playing with …
He's/She's wearing …
He's/She's in front of/behind/next to/near …
He's/She's on the left/on the right/in the middle.
He's/She's at the front/at the back/in the foreground/ in the background.

Asking
Who's this/that boy/girl on the left/who is wearing … ?
Which one/girl/boy/man/woman/guy?
Which one do you mean?

Explaining
The one with/who is …
The tall/good-looking one.

5 Work in pairs. Student A, go to page 137. Student B, go to page 143.

YOUR WORLD
6 In pairs, take it in turns to ask and answer questions about someone in the photo on page 89. Use phrases from the Speaking box. Describe the people and talk about their personality. Use the ideas below to help you.

seems calm   has a great sense of humour
is confident/shy/cheerful

He's/She's the kind of person who …

Unit 7 **94** I can explain who I am talking about.

For the teacher
• Teaching notes, page 211

On the Portal
• Photocopiable activity: *Identify them*

For the student
• Workbook, page 76

On the Portal
• Workbook: Lesson 7.6
• Extra Practice Activities: New Park video

7.7 Writing
A short story

1 What makes a friend a true friend?

2 Read the text. What do we find out about each friend in Flavia's story? Who are your real friends?

> 1 Last week I learned an interesting lesson about true friends. I was feeling stressed about my Science homework. I didn't understand it and I needed someone to explain it.
> 2 First, I asked my best friend Sienna to help. 'I'd explain it if I was free, but I'm quite busy.' Sienna and I get on well, and she's good at Science, so I was disappointed.
> 3 Next, I went to another friend who is also my neighbour. 'If I understood the homework, I'd help you,' said Harry, 'but it's too difficult.' Then I felt really stressed!
> 4 Just then a new classmate heard us. Lara is popular, but we don't speak often because she's quite loud and I'm a bit shy. I was surprised by her next words. 'I can help,' she offered.
> 5 Lara explained the Science homework to me carefully. Afterwards, we sat and chatted. We discovered we have a lot in common and the same sense of humour. It's been a great way to make a new friend!

3 Read Flavia's story again. Match the descriptions (1–5) with the events from the story (a–e).
1. [d] setting the scene
2. [c] the first event
3. [a] the second event
4. [e] the main event – the climax
5. [b] the solution or outcome

a Flavia's neighbour can't help her.
b Lara and Flavia become friends.
c Flavia's friend who is good at Science can't help her.
d Flavia has a problem.
e Flavia has a surprise offer of help.

4 Study the Writing box. Find examples of the phrases in Flavia's story.

WRITING — A short story

Starting your story and setting the scene
1 Last week I learned an interesting lesson about true friends.
Have you ever had a really unusual day?

Introduce your characters
2 My friend Sienna …   A new classmate …

Use direct speech
3 'I'd explain it if I was free, but I'm quite busy.'
'I'm sorry I can't help,' said Harry.

Main event – the climax (e.g. a surprise)
4 You'll never guess what happened next.   Then I had a real surprise.

End your story
5 All's well that ends well.   I never want to do that again!

5 Study the Language box. Write a few sentences about something strange/surprising that happened to you last week. Use the sequencers from the box.

LANGUAGE — Sequencers

We use sequencers to show the order of events in a story.
First, …
Next, …
Just then, …
Afterwards, …

I had a busy week. First, …

WRITING TIME

6 Write a story with the title *A friend in need*. It can be true or fictional.

1 Find ideas
Make notes about:
- the scene, the characters and the events.
- examples of direct speech.
- the ending.

2 Plan
Organise your ideas into paragraphs. Use Flavia's story to help you.

3 Write and share
- Write a draft story. Use the Language box and the Writing box to help you.
- Share your story with another student for feedback.
- Use the feedback from your partner and write the final version of your story.

4 Check
- Check language: did you use sequencers correctly?
- Check grammar: did you mostly use the Past Simple and some conditionals? Did you use relative clauses correctly?

Exercise 2
Sienna is good at Science. She is too busy to help Flavia. Harry is Flavia's neighbour. Harry finds the homework too difficult./Harry isn't good at Science. Lara is popular. She has a lot in common with Flavia. She has the same sense of humour as Flavia.

I can write a short story.

For the teacher
- Teaching notes, page 212

On the Portal
- Photocopiable activity: *Making new friends*

For the student
- Workbook, page 77

On the Portal
- Workbook: Lesson 7.7

Vocabulary Activator

WORDLIST 🔊 7.15

Word building (family)
great-grandfather (n)
great-grandmother (n)
great-grandparent (n)
half-brother (n)
half-sister (n)
stepbrother (n)
stepdaughter (n)
stepfather (n)
stepmother (n)
stepsister (n)
stepson (n)

Phrasal verbs
deal with (a problem) (v)
get along with (v)
get on with (v)
get together (v)
go out (with) (v)
grow up (v)
hang out with (v)
move away (v)

Word friends (relationships)
get to know someone
have an argument
have something in common
have the same sense of humour
see each other after school
share an interest in something
spend time with someone

Relations
(people)
best friend (n)
classmate (n)
mate (n)
stranger (n)
teammate (n)

(phrases with *friend(s)*)
be friends
have a friend
keep friends
make friends

Word friends
(phrases with *get*)
get a hot drink (for someone)
get a job
get a letter/a phone call/an email
get a pet
get better/worse
get bored/excited/upset
get dressed
get home
get old(er)
get ready

Extra words
arrive (v)
aunt (n)
biological (adj)
character (n)
complicated (adj)
cousin (n)
dilemma (n)
disagree (v)
disappointed (adj)
end-of-term party (n)
family meal (n)
fetch (v)
flight (n)
friendly (adj)
friendship (n)
generation (n)
hand-held console (n)
home town (n)
invitation (n)
likes and dislikes
long-lost (adj)
loud (adj)
marriage (n)
miss somebody (v)
neighbour (n)
nightmare (n)
opinion (n)
parent (n)
positive (adj)
recognise (v)
related by blood
relation (n)
relative (n)
reply (v)
rescue (v)
researcher (n)
rewind (v)
shared (adj)
similar (adj)
social identity (n)
step (n)
tell the whole story
thought (n)
uncle (n)
volunteer (v)
wedding (n)

1 Complete the sentences with words from the wordlist. Then, in pairs, say if the sentences are true for you.
 1 I want to *get* to know my classmates better.
 2 I *have* a lot of interests in common with my parents.
 3 I like to spend time *with* other people.
 4 I *get* upset when people forget my birthday.
 5 I prefer to keep old friends than to *make* new ones.
 6 My family *get/gets* together every weekend.
 7 I sometimes *have* arguments with classmates when they want different things.

2 Choose three phrases with *get* from the wordlist. Then, in pairs, share your phrases and make a short story with them.

3 Choose the correct option.
 1 No, I don't know that man. He's a complete *mate* / *stranger* to me.
 2 He doesn't live with his parents anymore – he moved *away* / *over* last year.
 3 She always gets his jokes – they have the *common* / *same* sense of humour.
 4 My grandmother grew *up* / *off* in this village.
 5 We need to talk about how to deal *off* / *with* this problem.

4 Complete the sentences with words from the wordlist. Then write a similar sentence. In pairs, complete each other's sentences.
 1 The opposite of 'friend' is *stranger*.
 2 A sister who has one parent different from you is your *half-sister*.
 3 Someone who is on the same side as you in a game of football is your *teammate*.
 4 My grandmother's dad is my *great-grandfather*.
 5 When a man marries a woman who has a son, the boy is the man's *stepson*.

5 🔊 7.16 **PRONUNCIATION** Listen to what happens when we say words together in speech.
 1 get together
 2 go out with someone
 3 grow up
 4 share an interest
 5 get dressed

6 🔊 7.17 **PRONUNCIATION** Listen again and repeat. Then, in pairs, practise saying the phrases.

For the teacher
- Audioscript, page 251

On the Portal
- **Photocopiable activities:** *Have you got…? Make a sentence*
- **Tests:** Unit 7 Test, Unit 7 Writing Test

For the student
- Workbook, pages 78–79

On the Portal
- **Workbook:** Self-check
- Wordlist
- **Extra Practice Activities:** Self-check

Revision

Vocabulary

1 Match phrases 1–6 with phrases a–f with a similar meaning.

1. _e_ get dressed
2. _d_ move away
3. _f_ grow up
4. _b_ go out with
5. _a_ get along with
6. _c_ hang out with

a communicate and spend time well together
b visit a fun place with friends
c spend time together
d go to live in a different place
e put your clothes on
f go from child to adult

2 Complete the text with the words below.

common   ~~great-grandfather~~   humour   interest
stepdaughter   stranger   time

We had a big family meal at my house last weekend. My mum's grandfather was there – my ¹_great-grandfather_. He was with a girl about my age. He said, 'This is my son's ²_stepdaughter_ from his second wife. Have you met her? Her name's Lara.' I said no. She was a ³_stranger_ to me. But we started talking and found that we had a lot in ⁴_common_. We also shared a(n) ⁵_interest_ in comedy films, and we had the same sense of ⁶_humour_! We spent a long ⁷_time_ talking, which was fun.

3 Write the correct word for each definition.
1. A brother you share one parent with. h_alf-brother_
2. Someone who is in the same team as you. t_eammate_
3. An informal word for 'friend'. m_ate_
4. When you solve a problem, you d_eal_ with it.
5. A person you share lessons with. c_lassmate_
6. When you spend time with a friend, you h_ang_ o_ut_ with him/her.

Grammar

4 Complete the Second Conditional questions with the correct form of the verbs in brackets. Then, in pairs, ask and answer the questions.
1. If your computer _stopped_ (stop) working, how _____ (you/deal) with the problem?
2. If your parents _____ (want) to get a new family pet, what animal _____ (you/choose)?
3. If a new student _____ (join) the class, how _____ (you/make) him or her feel welcome?
4. How _____ (you/help) a grandparent to get started if he or she _____ (want) to use social media for the first time?
5. What _____ (you/do) if a dog _____ (try) to follow you home?

5 Complete the sentences with relative pronouns.
1. My favourite school subject, _which_ is on Friday morning, is Art.
2. It's good to have a friend _who/that_ can stay positive in difficult situations.
3. A place _where_ I sometimes do my homework is on the sofa.
4. I came first in a singing competition, _which_ was a surprise for everyone.
5. We have to find a TV show _which/that_ everyone wants to watch.
6. My great-grandfather, _who_ is ninety-five years old, always beats me at chess.

6 Choose the correct relative pronoun. Then complete the sentences to make them true for you. In pairs, compare your sentences.
1. I like shops *where* / who _I like shops where_____.
2. I like playing games *which* / who _____.
3. A good friend is a person where / *who* _____.
4. A place which / *where* I like to hang out with friends _____.
5. The thing *that* / where helps me study best is _____.
6. I enjoy family meals who / *which* _____.

Speaking

7 In pairs, imagine you are looking at a family photo. Student A, go to page 137. Student B, go to page 143. Follow the instructions for Student A's 'family photo'. Then swap roles.

Student A: Talk about one person in the photo and say what they are doing.
Student B: Comment on that person. Then ask about another person in the photo.
Student A: Answer Student B's question. Then talk about and comment on another person.

Dictation

8 🔊 7.18 Listen. Then listen again and write down what you hear.

Exercise 4
1 would you deal
2 wanted; would you choose
3 joined; would you make
4 would you help; wanted
5 would you do; tried

Exercise 7
Sample answer:
A My sister Mary is here, on the right. She's wearing a red sweater.
B She looks friendly. And who is that boy on the left who is wearing blue trousers?
A His name is Harry. The one next to him is his dad. And the tall one next to Mary is my cousin Bob. He looks angry!

EXAM

Exercise 8
🔊 audioscript page 251

International Certificate Level 2, Listening and Writing, Section 2, (dictation)

97 Unit 7

BBC CULTURE
From generation to generation

Lessons from Grandad

Have you ever thought about what you get and learn from your elders? Take food, for example. Where does your food really come from? For example, think about modern milk production. Milk goes from a farm to a milk factory, where it is processed and put in milk bottles or cartons. Then someone buys it for you from a supermarket or a local shop. That's a lot of steps!

Mark Holland, from Surrey, didn't like the large number of steps involved in producing food. 'It seemed that the food was not as fresh as we thought. So, I decided to go to a farmer's market one day. My grandfather sells food from his farm there. The food is a little more expensive, but it is organic. This means it is more nutritious and there are no added chemicals in the food. It is much more delicious too. I spend a lot of time on my grandfather's farm. He shows me traditional methods of farming and cooking. Next year I want to study farming. I think with my grandfather's help and my studies, I can become a very successful farmer.'

Sarah became interested in organic food a few years ago. She enjoys hanging out with Grandad. 'One year he taught me how to make a vegetable salad. All the vegetables were from his garden. The salad was delicious – very different from the ones from supermarkets. This made me think about where our food comes from and how fresh it is. Now I'm a teenager I still visit Grandad and he teaches me so many things about food, like how to cook it and where it comes from. When I finish school, I want to become a chef and cook with food straight from my own market garden.'

> **nutritious** (adj) healthy and good for you to eat
> **organic** (adj) (of food) that has no added chemicals

1 **VISIBLE THINKING** In pairs, follow these steps.
   CONCEPT
   1 Look at the photo. What is the boy learning from his grandad? *gardening*
   2 Where do you get your food from? How fresh is it?
   CHALLENGE
   3 Is there a problem with food that comes from supermarkets?
   4 Can farmer's markets be a better choice than supermarkets?
   CHANGE
   5 Do you think you will choose to buy only organic food?

2 🔊 7.19 Read the article. Do you think people like Mark and Sarah can change how we buy food in the future?

3 Read the article again and mark the sentences true (T) or false (F).
   1 [F] Food in supermarkets usually comes straight from a farm.
   2 [T] Mark's grandfather sells his produce at a farmer's market.
   3 [F] Organic food is usually a little cheaper.
   4 [T] Mark gets to know traditional methods of farming.
   5 [T] Sarah learns about where food comes from with her grandad.
   6 [T] Sarah wants to cook with her own fresh food in the future.

4 In pairs, discuss the questions.
   1 Where do people in your country buy fresh food?
   2 Do you think modern and traditional methods can work together to produce healthy food?

BBC 98

For the teacher
- Teaching notes, page 213
- Videoscript, page 252

On the Portal
- Photocopiable activity: *Project worksheet: a digital presentation*

BBC ▶ Arctic life

5 ▶ 38 Look at the photo. What do you think the woman is teaching her granddaughter? Do you think they get on well? Watch Part 1 of the video and check your ideas.

6 ▶ 38 Watch Part 1 of the video again and complete the sentences with the words below.

> collect food   generations   hard life   sea

1 The ___sea___ freezes for half of the year in the Arctic.
2 Minnie doesn't think it is a ___hard life___ in her village.
3 Eva learns how to ___collect food___ from her grandmother.
4 The women in Minnie's family have collected food for ___generations___.

7 In pairs, discuss the questions.
1 Do you think you would find life in this village good? Why?/Why not?
2 Do you think the methods they use to find food are easy or difficult? Why?

8 ▶ 39 Watch Part 2 of the video and tick (✓) the correct sentences.
1 ✓ They make sure there is no sea water in the sea cave.
2 ☐ They have more than half an hour to work.
3 ✓ They find the food they are looking for.
4 ✓ When they hear the sea, they leave quickly.
5 ☐ The sea closes the ice hole.
6 ✓ Eva learns a traditional skill she can use.

9 In pairs or groups, discuss the questions.
1 What problems do you think the people in this village have?
2 How do you think the older generation help in this village?
3 What skills can older people teach us?

Exercise 5

▶ videoscript page 252

The woman (Minnie) is teaching her granddaughter (Eva) how to fish/collect food. Yes, they get on well.

Exercise 8

▶ videoscript page 252

PROJECT TIME

10 In groups of three, prepare a presentation about how people in remote places collect food. Follow these steps.

1 In groups, choose a remote place to focus on. Decide who can find the answers to these questions.
- Where is the place and what is it like?
- How do they find food? Is it a dangerous/traditional method?
- How do younger generations learn about traditional methods of collecting food?

2 Individually, create your part of the presentation.
- Find information and photos for your slides.
- For each slide, write a short text and add the photos.

3 In your group, create your presentation.
- Put all the slides together and think of a title for your presentation.
- Check and edit your presentation.
- Practise giving the presentation as a group.

4 Share your presentation with the class.
- Answer other students' questions.
- Listen to the other presentations. Ask questions.

99 BBC

Just justice

8

VOCABULARY
Crimes and criminals | Solving crimes | The law | Word building: negative adjectives | Investigating crimes

GRAMMAR
Present and Past Simple passive | have/get something done

SAFE NEIGHBOURHOODS

Let's stand up to crime

Hopefully, you haven't been unlucky and been the victim of a crime. But if you have, we have some tips and advice to help you. First, let's look at the type of crime some of you have experienced. Then click on the link to find out how you can stop the crime happening in the first place.

1 Rhea, Newcastle
I was a witness to a <u>bank robbery</u>. Two <u>robbers</u> ran into the bank and stole a lot of money. After robbing the bank, they got away on a motorbike. I spoke to the detective who's trying to solve the crime.

2 Mhairi, Glasgow
There have been a lot of <u>burglaries</u> in our area recently. Last month some <u>burglars</u> broke into our neighbour's house. The <u>thieves</u> stole her purse and some jewellery. She was really upset.

3 Jason, Bristol
<u>Pickpocketing</u> is a big problem in the city. Last night I was on a busy train when I felt someone's hand in my back pocket. I turned around quickly, but the <u>pickpocket</u> wasn't there. And neither was my wallet!

4 Humza, Coventry
I work in a small shop with a big problem: <u>theft</u>, or <u>shoplifting</u>, to be specific. The <u>shoplifters</u> steal all sorts of things. We're going to install security cameras to try to stop them.

5 Emma, Leeds
Some <u>vandals</u> ran through our neighbourhood last night. They damaged the swings in the children's park, broke a street light and threw a stone at a shop window. Why do people commit such stupid crimes? I don't understand <u>vandalism</u>.

Tips and advice **Read more**

8.1 Vocabulary

Crime

1 Read crime stories 1–5 and match them with photos A–E.
1 C   2 B   3 D   4 E   5 A

2 Read the stories again. Who do you think had the most unpleasant experience? In pairs, discuss your ideas.

3 🔊 8.1 Study Vocabulary box A. Find the words in the stories in Exercise 1 and check you understand them.

VOCABULARY A — **Criminals**

burglar   pickpocket   robber   shoplifter   thief   vandal

Unit 8 **100**

For the teacher
- Teaching notes, page 214
- Audioscript, page 252

On the Portal
- Vocabulary Memory Game
- Photocopiable activity: *Mime, define, draw*
- Test: Vocabulary Check 8

For the student
- Workbook, pages 80–81

On the Portal
- Workbook: Lesson 8.1
- Extra Practice Activities: Vocabulary

112

4 🔊 8.2 **WORD FRIENDS** Complete the sentences with the correct form of the verbs below. Use one of the verbs twice. Listen and check.

> break   break into   ~~commit~~   damage
> rob   solve   steal

1. A criminal is someone who _commits_ a crime and _breaks_ the law.
2. A shoplifter is someone who _steals_ things from a shop.
3. A bank robber is someone who _robs_ a bank.
4. A burglar is someone who _breaks into_ homes.
5. A vandal is someone who _damages_ buildings and other things.
6. A detective is someone who _solves_ crimes.
7. A thief is someone who _steals_ things from people.

5 🔊 8.3 Study Vocabulary box B. Find the crimes in the stories in Exercise 1 and complete the table. Listen and check.

VOCABULARY B ▸ Word building: crimes

Person	Crime
(bank) robber	_(bank) robbery_
burglar	_burglary_
pickpocket	_pickpocketing_
shoplifter	_shoplifting_
thief	_theft_
vandal	_vandalism_

6 🔊 8.4 Look at Vocabulary box B again and listen to a boy talking about crime. Write the examples of crimes and criminals you hear. What crimes have you heard or read about where you live? Discuss in pairs.

7 🔊 8.5 Study Vocabulary box C and complete the story below with the correct form of words from the box. Listen and check.

VOCABULARY C ▸ Solving crimes

> case   clue   detective   fingerprint   security camera
> suspect   witness

8 🔊 8.6 Study Vocabulary box D and choose the correct option in the newspaper headlines below. Listen and check.

VOCABULARY D ▸ The law

> court   fine   judge   lawyer   prison   punishment
> reward   sentence

1. £500 *punishment* / **reward** for information on local vandals
2. Ten-year prison *judge* / **sentence** for bank robbers
3. **Judge** / *Lawyer* decides shoplifter should work for the community
4. Train pickpocket gets a **fine** / *reward* of £250
5. Ex-burglar goes back to school to become a **lawyer** / *court*!
6. Vandals should go to *fine* / **prison**, says politician

YOUR WORLD

9 In pairs, discuss the questions.
1. What punishments would you give the criminals in the crime stories in Exercise 1?
2. Would you like to be a police officer/detective/lawyer/judge? Why?/Why not?

Exercise 6

🔊 audioscript page 252

bank robbery, burglary, shoplifting, vandalism, vandals, pickpocket, thief

---

I'm the lead ¹_detective_ investigating the recent bank robbery. It wasn't a difficult ²_case_. We interviewed several ³_witnesses_ and from their descriptions, I immediately thought of two possible ⁴_suspects_, so we brought them in for questioning. They said they had nothing to do with it, but I knew they were lying. We had two ⁵_clues_ that helped us solve the crime. First, the recording from the ⁶_security cameras_ showed their faces. Secondly, their ⁷_fingerprints_ were all over the bank. I arrested them. Then some police officers searched their flat and found the money from the robbery.

I can talk about crime and criminals.

8.2 Grammar

Present and Past Simple passive

1 What do you know about Sherlock Holmes? In pairs, make a list.

2 🔊 8.7 In pairs, do the quiz. Listen and check.

Exercise 2
🔊 audioscript page 252

The Sherlock Holmes QUIZ

1. The *Sherlock Holmes* detective stories were written 100 years ago by
   a Arthur Conan Doyle.
   b Agatha Christie.
2. Holmes had a famous assistant. What was his name?
   a Doctor Who
   b Doctor Watson
3. The stories were first published
   a in a book.
   b in a magazine.
4. Sherlock's flat is located at number 221B of a famous London street. It is
   a Sherlock Street.
   b Baker Street.
5. Which famous Sherlock Holmes quote is never really used by Sherlock Holmes?
   a 'Elementary, my dear Watson.'
   b 'My mind is like a racing engine.'

Exercise 4
build – built – built (irregular)
catch – caught – caught (irregular)
chase – chased – chased (regular)
hide – hid – hidden (irregular)
make – made – made (irregular)
see – saw – seen (irregular)
use – used – used (regular)
watch – watched – watched (regular)
write – wrote – written (irregular)

3 Study the Grammar box. Find more examples of the Present and Past Simple passive in the quiz.

> **GRAMMAR**   **The passive**
>
> **Present Simple passive**
> The quote is never really used by Sherlock Holmes.
>
> **Past Simple passive**
> The detective stories were written by a British author.

GRAMMAR TIME > PAGE 133

⚠️ **WATCH OUT!**
Use *by* + name/person to say who did the action.
The detective stories were written by a British author.

Exercise 6
2 were created
3 were written by/are written by
4 is/was used by
5 was changed
6 is read by
7 are sold

Exercise 7
Sample answer:
Enola Holmes is a book about Sherlock Holmes's younger sister. It was written by Nancy Springer and it was made into a film in 2020. On Enola's sixteenth birthday her mother disappears. Enola, who is very clever, tries to find her.

4 Write the Past Simple and past participle forms of the verbs below. Underline the verbs which are the same in the Past Simple and Past Participle. Use the irregular verbs list on page 136 to help you.

| ask | build | catch | chase | hide |
| make | see | use | watch | write |

ask – asked – asked

5 Complete the sentences with the past participle form of the verbs in brackets.
1 Security cameras are *used* (use) to find clues about many crimes.
2 The thief escaped but was *caught* (catch) when she fell.
3 Yesterday evening two car thieves were *chased* (chase) by police in fast cars.
4 Sometimes a recording from security cameras is *watched* (watch) by special detectives.
5 Last night the witnesses were *asked* (ask) questions by police officers.
6 This security camera is *hidden* (hide) so that shoplifters don't see it.

6 Complete the text with the Present or Past Simple passive form of the verbs in brackets. Add *by* where necessary.

> The *Nancy Drew* stories are among the most famous detective stories ever. The first stories about Nancy Drew [1] *were published* (publish) in the 1930s. Other, newer stories have appeared since then. The books [2] _____ (create) for teenagers. The *Nancy Drew* detective stories [3] _____ (write) several different authors. The name Carolyn Keene [4] _____ (use) by all the authors, but Nancy's name [5] _____ (change) in some countries. It may be surprising, but this old series [6] _____ (read) thousands of young people even today, and each year lots and lots of copies [7] _____ (sell).

YOUR WORLD

7 Tell the class about a detective story or film that you know.

Unit 8   **102**   I can use the Present and Past Simple passive.

For the teacher
- Teaching notes, page 215
- *Need support?* worksheet, page 239
- Audioscript, page 252

On the Portal
- Grammar presentation
- Photocopiable activity: *Quiz time*
- Test: Grammar Check 8

For the student
- Workbook, page 82
- Grammar Time, Student's Book, page 133

On the Portal
- Workbook: Lesson 8.2
- Extra Practice Activities: Grammar

8.3 Reading and Vocabulary
The right punishment?

1 Look at the photos and title of the article. Describe the photos. What do you think the article is about?

2 🔊 8.8 Read the article and check your answers to Exercise 1. What kind of court did Lisa and Ian choose? What countries have such courts?
A youth court. Countries in Europe, Asia and the USA.

3 Read the article again and choose the correct answer.
1 What did the police officer do that was surprising?
  a He arrested Lisa and Ian for stealing.
  b He sent Lisa and Ian to a youth court.
  c He asked Lisa and Ian to choose where to go.
  d He gave Lisa and Ian something from the shop.
2 Why did Lisa and Ian choose to go to a youth court?
  a They thought it was difficult to understand adults.
  b They believed their actions were legal.
  c They wanted to make their own choices.
  d They wanted to be heard by people of their own age.
3 Which of these statements is true about youth courts?
  a You listen to stories about all kinds of crimes.
  b You are heard by people who are a similar age.
  c You can choose a punishment that works for you.
  d You meet young people from around the world.
4 How did Lisa and Ian react to their punishment?
  a They agreed it was appropriate.
  b They were quite unhappy.
  c They wanted to change it.
  d They thought it was hard work.

4 🔊 8.9 Study the Vocabulary box. Find more adjectives with negative prefixes in the article and write the missing words. How do these prefixes change the meaning of an adjective?

VOCABULARY	Word building: negative adjectives
un-	unhappy, uninteresting, unimportant, uncomfortable, unkind, unfair, *unusual*
im-	impatient, *impossible*
il-	illogical, *illegal*
ir-	irregular, *irresponsible*

Adding the prefix makes the word mean the opposite to the original word.

EXAM
Exercise 3
B1 Preliminary for Schools, Reading, Part 3, (4-option multiple choice)

A fair punishment

Imagine that you're a police officer. What would you do if you saw some teenagers shoplifting? A kind police officer's decision helped Lisa and her brother Ian out of a difficult situation.

When Lisa was fifteen and Ian was seventeen, they were arrested for stealing from a shop. The police officer who caught them did an <u>unusual</u> thing: he gave them a choice. Did they want to go to a normal court, where an adult judge would decide their punishment? Or did they want to go to a youth court, where a group of young people would decide their punishment?

For Lisa and Ian, the answer was easy. They knew they had done something <u>illegal</u> and it was <u>impossible</u> to avoid punishment, but they hoped young judges might understand their situation better. That's why they chose to go to a youth court.

But what is a youth court? It's a place where the jury – the group of people who make decisions – is made up of people aged 12–19. Young people who are in trouble with the law have a chance to explain their story, be judged and get back on the 'right track'. There are now thousands of these courts around the world, including Europe, Asia and the USA. Of course, normal courts still deal with serious crimes.

At the court, Lisa and Ian, who were very nervous, were given three punishments. First, they both had to write an apology to the shop owner. Then they had to do forty hours of 'community service'. In other words, they had to help other people in their local area. Finally, they had to volunteer at the youth court themselves. The brother and sister both felt this was fair. They didn't want to be <u>irresponsible</u> any more. As volunteers, they have learned how the court works. They have both helped to choose fair punishments for other young people too.

YOUR WORLD
5 Do you think youth courts are a good idea? Why?/Why not?

I can understand an article about crime and punishments.

For the teacher
- Teaching notes, page 216
- *Need support?* worksheet, page 239

On the Portal
- Vocabulary Memory Game
- Photocopiable activity: Dominoes
- Test: Vocabulary Check 8

For the student
- Workbook, page 83

On the Portal
- Workbook: Lesson 8.3
- Extra Practice Activities: Vocabulary

8.4 Grammar
have/get something done

VIDEO ▶ A NEW LOOK

Abe: They're the photos for the poster for our film.
Eren: Wow! They're great. Is that Carla?
Abe: Yes.
Eren: So, who's that?
Abe: It's Carla too!
Eren: No way!
Abe: Yes, she wore a wig and make-up. In the film she's accused of a crime she didn't commit and she's on the run from the police. So, she changes her look. <u>She gets her hair cut short.</u> <u>She has it dyed blonde.</u> She has her eyebrows shaped and then <u>she gets her fingernails and her make-up done.</u>
Eren: How come her eyes have changed colour?
Abe: She put in coloured contact lenses.
Eren: She's so different! She looks like a rock star!
Abe: OK, I'm ready. Let's go to the park.
Eren: I've changed my mind. Let's go to the centre.
Abe: Why?
Eren: I want to change my look, to get my hair cut.

1 Look at the photo. What do you think Abe and Eren are doing?

2 ▶ 40 ◀)) 8.10 Watch or listen and check your ideas from Exercise 1. Why does Carla's character in the film change her look?

3 Do you like to change your appearance? What do you usually change – your hairstyle or your clothes?

4 Study the Grammar box. Find more examples of *have/get something done* in the dialogue.

> **GRAMMAR** *have/get something done*
>
> She **has her eyebrows shaped**.
> I want to **get my hair cut**.
> Are you going to **get your hair dyed**?
>
> GRAMMAR TIME > PAGE 134

⚠ WATCH OUT!
We use possessive adjectives (*my, your, his, her,* etc.) to talk about body parts.
I got **my** hair cut. NOT *I got the hair cut.*

Exercise 2
Abe and Eren are looking at the photos for the poster for the film that the friends have made. Carla's character changes her look because she's on the run from the police.

Exercise 6
2 haven't had my eyes tested
3 've already had my photo printed
4 have my bike stolen
5 have my bedroom cleaned

5 Match the sentence halves.
1 [e] The burglar broke the window
2 [f] He took a photo of the suspect
3 [a] If you put money in your back pocket,
4 [c] Your crime drawings are so good
5 [d] It would be a good idea
6 [b] After she got out of prison,

a you'll get it stolen.
b she had her name changed.
c you should have them published.
d to get a burglar alarm installed.
e so we had to get it fixed.
f and had it photocopied.

6 Complete the sentences with the correct form of *have something done*.
1 I *had my hair cut* (my hair/cut) last week.
2 I _____ (my eyes/not test) for ages.
3 I _____ (already/my photo/print) in the local paper twice.
4 I don't want to _____ (my bike/steal), so I always lock it up.
5 I'd love to _____ (my bedroom/clean), but I have to do it myself.

YOUR WORLD
7 In pairs, say if the sentences in Exercise 6 are true for you. Correct the false sentences.
I didn't have my hair cut last week. I had it cut about a month ago.

Unit 8 **104** I can use the construction *have/get something done*.

For the teacher
• Teaching notes, page 217
• *Need support?* worksheet, page 239

On the Portal
• Grammar presentation
• Photocopiable activity: *She's having her hair cut*
• Test: Grammar Check 8

For the student
• Workbook, page 84
• Grammar Time, Student's Book, page 134

On the Portal
• Workbook: Lesson 8.4
• Extra Practice Activities: Grammar, New Park video

8.5 Listening and Vocabulary
Crimes and criminals

Exercise 3
🔊 audioscript page 252

Exercise 4
🔊 audioscript page 252

EXAM

Exercise 6
International Certificate Level 2, Listening, Section 3, (note completion)

B1 Preliminary for Schools, Listening, Part 3, (gap fill)

Exercise 6
🔊 audioscript page 253

1 2 October/ 2nd October/ October 2nd
2 3.00/3/three; 5.00/5/five
3 (a) (digital) camera and (a) laptop
4 07836 198 477
5 20/twenty

Exercise 7
▶ videoscript page 253

1 Faye would be upset but she could live without it. Melissa, Shaun and Sarah would go to the police. Kenneth would buy a new one.
2 Faye would tell them to put it back or tell someone. Sarah and Melissa would tell an employee. Shauçn would mind his own business.
3 Sarah and Kenneth would call the police.

---

1 In pairs, describe the photo. How can social media help the police solve a crime like this? What about other crimes?

2 🔊 8.11 **WORD FRIENDS** Match the verbs with the nouns to make phrases about investigating crimes. Listen and check.
1 [c] search   a a witness
2 [e] arrest   b clues
3 [a] interview   c the area
4 [d] take   d fingerprints
5 [b] look for   e a criminal

3 🔊 8.12 Listen to the first part of a podcast. What do you think happened?

4 🔊 8.13 Listen to the second part of the podcast and check your ideas from Exercise 3.
The girl is talking about a burglary.

5 🔊 8.13 Listen again and number the events in the correct order.
a [6] The police arrested the burglar.
b [1] Katrina discovered her laptop was missing.
c [4] A friend told Katrina about a conversation in the park.
d [3] The police looked for clues in and near the house.
e [2] Katrina called the police.
f [5] Katrina and Mia started looking on social media.

6 🔊 8.14 Listen to the final part of the podcast and complete the notes.

> Date of burglary: ¹ _____
> Time of burglary: between ² _____ and _____ p.m.
> Items still missing: ³ _____
> Phone number: ⁴ _____
> Reward: ⁵ £ _____

VIDEO ▶ **WIDER WORLD**

7 ▶ 41 Watch five people answering the questions. What answers do they give?
What would you do if:
1 you had your phone stolen?
2 you saw someone shoplifting?
3 you saw someone vandalising something?

8 In pairs, ask and answer the questions in Exercise 7.
I'd call the phone company. Then I would tell all my friends and …

I can understand people talking about a crime.   **105** Unit 8

For the teacher
- Teaching notes, page 218
- Audioscript, pages 252–253
- Videoscript, page 253

On the Portal
- Photocopiable activity: *Caught red-handed!*

For the student
- Workbook, page 85

On the Portal
- Workbook: Lesson 8.5
- Extra Practice Activities: Vocabulary, BBC Vox Pop

117

8.6 Speaking
Keeping a conversation going

VIDEO ▶ IS SOMETHING WRONG?

Mum: It's so nice to go on a walk together. I love this park. You're quiet. <u>Are you OK?</u> <u>Is something wrong?</u>
Bea: <u>I'm fine</u>, Mum. <u>Honestly</u>.
Mum: Hmm … Come on, I can tell that you're worrying about something. It usually helps to talk.
Bea: <u>I don't know.</u>
Mum: <u>Go on, tell me.</u>
Bea: Well, some nasty comments were posted on my nature blog.
Mum: <u>Really?</u> <u>What do you mean?</u>
Bea: I shared my photo of that kingfisher we saw on the river. I thought it was amazing because it's hard to take good photos of birds when they're moving so fast.
Mum: <u>Right</u> …
Bea: Some people put nice comments like, 'So cute!'
Mum: That's nice!
Bea: But other people put things like 'Yawn. Boooring post!' Then one person said, 'A boring post by a boring person.' And I was really hurt.
Mum: Just ignore them! By the way, how many people liked your post?
Bea: I don't know, a few hundred?
Mum: Well, it seems to me most people agree with you.
Bea: Hmm, I see what you mean. 'Mum knows best', hey? After all, you're older and wiser … much older, in fact!
Mum: Hey! I'm not that old, OK?

SOUNDS GOOD! So cute! • Just ignore them! • By the way.

1 ▶ 42 🔊 8.15 Look at the photo. How do you think Bea feels? Watch or listen and check.

2 Do you think Bea's 'friends' showed respect in their online comments?

SET FOR LIFE

3 What can you do about negative comments on your social media? Discuss in pairs. Use these ideas to help you.
- ignore them
- block the person commenting
- if possible, speak to the 'commenter' in real life

Exercise 1
She's feeling sad because some people posted nasty comments on her blog.

4 Study the Speaking box. Find examples of the phrases in the dialogue.

SPEAKING — Keeping a conversation going

Inviting
Are you OK? Is something wrong?
Do you want to talk about it? Go on, tell me.

Encouraging
What do you mean? Really? Then what happened?
I'm sure (you were/did). Exactly.

Reassuring
Don't worry. I'm fine. Honestly.
Of course you can (do it). Right.

Responding
Definitely! Absolutely! I don't know.

5 🔊 8.16 Complete the dialogues with one or two words in each gap. Listen and check.
1 A: I like social media, but sometimes it's bad.
   B: What do you _mean_?
   A: When people post negative comments it's bad. I try to post positive comments.
2 A: I think thirteen is the right age to use most social media sites.
   B: Yes, _absolutely_! I think twelve is too young.

6 Discuss the statement in pairs. How many phrases from the Speaking box can you include in your conversation?
All social media is bad for friendship.

YOUR WORLD
7 In pairs take turns to tell your partner about something you like or dislike about social media. Invite your partner to comment.

I can keep a conversation going.

For the teacher
- Teaching notes, page 219

On the Portal
- Photocopiable activity: You can do it!

For the student
- Workbook, page 86

On the Portal
- Workbook: Lesson 8.6
- Extra Practice Activities: New Park video

8.7 Writing
An opinion essay

1. Give examples of rubbish you see in your everyday environment. Do you think leaving litter is a crime?

2. Read the essay. What is the writer's main opinion? Do you agree?

> 'Rubbish is bad for the environment. People who leave litter outdoors should pay a fine.' Do you agree? Explain your ideas.

> 1. We all agree that litter is bad for the environment. But personally, I believe that stronger punishments are needed **to** deal with the problem of rubbish. For example, many riverbanks and beaches are littered with plastic bottles and bags. This is a serious problem for river wildlife as well as ocean animals, as the plastic is carried out to sea. **As a result,** many animals are hurt or killed by pieces of plastic.
>
> 2. On the one hand, we must punish people who don't clean up after themselves. For example, if you do not put your litter in a bin, you should have to clean up other people's rubbish too! On the other hand, are such punishments enough? In my opinion, people would stop dropping litter if they had to pay a fine every time.
>
> 3. However, I do not think small fines will solve the problem. Although fines can make people think about the environment, it may not be enough **to** make them change their habits. **For this reason,** I would like to see bigger fines, **so as to** put a stop to littering.
>
> 4. In conclusion, I agree with serious fines for people who continue to drop litter **in order to** keep the environment clean and safe.

3. Study the Writing box. Complete the gaps with words and phrases from the essay.

WRITING — An opinion essay

Give your main reaction
1. In my opinion, …
   Personally, *I believe* that …

Balance opinions
2. On the one hand, …
   On the other hand, …

Add contrasting ideas
3. However, I think/do not think that …
   Although …

Summarise and conclude
4. Overall, …
   In general, …
   In conclusion,

4. Study the Language box. Find examples of the words and phrases in the essay.

LANGUAGE — Connectors of purpose and result

Connectors of purpose: *to, in order to, so as to*
Connectors of result: *for this reason, as a result*

5. Rewrite the sentences using the words in brackets. Use the Language box to help you.
   1. People should take their litter home to protect the environment. (as)
   2. They had to pay a fine so they are more careful now. (result)
   3. Animals are important, so people need to think about them. (reason)
   4. I believe fines are useful to help us keep the law. (order)

WRITING TIME

6. Write an opinion essay on the following question: 'Littering is a serious problem. People who drop litter should do unpaid community work.' Do you agree? Explain your ideas.

   1. **Find ideas**
      Make notes about:
      - litter in your local environment – think of examples
      - your opinion on community work. Is it a good punishment?
      - any other ideas to encourage people to behave responsibly
      - your conclusion

   2. **Plan**
      Organise your ideas into paragraphs. Use the essay in Exercise 2 to help you.

   3. **Write and share**
      - Write a draft essay. Use the Language box and the Writing box to help you.
      - Share your essay with another student for feedback.
      - Use the feedback from your partner and write the final version of your essay.

   4. **Check**
      - Check language: did you use connectors correctly?
      - Check grammar: did you use the passive correctly?

Exercise 2
The main opinion is that big fines will help people change their habits and reduce litter.

Exercise 5
1. People should take their litter home so as to protect the environment.
2. They had to pay a fine. As a result, they are more careful now./They had to pay a fine and they are more careful now as a result.
3. Animals are important. For this reason, people need to think about them./Animals are important. People need to think about them for this reason.
4. I believe fines are useful in order to help us keep the law.

I can write an opinion essay. **107** Unit 8

For the teacher
- Teaching notes, page 220
- Need support? worksheet, page 239

On the Portal
- Photocopiable activity: *I agree!*

For the student
- Workbook, page 87

On the Portal
- Workbook: Lesson 8.7

Vocabulary Activator

WORDLIST 🔊 8.17

Criminals
burglar (n)
pickpocket (n)
robber (n)
shoplifter (n)
thief (n)
vandal (n)

Word friends
(crime collocations)
break into homes
break the law
commit a crime
damage buildings
rob a bank
solve crimes
steal things

Word building
(crimes)
burglary (n)
pickpocketing (n)
robbery (n)
shoplifting (n)
theft (n)
vandalism (n)

Solving crimes
case (n)
clue (n)
detective (n)
fingerprint (n)
security camera (n)
suspect (n)
witness (n)

The law
court (n)
fine (n)
judge (n)
lawyer (n)
prison (n)
punishment (n)
reward (n)
sentence (n)

Word building
(negative adjectives)
illegal (adj)
illogical (adj)
impatient (adj)
impossible (adj)
irregular (adj)
uncomfortable (adj)

unfair (adj)
unhappy (adj)
unimportant (adj)
uninteresting (adj)
unkind (adj)
unusual (adj)

Word friends
(investigating crimes)
arrest a criminal
interview a witness
look for clues
search the area
take fingerprints

Extra words
accuse (v)
apology (n)
appear (v)
assistant (n)
author (n)
be in trouble with
catch (v)
chase (v)
choice (n)
community (n)
description (n)

elementary (adj)
engine (n)
eyebrow (n)
fair punishment
fingernail (n)
get away (v)
install (v)
investigate (v)
irresponsible (adj)
jewellery (n)
jury (n)
lie (v)
mind (n)
neighbourhood (n)
politician (n)
publish (v)
purse (n)
question (v)
quote (n)
recording (n)
series (n)
shop window (n)
stone (n)
street light (n)
swing (n)
wallet (n)

Exercise 1
1 prison, court
2 burglary, pickpocketing, robbery, shoplifting, theft
3 fine, punishment, sentence
4 detective, judge, lawyer

Exercise 4
Possible answers:
I/We could interview a witness/take fingerprints/search the area/look at security camera recordings.

1 Use the wordlist to find these things.
  1 two places where criminals are taken after they are arrested
  2 five crimes that involve stealing something
  3 three words for ways to pay for a crime
  4 three jobs

2 Answer the quiz questions with words from the wordlist. Then write one more question. In pairs, ask and answer each other's questions.

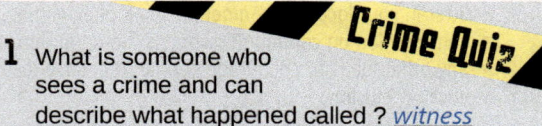

Crime Quiz
1 What is someone who sees a crime and can describe what happened called? *witness*
2 Which crime involves people breaking objects which are not their own? *vandalism*
3 Who is a person who helps with legal problems? *lawyer*
4 Who is the person who decides the punishment for a criminal? *judge*
5 Where are criminals sent as a punishment for their crimes? *prison*
6 What can detectives look for to help them understand a case? *clue(s)*

3 Match 1–8 with a–h to make phrases.
1 [e] arrest the   a law
2 [a] break the   b witness
3 [c] commit a   c crime
4 [b] interview a   d fingerprints
5 [g] rob a   e criminal
6 [f] search an   f area
7 [d] take   g bank
8 [h] steal   h things

4 In pairs, imagine you are detectives trying to find a criminal. Use your detective skills to suggest three things you could do. Use words from the wordlist.
We could look for clues.

5 🔊 8.18 **PRONUNCIATION** The underlined vowels in the suffixes of the words below are unstressed. Listen to their pronunciation (/ə/).

comfort**a**ble   import**a**nt   lawy**e**r   logic**a**l
punishm**e**nt   regul**a**r

6 🔊 8.19 **PRONUNCIATION** Underline the vowels with the /ə/ sound in the suffixes of the words below. Listen and repeat.

assistant   burglar   impatient
impossible   robber

For the teacher
- Audioscript, page 253

On the Portal
- Photocopiable activities: *Solve the clues, Who might say this?*
- Tests: Unit 8 Test, Unit 8 Writing Test

For the student
- Workbook, pages 88–89

On the Portal
- Workbook: Self-check
- Wordlist
- Extra Practice Activities: Self-check

Revision

Vocabulary

1 Complete the second sentence so that it means the same as the first one. Use the correct form of the underlined word.
1. <u>Robbers</u> can go to prison for a long time.
   People who commit _robbery_ can go to prison for a long time.
2. It isn't <u>possible</u> to read this book in one day.
   Reading this book in one day is _impossible_.
3. Police have arrested a <u>thief</u>.
   Police have arrested somebody for _theft_.
4. We didn't feel <u>comfortable</u> in our new car's seats.
   Our new car's seats were _uncomfortable_.
5. That woman has been a <u>burglar</u> in the past.
   That woman has committed _burglary_ in the past.
6. I couldn't see the <u>logic</u> in the detective's ideas.
   The detective's ideas seemed _illogical_ to me.

2 Complete the extract from a detective story with the words below.

> burglary case reward security
> suspect thief witness

Last week someone broke into another jewellery shop and stole the biggest diamond in London. It was only the latest crime in the most difficult ¹_case_ I've ever had. Like the other crimes, the ²_thief_ left no clues at all, and there were no ³_security_ camera recordings to look at. But I got lucky: a ⁴_witness_ came to see me! She was walking by the shop at the time of the ⁵_burglary_ and she described the person inside. But I still didn't have a ⁶_suspect_. So I made a poster with an artist's drawing, offering a large ⁷_reward_ for information.

3 Complete the news headlines with the Present Simple form of the correct verbs.

1. Building workers d_amage_ priceless painting in city art gallery
2. Detectives s_olve_ the crime of the century!
3. Armed men r_ob_ a bank and steal £1 million
4. Secret lives: the criminals who work by day and b_reak_ into homes by night
5. Police a_rrest_ bank robbers after long car chase

Grammar

4 Rewrite the sentences in the passive. Do not include the underlined subjects.
1. <u>They</u> investigated several internet crimes last year.
   Several internet crimes _were investigated last year_.
2. <u>We</u> don't use this building as a prison now.
   This building _isn't used as a prison now_.
3. <u>The city council</u> gave a lot of money to my neighbourhood to improve it.
   My neighbourhood _was given a lot of money to improve it_.
4. <u>People</u> don't play football very often in our park.
   Football _isn't played very often in our local park_.
5. <u>Nobody</u> saw the burglar when she entered the building.
   The burglar _wasn't seen when she entered the building_.

5 Complete the quiz questions with the Present Simple or Past Simple passive form of the verbs in brackets. Then match the answers below to the questions.

> Arthur Conan Doyle dogs Robin Hood
> Socrates Washington D.C.

1. Which ancient Greek philosopher (give) a death sentence? _was given_
2. Who (the Sherlock Holmes books/write) by?
3. Which American city (FBI headquarters/locate) in?
4. Which famous British thief (play) by Russell Crowe in a 2010 film?
5. What animals (use) to find illegal substances in airports?

6 Complete the dialogues with the correct form of *have something done* and the verbs in brackets.
1. A: Your hair looks great! When ¹_did you have it dyed_ (you/it/dye)?
   B: Yesterday.
2. A: The security camera isn't working.
   B: I know, we ²_____ (it/fix) soon.
3. A: Why do you keep your phone in your bag?
   B: I don't want to ³_____ (it/steal).
4. A: Who printed the crime photos? They're great!
   B: I ⁴_____ (not/them/print). I did them myself.
5. A: Your detective stories are really good!
   ⁵_____ (you/any of them/publish)?
   B: Not yet, but I'd like to.

Speaking

7 In pairs, turn to page 137 and follow the instructions to role play a dialogue. Then swap roles.

Dictation

8 🔊 8.20 Listen. Then listen again and write down what you hear.

Exercise 5
1 Socrates
2 were the Sherlock Holmes books written; Arthur Conan Doyle
3 are/is the FBI headquarters located; Washington D.C.
4 was played; Robin Hood
5 are used; dogs

Exercise 6
2 're going to have it fixed/'re having it fixed
3 have it stolen
4 didn't have them printed
5 Have you had any of them published

Exercise 7
Sample answer:
A You're quiet. Are you OK?
B I'm fine.
A Really? I don't think so. Tell me.
B I've lost my phone. I feel bad.
A Personally, I think you need to tell your parents. They will understand.
B OK, I see what you mean, thanks.
A Are you OK now?
B I'm fine now. Honestly. Thanks.

EXAM

Exercise 8

🔊 audioscript page 253

International Certificate Level 2, Listening and Writing, Section 2, (dictation)

SET FOR LIFE

You decide!

Should I play in the match instead of going to Elsa's birthday lunch?

For
- The team has never chosen me for a match before – it's fantastic that they asked me.
- They might be annoyed with me if I say 'no'.

Against
- I might play badly and that will be embarrassing.
- I don't know the people in the team very well.
- It's my best friend's birthday and she'll be sad if I don't celebrate her birthday with her.
- Everyone will talk about her birthday lunch the next day, and I'll feel bad that I wasn't there.

Exercise 3
1 Humans have an adult brain from the age of twenty-five.
2 Adults use the part of the brain that looks after facts; teenagers often use the part that looks after how they feel.
3 It is often important for teenagers to think about the long term too.

Exercise 4
🔊 audioscript page 253

Exercise 5
🔊 audioscript page 253

1 Read Harry's for and against lists. What would you do if you were in his situation?

2 In pairs, discuss the questions.
 1 What short-term decisions have you made today/this week/this year?
 2 What long-term decisions will you have to make in your life?
 3 Have you ever had to make a difficult decision? What was the situation? Why was it hard to decide what to do?

3 In pairs, look at the statements. Do you think they are T (true) or F (false)?
 1 [F] Humans have adult brains from the age of about fourteen.
 2 [F] Adults and teenagers make decisions in the same way.
 3 [T] It's important for teenagers to think about the long term when they make decisions.

4 🔊 8.21 Listen to an expert's talk on making decisions and check your answers in Exercise 3.

5 🔊 8.22 Listen to the next part of the talk and choose the correct option.
 1 Before you make a decision, make sure you know all the people / (facts).
 2 In a list of reasons for and against a decision, include (short-term) / good reasons and (long-term) / bad reasons.
 3 There isn't always only one right reason / (decision).
 4 You won't always have the (result) / decision that you hoped for.

6 Look again at Harry's lists in Exercise 1. Has he written down long-term (L) reasons or short-term (S) reasons? *short-term reasons*

Units 7–8 **110** I can make responsible decisions.

For the teacher
- Teaching notes, page 221
- Audioscript, page 253

On the Portal
- Photocopiable activity: *You decide!*

Make a decision

7 Read these extra reasons. Should they be in Harry's for (F) list or his against (A) list? Are they long-term (L) or short-term (S) reasons?

1	F	I've trained with the team for months, so I've worked hard for the opportunity.
2	F	If I don't agree to play in the match this time, they may not ask me again.
3	F	It's Ethan's birthday next month, and then Elsa's birthday will be old news.
4	F	It's good for my well-being and health to play a sport.
5	F	I'll get to know my teammates more quickly if I play in matches with them.
6	A	People don't stay friends if they don't make the effort to celebrate their birthdays together.
7	F	I want to get better at my sport and it's hard to do that if I don't play in matches.

They are all long-term reasons.

8 Give each of Harry's reasons in Exercises 1 and Exercise 7 a score from 1 (not at all important) to 10 (extremely important). Then compare the total score for all the 'for' reasons and all the 'against' reasons. What do you think Harry should do?

9 Read the Useful Phrases. Imagine you have to make a decision. In pairs, choose one topic and discuss some reasons for and against.
1 Should I give up my hobby so that I can spend more time studying?
2 Should I tell my friend's parents that he sometimes shoplifts?
3 Should I miss three months of school to be in a film?

10 Read the Useful Tips. Do you think these ideas will help you to make better decisions in the future? Why?/Why not?

SET FOR LIFE

11 In pairs, make a decision. Remember to think about short-term and long-term reasons. Follow these steps.

1 Choose one of the situations in Exercise 9 or think of your own ideas.

2 Write two lists, with reasons for and against. Use expressions from the Useful Phrases box to discuss your reasons.

3 Give each reason a score from 1 (not at all important) to 10 (extremely important). Use the total scores to help you make the decision.

4 Present your decision and reasons to the class.

USEFUL TIPS

When you make decisions, it's important to consider short-term and long-term reasons, and make the best decision with the information available.

- Make sure you know all the facts before you decide.
- Make lists of reasons for and against.
- Think about both long-term and short-term reasons.
- Choose the decision with the more important reasons.

USEFUL PHRASES

Reasons for and against
One long-term/short-term advantage is that …
In the long/short term, it's (not) a good idea because …
If you (didn't) … , you would(n't) …

What should influence a decision
That's a very important point.
That's the biggest reason for … -ing.
I don't think that should influence the decision very much.
That doesn't matter very much because …
I think … is a bigger issue than …

Lessons in life 9

VOCABULARY School subjects | Describing students | Learning and assessment | Collocations with *make* and *take* | Phrasal verbs

GRAMMAR Reported speech: statements | Word order in questions

Top five coolest lessons?

Do you ever want to learn outside the classroom? Would you enjoy studying subjects where you take a practical exam, not a written test?

If the answer is 'yes', you might like to move to Australia and Hawaii! In these places, it's important for pupils to be confident in water, so surfing lessons are a normal part of the school curriculum. As well as Language, Maths and History, many countries also have special lessons in subjects which they believe are important. In Scotland, traditional dance lessons are often offered to high school pupils. In some schools in the UK, it's possible to learn unusual new skills like bee-keeping or to have IT lessons in cyber security! And in the USA, some students spend one year creating a science discovery project.

Such a variety of choices is great for students, preparing them for either the world of work or further study.

9.1 Vocabulary
Education

Exercise 1
The five 'cool' lessons are: surfing lessons, traditional dance lessons, bee-keeping lessons, IT lessons in cyber security, science discovery lessons

1 Read the article and find the five 'cool' lessons. Then, in pairs, answer the questions.
  1. Do you agree that all these lessons are cool?
  2. Which would you add to your school curriculum? Why?
  3. Which would you not add? Why?

2 🔊 9.1 Study Vocabulary box A. What do you think of these subjects? What are your favourite subjects? In pairs, discuss your ideas.

VOCABULARY A — School subjects

Art Biology Chemistry Cooking D&T (Design and Technology) Drama Economics Geography History IT (Information Technology) Languages Literature Maths Music PE (Physical Education) Physics

3 Add the subjects from Vocabulary box A to the correct category in the spidergram. Can you add any more subjects?

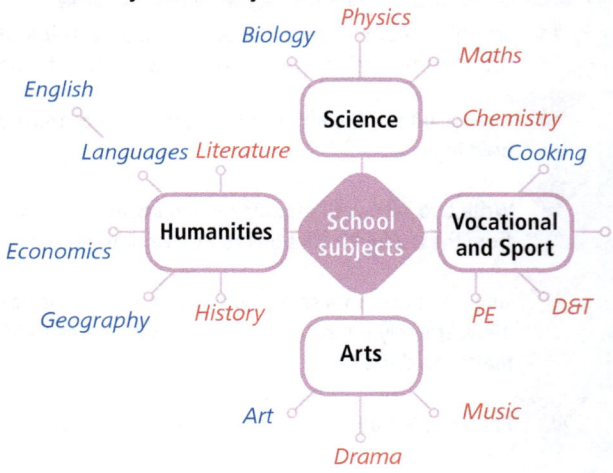

- **Science**: Biology, Physics, Maths, Chemistry
- **Humanities**: English, Languages, Literature, Economics, Geography, History
- **Vocational and Sport**: Cooking, PE, D&T
- **Arts**: Art, Music, Drama

Unit 9 112

For the teacher
- Teaching notes, page 222
- *Need support?* worksheet, page 240

On the Portal
- Vocabulary Memory Game
- Photocopiable activity: *Hidden words*
- Test: Vocabulary Check 9

For the student
- Workbook, pages 90–91

On the Portal
- Workbook: Lesson 9.1
- Extra Practice Activities: Vocabulary

124

4 Which subjects from Vocabulary box A are taught in your school? Would you add any of the skills below to the curriculum?

> Fashion design   Film-making   Gardening
> Karate   Photography

5 **I KNOW!** In pairs, make your own spidergram about School. Add the three categories below, and the examples. How many words can you add to each category?
1. Types of schools: *primary school*
2. People at school: *head teacher*
3. Places at school: *library*

6 Do you ever use spidergrams to learn facts? Which subjects do you think they are best for?

7 🔊 9.2 Study Vocabulary box B. Can you add more words describing students?

VOCABULARY B ▶ **Describing students**

Qualities of a good student: confident   creative   hard-working   intelligent   talented
Skills: critical thinking   general knowledge   problem-solving   teamwork

8 🔊 9.3 Complete the sentences with words from Vocabulary box B. Listen and check.
1. Students who are able to learn and understand things easily are *intelligent*.
2. It's useful to know information about the world around you. This is called *general knowledge*.
3. If you believe you can do things successfully, you are *confident*, which helps you to do well.
4. Students who are *creative* can use their imagination to find ideas in science subjects as well as arts.
5. *Critical thinking* is a useful skill because it teaches you to think clearly and ask the right questions.
6. If you are doing a task and can find a solution, you are good at *problem-solving*.
7. Students who are *hard-working* are never lazy and always try to do their best. This can help them do well in any future job.
8. If you can work well with others, you've learned the secret of *teamwork*. This is one of the most important skills you can have in life.

9 Read texts (1–3) quickly ignoring the gaps. Match the texts with photos A–C.

1. [B] My favourite lesson is IT. I love ¹*learning* about how computers work and how to fix problems. We also find out about the future of computers. Last term, we did a ²*project* about robots – we worked together and built our own robot.

2. [C] I enjoy studying Geography because our teacher makes the lessons fun. Although we have to ³*memorise* a lot of information, the classes are really interesting. There's one thing I don't enjoy: giving ⁴*presentations*! It's hard to stand up and talk in front of the class.

3. [A] I enjoy Food Preparation classes because I like the mix of science and cooking. We have written exams at the end of the course, and we also have ⁵*practical* exams, where we make food using a recipe.

10 🔊 9.4 Study Vocabulary box C. Complete the texts in Exercise 9 with the correct form of the words from the box. Listen and check.

VOCABULARY C ▶ **Learning and assessment**

Learning
learn   memorise   revise   study   curriculum
Types of assessment
online test   practical exam   presentation   project   speaking exam   written exam

YOUR WORLD

11 Which class activities and types of assessment are the most suitable for different subjects and learners? Discuss in pairs and give reasons.

I can talk about school life.   **113**   Unit 9

Exercise 5
Possible answers:
(Students will show this information as a spidergram, with words around the related bubbles.)
Types of schools: college, secondary school, university
People at school: classmates, form tutor, pupils, students, teachers
Places at school: canteen, computer room, corridor, playground, Science lab, sports hall, staffroom

Exercise 7
Possible answers:
Qualities of a good student: disciplined, organised, punctual
Skills: communication, note-taking, time-management

125

9.2 Grammar

Reported speech: statements

1 Look at the posts. What is a debating club?

Debating Club

- Jack: We're starting a debating club.
- Daisy: I'm looking for some good topics to discuss.
- Mrs Walker: That's a great idea!
- Tom: We need to advertise it.

2 🔊 9.5 Listen to Daisy talking about the debating club and look at the posts in Exercise 1 again. What do you notice about the verbs in bold above and the verbs in the recording?

3 🔊 9.6 Read the interview quickly. What topics are chosen for the debates?
interesting topics: a mix of serious and silly topics

MILL HOUSE SCHOOL NEWS BY KATE BRANDON

'New Debating Club!'
Interview with Peter Brown, Year 11 student.

Tell us about the new debating club. How did it all start?
Last term the pupils of Year 11 told their teachers that they wanted to start a debating club. The teachers said that they liked the idea, so now each week we run a debate.

What are the rules?
One team has to agree and the other team has to disagree. Then the audience decide which team is the winner.

What about the topics of debates?
The teachers said we needed interesting topics, so we made a list. We have a mix of serious and silly topics. Last week the audience said they wanted to discuss something lighter.

So, what topic did you choose?
'Pasta or Pizza: which is best?' Our teachers told us to research our speeches. The audience can ask us difficult questions, so it's important to have a good plan and ... stay calm.

How can you join the club?
Just come to our debate. The teachers told us that we could have as many members as we wanted. 'The more members, the more interesting debates!' they said. So, join us!

Exercise 2
🔊 audioscript page 253

The verbs change. (You don't need to explain how, but students may notice they change to past tense.)

Exercise 4
We like the idea. We want to discuss something lighter. Research your speeches. You can have as many members as you want.

4 Study the Grammar box. Find more examples of reported speech in the interview. Then change the reported statements to direct speech: what were each person's exact words?

GRAMMAR Reported speech: statements

Present Simple → Past Simple
'You need a list of interesting topics.'
Teachers said (that) we needed a list of interesting topics.

Present Continuous → Past Continuous
'We're starting a debating club.'
Pupils told their teachers (that) they were starting a debating club.

GRAMMAR TIME > PAGE 134

WATCH OUT!
We use *said (that)* or *told me/you/etc. (that)* to report someone's words.

5 🔊 9.7 Choose the correct option. Listen and check.

Max told Sara that he ¹*is planning* / **was planning** to join the debating club. Sara said that she ²*doesn't want* / **didn't want** to join. She said that she ³ **wasn't** / *isn't* keen on speaking in public and then added, 'I ⁴ **can't** / *couldn't* come anyway because I ⁵*went* / **go** to dance classes on Tuesday.' Then Max said that the next debate ⁶ *is* / **was** 'Pasta or Pizza'. Sara said that it ⁷*sounds* / **sounded** a lot of fun and she told him she ⁸ **wanted** / *want* to give it a try.

6 Complete the reported statements.
1 'Uniforms aren't important.'
Nicola said uniforms *weren't* important.
2 'I disagree.'
Jared said he *disagreed*.
3 We don't want to discuss sports.
They told me they *didn't want* to discuss sports.
4 I'm planning a speech about pasta.
Ethan said he *was planning* a speech about pasta.
5 Julia doesn't know what pizza to order.
Mum said Julia *didn't know* what pizza to order.
6 I'm not coming to the debate on Friday.
I told them I *wasn't coming* to the debate on Friday.

7 Write a sentence that someone has said in the past week. In pairs, take turns to report what that person said. Use *said* or *told*.

YOUR WORLD

Unit 9   114   I can report what people say.

9.3 Reading and Vocabulary
Learning effectively

How to train your brain!

In our Citizenship class, Mrs Jones told us there were seven secret ways to become confident students. First of all, she said students needed to 'think like teachers'. ¹ _c_ A researcher gave the same information to two different groups of students. The first group had to learn the information for a test. The second group had to learn the information to teach it to someone else. I was surprised that the second group learned best. ² _f_ Because they knew how to explain it clearly.

Secondly, Mrs Jones said that we had to write down some things we remembered after each lesson. Then we had to make more notes in the evening.

Mrs Jones said that the third secret was taking tests. Tests aren't really the end goal of learning. ³ _e_ And after a few tests you should be able to see that you've made some progress.

Secret four is called 'spaced practice'. One researcher told students to study a topic in short sections, for half an hour or one hour. Your brain can store this information easily! This means you need to take regular breaks from studying.

The fifth secret is strange: 'Don't focus!' Researchers think it's good to mix things up. If you move between different parts of topics, you will see connections and the whole topic will hopefully start to make sense.

However, my favourite secret is number six. ⁴ _b_ Mrs Jones said that students who usually worked in the same place needed to move. Your brain makes a connection between the place and the topic you're learning. So sitting in a fresh place makes a topic easier to remember.

And finally, secret seven is good for learning vocabulary. When you're not sure of the meaning of a word on your list, don't check it. Try to understand the meaning from the context in which the word is used. ⁵ _a_ Your brain remembers things better when it has to work hard.

1 Do you think people can change their intelligence? Why/Why not?

2 Read the article quickly and answer the questions.
   1 Who do you think is the writer?
   2 What is the writer's purpose?
   3 Sum up each of the seven secrets.

3 🔊 9.8 Read the text again. Complete the gaps with a sentence from the list. There is one extra sentence.
   a Think of things that are related to it.
   b It's 'study in different places'.
   c She told us about an interesting experiment.
   d Many people forget the next rule.
   e They're actually a good way for us to learn!
   f Why did they remember the information so well?

4 In pairs, write two questions about the article and ask the class.

5 🔊 9.9 **WORD FRIENDS** Complete the phrases with *make* or *take*. Sometimes both are possible. Listen and check.
   1 _take_ a test/an exam
   2 _make_ sense
   3 _take/make_ notes
   4 _make_ progress
   5 _make_ a connection
   6 _take_ a break

YOUR WORLD
6 Which of the seven secrets in the article is the best? Will you try any of these ideas? Discuss in pairs.

Exercise 2
1 a pupil/student at a school/in Mrs Jones' Citizenship class
2 to explain a lesson for other pupils/students who weren't in the same class
3 Possible answers:
   1 Think like a teacher.
   2 Make notes after the lesson.
   3 Take tests.
   4 Take a regular break./Do 'spaced practice'.
   5 Don't focus.
   6 Sit in a fresh/different place.
   7 Try to understand (meaning from) the context.

EXAM
Exercise 3
B1 Preliminary for Schools, Reading, Part 4, (gapped text)

I can understand an article about effective learning. **115** Unit 9

For the teacher
- Teaching notes, page 224
- *Need support?* worksheet, page 240

On the Portal
- Photocopiable activity: *Make or take?*
- Test: Vocabulary Check 9

For the student
- Workbook, page 93

On the Portal
- Workbook: Lesson 9.3
- Extra Practice Activities: Vocabulary

9.4 Grammar
Word order in questions

VIDEO ▶ AN INTERVIEW

Bea: Thanks for letting me interview you.
Carla: No problem. I know you need articles for the school news blog.
Bea: So, I've got a list of questions about your Portuguese course. <u>Is it OK to record the interview?</u>
Carla: Of course. Go ahead.
Bea: OK then. Have you done any online courses?
Carla: Yes, I've just finished an eight-week course in Portuguese.
Bea: That's so cool! <u>Why did you choose to learn Portuguese?</u>
Carla: Well, I know some Portuguese, but I wanted to practise speaking. We're going to Brazil in the summer, so I'd like to chat with my cousins.
Bea: Lucky you! Er, <u>who was your tutor?</u>
Carla: She was my dad's friend. She helped me a lot.
Bea: <u>Was it easy to learn a language online?</u>
Carla: Yes, and the lessons were interesting. I learned some salsa moves and I made things. Just a minute … <u>How cool is this?</u>
Bea: Wow! That headdress is amazing!
Carla: <u>Can I ask you a question now?</u> Why do you ask so many questions?
Bea: Because I'd like to be a journalist one day. <u>Do you want to listen to the interview?</u>
Carla: Sure.
Bea: Oh no! I don't believe it! I forgot to press 'Record'!
Carla: Really?

Exercise 3
2 Did you leave home late/at eleven this morning?
3 Are you going on holiday this year?
4 Have you been to the cinema recently?/Did you go to the cinema last week?
5 Are you having a party/doing anything for your birthday?

Exercise 4
2 Who had a Maths test this morning? What test did Class 12D have this morning?
3 Who in your class has read this book? What has everyone in your class read?
4 Who saw you when you were at the bus stop? When did your teacher see you?
5 Who is going to see that new film? What are all your friends going to see?

1 ▶ 43 🔊 9.10 Look at the photo. What do you think is happening in the photo? Watch or listen and check.

2 Study the Grammar box. Find more examples of questions in the dialogue.

> **GRAMMAR ▶ Word order in questions**
>
> **Yes/No questions**
> It is OK. → Is it OK?
> You have done some online courses. → Have you done any online courses?
> You enjoyed it. → Did you enjoy it?
>
> **Wh- questions**
> Why are you laughing?
> Why do you ask so many questions?
>
> **Subject questions**
> A: Who studied with you?   B: Lee studied with me.
>
> **Object questions**
> A: Who did you study with?   B: I studied with Lee.
>
> GRAMMAR TIME > PAGE 135

3 Write questions for these answers.
1 Yes, I had pasta for dinner last night.
   Did you have a hot meal for dinner last night?
2 No, I left home early this morning, not late.
3 Yes, we're going to Brazil for our summer holidays.
4 Yes, I saw two films at the cinema last week.
5 No, I'm not going to do anything for my birthday.

4 Write two questions for each answer. Make questions about the underlined words.
1 <u>The fire</u> started in the <u>Science lab</u>.
   What happened in the Science lab?
   Where did the fire start?
2 <u>Class 12D</u> had a <u>Maths</u> test this morning.
3 <u>Everyone</u> in my class has read <u>this book</u>.
4 The teacher saw me <u>when I was at the bus stop</u>.
5 <u>All my friends</u> are going to see <u>that new film</u>.

YOUR WORLD
5 In pairs, ask and answer the questions you wrote in Exercise 3. Some of your answers can be false. Guess if your partner's answers are true.

Unit 9 **116** I can make questions with the correct word order.

For the teacher
- Teaching notes, page 225
- *Need support?* worksheet, page 240

On the Portal
- Grammar presentation
- Photocopiable activity: *Ask and answer*
- Test: Grammar Check 9

For the student
- Workbook, page 94
- Grammar Time, Student's Book, page 135

On the Portal
- Workbook: Lesson 9.4
- Extra Practice Activities: Grammar, New Park video

128

9.5 Listening and Vocabulary

Conversations in the classroom

1 Teachers ask 300–400 questions every day! Do your teachers ask any of these questions? What other questions do they ask?
- Did you understand everything?
- What does … mean?
- What do you think about … ?

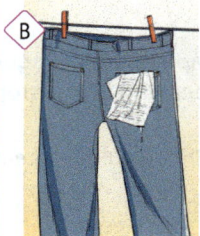

2 🔊 9.11 Listen to four dialogues and choose the correct answer.
1 What does the teacher want the girl to do before the test? *B*
2 Where are all the other students now? *A*
3 What happened to the boy's form? *B*
4 What were the students doing? *C*

3 🔊 9.11 Listen again. Which teacher asked the most questions? Why do you think he/she did that?
Teacher 3 asked the most questions. (He was joking with the student.)

4 🔊 9.12 Study the Vocabulary box and complete the sentences below with the phrasal verbs. Listen and check.

VOCABULARY — Phrasal verbs
calm down   fill in (a form)   get on   hand in/out
look over   look up   miss out

1 The teacher asked us all to *hand in* our homework on time.
2 Pupils who finish early should *get on* with some extra reading.
3 I'm definitely coming to the end-of-term party – I don't want to *miss out* on all the fun!
4 Make sure you *look over* all your answers before you finish.
5 You can *look up* any words you don't know in a dictionary.
6 We have to *fill in* this form with our name and phone number.
7 Ella was so nervous before her exam, so I told her to *calm down* and take a deep breath.

5 🔊 9.13 Choose the most appropriate answer to each question. Listen and check.
1 Who's ready to hand in their essay?
  a Yes, I will.   (b) I've just finished it.
  c No, it wasn't difficult.
2 Are we going to look over the test results now?
  a Yes, I will.   b No, it isn't.
  (c) Yes, we are.
3 Did the students get on quietly with their projects?
  (a) No, they didn't.   b No, there weren't.
  c Where were they?
4 Can everybody calm down, please?
  (a) Yes, Miss.   b No, he can't.
  c Thank you, Miss.

VIDEO ▶ WIDER WORLD

6 ▶ 44 Watch five people talking about their first school and first teacher. Note down one thing each person remembers about the school, and one about his/her teacher.

7 Write a few sentences about a memory from your primary school. In pairs share your memories.

I can understand short classroom conversations.

EXAM

Exercise 2
🔊 audioscript page 253

B1 Preliminary for Schools, Listening, Part 1, (visual multiple choice)

Exercise 5
🔊 audioscript page 254

Exercise 6
▶ videoscript page 254

Possible answers:
Jacqui: All Saints School, little and her favourite; Mrs Webster, who taught her how to sew
AJ: Grade school in small town, small classes; teacher who was great at explaining things
Sophie: Tiny school, about sixty pupils, very sweet and humble, learning better than in bigger schools; Mrs Buchanan, lovely, worked in reception class for years, everyone knew her well
Jonathan: International school in Rome/Italy, learned English and Italian; Miss Carlson, Liverpool FC fan, they argued about who was better team
Celia: Small school in Auckland/New Zealand, only a few hundred students, by the beach; Mr Norwell, lovely, in his fifties, taught Maths using pebbles

---

For the teacher
- Teaching notes, page 226
- *Need support?* worksheet, page 240
- Audioscript, pages 253–254
- Videoscript, page 254

On the Portal
- Vocabulary Memory Game
- Photocopiable activity: *Calm down!*

For the student
- Workbook, page 95

On the Portal
- Workbook: Lesson 9.5
- Extra Practice Activities: Vocabulary, BBC Vox Pop

9.6 Speaking
Exchanging information

VIDEO ▶ WHAT A COINCIDENCE!

Bea: I can't believe it's the last week of term. I can't wait to go on holiday.
Abe: Last week of the semester, you mean. And go on vacation!
Miyu: Excuse me? Would you mind … ?
Abe: Do you want me to take your photo?
Miyu: Thank you so much. Awesome! Maybe just one more.
Bea: Hey, I'm Bea. Have you been in England before?
Miyu: Hi, I'm Miyu. Well, this is my first time, but I've been here for a month now.
Abe: Really? Where are you from? Your accent sounds American.
Miyu: Yeah, you guessed it. I'm from the USA.
Abe: Me too! Which part of the States are you from?
Miyu: New York.
Bea: I'd love to go to New York City.
Miyu: Oh no, I'm not from New York City. I'm from a town in upstate New York, Syracuse.
Abe: No way! That's where I'm from!
Bea: That's so funny. How long are you staying for, Miyu?
Miyu: My brother and I are staying with a lovely host family for the summer because we're doing a Drama course at Grove College.
Bea: I don't believe it! That's where my mum works!
Miyu: What a coincidence!
Abe: What do you think of the UK?
Miyu: I really like it. Look, what are you guys doing right now? Would you like to get an ice cream?

SOUNDS GOOD! I can't wait! • You guessed it. • What a coincidence!

Exercise 2
1 Miyu asks Abe and Bea to take a photo of her.
2 Because they don't know one another/they're getting to know one another.
3 Abe and Miyu are both from Syracuse in (upstate) New York.

Exercise 5
Past experience: Well, this is my first time, but I've been here for a month now.
Present situation: I'm from the USA. My brother and I are staying for the summer. I really like it.

1 Have you ever met a tourist in your area? Did he/she ask you for any help?

2 ▶ 45 ◀)) 9.14 Watch or listen and answer the questions.
1 Why does Miyu speak to Abe and Bea?
2 Why do Abe and Bea ask a lot of questions?
3 What do Abe and Miyu have in common?

3 Do you think Miyu felt welcome when she met Abe and Bea? Why?/Why not?

SET FOR LIFE
4 Work in pairs. Imagine you have just met a visitor from another country. What friendly things can you say? Make a list.

5 Study the Speaking box. Match the questions with responses in the dialogue.

SPEAKING Exchanging information

Past experience
Have you been in England before?
Present situation
Where are you from? How long are you staying for?
What do you think of the UK?
Future plans
What are you (guys) doing now/later?
Would you like to get an ice cream?

6 ◀)) 9.15 Complete the dialogues with phrases from the Speaking box. Listen and check.
1 A: Would you like to get an ice cream?
   B: Yes. That would be great. Let's go.
2 A: How long are you staying for?
   B: Just a few weeks.
3 A: What do you think of the UK?
   B: Well, it's interesting, but I miss home.
4 A: Have you been in England before?
   B: Yes, I have. I love it here.

YOUR WORLD
7 In groups of three, role play the situation below.
Students A and B, you are friends. You meet Student C, who is a friend of Student A. Have a conversation using phrases from the Speaking box and Exercise 6.

I can exchange information in a conversation.

For the teacher
• Teaching notes, page 227

On the Portal
• Photocopiable activity: Sort them out

For the student
• Workbook, page 96

On the Portal
• Workbook: Lesson 9.6
• Extra Practice Activities: New Park video

9.7 Writing
A formal letter asking for information

1 Read the advert. Which course would you choose? Why?

Summer Courses
- English Revision
- English for Science
- English for Arts
- English for Humanities
- English for Vocational Studies

Would you like to improve your language skills this summer? Write to us explaining which course you are interested in and why. Let us know if you have any questions about our courses.

2 Read Georgia's letter in response to the advert in Exercise 1. What two things does she want to know?

3 Study the Writing box. Add more phrases from Georgia's letter.

WRITING — A formal letter asking for information

Greeting
1 Dear Mr/Mrs/Ms/Miss (surname),
Dear Sir/Madam,

Say why you are writing
2 I am writing to ask for/about …
I am writing to say (that) …

Ask for information
3 Would you mind … (+ -ing)?
Please could you …

Give information
4 My teacher said that …   My plan is to …
She also told me that …   I would like to …
I also hope to …

Before you finish
5 I look forward to your reply.
I look forward to hearing from you soon.

End your letter
6 Yours sincerely, (if you know the person's name)
Yours faithfully, (if you used Dear Sir/Madam)

4 Study the Language box. Find examples of the phrases in the letter. Then complete the sentences about you.

LANGUAGE — Talking about learning goals

- My aim is to (study/work on) …
- My plan is to (learn/stay) …
- I hope to (learn more about/find out about) …
- I would like to (improve/practise) …

---

33 Alexiou Street, Athens 104 36, Greece
20th October

1 Dear Sir/Madam,

2 I am writing to say that I am interested in the English for Science summer course. My aim is to study Science at university and this course will help me.

3 Please could you send me more information about the topics that are covered in the course? Also, would you mind telling me more about the accommodation with a host family – in particular, the price?

4 My English teacher said that my language skills were suitable for this course. However, she told me that I needed to improve my speaking skills. My plan is to stay with a host family as I would like to practise speaking every day. I also hope to learn more about British culture while I am staying there.

5 I look forward to hearing from you soon.

6 Yours faithfully,
Georgia Kallas

Exercise 2 more information about the topics in the course; more information about/the price of staying with a host family

WRITING TIME

5 Look at the advert in Exercise 1 again and choose a course. Write a letter in response to the advert, asking for information.

1 Find ideas
Make notes about:
- questions you would like to ask.
- information you will give.
- your learning goals.

2 Plan
Organise your ideas into paragraphs. Use Georgia's letter to help you.

3 Write and share
- Write a draft letter. Use the Language box and the Writing box to help you.
- Share your letter with another student for feedback.
- Use the feedback from your partner and write the final version of your letter.

4 Check
- Check language: did you use a range of phrases to talk about your learning goals?
- Check grammar: is the word order in questions correct?

I can write a formal letter asking for information. **119** Unit 9

For the teacher
- Teaching notes, page 228

On the Portal
- Photocopiable activity: A formal letter

For the student
- Workbook, page 97

On the Portal
- Workbook: Lesson 9.7

Vocabulary Activator

Revision Exercise 5

Possible answers:
1 Why did ancient Egyptians build pyramids? (for when they died)
2 Where do polar bears live? (in the Arctic/at the North Pole)
3 Who discovered radium? Marie and Pierre Curie
4 Is Rio de Janeiro the capital of Brazil? No, it's Brasilia.
5 Which countries are sending manned spacecraft into space now? the USA, Russia and China
6 How did Hannibal cross the Alps and beat the Romans in battle? He used elephants.

WORDLIST 9.16

School subjects
Art (n)
Biology (n)
Chemistry (n)
Cooking (n)
Drama (n)
D&T (Design and Technology) (n)
Economics (n)
Geography (n)
History (n)
IT (Information Technology) (n)
Languages (n)
Literature (n)
Maths (n)
Music (n)
PE (Physical Education) (n)
Physics (n)

Describing students
(qualities of a good student)
confident (adj)
creative (adj)
hard-working (adj)
intelligent (adj)
talented (adj)
(skills)
critical thinking (n)

general knowledge (n)
problem-solving (n)
teamwork (n)

Learning
curriculum (n)
learn (v)
memorise (v)
revise (v)
study (v)

Types of assessment
online test (n)
practical exam (n)
presentation (n)
project (n)
speaking exam (n)
written exam (n)

Word friends
(learning)
make a connection
make/take notes
make progress
make sense
take a break
take a test
take an exam

Phrasal verbs
calm down (v)
fill in (a form) (v)
get on (v)
hand in (v)
hand out (v)
look over (v)
look up (v)
miss out (v)

Extra words
aim (n)
bee-keeping (n)
Citizenship (n)
classroom (n)
club president (n)
course (n)
culture (n)
cyber security (n)
debate (n)
discovery (n)
driving (n)
environment (n)
fashion design (n)
final term (n)
food preparation (n)
fresh place (n)

gardening (n)
goal (n)
head teacher (n)
high school (n)
host family (n)
Humanities (n)
karate (n)
look forward to (v)
member (n)
option (n)
photograph (n)
popular (adj)
pupil (n)
research (n)
Science (n)
special lesson (n)
speech (n)
spidergram (n)
stay calm
store information
suitable (adj)
surfing (n)
traditional dance (n)
university (n)
vocational (adj)

1 Complete the sentences with words from the wordlist.
This subject teaches you to:
1 draw beautiful pictures. *Art*
2 play a character in a film. *Drama*
3 use a computer well. *IT (Information Technology)*
4 understand how money works. *Economics*
5 prepare food. *Cooking*
6 enjoy sport and stay fit. *PE (Physical Education)*

2 Choose two school subjects from the wordlist. In pairs, take turns to say why you are interested in these subjects.

3 Complete the sentences with words from the wordlist. Then change the sentences to make them true for you. In pairs, compare your learning routine.
1 I *take* a break from my homework every fifteen minutes.
2 I have excellent *general* knowledge: I know lots of facts about different things.
3 At school, I have *practical* exams in Music, which means I have to play the piano.
4 I've made *progress* this year in History. I'm much better at it.
5 I *make/take* tidy notes in lessons because I study well from them later.

4 Find words from the wordlist which match descriptions of the students. Then, in pairs, decide which three qualities are most important for good students.
1 He's really good at looking at information and making sense of it. *critical thinking*
2 She believes in herself and is not afraid to try. *confident*
3 She's great at thinking of new ideas and she also loves Art lessons. *creative*
4 He always works very hard! *hard-working*
5 She works very well with other students in a group. *teamwork*
6 He understands even difficult things really well. *intelligent*

5 9.17 **PRONUNCIATION** Listen to the sentences and underline the main stress in the phrasal verbs in bold.
1 Can you **look <u>over</u>** your work please?
2 **Calm <u>down</u>!** Everything will be OK.
3 Please **hand <u>in</u>** your work.
4 **Look <u>up</u>** that word in the dictionary.
5 Please **get <u>on</u>** with your homework!

6 9.17 **PRONUNCIATION** Listen again and repeat.

Unit 9

For the teacher
- Audioscript, page 254

On the Portal
- Tests: Unit 9 Test, Unit 9 Writing Test

For the student
- Workbook, pages 98–99

On the Portal
- Workbook: Self-check
- Wordlist
- Extra Activities: Self-check

Revision

Vocabulary

1 Choose the correct option.
1. My sister is very good *in* / *at* Chemistry: she's the best in her class.
2. Most people hate giving a *project* / *presentation* in front of other people.
3. My brother is *revising* / *studying* Medicine at university.
4. Could you fill *in* / *up* this form, please?
5. You've worked hard! Do you want to *take* / *make* a break?

2 Write the correct word for each definition.
1. A school subject where you learn to plan and build things. D*&T (Design and Technology)*
2. All the subjects that students study at school. c*urriculum*
3. A subject where you learn about great books. L*iterature*
4. A test where you show your skills by doing tasks in real-life situations. p*ractical* e*xam*
5. A school subject where you learn about animals and plants. B*iology*
6. Assessment where you write and upload answers by computer. o*nline* t*est*

3 Complete the text with the words below. Which tips would you follow?

look   make   memorise   miss   ~~revise~~   take (x2)

How to survive a test!

- Start to ¹*revise* a few days before, not the night before!
- Maybe the notes you made two months ago don't ² *make* sense. Write your notes again and use diagrams and colour to help you understand and ³ *memorise* the information.
- Always ⁴ *take* regular breaks when studying for a test.
- When you ⁵ *take* a test, don't go too fast! You might make a mistake, or ⁶ *miss* out something.
- Try to leave five minutes at the end so you can ⁷ *look* over your answers one more time.

Grammar

4 Read the dialogues and complete the sentences.
1. **Mum:** I'm cooking and I need some help.
   Lisa: I'm doing my homework. John is free: he can help.

Mum said she ¹*was cooking* and needed help. Lisa said that she ² *was doing* her homework, but that John ³ *was* free and that he ⁴ *could* help.

2. **Jo:** I'm enjoying Geography lessons this term. They are interesting.
   Tom: I agree. I'm making a lot of progress. But the teacher gives a lot of homework!

Jo said she ⁵ *was enjoying* Geography lessons that term and that they ⁶ *were* interesting. Tom agreed and said that he ⁷ *was making* a lot of progress, but that the teacher ⁸ *gave* a lot of homework.

5 Make questions with the words in brackets. Then, in pairs, answer the questions.
1. why / ancient Egyptians / build / pyramids / ?
2. where / polar bears / live / ?
3. who / discover / radium / ?
4. Rio de Janeiro / the capital of Brazil / ?
5. which countries / send / manned spacecraft into space now / ?
6. how / Hannibal / cross / the Alps and beat the Romans in battle?

6 Write questions to which the underlined words are the answers.
1. <u>My sister Emily</u> plays football.
2. <u>I revised for my Maths exam</u> last night.
3. I saw <u>Graham</u> at Sandra's birthday party.
4. The Geography lesson finished <u>at half past two</u>.
5. <u>It started raining</u> when we went outside.
6. <u>Everyone</u> is going to visit the zoo this weekend.

Speaking

7 Work in pairs. Student A: turn to page 137, Student B: turn to page 143, and follow the instructions to role play a dialogue. Then swap roles.

Dictation

8 🔊 9.18 Listen. Then listen again and write down what you hear.

Exercise 6
1. Who plays football?
2. What did you do last night?
3. Who did you see at Sandra's birthday party?
4. When/What time did the Geography lesson finish?
5. What happened when you went outside?/When did it start raining?
6. Who is going to visit the zoo this weekend?

Exercise 7
Sample answer:
A What's your name, please?
B Ben.
A And where are you from, Ben?
B Germany.
A What do you like to do in your free time?
B I love dancing and I also like reading books. I like travelling too.
A Interesting! Which countries have you visited?
B Italy, Spain and the USA.
A Right. So, what are your plans for the future?
B Well, I'm not sure, but I think I would like to be a doctor. I'm going to study Medicine.
A Thanks for talking to me, Ben. Enjoy your stay at the camp!

EXAM
Exercise 8
🔊 audioscript page 254

International Certificate Level 2, Listening and Writing, Section 2, (dictation)

BBC CULTURE — Different forms of education

Anna's school

I go to an alternative school which is different from the traditional schools my friends go to. First of all, our learning is more creative and interactive. We don't just sit in class and remember facts; we do a lot of practical stuff.

For example, today we had a Science lesson. We learned all about robots and then we built a model car on our own. It was fun – I enjoyed working alone because I could focus better. Then we took it in turns to choose a topic and give a presentation. We often do group work so we can learn from each other. It's fun, but the noise doesn't let me think sometimes.

Anyway, it's great that we have the freedom to do lots of practical activities. And the other interesting thing is that there are no tests – we just revise the material in our own time!

We only do academic subjects for a few hours a day. The rest of the day we do gardening, creative arts and crafts. Today we had singing and dancing – my favourites! We also have interesting discussions on different problems our world has and think of ways to help to make our world better in the future. One thing that they discourage at my school is using the computer. We aren't allowed to sit in front of a screen for a long time unless we're looking for information for a project. I don't like this, but I understand the reasons – we can do that at home.

Here the teachers are great – they are your friends. They don't just instruct you; they help you achieve your potential. I love that. I actually look forward to going to school!

achieve (v) succeed in doing something
discourage (v) try to make someone want to do something less often
in our own time (phr) – outside normal school hours
take it in turns (phr) one after another

Exercise 1
1 Possible answers:
In the first photo, the student is working on her own. In the second photo, she is working in a group.
3 a She has time to focus because it's quiet.
  b It can get noisy, so she can't think.

Exercise 2
1 traditional schools
2 She enjoyed working alone (because she could focus better)./She enjoyed learning about robots and building a car.
3 the students
4 when they are looking for information for a project
5 She sees them as friends.

---

1 🔊 9.19 **VISIBLE THINKING** In pairs, follow these steps.
YOUR VIEWPOINT
1 Look at the photos. How are the students learning in each one?
2 How do you like to learn? Do you prefer working in groups or alone?
THE WRITER'S VIEWPOINT
3 Read the article and answer the questions.
  a What does Anna think about learning on her own?
  b What doesn't she enjoy about working in groups?
WHAT DO YOU THINK NOW?
4 Which is better: group work or working on your own?

2 Read the article again and answer the questions.
1 What type of schools do Anna's friends go to?
2 Why did she find her Science lesson fun?
3 Who chose the topics of the presentations?
4 When can the students use computers at Anna's school?
5 How does Anna see her teachers?

3 In pairs, discuss these questions.
1 What do you think about tests?
2 How traditional do you think your school is? Why?
3 Would you like to go to a school like Anna's? Why?/Why not?

BBC 122

For the teacher
- Teaching notes, page 229
- Videoscript page 254

On the Portal
- Photocopiable activity:
  Project worksheet: a website

BBC ▶ Learning goals

4 Look at the photo. What kind of alternative school do you think it is? Discuss in pairs.

5 ▶ 46 Watch the video and check your answers to Exercise 4.

6 ▶ 46 Watch the video again and answer the questions.
1 Do the students at Ian's school work hard?
2 What do they do after the lessons finish?
3 What time does Ian get home?
4 Why does he go to bed right after dinner?

7 How is Ian's alternative school different from Anna's?

8 In pairs, discuss the questions.
1 The video says, 'Ian knows that you have to work hard if you want to be the best. But when you have a passion and a talent, you don't mind doing a little bit extra.' Do you agree? Why?/Why not?
2 Would you like to attend an alternative school? Why?/Why not?

Exercise 4
Possible answer: This might be a boys' school. It could be a sports school because all the students are wearing tracksuits with the same logo.

Exercise 5
▶ videoscript page 254

This is the Stoke City Football Academy. It's a school for young players who might play with the football club professionally one day.

Exercise 6
1 Yes, they do.
2 They have football training.
3 at about 8.30 in the evening
4 because he's tired

Exercise 7
Possible answer: Ian's school is based on learning about and training for football. Anna's is based on school subjects and practical activities.

PROJECT TIME

9 In groups of four, create a website for a new school. Follow these steps.

1 In groups, think about what information to include. Decide who can prepare this information.
• what students will learn at the school
• what the timetable will be
• what students will do after the lessons
• a day in the life of a student at the school

2 Individually, create your part of the website.
• Think about what information you want to give and write your text.
• Find or draw pictures to illustrate your section of the website.

3 In your group, put together your website. You can use a website template.
• Decide on a title, the layout and a logo.
• Position the text, the logo and the pictures.
• Check and edit your website.

4 Share your website with the class.
• Answer other students' questions.
• Look at the other websites. Ask questions.

Progress Check Units 1–9

Exercise 1
2 helpful
3 theft
4 illegal
5 management/managers
6 impatient

Vocabulary and Grammar

1 Complete the sentences with words formed from the words in brackets.
1 The new husband of my mother is my *stepfather* (FATHER).
2 The internet is very _____ (HELP) for students who need to find information for homework.
3 Police think there was a _____ (THIEF) in this office because important papers are missing.
4 You can be arrested if you do something that's _____ (LEGAL).
5 The _____ (MANAGE) of the transport company were sorry about the bus problems.
6 It doesn't help to be _____ (PATIENT) if you have to wait a long time for something.

2 Complete the text with one word in each gap.

Last year none of us could think ¹ *of* an idea for Grandma's eightieth birthday. Then one evening when we ² *were* watching television, my sister surprised us. She stood in front of the TV and said, 'I've ³ *just* thought of the perfect thing for Grandma!' Grandma loves rabbits, so we decided to ⁴ *have/get* a cake made in the shape of a rabbit. I knew a cake shop ⁵ *where* they designed cakes. Grandma said, 'It's ⁶ *the* best cake in the world!'

EXAM

Exercise 5
International Certificate Level 2, Speaking, Section 13, (role play)

3 Choose the correct answer.

My friend Gail and I ¹ *c* together at the weekend because we are doing an online course about preparing meals with healthy ² *c* . Students don't take tests, but teachers assess your ³ *b* on the course from the work you do. We had to prepare our own recipe and ⁴ *c* it for the other students, ⁵ *a* would then cook and taste it! I knew I would do this task better if I ⁶ *c* with someone else. Online courses are interesting and ⁷ *b* of them are free.

Exercises 7–8
🔊 audioscript page 255

EXAM

Exercise 8
B1 Preliminary for Schools, Listening, Part 2, (3-option multiple choice)

	a	b	c
1	meet	bring	get
2	flavours	parts	ingredients
3	description	performance	exam
4	follow	connect	upload
5	who	which	that
6	work	will work	worked
7	much	a lot	a little

124

Speaking

4 Match 1–7 with a–g to make a dialogue.
1 *d* A: Hi! My name's Juanita. What's yours?
2 *b* A: Have you stayed at this camp before?
3 *g* A: Where are you from?
4 *c* A: I'm from Spain. So, how long are you staying for?
5 *e* A: And what are your plans after the camp?
6 *a* A: That sounds interesting. So, the sports here are good. Do you agree?
7 *f* A: Let's meet up later. Would you prefer to meet in the games room or here?

a B: Definitely!
b B: No, this is my first time.
c B: Two weeks.
d B: Olga. Nice to meet you!
e B: I'm going on holiday with my family.
f B: I'd rather meet in the games room.
g B: Turkey, and you?

5 In pairs, do the speaking task. Go to page 143.

Listening

6 You are going to hear a police officer talking to school students about the crimes below. In pairs, discuss the questions.

burglary   pickpocketing   shoplifting

1 Which of the crimes is the easiest to stop happening? *pickpocketing*
2 For which crime is it the easiest to catch the criminal? *shoplifting*

7 🔊 PC1–9.1 Listen to the police officer and write his answers to the questions in Exercise 6.

8 🔊 PC1–9.1 Listen again and choose the correct answer.
1 Shoplifting is an easy crime to commit because
  a nobody ever looks at you in a shop.
  (b) shoplifters can easily take things and leave.
  c shop security is often not good enough.
2 The best way for shops to stay safe from shoplifters is to
  (a) record a video of people in the shop.
  b tell the police if there was a shoplifter.
  c watch people in the shop at all times.
3 It is difficult for police to catch burglars because
  a burglars make a mess in the house.
  b the police don't take fingerprints.
  (c) burglars are very careful during the burglary.

For the teacher
• Audioscript, page 255

On the Portal
• Photocopiable activities: Crossword, Choose and ask
• Tests: Units 1–9 Progress Test, Units 1–9 Progress Writing Test, Units 1–9 Progress Speaking Test

For the student
• Workbook: Exam Time 3 Units 1–9, pages 108–110

On the Portal
• Workbook: Exam Time 3 Units 1–9
• Extra Practice Activities: Use of English

4 You should tell police about a stranger near your house because
   a your house might not have strong enough security.
   (b) this person might be a burglar who is studying the house.
   c this person might tell a burglar about your house.

5 One of the few ways to catch a pickpocket is to
   (a) notice the pickpocket committing the crime.
   b think of a good plan to catch the pickpocket.
   c call for help after the crime.

6 It's easy to stay safe from pickpockets if you
   a stay near other people who can help you.
   (b) keep your personal things close to you.
   c stay away from someone who might be a pickpocket.

Reading

9 You are going to read an article about an environmentally friendly school. Look at the photo and the name of the school. In pairs, discuss what it might be like to go to this school.

10 🔊 PC1–9.2 Read the article about an environmentally friendly school. Complete the gaps with sentences a–f. There is one extra sentence. Listen and check.
   a One of these is project work, which is very important at Green School.
   b It's a tropical island with beautiful beaches.
   c Another example of a project managed by students is the 'Bio Bus'.
   d They look different to any classes I've ever seen before.
   e The results also find their way onto the school lunch menu.
   f This is a daily reality for students at Green School.
   g We hope they will agree and offer to show us around.

11 Would you like to be a student at Green School? Why?/Why not? Discuss in pairs.

Green School, Bali

1 Imagine what it would be like if your school were right next to a tropical forest! As you're listening to the teacher's instructions, you hear the sounds of wildlife such as exotic birds and insects. ¹ __f__ The school opened in 2008 in Bali, part of the Indonesian archipelago between the Pacific and Indian Oceans. ² __b__ My wife and I, like many Australians, love to have our holiday there.

2 We are teachers, so we're interested in knowing more about the school. On this year's holiday to Bali we hope to take some time away from the beaches to see it. We are going to write to the school to ask about the possibility of a visit. ³ __g__ The classrooms are made from local plants like bamboo, which are all found right there on the island. ⁴ __d__ There are large open spaces between them, and windows open to the outside on all sides.

3 Many of the subjects at Green School are the same ones which are taught in many schools around the world. But the curriculum gives special attention to certain types of learning. ⁵ __a__ The school believes that children should learn by studying about different, interesting topics. For example, students grow fresh fruit and vegetables in the school's gardens and then describe what they've done. ⁶ __c__ It started in 2015 and it's the school's environmentally friendly local transport. Students at Green School experience a different way of learning, and I do hope we can visit it!

EXAM
Exercise 10
B1 Preliminary for Schools, Reading, Part 4, (gapped text)

Writing

12 Go to page 143. Think about your answers to the questions. Then, in pairs, discuss your answers. Give reasons.

13 Write an opinion essay (100–150 words) on the following question: 'Students should decide what they learn.' Do you agree? Use the paragraph plan below to help you.
   • Paragraph 1: Introduce the topic and give your opinion.
   • Paragraph 2: Present some ideas which support students deciding what they learn.
   • Paragraph 3: Present some possible problems with students deciding what they learn.
   • Paragraph 4: Summarise your opinion.

Grammar Time

1.2

Present Simple and Present Continuous, state verbs

Present Simple
We use the Present Simple for facts, permanent situations and routines.
They **sing** in a band.
She **doesn't use** her tablet every day.

Time expressions
every day/week/month/year
once/twice/three times a month
on Mondays/weekdays/holiday
always/usually/often/sometimes/rarely/never

Present Continuous
We use the Present Continuous for actions that are happening at or around the moment of speaking.
They**'re playing** a computer game now.
I**'m recording** songs this week.

Time expressions
now, at the moment, this morning/afternoon, this year, these days

State verbs
State verbs often express opinions, preferences, mental states and perception. Some common state verbs are: *love, like, hate, prefer, want, need, understand, think, feel, hear, see*.

We don't normally use state verbs in continuous tenses, even if they refer to the moment of speaking.
I **don't need** any help at the moment, thank you.

1 Complete the text with the Present Simple or Present Continuous form of the verbs in brackets.

Kids my age ¹*love* (love) watching music videos on YouTube, and so do I. One of my favourites is *What Does The Fox Say?* by Ylvis. It's not a new song, but I ² _think_ (think) it's really cool. The music is great, and the video is fun to watch. In the video, there's a fancy dress party and all the people ³ _are wearing_ (wear) animal costumes. They are in a forest, and they ⁴ _are dancing_ (dance) and making strange animal sounds. If you ⁵ _don't know_ (not know) the song, look for it on YouTube. It's great!
Unlike me, my sister ⁶ _doesn't like_ (not like) music videos. She ⁷ _prefers_ (prefer) videos about shopping, where people ⁸ _buy_ (buy) things and then ⁹ _show_ (show) the viewers what's in their shopping bags. In fact, she ¹⁰ _is watching_ (watch) one at the moment – on *my* laptop!

2 Write a short text about your favourite music video. What's in it? Why do you like it? Use the text in Exercise 1 to help you.

1.4

Verb + -ing, verb + to-infinitive

Verb + -ing
After: *avoid, can't stand, enjoy, finish, look forward to, (not) mind, miss, practise, stop*
You can go out when you **finish tidying** your room.
We also use the *-ing* form after prepositions.
Don't leave **without saying** goodbye to your friends.

Verb + to-infinitive
After: *agree, allow, ask, choose, decide, forget, hope, learn, need, offer, plan, remember, try, want, would like/love*
Remember to call your parents when you arrive.

Verb + -ing or to-infinitive
After: *like, love, hate, prefer, start*
I **love taking**/**love to take** photos of cats.

1 Complete the sentences with the correct form of the verbs in brackets.
1 Martha's parents often allow her _to stay up_ (stay up) late at night.
2 I would love _to buy_ (buy) a new tablet – this one's too old.
3 Don't worry about me – I don't mind _waiting_ (wait).
4 Why don't you practise _playing_ (play) this song again?
5 Please try _to stay_ (stay) calm.

2 Choose the correct option.
Ella: What are you planning ¹ (to do) / doing at the weekend?
Josh: I don't know. I need ² (to write) / writing the French essay – finish ³ to write / (writing) it, in fact.
Ella: That doesn't sound very exciting.
Josh: I know! I can't stand ⁴ to write / (writing) essays! What about your weekend, then?
Ella: Well, I'm trying ⁵ (to earn) / earning some money, so I'm helping my uncle in his garden. He offers ⁶ (to pay) / paying me five pounds an hour. In fact, he wants me ⁷ (to bring) / bringing a friend to help us plant some trees. Would you like ⁸ (to join) / join us?
Josh: Really? Yes, I'd love ⁹ (to join) / join you!

3 In pairs, practise the dialogue in Exercise 2. Then make a similar dialogue using your own ideas. Try to use some of the verbs in the Grammar box above.

2.2

Past Simple: regular and irregular verbs

We use the Past Simple to talk about actions and situations that started and finished in the past. We often mention when these actions/situations happened.

Regular verbs
Regular verbs form the Past Simple with the ending -ed.
It snowed last night.
It didn't snow last night.
Did it snow last night?

Irregular verbs
Irregular verbs do not form the Past Simple with -ed.
Each verb has its own form. For a list of irregular verbs, see page 136.
We saw a storm yesterday.
We didn't see the storm.
Did you see the storm?

Time expressions
yesterday, two hours/days/weeks/years ago, in 2020, last week/year/night.

1 Complete the sentences with the Past Simple form of the verbs in brackets.
1. I _visited_ (visit) my aunt in August.
2. I last _saw_ (see) the rainbow two weeks ago.
3. It _rained_ (rain) a lot last summer.
4. We _took_ (take) many photos during the holidays.
5. Lisa _studied_ (study) for the Maths test last night.
6. I _had_ (have) fried eggs for breakfast yesterday.

2 Make questions in the Past Simple. Use the time expressions below. Then, in pairs, ask and answer the questions.

> yesterday   the day before yesterday
> last Monday/Friday/Saturday   last month   last summer
> a year ago   two years ago   five years ago

1. what / you / have / for lunch / ?
2. what films / you / see / ?
3. where / you / go / on holiday / ?
4. what sports / you / do / ?
5. what video games / you / play / ?
6. what mobile phone / you / have / ?

A: What did you have for lunch the day before yesterday?
B: I had a chicken sandwich and an apple.

3 Write five true sentences about yourself. Use the Past Simple and five different time expressions.

2.4

Past Continuous and Past Simple

We use the Past Continuous to describe an activity that was in progress at a particular time in the past. We also use it to describe a scene (e.g. in a story).
At six o'clock I was talking to friends online.
It was midnight. Outside, it was snowing.
She was doing her homework. She wasn't playing games.
They were swimming. They weren't running.
Was she sleeping? Yes, she was./No, she wasn't.

Past Continuous and Past Simple
We often use the Past Simple with the Past Continuous to talk about an action that happened while another one was in progress. We use the Past Continuous for the longer action that was in progress and the Past Simple for the shorter action.
I was walking in the forest when I saw a bear.
Anne called me while I was doing the Maths homework.

1 Complete the sentences with the Past Simple or Past Continuous form of the verbs in brackets.
1. When you _called_ (call), I _was taking_ (take) a shower.
2. It was a beautiful day. The sun _was shining_ (shine) and the birds _were singing_ (sing).
3. A: What _were you doing_ (you/do) at 10.00 p.m. on Wednesday?
   B: I'm not sure. I _wasn't sleeping_ (not sleep). I think I _was watching_ (watch) a film on TV.
4. A: _Were you playing_ (you/play) games on your phone when the teacher _came_ (come) into the classroom?
   B: No, I _wasn't_ ! I _was looking_ (look) for some information about Asia on the internet.

2 Complete the text with the Past Simple or Past Continuous form of the verbs below.

> appear   break   come   fall   hear
> hike   run   shout   try

Last winter I [1] _was hiking_ in the mountains with my friend Jake when we [2] _heard_ a strange sound. We were quite scared. There was lots of snow on the top of the mountain and it [3] _was coming_ down on us really quickly. It was an avalanche! 'Run!' Jake [4] _shouted_ . We [5] _were running_ when we both [6] _fell_ down the slope and Jake [7] _broke_ his leg! I [8] _was trying_ to call my dad on my mobile when a helicopter [9] _appeared_ in the sky. We were saved!

2.2
Exercise 2
Possible answers:
2. What films did you see (last month)?
3. Where did you go on holiday (last summer)?
4. What sports did you do (five years ago)?
5. What video games did you play (yesterday)?
6. What mobile phone did you have (five years ago)?

Grammar Time   **127**

Grammar Time

3.2
Present Perfect with ever, never, just, already and yet

We form the Present Perfect with *have/has* + the past participle of the main verb. For regular verbs, the past participle is the same as the Past Simple form. For irregular verbs, it is different. For a list of irregular verbs, see page 136.

We use the Present Perfect to talk about:
- life experiences, often with *ever* (in questions) and *never* (in negative sentences).
  Have you *ever tried* Mexican food?
  I*'ve never eaten* sushi.
- actions that finished a very short time ago, often with *just*.
  I'm not hungry. I*'ve just had* a sandwich.
- actions that were (or were expected to be) completed at an unspecified time with the past. We often use *already* in affirmative sentences and *yet* in negative sentences and questions.
  I*'ve already cooked* lunch.
  I *haven't cooked* lunch *yet*.
  Have you *cooked* lunch *yet*?

1 Complete the sentences with the correct form of the verbs in brackets.
1. Our pizza <u>has just arrived</u> (just/arrive). Let's eat!
2. Dave _____ (already/wash) the dishes, so we can relax.
3. A: _____ (you/have) lunch yet, boys?
   B: No, we _____ .
4. A: _____ (Lee/do) the shopping yet?
   B: Yes, she _____ (just/return) from the shops.
5. I _____ (never/try) Indian food.
6. Ian and Eva started making dinner two hours ago and they _____ (not finish) yet.

2 In pairs, ask and answer questions about the things below. Use the Present Perfect with *ever*.
1. try snails
2. cook a family dinner
3. make a cake
4. be to an expensive restaurant
5. upload a video on YouTube
6. watch a horror film

A: Have you ever tried snails? B: Yes, I have.

3 You are organising a party with a friend. Write him/her a note to say what you have already done and what you haven't done yet.

Hi Mark! I've already bought some crisps and nuts, but I haven't bought any soft drinks yet. …

3.2 Exercise 1
2 has already washed
3 Have you had; haven't
4 Has Lee done; has just returned
5 have never tried
6 haven't finished

3.2 Exercise 2
2 Have you ever cooked a family dinner?
3 Have you ever made a cake?
4 Have you ever been to an expensive restaurant?
5 Have you ever uploaded a video on YouTube?
6 Have you ever watched a horror film?

3.4 Exercise 3
2 She's had her skis for a year/ since last year.
3 She's had her jumper since last winter.
4 She's had her favourite book for three weeks.

3.4
Present Perfect with *for* and *since* | Present Perfect and Past Simple

Present Perfect with *for* and *since*
We often use the Present Perfect with *for* and *since* to talk about an action or situation that started in the past and still continues.

We use *for* to say how long something has continued, e.g. with *a week, a month, a year, a long time*.
They've owned this restaurant *for two years*.

We use *since* to say when something started, e.g. with *2019, March, last Tuesday, the day we met*.
I've had this laptop *since February*.

Present Perfect and Past Simple
We use the Past Simple when we say when a past action happened.
I went to this pizzeria *last Sunday*.

With the Present Perfect, we don't use a time reference. We are talking about things that have happened in our lives up to now.
I*'ve been* to this restaurant. It's really nice.

Be careful: when we want to give more details about an experience, we use the Past Simple.
I*'ve been* to this restaurant. I *went* there with my cousins last week.

1 Complete the sentences with *for* or *since*.
1. I've lived in this house <u>since</u> I was born.
2. I've known Tim <u>for</u> ten years.
3. I've had this bike <u>for</u> two months.
4. I haven't seen Jo <u>since</u> yesterday.

2 Make sentences using the correct form of the verbs.
1. Maria / get / her mobile phone / two years ago
   Maria got her mobile phone two years ago.
2. she / win / her skis in a skiing competition / last year
   She won her skis in a skiing competition last year.
3. she / make / her jumper herself / last winter
   She made her jumper herself last winter.
4. she / find / her favourite book in a park / three weeks ago
   She found her favourite book in a park three weeks ago.

3 How long has Maria had her things? Look at Exercise 2 again and write sentences using *for* or *since*.

Maria has had her mobile phone for two years.

128 Grammar Time

4.2

Comparatives and superlatives, too/not enough, (not) as … as …

Comparative
To compare two people, things, places, etc., we use the comparative form of the adjective (+ *than*).
His first film was funnier than the second one.
The book is more interesting than the film.

Superlative
To compare one person, thing, place, etc. in a group with the rest, we use *the* + the superlative form of the adjective.
Coming 2 America is the funniest film I've seen.
This is the most interesting book I've read.

too/(not) enough
We use:
- *too* + adjective to mean 'more than you need'.
  The screen is too dark. (= It's darker than it should be.)
- adjective + *enough* to mean 'just right'.
  The screen is bright enough. (= It's OK.)
- *not* + adjective + *enough* to mean 'less than you need'.
  The screen isn't bright enough. (= It should be brighter.)

(not) as … as
We can also use *not as* + adjective + *as* to compare two people, things, places, etc.
The film is as good as the book.
The cinema isn't as exciting as the theatre.

1 Write the comparative and superlative forms of the adjectives below. Then choose three comparative forms and three superlative forms and write true sentences.

> amusing   bad   big   difficult
> heavy   large   sad   strange

2 Complete the text with the words below.

> as comfortable as   bigger   cheaper   ~~closer~~
> comfortable enough   more expensive   the best
> the biggest   too expensive

I often go to the cinema and here are my three favourites. Multi-Film and MacroMovie are two typical multiplex cinemas. MacroMovie is ¹*closer* to the city centre and it has ² _____ screens (probably ³ _____ in the city), but it's also ⁴ _____ than the other cinemas, so I don't go there so often. The tickets are ⁵ _____ if you ask me … The seats in Multi-Film are ⁶ _____ the seats in MacroMovie, but the tickets are ⁷ _____ . I often choose Chaplin Cinema; maybe the chairs there aren't ⁸ _____ , but it's got ⁹ _____ sound quality.

3 In pairs, talk about three films you know. Use Exercise 1 to help you.
A: I think … is the funniest.
B: Yes, and it also has the best special effects.

4 Write a short paragraph comparing two actors or two TV programmes.

4.4

Quantifiers: *some, any, much, many, (a) few, (a) little, a lot of, lots of*

Countable and uncountable nouns
We use quantifiers with nouns to talk about quantity. Countable nouns refer to things we can count, e.g. *a bracelet, three bracelets*. Uncountable nouns refer to things we cannot count, e.g. substances and liquids (*rice, milk*), groups of things (*furniture, jewellery*) and abstract ideas (*love, peace*).

a lot/lots of, much and many
We use *a lot/lots of* with all nouns in affirmative sentences.
There's lots of cola for everyone.
I've got a lot of T-shirts.
We use *much* with uncountable and *many* with countable nouns, usually in negative sentences and questions.
How many T-shirts have you got?   How much cola is there?
I haven't got many T-shirts.   There isn't much cola.

some and any
We use *some* and *any* with countable and uncountable nouns. We use *some* in affirmative sentences and *any* in negative sentences and questions.
I've got some T-shirts.   There's some cola.
Have you got any T-shirts?   Is there any cola?
I haven't got any T-shirts.   There isn't any cola.

a few, few, a little, little
We use *a few* and *few* with countable nouns, and *a little* and *little* with uncountable nouns. The article *a* changes the meaning.
I've got a few T-shirts. (= some T-shirts)
I've got few T-shirts. (= not many T-shirts)
There's a little cola. (= some cola)
There's little cola. (= not much cola)

4.2
Exercise 1
amusing – more amusing (than) – the most amusing
bad – worse (than) – the worst
big – bigger (than) – the biggest
difficult – more difficult (than) – the most difficult
heavy – heavier (than) – the heaviest
large – larger (than) – the largest
sad – sadder (than) – the saddest
strange – stranger (than) – the strangest
Students' own answers

4.2
Exercise 2
2 bigger
3 the biggest
4 more expensive
5 too expensive
6 as comfortable as
7 cheaper
8 comfortable enough
9 the best

Grammar Time

1 Read the texts and choose the correct answers.

> I only wear sports clothes, so in my wardrobe there aren't ¹any smart dresses. I've got ² _____ T-shirts and ³ _____ hoodies. I haven't got ⁴ _____ jewellery – only ⁵ _____ bracelets.

> I like smart clothes, so in my wardobe there are ⁶ _____ suits and ⁷ _____ white shirts. I haven't got ⁸ _____ trainers – I hate sports shoes!

1 **(a)** any	b some	c much
2 **(a)** lots of	b a lot	c much
3 a a little	**(b)** a few	c any
4 **(a)** much	b many	c any
5 a a little	b little	**(c)** a few
6 **(a)** a few	b few	c any
7 **(a)** some	b any	c much
8 a much	b few	**(c)** any

2 Write a short paragraph about clothes and accessories you have got. Try to use different quantifiers from the Grammar box above.

5.2

Future forms: *will*, *be going to*, Present Continuous, Present Simple

Will
We use *will* for predictions or decisions made at the moment of speaking.
I don't think he'll win the competition.
Wait, I'll help you.

Be going to
We use *be going to* for plans and intentions, and for predictions based on things we know now.
I'm going to take up kayaking.
Look at the sky: it's going to rain.

Present Continuous
We use the Present Continuous to talk about fixed arrangements.
We're having a competition next month.

Present Simple
We use the Present Simple to talk about timetables and schedules.
My basketball training starts in October.

---

1 Choose the best option.
1 **I'm going to** / I'll buy a new tennis racket, so I'm looking for some offers online.
2 I'm sorry, I can't come with you on Tuesday. **We're visiting** / We'll visit my grandparents.
3 In our school, all extra-curricular classes *are starting* / **start** in October.
4 Susan looks really pale. She **isn't going to finish** / *doesn't finish* the race.
5 I've arranged an interview with Mr Saunders for our school magazine. He's **coming** / *going to come* tomorrow at 6.30.
6 A: I'm starving.
   B: I'm going to / **I'll** make you a sandwich.

2 Complete the questions with the words below. Then, in pairs, ask and answer the questions.

> going (x2)   having   meeting   will (x2)

1 What do think the weather _will_ be like tomorrow?
2 Are you _going_ to get a summer job during the holidays?
3 Are you _having_ any extra-curricular classes tomorrow?
4 Are you _meeting_ your friends in the evening?
5 Do you think e-books _will_ replace 'real' books in the future?
6 Are you _going_ to organise a birthday party any time soon?

A: What do you think the weather will be like tomorrow?
B: I think it will be rainy and windy.

5.4

First Conditional with *if* and *unless*

We use the First Conditional (*if* + Present Simple, *will*) to talk about something that may happen in the future as a result of an action or situation.

The *if* clause can come at the beginning of the sentence or after the main clause. When it is at the beginning, we use a comma between the two clauses.
If you like gymnastics, you'll love slacklining.
You'll love slacklining if you like gymnastics.

Unless
We can also use *unless* in First Conditional sentences. It means 'if not'.
You won't be good at slacklining if you don't practise.
You won't be good at slacklining unless you practise.

Time clauses with *when*
Notice the difference between a First Conditional sentence and a time clause with *when*.
I'll tell Jack about the competition if he comes. (Jack may or may not come.)
I'll tell Jack about the competition when he comes. (Jack will come and then I will tell him.)

1 Complete the First Conditional sentences with the correct form of the verbs in brackets.
1. We _will go_ (go) skiing at the weekend if it _snows_ (snow).
2. If she _comes_ (come) round, I _will show_ (show) her some skateboarding tricks.
3. Your team _won't win_ (not win) the match if they _don't change_ (not change) a few players.
4. If the train _isn't_ (not be) late, the footballers _will arrive_ (arrive) at Brighton at 5 p.m.
5. The training _won't start_ (not start) if the coach _is_ (be) ill.
6. If the rain _stops_ (stop), I _will go_ (go) jogging.

2 Rewrite the sentences. Use *if* or *unless*.
1. You won't get better unless you practise.
   You'll get better if you practise.
2. If we don't win, our coach will be very disappointed.
3. Unless Joe feels better, he won't come to basketball practice.
4. They won't choose her for the team if she isn't really good.
5. I won't join the gym unless I have more free time in the summer.

6.2
Modal verbs: must, have to, ought to, should

Obligation and prohibition
We use *must* and *have to* to express obligation. We use *must* when the speaker feels that something is necessary. We use *have to* when something is necessary because there is a rule or because another person says so (e.g. a teacher, a manager).
I must go now. I don't want to be late.
We have to wear a uniform at school.

We use *mustn't* to expresses prohibition.
You mustn't use your mobile phone during the flight.

Advice
We use *should/shouldn't* and *ought to* to give advice. The negative form of *ought to* is not very common.
You should/shouldn't take the train.
You ought to pack your bag now.

Lack of obligation
To say that something is not necessary, we use *don't have to*.
She doesn't have to work in July.

Notes on form
Must, *should* and *ought to* are modal verbs. They have the same form in all persons, singular and plural. To form questions, we use inversion. We don't normally use *ought to* in questions.
She *must/should/ought to* leave now.
Must/Should we leave now?
You *mustn't/shouldn't* leave now.

Have to has different forms (*I/you/we/they have to; he/she/it has to*). To form questions and negative sentences, we use *do/does* and *don't/doesn't*.
You *have to* wait here.
She *doesn't have to* work hard.
Do we *have to* go now?

1 Complete the second sentence so that it means the same as the first one. Use the verbs in brackets.
1. It is necessary for Joanna to wear a suit in the office.
   Joanna _has to wear a suit_ in the office. (has)
2. Is it a good idea for us to check out before breakfast?
   Should we check out before breakfast? (should)
3. Don't take your passport – it's not necessary.
   You _don't have to take your_ passport. (have)
4. You should buy new sunglasses.
   You _ought to buy new_ sunglasses. (ought)
5. Using a dictionary is not allowed in the exam.
   You _mustn't use a dictionary_ in the exam. (mustn't)
6. Is it necessary for Abe to take a sleeping bag?
   Does Abe have/need to take a sleeping bag? (does)

2 Choose the correct option.
1. Betty _____ clean her room today because she did it yesterday.
   a has to   b mustn't   **c doesn't have to**
2. My teacher says I _____ read books in English to learn new words.
   a should   b mustn't   c don't have to
3. We _____ to leave right now if we don't want to be late.
   a must   b should   **c ought**
4. Football players _____ touch the ball with their hands.
   a shouldn't   **b mustn't**   c have to

5.4
Exercise 2
2. Unless we win, our coach will be very disappointed.
3. If Joe doesn't feel better, he won't come to basketball practice.
4. They won't choose her for the team unless she's really good.
5. I won't join the gym if I don't have more free time in the summer.

Grammar Time **131**

Grammar Time

6.4

Modal verbs: *must, could, may/might, can't* (speculation)

We can use the modal verbs *must*, *could*, *may/might* and *can't* to speculate about the present or future. We use:

- *must* when we strongly believe that something is true.
  She **must** feel exhausted after the trip. (= I'm sure she feels exhausted.)
- *may/might* or *could* when we think that something is possibly true.
  It **may**/**might**/**could** be cold at night in the mountains. (= It's possible that it's cold.)
- *can't* when we strongly believe that something is not true.
  This rucksack **can't** weigh more than ten kilos – it's so small! (= I'm sure it doesn't weigh more than ten kilos.)

1 Complete the dialogues with the words below.

> might   can't   ~~must~~

A: Joe had a shower and went straight to bed. He ¹*must* be exhausted after his football practice.
B: He ² __can't__ be exhausted. He didn't go to football practice today, and he got up at 11 a.m.
A: Oh. Well, he ³ __might__ want to get some rest before his next football practice, then!

> can't   must   could

A: The water ⁴ __must__ be freezing – look, nobody's swimming.
B: No, it ⁵ __can't__ be freezing – not with this sunny weather. The water is always quite warm here.
A: I'm not going anyway. It ⁶ __could__ be muddy or full of seaweed ... Brr!

2 Complete the modal verbs in the email.

Hi Mark,

I'm writing about the cruise. I've thought about it, and I think it ¹*may* not be the best idea. First of all, the cruise in the Mediterranean ²m__ust__ cost a fortune – I'm sure we can't afford it. It ³c__ould__ also be a bit boring because we get to the harbour in the evening, and it's too late to go sightseeing. Just looking at the sea ⁴c__an't__ be very exciting!
Let's go sailing instead. I think it's more exciting – and it ⁵m__ust__ be healthier too! Let me know what you think.

Martha

7.2

Second Conditional

We use the Second Conditional (*if* + Past Simple, *would*) to talk about:

- unreal or imaginary situations in the present or future.
  If dogs **had** wings, they **would fly**. (= Dogs don't have wings, and they don't fly.)
- situations in the present or future that are not very likely.
  If I **had** some money, I **would buy** a new bike. (= I probably won't have money, and I probably won't buy a bike.)

We often use the phrase *If I were you* to give advice.
If I **were** you, I **would ask** someone for help.

We can use *were* instead of *was* in Second Conditional sentences.
If she **was**/**were** taller, she'd join the basketball team.

1 Complete the Second Conditional sentences about friendship with the correct form of the verbs in brackets.

A good friend:
1 *would help* (help) me if I *was/were* (be) in trouble.
2 __would give__ (give) me some money if I __didn't have__ (not have) any.
3 __would try__ (try) to help me feel better if I __was/were__ (be) ill.
4 __wouldn't be__ (not be) angry with me if I __did__ (do) something wrong.
5 __wouldn't complain__ (not complain) if I __wasn't/weren't__ (not be) in a good mood.

2 Make Second Conditional sentences.

1 how / you / behave / if / you / be / me / ?
  How would you behave if you were me?
2 Chris / not feel / so sad / if / his classmates / not laugh / at him
  _____
3 if / I / win / the match / my parents / be / very proud of me
  _____
4 Sarah / be / very disappointed / if / we / miss / her birthday party
  _____
5 if / you / work / harder / you / not fail / all your exams
  _____

7.2
Exercise 2

2 Chris wouldn't feel so sad if his classmates didn't laugh at him.
3 If I won the match, my parents would be very proud of me.
4 Sarah would be very disappointed if we missed her birthday party.
5 If you worked harder, you wouldn't fail all your exams.

7.4
Relative clauses

We use relative clauses to give information about people, things and places. We use *who* to refer to people, *which* to refer to things and *where* to refer to places.

Defining relative clauses

With defining relative clauses, the information we give is important and necessary. The sentence is not complete without it.
This is the woman who asked about you.
I ate the sandwich which was in the fridge.
This is the town where my dad grew up.

In defining relative clauses, we can use *that* instead of *who* and *which*.
This is the woman that asked about you.
I ate the sandwich that was in the fridge.

Non-defining relative clauses

With non-defining relative clauses, we give extra information. This information is not essential to identify the person, thing or place we are talking about. The sentence is still complete without it.
I saw Ed Davies, who lives in my street.
We saw Arrival, which is my favourite film.
He comes from Cornwall, where my mum grew up.

We use commas to separate the non-defining relative clause from the main clause.
Maria Kennel, who lives next door, is in my class.

1 Join the sentences using defining relative clauses. Which relative pronouns can be replaced with *that*?
1. That's the hospital. I was born there.
   That's the hospital where I was born.
2. This is the teacher. He teaches German at my brother's school.
3. Where's the pen? It was on my desk.
4. We visited the house. Shakespeare lived there.
5. Is that the tablet? Did your dad give it to you for your birthday?

2 Join the sentences using non-defining relative clauses.
1. Ian's house is on West Street. My school is there.
   Ian's house is on West Street, where my school is.
2. Fiona told me about Heath's birthday party. It was a surprise.
3. Mark's cousin went to our school. He is a doctor now.
4. The President Hotel is the oldest building in the town. We stayed there.
5. My great-grandmother lived in a village near Edinburgh. Edinburgh is the capital of Scotland.

8.2
Present and Past Simple passive

We use the passive:
- when we think that an action is more important than who does it.
- when we don't know who did the action that we are talking about.

Present Simple passive

We form the Present Simple passive with *am/is/are* + past participle.
The play is based on Agatha Christie's crime novel.
Shoplifters aren't always caught.
Where are these security cameras made?

Past Simple passive

We form the Past Simple passive with *was/were* + past participle.
The witness was interviewed yesterday.
He wasn't found guilty.
When were the criminals arrested?

If we want to say who did the action, we use *by*.
Shoplifters aren't always caught by store owners.
The witness was interviewed by Detective Bower.

1 Rewrite the sentences in the passive.
1. Someone damaged the school gate last night.
   The school gate *was damaged last night* .
2. People don't use CCTV cameras just for fun.
   CCTV cameras _____ .
3. Someone saw the suspect in Hyde Park on Sunday.
   The suspect _____ .
4. Did the police arrest the robbers?
   Were _____ ?
5. Do people find fingerprints on food and clothes?
   Are _____ ?
6. Someone stole my aunt's bag this morning.
   My aunt's bag _____ .
7. The police caught the criminals yesterday.
   The criminals _____ .
8. The thieves hid the stolen painting in the garage.
   The stolen painting _____ .

7.4
Exercise 1
2. That's the teacher who/that teaches German at my brother's school.
3. Where's the pen which/that was on my desk?
4. We visited the house where Shakespeare lived.
5. Is that the tablet which/that your dad gave you for your birthday?

7.4
Exercise 2
2. Fiona told me about Heath's birthday party, which was a surprise.
3. Mark's cousin, who is a doctor now, went to our school.
4. The President Hotel, where we stayed, is the oldest building in the town.
5. My great-grandmother lived in a village near Edinburgh, which is the capital of Scotland.

8.2
Exercise 1
2. aren't used just for fun
3. was seen in Hyde Park on Sunday
4. the robbers arrested (by the police)
5. fingerprints found on food and clothes
6. was stolen this morning
7. were caught yesterday
8. was hidden in the garage

Grammar Time 133

Grammar Time

8.4
Have/get something done

We use *have something done* to talk about things that we don't do ourselves but somebody else (usually a professional) does for us. The form is: subject + *have* + object + past participle.
I made my costume. (= I made it myself.)
I had my costume made. (= Somebody else made it for me.)
We can use *get something done* in the same way. It is more informal and we often use it in spoken English.
I got my costume made.

1 Complete the questions with the correct form of *have something done*. Then, in pairs, ask and answer the questions.
1 How often do you have your hair cut (you/your hair/cut)?
2 _____ (you/ever/your photo/take) by a professional photographer?
3 When was the last time you _____ (your computer or phone/service)?
4 Would you ever _____ (your hair/dye) blue or green?
5 _____ (your room/paint) in the near future?
6 Should _____ (people/their houses/clean) or should they clean them themselves?

2 Complete the email with the phrases below.

| it styled   ~~my dress made~~   my hair cut |
| my nails painted   some photos taken   them repaired |

✉

Hi Jessie,
How are you? How are the preparations for the end-of-year party going? I've already had ¹*my dress made*. I'm really lucky as my aunt works in a little clothing company and I had a discount. The dress is red and it's got little red roses at the front. I'm going to wear my red shoes. They are the same colour as the dress and I had ² _____ last week. Anyway, I don't want to have ³ _____ although it's a bit long now … My mum says it brings bad luck before the exams! I'm only going to have ⁴ _____ before the party. And I'm not going to have ⁵ _____ – I'll paint them myself. By the way, don't forget we're having ⁶ _____ on Monday for the album. Do you know what we should wear then?
Best,
Pam

8.4 Exercise 1
2 Have you ever had your photo taken
3 had your computer or phone serviced
4 have your hair dyed
5 Are you going to have your room painted
6 people have their houses cleaned

8.4 Exercise 2
2 them repaired
3 my hair cut
4 it styled
5 my nails painted
6 some photos taken

9.2 Exercise 1
2 Mia said (that) they didn't have to wear a uniform at her school.
3 The students said (that) they wanted to start a school debating club.
4 Ollie said (that) their Geography teacher gave them a lot of homework.
5 Nadia said (that) she was never late for class.

9.2
Reported speech: statements

We use reported speech to say what someone has said. When we report someone's words:
- we use *said* or *told*.
  'I'm tired,' he told me. →
  He told me/He said (that) he was tired.
- we change the pronouns and possessive adjectives.
  'We're waiting for our friends,' they said. →
  They said (that) they were waiting for their friends.
- we change the tense of the main verb in this way:
  Present Simple → Past Simple.
  'I want to study Biology,' she said. →
  She said (that) she wanted to study Biology.
  Present Continuous → Past Continuous.
  'I'm working on my project,' he said. →
  He said (that) he was working on his project.

1 Rewrite the sentences in reported speech.
1 'I'm writing an essay,' Ken said.
  Ken said (that) he was writing an essay.
2 'We don't have to wear a uniform at my school,' Mia said.
  _____
3 'We want to start a school debating club,' the students said.
  _____
4 'Our Geography teacher gives us a lot of homework,' Ollie said.
  _____
5 'I'm never late for class,' Nadia said.
  _____

2 Rewrite the sentences in direct speech.
1 Fred said he needed help with his homework.
  '*I need help with my homework*,' Fred said.
2 Mr Green said lessons always started at 9.00.
  '*Lessons always start at 9.00*,' Mr Green said.
3 Pete and Anna said they were thinking about joining the theatre club.
  '*We're thinking about joining the theatre club*,' Pete and Anna said.
4 I said I didn't know what was for homework.
  '*I don't know what's for homework*,' I said.
5 Jim said he was making a vlog about his town.
  '*I'm making a vlog about my town*,' Jim said.

9.4

Word order in questions

Yes/No questions

- Yes/No questions begin with an auxiliary verb (e.g. *be*, *have*) or a modal verb (e.g. *can*, *should*). To form questions, we use inversion: we put the auxiliary/modal verb before the subject.
  He *is* talented. → *Is* he talented?
  He *can* help us. → *Can* he help us?
- With verb forms that already have an auxiliary verb (e.g. Present and Past Continuous, Present Perfect, *be going to*, *will*), we simply change the order of the subject and the auxiliary.
  They*'re* leaving. → *Are* they leaving?
  She*'s* going to stay. → *Is* she going to stay?
- With the Present and Past Simple, we add an auxiliary verb (*do/does*, *did*) to form the question.
  He *studies* abroad. → *Does* he *study* abroad?
  They *passed* the test. → *Did* they *pass* the test?

Wh- questions

Wh- questions begin with a question word (e.g. *what*, *where*, *when*, *how*). After the question word, the word order is the same as in yes/no questions.
They are going to the park. → *Where* are they going?
He bought a laptop. → *What* did he buy?

Subject questions

Questions with *who* or *what* can be about the subject or object of the answer.

When they are about the subject, we use the same word order as in affirmative sentences. We don't use auxiliary verbs. Compare:
Who saw David? → *Nick* saw David. (Our question is about Nick. Nick is the subject.)
Who did Nick *see*? → Nick saw *David*. (Our question is about David. David is the object.)

1 Order the words to make questions. Then, in pairs, ask and answer the questions.

1. do / most useful / what / subjects / you / find / ?
   What subjects do you find most useful?
2. last month / you / how many / take / tests / did / ?
   How many tests did you take last month?
3. doing / at 5 p.m. / yesterday / what / you / were / ?
   What were you doing at 5 p.m. yesterday?
4. any homework / you / to / are / do / this evening / going / ?
   Are you going to do any homework this evening?
5. cheated / in a test / you / have / ever / ?
   Have you ever cheated in a test?

2 Write two questions for each answer. Use the question words in brackets.

1. My dad has bought me a new tablet. (who, what)
   Who has bought you a new tablet?
   What has your dad bought you?
2. Jessica is going to take a French exam next week. (who, when)
   Who is going to take a French exam next week?
   When is Jessica going to take a French exam?
3. Mark wants to study in Belgium. (who, where)
   Who wants to study in Belgium?
   Where does Mark want to study?
4. The accident happened in the Science lab. (what, where)
   What happened in the Science lab?
   Where did the accident happen?
5. Emily won the writing competition. (who, what)
   Who won the writing competition?
   What did Emily win?

Irregular Verbs

🔊 10.1

Infinitive	Past Simple	Past Participle	Infinitive	Past Simple	Past Participle
be	was | were	been	lay	laid	laid
become	became	become	learn	learned/learnt	learned/learnt
begin	began	begun	leave	left	left
break	broke	broken	lend	lent	lent
bring	brought	brought	let	let	let
build	built	built	lie	lay	lain
burn	burned/burnt	burned/burnt	lose	lost	lost
buy	bought	bought	make	made	made
can	could	been able to	meet	met	met
catch	caught	caught	pay	paid	paid
choose	chose	chosen	put	put	put
come	came	come	read	read	read
cost	cost	cost	ride	rode	ridden
cut	cut	cut	ring	rang	rung
do	did	done	run	ran	run
draw	drew	drawn	say	said	said
dream	dreamed/dreamt	dreamed/dreamt	see	saw	seen
drink	drank	drunk	sell	sold	sold
drive	drove	driven	send	sent	sent
eat	ate	eaten	set	set	set
fall	fell	fallen	shine	shone	shone
feed	fed	fed	show	showed	shown
feel	felt	felt	sing	sang	sung
fight	fought	fought	sit	sat	sat
find	found	found	sleep	slept	slept
fly	flew	flown	speak	spoke	spoken
forget	forgot	forgotten	spell	spelled/spelt	spelled/spelt
forgive	forgave	forgiven	spend	spent	spent
get	got	got	stand	stood	stood
give	gave	given	steal	stole	stolen
go	went	gone	sweep	swept	swept
grow	grew	grown	swim	swam	swum
hang	hung	hung	take	took	taken
have	had	had	teach	taught	taught
hear	heard	heard	tell	told	told
hide	hid	hidden	think	thought	thought
hit	hit	hit	understand	understood	understood
hold	held	held	wake	woke	woken
hurt	hurt	hurt	wear	wore	worn
keep	kept	kept	win	won	won
know	knew	known	write	wrote	written

136 Grammar Time

Student Activities

Unit 5 Revision Exercise 7

Student A

> - this evening: work on History project; then: watch TV
> - tomorrow: play football; after that: meet friends
> - next Saturday: go shopping; later: help my grandparents

Unit 6 Lesson 6.6 Exercise 7

Student A

> You're at the train station and your train is late. Call your friend and explain what's happening.

A: Hi, It's me. I'm at …

Student B

> Your friend calls from the station but it's noisy. You want to know what time she is arriving.

A: Hi, It's me. I'm at …

Unit 6 Revision Exercise 7

- Student A: Ask, 'Do you like the Mediterranean?'
- Student B: You didn't hear 'Mediterranean' very well. Ask for clarification.
- Student A: Clarify what you said.
- Student B: Thank Student A, say you understand and answer his/her question.

Then swap roles and role play a different situation where you ask for and give clarification.

Unit 9 Revision Exercise 7

Student A

You are an activity leader at a summer camp. You ask Student B questions about the things below because to help you to plan groups for social activities.
- personal details (name, nationality, etc.)
- present situation (school, interests, etc.)
- past experience (travel, films seen, etc.)
- future plans (study, work, etc.)

Unit 7 Lesson 7.6 Exercise 6

Student A

Describe a person in the photo below. Follow the instructions. Then swap roles.
- Choose a person in your photo to describe.
- Your partner/group should ask you questions.
- Answer the questions with one piece of information at a time.

A: Who are you thinking of?
B: A person who looks/is wearing …
A: Where is this person?
B: He's/She's behind/in front of …

Unit 7 Revision Exercise 7

Student A

Unit 8 Revision Exercise 7

You are friends. Student B looks a bit sad and isn't saying much.
- Student A: Check if Student B is OK.
- Student B: Say you are fine.
- Student A: Encourage Student B to speak.
- Student B: Explain your problem.
- Student A: Respond to the problem and reassure Student B.
- Student B: Thank Student B.
- Student A: Ask Student B if they feel better.
- Student B: Reassure Student A that you feel fine now.

SCIENCE

CLIL 1

Cooking and science

Heston Blumenthal is an English chef. He is important because he has made people think about the science of cooking. Heston uses complicated scientific techniques all the time in his cooking, and some of the equipment that he uses in his kitchen is from a science laboratory!

Science is part of all cooking. Every time we cook something, there is a chemical change. A chemical change means that we create a new substance. The process is irreversible – the ingredient cannot change back. To do this, we need energy – in cooking that means a high temperature. When we use heat during cooking, we change both the taste and the texture of the ingredients.

Here are some examples of chemical changes that happen when we cook. A cake looks and tastes very different before and after cooking. With the heat of the oven, it rises. This is because the baking powder ($NaHCO_3$) in the mixture changes at a high temperature. It produces carbon dioxide (CO_2) and the cake grows. But there was no CO_2 in the cake before! Another example is when we toast bread. The carbohydrates in the bread break to form carbon (C). This makes the bread brown and hard, a change in texture and colour. Proteins in meat and eggs change too. The protein molecules take the energy from the heat and change shape. The meat gets harder and red meat becomes brown. Clear egg whites become solid and white.

Chefs like Heston Blumenthal use their knowledge about chemical changes in food to create new tastes and textures. Heston's famous bacon-and-egg ice cream is made using liquid nitrogen!

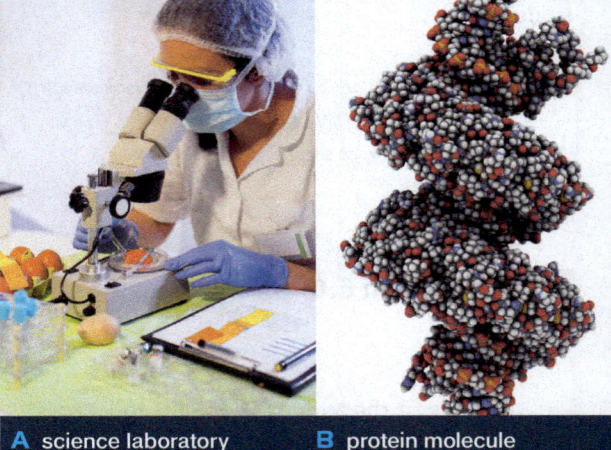

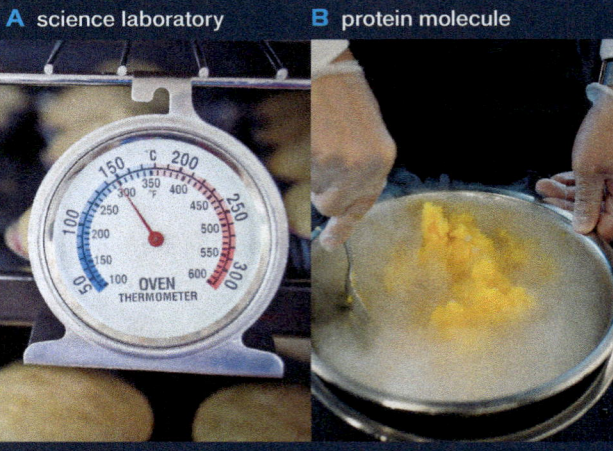

A science laboratory   **B** protein molecule

C high temperature   **D** liquid nitrogen

Exercise 2
1 He is a famous English chef. He makes people think about the science of cooking.
2 It means that we create a new substance (and the change is irreversible).
3 The heat from the oven changes the baking powder and produces carbon dioxide, which makes the cake rise/grow.
4 The carbohydrates in the bread break down to form carbon.
5 The protein molecules change shape. The meat gets harder and becomes brown. Clear egg whites become solid and white.
6 bacon-and-egg ice cream

1 In pairs, discuss the questions.
  1 Look at photos A–D. What do they show? How do you think they are linked to cooking?
  2 Why do you think some people say cooking is an art and others say it is a science?

2 🔊 10.2 Read the article and answer the questions.
  1 Who is Heston Blumenthal and why is he important?
  2 What does 'a chemical change' mean?
  3 What happens to make a cake rise?
  4 What happens when bread becomes toast?
  5 What happens when we cook meat and eggs?
  6 Which of Heston's dishes is made using liquid nitrogen?

3 In pairs, discuss the questions.
  1 What did you find most interesting in the article? Why?
  2 What other everyday activities can science help us with?

4 Think of a raw ingredient which changes when we cook it. Then, in pairs, take turns to describe the ingredient before and after cooking. Can your partner guess what it is?
  A: Before cooking they're round, white and hard. After cooking at a high temperature they're light, brown and break easily.
  B: Potato slices which become crisps!

5 (GO ONLINE) Use the internet to research another chemical change that happens to food during cooking. Make notes about these things.
  • what happens and why
  • examples of meals where this happens
  • any other interesting information

6 (SHARE IT) Prepare a short presentation. Write a paragraph about the chemical change. Add pictures and diagrams. Share your presentation with the class.

CLIL **138**

For the teacher
• Teaching notes, page 230

MUSIC

CLIL 2

David Bowie and space

1 David Bowie was one of England's greatest singers. He died in 2016, but for five decades, his music touched people all over the world. He was not only a singer, but also a songwriter and an actor. People remember him for his music, but also for the wonderful characters he created on stage, especially Ziggy Stardust. As a musician, he was always very imaginative and creative, and had his own unique style. He started singing pop songs, then rock, then glam rock and in the 2000s he even experimented with industrial and jungle styles.

2 One theme that Bowie used many times in his songs was space. His songs were often about going into space or aliens coming to visit Earth. Perhaps his most famous song about space is *Space Oddity*. It was released just before Apollo 11 landed on the moon on 20 July 1969. The lyrics of the song tell the story of a fictional astronaut, Major Tom, who goes on a space walk but loses contact with the astronauts in the space station and with the station on Earth.

3 *Space Oddity* became one of Bowie's signature songs. It also became famous again in 2013 for a very important reason. While on the International Space Station, the Canadian astronaut Chris Hadfield filmed himself singing *Space Oddity*. It was the first video ever shot in space. People remember Bowie for *Space Oddity*, but he also wrote many other space-themed songs, and they were very popular. Some of them are on his album *The Rise and Fall of Ziggy Stardust and the Spiders from Mars*.

1 Have you heard of David Bowie? What do you know about him? Do you know any of his songs?

2 Look at photos A–C. How do you think space and music might be connected?

3 🔊 10.3 Read the article quickly and check your ideas from Exercises 1 and 2. In which paragraphs (1–3) are photos A–C mentioned?
A `2`   B `1`   C `3`

4 Read the article again and complete the fact file.

David Bowie			
Born:	*1947*	**Died:** ¹	
Famous character:	²		
Types of music:	³		
Famous single:	⁴	**Released:** ⁵	
Famous album:	⁶		

5 In pairs, read about two songs that were played in space. Student A, read text A. Student B, read text B. Take turns to tell your partner about your song. Then find and listen to the songs online. Which one is better? Why?

> **A** *Across the Universe*, The Beatles
> This was the first song that was sent into space as a radio message on 4 February 2008. It was sent from a seventy-metre dish at the Deep Space Network near Madrid. It celebrated the fortieth anniversary of the song, the forty-fifth anniversary of the DSN and the fiftieth anniversary of NASA.

> **B** *Reach for the Stars*, will.i.am
> On 28 August 2012, NASA sent this song from Mars to Earth using a special device. NASA and will.i.am wanted to encourage young people to study Science. The song travelled 300 million miles and was the first song ever sent to Earth from another planet.

6 (GO ONLINE) Use the internet to find out more about a famous singer/songwriter from your country. Make notes about these things.
- his/her career
- why he/she became famous
- any other interesting information

7 (SHARE IT) Prepare a digital presentation. Write a paragraph about the singer/songwriter. Add pictures and some of his/her music. Share your presentation with the class.

Exercise 4
1 2016
2 Ziggy Stardust
3 pop, rock, glam rock, industrial, jungle
4 *Space Oddity*
5 1969
6 *The Rise and Fall of Ziggy Stardust and the Spiders from Mars*

For the teacher
- Teaching notes, page 230

GEOGRAPHY

CLIL 3

The International Date Line

A — International Date Line/IDL
B — Prime Meridian
C — Equator

Tonga and Samoa are two islands in the South Pacific. They are 557 miles apart. If you flew from Tonga to Samoa, the journey would take you two hours, but you would arrive twenty-two hours before you left! It might be 5 November when you leave Tonga and 4 November when you arrive in Samoa. Why? Because you would cross the International Date Line (IDL). This can be confusing for travellers and cause problems with hotel bookings!

The IDL – an imaginary line, not a real one – goes from north to south. There are two other important imaginary lines across the Earth: the Equator, which divides the world into the northern and southern hemispheres, and the Prime Meridian (which goes through London), dividing the world into the western and eastern hemispheres. The IDL is on the opposite side of the world to the Prime Meridian. The world is always turning and as we travel around the world (east or west), our days become shorter or longer. The IDL tells all the countries in the world where the beginning of one day and the end of another come together.

The IDL starts at the North Pole and goes down to the South Pole, and crosses through the Pacific Ocean. But it isn't a straight line – it has several zigzags in it! This is so that it is the same date in one country. For example, the line zigzags east to go through the Bering Straits so that Alaska and Russia are on different sides. The country of Kiribati used to be on the eastern side, but it decided to change to the western side. It wanted to be the first country in the world to celebrate the new millennium in 2000!

1 When it is Friday 11th December in New York City, USA, it is Saturday 12th December in Sydney, Australia. Why do you think the dates are different?

2 🔊 10.4 Read the article quickly and check your answers in Exercise 1. Label A–C on the maps.

3 Read the article again and mark the sentences T (true) or F (false).
   1 [F] It takes twenty-two hours to fly from Tonga to Samoa.
   2 [T] The IDL is on the other side of the world from the Prime Meridian.
   3 [F] The IDL goes in a straight line from north to south.
   4 [F] It is the same time and day in Russia and Alaska.
   5 [T] Kiribati is on the western side of the IDL.

4 What did you find most interesting in the article? Why?

5 Read about the history of the IDL. How was the problem of losing a day first discovered?

History of the IDL

In 1519 the explorer Ferdinand Magellan was the first person to sail round the world. During the journey, the crew kept careful records. When they got home, they discovered that they had lost a complete day. The date they had was a day behind the people in their country. This was the beginning of the idea of an international date line and in the seventeenth century it started to appear on maps. It became official in 1884, after an international meridian conference. However, there is still no law that says the IDL exists.

6 Why do you think the IDL is important? What would happen without it?

7 (GO ONLINE) Use the internet to find out about one of the other imaginary lines around the Earth. Make notes about these things.
   • where it goes
   • its purpose and when it was named
   • any other interesting information

8 (SHARE IT) Prepare a short presentation. Write a paragraph about the imaginary line you have chosen and add a map with labels. Share your presentation with the class.

Exercise 5
Possible answer: Magellan's crew discovered it when they returned from a journey round the world. The date on their records from the journey was one full day behind the date in their country.

For the teacher
• Teaching notes, page 231

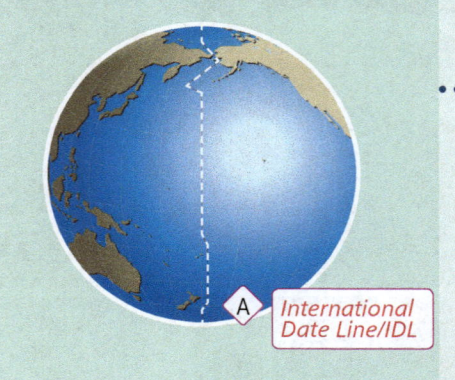

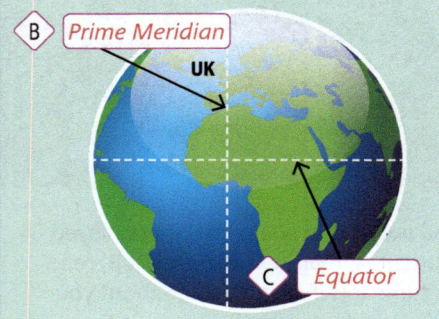

CLIL 140

SCIENCE

CLIL 4

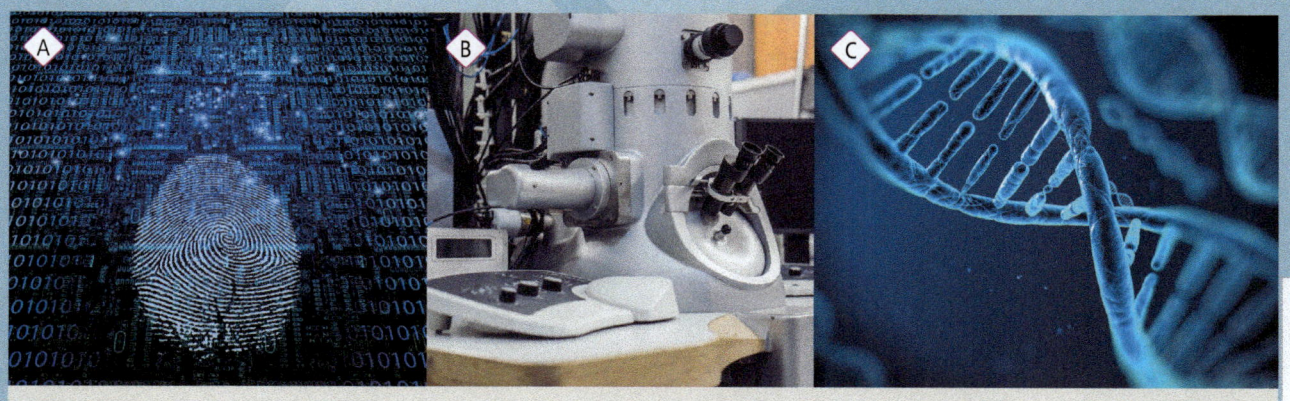

Forensics

The crime scene
When there is a crime, the police often use forensic scientists to help them to find the criminal. At nearly every crime scene there is some evidence that scientists can check. This might be blood, hair, fingerprints or other very small things that they can analyse. The forensic scientist uses special equipment in a police laboratory to carry out experiments. They use a powerful microscope (an electron microscope) to check both the evidence and samples from suspects. Forensic scientists also study dead bodies to find out how and when they died. This is called an autopsy, or post-mortem. All this information helps the police.

Fingerprints
Everyone has different fingerprints. These are the lines and circles on the tips of our fingers. When we touch something, we leave a print. Scientists can use special powder to copy these prints. These are compared to records of fingerprints to find out who left them.

DNA
DNA is like a genetic fingerprint. Everyone's DNA is different (apart from identical twins). So if a criminal leaves DNA at a crime scene, the forensic scientist can use it. DNA can be found in many things such as blood, hair, teeth, bone and saliva (from inside our mouths). We leave our DNA everywhere – on clothes and cups, in hairbrushes and on toothbrushes.

Exercise 1
1 Photo A: fingerprint
Photo B: (forensic) lab
Photo C: DNA
2 Students' own answers

Exercise 2
A forensic scientist is a scientist who helps the police to solve crimes by analysing blood, hair, etc.

Exercise 3
1 in a police laboratory
2 how and when they died
3 Fingerprints are the patterns of lines and circles on the tips of our fingers. A forensic scientist uses special powder to copy the prints, then checks them against records of fingerprints.
4 DNA is like a genetic fingerprint. It can be found in blood, hair, teeth, bone and saliva.

---

1 In pairs, discuss the questions.
  1 Look at photos A–C. What do they show? How do you think science can help detectives?
  2 What do you think a forensic scientist does?

2 🔊 10.5 Read the article quickly and check your answers in Exercise 1.

3 Read the article again and answer the questions.
  1 Where does a forensic scientist work?
  2 What can they find out about a dead person?
  3 What are fingerprints and how does a forensic scientist check them?
  4 What is DNA and where is it found?

4 In pairs, read the texts about evidence. Student A, read text A. Student B, read text B. Take turns to tell your partner about your text. How can the evidence you read about help forensic scientists?

A Hair Our hair falls out all the time and a criminal often leaves hair at a crime scene. Scientists can analyse hair and find out if the colour is natural and if it is an animal or human hair. They can also get an idea of the age and gender of the person. There are many different things a hair can tell the scientist! If the hair has a root, it can also give DNA.

B Shoes Shoes can leave prints. These can tell scientists about a criminal's size, the way they walk and the type of shoe that they wore. Shoes also leave dirt. Scientists can sometimes learn where the person lives or works, if they have pets, where they walk and even which field or path he/she has walked on.

5 Would you like to be a forensic scientist? Why?/Why not?

6 **GO ONLINE** Use the internet to find out how the police solved a famous crime using forensics. Make notes about the crime and the evidence.

7 **SHARE IT** Prepare a short presentation. Write a paragraph about the crime and the forensic work involved. Add pictures. Share your presentation with the class.

For the teacher
• Teaching notes, page 231

Student Activities

Unit 1 Lesson 1.5 Exercise 2

Do you need a digital detox?
Results
- **Mostly a:** You're obviously busy with other things in life and that's great. Have fun and enjoy real time with your friends!
- **Mostly b:** You know your mobile is there when you need it, but technology isn't the most important thing in your life.
- **Mostly c:** You're internet crazy! You love being online and checking messages from friends. Make sure you take time to do other things too.

Unit 1 Lesson 1.6 Exercise 5

Follow the instructions to role play a dialogue. Then swap roles.
- **Student A:** choose a situation from the list below. Then accept or reject Student B's solutions.
- **Student B:** listen to Student A and respond with a suitable suggestion.

- My QR code reader app doesn't work.
- I dropped my phone and it broke.
- There's no wi-fi signal in my room.
- My computer keeps crashing.

Unit 2 Lesson 2.6 Exercise 6

- I copied my homework from a friend.
- I didn't buy my friend a birthday present.
- I spent a lot of money on a concert/sports ticket.

A: State the problem. Add extra information if possible.
B: Ask about your partner's actions.
A: Explain your reasons.
B: Give your opinion or say if you understand now.

Unit 2 Revision Exercise 8

Follow the instructions to role play a dialogue. Then swap roles.
- **Student A:** Phone your friend. Apologise and say you don't want to go camping. Add extra information if possible.
- **Student B:** Accept your partner's apology and ask why they don't want to go camping.
- **Student A:** Explain your reasons. Add as many as you can.
- **Student B:** Accept your partner's explanation.

Unit 3 Lesson 3.6 Exercise 6

Digby's Restaurant Menu

Starters
Nachos with cheese
Mini pizzas
Toast with olive oil, garlic and fresh tomatoes

Main courses
Salmon with sweet potatoes
Hamburger with fries
Pasta with mushroom sauce

Desserts
Fruit salad with fresh cream
Pumpkin pie with vanilla ice cream
Chocolate cake

Drinks
Cola • Carrot and pear smoothie • Apple juice

Unit 3 Revision Exercise 8

SAM'S SNACKS MENU

SANDWICHES
Tuna • Salmon • Chicken •
Beef burger • Tofu burger

EXTRAS
Chips • Mushrooms •
Carrot and green pepper salad •
Olives • Pickles

DRINKS
Orange juice • Mango juice •
Pineapple juice • Mineral water • Tea

Progress Check Units 1–3 Exercise 5

1. You are on a walking trip in the mountains.
   - **Student A:** explain that you think you are lost. Apologise. It was your job to find the way, but the map app on your phone doesn't work.
   - **Student B:** respond to what Student A says.
   - Discuss a solution.

2. You are both at Student B's house. Student A is a guest. You are in the kitchen because you agreed to cook pizza.
   - **Student B:** explain that you have a problem with the recipe for the pizza. Explain the problem and apologise.
   - **Student A:** respond to what Student B says.
   - Discuss a solution.

Unit 5 Revision Exercise 7

Student B

- this evening: work out at gym; after that: cook dinner
- tomorrow: visit my uncle; then: do schoolwork
- next Saturday: watch football match; later: go to the cinema

Unit 7 Lesson 7.6 Exercise 5

Student B

Describe a person in the photo below. Follow the instructions. Then swap roles.
- Choose a person in your photo to describe.
- Your partner/group should ask you questions.
- Answer the questions with one piece of information at a time.

A: Who are you thinking of?
B: A person who looks/is wearing …
A: Where is this person?
B: He's/She's behind/in front of …

Unit 7 Revision Exercise 7

Student B

Unit 9 Revision Exercise 7

Student B

You are staying at the summer camp. Make up the information below about yourself and answer Student B's questions.
- personal details (name, nationality, etc.)
- present situation (school, interests, etc.)
- past experience (travel, films seen, etc.)
- future plans (study, work, etc.)

Progress Check Units 1–9 Exercise 5

1. In pairs, follow the instructions to role play a situation where you are making friends on a summer holiday course.
   - In pairs, decide where you are and what course you are doing.
   - Now work on your own. Imagine a new identity for yourself! Decide your new name and where you are from.
   - In pairs, talk about the holiday course experience and your future plans.

2. Think about your conversation. Did you:
   - listen carefully?
   - smile and show interest?
   - use a variety of different tenses correctly?
   - ask for clarification if you needed to?

3. Swap roles or work in new pairs and repeat the role play.

Progress Check Units 1–9 Exercise 12

	Yes	No	Maybe
1 Would you like to learn only by doing projects?	☐	☐	☐
2 Would you like to stop learning Maths?	☐	☐	☐
3 Would you like to learn outdoors?	☐	☐	☐
4 Would you like to learn to do creative and practical things with your hands?	☐	☐	☐
5 Would you like to decide what school subjects you learn?	☐	☐	☐

Student Activities 143

0 Welcome to New Park
Student's Book pages 6–11

Unit contents

Vocabulary
- Activities and interests | Home and furniture | Jobs | Everyday activities | Clothes and accessories | Countries and languages

Grammar
- *There is/are* with *some/any* | Possessive adjectives and possessive *'s* | Present Simple with adverbs of frequency | Present Continuous | *Was/were, there was/were* | Past Simple: regular verbs

Speaking
- Likes and dislikes | Talking about feelings

Check your progress with **Benchmark Young Learners Levels 4/5** or **Benchmark Test A/B1** on completing Unit 0.

For Online Classroom, go to the Portal.

0.1 INTRODUCING ABE

Activities and interests | Home and furniture | *There is/are* with *some/any* | Possessive adjectives and possessive *'s*

Lesson aims
- Students can talk about their activities and interests and describe their homes and the furniture in it.
- Students can use *there is/are* with *some/any*, possessive adjectives and possessive *'s*.

For the teacher
- Vocabulary Memory Game

For the student
- Workbook, page 2

Lead-in

Introduce yourself to the class (name, where from, where live, favourite hobby). Students work in pairs to do the same.

- **Setting lesson goals:** Write on the board: *I like reading books. There are some trees in my garden. There aren't any windows in my parents' garage.* Elicit similar sentences from students and say you will explore this language in the lesson.

Exercises 1–12
- Follow the instructions in the Student's Book.

Extra activity

Demonstrate the meaning of each preposition for Exercise 10 using, e.g. a mobile phone and two books. With **more confident** students, elicit the prepositions from the class instead.

- **FINISHED EARLY?** Ask students to write down their answers for Exercise 4.
- **Reviewing lesson goals:** Ask students to write on a piece of paper: two examples of activities and interests, a sentence about something they like or dislike, three examples of words for home and furniture, a sentence with *there is/are* with *some/any*, and a sentence with a possessive adjective or possessive *'s*. Ask them to leave their pieces of paper on your desk. Check, and if there are any recurring errors, find time to review the language.

0.2 INTRODUCING BEA

Present Simple with adverbs of frequency | Jobs | Everyday activities

Lesson aims
- Students can use the Present Simple with adverbs of frequency.
- Students can talk about jobs and everyday activities.

For the student
- Workbook, page 3

Lead-in

Tell the class about things you do most days, e.g. get up, make breakfast, come to work, etc. Students work in pairs or small groups to do the same. For feedback, get some volunteers to tell the class something interesting they found out about their partners.

- **Setting lesson goals:** Say and write: *I'm a teacher.* Then, give the class examples of five activities you always, usually, often, sometimes or never do. Include information about your job as well as your everyday activities (see Exercise 8 for ideas). Write these sentences on the board. Highlight the Present Simple verb forms and adverbs of frequency. Ask students to look through page 8 quickly to get an idea of the lesson aims.

Exercises 1–10
- Follow the instructions in the Student's Book.

Extra activity

To add words to the Vocabulary box in Exercise 6, put students into groups of four and give each group a different category of job to think about, e.g. outdoor jobs, jobs with uniforms, part-time jobs for teenagers or students. Elicit each group's ideas and write them on the board for students to copy in their notebooks.

- **FINISHED EARLY?** Ask students to write a description of their typical working day in their dream job in the future.
- **Reviewing lesson goals:** Ask students to use their Emoji response cards to show how confident they feel about using the language from the lesson. Make a note to revise any problem areas in a later lesson.

0.3 INTRODUCING EREN

Clothes and accessories | Present Continuous

Lesson aims
- Students can describe clothes and accessories.
- Students can use the Present Continuous.

For the teacher
- Vocabulary Memory Game

For the student
- Workbook, page 4

Lead-in

Ask: *What am I wearing?* Elicit students' ideas about your clothes and accessories. Help with any unfamiliar vocabulary. Then, students work in pairs to describe the clothes and accessories of someone in the class for their partner to guess.

- **Setting lesson goals:** Write on the board: *Eren is sitting in the living room with his grandad. Eren is wearing a hoodie.* Highlight the verb forms and explain that you are going to practise using the Present Continuous to talk about clothes and accessories.

Exercises 1–9 0.9 audioscript page 242
- Follow the instructions in the Student's Book.
- **FINISHED EARLY?** Ask students to write their answers to Exercise 9 using the adverbs of frequency from page 8.
- **Reviewing lesson goals:** Ask students to give themselves a mark 1–3 for each exercise (1 – easy to do, 2 – could do it with help, 3 – difficult to do). Read out the exercise numbers and ask students to hold up the number of fingers for each one. Make a note to revise any difficult points.

0.4 INTRODUCING CARLA

Countries and languages | Was/were | There was/were | Past Simple: regular verbs

Lesson aims
- Students can talk about which countries people are from and what languages they speak.
- Students can use past forms including *was/were*, *there was/were* and the Past Simple with regular verbs.

For the student
- Workbook, page 5

Lead-in

Bring into class photos of famous people students know. Write: *He's/She's from …* and *He's/She's …* and elicit the answers for each one, (e.g. *Robert Lewandowski is from Poland. He's Polish.*)

- **Setting lesson goals:** Show the class a photo of a child. Say, e.g. *This is Anita. She was six years old here. Her family lived in Germany, so Anita can speak German. There was a shop next to their house.* Highlight the target language and explain that you are going to practise this in the lesson.

Exercises 1–8 0.12 audioscript page 242
- Follow the instructions in the Student's Book.

Extra activity

When students have finished Exercise 1, look at the first example (Brazil/Portugal – Portuguese) and ask students to think of other countries where the name of the language may not be obvious, e.g. *Canada – English/French, Egypt – Arabic, Switzerland – French/German/Italian, Argentina – Spanish*.

- **FINISHED EARLY?** Ask students to write down their answers for Exercise 8.
- **Reviewing lesson goals:** Ask students to use their Traffic Light cards to show how confident they are about using past forms, countries and languages. Make a note to revise any problem areas.

0.5 REVISION

Lesson aims
- Students revise Unit 0.

For the student
- Workbook, page 5

Lead-in

Books closed. Read the headings from Lessons 0.1–0.4 at random, and elicit one or two examples for each heading (e.g. Activities and interests: *playing computer games*).

- **Setting lesson goals:** Books closed. Elicit the names of the four main characters and two facts about each one. Tell students they will revise what they have learned.

Exercises 1–5 0.13 audioscript page 242
- Follow the instructions in the Student's Book.
- **FINISHED EARLY?** Ask students to write down their answers to the quiz questions in Exercise 3.
- **Reviewing lesson goals:** Ask students to try to recall one or two more facts (that weren't included in the quiz) about each character.

1 Tech check

Student's Book pages 12–23

Unit contents

Vocabulary
- Technology
- Using technology
- Social media
- Opposites
- Time

Grammar
- Present Simple and Present Continuous, state verbs
- Verb + -ing, verb + to-infinitive

Speaking
- Problem-solving

Writing
- A description of your daily routine and online hobbies

Future skills
- Creativity: problem-solving

Exam
- International Certificate Level 1/2, Reading, Section 6, (open-ended question)
- A2 Key for Schools, Listening, Part 5, (matching)

For Online Classroom, go to the Portal.

1.1 VOCABULARY

Lifestyle

Lesson aims
- Students can talk about everyday technology.

For the teacher
- Vocabulary Memory Game
- Photocopiable activity: *Social media word friends*
- Test: Vocabulary Check 1

For the student
- Workbook, pages 6–7
- Extra Practice Activities: Vocabulary, BBC Vox pop

Lead-in

Books closed. Write the following gapped words on the board and ask students to complete them: l _ _ t _ p, g _ d g _ _ , b l _ _ , t _ l _ v _ _ _ _ _ , s _ _ r t p _ _ n _ (laptop, gadget, blog, television, smartphone). Elicit what topic connects the words (technology). Check comprehension of *gadget* by asking which of the words are for gadgets (laptop, smartphone).

- **Setting lesson goals:** Write the lesson aim on the board and read it out with students. Ask: *What technology do you use every day?*

Exercise 1
- **Peer learning:** Use the Think-Pair-Share technique. Give students half a minute to consider the questions on their own, then give them another minute to compare ideas in pairs. Elicit suggestions in open class, inviting comments from other students.

Exercise 2
- Elicit or pre-teach *everyday essentials* (things that we really need daily). Explain that Grace is writing about the most important gadgets for her. As students read, suggest that they find the gadgets Grace mentions, then consider the question. Elicit or explain the meaning of *waterproof, password*. Ask students to compare ideas in pairs before eliciting opinions in open class.

Exercise 3 🔊 1.1
- Read the information in the Vocabulary box as a class. Check students understand the new words. Set a time limit for students to complete the task. Then, play the audio for them to listen, repeat and check their answers. Pause after each word to check students' pronunciation.
- Suggest that students use the questions: *What is it? How do we use it?* to check their comprehension. Write these prompts on the board for support.

Exercise 4
- Set a time limit of two minutes, then get pairs to think of as many words as they can. Get pairs to swap their lists with another pair to check each other's work.

Exercise 5 🔊 1.2 audioscript page 242
- Tell students they are going to hear six short explanations of how we use a gadget. Play the first part of the audio, pausing after each definition to give students time to write their answers. Then play the second part of the audio for students to check their answers.
- **Peer learning:** When you play the first, gapped part of the audio, pause after each item, and allow students to compare ideas in pairs before moving on to the next definition. By encouraging peer support, students are more likely to figure out the correct answers.

Exercise 6
- Ask students to read the adjectives in the box, and check comprehension by eliciting an explanation in students' own words or an example to illustrate their meaning. Elicit two or three different ideas for each adjective.
- Then, students tell their partner which object would be the best present for them.

Exercise 7 🔊 1.3
- Go through the phrases and check understanding.
- When students have matched the icons and phrases, ask them to compare answers in pairs before you play the audio for them to check the answers, then play it again so they can practise the pronunciation.

Exercise 8 🔊 1.4 audioscript page 242
- Play the audio. Check the answers.

Exercise 9 🔊 1.5
- Check comprehension by eliciting an explanation of each phrase from a volunteer, in their own words. Students choose the correct options, then check each other's work. Then, play the audio for them to check again. Give them a minute to discuss which statements are true for them. Ask a different student to tell the class about their partner for each sentence.

Exercise 10
- Suggest that students read the text quickly first without completing any gaps, to get a general sense. This will help them complete the task more easily.
- **NEED SUPPORT?** Remind students that parts of each phrase are included in the text before or after each gap. Tell **less confident** students to look for words that also appear in the Word Friends phrases in Exercise 9, then consider if the phrase fits the text logically. Encourage **more confident** students to cover Exercise 9 and complete the task without looking back at the Word Friends.

Exercise 11 ▶ 5 videoscript page 242
- Pre-teach or elicit the following words and phrases from the video: *probably*, *colleagues*, *I guess*, *uni* (as the short form of *university*), *architect*.
- Ask students to close their books and play the video all the way through for them to watch. Then ask: *What's the video about?* (how people in their families use technology).
- Play the video again for students to do the task, then check answers as a class.

Exercise 12
- Give students a minute to read the example, then consider the question. Then put them in pairs or small groups to discuss the question.
- **FINISHED EARLY?** Ask students to think of famous characters from films, TV shows or books, and write five sentences about what they use technology for, e.g. *Marty McFly uses a special car to travel in time.*
- **Reviewing lesson goals:** Ask students to think about the lesson aim again. Encourage them give themselves a number from 1–5 to say how they feel about the lesson (1 – least to 5 – most confident) on a small piece of paper. Collect these, and if there are several 1s or 2s, find time to review the language from Lesson 1.1.

1.2 GRAMMAR

Present Simple and Present Continuous, state verbs

Lesson aims
- Students can use different tenses to talk about the present.

For the teacher
- *Need support?* worksheet, page 232
- Grammar presentation
- **Photocopiable activity:** *Find someone who …*
- **Test:** Grammar Check 1

For the student
- Grammar Time, Student's Book, page 126
- Workbook, page 8
- **Extra Practice Activities:** Grammar, BBC Vox Pop

Lead-in

Ask students: *Do you watch music videos? Which videos do you think are the best?* Elicit some responses, and invite comments from the rest of the class.
- **Setting lesson goals:** Write on the board a sentence in the Present Simple and one in the Present Continuous about yourself, for example: *I teach English in a school. I'm writing on the board.* Ask: *When do I do these things?* (Monday to Friday; right now). Elicit what students think the lesson will be about.

Exercise 1 🔊 1.6
- When students have discussed their ideas in pairs, elicit some predictions in class. Accept all suggestions even if they later turn out to be wrong. When students have finished, play the audio while they read again and check their ideas.

Exercise 2
- Ask: *Who usually writes the band's blog? Who's writing it today?* (Ziggy usually writes the blog. Evy is writing it today.) Write the two examples on the board. Elicit the names of the tenses, and what students remember about the rules of forming them. Then focus their attention on the Grammar box so they can check their ideas.
- Ask: *Which tense do we use for habits and repeated actions?* (Present Simple). *Which tense do we use for actions at or around the time of speaking?* (Present Continuous). Elicit the rules of forming statements and questions in both the present tenses.
- Ask students to find examples of the two present tenses first and compare their answers in pairs. Then ask them to identify the state verbs together.

Exercise 3 🔊 1.7
- Suggest that students look for time expressions or adverbs, which will help them decide whether the sentence is about habits and repeated actions or about actions around the time of speaking. Do the first sentence together as a class. Elicit that *at the moment* refers to an action at the time of speaking. Allow students to compare answers in pairs before you play the audio for them to check.

159

1 Tech check
Student's Book pages 12–23

Exercise 4
- Ask a volunteer for each question to explain why they used the given tense. Then, put them in pairs to ask and answer the questions.
- **NEED SUPPORT?** Prepare copies of the photocopiable worksheet on page 232. This version of the task tells students which tense to use in each sentence.

Exercise 5
- Suggest that students look for time expressions or adverbs to help them. Allow students to compare answers in pairs before you check as a class.

Exercise 6 ▶ 6 videoscript page 242
- Tell students that the speakers are going to mention sixteen sports or hobbies.
- Elicit the words and write them on the board. Play the video again to check.

Exercise 7
- 💬 **Monitoring learning:** Monitor the discussions and make a note of the most interesting ideas. Elicit these in open class feedback.
- **FINISHED EARLY?** Ask students to write questions in the Present Simple and Present Continuous about the two texts in Lesson 1.2. They can use these to test each other in pairs if time allows.
- 🎓 **Independent learning:** Ask students to look back at the exercises and give three stars to the most difficult tasks, one to the easiest. Students compare their ideas in groups of three.

1.3 READING AND VOCABULARY

Science competitions and projects

Lesson aims
- Students can understand a message and an email about Science competitions and projects.

For the teacher
- *Need support?* worksheet, page 232
- Vocabulary Memory Game
- **Photocopiable activity:** Match and create
- **Test:** Vocabulary Check 1

For the student
- Workbook, page 9
- Extra Practice Activities: Vocabulary

Lead-in
Write the word *science* on the board. Elicit from students what kind of things they learn about in Science classes and write up the most relevant ideas as a spidergram.
- 🎯 **Setting lesson goals:** Ask students to look through page 15 quickly and identify three new things they think they are going to learn or practise. Tell them to make a note of these. Get them to compare their ideas in pairs or small groups, then elicit suggestions in open class.

Exercise 1
- Check comprehension of *do a project* and *take part in a competition* by asking a different volunteer to explain each expression or illustrate its meaning by giving an example. Then, puts students in groups for the discussion.

Exercise 2 🔊 1.8
- Elicit or pre-teach: *prize, in danger, end-of-term, bat*. Point out that there are three texts, so one of the questions will match more than one text. Play the audio while students read to ensure they all progress at the same pace. Ask students to compare answers in pairs before checking as a class.

> **Background note**
> There are a number of different **Science competitions** in the UK for young people. The Longitude Explorer Prize was established in 2014 for participants aged 11–16. Each year there's a different theme. The prize is named in honour of the original Longitude Prize, established by the government in 1714 to encourage research into safer sea navigation.

Exercise 3
- **EXAM** International Certificate Level 1/2, Reading, section 6, (open-ended question)
- Allow each student to re-read the texts. The task is to find specific information in the texts. Suggest that students decide what kind of information each question is looking for (1 a certain group of people, 2 a name of a competition, 3 a specific age, etc.). Tell them next to scan the text to find the information, then study that section more carefully to decide which part of it answers the question.
- **NEED SUPPORT?** Prepare copies of the photocopiable worksheet on page 232. This task provides a different way of checking comprehension.

Exercise 4 🔊 1.9
- For extra challenge, you could do this task as a race to see which student finds all the adjectives most quickly. Drill the pronunciation.
- **NEED SUPPORT?** Less confident students could work in pairs to find the adjectives.
- 💬 **Monitoring learning:** As students pronounce each word, ask them to show how many syllables they hear by raising the appropriate number of fingers.

Exercise 5
- Write the following prompt on the board: *What makes it …?* As students discuss their ideas for each item, encourage them to answer the question using the appropriate adjective. (For example: *What makes a koala a strange animal? It only lives in one part of the world.*)

- For feedback, get some students to share one of their ideas with the class, without revealing which category it is an example for. The others should try to guess, and also guess why it was chosen.

Exercise 6
- Ask students: *Imagine that you have to do a Science project. What Science do you choose?* Give students a minute to think about their answer. This should then inform their subsequent pairwork discussions.
- Tell students to copy and complete the form in their notebooks. Encourage them to write at least three or four things about their idea for the project. These can be bullet points rather than complete sentences.
- Put students in pairs. Ask them to share their idea with their partner. For feedback, get some volunteers to tell the class. As a class, vote on the best suggestion.
- **FINISHED EARLY?** To expand the lexical set in Exercise 4, ask students to write some more synonyms and antonyms for the adjectives. Allow them to use a dictionary if necessary.
- **Reviewing lesson goals:** Ask students to check their predictions about the three learning goals that they made at the start of the lesson. Ask them to decide whether the lesson has covered what they expected, or if there is anything they would still like to learn more about.

1.4 GRAMMAR

Verb + -ing, verb + to-infinitive

Lesson aims
- Students can use verbs followed by the *-ing* form and/or the *to*-infinitive.

For the teacher
- **Photocopiable activity:** *I'm the same as you!*
- Grammar presentation
- **Test:** Grammar Check 1

For the student
- Grammar Time, Student's Book, page 126
- Workbook, page 10
- **Extra Practice Activities:** New Park video, Grammar

Lead-in
Elicit the names of the main characters from the video story (introduced in Lessons 0.1 and 0.2). Write the names on the board. Ask students to try to remember two facts about each person, then compare ideas in pairs. Elicit and make a note of the facts on the board. Ask the rest of the class to check and confirm or correct the information.

- **Setting lesson goals:** Write a couple of examples with verb + *-ing* and verb + *to*-infinitive on the board, e.g. *I enjoy reading books. I want to be a rock star.* Elicit what students think they will be learning about. Ask them to look briefly at page 16 to check their ideas.

Exercise 1
- Elicit what tense we use to describe the actions of people in photos (Present Continuous).
- You could elicit suggestions in open class, or put students in pairs or groups first to brainstorm ideas before collating suggestions together as a class.

Exercise 2 ▶ 7 ◀) 1.10
- Check comprehension of the following expressions from the video: *Is now a good time? I need to pack. There's something wrong. Don't forget. Safe journey!* Elicit when someone might use each one. Accept any reasonable suggestions.
- Read the questions, and check that students understand what information to listen for. Ask them to compare ideas in pairs before you check answers as a class.
- **NEED SUPPORT?** Play the video or audio again and pause after key moments to ask **less confident** students comprehension questions, e.g. *Where's Abe going soon?* (to the airport). *What do they have problems with?* (the sound). *What does Abe's video chat background show?* (a beach). *What's making the noise?* (Bea's mum is vacuuming.) *What does Bea ask Abe to bring her?* (a basketball shirt). *Where are they going to meet next?* (in the UK). Elicit answers before continuing the video or audio.

Exercise 3
- Explain that certain words are usually followed by one or the other verb form in the Grammar box, and a few words can be followed by either form.
- Split the class into two teams. Ask one team to find more examples of verbs with *-ing*, and the other to find examples with verbs + *to*-infinitive. Elicit the examples and build up a collated list on the board for students to copy.

Exercise 4
- Ask students to complete the task and compare answers in pairs before you check as a class.
- **NEED SUPPORT?** **Less confident** students can complete the task by studying the Grammar box. **More confident** students should cover the box and do it from memory.

Exercise 5
- Suggest that students find the verbs before each gap in order to help them decide which form they usually go with. When students have completed the text, ask them to compare answers in pairs before you check as a class.

Exercise 6
- Before students begin the task, review the technology collocations from Lesson 1.1. Write the following verbs on the board and ask students to come up with technology-related phrases that could follow them: *add, chat, connect, delete, follow, message, post, search, send, set, share, take, update, upload.* There is more than one collocation for each verb, so accept all correct suggestions.

1 Tech check
Student's Book pages 12–23

- Give pairs half a minute to decide on the gadget. Then give them plenty of time to discuss the tips and write them down. Suggest that they aim for four to six tips.
- Ask a number of pairs to share their tips with the class, without revealing what gadgets they are for. Ask the class to write their guesses about all the gadgets described, then check who guessed the most correctly at the end.
- **Monitoring learning:** Monitor the discussions and make a note of good examples of language to elicit in open class and of recurring errors for correction at the end of the activity.
- **FINISHED EARLY?** Ask students to choose five verbs from the Grammar box and write true sentences about themselves. Remind them to use the correct form: verb + *-ing* or verb + *to*-infinitive.
- **Reviewing lesson goals:** Ask students to use the Emoji response cards to show how confident they feel about the language from Lesson 1.4. Make a note to revise any language they seem to have issues with.

1.5 LISTENING AND VOCABULARY

Are you technology crazy?

Lesson aims
- Students can understand a radio programme about using technology.

For the teacher
- *Need support?* worksheet, page 232
- Photocopiable activity: *What do you do?*

For the student
- Workbook, page 11
- Extra Practice Activities: Vocabulary

Lead-in

Write *technology crazy* on the board, and check comprehension by eliciting an explanation. (If you're crazy about something, it means you really like it.) Ask: *Are you technology crazy?* Elicit some responses from volunteers, encouraging them to give reasons. Then write *digital detox* on the board, and elicit guesses about what students think it means.

- **Setting lesson goals:** Ask students to look through page 17 and decide which activity they are most looking forward to. Ask them to compare ideas in pairs or small groups.

Exercise 1

- **Peer learning:** Use the Think-Pair-Share technique. Before you elicit suggestions in open class, ask students to hold their thumbs up if the answer is yes, and thumbs down if the answer is no. Invite some opposing viewpoints, encouraging students to give reasons.

Exercise 2

- Check comprehension of *the minute* (*I wake up*), *have a free moment* and *all the time*. Ask a different volunteer to explain each phrase in their own words.

- Ask students to complete the quiz individually, then read the information on page 142. For feedback, ask a few volunteers to report back on what the quiz told them about themselves, and whether they agree, and why.

Extra activity

Put students in pairs to discuss what other questions the quiz could ask about digital habits (for example about video games). Ask them to write one or two more questions, with three answer options.

Exercise 3 🔊 1.11

- Read the information in the Vocabulary box as a class. Check that students understand what kind of words each group contains (units of time, exact time, parts of the day, different days, periods of time, frequency). Elicit this from students.
- Ask students to compare their answers in pairs before you play the audio for them to check.

Exercise 4

- Ask students to take turns to ask and to answer each question. Tell them to include their own answer to question 1 as well.
- When students have answered all the questions, ask for a show of hands for each possible answer in class, and invite some students to share their reasons with the class.

Exercise 5 🔊 1.12 audioscript page 242

- Ask students to read the task before you play the audio.
- **Monitoring learning:** Ask students to write the letter of the answer on a piece of paper and hold it up, everyone at the same time. This way you can check everyone's comprehension, not just of those students who volunteer to give an answer.

Exercise 6 🔊 1.13 audioscript page 243

- **EXAM** A2 Key for Schools, Listening, Part 5, (matching)
- Before students begin completing the exam task, ask them to brainstorm ideas in pairs or small groups for ways in which they could say the ideas in options a–e differently. Remind them that in the audio, speakers might often use different words to express the same ideas (for example, 'a running app' is a phone app that shows how fast or where a person runs), so paraphrasing is a key skill for exams. Remind students to listen for the meaning, not for the exact words that appear in the task.
- Play the audio twice. Ask students to mark the answers they are sure about the first time they listen. When you play the audio for the second time, ask them to check these answers and focus more closely on the more difficult items.
- As you check answers together, play the audio for the final time, and for each answer, ask students to try to recall the phrases the speakers used.
- **NEED SUPPORT?** Prepare copies of the photocopiable worksheet on page 232. This version of the task asks students to choose from two options to complete statements.

Exercise 7

- Read the example together, and check that students understand the task. Before students begin writing their

sentences, ask them to look back at Lessons 1.1 to 1.5 and elicit ways in which people in the texts/audio/video use technology.
- **FINISHED EARLY?** Ask students to look back at the Vocabulary box, and choose five time expressions, each from a different group, and make true sentences about themselves.
- **Independent learning:** Ask students to look back at Lesson 1.5 and make a note of one new word they learned (Exercise 3), one fact they didn't know about their partner before (Exercise 4) and one useful exam technique they used (Exercise 6).

1.6 SPEAKING

Problem-solving

Lesson aims
- Students can describe a problem, suggest solutions and respond to suggestions.

For the teacher
- Photocopiable activity: *Help! What should I do?*

For the student
- Workbook, page 12
- Extra Practice Activities: New Park video

Lead-in

Give students two minutes to brainstorm what kind of problems people might have with everyday technology. Elicit some suggestions.

Setting lesson goals: Write the word *problem-solving* on the board. Elicit an explanation for the meaning of the phrase (understanding a problem, then finding a solution for it). Then, ask students to try to predict what kind of language they will learn. Elicit some ideas, but accept all suggestions at this stage.

Exercise 1 ▶ 8 🔊 1.14

- Ask students if they remember what was happening in the video in Lesson 1.4 (Bea and Abe had a video call. Abe was packing for his trip to the UK.)
- Ask students to look at the photo but cover the dialogue. Give them a minute to discuss their ideas in pairs, before you elicit suggestions for the question. Accept any reasonable ideas.
- Play the video or audio all the way through for students to watch or listen. Check answers as a class.
- Focus on the Sounds Good! box. Ask students to find in the dialogue where speakers use each expression. Elicit or explain their meaning.

Exercise 2

- Ask students to study the Speaking box and discuss the meaning of the phrases as a class.
- Ask students to cover the dialogue, then to study the Speaking box again and try to identify who said each sentence: Bea or Abe. Ask them to check back in the text (in order: Abe, Abe, Bea, Abe, Abe, Bea, Abe, Abe, Abe, Bea), then find further examples for each heading. Elicit these in open class.

Exercise 3 🔊 1.15 audioscript page 243

- Play the audio, pausing after each problem. Ask: *What's the problem?* to get students to recall what they've heard. Give them a few moments in pairs to think of possible solutions, then elicit ideas from volunteers.
- **NEED SUPPORT?** For **less confident** students, write the following key words on the board: *app, cable, instructions, phone*. Ask students to match each key word to the speaker (1 *phone*, 2 *cable*, 3 *app*, 4 *instructions*). Then, ask them to recall what problem each speaker mentioned. Put students in pairs to brainstorm solutions, using expressions from the Speaking box.

Exercise 4

Creativity: problem-solving

This task helps students to develop their problem-solving skills. It will get them to consider and evaluate potential solutions and choose the best one. This is a valuable skill that will help students deal with issues at home, at school and in the workplace.

- Assign one of three corners of the room to the three options in the box, and the fourth corner to those who think something else should be the solution. Ask students to choose their preferred solution and stand in the assigned corner. Then, form pairs or groups of students who chose different ideas and give them two minutes to try to persuade their partner about the benefits of their choice over their partner's. Monitor the discussions, helping with any challenging language as necessary – and make sure there is a calm, constructive exchange of conflicting ideas.

Exercise 5

- Ask students to read the role play task, and check that they understand what to do. Elicit or pre-teach: *QR code (reader), keep crashing*. Also clarify that *broke* can refer to either physically breaking (e.g. having cracks or pieces falling off) or to a gadget no longer functioning. Students then do the role play. Monitor, and check that students use the appropriate expressions from the Speaking box on page 18.

Exercise 6

- Remind students of the various technology-related problems you brainstormed together at the start of the lesson. Ask students to work in pairs and choose one of the suggested solutions from Exercises 3–5 or suggest a solution of their own. Ask them to explain why they think this might be the best solution.
- **FINISHED EARLY?** Ask students to write a short description of a technology-related problem they couldn't solve, on a separate piece of paper. Remind them to include why the solutions they tried didn't work. Offer the problems to other volunteering students so they can try to come up with a better solution for next lesson. At the start of the next class, have the volunteers present the problem and their suggested solution to the class in one minute. Vote on the most creative or most effective solution.

1 Tech check

Student's Book pages 12–23

- 🎯 **Reviewing lesson goals:** Ask students to think back to their predictions about the lesson goals at the start of the class. Ask: *Did you learn what you expected to learn? Which ideas or expressions do you think will be most useful?* Then, ask students to give themselves a mark out of three for how confident they are about using this language (1 – not confident, 2 – confident but may need some help, 3 – very confident). If there are lots of 1s and 2s, find time to review and practise the language again.

1.7 WRITING

A description of your daily routine and online hobbies

Lesson aims
- Students can write a description of their daily routine and online hobbies.

For the teacher
- *Need support?* worksheet, page 232
- Photocopiable activity: *Correct connectors*

For the student
- Workbook, page 13

Lead-in

Ask students to work in pairs to describe and compare their daily routine on a normal school day and at a typical weekend. Remind them to look at Lesson 0.2 if they need support with language (Present Simple with adverbs of frequency and everyday activities).

- 🎯 **Setting lesson goals:** Books closed. Explain to students that the task at the end of the Writing lesson will be to write an article for a school website about their daily routine and online hobbies. Ask them to try to predict which verb tense they will mainly need to use, and what useful words they might need. Ask them also to say what they expect to be the most challenging thing about this task. Get students to make a note of their predictions so they can refer back to this at the end of the lesson.

Exercise 1

- Set a time limit of two minutes for students to work out their answers.
- Ask students to compare their ideas in pairs or small groups before you check the answer as a class.

Exercise 2

- Students match the focus of each paragraph. Ask them to compare their ideas in pairs before you check answers as a class.

Extra activity

- Ask: *Who is Zak?* (a teenage student in Manchester, in the UK). *Who do you think is going to read his article?* (other students). *How formal or informal is the article?* (neutral: not too formal, not too informal). *How do you know?* (possible answers: Zak writes from a personal perspective, but he isn't writing to a specific person; he doesn't use contractions or colloquial phrases, but he doesn't use very formal expressions, either.)

- 🎓 **Independent learning:** Tell students to memorise the four basic questions they must answer before they begin any writing task: *Who?* (the intended audience). *What?* (type of text). *Why?* (reason or purpose). *How?* (style and register).

Exercise 3

- Ask students to find the information in the text about Zak that completes each of the six sentences in the Writing box. Get them to compare their ideas in pairs.
- Next, ask students to complete the sentences for themselves.
- Ask them to work in pairs again, to compare their daily routine and online hobbies. Tell them to find one thing that's very similar, and one that's very different. Ask a few pairs to report back to the class about the similarities and differences.
- **NEED SUPPORT?** With **less confident** students, before they begin writing their own sentences, you could tell the class about yourself, completing each sentence.

Exercise 4

- When students have completed the Language box, ask them to compare answers in pairs before you check as a class.

Exercise 5

- Write the following questions on the board to help students: *Where do you live? What do you do on weekdays? What do you like doing in your free time? How much time do you spend online? What do you enjoy most about being online? How do you find time for what you do in real life and what you do online?*
- 🌐 **Peer learning:** When students have written their sentences, ask them to work in pairs to check each other's work, and suggest any improvements they think their partner should make. Remind them to check that any connectors are used in the way shown in Zak's article.
- **NEED SUPPORT?** Prepare copies of the photocopiable worksheet on page 232. This task asks students to choose the correct connector to complete each sentence, then to rewrite them.

Exercise 6

- Ask students to read the Writing Time box and check comprehension. Remind them to follow the instructions step-by-step to write their articles. Suggest that they tick off each stage as they have completed it, then move on to the next one in the list.
- **NEED SUPPORT?** If students do the writing task for homework, you could allow **less confident** students to focus on their online hobbies only and write a shorter text.
- **FINISHED EARLY?** Ask students to read Zak's article again and find as many similarities with their own lives as they can.
- 💬 **Giving feedback:** If you collect students' work for marking, you could reduce the amount of feedback by focusing only on some key areas. Mention two things that you really liked about the article. Avoid focusing on

correcting incorrect language beyond the student's level and focus on those elements that students are more likely to get right on a second attempt. A heavily marked piece of writing is more likely to discourage learners than to get your key points across.

- **Independent learning:** Ask students to think back to the writing task, and decide what, if anything, they found most challenging about it. Did they predict this correctly at the start of the lesson? Ask them to consider what they might try to do differently the next time they do a similar task. You could get students in pairs or small groups to exchange their ideas, and suggest possible solutions to each other.

BBC CULTURE

Screenagers

Lesson aims
- Students learn about how British and American teenagers typically use their mobile phones.

For the teacher
- Photocopiable activity: *Project worksheet: a digital presentation*

Lead-in

Books closed. Write *screenager* on the board. Ask students to work in pairs or small groups to brainstorm ideas for what the word might mean. Elicit and accept any suggestions. Ask students to open their books on pages 22–23, and check if the photos and headings confirm or contradict their ideas.

- **Setting lesson goals:** Give students half a minute to look through the lesson. Books closed, ask them to say what they think they are going to learn about. Write up their suggestions on the board. Then tell them the lesson aim, and check if any students have guessed correctly.

Exercise 1

- Ask students to describe the photo at the top of the page. You may want to do the same for the video screenshots on page 23. Ask if students think these young people are similar to or different from teenagers in their own country and explain why or how.

Exercise 2 1.20

- **Peer learning:** Write the question: *What makes you say that?* on the board. Put students in pairs. Ask them first to discuss questions 1a and 1b. When one of them has expressed an opinion, their partner should respond by asking: *What makes you say that?* This is to encourage them to think more deeply and try to find evidence (or further evidence) to support their views.
- Before students read the article and discuss questions 2a and 2b in a similar way, elicit or pre-teach: *own* (v), *keep in touch*, *ban* (v), *distraction*, *productive* and *resource* (n). Play the audio while they read the article, then ask them to discuss questions 2a and 2b.

Background note
A 2015 study in the UK compared schools that have banned the use of **mobile phones** with schools that haven't. They found that in schools with a phone ban in place, the exam scores of 16-year-old students increased by 6.4%, especially among low-performing students. Researchers believe that multitasking (using a mobile phone while completing another task) has a negative effect on learning.

However, mobile phones can also be beneficial by providing easy access to information, supplementing the lessons with digital materials and allowing students to use digital learning platforms and apps.

Exercise 3

- As you check each answer as a class, ask: *What makes you say that?* to elicit evidence from the text.

Exercise 4

- **Monitoring learning:** The focus of the activity is on fluency, so avoid error correction unless mistakes hinder understanding.

Exercise 5

- **Peer learning:** Use the Think-Pair-Share technique.

Exercise 6 9 videoscript page 243

- **With video:** Play the video. Allow students to compare ideas in pairs before you elicit the answer in open class.
- **Without video:** Print out copies of the videoscript. Ask students to read it and answer the question. When you check the answer, ask them to find evidence in the script.

Exercise 7 9 videoscript page 243

- **With video:** Play the video again. Allow students to compare ideas in pairs before you elicit the answers in open class.
- **Without video:** Ask students to read the videoscript again and do the task. Allow them to compare answers in pairs before you check as a class.

Exercise 8

- Assign one half of the classroom to YES and the other to NO. Read out each question and give students ten seconds to move to the side of the room that expresses their own opinion. Put students in pairs to discuss the questions. Wherever possible, pair up students with conflicting opinions on at least one of the questions. Remind them to use the question: *What makes you say that?* to elicit further evidence from their partner. For feedback, ask some volunteers to tell the class something interesting or unexpected that they found out about their partner.
- **PROJECT TIME** The project worksheets include step-by-step support for students. They also include teacher's notes on how to set up the projects with and without technology.
- **Independent learning:** Ask students to think back to the lesson and write down the most interesting or surprising thing they learned. Ask them to tell each other in pairs.

165

2 Wild and Beautiful

Student's Book pages 24–35

Unit contents

Vocabulary
- Word building: weather
- Weather and climate
- Adverbs of degree
- Camping
- In the wild

Grammar
- Past Simple: regular and irregular verbs
- Past Continuous and Past Simple

Speaking
- Criticising and explaining

Writing
- An article describing your local area and climate

Future skills
- Communication: understanding messages
- Self-management: self-control

Exam
- A2 Key for Schools, Reading and Writing, Part 3, (3-option multiple choice)
- International Certificate Level 1/2, Listening, Section 3, (note completion)/A2 Key for Schools, Listening, Part 2, (gap fill)

For Online Classroom, go to the Portal.

2.1 VOCABULARY

Weather and climate

Lesson aims
- Students can talk about the weather and climate.

For the teacher
- Vocabulary Memory Game
- Photocopiable activity: *What's the weather like in …?*
- Test: Vocabulary Check 2

For the student
- Workbook, pages 16–17
- Extra Practice Activities: Vocabulary

Lead-in

Books closed. Write *1 → 12* on the board. Say: *January*, then point to a student to elicit *February*. Each student should then point to another student to elicit the name of the next month. When you have reached *December*, erase the reminder, and write *A → Z* instead. Say: *April*, then elicit *August*, and so on, each month in alphabetical order until you reach *September*.

- **Setting lesson goals:** Write the following sentences on the board (making them true for your country): *July is usually hot in* [our country]. *It's cold in December.* Elicit ideas for what the focus of the lesson might be. Accept all reasonable suggestions, then ask students to look through pages 24–25 quickly to check their ideas.

Exercise 1

- Elicit or pre-teach: *sculpture*.
- **Peer learning:** Use the Think-Pair-Share technique. Also ask: *What's the connection between the two photos?*

Exercise 2

- Elicit or pre-teach: *represent, sea level, benefit, plant* (v) before students begin reading.
- Set a time limit of two minutes for students to quickly skim the text for general understanding.
- Then, suggest that they first scan the article to find the parts of the text that contain information about each question, then read these sections more closely to find the answers.
- Allow students to compare ideas with another pair before you check answers as a class.
- **Independent learning:** Encourage students to try to work out the meaning of: *climate change, temperature, cause, melt, affect, global warming, sink* (v), *roots, soil* and explain any of the more challenging words.

Exercise 3 2.1

- Read the information in Vocabulary box A as a class. Check students understand the new words. Set a time limit for students to complete the task. Then, play the audio for them to listen, repeat and check their answers. Pause after each word to check students' pronunciation.
- You can display the digital flashcards available on the Portal and ask students to repeat the words. Play a memory game. Display the digital flashcards available on the Portal in a random order and elicit the words.

Exercise 4

- Read the information in the Watch Out! box. Ask: *What's the weather like today?* and elicit an answer from a volunteer. You could write this on the board as a model. Remind students to use the correct form when they take turns to describe the weather. Students in pairs then describe two other days of the week.

Exercise 5 2.2

- Read the information in Vocabulary box B as a class. Check students understand the new words. Elicit or point out that they are all nouns. (We only use adjective forms in a similar way to those in Exercise 3 for three of the words: *breezy, showery, thundery* – but these aren't common.) Set a time limit for students to complete the task. Then, play the audio for them listen, repeat and check their answers. Pause after each word to check students' pronunciation.
- Write: *There is a light breeze today.* on the board, and highlight *There is* to show the correct structure used with the noun form.

Exercise 6 🔊 2.3 audioscript page 243
- Elicit or pre-teach: *forecast*.
- Ask students to study the gaps and decide in pairs what kind of words might complete each one, i.e. an adjective, a verb or a noun. Tell them also to look at the words before or after each gap for further clues about what kind of thing they describe. Then, ask them to look for the word in the box that fits each gap best. Play the audio for them to listen, repeat and check their answers. Pause after each word to check students' pronunciation.

Exercise 7
- 💬 **Giving feedback:** Monitor the pairwork, and check use of the correct forms of the new vocabulary from the lesson. As long as the meaning is clear, don't correct errors in the use of future forms, as these will only be covered in Unit 5. Make a note of any recurring errors, and go over them at the end of the activity with the class, ensuring anonymity.

Exercise 8 🔊 2.4 audioscript page 243
- Elicit which countries the cities are in (Poland, Spain, Turkey). Check that students know the names of the seasons by naming an appropriate month for each, and elicit what season it is in.
- Ask: *It's summer. What's the weather like in these cities?* Then, *It's winter. What's the weather like?* Accept any reasonable ideas. Then, tell students they are going to hear the forecast for a winter day. Play the audio, then elicit the answer.
- **NEED SUPPORT?** Ask **less confident** students to work together in groups of three. Each of them should choose one city and listen to its forecast, then compare what they heard together to decide on the answer.

Exercise 9 🔊 2.4 audioscript page 243
- Play the audio again, twice if necessary. Students write their answers in their notebooks. Tell them to write one word (a weather noun or adjective) or a number (a temperature) in each gap.
- **NEED SUPPORT?** Pause the audio after the forecast for each city so students have time to record their answers. **More confident** students could try to complete some of the gaps before you play the audio again. **Less confident** students could work in groups of three again – but they should each preferably choose a different city this time, if they are working with the same partners as in Exercise 8.

Exercise 10
- Assign each corner of the room to one of the seasons. Ask students to stand in the corner for their favourite season. Form pairs of students who chose opposite corners.
- Write the following prompts on the board as a grid for a table: [the name of the country] at the top, *spring, summer, autumn, winter* below it as column headings. On the left, write the following as row headings: *weather, hottest temperature, coldest temperature*.

Tell students they can use this table as a reminder for discussing the country's climate.
- Also write: *What kind of weather do you like?* so they don't forget to include this in their discussions.
- 💬 **Monitoring learning:** Ask some volunteers to report back to the class on something interesting or surprising they found out about their partner.
- **FINISHED EARLY?** Students choose three significant dates (e.g. their birthday, any major holidays, the first/last day of the school year), and write the forecast for the typical weather that day.
- 🎯 **Reviewing lesson goals:** Ask students to think back to the lesson goals and use their Traffic Light cards to show how confident they feel about the newly learned language (students show 'green' if they understand the topic, 'orange' when they need some help and 'red' when they feel they need re-teaching the language point).

2.2 GRAMMAR

Past Simple: regular and irregular verbs

Lesson aims
- Students can use the Past Simple to talk about past events.

For the teacher
- *Need support?* worksheet, page 233
- **Photocopiable activity:** *When did it happen?*
- Grammar presentation
- **Test:** Grammar Check 2

For the student
- Grammar Time, Student's Book, page 127
- Workbook, page 18
- **Extra Practice Activities:** Grammar

Lead-in

Ask: *What was the weather like yesterday?* Elicit the answer, and write it in the past tense on the board, e.g. *It was cloudy but warm.* Ask about a couple of other days in the past that students are likely to remember (e.g. the first day of the school year).
- 🎯 **Setting lesson goals:** Say and write the following on the board: *The rain <u>started</u> at twelve o'clock. It <u>didn't stop</u> until ten o'clock in the evening. The temperature <u>fell</u> eight degrees.* Highlight the past verb forms in the examples, and elicit what students think might be the focus of the lesson. Ask them to look briefly through page 26 to check their ideas.

Exercise 1
- Say five or six weather words from Lesson 2.1, and ask for a show of hands about which students enjoy that kind of weather. Make sure you include *storms* as the last item. For each word, ask a different student with their hand up to say why they like that kind of weather, and another with their hand down why they don't.

2 Wild and Beautiful

Student's Book pages 24–35

Exercise 2 🔊 2.5
- Read out the task, and check comprehension of *unusual* (not typical/normal). Play the audio as students read and locate the three pieces of information.
- **NEED SUPPORT?** To scaffold the activity for **less confident** students, write the following questions on the board: *What colour was the lightning? Where was the lightning? What kind of world record does the Catatumbo Lightning hold?*

Exercise 3
- Discuss the Grammar box with the class. Check that students understand that we often use the Past Simple with past time expressions, and also that some verbs are irregular so their past forms need to be memorised. Tell students that if there are any verbs they don't know the Past Simple form for, they can refer to the irregular verb list on page 136. Elicit that negatives and questions are formed the same way with regular or irregular verbs (*didn't* + infinitive; *Did* + subject + infinitive + ?).
- For each verb in the box, elicit and write on the board the Past Simple affirmative form, even where the text only contains a negative or question form. Highlight the regular verbs and the irregular verbs in different ways.

Exercises 4–5
- For each task, students rewrite the sentences individually, then compare answers in pairs before you check as a class.
- 💬 **Monitoring learning:** Ask students to decide which of the exercises was easier and invite a show of hands to find out. Elicit students' ideas about why one exercise might be easier than the other.

Exercise 6
- Students could complete the task as described. For feedback, elicit some sentences from volunteers.

Extra activity
As an alternative, students could make up false answers to some (but not all) of the sentences and then work in pairs to guess which of their partner's sentences are true.

Exercise 7
- Elicit what word we use to make questions in the Past Simple (*did*), and where this normally goes in a question (at the start of a *Yes/No* question; after the question word/phrase in a *Wh-*question) before students complete the task in their notebooks.
- Check that they all have the correct questions written down before you move on to Exercise 8.

Exercise 8 🔊 2.6 audioscript page 243
- For each question, students first write down sentence beginnings.
- For the second part of the task, explain that students are going to hear a radio programme where they're interviewing Mariana Fernandez, a young woman who experienced the storms in Venezuela. Play the audio in chunks, pausing after each piece of relevant information is given so students have time to record their answers. Play the audio again so they can check and confirm or correct their answers, before you check as a class.
- **NEED SUPPORT?** Prepare copies of the photocopiable worksheet on page 233. This version of the task gives students possible options to complete the answers with.

Exercise 9
- Tell the class about a storm you experienced yourself, answering the three questions, to give students a model for their own answers.
- Ask some volunteers to tell the class about what they found out about their partners.
- **FINISHED EARLY?** Ask students to write four questions with the Past Simple about the article in Exercise 2.
- 🔄 **Peer learning:** Ask: *What was the easiest thing about this lesson? Why? What was the most difficult thing? Why?* Students discuss their answers in pairs, before you wrap up as a class.

2.3 READING AND VOCABULARY

Life in a hot place

Lesson aims
- Students can understand an article about life in a hot place.

For the teacher
- *Need support?* worksheet, page 233
- Photocopiable activity: *Very good, absolutely awesome*
- Test: Vocabulary Check 2

For the student
- Workbook, page 19
- Extra Practice Activities: Vocabulary

Lead-in
Write the following on the board and ask students to put the places in order from coldest to hottest: [the students' own country], *the Sahara, the Antarctic, the Amazon jungle, Scotland, California, Alaska, Malta*. Encourage students to say why they think one place is colder/hotter than another. Accept any reasonable answers. Ask: *What other hot places on the planet do you know?*
- 🎯 **Setting lesson goals:** Ask students to look through the exercises on page 27 very quickly and try to predict how easy or difficult they are going to be. On a piece of paper, they should write down a difficulty score 1–3 for each one (1 – easy, 3 – difficult). Ask them to compare their scores with a partner, then remind them to keep this note until the end of the lesson.

Exercise 1
- Ask the question and elicit students' ideas with books closed first, then get them to compare their suggestions with those in the box.

Exercise 2
- Ask students to study the photo and read the text to get a general sense and answer the questions. Check the answers to the questions as a class.

> **Background note**
> **Death Valley** is a desert valley in the northern part of the Mojave Desert in California, in the US. It is one of the hottest places on the planet. The lowest point of North America (at 86 metres below sea level) is also in Death Valley. Death Valley has been a protected natural area since 1933, and designated a National Park since 1994.

Exercise 3
- Check comprehension of *fact* (something that's always true) and *opinion* (what some people think is true, but others might disagree). Get a different student to read out each sentence in red and ask for a show of hands to find out if students think it's a fact or an opinion. Ask a volunteer to give reasons.
- Ask students to read the text again to find more examples of facts and opinions.
- **NEED SUPPORT?** **Less confident** students could work together in pairs to find the examples. One of them looks for facts, the other for opinions.

Exercise 4 ◀)) 2.7
- **EXAM** A2 Key for Schools, Reading and Writing, Part 3, (3-option multiple choice)
- Elicit or pre-teach: *volcano crater, desert, open air, sand dune*.
- Explain that in this type of reading task the questions follow the order of information in the text. Ask students where the information about each answer can be found (for each question 1–4, in a separate paragraph). Also point out that there may often be a final question for which they need to study the whole text again (question 5).
- Remind students that only one answer for each question is true. They should study each relevant section closely and decide which statements are supported by the article, and which aren't. They should eliminate the most obviously incorrect answers first, then read again to choose from the remaining options.
- Ask students to check each other's work before you check as a class. For each answer, ask a different student to quote the evidence from the text that supports it.
- **NEED SUPPORT?** Prepare copies of the photocopiable worksheet on page 233. This version of the task reduces the number of options that students choose from.

Exercise 5 ◀)) 2.8
- Read the information in the Vocabulary box as a class. Check students understand the adjectives and understand what kind of words are missing (adverbs which say how strong the adjective is). Set a time limit for students to complete the task. Then play the audio for them to listen, repeat and check their answers. Pause after each phrase to check students' pronunciation.

Exercise 6
- When you check answers, ask students to say why each adverb is the correct one to use. Ask the rest of the class to confirm or correct each answer.

Exercise 7
- Model the task by asking a **more confident** student to choose one of the four points and give an answer. Check that they use adverbs of degree correctly. Write the example the student gave on the board, as a model.
- Give students a minute to gather their ideas, then put them in small groups to tell each other about the four prompts. You could choose to do this task as a writing or speaking task.

Exercise 8
- Give students time to write a paragraph about their area. Remind them to use the Past Simple and adverbs of degree, and to use Miguel's blog post in Exercise 2 as a model.
- **Peer learning:** Ask pairs to swap their paragraphs and check each other's work. They tell their partner two things they really liked about their writing, and, if appropriate, one thing that could be improved, suggesting a way to make this improvement.
- **FINISHED EARLY?** Ask students to cover Miguel's blog post, then try to remember what each of the adverb + adjective collocations in Exercise 5 refers to, before they read it again to check.
- **Reviewing lesson goals:** Ask students to look back at the notes they made at the start of the lesson. Were their predictions right? What turned out differently? Ask students to discuss this briefly with a partner, then ask a few volunteers to report back to the class.

2.4 GRAMMAR

Past Continuous and Past Simple

> **Lesson aims**
> - Students can use the Past Continuous and the Past Simple to talk about past events.
>
> **For the teacher**
> - Photocopiable activity: *What were they doing?*
> - Grammar presentation
> - Test: Grammar Check 2
>
> **For the student**
> - Grammar Time, Student's Book, page 127
> - Workbook, page 20
> - **Extra Practice Activities:** New Park video, Grammar, BBC Vox Pop

Lead-in

Ask students to recap the story so far. Ask: *Who's Abe/Bea/Carla/Eren?* Elicit at least one fact about each character. Ask: *What happened in the last episode?* (Bea helped Abe to install a new router.) Ask: *What happened in the episode before that?* (Abe packed his bags to leave for the UK and talked to Bea on video chat.)

2 Wild and Beautiful
Student's Book pages 24–35

- **Setting lesson goals:** Write on the board: *Abe was packing when he got the video call from Bea.* Highlight the past verb forms. Elicit what students think the lesson will focus on, then ask them to look through page 28 quickly to check their predictions.

Exercise 1 ▶ 10 🔊 2.9

- Write on the board: *What do you think happened to Abe?* Elicit students' ideas after they study the photo, with the dialogue covered. Then, ask students to close their books and play the video or audio all the way through for students to watch or listen. Check the answer as a class.
- **NEED SUPPORT?** Play the video or audio again and pause after key moments to ask **less confident** students comprehension questions, e.g. *What's the weather like outside?* (It's very windy/there's a gale.) *Why is Abe in a hurry?* (He took a cool photo, and he wants to download and check it before he posts it on his blog.) *What was the weather like then?* (It was sunny, but there were some clouds.) Elicit answers before continuing the video or audio.

Exercise 2

- Discuss the Grammar box with the class. Check if the students understand when to use the Past Continuous (to set the scene in the past; to talk about an action in progress in the past) and the Past Simple (to talk about single actions that happened in the past). Elicit how we form the Past Continuous. Students find further examples in the dialogue.
- **NEED SUPPORT?** Allow **less confident** students to work in pairs. One student could collect examples of the Past Simple, the other student, examples of the Past Continuous, then copy each other's lists.

Exercise 3

- Draw a wavy timeline on the board for the Past Continuous, then put a single mark through the line for the Past Simple. Read out one of the examples from the Grammar box while you're pointing out the relevant mark on the board.
- If necessary, do the first sentence together as a class, again using the timeline to illustrate the relationship of the tenses.
- Allow students to compare answers in pairs before you check as a class.

Exercise 4

- **Peer learning:** When students have completed the email, ask them to check each other's work in pairs, explaining any errors they find to their partners.

Extra activity

Students work in pairs to come up with the ending for the story in the email. Elicit some stories in open class, and vote on the best one.

Exercise 5 ▶ 11 videoscript page 244

- Draw the outline of a male face on the board. Check comprehension of *moustache* and *top lip* by asking a volunteer to draw these on. Also elicit or pre-teach: *sensible* (a good idea), *shave off*, *ludicrous* (very silly), *get some sun* (to enjoy the sunshine; to sunbathe), *paralysed* (used figuratively here: unable to do anything), *ferry*, *sugar cubes*.
- Play the video. Allow students to compare ideas in pairs before you check their notes as a class.

Exercise 6

- Tell the students a funny holiday story of your own (real or invented) to get them started and to provide a model.
- **Setting success criteria:** Elicit the most interesting details that students heard from their partners. Ask students to say what they think makes these details particularly enjoyable.
- **FINISHED EARLY?** Ask students to write a reply as Sara to the email from Exercise 4.
- **Reviewing lesson goals:** Ask students to think back to the lesson and indicate how confident they are about the grammar points (1. how we form the Past Continuous; 2. how we decide which past tense to use) by holding their thumb up for 'quite confident', and thumb down for 'not so confident'. Make a note to check the work of the **less confident** students.

2.5 LISTENING AND VOCABULARY

In the wild

Lesson aims
- Students can understand a conversation about outdoor activities.

For the teacher
- Vocabulary Memory Game
- *Need support?* worksheet, page 233
- **Photocopiable activity:** *Categorise and draw*

For the student
- Workbook, page 21
- **Extra Practice Activities:** Vocabulary

Lead-in

Books closed. Write *In the wild* on the board. Ask students to brainstorm ideas in pairs or small groups for what this expression might mean, and what they expect to learn about in the lesson. Elicit suggestions, then ask students to study the photos on page 29 and check their ideas.

- **Setting lesson goals:** Ask: *What activities do people do when they're outdoors?* Elicit what kind of activities students expect to hear about in the lesson. Ask them to look through the activities on page 29 to check their ideas.

Exercise 1

- Assign each half of the classroom to those who enjoy being outdoors and those who don't. Ask students to stand on the appropriate side, then form pairs from students on opposing sides.

Exercise 2 🔊 2.10 audioscript page 244

- Ask students to read the statements so they know what information to listen for. Play the audio for them to choose the correct answers. When you check answers, play the audio again, and ask students to recall what information they heard that confirmed each answer.

Exercise 3 🔊 2.11

- Read the information as a class. Check students understand the new phrases. Set a time limit for students to complete the task. Then play the audio for them to listen, repeat and check their answers. Pause after each word to check students' pronunciation. Make sure all students have recorded the correct answers as these will be needed to complete Exercise 4.

Exercise 4 🔊 2.12 audioscript page 244

- **EXAM** International Certificate Level 1/2, Listening, Section 3, (note completion)/A2 Key for Schools, Listening, Part 2, (gap fill)
- Explain that students are going to hear Poppy telling her friend Milo about her adventure holiday. Play the audio for students to complete the notes.
- **NEED SUPPORT?** Play the audio in chunks, pausing after each activity is mentioned so students have time to complete their notes. If you want to make the task more manageable for **less confident** students, you could draw attention to the first two questions in Exercise 5, and ask: *Which activities did Poppy not do?* Now students will only need to listen for the order of the five correct activities, without distractors.

Exercise 5 🔊 2.12 audioscript page 244

- Read out the questions. Ask **more confident** students to try to answer the questions from memory before they listen again to check.
- **NEED SUPPORT?** Prepare copies of the photocopiable worksheet on page 233. This version of the task asks students to match parts of the answers.

Exercise 6 🔊 2.13

- Read the information in the Vocabulary box as a class. Check students understand the new words. Set a time limit for students to complete the task. Then play the audio for them to listen, repeat and check their answers. Pause after each word to check students' pronunciation.

Exercise 7

- Do the task as a group race. Set a time limit, and check which group collected the most correct words.
- 📖 **Independent learning:** Ask students to make word cards for the new vocabulary. On one side, they should write the words for wild animals or elements of landscape, and on the other, draw or attach a picture illustrating its meaning. Students can use these word cards to practise recalling the vocabulary and to test themselves.

Exercise 8

- 💬 **Monitoring learning:** Students could write the answer for each sentence on a mini-whiteboard or a piece of paper. On the count of three, they should raise their answers all at the same time so you can check everyone's work. Make a note of any students who make more than one mistake, and provide further support for them.

Exercise 9

- Elicit some things you have learned about adventure camps in Lesson 2.5. Make notes on the board about activities and things to see/experience as prompts.
- 🤝 **Peer learning:** Once students have completed writing their paragraphs, ask for a show of hands to find out who likes/hates the idea, then pair up students with opposing views to read each other's work. Ask them to say one thing they agree with in their partner's paragraph.
- **FINISHED EARLY?** Students cover the page and try to make a list of the new words from the lesson. How many words can they remember?
- 🎯 **Reviewing lesson goals:** Ask students to use their Emoji response cards to show how confident they are with the language they learned in Lesson 2.5. Make a note to review any language that a number of students show an unhappy face for.

2.6 SPEAKING

Criticising and explaining

Lesson aims
- Students can criticise and explain when things go wrong.

For the teacher
- Photocopiable activity: *I didn't mean to …*

For the student
- Workbook, page 22
- Extra Practice Activities: New Park video, BBC Vox Pop

Lead-in

Write *apologising* on the board. Elicit phrases used for apologising from the students, and write these up on the board. Ask students in pairs to brainstorm situations in which people have to apologise. Elicit some situations.

- 🎯 **Setting lesson goals:** Write the following phrases on the board: *Why did you do that? I didn't realise … Never mind.* Elicit what students think the lesson will be about. Then, ask them to look at page 30 and check their ideas. Clarify what *criticising* (telling someone what they did wrong) and *explaining* (telling someone how or why they did something) mean.

2 Wild and Beautiful

Student's Book pages 24–35

Exercise 1 ▶12 🔊 2.14
- Ask students to study the photo and elicit who they can see in the scene (Abe and Bea) and where they are (in the garden). Give them a minute or two to brainstorm ideas about the questions before you elicit suggestions. Accept all reasonable ideas. Then play the video or the audio for students to check.
- Ask: *What did Bea ask Abe to do?* (to take the weeds out). *What did Abe do?* (He picked the flowers.)
- Elicit or explain *weeds* and *It's my fault*. Then, ask a different volunteer to explain the meaning of each phrase in the Sounds Good! box in their own words.

Exercise 2
- **Peer learning:** Use the Think-Pair-Share technique. When you elicit ideas in open class, accept all logical ideas but make sure that the fact that Bea didn't give Abe clear instructions and that Abe didn't listen carefully enough are mentioned.

Exercise 3

> **Communication: understanding messages**
>
> This task helps students to understand the importance of thoughtfully interpreting what others communicate, and how paying attention and asking clarifying questions helps us to make sure that we understand the most important points in a message.

- Ask students to find in the dialogue where Bea gives Abe instructions, then discuss why he didn't understand them properly. Ask: *Did Bea give clear instructions? Did Abe pay attention?* Elicit students' own ideas. Then, ask students to discuss the questions in Exercise 3. Elicit ideas and make notes on the board under the headings: *Clear instructions* and *Paying attention*.

Exercise 4
- Ask students to study the Speaking box and discuss the meaning of the phrases as a class. Then, draw their attention to *I didn't mean to …* and *I didn't realise …*. Ask students: *What is the difference between the two expressions?* Elicit that the first phrase focuses on what the speaker did wrong, while the second phrase explains what they think they misunderstood.
- Students work in pairs to find examples of the phrases in the dialogue.

Exercise 5 🔊 2.15
- Ask students to complete the dialogues individually, then compare answers in pairs before you play the audio for them to check their answers.
- **NEED SUPPORT?** Before you play the audio, pair **less confident** with **more confident** students and ask them to compare answers.

Exercise 6
- Ask Student A to choose one of the situations, then follow the instructions to have a conversation with Student B. Then, ask them to swap roles and choose a different situation to repeat the task.
- For feedback, get a different volunteering pair to act out their role play in front of the class for each of the three situations.

Exercise 7 ▶13 videoscript page 244
- Elicit or pre-teach: *debit card, be stuck* (somewhere), *student exchange, lecturer, lamentable, ladder, misplace, mental health hospital, locked ward, ladder, save the day*.
- Books closed. Play the video. Ask what all four speakers are talking about (problems). Elicit what problems students heard about, in their own words. Then, play the video again and ask them to do the task in Exercise 7.

Exercise 8
- **Giving feedback:** As students share their stories with each other, monitor their progress, and when you hear a student using a particularly good expression or language structure, write this on a piece of paper with a positive emoji and leave it on the student's desk. At the end, ask students who received your feedback to read out their examples.
- **FINISHED EARLY?** Ask students to imagine that they want a friend to help them with a task, and to write as clear instructions for them as they can.
- **Reviewing lesson goals:** Use the Traffic Light cards to find out how confident students feel about: 1. criticising; 2. giving explanations; 3. apologising and 4. accepting explanations and apologies. Make a note of any problem areas to review in the next lesson.

2.7 WRITING

An article describing your local area and climate

> **Lesson aims**
> - Students can write an article about their local area and climate.
>
> **For the teacher**
> - *Need support?* worksheet, page 233
> - Photocopiable activity: *Tell me anything*
>
> **For the student**
> - Workbook, page 23

Lead-in

Tell the class about the place where you grew up, its geography, climate and things to see or do. When you've finished, elicit the information students can remember from your description.

- **Setting lesson goals:** Once you've completed the Lead-in activity, ask students, with books closed: *What kind of text do you think we're going to learn to write today?* Elicit some ideas and write on the board. Then, explain that in this lesson students are going to learn to write an article about their local area and climate.

172

Exercise 1
- Lead a whole-class discussion. Encourage students to give reasons. Build up a list of arguments for and against visiting the area on the board.

Exercise 2
- When they've read the texts, ask students to discuss the questions in pairs or small groups.

Exercise 3
- Ask students to scan the article and find the relevant information about each point. Allow them to compare ideas in pairs before you check answers as a class.

Exercise 4
- Ask students to change the example sentences in the Writing box so they are true for their local area.
- **NEED SUPPORT?** More confident students can come up with their own sentences, as well.
- Elicit sentences, and ask for a show of hands to find out whether the class agrees they are true for their area.

Exercise 5
- Discuss the Language box as a class. Make sure that students notice that we use -*body* or -*one* for people, -*thing* for things, and -*where* for places. Ask students to find examples in the text. Explain that we normally use *some*- in statements to talk about one particular example, but we don't know or don't want to say exactly who, what or where. We use *any*- with the same meaning in negative sentences or questions. We use *every*- to talk about all the people, things or places in a given category.
- For the task, students could simply change the examples from the article to make them true for their own local area, or write their own.
- **NEED SUPPORT?** Prepare copies of the photocopiable worksheet on page 233. This version of the task asks students to choose the correct pronouns.

Exercise 6
- Ask students to read the Writing Time box and check comprehension. Remind them to follow the instructions step-by-step to write their articles.
- **NEED SUPPORT?** You could allow less confident students to write a shorter text of just two paragraphs.
- **FINISHED EARLY?** Ask fast finishers to check the article about Lima for the use of adjectives and try to replace them with more colourful synonyms. Using a wider variety of adjectives is a great way for students to make their writing interesting.
- **Reviewing lesson goals:** Use the Emoji response cards to find out how confident students feel about writing an article, and using indefinite pronouns. Make a note to revise any problematic areas again in a later class.

SET FOR LIFE

Keep calm and carry on

Lesson aims
- Students can keep calm when something bad happens.

Future skills
- Self-management: self-control

For the teacher
- Photocopiable activity: *Keep calm and carry on*

Lead-in
Pre-teach or elicit: *self-control*. Tell the class about a situation where you felt frustrated or upset, and you had to keep calm, to illustrate self-control. Ask students to brainstorm some further ideas for situations which require self-control, then elicit some suggestions in open class.
- **Setting lesson goals:** Write the lesson aim on the board and read it out with students. Elicit one or two examples of how one can keep calm in a difficult situation.

Self-management: self-control
Self-control is the ability to manage one's behaviour and emotions to achieve a task or to find a solution to a problem. This lesson asks students to reflect on the causes of their emotions and focuses on developing their ability to use a variety of strategies to manage their emotions.

Exercises 1–8 2.20–2.21 audioscripts pages 244–245
- Follow the instructions in the Student's Book.

Exercise 9
- Read the Useful Tips as a class. Put students in pairs or small groups to discuss the questions.

Exercise 10
- Put students in pairs and read through the steps together. Give them half a minute to agree on which situation they will discuss.
- Ask for a few volunteering pairs to act out their dialogue for the class or to play the recording they made.
- Ask the class to give their opinion of Student B's advice and Student A's actions.
- **SELF-REFLECTION** Ask students to think about the way they worked together in Exercise 10, and to discuss these questions: *How did you feel when you practised the dialogue? Did you find it easy to keep calm? How much did your partners help you to find a positive solution?* Elicit ideas and write the best ones on the board.
- **Reviewing lesson goals:** Ask students to read the lesson aim again. Then, elicit any Useful Tips that they remember. Then, ask students: *Which tip will you try to use in the future?* Ask students to share their ideas in pairs or small groups.

3 Tasty treats

Student's Book pages 36–47

Unit contents

Vocabulary
- Food
- Cooking
- Flavours
- Word building: food
- Collocations about food
- Describing food

Grammar
- Present Perfect with *ever*, *never*, *just*, *already* and *yet*
- Present Perfect with *for* and *since*
- Present Perfect and Past Simple

Speaking
- Ordering food

Writing
- An email to a friend

Future skills
- Collaboration: task management

Exam
- International Certificate Level 1/2, Reading, Section 7, (note completion)
- International Certificate Level 1/2, Listening, Section 3, (note completion)/B1 Preliminary for Schools, Listening, Part 3, (gap fill)

For Online Classroom, go to the Portal.

3.1 VOCABULARY

Food and drink

Lesson aims
- Students can talk about food and drink.

For the teacher
- Vocabulary Memory Game
- *Need support?* worksheet, page 234
- **Photocopiable activity:** *Food choices*
- **Test:** Vocabulary Check 3

For the student
- Workbook, pages 26–27
- **Extra Practice Activities:** Vocabulary

Lead-in

Ask: *What's your favourite food?* and elicit a few examples from students. Find out if there are any favourites that are particularly popular among the class and ask a volunteer to say why they think they're popular.

- **Setting lesson goals:** With books closed, tell the class they are going to learn about food and drink. Elicit some suggestions for what language or topics students expect to cover in the lesson, then ask them to check their ideas on pages 36–37.

Exercise 1

- Ask students to study the photos, then discuss their answers to the questions in pairs.

Exercise 2 3.1

- As students do the matching task, remind them that they shouldn't try to understand every word, just focus on finding enough information to decide on their answers. Play the audio to check answers.

Exercise 3 3.2

- Read the information in Vocabulary box A as a class. Elicit or pre-teach the meaning of the table headings. Check students understand the new words. Set a time limit for students to complete the task. Then, play the audio for them to listen, repeat and check their answers. Pause after each word to check students' pronunciation.

Background note

In botanical terms, **mushrooms** belong to the kingdom of fungi – a group separate from both plants and animals, although they share some characteristics of both. In cooking, though, we usually consider them vegetables.

A fruit is the edible part of a plant formed from its flowers or spores. In this sense, **peppers and chillies** are also types of fruit – although we also consider these vegetables.

Exercise 4

- Do the activity as a race. Each group scores a point for a correct word in the correct group, zero points for a correct word in the wrong group, and gets a point deducted for any word that isn't a word for a kind of food. The group with the most points wins.
- **Independent learning:** Suggest that students start a visual dictionary for any words that are easier to illustrate than to explain (e.g. words for food). They could either draw images or find pictures online and add these to their dictionary notebooks. There are many free digital tools that allow users to store text (e.g. words, definitions, example sentences) together with media files (e.g. pictures, videos).

Exercise 5

- Give students two or three minutes to complete the task and compare answers in pairs.

Extra activity

You could ask students to repeat the task, choosing the odd word again from the three that are left in each group. As the most obvious answer has already been eliminated, students will need to use their creative thinking to identify a characteristic to set this second choice apart from its group. Accept any answers that students can justify.

Exercise 6 3.3

- Elicit or pre-teach: *toppings*. Ask students to quickly read the text for general sense, then read it again more carefully to fill in the gaps. Play the audio for students to check their

answers. To check comprehension, elicit the names of the top ten toppings again – now in the correct ranking order, not in the order they are mentioned in the text.
- Ask students to compare their favourite toppings in pairs.

Extra activity

Play a game to revise food vocabulary. Say: *I went to the supermarket and I bought an apple.* Tell students that each player in turn should repeat what others have said, and add another item beginning with the next letter in the alphabet. Model this with a **more confident** student. Encourage students to help one another if they forget any of the items that have been said before or if they have difficulty thinking of an item with the next letter. Try to keep the activity going until students reach the letter *y*.

Exercise 7 3.4

- Read the information in Vocabulary box B as a class. Check students understand the new words, then play the audio for them to listen and repeat. Pause after each word to check students' pronunciation.
- Put them in pairs to discuss the questions.

Exercise 8 3.5

- Read the information in Vocabulary box C and the Watch Out! box as a class. Check students understand the new words, then play the audio for them to listen and repeat. Pause after each word to check students' pronunciation.
- Put students in pairs to brainstorm other ice cream flavours, then to say which ones they love or can't stand.
- For feedback, ask for a show of hands for each flavour in the box, and ask a different student to say why they like or dislike it.

Exercise 9 3.6 audioscript page 245

- Pre-teach: *fake*.
- Explain that students are going to hear two friends discussing ice cream flavours. Tell them they will hear six flavours mentioned and that some of the flavours have two different ingredients, like *chocolate and mint*. Play the audio. Elicit answers. Then, ask students to say which flavour the speakers called unusual, and which was not a real flavour. Play the audio again for them to check their ideas.
- **NEED SUPPORT?** Prepare copies of the photocopiable worksheet on page 234. This version of the task gives students gapped notes to complete.

Exercise 10

- Ask students to identify one food for each meal, and one as a snack, then compare their ideas in pairs. Remind them to use words from Vocabulary boxes A, B and C. Elicit some responses in open class.
- **FINISHED EARLY?** Ask students to write sentences about their dream breakfast, lunch or dinner.
- **Reviewing lesson goals:** Ask students to use their Emoji response cards to show how confident they feel about the language in each Vocabulary box. Make a note to review any of the language that several students feel less happy about in a later lesson.

3.2 GRAMMAR

Present Perfect with *ever*, *never*, *just*, *already* and *yet*

Lesson aims
- Students can use the Present Perfect to talk about experiences.

For the teacher
- **Photocopiable activity:** *Have you ever …?*
- Grammar presentation
- **Test:** Grammar Check 3

For the student
- Grammar Time, Student's Book, page 128
- Workbook, page 28
- **Extra Practice Activities:** Grammar, New Park video, BBC Vox Pop

Lead-in

Tell the class what you had for breakfast in the morning. (You can invent details if necessary to give students a good model.) Ask: *What did you have for breakfast this morning?* Get students to find someone in the class who had the same breakfast.

- **Setting lesson goals:** Write the following on the board: *I've already tried an English breakfast. Have you tried it yet? I've never had brown sauce.* Highlight the verb forms, and elicit that this tense is called the Present Perfect. Ask: *Do we use this tense to talk about the present?* (No, we use it to talk about the past.) Explain that in this lesson students will learn how to use this tense to talk about past experiences.

Exercise 1

- Elicit students' ideas for what a full English breakfast might consist of. Make a note of their suggestions on the board. Leave this up when you do Exercise 2. Also ask students to describe the typical breakfast in their country.

Background note

A **full English breakfast** usually consists of fried or scrambled eggs, sausages, bacon, baked beans, fried mushrooms and tomatoes. It's served with toast. Most people drink tea with milk to accompany their English breakfast. People don't normally eat a full fried breakfast too often.

Exercise 2 14 3.7

- Ask students to study the photo and say who they can see (Abe and Bea) and where they are (in the kitchen). Ask students to describe any further details in the photo, then elicit what they can remember about the two friends from previous episodes of the video story.
- Play the video or audio and ask students to check which of their suggestions for a full English breakfast (on the board from Exercise 1) are mentioned. Then, play the audio or video again for students to answer the first two questions. Allow them to compare ideas in pairs before you check answers as a class.

3 Tasty treats
Student's Book pages 36–47

- Ask for a show of hands to find out who likes or doesn't like Bea's breakfast. Put students with opposing views in pairs to explain their reasons to each other, then elicit some of these in open class feedback.

Exercise 3

- Discuss the Grammar box with the class. Elicit how we form the Present Perfect: *have/has* + past participle in statements, *haven't/hasn't* + past participle in negatives, *Have/Has* + subject + past participle in questions. Explain that for regular verbs the past participle form is the same as the Past Simple form, but for irregular verbs it's often different! Tell students that if there are any verbs they don't know the past participle of, they can refer to the irregular verb list on page 136.
- Point out the position of *ever, never, just* and *already* (between *have/has* and the main verb) and *yet* (at the end of the sentence).
- Explain that we use the Present Perfect to talk about past experiences generally, when we don't mention a specific time for when they happened. We also use it to talk about actions completed any time before the time of speaking. When we add *just*, we refer to actions completed shortly or immediately before the time of speaking.
- Ask students to find further examples in the dialogue.

Exercise 4

- Students make sentences and questions, then compare their answers in pairs before you check as a class.
- **NEED SUPPORT?** Before students start making sentences and questions, ask them to identify the verb in each line of prompts, then elicit its past participle and write this on the board for reference. Do the first sentence together as a class to provide **less confident** students with a model.

Exercise 5 🔊 3.8

- Follow the instructions in the Student's Book.

Extra activity

Ask students to practise acting out the dialogue in pairs.

Exercise 6 ▶ 15 videoscript page 245

- Pre-teach: *soft shell crab, appetising, cuisine.*
- Play the video, and ask students to make notes, then compare their notes in pairs to answer the questions. Elicit answers in open class.
- **NEED SUPPORT?** For **less confident** students, write the names of the dishes on the board (*bangers and mash, bánh mì, fish and chips, sashimi, shepherd's pie, sushi*), and ask students to identify which speaker mentioned them. Elicit further details they said about them.

Exercise 7

- Give students a minute to think of places where people enjoy eating out in their area. Ask them also to think of the answers to the three points in Exercise 6.
- Then put them in pairs to ask and answer each other's questions.

- 💬 **Giving feedback:** As you monitor their discussions, make a note of the most interesting ideas and good examples of the use of the Present Perfect on separate pieces of paper, and place them on students' desks as positive feedback (e.g. 'Eco-friendly dishes': interesting point; You said: 'I've never eaten a better burger in my life.': good use of grammar).
- **FINISHED EARLY?** Ask students to think of typical dishes from their country and to write short explanations to say what they are and when they are usually eaten. Encourage them to use a dictionary for any words they don't know.
- 🎯 **Reviewing lesson goals:** Ask students to look back at the exercises on the page. For each one, ask students to use their Traffic Light cards to show how confident they feel about them. Make a note of any language with several red cards shown and review it in the next lesson.

3.3 READING AND VOCABULARY

Super healthy foods

Lesson aims
- Students can understand an article about superfoods.

For the teacher
- *Need support?* worksheet, page 234
- **Photocopiable activity:** *Sugar and spice*
- **Test:** Vocabulary Check 3

For the student
- Workbook, page 29
- **Extra Practice Activities:** Vocabulary

Lead-in

Write the following questions on the board: *What's the healthiest food you've ever eaten? Why do you think it's healthy?* Give students a minute or two to discuss in pairs or small groups. Elicit some ideas in open class, inviting comments from other students.

- 🎯 **Setting lesson goals:** Write *superfoods* on the board and elicit ideas for what the word might mean. Accept any reasonable ideas. Next, write *health → healthy* and *full of sugar* on the board. Explain that students are going to read an article about superfoods, about forming adjectives from nouns and about common collocations (words that often appear together).

Exercise 1

- 👥 **Peer learning:** Use the Think-Pair-Share technique to find out which superfood students in the class like best. Ask for a show of hands for each photo.

Exercise 2 🔊 3.9

- Play the audio as students read the text to choose the correct answer. Allow them to compare ideas before you check the answer as a class.
- Elicit or pre-teach: *multitask* (v), *abstract ideas, medicine, treats* (n), *strengthen.*

Exercise 3

- **EXAM** International Certificate Level 1/2, Reading, section 7, (note completion)
- Suggest that students first find the relevant part of the article that has the information about each sentence, then study this part more closely to work out what words could complete each statement. Allow students to compare answers in pairs before you check as a class.
- **NEED SUPPORT?** Prepare copies of the photocopiable worksheet on page 234. This version of the task asks students to match the sentences with the missing information.

Exercise 4 🔊 3.10

- Follow the instructions in the Student's Book. When you check answers, remind students that adding -y is only one way of forming adjectives from nouns. (Other ways include adding the suffixes -able, -al and -ous.) Highlight the spelling changes (dropping the -e from the end of the word, and doubling the final single consonant in short words).
- **NEED SUPPORT?** Tell **less confident** students that the adjectives appear in the same order in the article. **More confident** students could cover the text and try to form the adjectives themselves before they check their answers in the text.

Exercise 5

- Suggest that students look back at the various foods they discussed in Lesson 3.1 before they begin this task. Then, put them in pairs to ask and answer questions. Monitor students' progress and keep the activity going until each student has made four or five contributions.

Exercise 6 🔊 3.11

- Go through the phrases and check understanding. Ask students to complete the task and compare ideas in pairs before you play the audio for them to check their answers. Play it again for students to listen and repeat, and practise pronunciation. Then, put students in pairs and say if the statements are true for them. For feedback, ask some students to report back on what they learned about their partner.

Exercise 7

- Ask students to make two lists of at least five or six items each. Set a time limit for this stage of the task.
- Then form groups and ask students to compare their lists with each other.
- **NEED SUPPORT?** You could allow **less confident** students to compile their lists together before they begin their discussions. You could ask **more confident** students to give reasons why they consider a certain food healthy or unhealthy.
- **FINISHED EARLY?** Ask students to look at the adjectives in Exercise 4 and think of an example of a food that each could be used to describe.
- 🎯 **Reviewing lesson goals:** With books closed, ask: *What are superfoods?* and elicit an explanation in the students' own words. Then, ask them to show how confident they feel about the vocabulary in the lesson by showing a thumb up for 'quite confident' and a thumb down for 'not very confident'.

3.4 GRAMMAR

Present Perfect with *for* and *since*; Present Perfect and Past Simple

Lesson aims
- Students can use the Present Perfect and the Past Simple to talk about experiences.

For the teacher
- *Need support?* worksheet, page 234
- **Photocopiable activity:** *She's lived here all her life*
- Grammar presentation
- Test: Grammar Check 3

For the student
- Grammar Time, Student's Book, page 128
- Workbook, page 30
- **Extra Practice Activities:** Grammar

Lead-in

Write *fruit smoothie* and *milkshake* on the board. Check comprehension by eliciting an explanation in the students' own words. Assign one half of the classroom to each drink and give the class ten seconds to choose one half. Pair up students from each half and give them two minutes to convince their partner that their choice is the better drink.

- 🎯 **Setting lesson goals:** Write on the board: *Have you ever drunk a mango smoothie? I drank a mango smoothie last summer.* Highlight the verb forms and elicit which tenses they are. Write: *I've been a language teacher since* [the year you started work]. *I've taught English for* [number of] *years*. Highlight the Present Perfect forms and *since* and *for*. Elicit what students expect the lesson will focus on, then ask them to check their ideas by looking through page 40 quickly.

Exercise 1

- 🌐 **Peer learning:** Use the Think-Pair-Share technique.

Exercise 2 🔊 3.12

- Elicit or pre-teach: *especially*, *owner*.
- Play the audio as students read the text. Then, give them a minute or two to work out the answers in pairs before you check as a class.

Exercise 3

- Quickly elicit the rules for forming the Present Perfect. Then discuss the Grammar box with the class. Check that they understand the difference between using *for* and *since* by doing the task in the Student's Book. Elicit what time phrases in each group have in common (a: specific points in time; b: periods of time).
- Also check students understand that we use the Past Simple with a specific time reference, but the Present Perfect when we talk about experiences in general, without saying when in the past they happened.

177

# 3 Tasty treats

Student's Book pages 36–47

Exercise 4
- Do the task as a race. Set a time limit. The student who finds the most correct examples wins.
- **NEED SUPPORT?** Allow **less confident** students to work in pairs.

Exercise 5
- Ask students to work individually, then to compare answers in pairs before you check as a class.
- **NEED SUPPORT?** Prepare copies of the photocopiable worksheet on page 234. This version asks students to do a gap-fill task.

Exercise 6 3.13
- Ask students to work individually, then to compare answers in pairs before you play the audio for them to check the answers.

Extra activity
Write on the board: *We've been on holiday since yesterday.* Then, write the following prompts underneath, one at a time: *not, for, last week, already, yet, ?*. For each prompt, ask students to rewrite the sentence to include the item – making any other changes as necessary. Elicit the first answer (e.g. *We haven't been on holiday since the day before yesterday.*) before you write up the next prompt.

Exercise 7
- Ask a **more confident** student to ask you the example questions in the Student's Book and give your own answers to them, to model the conversation. Then, ask students to write six questions: three in the Present Perfect about experiences (which don't all have to be about eating or drinking), and three follow-up questions in the Past Simple.
- **Monitoring learning:** Ask students to raise a hand when they have written all six questions they want to use. Then, instruct them to move on to the conversation stage. Walk around the class, listening to discussions, and make a note of any recurring errors in the use of the tenses to review with the class in a later lesson. As the focus is on fluency as much as accuracy, limit error correction to the minimum.
- **FINISHED EARLY?** Ask students to use the information in the blog post to write five true sentences about Ashley in the Present Perfect.
- **Peer learning:** Ask students to look back at the exercises on page 40 and decide which exercise was the easiest, and which was the most difficult. Ask them to compare their ideas in pairs and try to say why they found them easy/difficult.

3.5 LISTENING AND VOCABULARY

A dream cake

Lesson aims
- Students can understand people describing food.

For the teacher
- Vocabulary Memory Game
- Photocopiable activity: *Food adjectives*

For the student
- Workbook, page 31
- Extra Practice Activities: Vocabulary, BBC Vox Pop

Lead-in
Bring into class a photo of your birthday cake (or just a birthday cake photo from the internet) and show it to the students. Ask the class to describe it, and to say what they like or don't like about it. Elicit what type of cake students like best.
- **Setting lesson goals:** Write on the board: *I can understand people describing food*. Elicit students' ideas about what kind of language they expect to learn in the lesson, then ask them to check their predictions by looking through page 41.

Exercise 1
- **Peer learning:** Use the Think-Pair-Share technique. Encourage students to give reasons.

Exercise 2 3.14
- Read the information in the Vocabulary box as a class. Check students understand the new words by asking them to give examples of any food or drink they could describe using each adjective. Then, play the audio for them to listen and repeat. Pause after each word to check students' pronunciation.
- Set a time limit and ask students to add as many more adjectives to the box as they can. The student who added the most correct words wins.

Exercise 3 3.15
- Follow the instructions in the Student's Book.
- **NEED SUPPORT?** **Less confident** students could do the task in pairs.

Exercise 4 3.16 audioscript page 245
- Ask students to read the statements first, and make sure they understand them. Ask them also to try to think about which element in each statement may be the most likely to decide whether the information is correct or not. (For example, in 1, we already know that Gianni is the speaker and that he's talking about a cake, so the most likely element to focus on is *where* exactly he saw the cake.)
- Elicit or pre-teach: *car show, massive*.
- Play the audio twice, allowing time between for students to mark their answers. Check answers as a class.

Exercise 5

- Remind students that trying to predict what kind of information is missing in a gap-fill task is a useful exam skill, and that it will prepare them for Exercise 6.
- **Monitoring learning:** When students have completed the task in pairs, get feedback from the whole class by asking students to raise an open palm where they think the answer is a word, and a closed fist where it is a number.

Exercise 6 3.17 audioscript page 245

- **EXAM** International Certificate Level 1/2, Listening, Section 3, (note completion)/B1 Preliminary for Schools, Listening, Part 3, (gap fill)
- Elicit or pre-teach: *icing, filling, runner(s)-up, cost, closing date*.
- Play the audio for the first time. Remind students that the information is heard in the same order as it appears in the notes. Ask students to complete the gaps they are sure about. When they listen for the second time, tell them to check the answers they have already written, and listen more closely to work out the more difficult items.
- When students have discussed answers in pairs, check as a class. Play the audio again and pause at the relevant pieces of information.
- **Peer learning:** Before playing the audio for the second time, ask students to check each other's answers in pairs, and where they differ, ask them to try to recall together exactly what information they heard in the audio.
- **NEED SUPPORT?** You could make the task less challenging by pausing the audio on the first listening once the information about each statement is heard so **less confident** students have more time to process it.

Exercise 7 16 videoscript page 245

- Elicit or pre-teach: *crumble, crust, whipped cream, moist, layer*.
- As students watch or listen, remind them that cakes often have more than one layer or flavour, and they should make notes of all the flavours mentioned.

Exercise 8

- Play the video again or describe your own best cake experience, so students have models of describing cakes. Put students in pairs and give them three minutes to do the task.
- **FINISHED EARLY?** Ask students to think of some literary characters, and invent a special cake for them, and think of reasons why it would be appropriate for them.
- **Independent learning:** Ask students to look back at Lesson 3.5, and for each exercise on the page, give themselves a mark of 1–5 depending on how well they feel they did (1 – worst, 5 – best). Ask them to review exercises they marked 1 or 2.

3.6 SPEAKING

Ordering food

Lesson aims
- Students can order food in a café or restaurant.

For the teacher
- *Need support?* worksheet, page 234
- Photocopiable activity: *What's in it?*

For the student
- Workbook, page 32
- Extra Practice Activities: New Park video

Lead-in

Write *café, fast-food restaurant, juice bar, takeaway, restaurant* on the board. Ask students to discuss in groups how often they go out to each type of place, and what they eat or drink there.

- **Setting lesson goals:** Write *ordering food in a café or restaurant* on the board. Check that students understand. Then, ask students to use their Emoji response cards to show how confident they feel about doing this, first in their own language, then in English. Tell them they are going to learn how to do this in English.

Exercise 1

- Ask pairs to list their examples of American foods in ranking order. When you elicit answers, apply a very broad definition of what food is considered 'American'. Ask the class to vote for each suggestion and tally the votes on the board to find out about the class's favourite American food.

Exercise 2 17 3.18

- Ask students to study the photo and say who is in it (Bea, Bea's mum (Penny), Abe), and what they are doing (Bea/Penny are having a meal/ordering food. Abe is serving their food.).
- Play the video or audio while students read the dialogue and make notes of Bea's and Penny's order. Allow students to compare answers in pairs before you check answers as a class.
- Ask students to find how speakers use the phrases in the Sounds Good! box, then write the following synonyms on the board for the students to match with the phrases: *Of course.* (Sure thing.), *Wait a moment!* (Hold on!), *Of course not!* (You must be joking!).
- **NEED SUPPORT?** Play the video or audio again and pause after key moments to ask **less confident** students comprehension questions, e.g. *Are Bea and Penny going to have different starters?* (No, they're going to share.) *Why doesn't Penny want to eat a burger?* (She's vegetarian.) *Are there good vegetarian dishes on the menu?* (no, only salad and dessert). Elicit answers to these before continuing the video or audio.

3 Tasty treats

Student's Book pages 36–47

Exercise 3
- Ask students to study the Speaking box and discuss the meaning of the phrases as a class.
- Students work in pairs to find examples of the phrases in the dialogue.

Exercise 4
- When students have completed the matching task, ask them to compare ideas in pairs before you check answers as a class.
- **NEED SUPPORT?** Prepare copies of the photocopiable worksheet on page 234. This version of the task reduces the number of options students are asked to choose from.

Exercise 5

> **Collaboration: task management**
>
> This task helps students to learn how to work together more efficiently by coordinating their actions. It will highlight how breaking down more complex projects into more manageable tasks, then allocating each task to the most suitable person will ensure their success at school or in the workplace.

- Read the task together as a class.
- Ask students to brainstorm what kind of events they could be working together on (a special meal, a party, a trip, etc.) and choose an idea together.
- Ask students to go through the three points and discuss why each one is important for working together.
- Ask each group to draw up a list of 6–8 tasks to do for their chosen event.
- Ask them to discuss together and agree which of them would be most suitable for each task, and why.
- For feedback, ask each group to report back on their plan to the class, describing how they decided on the list of tasks and the distribution of tasks among the team members.

Exercise 6
- Form pairs or groups of three (no more than four). In each group, one person should play the waiter, the others should play customers, ordering at least three items each from the menu. Remind them to use phrases from the Speaking box. When they have all ordered, ask them to swap roles so someone else plays the waiter, and repeat the activity.
- For feedback, ask one or two volunteering pairs or groups to act out their dialogues in open class. Ask the rest of the class to listen carefully and make notes of what's being ordered – then elicit this at the end of the performance.
- **Setting success criteria:** Before students begin, elicit what are the most important things for speakers to include (waiter: welcoming customers, giving out the menu, checking if they're ready to order, asking about each heading in the menu; customers: responding to the waiter's questions; both: using polite expressions), and write these prompts on the board as reminders. When students have completed the task, ask them to check whether they have included all these key points in their answers.
- **FINISHED EARLY?** Ask students to write items for the menu of their imaginary café or restaurant. Encourage them to think of a theme and to include a good variety of dishes.
- **Reviewing lesson goals:** Ask students to use their Emoji response cards first to show how confident they felt about ordering food in English at the start of the lesson, and how confident they feel now. Include some more practice of this skill if the cards don't show sufficient improvement.

3.7 WRITING

An email to a friend

Lesson aims
- Students can write an email to a friend.

For the teacher
- Photocopiable activity: *Hi!*

For the student
- Workbook, page 33

Lead-in

Elicit as many different ways of keeping in touch with friends (e.g. chatting on the phone, messaging on social media, emailing, speaking to each other in person) as students can think of. Ask them to decide which of these ways is the most/least popular among their age group and why.

- **Setting lesson goals:** With books closed, elicit features of emails from students by asking: *How do you start an email? What kind of language do you use? How long is a typical email to a friend? How do you end the email? Do you sign your name, and if you do, how? What else is typical of an email to a friend?* Ask students to look through page 43 briefly and explain that you are going to practise writing an email to a friend.

Exercise 1
- Ask pairs to write a list together, then put them together with another pair to compare ideas.

Exercise 2
- When students have completed the matching exercise, check answers as a class. Then, say each word for students to repeat, to practise pronunciation.

Extra activity

To re-check comprehension, mime the actions with your hand and elicit the word for each. You could ask students to make four cards with the verbs on them and raise the correct word each time you mime one of them. Repeat a few times until all students consistently identify all four verbs.

Exercise 3
- Elicit or pre-teach: *celebrate, yummy*.
- When students have read the email, ask them to compare it with the list they wrote for Exercise 1.
- Ask students to find the following phrases in the email, then elicit their meaning in the students' own words: *I can't tell you how good it is!* (It's so good it's difficult to find words to describe it.); *I was wondering if …* (I'd like to know if …).

Exercise 4
- Before students begin, clarify that the task is to number the things 1 to 4 in the order they appear in the email, not to match them to the paragraph numbering. ('Elsie thanks her friend and comments on her friend's news' covers both paragraphs 1 and 2.)
- Ask students to compare their answers in pairs before you check as a class.

Exercises 5–6
- Make sure students understand the term *imperative*.
- Follow the instructions in the Student's Book.

Exercise 7
- Ask students to read the Writing Time box and check comprehension. Remind them to follow the instructions step-by-step to write their articles. Suggest that they tick off each stage as they complete it, then move on to the next one in the list.
- **NEED SUPPORT?** **Less confident** students could write a shorter email of just one paragraph. **More confident** students could include two recipes.
- **FINISHED EARLY?** Ask students to write a short reply to Elsie from Shannon, accepting the invitation.
- **Reviewing lesson goals:** Ask students to use the Traffic Light cards to show how confident they feel about using the following: verbs for cooking processes (Exercise 2), sequencers (Exercise 5), language for informal emails (Exercise 6), and make a note to review any problematic language in a later lesson.

BBC CULTURE

Fantastic food

Lesson aims
- Students learn about what food is popular in the UK.

For the teacher
- Photocopiable activity: *Project worksheet: a digital poster*

Lead-in
Book closed. Ask students to brainstorm examples of famous dishes from the UK in groups. Elicit suggestions and write them up on the board.
- **Setting lesson goals:** Ask: *What food do you think is most popular in the UK?* Focus attention on the examples on the board and elicit if students think they include the most popular dishes. Tell the class they are going to learn more about this in this lesson.

Exercise 1 🔊 3.23
- Ask students to describe the photo at the top of the page, but to cover the article below it. Ask: *Where do you think this kind of food originally comes from?* (the Indian subcontinent). *Why do you think it's here in this lesson?* (because Indian food is very popular in the UK).
- Ask students to discuss questions 1 and 2 in pairs, then elicit some ideas in open class, inviting comments from the rest of the class.
- Next, ask students to brainstorm ideas about questions 3 and 4 in pairs again, then elicit some suggestions, accepting any reasonable ideas.
- Finally, play the audio while students read the article to check their ideas from their previous discussion. Ask them to compare their answers to the questions with another pair before you check as a class.

> **Background note**
> **Chicken tikka masala** is a combination of the recipes for two popular dishes: chicken tikka (roasted, marinated chunks of spiced chicken) served with the creamy sauce for butter chicken. It was most likely created by a Bangladeshi chef in Britain sometime in the 1960s to cater for the tastes of his local customers. Chicken tikka masala is very popular in the UK.

Exercises 2–4
- Follow the instructions in the Student's Book.

Exercise 5 ▶ 18 videoscript page 246
- **With video:** Play the video.
- **Without video:** Ask students to read the videoscript and do the task.
- **With/Without video:** Allow students to compare answers in pairs before you check as a class.

Exercise 6
- Follow the instructions in the Student's Book.

Exercises 7–8 ▶ 19 videoscript page 246
- **With video:** For each exercise, play the video.
- **Without video:** For each exercise, ask students to read the videoscript and do the task.
- **With/Without video:** Allow students to compare answers in pairs before you check as a class.

Exercises 9–10
- Monitor the pairwork and make a note of the most interesting ideas to elicit in open class at the end of the activity.
- **PROJECT TIME** The project worksheets include step-by-step support for students. They also include teacher's notes on how to set up the projects with and without technology.
- **Peer learning:** Ask students to think back to the lesson and write down three things they learned about food in the UK. Ask them to tell each other in small groups.

4 Entertain us!

Student's Book pages 50–61

Unit contents

Vocabulary
- Types of film
- Word building: entertainment
- Film and TV
- Collocations: music
- Compound nouns

Grammar
- Comparatives and superlatives, too/(not) enough, (not) as … as
- Quantifiers

Speaking
- Talking about preferences

Writing
- A review on a blog

Future skills
- Self-management: planning
- Leadership: empowering others

Exam
- A2 Key for Schools, Reading and Writing, Part 4, (3-option multiple-choice gap fill)
- B1 Preliminary for Schools, Listening, Part 4, (3-option multiple choice)

For Online Classroom, go to the Portal.

4.1 VOCABULARY

Film and TV

Lesson aims
- Students can talk about films and television.

For the teacher
- Vocabulary Memory Game
- Photocopiable activity: *That's entertainment*
- Test: Vocabulary Check 4

For the student
- Workbook, pages 38–39
- Extra Practice Activities: Vocabulary, BBC Vox pop

Lead-in

Ask: *What's your favourite film?* Get students to compare ideas briefly in small groups, then write some examples on the board. Leave the titles on the board.

Set a time limit and ask students to work in groups to name famous films from non-English-speaking countries. The group that can name the most examples wins.

- **Setting lesson goals:** Ask students to look at the film titles listed on the board, and write the following questions on the board: *What kind of films are these? Who worked on them? Who usually watches them?* Tell students to look through pages 50–51 and find the exercises which will help them answer these questions.

Exercise 1

- Ask: *Which country do you think makes the most films each year?* Elicit suggestions. Then, write *Bollywood* on the board. Elicit what, if anything, students know about it.

Exercise 2

- Ask students to read the text and check their ideas. Then, give them two or three minutes to discuss their answers to the questions before you elicit them as a class.

Exercise 3 ◀)) 4.1

- Read Vocabulary box A as a class. Check that students understand what each type of film is by eliciting an example. Set a time limit for scanning the text for the words mentioned. Play the audio to practise pronunciation.

Exercise 4

- Do the activity as a race. Set a time limit. The student who can add the most film types wins.
- **NEED SUPPORT?** Less confident students can do this in pairs.

Extra activity

Focus on the titles on the board from the lesson Lead-in. Elicit what type of film each example is.

Exercise 5 ◀)) 4.2 audioscript page 246

- Explain that students will hear short extracts from different types of (made-up) films, and their task is to recognise the genre. Suggest that they listen to the dialogue as well as to any sound effects to find clues. Play the first extract and read the example answer, to make sure students understand the task. Elicit what clues help to decide the answer (music, dancing). Then, play the rest of the audio, pausing after each extract to give students time to write their answers.

Exercise 6 ◀)) 4.3

- Read Vocabulary box B as a class. Check students understand the new words and how the words in each row relate to each other.
- Set a time limit for students to read through the review quickly without filling in gaps to get a general sense.
- Ask students to look at each gap and decide what kind of word is missing: a verb to describe an action, a noun for a thing or activity or a noun for a person.
- When students have completed the task, play the audio for them to listen and check their answers, then say the words in the box again, and ask students to repeat them and practise pronunciation.
- **NEED SUPPORT?** Less confident students could work together in pairs to do the task. More confident students could cover Vocabulary box B and try to complete the gaps from memory.

Exercise 7 🔊 4.4
- Read Vocabulary box C as a class. Check students understand the new words. Set a time limit for students to read through the text quickly to get a general sense.
- Ask students to complete the task, then compare answers in pairs before you check as a class. Play the audio for them to listen and check their answers.
- 🎓 **Independent learning:** Elicit as many ideas as you can from students for memorising and storing new vocabulary (e.g. translations, example sentences, pictures that illustrate the meaning, spidergrams, word cards in thematic envelopes). Write these ideas up on the board. Explain that each student might find a different approach the most effective for themselves. Encourage students to experiment with the various methods.

Exercise 8
- Read through the questions as a class, and check that students understand them. Then, put students in pairs to discuss the topic. Encourage students to add reasons or examples to their answers.
- For feedback, ask some volunteers to tell the class about one of their partner's preferences or answers that surprised them.

Exercise 9 ▶ 20 videoscript page 246
- Pre-teach: *sitcom, housemates, depict, numerous*.
- Play the video and ask students to make notes.
- Ask students to compare notes in pairs before you check the answers as a class.

Exercise 10
- Give students a minute or so to think about their own answers, then put them in pairs to discuss their favourite films and TV series.
- As a variation, you could ask students to tell their partners about their favourites without giving the title of the series and see if their partner can guess them.
- 💬 **Monitoring learning:** Check that students are using the task prompts correctly and make a note of any persistent errors to go over with the class.
- **FINISHED EARLY?** Ask students to write an example for each type of film in Vocabulary box A and write one thing about each example (for example, the people who worked on it, or the story, or any awards it's won).
- 🎯 **Reviewing lesson goals:** Ask students to reflect on Lesson 4.1 and use their Emoji response cards to show how confident they feel about using the language in each Vocabulary box. Make a note to yourself about revising any challenging vocabulary if there are several unhappy emojis around the class.

4.2 GRAMMAR

Comparatives and superlatives, *too/(not) enough*, *(not) as ... as*

Lesson aims
- Students can use the comparative and superlative of adjectives to describe things.

For the teacher
- *Need support?* worksheet, page 235
- **Photocopiable activity:** *Black Widow is better than Spider-man*
- Grammar presentation
- **Test:** Grammar Check 4

For the student
- Grammar Time, Student's Book, page 129
- Workbook, page 40
- **Extra Practice Activities:** Grammar, BBC Vox Pop

Lead-in
First, tell the class about your last film experience. Ask: *What was the last film you saw? Where did you see it?* Put students in small groups to tell each other.
- 🎯 **Setting lesson goals:** Write the following sentences on the board: *TV shows are <u>better than</u> films. Science-fiction series are <u>the best</u>.* Ask for a show of hands to see who agrees. Highlight the comparative and superlative forms, and read the lesson aims from the bottom of page 52.

Exercise 1
- Read the question. Assign each half of the classroom to each alternative, and give students ten seconds to stand on the side they tend to agree with more. Pair up students with opposing views, and give them a minute to explain their reasons. Elicit some ideas in open class feedback.

Exercise 2 🔊 4.5
- Check comprehension of *3-D*. Ask: *Have you seen a 3-D film? Did you like it?* Elicit answers from volunteers. Then elicit ideas for what *4-D* means. Accept any reasonable suggestions.
- Then, play the audio as students read the text and choose the correct options.

Background note
3-D films create an illusion of spatial three-dimensionality, usually with the help of special glasses worn by the audience. They trick the brain into believing the eyes are viewing the image from slightly different angles – creating the illusion of space. The technology was invented in 1915, but 3-D films first became popular in the 1950s, then enjoyed a second period of popularity in the 2000s and 2010s.

4-D is a marketing term for films that combine 3-D presentation with physical effects for a more immersive experience.

4 Entertain us!

Student's Book pages 50–61

Exercise 3
- Discuss the Grammar box with the class. Elicit or explain that we form comparatives by adding the *-er* suffix to short adjectives or by adding *more* before longer adjectives. We use it with the preposition *than* to compare two things to each other. We can also use (*not*) *as* + base adjective + *as* to compare two things.
- We form superlatives by adding the *-est* suffix to short adjectives or by adding *most* before longer adjectives. We usually use it with the definite article to say which thing stands out from a given point of view from a particular category (e.g. *the best film in the 2020s*).
- Point out the spelling rules (doubling of the final single consonant in short adjectives, dropping the final *-e*, and replacing the final *-y* with *-i* before adding the *-er/-est* suffix) and that some adjectives have irregular comparative and superlative forms (*good, better, best; bad, worse, worst*, etc.).
- Check comprehension of *too* + adjective and (*not*) + adjective + *enough* and highlight the correct word order.
- Ask students to find further examples in the article.

Extra activity
Play a game to practise comparatives and superlatives. Ask students to stand. Throw a ball to a student and say an adjective. They have five seconds to respond with its comparative form, then to throw the ball to another student to do the same with the superlative, then to start a new round by saying an adjective. Any student who completed their task can sit down. Continue playing until all the students are seated.

Exercise 4
- Elicit what preposition we use with comparatives (*than*). Suggest that students look for this preposition to decide which sentences require the comparative form.
- Ask students to compare answers in pairs before you check as a class.

Exercise 5
- Read the example together and check that the task is clear. Remind students that in some cases they might need to use different words, not just different forms of the words from the first sentence, to express the same idea.
- **NEED SUPPORT?** Before students begin the task, ask them to find the adjective in the first sentence in each pair, and elicit its base, comparative and superlative forms. Also elicit the opposite of each adjective – when eliciting the opposite of *boring*, guide students towards *interesting*. Record these on the board.
- **NEED SUPPORT?** Prepare copies of the photocopiable worksheet on page 235. This version of the task gives students possible options to choose from.

Exercise 6 ▶ 21 videoscript page 247
- Tell students the speakers will compare three pairs of things.
- First, play through the whole video and elicit which pairs of things are compared, and how many speakers give their opinions (theatre and cinema, 4; comedies and documentaries, 2; books and films, 1). Then, play the video again and ask students to make notes on which thing each speaker prefers and what reason they give for their opinion.
- Ask students to compare answers in pairs before you check them as a class.

Exercise 7
- Give students enough time to think about and write their six sentences. As they're working, monitor their progress, and provide help to students who need it.

Extra activity
Ask students to mingle, and for each of their preferences, find someone in the class who agrees with it, then to briefly discuss whether they mentioned the same reasons. Get some students to report back on those who shared their preferences.
- **FINISHED EARLY?** Ask students to look back at the types of films on page 51 and write six sentences comparing three pairs of film genres, using the comparative forms or (*not*) *as … as*.
- **Reviewing lesson goals:** Read out the target language structures: 1. comparatives; 2. superlatives; 3. (*not*) *as … as*; 4. *too*; 5. (*not*) *enough* – and ask students to raise their hand with the thumb up if they're reasonably confident about using it, or with the thumb down if they need more help. Make a note to revise any problematic areas in a later lesson as necessary.

4.3 READING AND VOCABULARY

How do you listen to music?

> **Lesson aims**
> - Students can understand a post on a music blog.
>
> **For the teacher**
> - *Need support?* worksheet, page 235
> - Photocopiable activity: *She's a star*
> - Test: Vocabulary Check 4
>
> **For the student**
> - Workbook, page 41
> - Extra Practice Activities: Vocabulary

Lead-in

Ask: *What's the best way to listen to music?* Elicit as many ideas for possible answers as students can think of.
- **Setting lesson goals:** Ask: *Do you read any music blogs? What do bloggers write about?* and elicit some ideas from students. Then, write the lesson aim on the board.

Exercise 1
- **Peer learning:** Use the Think-Pair-Share technique.

Exercise 2
- Set a time limit to encourage students to skim the text rather than read for details. Tell them also to ignore the gaps for now.

Exercise 3 🔊 4.6

- **EXAM** A2 Key for Schools, Reading and Writing, Part 4, (3-option multiple-choice gap fill)
- Ask students to cover the options in Exercise 3 and to read through the text again, looking more carefully at the parts of the text before and after each gap. Ask them to think about what might logically complete each gapped sentence before looking at the options provided and choosing the one that best matches their own idea.
- Do the first gap together as a class. Suggest that students go through all the gaps the same way.
- Remind them to read through the completed text again to make sure that each option they have chosen fits the sentence both logically and grammatically.
- Play the audio for students to listen and check their answers.

Exercise 4

- Ask students to read the blog post again and find the answers to the questions. Suggest that they think of a different way of expressing the same idea. In tasks like this, speakers often use paraphrasing – so the task involves looking for the key ideas in the questions, not the exact words. Demonstrate this with the first question. Ask students what words André uses to say *reach different people* (find a new audience).
- When you check answers, ask students to quote the relevant part of the text that supports their chosen answer.
- **NEED SUPPORT?** Prepare copies of the photocopiable worksheet on page 235. This version of the task reduces the number of options for each question.

Exercise 5 🔊 4.7

- Go through the phrases and check understanding. Ask students to complete the task and compare ideas in pairs before you play the audio for them to check their answers. Play it again for students to listen and repeat, to practise pronunciation.

Extra activity

Do a quick class survey. Ask students to write a question about each phrase in the box, then mingle around the class and speak to at least three other students to find out their answers. Ask students to report back to the class with the results to find out the most popular ways among the class to enjoy music. You could also brainstorm other ways of enjoying music (e.g. buying CDs or vinyl records, playing in a band, dancing in a music club), and include these in the survey as well.

Exercise 6

- Put students in pairs to discuss the questions. Encourage them to use the phrases from Exercise 5.
- 💬 **Monitoring learning:** Monitor students' discussions. As the focus is on fluency, limit error correction to the minimum.
- **FINISHED EARLY?** Ask students to write their own response to the blogger, using the posts from Damon, André and Carmela as models.

- 🎯 **Reviewing lesson goals:** Ask students to hold up their Traffic Light cards to show how they feel about Exercise 4. Look at the results and if there are lots of reds, find time to review the technique to do this type of exercise.

4.4 GRAMMAR

Quantifiers: *some, any, much, many, (a) few, (a) little, a lot of, lots of*

Lesson aims
- Students can talk about quantities.

For the teacher
- **Photocopiable activity:** *Similarities and differences*
- **Grammar presentation**
- **Test:** Grammar Check 4

For the student
- **Grammar Time**, Student's Book, page 129
- **Workbook**, page 42
- **Extra Practice Activities:** Grammar, New Park video

Lead-in

Ask: *Have you ever made a video or taken an interesting photo with your phone? What was in it? Who did you show it to? How/Where did you make the video or take the photo?* Elicit some responses from volunteers.

- 🎯 **Setting lesson goals:** Write: *some, a few, not any,* and *lots of* on the board. Ask: *What do we use these expressions to talk about?* (quantities). Ask students to order the expressions from the least to the most amount.

Exercise 1

- Ask students to read the poster for the Take 3 Video Challenge, then try to predict what this episode of the story will be about. Ask them to look at the photo and describe the people in it and imagine what they're doing.

Exercise 2 ▶ 22 🔊 4.8

- Play the video or the audio for students to check their predictions about the story. Ask them to work in pairs to answer the questions.

Exercise 3

- Elicit some examples of countable and uncountable nouns students are already familiar with (e.g. food words as well as *money, information, furniture, advice*). Elicit that we only use indefinite articles and plural forms with countable nouns, while uncountable nouns only have one form.
- Study the Grammar box together as a class. Ask students to study the examples in the box, and elicit what form is used after the quantifiers (countable: always plural; uncountable: always singular).
- Elicit that these quantifiers are used to express unspecified quantities. We normally use *some* in statements, and *any* in negatives and questions.

4 Entertain us!

Student's Book pages 50–61

- Ask students if there is any difference between *a lot of* and *lots of* (there isn't any difference). Ask about the difference between *few* and *a few* and *little* and *a little* (*few* and *little* mean 'a very small number' but *a few* and *a little* mean 'some').
- Compare *I've got a little money* (this has a fairly positive meaning – i.e. *I've got some money*) and *I've got little money* (this has a negative meaning – i.e. *I'm poor*).
- Ask students to find the examples in the dialogue and identify the speaker for each one.

Exercise 4 4.9
- Ask students to complete the task and compare answers in pairs before you play the audio for them to check.

Exercise 5
- Ask students to complete the task. Remind them that there may be more than one possible answer for some gaps. Ask students to compare answers in pairs before you check as a class.

Exercise 6
- Give students some time to think about the questions in Exercise 5, then put them in pairs to compare their answers to each question. Ask them to find similarities and differences. Ask a few volunteers to report back on the similarities and differences they found with their partners.
- **FINISHED EARLY?** Ask students to write a sentence with each of the quantifiers from Lesson 4.4 about films or videos they've seen, for example: *There are a lot of famous actors in Dune. Few films are as successful as Titanic.*
- **Peer learning:** Ask students to look back at the exercises on page 54, and decide which one was the easiest, and which was the most difficult. Ask them to brainstorm ideas in pairs or small groups for how they could practise getting better at the most difficult tasks.

4.5 LISTENING AND VOCABULARY

The June Festival

Lesson aims
- Students can understand an interview about a festival.

For the teacher
- *Need support?* worksheet, page 235
- Photocopiable activity: *bed + room = bedroom*

For the student
- Workbook, page 43
- Extra Practice Activities: Vocabulary

Lead-in
Write the word *festival* on the board. Elicit the names of some famous festivals from around the world and from the students' own country. Elicit also some information that students know about each festival mentioned.

- **Setting lesson goals:** Say: *Imagine you have to describe a local festival to a visitor from an English-speaking country. What kind of information do you have to tell them?* Elicit ideas. For example, when it is, where people celebrate it, what they wear, what activities they do, what food/drink is connected to the festival. Accept all relevant ideas. Ask students to look through page 55 briefly and check if the lesson will cover their suggestions.

Exercise 1
- **Peer learning:** Use the Think-Pair-Share technique. When you elicit ideas in open class, encourage students to give reasons. Ask them to say what the festival is, what it celebrates and what kind of things people do to celebrate it.

Exercise 2 4.10 audioscript page 247
- Play the audio, then elicit the answer.
- Ask further comprehension questions: *How old is Bruno?* (16). *Where was he born?* (in the USA). *What languages does Bruno speak?* (English and Portuguese).

Exercise 3 4.11 audioscript page 247
- **EXAM** B1 Preliminary for Schools, Listening, Part 4, (3-option multiple choice)
- Check that students know that *vacation* is the American English word for a *holiday*. Also elicit or pre-teach: *dress-up, fancy dress, checked* (used to describe a pattern on clothing), *freckles*.
- Before they listen, ask students to read through the questions and start thinking about what kind of information or key words they should be listening for. Remind them that the questions follow the order in which information is heard in the audio. If they can't work out the answer to a particular question, they should at least try to eliminate the option they think is incorrect and move on so they don't miss the next question. The second time they listen, they should listen more carefully to the skipped items and make their choice. Point out that in an exam, they should never leave a multiple-choice question unanswered. If they don't know the answer after they've heard the dialogue twice, then (and only then) they should guess.
- Check answers as a class.
- **NEED SUPPORT?** Prepare copies of the photocopiable worksheet on page 235. This version of the task reduces the number of options.

Background note
Festas Juninas (also known as Festas de São João) is a festival celebrated in Brazil on or around 24 June. This period signals the end of the rainy season, and people living in the countryside give thanks for the rains that make their soil fertile. The square dance tradition of quadrilha is usually accompanied by a traditional musical style called forró.

Exercise 4 🔊 4.12

- Read the information in the Vocabulary box as a class. Write the compound nouns on the board to clarify that the two words are regarded as a single noun. Form groups. Set a time limit. Accept all compound nouns that are meaningful.
- Play the audio for students to check their answers, then play it again so they can listen, repeat and practise their pronunciation paying attention to stress.

Exercise 5

- Brainstorm some ideas for events or festivals as a class. Ask students to write three or four sentences, and remind them to use the compound nouns from Exercise 4. Elicit some sentences from volunteers.
- **NEED SUPPORT?** **Less confident** students can work in pairs.

Exercise 6

- Give students half a minute to read the task and think about their own answers before you put them in pairs to discuss and agree their priorities together. Remind them to cover all seven things in the list and encourage them to give reasons for their answers. Ask them also to think what else might be important for a good festival. Monitor their progress, and once all the pairs have covered the things in the list, elicit some suggestions in open class, inviting other students to agree or disagree, saying why.
- **FINISHED EARLY?** Ask students to use the compound nouns from Exercise 4 to write sentences about things they like or don't like.
- **Reviewing lesson goals:** Ask students to read the lesson aim again. Ask them to raise their hands to show how they feel about the lesson: with the thumb up if it was fairly easy, and with the thumb down if they had difficulties. If there are lots of thumbs down, find time to review the lesson.

4.6 SPEAKING

Talking about preferences

Lesson aims
- Students can talk about preferences.

For the teacher
- Photocopiable activity: *I'd rather not*

For the student
- Workbook, page 44
- Extra Practice Activities: New Park video

Lead-in

Ask students to express their preferences for the following pairs of things: *summer or winter; in your free time: going out or staying in; streaming music or going to live events; dancing or singing; cinema or TV*. For each pair, assign one half of the classroom to one option, and the other half to the other option. Give students ten seconds to move each time. After each decision, ask students to tell the others on their side one reason for their choice.

- **Setting lesson goals:** Elicit ways that students already know to express their preferences (for example: *I like … better than …; I enjoy … but I don't enjoy …*). Explain that in this lesson you're going to practise other ways of talking about preferences.

Exercise 1

- Give students half a minute to choose two activities from the box, then mingle around the class to try to find someone who has a similar opinion to theirs. Remind them to use: *What about you?* or *What do you prefer?* to ask the other person about their preference, and to give reasons.

Exercise 2 ▶ 23 🔊 4.13

- Elicit what happened in the last episode of the story (the friends decided to enter the Take 3 Video Challenge and make a video together). Check that they remember what Bea's idea was (a character who wants to be a star but she isn't good at anything). Explain that in the current episode, the friends are filming the scene.
- Ask students to look at the photo but cover the dialogue, and brainstorm ideas in pairs about what the characters played by Eren and Carla are doing. Ask them to compare ideas with another pair before you play the video or audio for them to check their ideas.
- Ask students to find where speakers use the phrases in the Sounds Good! box and elicit their meaning.
- **NEED SUPPORT?** Play the video or audio again and pause after key moments to ask **less confident** students comprehension questions: *Who plays the character that Bea suggested last time?* (Carla). *What's the name of Carla's character?* (Gloria). *What's the name of Eren's character, and what does he do?* (Van Dixon, artist agent). *What talent does Gloria have?* (She can read Van Dixon's mind.) Elicit answers to these before continuing the video or audio.

Exercise 3

- Ask students to read the dialogue again and discuss the questions together. Elicit the answers from volunteers and ask the class to confirm or amend the answer, as necessary.

Exercise 4

> **Self-management: planning**
>
> This task helps students to develop their ability to set realistic goals and plan activities ahead of time. This is a valuable skill that will enable students to take control of whatever is needed to achieve their objectives.

- **Peer learning:** Use the Think-Pair-Share technique. For feedback, elicit ideas from volunteers for discovering one's own strengths and weaknesses.

4 Entertain us!

Student's Book pages 50–61

Exercise 5
- Ask students to study the Speaking box and discuss the meaning of the phrases as a class. Set a time limit for students to find the phrases.
- Point out that we use the two verbs in a slightly different structure: *I'd rather* is followed by the infinitive, while *I'd prefer* is followed by the *to*-infinitive.
- Students work in pairs to find Carla's reasons in the dialogue.

Exercise 6
- First, ask students to expand the prompts into questions. Allow them to compare their ideas in pairs before you check the questions they formed as a class.
- Next, ask students to discuss the questions in pairs, choosing one of the two things suggested in the brackets. Encourage them to also say why.
- For feedback, ask some volunteers to tell the class about some of their partner's preferences, quoting the reasons they have given.
- **FINISHED EARLY?** Ask students to write a mini-dialogue with two friends discussing plans for the weekend, using the phrases for talking about preferences.
- **Peer learning:** Ask students to decide what the most difficult part the lesson was for them, then brainstorm ideas together for overcoming that difficulty.

4.7 WRITING

A review on a blog

Lesson aims
- Students can write a review on a blog.

For the teacher
- *Need support?* worksheet, page 235
- Photocopiable activity: *A spectacular film*

For the student
- Workbook, page 45

Lead-in

Ask for a show of hands for the following questions: *Have you ever been to the cinema? Have you ever seen a film in 3-D? Have you ever been to a live music event? Have you ever been to the theatre?* For each question, pick one or two students to say what/who they saw.

- **Setting lesson goals:** Write *a review* on the board. Elicit the meaning (an article in a newspaper or magazine that gives an opinion about a new book, play, film, etc.). Ask: *Do you read reviews? What was the last review you read? Was it positive or negative?* Explain that in this lesson students are going to learn how to write a review of a play, film or a live performance.

Exercise 1
- You could ask a couple of volunteers to talk about their experience in open class. Alternatively, you could ask for a show of hands to find out who's seen a play or musical, then form groups for each of them to tell others about their experience.

Exercise 2
- Read out the questions, then ask students to read the review to find the relevant pieces of information. Clarify the meaning of *routine* (here: a set of movements that form part of the performance), *catchy* (pleasant to hear and easy to remember) and *particularly* (more than the others). Ask students to compare their answers in pairs before you check as a class.

Exercise 3
- Read the phrases in the Writing box together and check that students understand them. Then, set a time limit for students to find the examples in the review. Check answers as a class.

Exercise 4
- Ask students to scan for further examples of phrases to describe the performance. Allow them to compare ideas in pairs before you check answers as a class.

Exercise 5
- Read the information in the Language box together and check understanding. Explain that adjectives and adverbs are a great way of making your writing more interesting for the reader. Write the following examples on the board: *All the actors gave brilliant performances. All the actors performed brilliantly.* Highlight the adjective and adverb, then elicit or explain that we use adjectives to describe nouns, and adverbs to modify verbs, adjectives or other adverbs.
- Give students some time to find examples of adverbs in the review and say what each adverb refers to.
- Then, ask students to write four sentences about films or live performances they have seen using an adverb, and elicit some of these sentences for feedback.
- **NEED SUPPORT?** Prepare copies of the photocopiable worksheet on page 235. This task provides students with sentences to complete.

Exercise 6
- Ask students to read the Writing Time box and check comprehension. Remind them to follow the instructions step-by-step to write their reviews. Suggest that they tick off each stage as they complete it, then move on to the next one in the list.
- **NEED SUPPORT?** **Less confident** students could write a shorter text, with just one or two sentences for each point in the Writing box.

Extra activity

Put up the reviews on the board or the classroom wall for all students to read. Ask each student to pick a film or live performance reviewed by another student, and say why they would choose that to see themselves.

- **FINISHED EARLY?** Ask students to make a list of the best films, theatre performances, music events, TV shows, etc. they've ever seen, and write at least one reason why they liked them.

- **Peer learning:** With books closed, ask students to recall what information should be included in a good review, and list at least five phrases they remember from the Writing box. Ask them to work together to recall as many details from the lesson as they can, and help each other with suggestions or constructive feedback.

SET FOR LIFE

Team up!

Lesson aims
- Students can lead a team of people.

Future skills
- Leadership: empowering others

For the teacher
- Photocopiable activity: *Team Up!*

Lead-in

Ask: *Do you prefer to work on your own or as a member of a team? Why?* Use the Think-Pair-Share technique to engage all the students in the class.

- **Setting lesson goals:** Pre-teach or elicit: *leadership*. Ask students to give examples of skills or qualities that make a good leader for a team. Explain that in this lesson, you will explore the best ways to lead a team.

Leadership: empowering others

Empowering others is the ability to help others to complete their task to a high standard, while they are encouraged to make their own decisions. It is also about ensuring team members have the support they need to succeed. This lesson explores why it is important to be aware of team members' individual strengths, weaknesses and preferences, and how team leaders can support their collaboration by assigning each team member the tasks that suit them best.

Exercise 1
- Elicit or pre-teach: *charity*, *volunteer*, *raise money*.

Exercise 2
- Ask students to read the advert and email and elicit what the first task is (choosing the type of event), and what other decisions the team have to make (where to organise the event; what jobs volunteers will need to do).

Exercises 3–7   4.18–4.19 audioscript page 247
- Follow the instructions in the Student's Book.
- **NEED SUPPORT? Less confident** students could be paired up with **more confident** students who can help them complete the task.

Exercise 8
- Ask students to read the jobs list, and check understanding. Then, explain that the task is to select the most suitable person from the list of volunteers for each of the six jobs. Remind students that each volunteer should only be given one job.
- Put them in pairs to discuss the task and remind them to use the language from the Useful Phrases box. As you monitor their discussions, check that they are using the phrases correctly.
- Put pairs together with another pair to compare ideas before you elicit suggestions in open class. Ask students to explain their reasons for assigning each task to a particular person.

Exercise 9
- Read the Useful Tips as a class and check comprehension. Elicit or explain: *vote*, *spread* (something) *fairly*. Ask students to suggest any similar tips, based on their discussions in Exercise 8.
- Give students in pairs plenty of time to discuss the three questions.
- **Monitoring learning:** Monitor students' progress and encourage them to move on if they seem to get stuck on any particular question. Make a note of the most interesting ideas and elicit these at the end of the activity as feedback.

Exercise 10
- Put students in groups of four or five and read through the steps together. The exercise essentially involves role-playing the situation from the advert, email and audio on page 60.
- First, ask each group to choose a team leader. Remind them that they can vote on decisions together, but it is the team leader's responsibility to make sure every task is assigned to the person best suitable for it, and to check that the task is being completed.
- Next, ask the groups to make a list of at least as many tasks as there are students in their group.
- Students should describe their real-life skills and qualities when they decide on the best person for each task.
- Remind students to use the Useful Phrases and to follow the advice in the Useful Tips.
- Ask each group to present their plan to the class, explaining why each team member was assigned to a particular task. Set a time limit of three minutes for each group presentation.
- **SELF-REFLECTION** Ask students to think about the way they worked as a team in Exercise 10. Ask: *Did you like working in a group? Is it easier to work with others or on your own? Did your partners help you and how? Did you help your partners and how?* Invite students to share their ideas.
- **Reviewing lesson goals:** With books closed, elicit ideas from the lesson about what makes a good team leader. Ask students to decide what they found to be the most useful thing they have learned.

5 To the limit

Student's Book pages 62–73

Unit contents

Vocabulary
- Sports equipment
- Sporting events
- Sports collocations
- Fitness and training
- Word building: sport

Grammar
- Future forms: *will*, *be going to*, Present Continuous and Present Simple
- First Conditional with *if* and *unless*

Speaking
- Talking about plans

Writing
- Short messages

Future skills
- Social responsibility: ethical competence

Exam
- A2 Key for Schools, Reading and Writing, Part 2, (multiple matching)
- A2 Key for Schools, Listening, Part 3, (3-option multiple choice)

For Online Classroom, go to the Portal.

5.1 VOCABULARY

Sport

Lesson aims
- Students can talk about sports equipment and sporting events.

For the teacher
- Vocabulary Memory Game
- **Photocopiable activity:** *Sports*
- **Test:** Vocabulary Check 5

For the student
- Workbook, pages 48–49
- **Extra Practice Activities:** Vocabulary

Lead-in

Play a game. Ask the class to stand up, then throw a ball to a student. They have to name a sport in English, throw the ball to another student still standing, then sit down. If a student can't name a sport or repeats one already used, they remain standing and continue playing. Keep going until all but one students are seated.

- **Setting lesson goals:** Books closed. Write *sport* in the middle of the board. Elicit topic areas students expect to cover (e.g. types of sports, equipment, venues, events, sportspeople) and draw a spidergram with the suggestions. Get students to copy the spidergram in their notebooks. Then ask students to look through pages 62–63 quickly to see which of their ideas are mentioned.

Exercise 1

- Read the group headings, and check understanding. Then, set a time limit and do the activity as a race. The student who writes the most words in the correct groups within the timeframe wins.
- **NEED SUPPORT?** **Less confident** students can team up in pairs and do the activity together.

Exercise 2 🔊 5.1

- Read the information in Vocabulary box A as a class. Check students understand *equipment* and the new words. Ask them to do the matching task in pairs. Then, play the audio for them to listen, repeat and practise their pronunciation.
- Play a memory game. Display the digital flashcards available on the Portal in a random order and elicit the words.

Exercise 3

- First, ask students to do the quiz and compare their answers in pairs before you quickly check this in class. Then, ask them to continue working in pairs to discuss the questions from the exercise task. Ask a few volunteers to report back to the class about what they found out about their partners.

Exercise 4

- Set a time limit to encourage scanning rather than detailed reading. Allow students to compare answers in pairs before checking as a class.

Exercise 5

- Elicit or pre-teach: *spin* (v), *hurdles*, *final score*. Ask students to decide on their answers for the first two questions individually, then compare ideas in pairs, and brainstorm further examples of sporting records together. Elicit a few of these sporting records for feedback, then have the class vote on the most impressive record mentioned.

Exercise 6 🔊 5.2 audioscript page 248

- Play through the audio and elicit which sports Sandi mentions. Then, elicit which two of these are not given as examples of Olympic sports.
- **NEED SUPPORT?** Write the names of the sports mentioned in the recording on the board for **less confident** students.

Extra activity

Set a time limit and ask students to work in pairs to make a list of as many Olympic sports as they can think of. The pair with the most Olympic sports correctly listed wins.

Exercise 7 🔊 5.3

- Read the information in Vocabulary box B as a class. Check students understand the new words. Set a time limit for the gap-fill task. Then, play the audio for them

to listen and check, then again to listen and repeat the words. Check their pronunciation.
- 🎓 **Independent learning:** Ask students how they usually store new vocabulary and elicit other ways of doing this (by topic, in spidergrams, etc.). Tell students to experiment to find out what works for them.

Exercise 8 🔊 5.4
- Ask students to complete the collocations individually, then to compare answers in pairs before you play the audio for them to check their answers.

Exercise 9
- Assign each half of the classroom to the two options in question 1 and give ten seconds for students to choose a side. As much as possible, pair up students with opposing preferences. Set a time limit. Ask them to discuss the questions together.
- 🎯 **Setting success criteria:** Before they begin the task, write this answer on the board: *I prefer team sports because they're fun.* Elicit if this is a correct answer to question 1 (yes), and if it is a satisfactory answer to the person who's asking (probably not). Elicit reasons (there isn't enough detail; it isn't specific enough; it's not interesting) and stress how important it is to expand our answers by adding examples, reasons or interesting details.
- **FINISHED EARLY?** Ask students to write a paragraph with the title *My greatest sporting success*. They can write a real or an invented story.
- 🎯 **Reviewing lesson goals:** Ask students to look back at their spidergrams. Ask them to use their Emoji response cards to show how confident they feel about using the words in each Vocabulary box. Make a note to revise any problematic language.

5.2 GRAMMAR

Future forms: *will*, *be going to*, Present Continuous, Present Simple

Lesson aims
- Students can talk about plans, predictions, arrangements and timetables.

For the teacher
- **Photocopiable activity:** *Future chat*
- **Grammar presentation**
- **Test:** Grammar Check 5

For the student
- **Grammar Time, Student's Book, page 130**
- **Workbook, page 50**
- **Extra Practice Activities:** Grammar, New Park video

Lead-in
Elicit the names of the four main characters in the on-going video story (Abe, Bea, Carla, Eren). Write the following on the board: *tennis*, *fitness class*, *running*, and ask them to try to match the sports with the characters. They can use one of the activities twice. Elicit students'

ideas before revealing the answer (Bea and Carla: fitness class, Eren: tennis, Abe: running).
- 🎯 **Setting lesson goals:** Books closed. Write on the board: *China will win the most medals at the next Olympics. I'm going to join a gym this week. I'm meeting my friends at 9 to go for a walk. Your next lesson starts at 11.45.* Highlight the verb forms. Explain that all these forms are used to talk about the future. Elicit what students think the difference is between the examples, then tell them that this will be the focus of Lesson 5.2.

Exercise 1
- Put students in groups to discuss the questions. Elicit some ideas from volunteers for feedback.

Exercise 2 ▶ 24 🔊 5.5
- Ask students to look at the photo and elicit what they think is happening in the scene. Elicit or pre-teach: *train* (v), *skip* (v), *manage* (to do something), *tough*.
- Play the video or audio as students read the dialogue and find the answers to the questions. Ask them to compare ideas in pairs before you check answers as a class.
- Tell the class the speakers use two different adjectives to say that an activity is difficult, and ask them to find these (*hard*, *tough*).

Exercise 3
- Discuss the Grammar box with the class. Check or clarify: *prediction*, *decision*, *arrangement* and *timetable*. Point out that we use different verb forms to express different ideas about the future. Discuss the difference between *a plan* and *an arrangement* (an arrangement is a plan involving someone else) and explain that we use the Present Simple for timetables.
- Ask students to find all the examples in the dialogue. Elicit why a particular form is used in each case.

Exercise 4
- Ask students to complete the task individually, then check each other's answers in pairs before you check as a class.

Exercise 5 🔊 5.6
- When students have chosen their answers, ask them to check their answers in pairs before you play the audio for them to check again.

Extra activity
Ask students to work in pairs and practise role-playing the dialogue together.

Exercise 6
- Before students begin, elicit what function each sentence is aimed to fulfil (1 decision made at the moment of speaking, 2 prediction, 3 plan, 4 prediction based on things we know now, 5 arrangement, 6 timetable). Give them two or three minutes to write their sentences.

5 To the limit

Student's Book pages 62–73

- Alternatively, suggest that students make some but not all of their sentences untrue. Put them in pairs to read their sentences for their partner to guess which sentences are true or false.
- **FINISHED EARLY?** Ask students to write sentences with all four future forms about an event that they are looking forward to. Remind them to think about why a particular future form is the correct choice in each case.
- **Reviewing lesson goals:** Ask students to use their Emoji response cards to show how confident they feel about using future forms. Read out the future forms and their functions from the Grammar box, and ask students to lift the appropriate card for each one. Make a note to review any language that several students appear to be unhappy about.

5.3 READING AND VOCABULARY

Sports and hobbies

Lesson aims
- Students can understand an article about fitness and training.

For the teacher
- Vocabulary Memory Game
- *Need support?* worksheet, page 236
- **Photocopiable activity:** *Running up that hill*
- **Test:** Vocabulary Check 5

For the student
- Workbook, page 51
- **Extra Practice Activities:** Vocabulary, BBC Vox Pop

Lead-in

Set a time limit. Ask students to make a list of as many sports mentioned in the previous lessons as they can remember. Elicit the words and write them on the board. Leave this up for Exercise 1.

- **Setting lesson goals:** Remind students of their discussions at the beginning of Lesson 5.2 about ways of keeping fit. Elicit some of these ideas again. Explain that in this lesson, they are going to read about people doing different activities to keep fit.

Exercise 1
- **Peer learning:** Ask students to study the list of sports on the board from the Lead-in activity, then use the Think-Pair-Share technique to find out their ideas about the question.

Exercise 2 5.7
- Ask students to study the three photos. Ask: *What sports do they show? What do you know about these sports? How hard are they to do?* Elicit students' ideas.
- Then, play the audio for students to read the whole text to check their ideas. Elicit their responses to the questions in the book.

Background note
There are three distinct competitive gymnastic events in the Olympic Games – each of which is organised by its own, separate federation. **Artistic gymnastics** (or simply gymnastics) consists of floor, vault, uneven bars and beam for women; floor, vault, parallel bars, horizontal bar, rings and pommel horse for men. **Rhythmic gymnastics** is a women-only event, consisting of exercises with five different types of apparatus: ball, hoop, ribbon, clubs and rope. The third Olympic gymnastic event is trampolining.

Exercise 3
- **EXAM** A2 Key for Schools, Reading and Writing, Part 2, (multiple matching)
- Ask students to read the questions first, and in pairs brainstorm ways of expressing the same ideas in different words (for example: 1 *get better* → *learn new skills*). Remind them that the text often uses paraphrasing, so they should read the text for ideas, not exact words. Also remind them that this is a matching task, so the questions aren't in the same order as the information in the article. When you check answers as a class, ask students to quote the part of the text that supports their answers.
- **NEED SUPPORT?** Prepare copies of the photocopiable worksheet on page 236. This version of the task reduces the number of options to choose from.

Exercise 4 5.8
- Read the information in the Vocabulary box as a class. Check that students understand the new words. Encourage them to work out their meaning from the article. Elicit which words are nouns and which are verbs. Then, set a time limit for the sentence completion task. Play the audio for students to listen and check their answers. Then, read out the words in the box and ask students to repeat the words to practise pronunciation.

Exercise 5
- Put students in pairs to compare their answers. Ask them to change the false statements to make them true. Encourage them to add reasons or examples to their responses as well. For feedback, ask a few students to report back on any similarities or differences they identified with their partner.

Extra activity
To review the sports-related vocabulary from Unit 5, ask students to prepare 12 word cards with any words from the Vocabulary boxes on pages 62, 63 and 65. Collect the sets of word cards, and give each set to a different student. Put students in pairs to play a game. Players take turns to look at a word from their set, and without saying anything, mime it for their partner to guess. Which pair can guess each other's words the quickest?

Exercise 6 ▶ 25 videoscript page 248
- Elicit or pre-teach: *insight, large-scale, CV*. Read the task, and elicit students' ideas about what volunteers might be needed for at sporting events (e.g. directing people to their seats, giving out information, helping security services to monitor the crowd). Ask them also to say why people might be interested in volunteering and accept any valid suggestions.
- Play the video, then check answers.

Exercise 7
- Read out the example and check that the task is clear. Put students in pairs to discuss it.
- Alternatively, ask students to mingle and interview at least five other students about their preferences and reasons.
- For feedback, ask students to report back on what they found out about their partner or the other students they interviewed.
- **FINISHED EARLY?** Ask students to write a paragraph about their favourite hobby, describing their activities, and why they like it. They can use the paragraphs in Exercise 2 as a model.
- **Peer learning:** Ask students to look back at page 65 and for each exercise, give themselves a score between 1 and 5 (5 – did very well, 1 – found it too difficult), then compare their scores in pairs, and give each other advice on what to try doing differently next time to improve their scores.

5.4 GRAMMAR

First Conditional with *if* and *unless*

Lesson aims
- Students can use the First Conditional to talk about possible situations in the future.

For the teacher
- *Need support?* worksheet, page 236
- Photocopiable activity: *What if …?*
- Grammar presentation
- Test: Grammar Check 5

For the student
- Grammar Time, Student's Book, page 130
- Workbook, page 52
- Extra Practice Activities: Grammar, BBC Vox Pop

Lead-in
Books closed. Ask students if they know any popular new sports that there aren't any organised sporting events for, e.g. bungee jumping. Write their suggestions on the board. Add *slacklining* and elicit students' ideas for what this sport might involve. Accept any suggestions. Tell students they will find out more during this lesson.
- **Setting lesson goals:** Write the following sentences on the board: *If you work hard, you'll do well. If you don't train enough, you won't win.* Explain that this structure is called the First Conditional, and in this lesson they will practise using it.

Exercise 1
- Read the words in the box and check understanding. Ask students to point to the rope in the picture, then get them to stand up and mime the actions for each of the four verbs. Ask a volunteer to describe what the girl is doing in the photo. Then, ask for a show of hands to find out which students think they could do the activity. Elicit reasons from one or two students who raised their hand, as well as from those who didn't.

Exercise 2 🔊 5.9
- Play the audio as students read the text and find out the meaning of *slackline* and check their suggestions from the Lead-in.

Exercise 3
- Discuss the Grammar box with the class. Elicit that a First Conditional sentence is made up of two parts: *if* + Present Simple, *will* + infinitive.
- Then, look at the difference between *if* and *unless*. Write: *You won't pass your exams* unless *you work hard. You won't pass your exams* if *you don't work hard.* Highlight *unless* and *if*. Elicit that *unless* has the meaning *if not*, so we use *unless* in the first sentence and *if* in the second sentence.
- Ask students to find examples in the advert. Highlight the use of the comma when the *if* clause comes first, and the omission of comma when the main clause is first.

Exercise 4
- When students have completed the matching task, allow them to compare answers in pairs before you check as a class.
- **NEED SUPPORT?** Before students begin, elicit which sentence halves contain the condition (*if/unless*) clause (1, a, b, d), and which the main clause (2, 3, 4, c). This should reduce the number of possible matches.

Exercise 5 🔊 5.10
- Read the information in the box as a class. Then, ask students to complete the task, and raise a hand when they have finished. When all (or most) of the class have finished, play the audio for them to check their answers.
- **NEED SUPPORT?** Prepare copies of the photocopiable worksheet on page 236. This version of the task tests the First Conditional with a simplified task.

Exercise 6 ▶ 26 videoscript page 248
- Pre-teach: *depending* (*on*), *basically*. Explain that students will hear one person completing sentences 1 and 2, and three different people completing sentence 3.
- You could do the task orally or in writing.
- **NEED SUPPORT?** For **less confident** students, pause the video after each sentence and check the answer before moving on.

5 To the limit

Student's Book pages 62–73

Exercise 7

- Elicit what verb form students will need to use (the future form with *will*). Give them three minutes to write their own endings. Put them in pairs to compare answers. Are they similar or different? For feedback, ask a few volunteers to report back on something interesting or surprising they learned about their partners.
- **FINISHED EARLY?** Ask students to write a different beginning of their own for the four sentence endings a–d in Exercise 4. Encourage them to write about something different from the topic of slacklining.
- **Independent learning:** Books closed. Write the following prompts on the board: *if, unless, won't*. Ask students to write one First Conditional sentence with each prompt, then check if their examples are correct by looking at the Grammar box on page 66, or the more detailed Grammar Time explanations on page 130. Then, ask them to raise their hand with their thumb up if they feel confident about using the structure, and their thumb down if they don't. Make a note to revise the First Conditional if several students are reporting problems.

5.5 LISTENING AND VOCABULARY

A fascinating footballer

Lesson aims
- Students can understand a conversation about sports personalities.

For the teacher
- *Need support?* worksheet, page 236
- Photocopiable activity: *Complete the gaps*

For the student
- Workbook, page 53
- Extra Practice Activities: Vocabulary

Lead-in

Ask: *Who's the most famous sportsperson in your country? What is he/she famous for?* Use the Think-Pair-Share technique to find out students' opinions.

- **Setting lesson goals:** Ask students to recall slacklining from Lesson 5.4. Elicit the noun for the activity, the noun for the person who does it, and the verb form (*slacklining, slackliner, slackline*). Explain that in this lesson students are going to explore similar word families about the topic of sport and listen to a conversation about sports personalities.

Exercise 1

- Put students in small groups to compare their favourites. Remind them to give reasons. For feedback, elicit a few examples in open class.

Exercise 2

- Ask students first to scan the Fact Box to find the information about each statement, then study it more closely to decide whether they match or not. Allow them to compare answers in pairs before you check as a class.

- **NEED SUPPORT?** Ask further comprehension questions about the Fact Box to help **less confident** students decide about the statements, e.g. *When did the BBC Sports Personality of the Year Award start?* (1954). *How can you win the award if you're not British?* (if you live and play sport in the UK). *Who won more than once?* (Andy Murray, three times).

Exercise 3

- Ask students to brainstorm ideas in pairs or small groups. Elicit some suggestions in open class. Accept any reasonable ideas.

Exercise 4 5.11 audioscript page 248

- **EXAM** A2 Key for Schools, Listening, Part 3, (3-option multiple choice)
- Play the audio through without pausing for students to check if their ideas from Exercise 3 are mentioned. Then, ask students to read the questions to find out what information they should listen for. Remind them that the questions follow the order of information in the audio. Play the audio again for students to complete the listening task. Play the audio for a final time for students to check the answers they have already selected, and to listen more carefully for the remaining items. Remind them that they should not leave any questions unanswered. Check answers as a class.
- **NEED SUPPORT?** Prepare copies of the photocopiable worksheet on page 236. This version of the task reduces the number of options to choose from.

Exercise 5 5.12

- Read the information in the Vocabulary box as a class. Check that students understand any new words. Play the audio for them to listen and repeat the words. Check their pronunciation. Point out that the score 5–0 is read as *five-nil*. In football scores, we use *nil*, not *zero* or *nought*. Set a time limit for students to identify the type of words in the examples. Check answers as a class.

Exercise 6

- Ask students to complete the table, then to compare answers in pairs before you check as a class.
- **NEED SUPPORT?** **Less confident** students can use a dictionary to help them to complete the table.

Exercise 7 5.13

- Ask students to read the text quickly to get a general sense, then to study the gaps and decide if the missing word is a verb, a noun for an action or a noun for a person. Then, ask them to complete the gaps. Play the audio for students to check their answers.

Exercise 8

- Read the task together as a class, and check students understand what to do by asking: *How many people do you need to choose?* (three). *What are you choosing them for?* (for the Sports Personality of the Year award). Set a time limit for the discussions. Monitor groups'

progress and remind them to agree on three candidates for the imaginary award, and also to make notes of their reasons.
- Give each group two minutes to present their nominations and ask them to list the names on the board. Once all groups have presented their candidates, have a class vote on the winner.

Extra activity
Book closed. Ask students to test each other's word building skills in pairs by taking turns to say a verb or a noun from the lesson and to elicit the other forms from their partner.
- **FINISHED EARLY?** Ask students to select at least five words from Exercises 5 and 6 and to write a paragraph telling a story about a real or invented sportsperson.
- **Reviewing lesson goals:** Ask students to use their Traffic Light cards to show how confident they feel about Exercises 4, 5 and 6, and make a note to practise similar listening tasks if several students appear to have problems.

5.6 SPEAKING
Talking about plans

Lesson aims
- Students can ask and talk about plans.

For the teacher
- *Need support?* worksheet, page 236
- Photocopiable activity: *Tell me your plans*

For the student
- Workbook, page 54
- Extra Practice Activities: New Park video

Lead-in
Elicit what students remember about the video story so far. If necessary, allow them to flick through the previous lessons quickly to remind them. Don't spend more than a couple of minutes on this activity – the aim is only to refresh students' memories about the story, not to recall every detail.
- **Setting lesson goals:** Ask students to think about their plans for the coming weekend. Elicit what language they can use to talk about them (*be going to* for plans, Present Continuous for arrangements already made, *will* for decisions made at the time of speaking). Explain that in this lesson students are going to practise this language as well as other useful phrases to ask and talk about plans.

Exercise 1
- Ask students to study the photo, then to describe it and discuss the questions in pairs. Elicit some suggestions in open class for feedback.

Exercise 2 ▶ 27 ◄)) 5.14
- Pre-teach or elicit: *hang out with*. Play the video or audio for students to check their ideas. Then, set a time limit for them to do the matching task. Ask them also to find

which speaker uses each of the phrases in the Sounds Good! box (Abe, Eren). Elicit what each phrase means, and another situation where each phrase might be appropriate (e.g. *What did you do on holiday? Nothing special. We're meeting at 6 outside the cinema. Can you make it?*).
- **NEED SUPPORT?** Prepare copies of the photocopiable worksheet on page 236. This version of the task reduces the number of options to choose from.

Exercise 3

> **Social responsibility: ethical competence**
> This exercise focuses on flexibility and empathy towards the needs of others. This is a valuable skill that will help students to work and live as part of a community, and to be able to make the necessary compromises when at home, at school or in the workplace.

- Give students four minutes to discuss their experiences in pairs. Ask them to focus on the reasons why they decided to change their plans, then evaluate the reasons given. For feedback, elicit what students consider to be good reasons for changing plans, and draw up a list of these on the board.
- **NEED SUPPORT?** To help students get started, you might like to write the following suggestions on the board: *an emergency, to help a friend in trouble, to support a friend facing a challenge*. When students have discussed their own ideas, add their suggestions to this list.

Exercise 4
- Read the information in the Speaking box as a class.
- Ask students to work in pairs. Suggest that one student in each pair finds examples of asking about plans, and the other student, examples of answering and following up. Then, ask them to match the questions and responses. Check answers as a class.

Exercise 5 ◄)) 5.15
- Ask students to look through the lines of dialogue and decide which of them ask and which respond to someone asking about plans. Encourage them to try to find matching pairs, then decide on the logical order of exchanges. Allow students to compare their ideas in pairs before you play the audio for them to check.

Extra activity
Ask students to practise acting out the dialogue in pairs.

Exercise 6
- Give students a couple of minutes to think about their plans for each of the prompts and make notes for themselves. Then, put them in pairs to ask and answer questions. Remind them to use the expressions from the Speaking box.

5 To the limit

Student's Book pages 62–73

- 💬 **Giving feedback:** Monitor the pairwork and make a note of any particularly good uses of language. Write these on the board after the activity for students to copy in their notebooks.

Extra activity

Ask students to act out their mini-dialogues in pairs and use their mobile devices to record them as short videos. Ask a few volunteers to share the videos with the class. Ask the class to listen and make notes on what plans are mentioned.

Exercise 7

- Ask some volunteers to report back to the class about their partner's plans. Ask the class to listen and make notes on what plans are mentioned.
- FINISHED EARLY? Ask students to write sentences using the future forms from Lesson 5.2 and the expressions from Lesson 5.6 about their plans for the next school holiday.
- 🔄 **Peer learning:** Ask students to look back at the exercises in Lesson 5.6 and mark them according to the level of difficulty (three stars for most difficult, one star for easiest), then compare their marks with a partner, see if they agree or disagree and say why. Ask for a show of hands to find out which exercise most students found difficult, and make a note to practise more of that type of activity in later lessons.

5.7 WRITING

Short messages

> **Lesson aims**
> - Students can write a short message to thank, congratulate and make a request.
>
> **For the teacher**
> - Photocopiable activity: *Would you mind ...?*
>
> **For the student**
> - Workbook, page 55

Lead-in

Elicit the names of popular apps or social media which young people use for sending messages. Ask for a show of hands to find out which of them are the most popular.

- 🎯 **Setting lesson goals:** Books closed. Ask: *How do you greet someone you know well? How do you say thanks? How do you congratulate them on something? How do you ask them to help you or do something for you? How do you say goodbye to a friend?* It's enough to elicit just one or two responses to each function. Explain that in this lesson students are going to practise using a wider variety of ways to express these ideas.

Exercise 1

- 🔄 **Peer learning:** Remind students about your earlier discussion of apps and social media. Ask them also to think about other ways of sending messages. Then, use the Think-Pair-Share technique. Ask students to rank different ways of sending messages from fastest to slowest.

Exercise 2

- Ask students to quickly skim the three messages and elicit who Dev, Alison and Mo are writing to. Then ask them to read the texts more carefully and find the answers to the questions. Allow them to compare ideas in pairs before you check answers as a class.

Exercise 3

- Ask students to find the answers in the messages. When you check as a class, ask students to quote the relevant parts of the messages that support their answers.
- NEED SUPPORT? Allow **less confident** students to work in pairs to complete this task.

Exercise 4

- When students have found all the phrases in the texts, ask if they ever write messages in English. If students say they do, ask them which form of greeting and ending they usually use.

Extra activity

Tell students to rewrite one of the messages, using a different way of greeting, congratulating someone, thanking, making a request and ending the message, e.g. *Hi there, Well done, everyone! And thanks for all your help. Could we train together this weekend? All the best, Alison.*

Exercise 5

- Read the information in the Language box together and check understanding. Point out that each of the phrases with prepositions are followed by the *-ing* form of the verb. Set a time limit for students to find further examples.
- You could ask students to do the sentence completion task orally in pairs, or they could write first and then compare their sentences in pairs.

Exercise 6

- Ask students to read the Writing Time box and check comprehension. Remind them to follow the instructions step-by-step to write their messages. Suggest that they tick off each stage as they have completed it, then move on to the next one in the list.
- NEED SUPPORT? **Less confident** students could write one or two messages instead of three.
- FINISHED EARLY? Ask students to choose Dev's, Alison's or Mo's message and write a reply.
- 🎓 **Independent learning:** Ask students to use their Emoji response cards to report back on how confident they feel about using the target language: the five different functions in the Writing box and the structure in the Language box. Make a note of reviewing any language points several students appear to have problems with.

BBC CULTURE

Sporting tradition

> **Lesson aims**
> - Students learn about sporting traditions in Australia and in Scotland.
>
> **For the teacher**
> - Photocopiable activity: *Project worksheet: a video podcast*

Lead-in

Elicit the names of traditional sports from English-speaking countries around the world, e.g. cricket, rugby, golf, American (gridiron) football, baseball, softball, lacrosse, field hockey. Spend no more than a couple of minutes on this.

- **Setting lesson goals:** Books closed. Write *Aussie Rules* and *Highland Games* on the board. Elicit which English-speaking countries these terms might refer to, and anything students might know about each topic. Encourage them to speculate if they don't know too much. Explain that in this lesson, students will learn more about sporting traditions in Australia and in Scotland.

Exercise 1 🔊 5.19

- Ask students to describe the photo at the top of page 72. Ask: *What's happening? Which sport do you think this is? What does it remind you of?*
- **Peer learning:** Use the Think-Pair-Share technique to elicit students' ideas about question 1 and invite comments from the rest of the class.
- Then, ask them to discuss questions 2 and 3, and elicit suggestions for the country's national sport. Ask the rest of the class to agree or disagree and give reasons.
- Ask students to work in pairs for question 4.

Exercises 2–4

- Pre-teach: *commonly known, physical contact, equally popular*.
- Follow the instructions in the Student's Book.

> **Background note**
> **Association football** (soccer) is the most popular sport around the world.
> **Rugby** was first played at Rugby School in the north of England in the 1840s. Today, there are three different versions: Rugby Union, Rugby League and Rugby Sevens.
> **American and Canadian football** are popular in North America. There, players wear protective helmets and shoulder pads, as there is more physical contact.
> Australian rules for football also evolved from rugby. Finally, **Gaelic football** is yet another different sport, mainly popular in Ireland.

Exercise 5 ▶ 28 videoscript page 249

Elicit or pre-teach: *bagpipes, gather*.

- **With video:** Play the video, then ask students to compare ideas in pairs before you check answers as a class.
- **Without video:** Hand out copies of the videoscript. Ask students to find answers to the following questions: *What musical instruments are mentioned?* (bagpipes, drums). *What is the most popular event in the games?* (caber toss). *Where is the biggest Highland Games event held?* (in North Carolina, in the USA). *Why is the event important to people?* (it celebrates their Scottish identity).

Exercise 6 ▶ 28 videoscript page 249

- Ask students to try to complete the sentences from memory. Check their answers.

Exercise 7 ▶ 29 videoscript page 249

- **With video:** Play the video and elicit the answer.
- **Without video:** Hand out copies of the videoscript and ask students to find the answer.
- Write *caber* (*toss*) on the board to clarify spelling. Elicit or explain that the verb *toss* is a synonym of *throw*.

Exercise 8 ▶ 29 videoscript page 249

- Pre-teach: *unique blend, ancestors*.
- **With video:** Play the video again. Ask students to choose their answers individually, then compare ideas in pairs before you check answers as a class.
- **Without video:** Ask students to read the videoscript, and find and underline the parts of the text that support their answers. Ask them to compare ideas in pairs before you check answers as a class.
- Elicit what the 'heavy events' are (*stone shot, hammer throw* and *tossing the caber*).

Exercise 9

- Follow the instructions in the Student's Book.

Exercise 10

- **PROJECT TIME** The project worksheets include step-by-step support for students. They also include teacher's notes on how to set up the projects with and without technology.
- **Reviewing lesson goals:** Books closed. Ask students to work in pairs to test each other to see what their partner remembers about Aussie Rules football and the Highland Games. They take turns to ask their partner two questions about each topic, four in total. Remind them they can only ask questions they would be able to answer themselves. Give them a couple of minutes to think of their questions before they begin testing each other. For feedback, ask students to hold up the appropriate number of fingers for each question out of four they answered correctly.

6 Explore more

Student's Book pages 74–85

Unit contents

Vocabulary
- Types of holidays
- Going on holiday
- Holiday equipment and accommodation
- Traffic and transport
- Travel: confusing words

Grammar
- Modal verbs: *must, have to, ought to, should*
- Modal verbs: *must, could, may/might, can't*

Speaking
- Understanding a conversation

Writing
- An email about travel arrangements

Future skills
- Communication: understanding the context
- Social responsibility: environmental competence

Exam
- International Certificate Level 2, Reading, section 6, (open-ended question)
- International Certificate Level 2, Listening, section 3, (note completion)/B1 Preliminary for Schools, Listening, Part 3, (gap fill)

For Online Classroom, go to the Portal.

6.1 VOCABULARY

Holidays and travel

Lesson aims
- Students can talk about holidays and travel.

For the teacher
- Vocabulary Memory Game
- **Photocopiable activity:** *Words and definitions*
- **Test:** Vocabulary Check 6

For the student
- Workbook, pages 58–59
- **Extra Practice Activities:** Vocabulary, BBC Vox pop

Lead-in

Tell the class briefly about your last holiday. Say where you went, what kind of holiday it was, and mention one or two things you did there. Ask: *What was your last holiday like?* Put students in pairs or small groups to discuss.

- **Setting lesson goals:** Books closed. Write the following words on the board: *beach, suitcase, hotel*. Elicit their meanings and students' ideas about what topic the unit is about. Then, ask them to look through pages 74–75 quickly to check their ideas.

Exercise 1 🔊 6.1

- Read the information in Vocabulary box A as a class. Check students understand the new words. Play the audio for students to listen and repeat the phrases. Encourage students to copy the stress and intonation as well as the sounds.
- Ask students to do the matching task. Allow them to compare answers in pairs before you check as a class.

Exercise 2

- Pre-teach: *everything is included, in the sun, needn't*. Ask students to read the blog post and then discuss the question in pairs. Encourage them to give reasons when they discuss their preferences.

Exercise 3 🔊 6.2

- Read the phrases together as a class. Check students understand the phrases. Set a time limit for students to find the phrases in the blog post. Check answers and elicit in which paragraph (1–5) each phrase appears. Then ask students to choose the correct options. Play the audio for them to check their answers. When you have checked sentence 4, read the Watch Out! box together as a class before you move on.
- **NEED SUPPORT?** **Less confident** students can work together in pairs to complete the tasks.

Exercise 4 🔊 6.3

- Read the information in Vocabulary box B as a class. Check students understand the new words. Explain that *rucksack* and *backpack* have the same meaning, but the former is mainly used in British English while *backpack* is used by both British English and American English speakers. Play the audio for students to listen and repeat the words, to practise pronunciation.
- Put students in pairs to test each other on the words. Each word correctly guessed earns a point. The student with more points wins.
- **NEED SUPPORT?** You could pair up **less confident** students with a **more confident** partner, and instead of taking turns, get the **more confident** student to come up with the definition for the other student to guess.

Exercise 5 🔊 6.4 audioscript page 249

- Play the first part of the audio and do the first dialogue together as a class. Then, play the rest of the audio for students to complete the task. Pause after each dialogue so they have time to record their answers. Allow them to compare answers in pairs before you check as a class. Elicit or explain *spare (batteries)*, if necessary.

Exercise 6 🔊 6.5

- Read the information in Vocabulary box C as a class. Ask: *Which words are verbs?* (check in/check out). *Which words are nouns?* (all the others). Set a time limit for students to complete the gap-fill task. Play the audio for them to check their answers.

- 📚 **Independent learning:** Tell students that using word cards is a great way of memorising vocabulary. They should write a new word/phrase on one side, and a prompt (e.g. a definition, a picture, a gapped sentence, etc.) on the other. To practise, they look at the prompt side and try to recall the word. If they answer incorrectly, they put the card back at the bottom of the deck, and keep going until they recall all the words.

Exercise 7 ▶ 30 videoscript page 249

- Read the task and put students in pairs to brainstorm ideas for what speakers might say about each type of holiday.
- Play the video, pausing after each speaker to give students time to record their answers.
- Ask students to compare ideas in pairs before you check as a class. You may need to elicit or explain: *suntan lotion* (another word for *sun cream*), *anti-mosquito products, insects, medicine, camera* (for taking still photos), *brimmed hat, (get) sunstroke, visa, valid, cheque, all your essentials*.

Exercise 8

- Put students in pairs to exchange their travel stories.
- 💬 **Monitoring learning:** Listen to the discussions and make a note of any questions that seem to cause some students difficulties. Make a note to revise the relevant language point in a later lesson.
- **FINISHED EARLY?** Ask students to choose a total of six words from the three Vocabulary boxes and two phrases from the Word friends list, and write a paragraph in the style of the blog about a type of holiday.
- 📚 **Independent learning:** Ask students to look back at each exercise on pages 74–75 and indicate how difficult they found it by using their Emoji response cards. Make a note to revise any language that several students appear to have problems with.

6.2 GRAMMAR

Modal verbs: *must, have to, ought to, should*

Lesson aims
- Students can talk about obligation, prohibition and advice.

For the teacher
- Photocopiable activity: *Holiday advice*
- Grammar presentation
- Test: Grammar Check 6

For the student
- Grammar Time, Student's Book, page 131
- Workbook, page 60
- Extra Practice Activities: Grammar, BBC Vox Pop

Lead-in

Play a game to review the video story so far. Set a time limit for students to race to write down as many details from previous lessons as they can remember. Then, put them in pairs to check each other's answers and to find out who remembered the most about the story.

- 🎯 **Setting lesson goals:** Elicit some rules that students have to follow at their school (e.g. what time they must arrive, if they are allowed to use mobile phones). Don't worry about the use of modal verbs – this point will be covered later. Explain that in this lesson, students will learn ways to express obligation (things they have to do), prohibition (things they can't do) and advice (things that would be a good idea to do). Use the school rules elicited to give an example of each function.

Exercise 1

- Ask students to study the photo and brainstorm ideas about the question in pairs or small groups. Accept any ideas at this point.

Exercise 2 ▶ 31 🔊 6.6

- Play the video or the audio while students read the dialogue to check their ideas. Elicit the things Abe needs for his trip and write these on the board.

Exercise 3

- Discuss the Grammar box with the class. Clarify the meaning of the functional headings (*obligation, prohibition, advice*). Then explain that *must, ought to* and *should* are modal verbs. Elicit that modal verbs have only one form for all persons, and they are followed by the infinitive (without *to*). Write: *We should run.* Ask students to transform this sentence into a question and a negative and elicit that we make questions by inverting the modal verb and the subject, and negatives by adding *not* to the modal verb. Point out that *ought* is similar to *should*, but is followed by *to* (its negative and question forms are rarely used).
- Explain that *have to* is similar to *must* but it's not a model verb. Elicit that we use *has to* for the third person singular, and we need the correct form of *do* for each person as an auxiliary to make questions or negatives. Write on the board: *She has to go.* Elicit the question and negative form (*Does she have to go? She doesn't have to go.*).
- Elicit the difference between *have to/must* (it's necessary) and *mustn't* (it's not allowed). Explain that to say that something is unnecessary we use *don't have to*. Point out that *should/ought to* (it's a good idea) are used for giving advice and giving suggestions. Ask students to think of their own example with each of the verbs.
- Students find examples in the dialogue.

Exercise 4

- Follow the instructions in the Student's Book.

Exercise 5 🔊 6.7

- Ask students to read the advert quickly first to get a general sense, then read it again, and fill in the gaps. Suggest that they complete the easier gaps first, then study the relevant sentences more closely to decide on the more challenging ones. Play the audio to check answers.

199

6 Explore more

Student's Book pages 74–85

- **NEED SUPPORT?** Pair **less confident** students with **more confident** partners and allow them to discuss and decide on the answers together. Suggest that before completing the gaps, they should try to decide if the sentence with the gap expresses an obligation, a prohibition, advice or a lack of obligation.

Exercise 6 ▶ 32 videoscript page 249
- Elicit or pre-teach: *show up*, *make sure*. Clarify that both speakers will try to complete all three sentences, so students are going to hear six endings.
- Play the video and ask students to write the gist of the endings the speakers say. Pause after each sentence to allow students time to write their answers.

Extra activity
As an alternative, play the entire video, at normal speed, without pauses. Put students in groups of three to reconstruct all six endings word for word, as well as they can. Don't give them any more assistance. Finally, play the sentences again for students to check their reconstructions.

Exercise 7
- Follow the instructions in the Student's Book.
- **FINISHED EARLY?** Ask students to write sentences about travelling on foot or by bicycle. Ask them to include rules (obligations, prohibitions) and their own advice, using modal verbs from Exercise 3.
- **Peer learning:** Books closed. Write the four modal structures on the board: *must*, *have to*, *ought to*, *should*. In pairs, ask students to take turns to recall as much as they can remember about the rules for using this language. When they have finished, ask them to check their ideas in the Grammar box on page 76 or in Grammar Time on page 131.

6.3 READING AND VOCABULARY

Getting around Venice

Lesson aims
- Students can understand an article about traffic and transport.

For the teacher
- Vocabulary Memory Game
- *Need support?* worksheet, page 237
- Photocopiable activity: *Draw it!*
- Test: Vocabulary Check 6

For the student
- Workbook, page 61
- Extra Practice Activities: Vocabulary

Lead-in
Name a variety of destinations and elicit from students the best way to travel there (e.g. by air/plane, by sea/ship, by road/land/car/bus/train, on foot). For example: Las Vegas, the Antarctic, [the capital city of the students' country or of a neighbouring country], the city park, London, Istanbul,

and so on. Include Venice. Spend no more than two minutes on this activity.

- **Setting lesson goals:** Books closed. Write on the board: *getting around*. Elicit a definition for the phrase and ask students to give examples of how people get around a typical city or town. Write the lesson aim on the board and read it with students. Ask students questions to check understanding, e.g. *In what kinds of texts can you read about traffic and transport? Who usually reads these kinds of texts? What information do you expect to find in them?*

Exercise 1
- Ask students to look at the photo, then put them in pairs to describe it and discuss the questions. Elicit some answers from volunteers.

> **Background note**
> Millions of tourists visit **Venice** every year. While this is good for the tourism economy, it also causes overcrowding and pollution. Many locals are campaigning for rules to limit tourists' access to historical centres or to ban large cruise ships from entering.

Exercise 2 🔊 6.8
- Play the audio while students skim the text and identify the type of text it is.
- **Monitoring learning:** Elicit the answer by asking students to write the letter on a piece of paper, and hold it up, all at the same time.

Exercise 3
- **EXAM** International Certificate Level 2, Reading, Section 6, (open-ended question)
- Ask students to read the questions and check that they understand them. Then, ask them to scan the text to find the sentences that give information about each question. Suggest that they study these parts of the text more carefully to decide on their answer. Ask students to check answers in pairs before you check as a class.
- **NEED SUPPORT?** Prepare copies of the photocopiable worksheet on page 237. This task replaces open-ended questions with a sentence completion task.

Exercise 4 🔊 6.9
- Read the information in the Vocabulary box as a class. Check students understand the new words. Set a time limit for students to complete the gap-fill task. Play the audio for them to check their answers.

Exercise 5
- Ask students to think about how they will need to change the sentences to make them true for them, then put them in pairs to compare their answers. For feedback, ask a few volunteers to tell the class about something interesting or surprising they found out about their partners.

Extra activity

Play a game. Write these headings on the board: *Country*, *City*, *Form of transport*, *Holiday activity*. Pick a letter by closing your eyes and pointing somewhere on a random page in the book with a pencil. Give students a minute to write as many examples for each heading with that letter (e.g. *V: Venezuela, Venice, vaporetto, volleyball on the beach*) as they can. Each correct word scores a point. Repeat with other letters. The student with the highest score wins.

Exercise 6
- Students discuss in pairs. For feedback, ask a few volunteers to share their partner's experiences.

Exercise 7
- Ask students to make notes of how they think each member of their family gets or would get around in a big city.
- Form pairs and ask students to use their notes to tell each other about their families.
- **FINISHED EARLY?** Ask students to think back to the past week, ten-day period or month, and try to estimate how much time (in minutes) they spent using different ways of getting around (e.g. my parents driving me = 50 minutes, travelling by bus = 2 hours, walking = 3 hours, etc.) and write down the estimates in a table.
- **Peer learning:** Books closed. Ask students to write three true statements and a false one about traffic, transport, or about Venice, then have their partner guess which statement is false. Ask students to show how confident they feel about what they have learned today by raising their hand with the thumb up for 'confident' and the thumb down for 'not really sure'. Make a note to include more practice of reading articles if students indicate concern.

6.4 GRAMMAR

Modal verbs: *must, could, may/might, can't* (speculation)

Lesson aims
- Students can speculate about the present.

For the teacher
- *Need support?* worksheet, page 237
- Photocopiable activity: *He must be …*
- Grammar presentation
- Test: Grammar Check 6

For the student
- Grammar Time, Student's Book, page 132
- Workbook, page 62
- Extra Practice Activities: Grammar

Lead-in

Write *camping trip* on the board and ask students to brainstorm ideas in pairs about what kind of things they would need to take with them on a camping trip. Elicit all suggestions in open class.

- **Setting lesson goals:** Show students the photo on page 78 but cover the rest of the page. (Alternatively, bring into class a photo of any object that's difficult to identify, and use that for the activity.) Ask: *What do you think this is?* Accept any suggestions, no matter how far-fetched, and don't expect students to use the modal verbs they are going to cover later in the lesson. Explain that in this lesson students are going to learn ways of speculating (trying to guess something without knowing all the facts or details) about things.

Exercise 1
- If they haven't guessed yet, tell students the object is a type of tent.
- **Peer learning:** Use the Think-Pair-Share technique to elicit their ideas about the questions.

Exercise 2 🔊 6.10
- Write *advantages* and *disadvantages* as headings on the board. Play the audio while students read the blog post and comments. Ask students to brainstorm answers in pairs, then elicit them, writing each suggestion under the appropriate heading. Ask: *What other advantages or disadvantages could there be?* to elicit students' own ideas.

Exercise 3
- Discuss the Grammar box with the class. Elicit what you discussed about the form and use of modal verbs in Lesson 6.2. Ask students to study the examples and elicit or explain that we use *must* to say we are certain about something, *could*, *may* or *might* to say we think our idea is possible but we aren't completely sure, and *can't* to say that we are certain about something not being true.
- Set a time limit for students to find further examples in the texts.

Exercise 4
- Ask students to complete the task, then compare answers in pairs. When you check answers as a class, ask students to say why they chose each modal verb.

Exercise 5
- Ask students to read the first sentence in each pair and decide if the speaker is sure that something is true, sure that something isn't true or thinks that something is possible but isn't sure. This will help them decide the correct modal verb. Discuss the example together. Remind students that *may*, *might* and *could* are usually interchangeable.
- **NEED SUPPORT?** Prepare copies of the photocopiable worksheet on page 237. This version of the task provides the words to complete the sentences with.

Extra activity

Ask students to find online some photos where the object or place is difficult to recognise and bring them into class. Put them in groups to show each other their photos. Their partners should use the modal verbs in Exercise 3 to speculate and try to guess what the photos show.

201

6 Explore more

Student's Book pages 74–85

Exercise 6
- Put students in pairs and ask them to take turns to choose a place and speculate about it. Encourage them to add their own ideas to their partner's speculation before moving on to discussing the next holiday accommodation idea.

Extra activity
Ask students to choose the accommodation they'd most like to stay in, then work in pairs to tell each other about their choice and their reasons.

- **FINISHED EARLY?** Ask students to choose either the photo on page 77 or on page 91, and without reading the text on the page, write five sentences using modal verbs of speculation about the image.
- **Independent learning:** Write the target modal verbs (*must*, *may*, *might*, *could*, *can't*) on the board. Ask students to use their Emoji response cards to show how confident they feel about using this language and make a note to review the grammar if a number of students indicate problems.

6.5 LISTENING AND VOCABULARY

Jess lives the dream!

Lesson aims
- Students can understand a radio interview about travelling.

For the teacher
- *Need support?* worksheet, page 237
- Photocopiable activity: *Complete the gaps*

For the student
- Workbook, page 63
- Extra Practice Activities: Vocabulary

Lead-in

Write the word *travel* on the board. Ask students to stand, then throw a ball to one student to elicit a travel-related word or phrase beginning with A. If they can say one, then throw the ball to another student, and sit down. The next student should say a word or phrase beginning with B, then C and so on alphabetically. Students can 'pass' (miss a turn) and throw the ball to someone else for the next letter, but then they must remain standing. Continue until all students are seated or when they run out of words.

- **Setting lesson goals:** Write the lesson aim on the board and ask students if they have heard any programme on the radio about travelling. Briefly elicit a few things they remember. Also elicit ideas for what someone might talk about when being interviewed about travelling. Accept any reasonable ideas.

Exercise 1
- Elicit the modal verbs for speculation from Lesson 6.4. Then, ask students to study the picture, and, in pairs, brainstorm ideas about it. Elicit a few ideas in open class, inviting the rest of the class to agree or disagree and to say why.

Exercise 2 6.11 audioscript page 250
- Play the audio and ask students to tell each other the answer in pairs, then elicit in open class. Check comprehension by asking: *What's special about the young people who travel with Mike?* (They can't see./They're blind.)
- Elicit students' ideas about what kind of help these travellers might need.

Exercise 3 6.12 audioscript page 250
- Elicit or pre-teach: *sight*, *it depends*, *frustrating*.
- Play the audio for students to complete the task. As you check answers, play the audio again, pausing at the relevant points, and elicit the words that speakers use to express the ideas in the statements.
- **NEED SUPPORT?** To help **less confident** students, pause playback after the relevant information about each statement is heard, so they have more time to decide on their answers.

Extra activity
Prepare photocopies of the audioscript and ask students to find and underline the information about each true/false statement and to rewrite the false statements to correct them.

Exercise 4 6.12 audioscript page 250
- Ask students to read the task, and check that they understand what to do before you play the audio again. Put them in groups of three to compare ideas. Then, elicit answers in open class.
- **NEED SUPPORT?** You could form groups of three before they begin and allow **less confident** students to split up the task between them, with each student listening only for one of the three points. They could then report back to their group about their answers.

Exercise 5 6.13 audioscript page 250
- **EXAM** International Certificate Level 2, Listening, section 3, (note completion)/B1 Preliminary for Schools, Listening, Part 3, (gap fill)
- Ask students to read the text quickly. Allow them to brainstorm ideas in pairs about what kind of information they think is missing in each gap. Explain that making such predictions is also a key step in completing the listening task.
- Play the audio, and ask students to complete the text. Tell them that if they didn't hear a particular answer, they should not spend too much time trying to figure it out but move on to the next gap. Play the audio for a second time for students to check the answers they already have, and to listen more carefully for the answers to any missing items. Then, check answers as a class.
- **NEED SUPPORT?** Prepare copies of the photocopiable worksheet on page 237. This version of the task provides more support for the gap-fill task.

Exercise 6
- 🌐 **Peer learning:** Use the Think-Pair-Share technique.

Exercise 7 🔊 6.14
- Read the information in the Vocabulary box as a class. Ask students to try to explain the differences in meaning in their own words. (An *excursion* is an organised day trip to go to see something. A *journey* is the act of getting from one place to another. *Travel* (noun) is a general word often used to talk about different forms of transport. *Travel* (verb) means to go somewhere different. A *trip* is usually a holiday or a short visit somewhere. A *voyage* is a long journey by sea.) Set a time limit for students to do the task, then play the audio to check answers. Read out the words from the box, and ask students to repeat, to practise pronunciation.

Exercise 8
- Read the task and examples as a class. Check that students understand what to do. Put them in pairs, first to make a shortlist of five or six possible trips and excursions, then to discuss their advantages and disadvantages. Put two pairs together in a group of four to compare ideas and agree on which trips and excursions are the best. Elicit the top suggestions in open class, inviting students to say if they agree or disagree, and why.
- **FINISHED EARLY?** Ask students to write sentences about the best/worst, the most interesting/boring, the longest etc. excursions, journeys, trips or voyages they've ever had.
- 🎓 **Independent learning:** Ask students to look back at the lesson and use their Traffic Light cards to show how confident they feel about each exercise.

6.6 SPEAKING
Understanding a conversation

Lesson aims
- Students can clarify what they have said and ask for clarification.

For the teacher
- Photocopiable activity: *Sorry, what did you say?*

For the student
- Workbook, page 64
- Extra Practice Activities: New Park video

Lead-in
Tell the class briefly about a time when you got lost. Put students in small groups to share their stories with each other.
- 🎯 **Setting lesson goals:** Ask students: *When I say something and you don't understand, what do you do?* Elicit students' ideas (e.g. ask another student if they have heard it better; start the task and try to figure things out), and also elicit what expressions they could use. Explain that in this lesson you are going to practise ways of asking for and giving clarification. (You may need to pre-teach the word: *clarification*.)

Exercise 1
- Ask students to look at the photo. Elicit where they think Carla is, or what her problem might be (She's trying to get directions on the phone to go somewhere.). Accept any reasonable ideas. Then, read the task together. Put students in pairs to brainstorm ideas about how they find their way around a place. Elicit suggestions in open class and make notes of the relevant ideas on the board.

Exercise 2 ▶ 33 🔊 6.15
- Before you play the video or audio, ask students to read the three questions and check that they understand what information to listen for. Play the dialogue. Allow students to compare ideas before you check answers as a class. Then, ask students to look at the phrases in the Sounds Good! box, and ask them to explain in their own words in what situations these might be used.
- **NEED SUPPORT?** Play the video or audio again and pause after key moments to ask **less confident** students comprehension questions, e.g. *What is Carla doing in London?* (visiting/staying with her grandma). *Where does she invite Bea?* (to see the Hyperloop at the Transport Museum). *What transport does Bea recommend?* (the tube/underground). *Which line should Carla take?* (the Piccadilly line). Elicit answers before continuing the video or audio.

Exercise 3
- Put students in pairs to discuss the questions, then elicit opinions in open class. Invite comments from other students and encourage them to give reasons.

Exercise 4

> 🧍 **Communication: understanding the context**
>
> The task raises students' awareness of the importance of co-operating with other speakers to check comprehension of the information being conveyed. It will get them to practise what they need to do as active listeners to check what another person is saying, then to probe further to get more information. This is a valuable skill wherever communication and co-operation is important – at school, in the workplace or in society.

- Put students in pairs to brainstorm ideas. Then, put them together with another pair to compare ideas in groups of four. Then, elicit suggestions in open class. Ask the class to decide which ideas they like best.

Exercise 5
- Ask students to study the Speaking box and discuss the meaning of the phrases as a class. Students work in pairs to find examples in the dialogue.

6 Explore more

Student's Book pages 74–85

Exercise 6
- Ask students to complete the dialogue, then compare ideas in pairs. Check answers as a class before you get students to practise acting out the dialogue in pairs. Then, ask a volunteering pair to perform the dialogue in open class. Ask them not to read the dialogue but do this from memory.
- **NEED SUPPORT?** Allow **less confident** students to do the completion stage of the task together in pairs.

Exercise 7
- Put students in pairs. Ask them to agree which of them will play Student A and which Student B. Then, ask them to turn to page 137 and read their respective role cards before they start practising their dialogues.
- **Setting success criteria**: Monitor as students practise the role play, and make a note of particularly good use of language. Encourage those pairs to perform their dialogue for the class.
- **FINISHED EARLY?** Ask students to make a list of situations, other than the place being noisy, where the expressions from the Speaking box might need to be used. Elicit these ideas in open class when you have the time, making the link to the expressions clear to other students as well.
- **Reviewing lesson goals:** Play a game. Put students in a circle. Say something quietly to the student next to you so your sentence is difficult to hear. Allow the student to ask for clarification only once, using one of the phrases from the Speaking box on page 80, and then you repeat the sentence. Ask students to pass the sentence (as they heard it) around the circle in the same way. Each time, the next student can only ask for clarification once, then they have to pass on the message. When the message has made it round the class, elicit it from the last student, then write it and the original sentence on the board to compare. This should highlight why asking for clarification is a key communication skill.

6.7 WRITING

An email about travel arrangements

Lesson aims
- Students can write an email about travel arrangements.

For the teacher
- *Need support?* worksheet, page 237
- Photocopiable activity: *Remember your passport!*

For the student
- Workbook, page 65

Lead-in
Books closed. Write *travel arrangements* on the board, and check comprehension of the phrase. Elicit what kind of information might be included in travel arrangements (type of transport, when and where to meet, timetables, routes, etc.), and make notes in a spidergram for students to copy.

- **Setting lesson goals:** Elicit what students remember about writing informal emails from Unit 3. Ask: *How do you start your email? What kind of language do you use when you write to a friend? How do you finish your email?* Once you have elicited answers, ask students to look at the two emails on page 81 to check their ideas. Explain that in this lesson they will practise writing emails about travel arrangements.

Exercise 1
- Spend no more than a couple of minutes on eliciting dream destinations, and students' reasons for going there. You could have a class vote to see which European destination is most popular.

Exercise 2
- Ask students to read the questions so they know what information to look for, then to scan the emails for the relevant information. Allow them to compare answers in pairs before you check as a class.

Exercise 3
- Read the phrases in the Writing box together and check that students understand them. Then, set a time limit for students to find the examples in Jo's email. Check answers as a class.

Exercise 4
- Read the information in the Language box together, and check understanding. Explain that although we are talking about the future, we use the Present Simple. Elicit what other language structure is used similarly (the *if*-clause, in the First Conditional), and point out that the rules for using a comma are similar, too. Then, set a time limit for students to find the examples in Jo's email.

Exercise 5
- Give students five minutes or so to write their sentences. Ask them to use each connecting word or phrase at least once.
- **Peer learning:** Ask students to read each other's work in pairs. Ask them to mention at least one thing they like about their partner's sentences and suggest one thing their partner could improve next time. Then, ask a few volunteers to share their partner's best (most interesting, funniest, most surprising, etc.) sentence with the class.
- **NEED SUPPORT?** Prepare copies of the photocopiable worksheet on page 237. This version of the task offers more support for writing the sentences.

Exercise 6
- Ask students to read the Writing Time box and check comprehension. Remind them to follow the instructions step-by-step to write their emails. Suggest that they tick off each stage as they complete it, then move on to the next one in the list.
- **NEED SUPPORT?** **Less confident** students could write a shorter text with one or two sentences for each paragraph.

204

- **FINISHED EARLY?** Ask students to write an email to Jill saying if they'd prefer to go via Turin or Lyon, and why.
- **Independent learning:** Ask students to study the Writing box and the Language box, and to use the Emoji response cards to indicate how confident they feel about each learning point. Make a note to revise any problem areas if several students appear to be unhappy.

SET FOR LIFE

Eco-friendly travel

Lesson aims
- Students learn to plan an eco-friendly holiday.

Future skills
- Social responsibility: environmental competence

For the teacher
- Photocopiable activity: *Eco-friendly travel*

Lead-in

Elicit modes of transport, and write them on the board (e.g. car, bus, bicycle, walking, plane). Ask: *How often do you use each form of transport?* Ask students to compare their answers in pairs. Then, re-order the modes of transport from most commonly used to least commonly used. Leave this up on the board for the next activity.

- **Setting lesson goals:** Write *eco-friendly travel* on the board. Elicit what students think the expression might mean. Then, ask students to look at the modes of transport listed on the board, and put them in ranking order from most eco-friendly to least eco-friendly. Write up this list next to the one from the Lead-in. Ask students to say whether the most commonly used modes of transport are the most eco-friendly. Then, explain that in this lesson they will explore ways to become more environmentally conscious travellers.

Social responsibility: environmental competence

Environmental competence involves being aware of environmental issues, particularly those that are immediately relevant to students' lives, and showing a concern for the well-being of the planet. This lesson discusses the impact of transport and travelling on the environment and looks at strategies aimed at reducing the negative effect of travel, promoting more sustainable behaviours.

Exercise 1

- **Peer learning:** Use the Think–Pair–Share technique. Elicit views from a number of students in open class and encourage the rest of the class to say if they agree or disagree with the reasons given.

Exercise 2 6.19 audioscript page 250

- Pre-teach *air pollution, greenhouse gases, public transport, engine*.
- Play the dialogue and ask students to make a list of all the types of transport the speakers mention. Then, play the dialogue again, and ask students to identify the two types that Charlie is using. Check answers as a class.

Exercises 3–5 6.19 audioscript page 250

- Follow the instructions in the Student's Book.
- **Monitoring learning:** Monitor the discussions, checking the appropriate use of the Useful Phrases. Make a note to revise any problematic phrases later but avoid interrupting the activity.

Exercise 6

- Ask students to complete the questionnaire individually, then to compare their answers in pairs. Ask them to decide which student is more eco-friendly, and to give reasons.

Exercise 7

- Read the Useful Tips together as a class. Ask students to suggest any similar tips of their own. Then, ask students in pairs to discuss ideas for improving their travel habits from the questionnaire. Elicit some suggestions in open class.

Exercise 8

- Put students in groups of three or four, then ask them to read the steps carefully.
- Ask each group to brainstorm possible destinations and agree on one. Set a time limit for this step.
- Next, ask students to make a list of possible ways to travel to their destination. They should take into account how far it is, and how eco-friendly the options are.
- After this, groups should also agree how they could travel around at their destination, again considering the environmental factors.
- Once each group has agreed a plan, ask them to present it to the class. Give each group no more than two minutes to present their ideas. Have the class vote on the most eco-friendly plan.
- **SELF-REFLECTION** Ask students to think about how well they worked together in Exercise 8 and discuss these questions: *Did you enjoy working in groups when planning a holiday together? Did you find it easy or difficult to work together? Why?* Elicit ideas and discuss with students what they could do better next time.
- **Reviewing lesson goals:** With books closed, elicit tips for eco-friendly travel and holidays. Ask the class to vote on the best advice from the lesson.

7 People power

Student's Book pages 88–99

Unit contents

Vocabulary
- Word building: family
- Phrasal verbs
- Collocations: relationships
- Relations
- Collocations with *get*

Grammar
- Second Conditional
- Relative clauses

Speaking
- Identifying people in a group

Writing
- A short story

Future skills
- Communication: understanding messages

Exam
- International Certificate Level 2, Reading, Section 7, (note completion)
- B1 Preliminary for Schools, Listening, Part 4, (3-option multiple choice)

For Online Classroom, go to the Portal.

7.1 VOCABULARY

Family and friends

Lesson aims
- Students can talk about relationships with their family and friends.

For the teacher
- Vocabulary Memory Game
- **Photocopiable activity:** *Complete and answer*
- **Test:** Vocabulary Check 7

For the student
- Workbook, pages 70–71
- **Extra Practice Activities:** Vocabulary

Lead-in

Play a game. Elicit words for members of the family and write these on separate pieces of paper. Make as many of these cards as there are students in the class. Use sticky tape to attach a random word to each student's back. Ask students to mingle and ask their classmates questions to find out what the word is on their backs. The others can only give yes/no answers. For example: *Am I a man?* (No.) *Have I got grandchildren?* (Yes.) *Is my word 'grandmother'?* (Yes.) Play until all students have guessed their word.

- 🎯 **Setting lesson goals:** Books closed. Remind students of the game you've just played and explain that you're going to explore the topic of family and friends in more detail.

Exercise 1

- Elicit or pre-teach: *relations*. Give students a few moments to think about their answers, then put them in pairs or small groups to tell their partners about their families.

Exercise 2 🔊 7.1

- Elicit or pre-teach: *biological parents* (parents you're connected to through birth rather than adoption or one parent's re-marriage), *generation*. Ask students to study the diagram and fill in the missing numbers. Allow them to compare answers in pairs before you play the audio for them to check.

Exercise 3 🔊 7.2

- Read the information in Vocabulary box A as a class. Play the audio for students to listen, repeat and practise their pronunciation. Then, ask them to complete the explanations in pairs, and check as a class.

Exercise 4 🔊 7.3

- Write on the board: *carry on, give up*. Elicit their meanings, then explain that they are examples of phrasal verbs.
- Read the information in Vocabulary box B as a class. Explain that phrasal verbs are made up of a verb and one or more words, often prepositions. Check understanding of the new phrasal verbs. Set a time limit for the completion task. Play the audio for students to check their answers.

Extra activity

Play a game to review the phrasal verbs. Ask students in pairs to make eight pairs of cards. On one card in each pair, they should write the main verb (*deal, get,* etc.), and on the other, the particles (*with, on with,* etc.). Ask them to lay the two sets on the table separately, face down. In each turn, a player turns over a verb and a particle card. If they match, they must say a correct sentence with the phrasal verb. If they can do this, they get to keep the pair of cards and turn over another pair. If the pair doesn't match or they can't say a sentence, they must turn the cards back down, and the other player continues. The game goes on until all the cards have been collected. The player with the most cards collected wins.

Exercise 5

- Elicit or explain: *include*. Put students in pairs to compare their answers to the quiz. For feedback, ask some students to report back on how many similarities and differences they found.

Exercise 6 🔊 7.4

- Read the phrases as a class, and check students understand them. Ask students to complete the texts individually and compare answers in pairs before you play the audio for them to check.

Exercise 7

- Assign each half of the classroom to those who agree with Stefan, and those who disagree. Give students ten seconds to choose a side. As much as possible, make pairs from students with opposing views, then ask them to discuss their opinions. As you monitor, make a note of the most interesting ideas and elicit these in open-class feedback.
- **Peer learning:** As a variation on this activity, you could introduce the idea of a debate. Before students begin discussing an issue with two opposing sides, they simply toss a coin to decide who will argue *for*, and who will argue *against* the proposition. This is a technique to help students better anticipate counter-arguments from their partner.
- FINISHED EARLY? Ask students to choose at least two phrasal verbs from Exercise 4 and two of the phrases from Exercise 6 and write sentences about their own friends.
- **Independent learning:** Ask students to think about the lesson and reflect on their learning. Give them questions to answer in their notebooks, e.g. *Do I know how to describe members of my family? Do I know how to use phrasal verbs to talk about relationships? Do I know how to describe my relationships with friends?*

7.2 GRAMMAR

Second Conditional

Lesson aims
- Students can use the Second Conditional to talk about unreal or imaginary situations.

For the teacher
- *Need support?* worksheet, page 238
- Photocopiable activity: *Tell your group why*
- Grammar presentation
- **Test:** Grammar Check 7

For the student
- Grammar Time, Student's Book, page 132
- Workbook, page 72
- Extra Practice Activities: Grammar, New Park video, BBC Vox Pop

Lead-in

Play a game to review the video story so far. Ask all students to stand up. Throw a ball to a student, who must say a sentence about one thing that happened in the story. If the statement is correct, they can throw the ball to another student still standing to do the same, and then they sit down. Continue playing until all students are seated.

- **Setting lesson goals:** Write the following on the board: (1) *If we go to the park after school, I will show you how to do slacklining.* (2) *If I won a million Euros, I would move to Indonesia.* Check students' comprehension: *In (1), are we going to the park later?* (probably). *In (2), do I expect to win a lot of money?* (No.) Remind students that they learned about the First Conditional (1) in Unit 5, and in this lesson, they will find out more about the Second Conditional (2).

Exercise 1

- Ask students to brainstorm some ideas in pairs or small groups before you elicit suggestions in open class. Accept any reasonable ideas.

Exercise 2 34 7.5

- Play the video or audio for students to check their ideas. Then, elicit the answer to the question.
- NEED SUPPORT? Pause playback regularly to ask **less confident** students comprehension questions: *Why does Abe think he can't go to the party?* (He has to meet his mum at the airport.) *How would Abe feel if he didn't go to the airport?* (He'd feel bad.) *What time does the plane arrive?* (at nine). *What time does the party start?* (at eight). *Where does Abe go?* (to the airport).

Exercise 3

- Discuss the Grammar box with the class.
- Explain that in the Second Conditional, we use the Past Simple in the *if*-clause, and we use *would* (usually contracted to *'d*) + verb in the main clause. As in the First Conditional, we only use a comma when the *if*-clause comes first. Elicit or explain that the Second Conditional is used to describe unreal or imaginary situations – things that could, but aren't likely to, happen.
- To check comprehension of the language point, elicit the differences from the First Conditional.
- Point out that when using the Second Conditional, it is more formal to use *were* instead of *was*, e.g. *If it were (was) warmer, I would go swimming.* Explain that in informal speech it is fine to use *was*.
- Set a time limit for students to find further examples in the dialogue, then check as a class.

Exercise 4 7.6

- Do the first sentence together as a class, and write the completed sentence on the board so students have a model. When students have completed the task, ask them to compare answers in pairs before you play the audio for them to check.
- **Giving feedback:** Use the Basketball technique. Ask a student a question using the Second Conditional and throw them a ball, e.g. *If you found money in the street, would you keep it?* The student answers the question and then asks a question and throws the ball to another student to answer. Once several students have asked and answered questions, stop the game and give feedback to the class on any general mistakes.
- NEED SUPPORT? Prepare copies of the photocopiable worksheet on page 238. This version of the task provides students with options to choose from.

Exercise 5

- Write *party* and *airport* on the board. Ask for a show of hands for each decision. As much as possible, get students to work with a partner who would make a different choice. Ask them to give reasons for their decisions.

7 People power

Student's Book pages 88–99

- 💬 **Monitoring learning:** As you listen to students' discussions, make a note of the best arguments for or against each option. Elicit these in open class at the end of the pairwork activity.

Exercise 6 ▶ 35 videoscript page 251
- Pre-teach: *mean* (adj), *send somebody to voice mail, drop (everything), a date, make something up.*
- Play the video, and pause after each section so students have time to record the four sentence endings. Note that there are only three endings offered for 1 (Craig and Rebecca talk about her answer together but he doesn't give his own answer), and two for 4 (only Jamie and Liam answer). Elicit the sentence endings.
- **NEED SUPPORT?** Allow **less confident** students to work in pairs to complete the task.

Exercise 7
- Follow the instructions in the Student's Book.
- **NEED SUPPORT?** Allow **less confident** students to write down their sentence endings before you put them in pairs for the discussion stage.
- **FINISHED EARLY?** Ask students to write four or five sentences with the Second Conditional describing an imaginary chain of events, in which each next sentence uses the result clause from the previous one as a condition clause. For example: *If I had money, I'd buy a car. If I bought a car, I'd drive it to the ocean. If I drove to the ocean, I'd swim in it. If I swam in the ocean, I'd avoid the sharks.*
- 🎓 **Independent learning:** Ask students to look back at the lesson and use their Traffic Light cards to show how confident they feel about using the Second Conditional. Make a note to review the language point if several students choose the red card.

7.3 READING AND VOCABULARY

Making friends

Lesson aims
- Students can understand an article about friendship.

For the teacher
- Vocabulary Memory Game
- *Need support?* worksheet, page 238
- Photocopiable activity: *Friends*
- Test: Vocabulary Check 7

For the student
- Workbook, page 73
- Extra Practice Activities: Vocabulary

Lead-in
Review expressions with *make* + noun. Set a time limit and ask students to work in groups of four to write a list of as many expressions with *make* as they can. Elicit the expressions, and check comprehension of the more challenging examples by eliciting an example sentence from the person who suggested it.

- 🎯 **Setting lesson goals:** Books closed. Write *making friends* on the board, and elicit ideas for what students would expect to read about in an article on the topic. Accept all reasonable suggestions. Read the lesson aim as a class.

Exercise 1
- 🌐 **Peer learning:** Use the Think-Pair-Share technique.

Exercise 2 🔊 7.7
- Ask students to cover the exercise, then play the audio as they read. Pause after each paragraph and ask students to summarise its main point in pairs. When they have read the complete text, ask them to match the headings, and compare ideas in pairs. Then, check answers as a class.

Exercise 3
- **EXAM** International Certificate Level 2, Reading, Section 7, (note completion)
- Remind students that there may be different ways to complete each sentence but that they are only allowed to use words from the text. They can make small changes to the form of the word to fit the sentence. For each sentence, they should first scan the text to find where the missing information appears. Then, they should study it closely, and decide how to add it to the sentence so that it fits grammatically and expresses the same idea as the text.
- Allow students to compare answers in pairs before you check as a class.
- **NEED SUPPORT?** Prepare copies of the photocopiable worksheet on page 238. This version of the task provides students with options to choose from.

Exercise 4 🔊 7.8
- Read the information in the Vocabulary box as a class. Check students understand the new words. Encourage them to work out their meaning from the text. Play the audio for students to listen and repeat and practise pronunciation.

Exercise 5 🔊 7.9
- Set a time limit for the sentence completion task. Ask students to compare their answers in pairs before you play the audio for them to check.

Exercise 6
- Put students in pairs to brainstorm ideas for two minutes. Then, put each pair together with another pair to compare ideas in groups of four.

Extra activity
Ask groups to use their ideas to produce a poster for the Dos and Don'ts of Friendship. Display all the posters around the class, and have a class vote on the best poster and on the most useful piece of advice.

- **FINISHED EARLY?** Ask students to use the words from the Vocabulary box in Exercise 4 to write true sentences about themselves.
- **Reviewing lesson goals:** With books closed, elicit the five steps to friendship described in the text the students have read. They can use their own words to summarise the advice. Ask them to look back at the article to check how accurate their summaries were.

7.4 GRAMMAR
Relative clauses

Lesson aims
- Students can use defining and non-defining relative clauses to describe people, things and places.

For the teacher
- *Need support?* worksheet, page 238
- **Photocopiable activity:** *The student who ...*
- Grammar presentation
- **Test:** Grammar Check 7

For the student
- Grammar Time, Student's Book, page 133
- Workbook, page 74
- Extra Practice Activities: Grammar

Lead-in

Draw a simple house on the board. Say and write: *This is the house that Jack built*. Say: *man*, then say and write: *This is the man who lives in the house that Jack built*. To play the game with the class, continue to give one-word prompts which students have to add to the sentence last created – in whatever way they can (that is, it doesn't necessarily have to involve a relative clause). Each time, get a different volunteer to say the expanded sentence. Keep going for a few more rounds or until the sentence becomes too complicated to continue.

- **Setting lesson goals:** Highlight the relative clause and the relative pronoun in the original sentence from the Lead-in. Explain that we use this structure called a relative clause to add further information, and that this will be the focus of the lesson.

Exercise 1
- **Peer learning:** Use the Think-Pair-Share technique.

Exercise 2 7.10 audioscript page 251
- Elicit or explain: *rescue*, *flood*. Match the first quiz question and answer together as a class (1 g) to clarify what the task is. You may also need to explain: *handheld*. Ask students to do the task and compare answers in pairs before you play the audio for them to check.

Exercise 3
- Give students time to think of their own answers, then put them in pairs to compare ideas. There is no need to insist on using relative clauses at this stage, although some students will probably do so by modelling their answers on the sentences in Exercise 2.

Exercise 4
- Discuss the Grammar box with the class. Explain that there are two kinds of relative clauses. We use defining relative clauses to specify who or what we are talking about, and without the relative clause, the sentence would not be meaningful. We use non-defining relative clauses to add relevant or interesting details, but the sentence would still be meaningful without this information. Write the following examples on the board: (1) *My brother who has long hair works in a bank.* and (2) *My brother, who has long hair, works in a bank.* Ask *How many brothers do I have in each situation?* (more than one in 1, one in 2). Explain that defining relative clauses tell us exactly which person or thing we are talking about (as in example 1). Point out the difference in the use of commas.
- Explain that the relative clause is linked to the main part of the sentence with a relative pronoun: *who* for a person, *which* for a thing, *where* for a place and *whose* for a possession. In defining relative clauses, *that* can replace *who* or *which*. Point out the advice in the Watch out! box and remind students that we don't use *that* as a relative pronoun in non-defining relative clauses. Point out also that we never use *what* as a relative pronoun.
- Ask students to work in pairs to find the examples in Exercise 2 and decide if they are defining or non-defining clauses. Then, check answers as a class.

Exercise 5
- Ask students to do the task individually, then compare answers in pairs before you check as a class.
- **NEED SUPPORT?** Prepare copies of the photocopiable worksheet on page 238. This version of the task provides gaps for students to fill in.

Exercise 6
- Before students begin, ask them to work in pairs to decide which element of the sentence the relative clause should refer to (*Mrs Morris, the bike, Number 24, Park Street, Mr Jones, our school*). Then, ask them to write the sentences. Allow them to compare answers in pairs before you check as a class.
- **NEED SUPPORT?** Allow **less confident** students to work together in pairs for the writing stage of the task as well.

Exercise 7
- Model the activity by telling the class about your own favourites, using relative clauses to make one true and one false statement. Get the class to guess which of your statements is false. Then, give students a couple of minutes to write their own sentences. Put them in pairs to do the guessing task together.

Extra activity
Alternatively, ask students to mingle and speak to a number of other students. Ask: *How many of the people you spoke to guessed your sentences?*
- **FINISHED EARLY?** Ask students to prepare a few more questions for the quiz in Exercise 2 (for example: a film that you've seen more times than any other, a celebrity who annoys you the most).

209

7 People power

Student's Book pages 88–99

- **Independent learning:** Ask students to use their Emoji response cards to indicate how confident they feel about using relative clauses. Make a note to revise the language point if several students appear to be unhappy.

7.5 LISTENING AND VOCABULARY

A helpful friend

Lesson aims
- Students can understand a conversation about helping people in need.

For the teacher
- *Need support?* worksheet, page 238
- Photocopiable activity: *Get*

For the student
- Workbook, page 75
- Extra Practice Activities: Vocabulary, BBC Vox Pop

Lead-in

Ask: *When did you last help someone? What did you help them with?* Put students in pairs or small groups to discuss their experiences. For feedback, ask a few volunteers to tell the class something interesting or surprising that they learned about their partner.

- **Setting lesson goals:** Ask students to quickly look through page 93, and in pairs tell their partner which exercise they expect to be the easiest and the most challenging. Tell them to make a note of this to refer back to at the end.

Exercise 1

- **Peer learning:** Use the Think-Pair-Share technique. Try to elicit reasons for both sides of the argument. Keep the discussion light, as many people are sensitive about other people's different attitudes towards pets.

Exercise 2

- Ask students to study the photos, and get a different volunteer to describe each one: *Who's/What's in the photo? What are they doing?* Then, elicit other ways of dogs helping people, and write the suggestions on the board.

Exercise 3

- Ask students to study the questions, and to use these to try to predict the content of the audio. Remind students that doing so before they begin a listening task is a useful exam skill. Ask students to compare ideas in pairs.

Exercise 4 🔊 7.11 audioscript page 251

- **EXAM** B1 Preliminary for Schools, Listening, Part 4, (3-option multiple choice)
- Pre-teach: *disabled, wheelchair, assistance dog, slippers*, and explain *cerebral palsy* (see Background note).
- Remind students that the order of questions follows the order of information in the audio. Suggest that they use the questions to guide them. If they can't get the answer to a question, they should move on to the next one. When they listen for the second time, they should focus more closely on the difficult questions. At the end, if there are any questions they really couldn't decide on, they should eliminate the option that's most likely wrong, and then just guess. In a multiple choice task, they should never leave a question unanswered.
- Check answers as a class.
- **NEED SUPPORT?** Before you check answers as a class, allow **less confident** students to compare their answers with a partner.

Background note

Cerebral palsy is a permanent movement disorder that appears in early childhood. It is caused by abnormal development or damage to the parts of the brain that control movement, balance and posture. It affects more than 17 million people worldwide. Since 2012, 6 October has been assigned as World Cerebral Palsy Day to raise awareness of the condition.

Exercise 5

- Ask students to study the questions and options, then decide what kind of information they should focus on. Remind them that doing so before they begin a listening task is another useful exam technique. Ask students to compare ideas in pairs before you check as a class.

Exercise 6 🔊 7.12 audioscript page 251

- **EXAM** B1 Preliminary for Schools, Listening, Part 4, (3-option multiple choice)
- Play the audio twice for students to complete the task. Remind them to use the same techniques they applied in Exercise 4.
- **NEED SUPPORT?** Prepare copies of the photocopiable worksheet on page 238. This version of the task reduces the number of multiple choice options.

Background note

Asperger's syndrome is a neuro-developmental disorder on the autism spectrum. People with this condition often have difficulties in social interaction, especially in interpreting or using non-verbal communication, and often exhibit repetitive behaviour. However, Asperger's doesn't normally affect intelligence or language development. Many people with Asperger's have remarkable focus and persistence, an increased attention to detail and an acute ability to recognise patterns.

Exercise 7 🔊 7.13

- Read the information as a class. Set a time limit for the matching task. Ask students to compare answers in pairs before you play the audio for them to check. Play it again and ask students to repeat the phrases to practise pronunciation.

- **Independent learning:** Suggest that students find and make notes of further examples for each meaning of the verb *get*, e.g. *buy – get a new computer; arrive/reach – get to the airport; receive – get a present; bring/fetch – get something from your room; become – get sick*). Expanding the range of phrases they can use with a particular verb will help them to make their speech and writing more varied and expressive.

Exercise 8
- Ask students to do the task individually, compare answers in pairs, then check answers as a class.

Exercise 9 ▶ 36 videoscript page 251
- Pre-teach: *vet(erinarian)*, *cast* (that you wear on a broken limb).
- Play the video, then elicit the answers to the questions.

Exercise 10
- Give students half a minute to read the task and think of their own experiences. Then, put them in pairs to share their stories. **More confident** students could discuss more than one of the situations. For feedback, ask a few volunteers to share the most interesting stories they heard from their partners.
- **FINISHED EARLY?** Ask students to write true sentences about their family or friends using the collocations with *get* from Exercise 7.
- **Reviewing lesson goals:** Ask students to look back at their notes from the beginning of the lesson. Were they right about which exercise was the easiest or most difficult?

7.6 SPEAKING

Identifying people in a group

Lesson aims
- Students can explain who they are talking about.

For the teacher
- Photocopiable activity: *Identify them*

For the student
- Workbook, page 76
- Extra Practice Activities: New Park video

Lead-in
Elicit everything students can remember about Eren from the video story. Don't spend more than a couple of minutes on this.
- **Setting lesson goals:** Find and bring into class some group photos of you from childhood or your teenage years (for example, from parties with friends, class photos from school). If you don't want to share photos of yourself, find some photos of famous people from an earlier age online. Show the photos to the class and ask students to try to guess which person in the photo is you (or the famous person). To make it more challenging, choose photos that aren't labelled and where you're not too easy to recognise. When they have guessed correctly or you have revealed the answers, explain that in this lesson you're going to practise expressions for identifying people.

Exercise 1
- Ask students to cover the dialogue and study the photo, then elicit: *Who do you think this man is?* (Eren's grandfather). *Where are they now?* (in their living room/at home). *What is he doing?* Accept any reasonable ideas.

Exercise 2 ▶ 37 🔊 7.14
- Ask students to read the questions before you play the video or audio so they know what information to look for. Ask them to compare ideas in pairs before you elicit answers in open class. Also elicit the meaning of the phrases in the Sounds Good! box from volunteers (*What are you up to?* is an informal way of asking what someone is doing or planning to do).
- **NEED SUPPORT?** Play the video or audio again and pause after key moments to ask **less confident** students comprehension questions, e.g. *What is grandad watching?* (a programme about music in the 1970s). *Why is he interested in this?* (He used to go to live performances then.) *What is he wearing in the scene?* (a flowery shirt). Elicit answers before continuing the video or audio.

Exercise 3

> **Communication: understanding messages**
> This exercise highlights the importance in playing a constructive, active role in listening to another person, and making sure we understand the message they are trying to communicate. It will get students to evaluate different strategies for expressing interest and helping the flow of communication. This is a valuable skill wherever communication is essential: in everyday life, at school and in the workplace.

- Put students in pairs for the discussions. Ask them to make notes of the most important points. For feedback, elicit ideas from a number of pairs, and invite the rest of the class to respond. Write the key conclusions on the board.

Extra activity
Before starting the discussions, students could think about how Eren shows interest in the dialogue with his grandad.

Exercise 4
- Read the information in the Speaking box as a class. Elicit what tense we normally use to describe scenes in photos (Present Continuous). Set a time limit for students to find the examples in the dialogue. Check as a class.

Exercise 5
- Put students in pairs. Ask each student to follow the instructions and describe a person. Their partner should try to guess which person in the photo is being described.

7 People power

Student's Book pages 88–99

Exercise 6
- Ask students to work with a different partner, then take turns to choose and describe someone in the photo on page 89. Their partner should try to guess which person is being described.

Extra activity
This activity could be repeated using any other group photo available. Students could bring their own photos into class to talk about.

- **FINISHED EARLY?** Books closed. Students should try to recall and write down what information Eren's grandad gives about himself, Harry and Grandma when he describes them – then look back in the dialogue to check.
- **Reviewing lesson goals:** Ask students to read the lesson aim. Then, encourage students to write a number from 1–5 on a piece of paper to say how they feel about the phrases in the Speaking box (1 – easy to 5 – difficult). Elicit their reasons for their answers. They can put it on your desk as they leave the classroom. Study the results and if there are lots of 4s and 5s with similar reasons, find time to review the new language from the lesson.

7.7 WRITING

A short story

> **Lesson aims**
> - Students can write a short story.
>
> **For the teacher**
> - Photocopiable activity: *Making new friends*
>
> **For the student**
> - Workbook, page 77

Lead-in
Write *famous friends* on the board. Elicit some famous examples of friends from films, books, TV shows, and so on (for example: Sherlock Holmes and Dr Watson; Harry Potter, Ron and Hermione; C-3PO and R2-D2). Ask: *What makes them good friends?* Accept any relevant examples or suggestions.

- **Setting lesson goals:** Book closed. Elicit students' ideas about short stories. Ask: *What does the author usually write about at the start of a story?* (e.g. where it happens, who's in it, what the situation is). *How many characters are there in a short story?* (usually just a few). *What makes a good ending for a short story?* (something surprising, a good lesson to learn, something emotional). Explain that in this lesson, students are going to practise writing a story.

Exercise 1
- **Peer learning:** Use the Think-Pair-Share technique to elicit students' ideas. Make notes of the key qualities of a true friend on the board.

Exercise 2
- Ask students to read the story quickly and check which, if any, of the qualities on the board are mentioned. Elicit the names of the people described in the story (Sienna, Harry, Lara), then elicit how they are described by Flavia. Ask students to vote on which of them is a true friend to Flavia, then ask one or two volunteers to give reasons.

Exercise 3
- Ask students to read the story more carefully. Remind them that the five descriptions summarise the focus of each paragraph in the story, so it might be easier for them to match the events in a–e with what is in the paragraphs. Allow students to compare answers in pairs before you check as a class.

Exercise 4
- Read the phrases in the Writing box together and check that students understand them. Then, set a time limit for students to find the examples in the story. Check answers as a class.
- Focus attention on the examples for using direct speech and elicit that we use quotation marks around the exact words a person says/said. (Both single and double quotation marks are commonly used in English, but remind students not to mix the two styles within the same text. In written English, quotation marks are always shown at the top of the line.)

Exercise 5
- Read the information in the Language box together, and check understanding. Ask students to find where in the story each sequencer is used. Then, ask students to write sentences about their experiences.
- **NEED SUPPORT?** To support **less confident** students, write the following sentence prompts on the board, which students can then complete for themselves: *First, I went … Next, I decided to … Just then, a friend … Afterwards, we …*

Exercise 6
- Ask students to read the Writing Time box and check comprehension. Remind them to follow the instructions step-by-step to write their stories. Suggest that they tick off each stage as they complete it, then move on to the next one in the list.

Extra activity
Ask some volunteers to read their stories for the class, and have the class vote on the best one.

- **NEED SUPPORT?** **Less confident** students could write a shorter text with one or two sentences for each paragraph.
- **FINISHED EARLY?** Books closed. Ask students to practise re-telling Flavia's story orally, in their own words.
- **Peer learning:** Books closed. Ask students to recall and tell each other in pairs the things they have learned in this lesson about writing a story. When they feel they have covered all the key learning points, ask them to look back on page 95 to check their ideas.

BBC CULTURE

From generation to generation

Lesson aims
- Students learn about what older generations can teach them.

For the teacher
- Photocopiable activity: *Project worksheet: a digital presentation*

Lead-in

Tell the class about something you learned from your parents or grandparents (this could be a food recipe, a life skill or some other way in which they shaped who you are today). Put students in small groups to tell each other what they have learned from older generations themselves. For feedback, ask a few volunteers to share something interesting they have learned about their partners.

- **Setting lesson goals:** Give students no more than a minute to look through pages 98–99, then ask them to close their books, and try to complete the following sentence: *Today we are going to learn …* in as many different ways as they can. Ask them to compare ideas in pairs before you elicit some suggestions in open class.

Exercise 1

- Ask students to study the photo on page 98, then brainstorm ideas in pairs about questions 1 and 2. Elicit some ideas from a few pairs, and invite the rest of the class to comment.
- Next, ask pairs to discuss their opinions about questions 3–5. Put them together with another pair to compare ideas in a group of four before you elicit answers in open class. Stress that there are no correct answers, so encourage them to express their disagreement. Encourage all contributors to give reasons for their views.

Exercise 2 7.19

- Pre-teach: *elders* (older people in your family or community), *process* (v) and read the glossary box together. Play the audio as students read the text.
- **Peer learning:** Use the Think-Pair-Share technique to elicit students' views.

Exercise 3

- Ask students to read the statements first, then scan the text to find the relevant information about each one. Suggest that they study that part of the text more closely to decide if it says the same thing as the statement or something different. Allow students to compare answers in pairs before you check as a class.

Exercise 4

- Give students three minutes or so to discuss the questions in pairs.
- **Monitoring learning:** As you listen to students' discussions, make a note of those ideas that you'd like the rest of the class to respond to. At the end of the pairwork activity, elicit these ideas, and encourage other students to say if they agree or disagree and why.

Exercise 5 38 videoscript page 252

- Ask students to study the photo on page 99 and brainstorm ideas in pairs before you elicit their suggestions.
- **With video:** Play the video for them to check their ideas.
- **Without video:** Use extracts from the script to help students complete the task. First, read what one of the characters says: 'People say it is a hard life here but it seems normal for me. It's not a hard life. It's a beautiful life.' Then, read out the following sentences: *Minnie is teaching her granddaughter Eva how to fish. The women in her family have collected food like this for generations. Today is Eva's first time.* Elicit and check the answers.

Exercise 6 38 videoscript page 252

- Ask students to complete the sentences before you play the video or ask them to read the videoscript again to check their answers.

> **Background note**
> **The Arctic** is the region around the North Pole. Unlike the Antarctic, the Arctic is not a continent, but a polar ocean surrounded by the northern parts of the continents of North America, Europe and Asia. About 4 million people live in the Arctic.

Exercise 7

- Follow the instructions in the Student's Book.

Exercise 8 39 videoscript page 252

- Explain *shellfish* (any edible sea animal that has a shell, e.g. crabs, lobsters, oysters). Ask students to read the sentences first to find out what information they are looking for.
- **With video:** Play the video for students to watch, listen and choose the correct sentences.
- **Without video:** Ask students to read the videoscript, find and underline the information about each sentence, then decide which ones are correct.
- Check answers as a class.

Exercise 9

- Give students three minutes to discuss the questions in pairs or small groups. For feedback, elicit some ideas from volunteers, inviting comments from the rest of the class.

Exercise 10

- **PROJECT** The project worksheets include step-by-step support for students. They also include teacher's notes on how to set up the projects with and without technology.
- **Reviewing lesson goals:** Write on the board: *Today I have learned about/how to/that …* and ask students to complete the sentence in as many different ways as they can. Ask them to think back to their sentences at the start of the lesson, and to compare ideas in pairs.

8 Just justice

Student's Book pages 100–111

Unit contents

Vocabulary
- Crimes and criminals
- Solving crimes
- The law
- Word building: negative adjectives
- Investigating crimes

Grammar
- Present and Past Simple passive
- *have/get something done*

Speaking
- Keeping a conversation going

Writing
- An opinion essay

Future skills
- Social responsibility: ethical competence
- Critical thinking: evaluating arguments and options

Exam
- B1 Preliminary for Schools, Reading, Part 3, (4-option multiple choice)
- International Certificate Level 2, Listening, Section 3, (note completion)/B1 Preliminary for Schools, Listening, Part 3, (gap fill)

For Online Classroom, go to the Portal.

8.1 VOCABULARY

Crime

Lesson aims
- Students can talk about crime and criminals.

For the teacher
- Vocabulary Memory Game
- **Photocopiable activity**: *Mime, define, draw*
- **Test**: Vocabulary Check 8

For the student
- Workbook, pages 80–81
- Extra Practice Activities: Vocabulary

Lead-in

Elicit and write the titles of some popular crime TV shows on the board. Ask students in pairs to discuss if they like these kinds of TV dramas, and why.

- **Setting lesson goals:** Books closed. Write *crime* in the middle of the board. Elicit what kind of topics or themes students expect to cover, and add them to the board as a spidergram. Give students in pairs another two minutes to copy and expand the spidergram with their own ideas.

Exercise 1

- Ask students to cover the texts and work in pairs to describe each photo. Then, ask them to skim the texts and match. Check answers as a class.

Exercise 2

- Ask students to read the stories more carefully, and first identify what was taken or damaged in each case (1 a lot of money, 2 purse and jewellery, 3 wallet, 4 all sorts of things/items from the shop, 5 broken swings, street light and shop window).
- **Peer learning:** Use the Think-Pair-Share technique to discuss the question. Encourage students to give reasons why they think a particular experience is more unpleasant than another.

Exercise 3 🔊 8.1

- Read the information in Vocabulary box A as a class. Check students understand the new words, and that they are all examples of criminals. Play the audio and ask students to repeat the words, to practise their pronunciation. Set a time limit for students to find the story which mentions each criminal. Check as a class.

Exercise 4 🔊 8.2

- Check that students understand the differences in meaning between the words in the box: *break into* focuses on the act of illegally entering somewhere, e.g. a bank or a home. *Rob* collocates with the place in which the crime takes place, e.g. *rob a bank, rob a post office*, and *steal* with the items taken during the crime, e.g. *steal money, steal jewellery*.
- Read out the verbs in the box for the class and ask them to repeat the words to practise their pronunciation. Pay special attention to the stress on the second syllable in *commit*.
- Ask students to complete the sentences individually, then compare answers in pairs before you play the audio for them to check their answers.

Exercise 5 🔊 8.3

- Read the information in Vocabulary box B as a class. Read the example (*bank robbery*) together as a class to give students a model for the task. Ask students to complete the table, then compare answers in pairs before you play the audio for them to check. Play the audio again, and ask students to repeat the words, to practise their pronunciation.

Extra activity

Elicit the corresponding verb for each pair of nouns in the table. Note that *pickpocket* or *thieve* are very rarely used as verbs, and we usually use *steal* instead.

Exercise 6 🔊 8.4 audioscript page 252

- Read the task together as a class, and check comprehension. Play the audio for students to write down

the words mentioned from Vocabulary box B. Ask them to compare ideas in pairs before you check as a class.
- Give students two or three minutes for their discussions about crime where they live. Elicit a few ideas from volunteers, then ask the class to say which of the crimes they consider the most serious, and why.
- **NEED SUPPORT?** To give **less confident** students a more concrete target for the task, tell them that the speaker uses four words for crimes, and three words for criminals.

Exercise 7 8.5

- Read the information in Vocabulary box C as a class. Point out that all these words are nouns. Ask students to read the text first without filling in any gaps, to get a general idea. Then, they should complete the text, then compare ideas in pairs before you play the audio for them to check their answers. Point out the stress on the second syllable in de*tect*ive and se*cur*ity camera.
- Check comprehension of the new vocabulary by asking students questions, e.g. *What do we call people who we think committed a crime?* (suspects). *Who are people who saw someone else commit a crime?* (witnesses). *What's the word for an object or a piece of information that helps us solve a crime?* (clue).
- Elicit or explain: *lead* (adj), *investigate*, *interview* (v), *have nothing to do with* (*something*), *arrest* (v), *search* (*a place*).
- **NEED SUPPORT?** **Less confident** students could complete the task in pairs, then compare ideas with another pair.

Exercise 8 8.6

- Read the information in Vocabulary box D as a class. Read out the words and ask students to repeat, to practise their pronunciation.
- Do the first headline together as a model. Check comprehension of *punishment* (something that happens because of something bad you have done) and *reward* (money you receive for something you do). Set a time limit for completing the task. Ask students to compare ideas in pairs before you play the audio for them to listen and check. Ask **more confident** students to use their own words to explain the difference between any pairs of words that the class found more challenging. Help with explanations as necessary.

Exercise 9

- Ask the class to look at Exercise 8 and elicit the forms of punishment mentioned. Elicit other possible forms of punishment (community work, therapy sessions, etc.). Write these up on the board. After students have decided on suitable punishments for the crimes, elicit some suggestions in open class, and find out who suggested the strictest or most lenient penalties.
- Ask for a show of hands for each job mentioned in question 2, and form pairs of students with different views.
- Give pairs another minute to discuss their reasons for wanting or not wanting to pursue a career in law enforcement.

- **FINISHED EARLY?** Ask students to choose one of the headlines from Exercise 8 and write the story.
- **Reviewing lesson goals:** Ask students to look back at the spidergrams they created in their notebooks at the start of the lesson, and check whether they have covered the areas they expected to. Write the following on the board, and ask students to complete the statements for themselves: *Now I know … I don't really understand … I'd still like to find out …*

8.2 GRAMMAR

Present and Past Simple passive

Lesson aims
- Students can use the Present and Past Simple passive.

For the teacher
- *Need support?* worksheet, page 239
- **Photocopiable activity:** *Quiz time*
- **Grammar presentation**
- **Test:** Grammar Check 8

For the student
- **Grammar Time, Student's Book, page 133**
- **Workbook, page 82**
- **Extra Practice Activities:** Grammar

Lead-in

Review crime vocabulary from Lesson 8.1 by playing vocabulary tennis. Put students in pairs. They should take turns to say new words from the previous lesson. If either of them hesitates for longer than five seconds or repeats a word already mentioned, their partner scores a point. Continue playing for a couple of minutes or until the pairs run out of words.
- **Setting lesson goals:** Write the following two sentences on the board, and highlight the passive verb forms: *Crimes <u>are solved</u> by the police. The world's first detective story <u>was written</u> in 1841.* Explain that this verb form is the passive, and that students will learn more about it in the lesson.

Exercise 1

- Write the name *Sherlock Holmes* on the board, and give students in pairs two minutes to brainstorm and make notes on what they know about him. They might include information not only about Conan Doyle's stories but the various film or TV adaptations. Elicit some of this information in open class, but don't confirm answers at this stage. Tell students they are now going to get a chance to test their knowledge.

Exercise 2 8.7 audioscript page 252

- Give students in pairs two minutes to complete the quiz. Then, play the audio for them to check their answers. Ask if any of the information surprised them, and check who got all five questions right.

215

8 Just justice

Student's Book pages 100–111

Background note
Sherlock Holmes is a fictional private detective created by Scottish author Arthur Conan Doyle. The character first appeared in the story *A Study in Scarlet* in 1887. Over the next forty years, Conan Doyle wrote four novels and another fifty-seven short stories about Sherlock Holmes. Sherlock Holmes holds the Guinness World Record for the most portrayed literary human character in film and TV.

Exercise 3
- Study the Grammar box together as a class. Explain that we often use the passive when we don't know or it's not important who did the action. We can add this information by using the preposition *by*. Point out the advice in the Watch Out! box.
- Rewrite the example sentences on the board with active forms (e.g. *Sherlock Holmes never really uses the quote.*), and point out that the object of the active sentence (*the quote*) becomes the subject of the passive sentence.
- Explain that both the Present Simple passive and the Past Simple passive are formed by using the correct form of *be* (*am/are/is* and *was/were*, respectively) and the past participle. Remind students that some verbs have irregular past participle forms which may or may not be the same as their irregular Past Simple forms. Set a time limit for students to find the examples in the quiz.

Exercise 4
- Write three table headings on the board: *infinitive/Past Simple/past participle*, ask students to copy it into their notebooks, then write their answers in the table and underline the relevant verbs. For feedback, elicit all the forms in open class. Don't write them up on the board, as this would make Exercise 5 too easy.
- **NEED SUPPORT?** **Less confident** students could work together in pairs to complete the forms. Encourage students to complete as many of the verbs as they can themselves before they check the more difficult forms in the irregular verbs list on page 136.

Exercise 5
- Follow the instructions in the Student's Book. You could give students twenty seconds to try to memorise the table they have just completed, then ask them to cover it, and complete the sentences. When they have finished, ask them to check their answers in the table.

Exercise 6
- Ask students to read the text quickly without completing any gaps, to get a general sense. Elicit what else, if anything, they know about *Nancy Drew* stories. Suggest that before they fill in the gaps, they look for time expressions that might help them decide whether a sentence refers to the present or the past. Then, ask them to complete the text. Allow students to compare answers in pairs before you check as a class.

- **NEED SUPPORT?** Prepare copies of the photocopiable worksheet on page 239. This version of the task offers options to choose from.

Exercise 7
- Give students a minute to think of a detective story and to make notes. Then, give each volunteer two minutes to describe the story in their own words, but without naming the story. Can the class guess which story is being described?
- **FINISHED EARLY?** Ask fast finishers to look through page 102, find every verb (in instructions, exercises and texts), then expand the table from Exercise 4 with the infinitive, Past Simple and past participle form of each one (e.g. *know – knew – known* from the instructions for Exercise 1).
- **Independent learning:** Ask students to use their Emoji response cards to show how confident they feel about using the passive forms. Make a note to revise the language point in a later lesson if several students indicate concerns.

8.3 READING AND VOCABULARY

The right punishment?

Lesson aims
- Students can understand an article about crime and punishments.

For the teacher
- Vocabulary Memory Game
- *Need support?* worksheet, page 239
- **Photocopiable activity:** *Dominoes*
- **Test:** Vocabulary Check 8

For the student
- Workbook, page 83
- **Extra Practice Activities:** Vocabulary

Lead-in

Ask students to test each other in pairs by taking turns to name a crime or a criminal, and elicit the matching other noun from their partner (e.g. *thief – theft*, or vice versa).

- **Setting lesson goals:** Elicit the words for crimes from the Lead-in, and write these on the board. Then write: *The right punishment?* Ask: *What's the right punishment for each crime?* Elicit suggestions and encourage students to give reasons. Explain that in this lesson you are going to read an article about crime and punishments.

Exercise 1
- Ask students to study the photo and title, but cover the text. Elicit a description of the photo, then predictions about the text. Accept any reasonable ideas, but don't reveal the answer yet.

Exercise 2 🔊 8.8
- Play the audio while students read the text to check their ideas. Discuss the questions together as a class.

Background note
Youth courts in the US were first introduced in Texas in the early 1980s. By the 2000s, there were over 1,252 youth courts in forty-five states around the country. Youth courts allow juvenile offenders to take responsibility for their actions and make amends without ending up with a criminal record. A 2016 study confirmed the effectiveness of the programme, which has significantly reduced repeat offences.

Exercise 3
- **EXAM** B1 Preliminary for Schools, Reading, Part 3, (4-option multiple choice)
- Remind students that the questions follow the order of information in the text. Once they have found the relevant part of the text, explain that they should study it closely. It might be helpful to eliminate the more obviously incorrect options first, then choose the final answer. When students have completed the task, check answers as a class. Ask students to quote the part of the text that supports their answer. Explain that multiple choice questions do not always focus on specific facts, but at higher levels, the questions may also be about the people's feelings and attitudes.
- **NEED SUPPORT?** Prepare copies of the photocopiable worksheet on page 239. This version of the task reduces the number of multiple choice options.

Exercise 4 🔊 8.9
- Read the information in the Vocabulary box. Check that students understand that we can form the opposite of certain adjectives by adding a prefix before them.
- Set a time limit for students to find and add the negative adjectives to the table. Play the audio to check answers. You could elicit some further examples that students might already be familiar with.
- Explain that each adjective can only be used with one of these prefixes. The *un-* prefix is the most common and can be followed by an adjective beginning with any sound. Elicit or explain that *il-* and *ir-* prefixes can only be followed by adjectives beginning with *l* or *r*, respectively, and *im-* by adjectives beginning with *m*, *b* or *p*. Before other sounds, we use the *in-* prefix (but there are no examples of this in the article).
- Remind students that there is no clear-cut rule for when we should use *un-* or the other prefixes, so this will need to be learned for each adjective. You might like to suggest that students look up and record the appropriate negative prefix for each new adjective they learn.

Exercise 5
- Split the class into two teams. One should argue for, the other against youth courts. Ask each team to brainstorm persuasive arguments for two or three minutes and make notes.

- **Setting success criteria:** Write the following prompts on the board: *Yes, but …; You may be right, but did you think about …?; I'm not sure I agree, because …; Yes, that's a good point!* Encourage students to use at least two of these phrases in the next stage of the activity.
- Encourage students to use the arguments they noted, but also to listen carefully to their opponents and respond to their counter-arguments.

Extra activity
To increase the level of challenge, you could instruct students to switch sides whenever you say in the middle of the activity: *Switch!* Ask them not to repeat arguments their former opponents have already used, but to make new points.

- **FINISHED EARLY?** Ask students to choose five adjectives from Exercise 4 and write sentences with them that illustrate their meaning.
- **Independent learning:** Ask students to think back to the lesson and decide what the most useful learning point was for them. Ask them to use the Emoji response cards to show how confident they feel about understanding an article about crime and punishments.

8.4 GRAMMAR

have/get something done

Lesson aims
- Students can use the construction *have/get something done*.
- **For the teacher**
- *Need support?* worksheet, page 239
- **Photocopiable activity:** *She's having her hair cut*
- Grammar presentation
- **Test:** Grammar Check 8
For the student
- Grammar Time, Student's Book, page 134
- Workbook, page 84
- **Extra Practice Activities:** Grammar, New Park video

Lead-in

Write on the board: *changing your appearance*. Elicit ideas from students for ways people change the way they look, and make notes of these on the board.

- **Setting lesson goals:** Write the following two sentences on the board: *I have cut my hair. I have my hair cut.* Ask students to say who they think cut my hair in each case: me or someone else? Explain that the structure in the second example will be the focus of this lesson.

Exercise 1
- Ask students to study the photo but cover the dialogue. Elicit ideas about what the boys are doing in the scene. Accept all suggestions.

8 Just justice

Student's Book pages 100–111

Exercise 2 ▶ 40 🔊 8.10
- Play the video or audio for students to check their ideas. Did any students guess correctly? Elicit the answer for the question in open class.

Exercise 3
- Put students in group of four to discuss the questions. For feedback, ask one student from each group to tell the class the most interesting or surprising thing they found out about their partners.

Exercise 4
- Discuss the Grammar box as a class. Explain that we use this construction to talk about when we arrange somebody else to do a job for us. Explain that in informal contexts, *get/gets* can replace *have/has*. The construction *have/get something done* can also be used in any tense: present, past or future. As with the passive, we can use *by* to name the person who does the action, though this isn't very common. Check comprehension of the usage by asking students to read the examples and say who performs each action (a professional, not Carla or Eren).
- Set a time limit for students to find more examples.

Exercise 5
- Do the first matching pair together as a class, as a model. Students do the task, then compare ideas in pairs before you check answers as a class.
- **NEED SUPPORT?** Allow **less confident** students to work with a **more confident** partner who can help them complete the task.

Exercise 6
- Ask students to complete the sentences, then compare answers in pairs before you check as a class.
- **NEED SUPPORT?** Prepare copies of the photocopiable worksheet on page 239. This version of the task specifies the tense needed.

Exercise 7
- Give students a minute or so to read the completed sentences and decide how they would need to change them for themselves.
- **NEED SUPPORT?** **Less confident** students could write their sentences down before comparing them with a partner. **More confident** students could do the task orally.
- **FINISHED EARLY?** Ask students to cover the sentence beginnings 1–6 in Exercise 5 and use the endings a–f to write their own sentences.
- 🎓 **Independent learning:** Ask students to use the Traffic Light cards to show how confident they feel about using *have/get something done*. Make a note to revise the language point in a later lesson if several students indicate concern.

8.5 LISTENING AND VOCABULARY

Crimes and criminals

Lesson aims
- Students can understand people talking about a crime.

For the teacher
- **Photocopiable activity:** *Caught red-handed!*

For the student
- Workbook, page 85
- **Extra Practice Activities:** Vocabulary, BBC Vox Pop

Lead-in
Choose words from Lessons 8.1–8.4 to revise, and write each one on a slip of paper. In open class, give a definition for each word. The first student to guess the word correctly wins the slip of paper. The student with the most slips is the winner.
- 🎯 **Setting lesson goals:** Elicit situations in which people talk about crime (e.g. interview with a crime expert, witnesses making a statement for the police, victims reporting a crime). Explain that in this lesson students will listen to people talking about a crime.

Exercise 1
- Give students two minutes to describe the photo in as much detail as they can. Ask them not only to include visible details, but also speculate on what happened. Elicit answers in open class.

Exercise 2 🔊 8.11
- Do the first matching pair as an example. Set a time limit for students to complete the matching. Warn them that some of the verbs might match with more than one noun. Then, play the audio for them to check their answers. To check that students understand the collocations, ask volunteers to illustrate their meaning by saying a sentence for each of them.

Exercise 3 🔊 8.12 audioscript page 252
- Elicit or explain: *podcast*, *first up* (a phrase used to introduce the first person/topic). Play the audio, and give pairs one minute to brainstorm ideas about what might have happened. Elicit suggestions, but don't reveal the answer yet.

Exercise 4 🔊 8.13 audioscript page 252
- Pre-teach: *pretend*, *it's a pity*. Play the audio for students to check their ideas. Elicit what things were taken (laptop, smartwatch, digital camera).

Exercise 5 🔊 8.13 audioscript page 252
- Put students in pairs to discuss what they think the logical order for the events would be. Then, play the audio for students to check their ideas and work out the correct sequence of events.

Exercise 6 🔊 8.14 audioscript page 253
- **EXAM** International Certificate Level 2, Listening, Section 3, (note completion)/B1 Preliminary for Schools, Listening, Part 3, (gap fill)
- Explain that in this type of listening task, students have to listen for specific details in the audio. Warn them that there may also be irrelevant details, but each answer will appear in the audio, and they should write them down as accurately as possible. Remind them that sometimes the answer will be a number, not words. Play the audio twice, without pauses, and ask students to complete the task individually. Check answers as a class.
- **NEED SUPPORT?** Before **less confident** students listen to the audio, ask them to discuss in pairs what kind of information is missing in each gap.

Exercise 7 ▶ 41 videoscript page 253
- Elicit or pre-teach: *attached to (something), approach, authority (referring to a person), cashier, inform, mind (somebody's) own business*.
- Play the video for students to complete the task, pausing after each speaker to allow them time to record their answers.
- **NEED SUPPORT?** To make the task more manageable, tell **less confident** students that five speakers answer the first question, four the second and only two the third.

Exercise 8
- Put students in pairs or small groups to give their own answers to the questions, and to compare their ideas. Ask them to consider also what would happen next.
- **Monitoring learning:** Listen to students' discussions, and make a note of the most interesting ideas and the best use of language to elicit in open class for feedback at the end of the activity.
- **FINISHED EARLY?** Ask students to imagine they are police officers who have just arrived at the scene shown in the photo on page 105. Ask them to write a short police report about details of their observations, and the actions they have taken or intend to take.
- **Independent learning:** Ask students to think about the lesson and reflect on their learning. Give them questions to answer in their notebooks, e.g.: *Can you understand people talking about a crime? In what situations do people describe details of a crime? Why is it important to inform the police about any crime you witnessed? Which exercises did you find difficult, and why?* Lead a class discussion.

8.6 SPEAKING
Keeping a conversation going

Lesson aims
- Students can keep a conversation going.

For the teacher
- Photocopiable activity: *You can do it!*

For the student
- Workbook, page 86
- Extra Practice Activities: New Park video

Lead-in
- Write the following questions on the board: *What kind of things do you usually post online? How do other people respond? How do you feel about this? Do you often comment on other people's posts? How do they react?* Put students in pairs or small groups to discuss the questions. Elicit some ideas from volunteers. This may be a sensitive topic for some students, so avoid pressuring anyone into contributing.
- **Setting lesson goals:** Books closed. Write *keeping a conversation going* in the middle of the board, and check comprehension. Elicit different ways that people keep conversations going – both verbal and non-verbal. Spend no more than two minutes on this activity, then tell the class this is going to be the focus of the lesson.

Exercise 1 ▶ 42 🔊 8.15
- Ask students to study the photo but cover the dialogue. Ask them to say who's in the photo, where they think they might be, then how each of them might be feeling. Encourage them to give reasons to justify their predictions, but don't reveal the answers. Play the video or audio for students to check their ideas.
- Check understanding of the phrases in the Sounds Good! box. Explain that we use *by the way* to introduce a comment or question not directly related to what you have been talking about.
- **NEED SUPPORT?** To help students process the dialogue more easily, ask further comprehension questions, e.g.: *How does Penny know that Bea's upset?* (She's too quiet.) *Why is Bea upset?* (because of nasty comments on the nature blog). *What's Penny's advice about the nasty comments?* ('Just ignore them.'). Elicit answers before continuing the video or audio.

Exercise 2
- Play the video or audio, or ask students to read the dialogue again, if necessary. Ask them to say what Bea posted online (a photo of a kingfisher). Ask: *What words can you use to describe two types of comments?* (nice and nasty). Write the words on the board, then elicit examples of both types of comments Bea received (nice: *'So cute!'*; nasty: *'Yawn. Boooring post!', 'A boring post by a boring person.'*). Elicit students' opinions about the question in Exercise 2.

Exercise 3

Social responsibility: ethical competence

This task helps students to apply ethical reasoning and standards to make decisions in complex situations. It will highlight the importance of behaving responsibly on social media and allow them to discuss strategies for dealing with potentially harmful communication. This is a valuable life skill and increasingly important in the modern world.

8 Just justice

Student's Book pages 100–111

- Read the three suggestions as a class and have a class vote on which of them are the most or least effective. Elicit some reasons for students' opinions. Then, put them in pairs to discuss the issue, and encourage them to come up with other suggestions. Elicit ideas in open class, and as a class, agree on the most effective approaches together.

Exercise 4

- Read the Speaking box together as a class. Set a time limit for finding the examples in the dialogue. Ask students to suggest other phrases that fulfil the same functions to keep a conversation going, and write these up on the board for the class to copy in their notebooks.

Exercise 5 🔊 8.16

- Ask students to read and complete the mini-dialogues, then play the audio for them to check answers.

Extra activity

You could lead a class discussion about what students feel is the right age to use social media.

Exercise 6

- Give students a minute to consider the statement and collect some arguments both for and against the proposition. Remind them that anticipating their partner's counter-arguments is a useful skill for debating an issue.
- **Peer learning:** Put students in groups of three. Ask two students in each group to start discussing the topic. Remind them to use the phrases in the Speaking box. Ask the third person in each group to observe their partners, and make a note of each phrase used, and feed in more phrases when the speakers get too repetitive. After a minute or two, ask students to swap roles, so the observer becomes part of the discussion, and another student takes over observing.
- Ask some volunteers to share with the class any interesting ideas they heard from their partners.

Exercise 7

- Give students half a minute to think about at least one positive and one negative aspect of social media, then put them in pairs to discuss their ideas together. Remind students to use the phrases from the Speaking box. Elicit some ideas in open class for feedback, and invite the rest of the class to comment.
- **FINISHED EARLY?** With books closed, ask students to think back to the video story, and try to re-tell what happened in this episode in their own words.
- **Independent learning:** Ask students to think back to their discussion tasks in Exercises 6 and 7. Ask them to reflect on whether they used a wide variety of the phrases to keep the conversation going, then give themselves a score from 1 to 5 (1 – didn't use any, 5 – used a good variety of phrases), write it on a piece of paper and hold it up for you to see. Make a note to practise conversation tasks more if there are a lot of low scores.

8.7 WRITING

An opinion essay

Lesson aims
- Students can write an opinion essay.

For the teacher
- *Need support?* worksheet, page 239
- Photocopiable activity: *I agree!*

For the student
- Workbook, page 87

Lead-in

Write the following statements on the board: *Graffiti is vandalism./Graffiti is art*. To decide who's going to argue for each statement, pairs should toss a coin. Remind students to use phrases from the Speaking box on page 106. Elicit some ideas in open class, inviting comments from the class. Make a note of some of the best arguments mentioned on the board.

- **Setting lesson goals:** Books closed. Focus attention on the opinions on the board and explain that in this lesson students are going to learn how to write up their opinions about an issue in a formal essay.

Exercise 1

- Ask students to work in pairs to describe the photo, then spend a minute or so thinking of examples of rubbish in their environment. Ask them also to discuss their views about the question. Elicit some examples and opinions in open class. Invite the class to comment.

Exercise 2

- Ask students to skim the essay quickly to find out the writer's opinion. Elicit this in open class, then ask for a show of hands to see who agrees. Elicit some reasons from volunteers who agreed and who disagreed.

Extra activity

Ask students to read the essay more carefully, and to make notes under the following headings: *examples of litter in the environment, problems caused by rubbish, suggestions to solve the problem*. Write these headings on the board to help students. Ask them to compare their notes in pairs or small groups, then elicit answers in open class to check.

Exercise 3

- Read the phrases in the Writing box together and check that students understand the words and phrases. Then, set a time limit for students to find the examples in the essay and complete the gaps. Check answers as a class.
- Ask students to find examples of the passive in the essay (*stronger punishments are needed, riverbanks and beaches are littered with plastic, plastic is carried out to sea, animals are hurt or killed*). Remind them that the passive is often used in impersonal, formal writing, such as essays.

Exercise 4
- Read the information in the Language box together, and check understanding. Set a time limit for students to find the examples. Make sure students notice that connectors of purpose are followed by a verb phrase (with the verb in the infinitive), while connectors of result are normally followed by a clause.

Exercise 5
- Ask students to write their sentences in their notebooks. Remind them that the rewritten sentence should have the same meaning as the one in the book. Check answers as a class.
- **NEED SUPPORT?** Prepare copies of the photocopiable worksheet on page 239. This version of the task provides more scaffolding for the rewriting task.

Exercise 6
- Ask students to read the Writing Time box and check comprehension. Remind them to follow the instructions step-by-step to write their essays. Suggest that they tick off each stage as they complete it, then move on to the next one in the list.
- **NEED SUPPORT?** **Less confident** students could be allowed to write a shorter text: one or two paragraphs describing their opinion.
- **FINISHED EARLY?** Ask students to look back at previous lessons in Unit 8, and write sentences about any of the texts or stories, using connectors of purpose or result (e.g. *Penny gave good advice to Bea. As a result, Bea started to feel better.*)
- **Independent learning:** Ask students to use their Emoji response cards to show how confident they feel about writing opinion essays. Make a note to practise writing opinion essays again if a number of students need this.

SET FOR LIFE

You decide!

Lesson aims
- Students can make responsible decisions.

Future skills
- Critical thinking: evaluating arguments and options

For the teacher
- Photocopiable activity: *You decide!*

Lead-in
- Assign each half of the classroom to one of two options (indicating with your hand which side is which option for each round). Students have ten seconds to move to the side of their preference in each round. Use ideas like *tea or coffee*, *summer or winter*, *dog or cat*, and so on. At the end, ask students which decision they found the most difficult to make.

- **Setting lesson goals:** Ask students to recall the episodes from the video story when any of the characters had to make a decision (e.g. in 5.6, the friends decide to attend Eren's tennis match, in 7.2 Abe decides whether to go to a party or to meet his mum at the airport, in 8.4 Eren decides to change his look). Allow students to look back in the book if they have trouble remembering. Make notes of the decisions on the board, then ask the class to decide together which of these was the easiest and most difficult decision. Explain that the lesson will focus on making decisions.

> **Critical thinking: evaluating arguments and options**
> In this lesson students will learn that in order to make responsible decisions, they have to weigh up the relative merits of each option being considered and be able to decide which considerations are important.

Exercises 1–8 8.21– 8.22 audioscripts page 253
- Follow the instructions in the Student's Book.

Exercise 9
- Read the Useful Phrases box as a class, and check comprehension.
- Depending on how much time you have available, allow students to choose one, two or three situations to discuss. Elicit some ideas about each situation in open class, inviting comments from different students.

Exercise 10
- Read the Useful Tips together as a class. Ask students to suggest any similar tips of their own. Then, ask students in pairs to discuss ideas for making better decisions. Elicit some suggestions and reasons in open class.

Exercise 11
- Put students in pairs, then ask them to read the steps carefully. Ask each pair to choose a situation to analyse, either from Exercise 9 or their own ideas.
- Next, ask students to draw up their lists of arguments, then evaluate them in the way they did in Exercises 6–8.
- For each situation, ask a volunteering pair to present their decision and their reasons for choosing it. Invite comments from the class.
- **SELF-REFLECTION** Ask students to think about the way they worked together in pairs in Exercise 11 and discuss these questions: *Did you enjoy this task? Why?/Why not? Did you work together well with your partner? How could you work better next time?* Elicit ideas and write the best ones on the board.
- **Reviewing lesson goals:** Ask students to show whether they feel more comfortable about making responsible decisions than at the start of the lesson by holding up their hand with the thumb up, and with the thumb down if they don't feel more comfortable.

9 Lessons in life

Student's Book pages 112–123

Unit contents

Vocabulary
- School subjects
- Describing students
- Learning and assessment
- Collocations with *make* and *take*
- Phrasal verbs

Grammar
- Reported speech: statements
- Word order in questions

Speaking
- Exchanging information

Writing
- A formal letter asking for information

Future skills
- Social responsibility: multicultural competence

Exam
- B1 Preliminary for Schools, Reading, Part 4, (gapped text)
- B1 Preliminary for Schools, Listening, Part 1, (visual multiple choice)

Check your progress with **Benchmark Young Learners Levels 4/5** or **Benchmark Test A/B1** on completing Progress Check 1–9.

For Online Classroom, go to the Portal.

9.1 VOCABULARY

Education

Lesson aims
- Students can talk about school life.

For the teacher
- Vocabulary Memory Game
- *Need support?* worksheet, page 240
- **Photocopiable activity:** *Hidden words*
- **Test:** Vocabulary Check 9

For the student
- Workbook, pages 90–91
- **Extra Practice Activities:** Vocabulary

Lead-in

Play a game. Ask students to write down the letters of the alphabet, A to Z, and check this quickly. Put students in pairs. Set a time limit and ask students to write as many words related to schools or education for each letter as they can. The pair that writes the most words wins.

- **Setting lesson goals:** Write the lesson heading: *education*, and the following three themes on the board: *school subjects*, *describing students*, *learning and assessment*. Check that students understand the meaning of *subjects* and *assessment*. Elicit some words for each theme that students are already familiar with. Then, tell the class that in this lesson, you are going to expand these themes with some new vocabulary.

Exercise 1

- Ask students to study the photo, then elicit suggestions for how it might be linked to the topic of schools and education. Accept any reasonable ideas. Then, ask students to read the article and check their ideas.
- Ask students to scan the text to find the five 'cool' lessons as a race. Without saying the answers, they should raise their hands as soon as they have found all five. Keep waiting until all, or at least most, of the students have located the words, then check answers. Then, put students in pairs to discuss the three questions. Explain *curriculum* (a teaching programme).

Exercise 2 9.1

- Read the information in Vocabulary box A as a class. Check comprehension by asking students to give examples of the kind of things they learn in each subject. Play the audio for students to listen and repeat, and to practise pronunciation. Ask students to decide which three subjects they like best, and which subject they like least, then compare their preferences with a partner, saying why. For feedback, ask a few volunteers to tell the class something surprising they have learned about their partners.

Exercise 3

- When students have added the words to the spidergram, ask them to compare ideas in pairs. Then, elicit whether students study any school subjects not included in the box in Exercise 2. They add these to the relevant part of the spidergram. You may need to supply translations for the names of these local subjects.

Exercise 4

- Elicit the answer to the first question from the class, then ask for a show of hands for each subject in the box that students would consider adding to the school curriculum. Get a few volunteers to say why.

Exercise 5

- Books closed, ask students to play vocabulary tennis to revise school-related vocabulary. Put pairs of students together to play against another pair. Teams must take turns to say words in the category you name, but either team member can do this. If a team hesitates for longer than four seconds or repeats a word already mentioned, the other team scores a point. Keep going until students start running out of words, then name the next topic, and continue the game. Ask students to write up the words from the game in their spidergrams.

Exercise 6

- **Peer learning:** Use the Think-Pair-Share technique.

Exercise 7 9.2

- Read the information in Vocabulary box B as a class. Check comprehension by eliciting an explanation for

222

critical thinking, *general knowledge*, *problem-solving* and *teamwork* in the students' own words. Explain the meanings further if necessary. Play the audio for students to listen and repeat, and to practise pronunciation. Elicit a few more ideas from students and write the extra words on the board.

Extra activity
Ask students to think about how they would describe their own strengths, and which of the skills mentioned in Exercise 7 they would like to improve. Put them in pairs or small groups to discuss. As talking about potential weaknesses may be a sensitive subject for some learners, elicit ideas from volunteers, but avoid nominating students to contribute.

Exercise 8 9.3
- When students have completed the sentences, ask them to compare answers in pairs before you play the audio for them to check.

Exercise 9
- When students have completed the matching task, ask them to compare answers in pairs before you check as a class.

Exercise 10 9.4
- Read the information in Vocabulary box C as a class. Elicit the difference between the verbs under the *Learning* heading: we *learn* something new; we *memorise* the exact wording of e.g. a poem; we *revise* for a test; *study* is a general word that encompasses the meanings of *learn*, *memorise* and *revise*. The word *curriculum* is a formal noun referring to a teaching programme.
- Discuss the words under the *Types of assessment* heading: we do an *online test* on our own computers, connecting to the teacher/examiner remotely; a *practical exam* is where we have to produce a piece of work, or perform an experiment; a *presentation* is a longer talk on a given subject, often supported by visuals; a *project* is often an extended piece of work we produce individually or in pairs or groups, and present for assessment; a *speaking exam* (also called an *oral exam*) is often used to test our language ability through communication; and in a *written exam* we are each given a question paper and write the answers within a specified time limit.
- Set a time limit for the gap-fill task. When students have completed it, ask them to compare answers in pairs. Then, play the audio for them to check.

Exercise 11
- Put students in pairs to discuss the question.
- **NEED SUPPORT?** Prepare copies of the photocopiable worksheet on page 240. The task provides extra scaffolding for the discussion.
- **FINISHED EARLY?** Ask students to write their dream timetable for a school week. What subjects will they include, and how many times a week? How many classes would they have in a day?

- **Independent learning:** With books closed, set a time limit for students to list as many words as they can remember from the lesson for the three vocabulary topics: *school subjects*, *describing students*, *learning and assessment*. Then ask them to look back at pages 112–113 to check their answers.

9.2 GRAMMAR

Reported speech: statements

Lesson aims
- Students can report what people say.

For the teacher
- Photocopiable activity: *She said that …*
- Grammar presentation
- Test: Grammar Check 9

For the student
- Grammar Time, Student's Book, page 134
- Workbook, page 92
- Extra Practice Activities: Grammar

Lead-in
Play a game. Write your message on a piece of paper and show it to a student. Make the message relatively long and detailed, e.g. *The head teacher asked me to tell everyone that the PE lesson will not be in the gym at half past ten, but on the sports ground at two, after lunch, and that students should be there fifteen minutes early.* Students must now try to write down the message from memory, then pass on the message to the next student around the class the same way. They aren't allowed to copy the messages, and each time they must try to write down the message from memory as completely as possible. When the message reaches the last student, ask them to say what they think it was – then reveal the original message so students can compare.

- **Setting lesson goals:** Write the following sentences on the board: *Sally: 'I'm hungry.' Sally said she was hungry.* Highlight the target structure and explain that we use reported speech to say what someone else has said, and that this is what students are going to learn about in the lesson.

Exercise 1
- Ask students to read the posts quickly, then elicit suggestions about the question. Accept any reasonable ideas.

Exercise 2 9.5 audioscript page 253
- Play the audio for students to check their ideas. Then, ask them to compare the texts in Exercise 1 to what they heard. Elicit how the verbs changed in the recording. Explain that this tense shift to the past is a key element of reported speech. Write both the original and reported verb forms on the board.

9 Lessons in life

Student's Book pages 112–123

Exercise 3 🔊 9.6
- Play the audio while students read the interview. Elicit the answer to the question.

Exercise 4
- Discuss the Grammar box together as a class. Point out the tense shift students noticed during Exercise 2. Explain that this construction is used to report what someone else said – from the point of the speaker reporting their words. This change in perspective explains why elements of the statement change. Point out the advice in the Watch Out! box. Make sure students understand that we must always use a direct object with *tell/told* (*told me*) and we use *say/said* with no direct object or an indirect object (*said to me*). When students have found the examples in the interview, elicit the words of the original speakers in direct speech. Write these on the board (with quotation marks) so students can notice the changes again.

Exercise 5 🔊 9.7
- Ask students to complete the exercise, then to compare answers in pairs before you play the audio for them to check. Remind students that when we quote someone's words exactly as they said them, we use quotation marks, and we don't change the verb tenses.

Extra activity
Put students in pairs, and ask them to write and role play the dialogue between Max and Sara, based on the text in Exercise 5.

Exercise 6
- Ask students first to identify which word or words from the original sentences are missing from the reported statements, then think about how they will need to change to match the past reported verbs. When they have completed the sentences, allow them to compare ideas in pairs before you check answers as a class.
- **Giving feedback:** Use the Basketball technique. Say a sentence, and elicit the reported statement from a student that you throw the ball to, e.g. *I went to the cinema with my daughter yesterday.* → *The teacher said she went to the cinema with her daughter yesterday/the day before.* The student then says a new sentence, throws the ball to another student and elicits the reported speech. Once several students have taken a turn, stop the game and give feedback to the class on any general mistakes.

Exercise 7
- Write an example on the board: *'You don't need an umbrella when you go out.'* (*my mum*). Elicit the reported statement from a more confident student and write it also on the board: *Your mum told you (that) you didn't need an umbrella when you went out.*
- Now, ask each student to write a quote in direct speech, real or invented. Put them in pairs to report each other's statements.
- Alternatively, ask students to mingle and get as many others to try to report their sentence as they can. To make the task more varied, you could get students to swap sentences after each round, so they always get their previous partner's sentence reported by the next person.
- **FINISHED EARLY?** Ask students to choose some sentences from the texts in Exercise 9 on page 113, and rewrite them in reported speech.
- **Independent learning:** Ask students to use their Emoji response cards to indicate how confident they feel about using reported statements. Make a note to revise the language point if a number of students express concern.

9.3 READING AND VOCABULARY

Learning effectively

Lesson aims
- Students can understand an article about effective learning.

For the teacher
- *Need support?* worksheet, page 240
- **Photocopiable activity:** *Make or take?*
- **Test:** Vocabulary Check 9

For the student
- Workbook, page 93
- **Extra Practice Activities:** Vocabulary

Lead-in
Write the following on the board: *You have an important test next week. How do you prepare?* Form pairs or small groups to brainstorm different ways of preparation (e.g. making a study plan for the week, memorising as much as possible shortly before the exam, studying with others) and ask them to discuss why they think this is a good way for them to study. Elicit some ideas for feedback in open class, and invite comments from the other students.
- **Setting lesson goals:** Write *effective learning* on the board. Check comprehension of the phrase. Elicit students' ideas for what they would expect to learn about this topic. Accept any suggestions. Tell students that in this lesson they will read an article about effective learning.

Exercise 1
- **Peer learning:** Use the Think-Pair-Share technique.

Exercise 2
- Tell students to ignore the gaps as they skim the article, then work in pairs to answer the questions. Ask them to compare answers with another pair before you check as a class. Make a list of the seven secrets in bulletpoint form on the board. Leave this up until the end of the lesson, as the list will be needed for Exercise 6.

Exercise 3 🔊 9.8
- **EXAM** B1 Preliminary for Schools, Reading, Part 4, (gapped text)
- Explain to students that in a gapped text task, they should look for logical and grammatical clues in the

sentences before and after each gap. The sentence before the gap usually introduces the topic of the missing sentence in some way. The sentence after the gap often has linking words or pronouns referring back to the missing sentence. Finding these clues is the key to solving the task.
- Do the first gap together as a class to demonstrate how the exam technique works (the sentence before the gap uses the pronoun *she* to refer back to *Mrs Jones* – sentence c repeats the same pronoun; sentence c mentions an experiment – what follows the gap is a description of an experiment).
- Suggest that students first complete the gaps they are most confident about, which reduces the number of possibilities for the more difficult gaps. When they have chosen the answer for every gap, they should re-check that the extra sentence really doesn't fit any of the gaps, and that the completed text is both logical and grammatically correct.
- When students have completed the reading task, ask them to compare answers in pairs before you play the audio for them to check their answers.
- **NEED SUPPORT?** Prepare copies of the photocopiable worksheet on page 240. The first task should be done before students complete Exercise 3. The second task provides extra scaffolding for the gapped text task.

Background note
Citizenship has been a compulsory subject in England since 2001. The subject covers four main areas: politics (awareness about political issues, national and international organisations and how democracy works); financial awareness (including money management skills); volunteering and charity; law and justice.

Exercise 4
- Ask students to choose two parts of the text they found interesting, then write a question about each part. Remind them that the question shouldn't be too easy or obvious, but it should be one they would themselves be able to answer. Ask a few volunteering pairs to read out their questions, then elicit the answers from the rest of the class.
- If you would like to practise exam-type comprehension questions, you could do the same activity but specify the task type students should write questions for, e.g. true or false, multiple choice (with three or four answer options) or sentence completion (where students write sentences about the text but leave out factual information).

Exercise 5 🔊 9.9
- Ask students to find examples of the collocations with *make* or *take* in the article and complete the phrases. Allow them to check answers in pairs before you play the audio for them to check.

Extra activity
Ask students to write sentences about their own learning habits, using the collocations.

Exercise 6
- Refer back to the notes about the seven secrets on the board (from Exercise 2). Ask students to discuss them in pairs and come to an agreement about ranking them in order of usefulness. Ask them to give reasons. Then, ask them to identify all the ideas they would be keen to try, and say why.
- Put them together with another pair to compare ideas in groups of four. Then, ask for a show of hands for each 'secret' to find out which one is considered the best by most students. Ask one or two students to give reasons.
- **FINISHED EARLY?** Ask students to write a plan in their notebooks about how they'll use the learning technique they chose in Exercise 6. Suggest that they describe what situations it might be useful in, and why they chose it.
- **Independent learning:** Ask students to think back to the lesson, and choose one thing they found the most interesting, and one thing they found the most useful learning point about effective learning. Ask them to make a note of these at the end of their lesson notes in their notebooks.

9.4 GRAMMAR

Word order in questions

Lesson aims
- Students can make questions with the correct word order.

For the teacher
- *Need support?* worksheet, page 240
- **Photocopiable activity:** *Ask and answer*
- **Grammar presentation**
- **Test:** Grammar Check 9

For the student
- Grammar Time, Student's Book, page 135
- Workbook, page 94
- **Extra Practice Activities:** Grammar, New Park video

Lead-in

Play a version of Twenty Questions. Think of a person or a thing. Ask the class to stand up. Any student can ask you a *yes/no* question, but once you have answered it, they must sit down. Give only *Yes* or *No* answers. Keep going until someone can guess the person or thing you thought of. Only students still standing can ask a new question. Can they guess before they are all seated?
- **Setting lesson goals:** Write the lesson aim on the board. With books closed, elicit some examples of questions (*yes/no* and *wh-*questions), and the rules in the students' own words. Tell them that this is the language point you're going to review in the lesson.

9 Lessons in life
Student's Book pages 112–123

Exercise 1 ▶ 43 🔊 9.10

- Ask students to study the photo and ask: *Who is in the photo?* (Bea and Carla). *Where are they? What are they doing? What do you think is happening?* (students' own answers). Accept any suggestions. Then, play the video or audio for the students to check their ideas.
- **NEED SUPPORT?** To help **less confident** students, pause the video or audio regularly to ask comprehension questions, e.g. *What is Bea interviewing Carla about?* (her Portuguese course). *What's Bea's dream?* (to become a journalist). *What goes wrong with the interview?* (Bea forgets to record it.) Elicit the answers before you continue playback.

Exercise 2

- Discuss the Grammar box together. Elicit or explain the general rule: the auxiliary normally moves before the subject, and if we use no auxiliary in statements (Present Simple or Past Simple), we add the correct form of *do*. However, in subject questions the word order isn't inverted, and we don't add an auxiliary. Write the following on the board: Questions: (question word) + auxiliary from statement (or *do* if no auxiliary) + subject + main verb – e.g. *Where did you go? When will he be here?*
- To explain the difference between subject and object questions write on the board: *Shakespeare wrote Hamlet*. Elicit that Shakespeare is the subject of the sentence and Hamlet is the object. Explain that if we ask a question about the object, we must use an auxiliary (*What did Shakespeare write?*), and if we ask about the subject, we mustn't (*Who wrote Hamlet?*).
- Set a time limit for students to find examples in the dialogue. Then, elicit one or two further examples of their own for *yes/no*, *wh-*, object and subject questions. Also elicit the *wh*-question words (who, what, which, why, how, when, where, whose), and list them on the board. Remind students that the *w* is silent in *who* and *whose*.

Exercise 3

- Look at the example question together. Give students sufficient time to write their questions. Remind them to check that the statements answer them correctly. Check as a class.
- **NEED SUPPORT?** Prepare copies of the photocopiable worksheet on page 240. This task asks students to order words to produce the questions.

Exercise 4

- Read the examples together. Ask a **more confident** student to make one question for sentence 2 and write it on the board as an extra example (*Who had a Maths test this morning?*). When students have written their questions, ask them to test these in pairs by taking turns to read their questions and answering them, trying to avoid giving the answer in the book.
- **NEED SUPPORT?** Allow **less confident** students to write one question for each answer.

Extra activity

Play a game to practise question formation. Put students in groups of four. Choose one player who must think of a person, an object or a place. The others take turns to ask questions, to which the player may only answer *yes* or *no* (or *I don't know*). The team can only ask 21 questions to guess who or what the first player thought of. (To make it more challenging, the player doesn't have to answer if a question is grammatically incorrect, but the person who asked the question loses a turn.) Can they guess? If time allows, repeat with a different player answering the questions.

Exercise 5

- Ask students to work with a different partner and take turns to ask and answer the questions from Exercise 3. The person asking the questions tries to guess which answers are false.
- **NEED SUPPORT?** Allow **less confident** students some time to write down their answers before they begin the pairwork stage.
- **FINISHED EARLY?** Ask students to think of and write six interview questions they would like to ask their favourite famous person. Remind them to include different types of questions: *yes/no* questions, *wh*-questions, subject and object questions.
- 🎓 **Independent learning:** Read out the four headings from the Grammar box for the types of questions and ask students to raise their hand with the thumb up if they think they understand the rules, and the thumb down if they are not sure. Make a note to revise any language points that students express concerns about.

9.5 LISTENING AND VOCABULARY

Conversations in the classroom

Lesson aims
- Students can understand short classroom conversations.

For the teacher
- Vocabulary Memory Game
- *Need support?* worksheet, page 240
- **Photocopiable activity:** *Calm down!*

For the student
- Workbook, page 95
- **Extra Practice Activities:** Vocabulary, BBC Vox Pop

Lead-in

Put students in pairs and ask them to take turns to ask each other questions to which they think their partner will answer 'yes'. Remind them to give truthful answers. Each question eliciting a 'yes' answer scores a point. Set a time limit, but make sure each student in a pair has had the same number of opportunities. The winner in each pair is the person who has scored the most points.

- 🎯 **Setting lesson goals:** Ask students: *Who do you think asks more questions in the classroom: students or the teacher?* Elicit opinions. Then, elicit a few

226

examples of the kind of questions heard in the English classroom. Read out the lesson goal from the bottom of page 117.

Exercise 1
- Ask students to read the task, then elicit further examples of the kind of questions teachers often ask them.

Exercise 2   9.11 audioscript page 253
- **EXAM** B1 Preliminary for Schools, Listening, Part 1, (visual multiple choice)
- Ask students to study the sets of pictures for each question, and in pairs, briefly describe what each picture shows. Studying the options before the listening task begins is a good way to prepare for what kind of clues students should expect to hear in the audio. Don't spend more than a minute or two on this stage – in a real exam situation there's usually less time for this. Elicit or pre-teach: *spill* (v).
- Play the audio, pausing briefly after each dialogue to give students time to decide their answers.
- Play the whole audio through without pausing for a second time, so students can check and finalise their answers. Then, check as a class.
- **NEED SUPPORT?** If the class haven't had much experience with this type of task before, play the first dialogue, and after some thinking time, ask for a show of hands to see how many students got the answer right. Ask a volunteer with the correct answer to explain what helped them to decide.

Exercise 3   9.11 audioscript page 253
- Play the dialogues again, without pausing. Ask students to discuss the answers to both questions in pairs before you elicit them in open class.

Exercise 4   9.12
- Read the information in the Vocabulary box as a class. Check that students remember what phrasal verbs are (phrases made up of a verb and one or more short words, often a preposition, whose meaning is usually different from the meaning of the root verb). Set a time limit for the sentence completion task, then allow students to compare answers in pairs before you play the audio for them to check.
- **NEED SUPPORT?** Prepare copies of the photocopiable worksheet on page 240. This version of the task provides options to choose from for each sentence.

Exercise 5   9.13 audioscript page 254
- Remind students to think carefully about the purpose of each question. This should help them to choose the correct answer. Allow them to compare ideas in pairs before you play the audio for them to check.

Exercise 6   44 videoscript page 254
- Pre-teach: *sew*, *grade school* (the North American word for *primary school*), *humble*, *reception class* (first year of primary school in the UK, for ages 4–5), *pebbles*.

- Play the video, and ask students to note down one thing about the school, and one about the teacher, for each speaker.
- Ask students to compare ideas in small groups before you check as a class. Ask them also to say which school they found more interesting, and why.

Exercise 7
- Ask students to write three to six sentences about their primary school experiences, using the video clips from Exercise 6 as a model. Put students in pairs or small groups to share their stories.
- **Monitoring learning:** Listen to the discussions and make a note of any particularly interesting ideas or great use of language and elicit some of these for open-class feedback at the end of the activity.
- **FINISHED EARLY?** Ask students to think of a well-known story of a character in a book or film at a school (for example, Bart Simpson at Springfield Elementary, or Billy Batson in *Shazam!*), and make up some sentences about the character's school experiences.
- **Independent learning:** Ask students to use their Emoji response cards to show how confident they feel about understanding classroom conversations. Make a note to revise language from the lesson, if a number of students indicate concern.

9.6 SPEAKING
Exchanging information

Lesson aims
- Students can exchange information in a conversation.

For the teacher
- Photocopiable activity: *Sort them out*

For the student
- Workbook, page 96
- Extra Practice Activities: New Park video

Lead-in

Write the name *Abe* on the board. Elicit what students remember about his background (where he's from, where he lives now, what kind of things he enjoys doing).
- **Setting lesson goals:** Ask students to study the photo and cover the dialogue. Elicit ideas about what's happening in the scene, and who the person with Abe and Bea might be. Explain that in this lesson you are going to practise exchanging information. Elicit what kind of information the characters may be exchanging in this scene and accept any reasonable suggestions.

Exercise 1
- Ask students to first share their stories in pairs or small groups, then elicit some experiences from volunteers in open class.

9 Lessons in life

Student's Book pages 112–123

Exercise 2 ▶ 45 🔊 9.14
- Play the video or audio and ask students to work in pairs to answer the questions. Check answers as a class.
- Ask students to read the first four lines again. Elicit their ideas for why Abe is correcting what Bea is saying (Bea is using British English phrases: *term, holiday*, and Abe is suggesting their American English equivalents: *semester, vacation*).
- Check understanding of the phrases in the Sounds Good! box. Clarify that the meaning of *I can't wait!* is similar to *I'm looking forward to it!*, but it's more informal.

Exercise 3
- **Peer learning:** Use the Think-Pair-Share technique.

Exercise 4

> **Social responsibility: multicultural competence**
> This task highlights the value of being open to cross-cultural situations and showing sensitivity to different cultural values and experiences. It will get students to consider a range of suitable expressions to use in everyday situations with people from other cultures. This is a valuable skill that will enable students to be better prepared in multicultural contexts.

- Put students in pairs to brainstorm ideas for responding to visitors from other countries and to make a list. Then, put pairs together with another pair in groups of four. Give them large sheets of paper to write up their lists together. At the end, display all the lists, and have the class vote on the best one.
- **Peer learning:** While each group is working on a poster, tell them that they can appoint a 'spy' who can go around the class to look at the ideas from other groups, then report back with their intel in case the group decides to incorporate these extra ideas in their own list.

Exercise 5
- Ask students to read the Speaking box, then to find the responses in the dialogue. **More confident** students could try to recall the responses from memory before they look back in the dialogue to check. Ask students to compare ideas in pairs before you check as a class.

Exercise 6 🔊 9.15
- When students have matched the phrases, play the audio for them to check answers.

Exercise 7
- Read the role-play instructions as a class. Check understanding. Then, form groups of three, and ask students to practise their conversations. Remind them to use the phrases from the Speaking box and Exercise 6. Encourage them to speak from memory, as much as possible, without looking in the book or their notes. Get a few volunteering groups to perform their conversation in open class. Ask the class to listen and record what information is being exchanged.

- **NEED SUPPORT?** Allow **less confident** students to write down their lines before they begin practising.
- **FINISHED EARLY?** Ask students to make a list of facts about Abe, Miyu and Bea – based on the conversation on page 118. If time allows, they could look back at previous episodes as well to expand their fact files about the characters, or to produce a similar fact file for Carla and Eren.
- 🎓 **Independent learning:** Ask students to use their Traffic Light cards to show how confident they feel about the language for exchanging information. Make a note to revise any language that proves challenging for students.

9.7 WRITING

A formal letter asking for information

> **Lesson aims**
> - Students can write a formal letter asking for information.
>
> **For the teacher**
> - Photocopiable activity: *A formal letter*
>
> **For the student**
> - Workbook, page 97

Lead-in

Give students two minutes to write a list of all the different kind of texts they write in their everyday lives (e.g. *messages on social media, text messages, answers to written tasks, school notes, shopping lists, messages to family members*). Elicit suggestions from around the class and ask for a show of hands for each text type to see which ones are the most common.

- 🎯 **Setting lesson goals:** With books closed, elicit situations where people might have to write a formal letter or email. Accept any relevant ideas (e.g. *job application, holiday booking, complaint*). Explain that in this lesson students are going to practise writing a letter to ask for information.

Exercise 1
- Ask students to read the advert, then ask for a show of hands for each course. Get a different volunteer to explain their reasons for each course selected. If there are any courses not chosen by any students, ask a volunteer to try to explain why that option might be less popular with students.

Exercise 2
- First, ask students to scan Georgia's letter quickly to find out which course she has decided to apply for (English for Science), and why (She wants to study Science at university.). Then, ask students to read the letter again more carefully and find the two pieces of information Georgia is asking about. Check answers as a class.

Exercises 3–4
- Follow the instructions in the Student's Book.

Exercise 5
- Ask students to read the Writing Time box and check comprehension. Remind them to follow the instructions step-by-step to write their letters. Suggest that they tick off each stage as they complete it, then move on to the next one in the list.
- **NEED SUPPORT?** **Less confident** students could write a shorter letter by leaving out the paragraph where they give information.
- **FINISHED EARLY?** Ask students to complete the sentences in Exercise 4 from somebody else's point of view (this could be a friend, a family member, a teacher, or a famous person). The sentences don't necessarily have to be factually correct.
- **Independent learning:** Ask students to look at the letter they have written, and give themselves a grade (using whatever system is used in their own school, e.g. A for best, F for unsatisfactory). Ask them also to write a short explanation of why they decided on this grade. Ask them also to make a note of one thing they would like to improve on the next time they do a similar task.
- **Peer learning:** Write the following on the board: *Today I learned how to … I will need more practise in … What I enjoyed most was …* Ask students to think back to Lesson 9.7 and complete the sentences for themselves, then compare their answers in pairs or small groups.

BBC CULTURE

Different forms of education

Lesson aims
- Students learn about different kinds of schools that some teenage students go to.

For the teacher
- Photocopiable activity: *Project worksheet: a website*

Lead-in
Tell students about the school you went to when you were their age. Describe the school subjects and a typical school day. Allow students to ask you questions. Don't spend more than a couple of minutes on your description. Elicit some similarities and differences in comparison with the students' own school. Ask one or two volunteers to give reasons.
- **Setting lesson goals:** Write *alternative school* on the board. Elicit ideas for what the phrase might mean (a school which follows a different curriculum from typical, everyday schools; a school where students learn things in a different way). Ask if students know any alternative schools in their area or country, and elicit some things they know about these. Explain that in this lesson you are going to explore this topic further.

Exercise 1 🔊 9.19
- Put students in pairs to study and describe the photos at the top of page 122 together. Elicit and accept any suggestions in open class. Ask: *What makes you say that?* to elicit students' own justifications.
- **Peer learning:** Use the Think-Pair-Share technique to elicit ideas about question 2.
- Elicit or pre-teach: *alternative, traditional, creative, interactive, practical, academic, instruct, potential* (n). Write these key words on the board. Play the audio as students read the article to answer question 3. Ask students to discuss the writer's viewpoint in pairs, then compare ideas with another pair before you elicit some responses in open class feedback.
- For question 4, assign each half of the classroom to the options, give students ten seconds to choose a side. Form new pairs of students on opposite sides, and give them a minute to explain their reasons to each other.

Exercises 2–3
- Follow the instructions in the Student's Book.

Exercise 4 ▶ 46 videoscript page 254
- Follow the instructions in the Student's Book.
- **With video:** Play the video for students to check their ideas.
- **Without video:** Give students photocopies of the videoscript to check their ideas.

Exercise 5 ▶ 46 videoscript page 254
- First, ask students to read the questions so they know what information to look for.
- **With video:** Play the video and ask students to make notes about their answers.
- **Without video:** Ask students to find and underline the information about each question in the videoscript.

Background note
Football academies combine a traditional (although sometimes reduced) academic education with football skills training. These programmes are most common in Europe, Latin America and the Middle East. North American professional sports teams tend to rely more on talent emerging through college via athletic scholarships and the draft system.

Exercises 6–7
- Follow the instructions in the Student's Book.

Exercise 8
- **PROJECT TIME** The project worksheets include step-by-step support for students. They also include teacher's notes on how to set up the projects with and without technology.
- **Peer learning:** Write on the board: *Today I have learned about/how to/that …* and ask students to complete the prompts in as many different ways as they can. Ask them to compare ideas in pairs.

CLIL

CLIL 1 Science — page 138

Cooking and science

Lesson aims
- Students learn about the chemical processes involved in cooking.

Lead-in

Write *science* on the board, and elicit examples of different sciences (e.g. chemistry, physics, geology, biology) and use these to draw a spidergram. Ask students to brainstorm examples of the kind of things they can learn in each science. Elicit and write these in the spidergram.

- **Setting lesson goals:** Write the lesson title on the board: *Cooking and science*. Elicit ideas for how the two might be connected. Accept any reasonable suggestions.

Background note

Molecular gastronomy is a food science that views cooking as a chemical process. British celebrity chef, Heston Blumenthal, is often associated with molecular gastronomy. Blumenthal's first restaurant, The Fat Duck, is considered to be one of the best restaurants in the UK, offering dishes like scrambled egg ice cream.

Exercise 1
- Follow the instructions in the Student's Book.

Exercise 2 10.2
- Elicit or pre-teach: *substance, process* (n), *irreversible, texture, solid*. Play the audio as students read the text and find the answers to the questions. Allow them to compare answers in pairs before you check as a class.

Exercise 3
- **Peer learning**: Use the Think-Pair-Share technique.

Exercise 4
- Elicit or explain: *raw ingredient*. Give students half a minute to think of an example, then put them in pairs to do the guessing activity. Elicit some examples from volunteers.

Exercises 5–6
- Before students begin, you could brainstorm some ideas together (e.g. bread or cakes rising, sugar turning to caramel), so students have something more concrete to research. Ask each student to choose one chemical change and then research and prepare a three-minute digital presentation. Remind them to make notes about each point in Exercise 5 and to follow the steps in Exercise 6.
- **Peer learning:** Ask students to think of three things they learned about cooking and science. Put them together in small groups to compare ideas.

CLIL 2 Music — page 139

David Bowie and space

Lesson aims
- Students learn about David Bowie, an influential singer/songwriter.

Lead-in

Put students in groups and ask them to tell each other about their favourite pop/rock musician. Ask students to think of their favourite song by that artist and tell their partners what the song is about.

- **Setting lesson goals:** Write the lesson title *David Bowie and space* on the board. Elicit some ideas of what the lesson will be about. Accept any reasonable suggestions.

Background note

David Bowie is regarded as one of the most important popular music artists of the 20th century. He was only 15 when he started playing in a band. His breakthrough album was *The Rise and Fall of Ziggy Stardust and the Spiders from Mars* in 1972. The 25 studio albums released in his lifetime have sold over 140 million copies worldwide, making him one of the best-selling music artists of all time.

Exercises 1–2
- Follow the instructions in the Student's Book.

Exercises 3–4 10.3
- Elicit or pre-teach: *imaginative, unique, experiment* (v), *aliens, fictional, lose contact, astronaut*.
- Follow the instructions in the Student's Book.

Exercise 5
- **Peer learning:** While students read their texts, encourage them to think about their intended audience (their partner) and what their partner will want to know about it.
- Play the two songs. Ask for a show of hands, and elicit reasons from volunteers for their preference.

Exercises 6–7
- Brainstorm some examples of famous singer/songwriters in the students' country as a class. Ask each student to choose one artist and then research and prepare a three-minute digital presentation. Remind them to make notes about each point in Exercise 6 and to follow the steps in Exercise 7.
- **Peer learning:** Ask students to test each other in pairs about what they remember from the lesson. They take turns to ask and answer their partner's questions.

CLIL 3 Geography — page 140

The International Date Line

Lesson aims
- Students learn about the most significant lines used in mapping the world.

Lead-in

Look up the coordinates for the students' town and write them on the board (e.g. *51.5072° North, 0.1276° West* for London). Elicit what these numbers are, and how they point to a location on the map. Elicit students' ideas about where the place might be before revealing that it is their own town.

- **Setting lesson goals:** Write *IDL* on the board and elicit ideas for what the abbreviation might stand for. Then, tell students it's the International Date Line, and elicit suggestions of what that might be. Accept any reasonable ideas.

Background note

To define the location of any point on Earth, you need two coordinates: its latitude (its position in relation to the Equator, north or south) and its longitude (its position in relation to the **Prime Meridian**, east or west). The Equator is simply the line farthest from each pole. The Prime Meridian is also called the Greenwich Meridian because it passes through the Royal Observatory in Greenwich, London.

Exercise 1
- **Peer learning:** Use the Think-Pair-Share technique.

Exercise 2 10.4
- Elicit or pre-teach: *imaginary, Equator, hemisphere* (one half of the earth, especially the half above or below the Equator), *divide, (North/South) Pole, celebrate*. Play the audio as students read the text to check their ideas and label the maps. Check answers.

Exercises 3–4
- Follow the instructions in the Student's Book.

Exercises 5–6
- Elicit or pre-teach: *explorer, sail round the world, keep records*. Ask students to read the text, then put them in pairs to complete both tasks. Check answers as a class.

Exercises 7–8
- Brainstorm examples of other imaginary lines around Earth (e.g. Tropic of Cancer, Tropic of Capricorn, Arctic Circle, Antarctic Circle). Then, ask each student to choose one to research and prepare a three-minute presentation. Remind them to make notes about each point in Exercise 7 and to follow the steps in Exercise 8.
- **Independent learning:** Ask students to decide what they found most interesting or most surprising about the lesson, then to tell a partner.

CLIL 4 Science — page 141

Forensics

Lesson aims
- Students learn about the role of science in criminal investigations.

Lead-in

Ask: *Do you watch crime or detective series? How do detectives usually find and catch the criminals?* Elicit students' ideas and experiences, and invite comments from others.

- **Setting lesson goals:** Write *forensics* on the board and elicit ideas from students for what it might mean. Accept all suggestions, then ask them to look through page 141 quickly to check their ideas.

Background note

Fingerprints were first used in India by Sir William Herschel in 1858 for identification. Within the next few decades, application of the science became common around the world. The first criminal fingerprint identification was made in 1892 by Juan Vucetich in a murder case.

Forensic **DNA** (abbreviation for *deoxyribonucleic acid*) analysis was first used in Britain in 1984. These days, most law enforcement agencies maintain a DNA database of known criminals to speed up identification.

Exercise 1
- **Peer learning:** Use the Think–Pair–Share technique.

Exercises 2–3 10.5
- Elicit or pre-teach: *crime scene, evidence, fingerprints, laboratory, (finger)tips, identical twins, saliva*. Play the audio as students read the text to check their ideas, then answer the questions. Ask students to compare answers in pairs before you check as a class.

Exercises 4–5
- Follow the instructions in the Student's Book.

Exercises 6–7
- Ask students to research and prepare a three-minute presentation of a famous crime case (recent or historical). Remind them to make notes about points in Exercise 6 and to follow the steps in Exercise 7.
- **Reviewing lesson goals:** Books closed. Write *fingerprints, DNA, hair, shoes* on the board. Ask students to take turns to tell each other how each one can be used as evidence in criminal investigations. They then check their ideas on page 141.

1 Need support? worksheets

1.2 Grammar — Exercise 4

Make questions about the text, using the verb tense given in brackets. Ask and answer the questions in pairs.

1. Evy / normally / write / the band's blog / ? (Present Simple)
2. the band members / usually / travel / on Saturday afternoons / ? (Present Simple)
3. the band / play / a lot of concerts / these days / ? (Present Continuous)
4. the skateboarders / perform / in a competition / today / ? (Present Continuous)
5. Sara / wear / a helmet in the photo / ? (Present Continuous)
6. Sara / know / lots of awesome tricks / ? (Present Simple)

1.3 Reading and Vocabulary — Exercise 3

Read the texts and match sentences 1–4 with the missing information a–d.

A
1. Kieran is part of a _____.
2. The maximum prize in the competition is _____.

B and C
3. Lorraine wants to help _____.
4. Angie suggests putting _____ in the box.

a. animals that are in danger
b. £25,000
c. a waterproof camera
d. Science and Technology Group/SGT

1.5 Listening and Vocabulary — Exercise 6

🔊 1.13 Listen to the second part of the programme. Choose the correct answer to complete the sentences about the way the people use the technology.

1. *Mum / Lara* uses the phone alarm and checks messages.
2. *Dad / Mum* reads the news on a tablet.
3. *Dad / Lara* downloads and uses a running app.
4. *Lara's brother / Dad* looks at funny video clips and laughs.
5. *Lara / Everyone* often shares photos.

1.7 Writing — Exercise 5

Choose the correct connector to complete the sentences. Then, rewrite the underlined part of each sentence so they are true for you.

1. *Although / Because* I really enjoy going to football matches, I only do this once a year.
2. I often play golf on my computer, *and / but* I never do it in real life.
3. In the evenings, I go online *so / also* I can chat to my friends.
4. I'm a big fan of building games. *However, / As well as* I don't like fighting games.
5. I often post things on social media, and I sometimes share photos, *so / too*.

Need support? worksheets

2.2 Grammar — Exercise 8

For each question in Exercise 7, write the beginning of the answer, with the main verb. Then listen to the interview and choose the correct information below to complete each sentence 1–5. There are two extra pieces of information.

1 *Mariana met* _____.
2 _____.
3 _____.
4 _____.
5 _____.

> three storms   on different nights   two weeks ago
> storms   a scientist   thunder   on their website

2.3 Reading and Vocabulary — Exercise 4

Read the whole article and choose the correct answer.

1 Miguel says that the temperature
   a makes you feel tired.
   b is normal for the time of year.
2 The volcano crater was
   a really unusual.
   b not very big.
3 One night in the desert Miguel
   a slept in the open air.
   b saw something special in the sky.
4 According to Miguel, sand dunes
   a can make noises.
   b can be used for sport.

Answer question 5 in your Student's Book.

2.5 Listening and Vocabulary — Exercise 5

🔊 2.12 Listen again and match sentence beginnings 1–4 with the endings a–d.

1 Poppy didn't sleep outside because ____.
2 She didn't listen to the wildlife because ____.
3 There weren't any spiders in the camp because ____.
4 In the cave, ____.

a she slept really well.
b she saw hundreds of bats.
c the nights were cold.
d it was too cold for them to come out.

2.7 Writing — Exercise 5

Study the Language box on page 31. Choose the correct indefinite pronoun to complete the sentences.

1 *Anybody / Everybody* knows that our country has lots of mountains.
2 In our town, you can find great music and food *everywhere / everything*.
3 When you hear strange noises and music, you often realise that *somebody / anything* is dancing.
4 If you want to visit *somewhere / everywhere* outside our town, the best thing is to take a bicycle.
5 There isn't *anywhere / something* better than our town!

3 Need support? worksheets

3.1 Vocabulary — Exercise 9

🔊 3.6 Listen to two friends speaking about ice cream. Complete the notes with the flavours they mention.

Favourite flavours: strawberry and ¹_____
honey and ²_____
Unusual flavours: ³_____ and blue cheese
⁴_____
chocolate and ⁵_____
Fake flavour: ⁶_____ and _____

3.3 Reading and Vocabulary — Exercise 3

Read the article again and complete the sentences with phrases below. There are two extra phrases.

| chocolate cake   ~~chocolate regularly~~   crunchy snack |
| give you energy   healthier for you   health problems |
| positive effect on the brain   recipes   shy or nervous |

1 Your memory can improve if you eat *chocolate regularly*.
2 Dark chocolate is better for you than _____.
3 Salmon can stop you having _____.
4 Pickles are good in burgers or on their own as a _____.
5 You should eat pickles if you are _____.
6 Eating raw pumpkin seeds is _____.
7 You can add garlic to all sorts of _____.

3.4 Grammar — Exercise 5

Complete the sentences with the correct Present Perfect form of the verb in brackets and *for* or *since*.

1 I haven't _____ (have) a chocolate bar _____ a month.
2 My family has _____ (own) this café _____ 2010.
3 We haven't _____ (eat) any food _____ breakfast time.
4 This cookery programme has _____ (be) on TV _____ a few months.
5 Have you _____ (see) the cookery teacher _____ last lesson?
6 They've _____ (be) at the juice bar _____ half an hour.

3.6 Speaking — Exercise 4

Match questions 1–5 with answers a–e. There are two possible answers; choose the correct one. Use the Speaking box to help you.

1 Are you ready to order?   c / e
2 Could we share a dessert?   a / e
3 Have you got any fresh fruit?   a / b
4 What can I get you to drink?   b / d
5 Would you like chips with that?   d / e

a Yes, we have pineapple or melon.
b a fresh orange juice, please.
c Yes, can I have a chicken curry?
d No, not for me, thanks.
e Yes, of course we can.

Need support? worksheets

4.2 Grammar — Exercise 5

Choose the correct answer so the second sentence means the same as the first.

2. Our town isn't big enough for a theatre.
   Our town is *too small / smaller* for a theatre.
3. The film is funnier than the book.
   The book isn't *as funny as / funny enough* the film.
4. The main character in the film is too boring.
   The main character in the film isn't *more interesting / interesting enough*.
5. The French thriller isn't as scary as the Danish thriller.
   The Danish thriller is *scarier than / too scary for* the French thriller.

4.3 Reading and Vocabulary — Exercise 4

Read the blog post again and choose the correct name.

1. *Damon / André* thinks you reach different people on streaming services.
2. *Damon / Carmela* has similar views to the blogger.
3. *André / Carmela* plays an instrument and also sings.
4. *Damon / André* likes going to concerts.
5. *André / Carmela* makes his/her own music.

4.5 Listening and Vocabulary — Exercise 3

🔊 **4.11 Listen to the second part of the interview and choose the correct answer.**

1. Why is the festival special for Bruno?
   a. He enjoys the winter in Brazil.
   b. He likes being with his family.
2. How are the costumes different now?
   a. Girls often wear the same type of clothes as boys.
   b. Many boys don't wear checked shirts anymore.
3. What happens in one funny race?
   a. People in the race get a secret message.
   b. Runners hold a spoon with an egg in it.

Answer questions 4 and 5 in your Student's Book.

4.7 Writing — Exercise 5

Complete the text with the adverbs below.

> brilliantly   fast   happily   incredibly   particularly   well

I loved the new *Dune* film. All the actors played their parts very ¹_____, but I ²_____ liked Timothée Chalamet in the role of young Paul Atreides. He played the hero ³_____. *Dune* takes place on alien planets, but it all looks ⁴_____ real. The action didn't move very ⁵_____, so *Dune* is a very long film, but I would ⁶_____ watch it for a few more hours.

5 Need support? worksheets

5.3 Reading and Vocabulary — Exercise 3

Read the article again. Choose the correct name.

1 *Carrie / Ryan* follows the sport online to get better.
2 *Carrie / Suzy* mentions a favourite piece of equipment.
3 *Ryan / Suzy* trains with a family member.
4 *Carrie / Suzy* mentions she would like to get involved in competitive sport.
5 *Carrie / Ryan* mentions how training starts and finishes.
6 *Ryan's / Suzy's* coach warns younger people not to train too much.

5.4 Grammar — Exercise 5

5.10 Read the sentences and choose the correct verb forms. Listen and check.

1 If they *close / will close* the sports centre, we *aren't / won't be* able to play handball for ages.
2 I *won't stop / don't stop* playing badminton if they *close / will close* it.
3 We *don't have / won't have* karate lessons unless the teacher *finds / doesn't find* a new classroom.
4 I *'ll go / go* swimming every week if they *build / will build* a pool at the new centre.
5 If there *are / will be* tennis courts, I *take up / 'll take up* tennis.
6 We *'ll join / join* the new gym if it *isn't / won't be* too expensive.

5.5 Listening and Vocabulary — Exercise 4

5.11 Listen and choose the correct answer.

1 Callum thinks Marcus Rashford is
 a the best English football player.
 b not as good as another player.
2 When Marcus Rashford plays for Manchester United, he wears the number
 a ten.
 b eleven.
3 Megan thinks the winner of the BBC award should be
 a the best athlete.
 b the best person.
4 How many free meals did Marcus Rashford's charity pay for?
 a 400,000
 b 3 million

Answer question 5 in your Student's book.

5.6 Speaking — Exercise 2

27 5.14 Watch or listen and check your answers to Exercise 1. Then choose the correct name.

1 *Abe / Bea* is going to hang out with a friend.
2 *Abe / Eren* is going to play a sports match.
3 *Bea / Carla* is going to spend time with her family.
4 *Carla / Abe* is going to watch a sport event.

Need support? worksheets

6.3 Reading and Vocabulary — Exercise 3

Read the text again. Complete the sentences with no more than two words.

1 Water buses are _____ _____ to take you everywhere.
2 Gondolas are best for _____ _____.
3 If there's no bridge, you can cross the Grand Canal by _____.
4 If you travel around on a rented boat, you might get into a _____ _____ or have _____ _____.
5 The best and _____ way to see Venice is on foot.

6.4 Grammar — Exercise 5

Complete the sentences with the verbs below.

| can't   can't   could   might   must   ~~must~~ |

2 They're very quiet. Perhaps they're sleeping.
  They're very quiet. They _____ be sleeping.
3 I'm sure this isn't the same campsite.
  This _____ be the same campsite.
4 Dad thinks this is your ticket, but your ticket is in your hand.
  This _____ be your ticket because your ticket is in your hand.
5 I'm sure the map is on the table. I put it there.
  The map _____ be on the table. I put it there.
6 Here's a guidebook, but perhaps it's the wrong one.
  Here's a guidebook, but it _____ be the wrong one.

6.5 Listening and Vocabulary — Exercise 5

🔊 6.13 Listen and complete Jess's story with one or two words or a number. The first letter is given.

Activity camp information form

Name: [1] Jess
Age: [2] 1_____
Where from: [3] N_____ Z_____
Disability: [4] b_____
Likes: [5] a_____
Recent holidays: went on a [6] s_____ h_____ last year
Activity camp achievement: climbed a [7] m_____

6.7 Writing — Exercise 5

Complete the sentences with future time clauses so they are true for you.

1 I'll go cycling when _____ .
2 I'll _____ after I leave school.
3 Before I'm old, I'll definitely visit _____ .
4 I won't stop studying English until I can _____ .
5 I'll _____ as soon as I get home today.

7 Need support? worksheets

7.2 Grammar — Exercise 4

🔊 7.6 **Choose the correct verb form to complete the sentences. Listen and check.**

1 If I *have / had* enough time, I *helped / would help*.
2 If you *listened / would listen* carefully, you *understood / would understand*.
3 *Would / Will* you go to the beach if you *were / would be* free today?
4 He *wouldn't come / didn't come* here if he *wouldn't want / didn't want* to.
5 What *would / did* you do if you *would earn / earned* a lot of money?
6 *I'd phone / I'll phone* your dad if I *was / were* you.

7.3 Reading and Vocabulary — Exercise 3

Read the article again and complete the sentences with the phrases below. There is one extra phrase.

> a mirror   can't stand   conversations   friendship
> make time   send messages   three

1 The article tells us that there are five steps to _____.
2 For the first step, you may share information about things you like or _____.
3 When you've shared information, it's easier to have _____.
4 If both friends often listen and support each other, they have reached step _____.
5 A friend who supports your social identity acts like _____.
6 If you and your friend are in different places, you can call or _____.

7.4 Grammar — Exercise 5

Complete the sentences with *who*, *that*, *which*, or *where*.

1 Holly has a good friend _____ lives next door.
2 In Gran's house there's a picture _____ is 100 years old.
3 This is the camera _____ my dad uses on holiday.
4 There's a park _____ children play.

7.5 Listening and Vocabulary — Exercise 6

🔊 7.12 **Listen and choose the correct answer.**

1 A puppy trainer
   a teaches young dogs special skills.
   b finds new homes for unwanted dogs.
2 When the dogs left, Tilly felt
   a sad.
   b happy for them.
3 Who trained Prince?
   a Tilly on her own.
   b Tilly and her step-mum together.
4 What is the main thing we learn about assistance dogs from Tilly's account?
   a They take a long time to learn things.
   b They can help with a wide range of needs.

Need support? worksheets

8.2 Grammar — Exercise 6

Choose the correct answer to complete the text with the Present or Past Simple passive.

The *Nancy Drew* stories are among the most famous detective stories ever. The first stories about Nancy Drew [1] *are / were* published in the 1930s. Other, newer stories have appeared since then. The books [2] *created / were created* for teenagers.

The *Nancy Drew* detective stories [3] *were written by / wrote by* several different authors. The name Carolyn Keene [4] *was used / was using* by all the authors, but Nancy's name [5] *changed / was changed* in some countries. It may be surprising but this old series [6] *is / was* read by thousands of young people even today, and each year lots and lots of copies [7] *sold / are sold*.

8.3 Reading and Vocabulary — Exercise 3

Read the article and choose the correct answer.

1. What did the police officer do that was surprising?
   a. He arrested Lisa and Ian for stealing.
   b. He asked Lisa and Ian to choose where to go.

2. Why did Lisa and Ian choose to go to a youth court?
   a. They believed their actions were legal.
   b. They wanted to be heard by people of their own age.

3. Which of these statements is true about youth courts?
   a. You are heard by people who are a similar age.
   b. You can choose a punishment that works for you.

8.4 Grammar — Exercise 6

Complete the sentences with the correct form of *have something done*. Use the verb tense in brackets.

1. I _____ (my hair/cut) last week. (Past Simple)
2. I _____ (my eyes/not test) for ages. (Present Perfect)
3. I _____ (already/my photo/print) in the local paper twice. (Present Perfect)
4. I don't want to _____ (my bike/steal), so I always lock it up. (Present Simple)
5. I'd love to _____ (my bedroom/clean), but I have to do it myself. (Present Simple)

8.7 Writing — Exercise 5

Complete the second sentence, using a phrase with the word in brackets, so it means the same as the first sentence. Use the Language box on page 107 to help you.

1. People should take their litter home to protect the environment.
   People should take their litter home _____ protect the environment. (as)

2. They had to pay a fine, so they are more careful now.
   They had to pay a fine. _____, they are more careful now. (result)

3. Animals are important, so people need to think about them.
   Animals are important. _____, people need to think about them. (reason)

4. I believe fines are useful to help us keep the law.
   I believe fines are useful _____ help us keep the law. (order)

9 Need support? worksheets

9.1 Vocabulary — Exercise 11

Look at the ideas below and decide which class activities and which types of assessment are the most suitable for different subjects. Discuss in pairs and give reasons.

School subjects	Classroom activities	Types of assessment
English	group presentations	written exam
Literature	role play	speaking exam
History	note-taking	presentation
Maths	project work	project
Science	experiments	online test
PE	games	practical exam
IT	spidergrams	

Can you add other ideas to the lists?

_____

9.3 Reading and Vocabulary — Exercise 3

🔊 9.8 Match the words 1–4 to the things a–d.

1 she   a the word
2 Why   b tests
3 they   c Mrs Jones
4 it   d because

Read the text again. Complete the gaps with a sentence from the list. Use the words in bold. There is one extra sentence.

a Think of things that are related to **it**.
b It's 'study in different places'.
c **She** told us about an interesting experiment.
d Many people forget the next rule.
e **They**'re actually a good way for us to learn!
f **Why** did they remember the information so well?

9.4 Grammar — Exercise 3

Order the words to make questions for the answers.

2 this morning / home / Did / late / leave / you / ?
   No, I left home early this morning, not late.
   _____

3 on holiday / you / going / Are / this year / ?
   Yes, we're going to Brazil for our summer holidays.
   _____

4 the cinema / go / last week / you / Did / to / ?
   Yes, I saw two films at the cinema last week.
   _____

5 your birthday / a party / for / you / going / Are / to have / ?
   No, I'm not going to do anything for my birthday.
   _____

9.5 Listening and Vocabulary — Exercise 4

🔊 9.12 Study the Vocabulary box on page 117 and choose the correct phrasal verb to complete the sentences below. Listen and check.

1 The teacher asked us all to *fill in* / *hand in* our homework on time.
2 Pupils who finish early should *get on* / *calm down* with some extra reading.
3 I'm definitely coming to the end-of-term party – I don't want to *look over* / *miss out* on all the fun!
4 Make sure you *hand out* / *look over* all your answers before you finish.
5 You can *look over* / *look up* any words you don't know in a dictionary.
6 We have to *hand out* / *fill in* this form with our name and phone number.
7 Ella was so nervous before her exam, so I told her to *get on* / *calm down* and take a deep breath.

Need support? worksheets answer key

UNIT 1

1.2 Grammar
Exercise 4
1 Does Evy normally write the band's blog?
2 Do the band members usually travel on Saturday afternoons?
3 Is the band playing a lot of concerts these days?
4 Are the skateboarders performing in a competition today?
5 Is Sara wearing a helmet in the photo?
6 Does Sara know lots of awesome tricks?

1.3 Reading and Vocabulary
Exercise 3
1 d 2 b 3 a 4 c

1.5 Listening and Vocabulary
Exercise 6
1 Lara 2 Mum 3 Dad
4 Lara's brother 5 Everyone

1.7 Writing
Exercise 5
1 Although 2 but 3 so 4 However,
5 too
Students' own answers

UNIT 2

2.2 Grammar
Exercise 8
1 Mariana met a scientist.
2 Professor Mendes studied storms.
3 Mariana went to Lake Maracaibo two weeks ago.
4 She saw three storms.
5 She put the photos on their website.

2.3 Reading and Vocabulary
Exercise 4
1 a 2 a 3 b 4 b

2.5 Listening and Vocabulary
Exercise 5
1 c 2 a 3 d 4 b

2.7 Writing
Exercise 5
1 Everybody 2 everywhere 3 somebody
4 somewhere 5 anywhere

UNIT 3

3.1 Vocabulary
Exercise 9
1 vanilla 2 mango 3 pear 4 pepper
5 chilli 6 salt, vinegar

3.3 Reading and Vocabulary
Exercise 3
2 chocolate cake 3 health problems
4 crunchy snack 5 shy or nervous
6 healthier for you 7 recipes

3.4 Grammar
Exercise 5
1 had, for 2 owned, since 3 eaten, since
4 been, for 5 seen, since 6 been, for

3.6 Speaking
Exercise 4
1 c 2 e 3 a 4 b 5 d

UNIT 4

4.2 Grammar
Exercise 5
2 too small 3 as funny as
4 interesting enough 5 scarier than

4.3 Reading and Vocabulary
Exercise 4
1 André 2 Carmela 3 Carmela
4 Damon 5 Carmela

4.5 Listening and Vocabulary
Exercise 3
1 b 2 a 3 b

4.7 Writing
Exercise 5
1 well 2 particularly 3 brilliantly
4 incredibly 5 fast 6 happily

UNIT 5

5.3 Reading and Vocabulary
Exercise 3
1 Ryan 2 Carrie 3 Ryan 4 Suzy 5 Carrie
6 Suzy's

5.4 Grammar
Exercise 5
1 close, won't be 2 won't stop, close
3 won't have, finds 4 'll go, build
5 are, 'll take up 6 'll join, isn't

5.5 Listening and Vocabulary
Exercise 4
1 b 2 a 3 b 4 b

5.6 Speaking
Exercise 2
1 Bea 2 Eren 3 Carla 4 Abe

UNIT 6

6.3 Reading and Vocabulary
Exercise 3
1 too wide 2 sightseeing trips
3 traghetto 4 traffic jam, an accident
5 safest

6.4 Grammar
Exercise 5
2 could/might 3 can't 4 can't 5 must
6 could/might

6.5 Listening and Vocabulary
Exercise 5
2 16 3 New Zealand 4 blind
5 adventure 6 sailing holiday 7 mast

6.7 Writing
Exercise 5
Students' own answers

UNIT 7

7.2 Grammar
Exercise 4
1 had, would help 2 listened, would understand 3 Would, were 4 wouldn't come, didn't want 5 would, earned
6 I'd phone, were/was

7.3 Reading and Vocabulary
Exercise 3
1 friendship 2 can't stand
3 conversations 4 three 5 a mirror
6 send messages

7.4 Grammar
Exercise 5
1 who 2 which/that 3 which/that 4 where

7.5 Listening and Vocabulary
Exercise 6
1 a 2 a 3 b 4 b

UNIT 8

8.2 Grammar
Exercise 6
1 were 2 were created 3 were written by
4 was used 5 was changed 6 is
7 are sold

8.3 Reading and Vocabulary
Exercise 3
1 b 2 b 3 a

8.4 Grammar
Exercise 6
1 had my hair cut
2 haven't had my eyes tested
3 have already had my photo printed
4 have my bike stolen
5 have my bedroom cleaned

8.7 Writing
Exercise 5
1 so as to 2 As a result 3 For this reason
4 in order to

UNIT 9

9.1 Vocabulary
Exercise 11
Students' own ideas

9.3 Reading and Vocabulary
Exercise 3
Lead-in: 1c, 2d, 3b, 4a
Main task: 1 c, 2 f, 3 e, 4 b, 5 a

9.4 Grammar
Exercise 3
2 Did you leave home late this morning?
3 Are you going on holiday this year?
4 Did you go to the cinema last week?
5 Are you going to have a party for your birthday?

9.5 Listening and Vocabulary
Exercise 4
1 hand in 2 get on 3 miss out 4 look over
5 look up 6 fill in 7 calm down

Student's Book audioscripts and videoscripts

UNIT 0

🔊 0.9 Unit 0, 0.3, Exercise 8

L = Louka M = Max

L: Hey, Max. How are things? You look a bit nervous.
M: No, I'm not. I'm excited because I've got a big tennis match tomorrow.
L: What do you mean? There aren't any matches tomorrow. They're on Sunday!
M: Oh, you're right. Phew! I feel more relaxed already.
L: Good. In fact, there's a party tomorrow evening. Do you want to come?
M: Sure. I'd love to go to a party …
L: So what's the problem?
M: Tomorrow's Saturday, so I can't come. I don't want to feel tired on Sunday morning!

🔊 0.12 Unit 0, 0.4, Exercise 7

I = Interviewer E = Ella

I: Did you enjoy your summer holiday?
E: Yes, I did, thanks. I stayed with my cousins in Sopot in Poland. We walked along the beach every day. I loved it!
I: So, did you learn any Polish?
E: No, I didn't. Well, maybe a few new words. I speak Polish quite well anyway, because my mum's from Poland. But I learned some German when I was there because a very nice German family live next door to my cousins. It was a really good holiday.

🔊 0.13 Unit 0, 0.5, Exercise 2

Eren and his friend Abe are in Eren's garden with Abe's cousin Bea and her friend Carla. The weather is beautiful today. It's sunny and quite warm, so they're happy to be outside. There are a few places for young people to go in town, but on a day like this they don't mind sitting in the garden. They're chatting about school and their plans for the weekend. Bea is very excited because she is visiting her family in Brighton. Eren is annoyed when he finds out that there is a test in Maths on Monday.

UNIT 1

🔊 1.2 Unit 1, 1.1, Exercise 5

1 This is a *remote control*. You use it to change the channels or the sound volume on a TV.
2 This is a *charging cable*. You use it to charge the battery in your mobile phone.
3 This is a *password*. You use it to keep personal information safe online.
4 This is a *wi-fi router*. You use it to connect your phone or computer to an internet service.
5 This is a *power bank*. You use it to power up the battery on your mobile phone when you're not at home.
6 These are *wireless earbuds*. You use them to listen to music on your phone, tablet or computer.

🔊 1.4 Unit 1, 1.1, Exercise 8

1 I need to connect to the wi-fi router. Do you know the password?
2 Hang on, I'll send you a link to the website.
3 I often take a screenshot of important information on my phone.
4 I never share a link if I don't know it's safe to do so.
5 I often set a new password for my social media accounts.

▶ 5 Wider World, Unit 1, 1.1, Exercise 11

P = Presenter R = Roshni C = Cecile A = Adrian

P: In these videos we talk to people in the streets of London and ask them about their opinions on different topics. London is a huge and exciting city. Lots of people live here. And even more visit it every year from all over the world. Let's see who we're meeting today and what they tell us. Who in your family uses technology the most? What do they use it for?
R: I think my dad uses technology the most. He is always on his computer or his iPad, emailing people at work and he's always using his phone, much more than I do probably, just phoning other work colleagues, I guess.
My mum uses technology, but she only really uses her computer to watch programmes online. She doesn't know that much about how to use a computer. And then I guess I use my phone and my computer a lot to do uni work and write essays and that's about it.
C: So, my boyfriend uses technology a lot for everything. He does use his computer or tablet or smartphone for anything, starting from the weather.
A: My older brother, my oldest brother uses the most technology. He is an architect and all his architecture and design programs.

▶ 6 Wider World, Unit 1, 1.2, Exercise 6

P = Presenter H = Holly C = Chee R = Reema A = Akshay M = Mary An = Annette

P: What sports do you like?
H: I like all sorts of things, really. I'm, like, on my way actually to a yoga class right now, and I recently joined a health club near my home, so I'm doing classes like spinning, the circuits, step classes and stuff like that.
C: I quite like jogging, and, or strolling. It depends what mood I'm in. But I like exploring the green and that kind of calms me down and relaxes me quite a lot. I quite like badminton. I haven't played it in a long time, though. It does get my heart rate going. I'm not perfect at it, but it makes me happy, and I also enjoy bouldering, which is like rock climbing but it's like man-made rocks, does that make sense? And yeah, that's quite fun.
P: What do you like to do in your free time?
R: I love baking. So that's what I try and do over weekends or whenever I have the free time and I love to sing. I try and do that once a week where I, where I have a group of guys who love doing the same and we get together once a week and spend, like, a couple of hours singing. Yeah.
A: And as she loves baking, I love eating the stuff that she bakes.
P: What sport would you like to learn?
M: I'd love to learn self-defence, some kind of self-defence sport. But I've never really pursued that dream, so maybe I'll do that in the future.
An: I really would like to learn volleyball.
P: What new sports would you like to try?
C: So I'd really like to try skydiving. That's, oh, I'm really scared of heights, actually, but I'd really be proud of myself if I tried skydiving.
H: I'd like to try water skiing. I've never done it but it looks very difficult, so I'm not sure how good I'd be.

🔊 1.12 Unit 1, 1.5, Exercise 5

P = Presenter

P: And hello from Gold Radio! Now, a report today says that families are spending less time together because they're always on their phones or tablets. In the studio, I've got Lara. Lara, you live with your mum and older brother. Tell me, is this true in your house?

1.13 Unit 1, 1.5, Exercise 6

P = Presenter L = Lara

L: Well, I think we're the same as most other families. We love our screens and all enjoy using our smartphones at home. We've all got one. On a school day I use the alarm on my phone, so the minute I wake up, I see my phone and … er, I check my messages. Then I get up. My phone goes everywhere with me because I listen to music on it.
P: And what about your mum and dad?
L: Mum prefers her tablet. She often reads the news on it. My dad's training for a race and he downloads apps on his phone to show him how fast he runs or where he runs.
P: Your brother's older. Does he still use his phone or tablet a lot?
L: Yeah, definitely. He loves looking at funny video clips. He often sits with his earphones in and laughs. Mum gets a bit angry when she asks him something and he doesn't answer.
P: So, do you think you talk less at home because of the technology?
L: No, not at all. We never message at mealtimes. But in the evening we like watching funny videos and we often share photos. It's a big part of our daily life and I think it's something that we all enjoy.

1.15 Unit 1, 1.6, Exercise 3

1 My phone isn't working.
2 I can't find the cable for my phone.
3 I can't get this app to work.
4 The instructions are in Japanese.

1.19 Unit 1, Revision, Exercise 8

Too much technology can be bad for you. Once a week, I switch off my phone, my computer and all my other electronic things. Then I spend the next hour or two away from screens. It's good for me!

9 BBC Culture, Exercises 6 and 7

Disconnecting

Today's teenagers spend a lot of time online. During the day, how often do you look at a phone, or another device? But it's not just teenagers, of course! The average British person spends around three hours on their phone every day. Is it something that we just can't stop?

Matt thinks that he uses his phone too much. Natalie is worried about the same thing.

'I realised it was the first thing I do and the last thing I do – in the morning and before I go to bed.'

But are smartphones really a serious problem? Scientists are trying to find the answer to this question.

This is Professor Nancy Cheever from the University of California. In Professor Cheever's experiments, people have to give her their phones and then watch a video. In secret, Professor Cheever sends text messages to their phones. It isn't easy to concentrate on the video! A computer shows how far each person's stress levels go up.

'This is awful!'

Maybe we should be worried about it.

Matt and Natalie are having a break from their phones and from the Internet. They're staying in a remote valley in Wales. Everybody's phones and digital devices go in a box.

But how do they feel the next morning?

'My mind thought, Oh, I'd better just check my phone. Like, what's going on? You know. I might have a text message or something.'

The group do relaxing, healthy activities to stop them thinking about their phones. They also do some group exercises. Today, everybody can have their devices back again.

'This is so strange! Hi, darling!'

How are they feeling?

'I didn't want it back and I thought I would be looking forward to this moment, but I didn't want this moment to happen so soon. No. I guess I don't need it.'

But the next day …

Perhaps we should take more breaks from technology to change our bad habits.

UNIT 2

2.3 Unit 2, 2.1, Exercise 6

1 The weather forecast for today is for heavy rain. The weather forecast for Tuesday is for heavy snow and strong winds. The weather forecast for Sunday is for some high temperatures in the middle of the day, but quite low temperatures at night.
2 It will be ten degrees Celsius in the daytime, but it will be minus five degrees at night. It will be wet on Monday, but it will be dry on Tuesday. It will be cool on Wednesday, but it will be warm on Thursday. It will be boiling hot this week, but it will be freezing cold next month.
3 It's warm and the temperature is rising in the west, but in the east the temperature is falling.
4 The weather was good, but it's bad now. It's going to be fine tomorrow.
5 Australia has a hot climate. The UK has a mild climate. Iceland has a cold climate.

2.4 Unit 2, 2.1, Exercises 8 and 9

And now let's look at the winter weather in Europe. In Krakow, Poland, it's a very cold day with a temperature of minus two degrees. There is some ice on the roads, so be careful. And it's a good day in Barcelona, which is sunny at the moment. It's quite warm. The temperature is a comfortable nineteen degrees now. There is the possibility of some light rain later. And finally, Istanbul in Turkey is very cloudy today, with some fog that is causing a few problems at the airport. The temperature is around seven degrees at the moment. This evening it could be cool, so don't forget to keep warm. And that's all from us until …

2.6 Unit 2, 2.2, Exercise 8

R = Roberto M = Mariana

R: First up on tonight's programme, Mariana Fernandez tells us more about a very strange storm. Mariana?
M: Well, last year I met a scientist who studied storms. His name was Professor Mendes. He was very interested in Catatumbo Lightning, which happens over Lake Maracaibo in Venezuela. Two weeks ago I visited Professor Mendes to see the lightning for myself. I arrived on a dark night and we watched the clouds, but sadly, we didn't see a storm. Luckily, I stayed there for five days and I saw storms on three different nights. In fact, storm clouds gather there most nights and there are about one million lightning strikes a year! Also, until recently, people thought that Catatumbo storms were different from other storms because they didn't hear thunder. I didn't hear any thunder myself. However, the storms happen over the middle of the lake, so they're far away. Professor Mendes explained that you can only hear thunder if you are near a storm. This is also the reason why the lightning looks pinkish-orange: because it is so far away. I took some awesome photos. Of course, you can't see them on the radio, but yesterday I put some photos up on our website for viewers to enjoy.
R: Well, Mariana, that is all …

11 Wider World, Unit 2, 2.4, Exercise 5

P = Presenter N = Neal C = Cecile A = Affie J = James

P: Tell me about something funny that happened to you on holiday.

N: On a family holiday in Belgium, when I was maybe twelve or thirteen, my dad, who has always had a moustache, thought it would be sensible to shave it off, and he came into the room where we were all sitting and it turns out he basically has no top lip, and he was terrifying and we all ran into the room, shut the door, and he was just left on his own. And for the rest of the holiday, no one could really look at him or take him seriously 'cause he looked ludicrous, and then it took him at least two months to grow it back.

C: A few years ago I went on holiday to Mauritius to get some sun, but the weather was awful and it rained every day, so I just stayed most of my time in the hotel, which was a bit of a shame.

A: When I was about to take my first flight on my own, they changed my gate. I had no idea where I was. It was a huge airport in Munich. I was paralysed. I was running everywhere, asking everyone, 'Where is my gate?' And it turned out it was just in front of me, and I was just running around the airport with no idea where should I go, when I was actually in the right place.

J: I remember when I was four or five on a ferry to France on a summer holiday with my parents and I, apparently, got lost. They had to speak over the speaker phone to try and find me, the whole ship was looking for me and they found me in a cupboard with a bowl of sugar cubes, just sat there eating sugar cubes.

2.10 Unit 2, 2.5, Exercise 2

Would you like to wake up to the sound of wildlife all around you? Then join us at the Wild Adventure Activity Camp for thirteen- to seventeen-year-olds. Our summer camps are all about being outdoors. That's why our camps are all in different beautiful places. You can stay in the forest, near the beach or at the top of a mountain – we let you decide. Come and learn how to make a fire and cook a meal outside. Have fun sleeping under the stars and discover plants and animals that live around us. So what are you waiting for? It's time to find your wild side!

2.12 Unit 2, 2.5, Exercises 4 and 5

M = Milo P = Poppy

M: Are these your photos from Wild Adventure?

P: Yes, it was amazing. That's the sunset on the second day, so Tuesday. We made a fire and told stories when it was dark!

M: Cool. Did you really sleep outside?

P: No. We learnt how to make a shelter when we got there on Monday, but it was cold at night, so we slept in tents in the end. A girl in my tent liked listening to the wildlife in the forest, but I didn't hear a thing. I slept so well.

M: Ugh, it looks freezing!

P: Yes, but at least it wasn't raining. On Thursday night there weren't any clouds and we watched the stars. It was awesome.

M: And were there lots of spiders?

P: No, I think it was too cold for them. Honestly, Milo, it was so good to do something different every day. On Wednesday we walked up a path into the mountains to look for wild animals. Then we ate near a waterfall.

M: Did you see any bears?

P: No, don't be silly! But we found a cave where hundreds of bats were living.

M: Ah, now that sounds fun. I like bats.

P: It was. But the best day was the last day. We discovered unusual plants in the forest that you can use for medicine.

M: Great … Er, have you got something for a headache?

13 Wider World, Unit 2, 2.6, Exercise 7

P = Presenter Co = Corrine G = Geoff Ch = Chee A = Andrew

P: Tell me about a time when you had a problem.

Co: The problem yesterday when I needed to take the train to Nottingham from Bedford, but when I got to the train station, I realised I had left my debit card at home, so I couldn't pay for a ticket and I also couldn't pay for a bus back to my house. So, I was stuck in a train station and I really had to get to Nottingham that day. So, I had to wait there in the train station for about three hours until my parents came and gave me some money on their way back from work and then I could buy tickets and get to Nottingham.

G: I was staying in France on a student exchange, as, as a lecturer rather than as a student and participated in the local marathon. Having completed the marathon in a, in a lamentable time of about four and a half hours, I eventually went back to the house where I was staying and found that I was locked out. So, having done a marathon, which completely exhausted me, it was then necessary for me to find a ladder and try to get into the house through, up the ladder and into an upstairs window. It was not an easy task.

Ch: I had misplaced my keys, and these are really important keys. These are keys for work, and I work in a mental health hospital where it's a locked ward. So, I had difficulty trying to get into hospital. Again, I was running late, which seems to be a habit of mine, really bad habit, but eventually I managed to convince one of my colleagues to lend me their keys and they saved the day, and I was fine. No one noticed that I was late.

A: I've had problems with people thinking I'm not taking things seriously, when I am.

2.19 Unit 2, Revision, Exercise 9

Yesterday the weather was very nice. I met my friend and we went for a walk. But when we were coming back, it started to rain and we got wet.

2.20 Unit 2, Set for Life, Exercise 3

S = Sam J = Jess

S: I don't believe it, Jess! Look at my bike!

J: Oh no, Sammy! Bad luck!

S: I always have such bad luck. It isn't fair. Nothing ever goes right for me!

J: I'm sorry.

S: What am I going to do? I can't get to school in the mornings without my bike!

J: Why don't you go on the bus with your sister?

S: No way! It's so slow. My sister leaves home forty minutes before me in the morning.

J: Why don't you buy some new wheels? How much do they cost?

S: I don't want to pay for new wheels. They'll probably disappear too, like the old ones. As I said, nothing *ever* goes right for me!

J: Well, first, think about getting the bike back home. Can you carry it?

S: Perhaps the best thing is to leave it here outside the library, so someone can take the rest of it.

J: You don't want that!

S: You just don't understand, Jess. I loved that bike, but it'll never be the same now. I don't want it any more.

🔊 2.21 Unit 2, Set for Life, Exercises 5 and 6

S = Sam J = Jess

J: Come on, Sam! You need to keep calm. Breathe slowly and think again about what to do.
S: Sorry, Jess. You're right. Losing the bike wheels isn't the end of the world. Actually, it's lucky that I still have the main part of the bike. Someone stole my friend Tom's bike once. It cost him four hundred euros to get a new one. At least new wheels aren't very expensive.
J: So what are you going to do?
S: I guess I can carry it home. It's only a kilometre – and the bike's lighter now than it was before!
J: How are you going to get to school in the morning?
S: On the bus. It's a slow, boring journey, so I want to be back on my bike soon. Maybe I can do jobs for my mum to get the money for new wheels. And I can lock the wheels to the rest of the bike in the future. That way, it's unlikely that anyone will steal them again.

UNIT 3

🔊 3.6 Unit 3, 3.1, Exercise 9

B = Boy G = Girl

B: Mmm, I love ice cream!
G: Mm, me too. My favourite flavour's strawberry and vanilla. What's yours?
B: Honey and mango.
G: Really? That's an unusual flavour.
B: That's nothing. One time I tried pear and blue cheese!
G: No! What was it like?
B: It wasn't very good.
G: One time my dad ordered pepper flavoured ice cream.
B: Pepper?!
G: Yes, honestly. It was interesting – you know, hot and cold at the same time. And in the same shop they sold lots of unusual flavours like chocolate and chilli.
B: Ooh! That sounds good!
G: My mum had salt and vinegar flavour!
B: Really?
G: No, that one's not true, but the other ones are!

▶ 15 Wider World, Unit 3, 3.2, Exercise 6

P = Presenter H = Holly C = Corrine A = Akshay
R = Reema

P: Where do you like to eat with friends?
H: I really like a sushi restaurant in Covent Garden. They do amazing sashimi and soft shell crab. So, I've been there quite a few times actually. It's probably my favourite one.
P: Why do you like it?
H: It's very fresh. You can tell it's all been made, like, there and then. It's really presented lovely with lovely colours and lovely things on the plates. Looks very appetising.
P: When were you there last time?
H: Probably I was there last about three weeks ago.
P: Where do you go for Vietnamese food? What's it like? How often do you go there?
C: For Vietnamese food I go to a café in London here in Finsbury Park, where I used to live, and they have food like Bánh mì, which is baguettes filled with different meat and vegetables. I go to this café maybe once a month, whenever I'm in London.
P: What food from other countries have you tried?
A: On our last trip to Thailand we tried nothing but Thai food because were in Thailand, and now that we're here we would love to just have as much classic British food as we can, so I'm really looking forward to bangers and mash and shepherd's pie.
R: Fish and chips.
A: And fish and chips, yes. I think we haven't tried any African cuisines as such. We've tried we've definitely had Japanese, southeast Asian in general. We haven't had a lot of Australian specific stuff, so those are on the list now.

🔊 3.16 Unit 3, 3.5, Exercise 4

My dad often takes me to car shows. We've been to places like Boston and Washington, and a few years ago there was an amazing show in New York. When we went in, there was this massive cake in the shape of a big yellow car. The top of the cake was like a Transformer robot from the movie. The baker from the cake shop was there and he told people about his baking. He and his team worked for four days to make the cake! It was really big, about three metres high, so there wasn't enough space in the shop and they made it outside! I was there when they cut the cake. There was plenty for everyone because it weighed about seven hundred kilos! I tried a piece. It was really tasty and sweet, but it wasn't very fresh. It had been there for a few days, so it was a little bit dry.

🔊 3.17 Unit 3, 3.5, Exercise 6

Today's competition is very special: you can win a cake from Zany Cake Bakery for your birthday. In fact, you can design the cake yourself, then they choose a winner … and make your ideal cake! Anyone can enter the competition. You need to draw a picture of your perfect cake. Then send an email of your drawing to this address: orders@zanycake.com; that's 'zanycake' – all one word, no spaces.

The team at Zany Cake Bakery are very clever. They can make any cake you dream of! And remember, their birthday cakes usually sell for fifty euros, so this is an amazing prize. So what next? You've designed your cake and you've attached your picture to an email. There are two more things you need to do. First, choose a flavour. You can choose chocolate, coffee or vanilla. The chocolate one has fresh cream in the middle; the coffee one has tasty butter icing; and the vanilla one has a delicious strawberry jam filling. After that, there's one more important piece of information: tell them your birthday! Don't forget!

Finally, the closing date of the competition for all you cake-lovers. Send your entry by the end of this month – that's Friday the thirty-first of January.

One more thing: there's a special runners-up prize for five people: twelve fantastic cupcakes in your favourite flavour. So start drawing now!

▶ 16 Wider World, Unit 3, 3.5, Exercise 7

P = Presenter N = Nympha M = Miguel J = Jamie L = Liam

P: What's the best cake you've ever had?
N: I had a terrific cake, it was with a crumble crust, a little bit of whipped cream and then some very sweet strawberries on top of it. Delicious. It tasted very sweet. It was a little bit of heaven in my mouth.
M: The best cake I ever had would be something with chocolate and whipped cream and lots of calories.
J: There was like chocolate icing on the top and then it was very moist chocolate cake underneath it, and then there was a layer of raspberry jam in between another layer of chocolate icing. So, you had chocolate icing, chocolate cake, raspberry jam and chocolate icing, then more chocolate cake, and then more chocolate icing. I haven't been able to count all those different layers, but it was bellissima. Tasted like heaven. And raspberry and chocolate.
L: The best cake I have ever had was the same chocolate cake I would have every year growing up made by my mother. It was a moist chocolate, dark chocolate cake, really delicious, really soft, delicious chocolate.

🔊 3.22 Unit 3, Revision, Exercise 9

I know a lot about food because I cook it, I eat it and I write about it. I've eaten many meals in many restaurants. But I've never eaten anything better than a simple boiled egg.

▶ 18 BBC Culture, Exercise 5
Indian food Liverpool style, Part 1

This is Anjum Anand. She's a food writer and a chef born in London, but of Indian origin. In this series she travels to different cities in the UK to find a wide range of Indian food and flavours. She also teaches inexperienced cooks how to make great Indian food.

In this programme she's in Liverpool, where there's a large community from the Southern Indian state of Kerala. She meets Lynn Mitchell, who works for a hospital in the city. The plan is to take part in a local farmers' market to raise money for charity. Lynn wants to sell Indian food at the market. The problem is that Lynn has never cooked Indian food, so it's going to be a real challenge.

Kerala is in the south-west of India and is a popular holiday destination for British people. A lot of Keralan people have come to Liverpool in the last ten years to look for work. There are now over one thousand families there. Anjum is going to teach Lynn three traditional Keralan dishes – coconut chicken with ginger, which has a lovely, sweet flavour, delicious salmon wraps with curry leaves and finally, rice noodles. Keralan specialities include a lot of fruit and fish. The cuisine is very light and healthy compared to other Indian food.

In Liverpool it's easy to find the ingredients for these dishes – Anjum can find all the fruit, vegetables and spices that she needs in special Keralan shops.

▶ 19 BBC Culture, Exercises 7 and 8
Indian food Liverpool style, Part 2

First, Lynn chops and fries up all the ingredients. When the dishes are ready, Anjum tries them. They are really tasty! Lynn hasn't made any mistakes yet.
'Mmm, that's amazing!'
'That's perfect!'
'Oh fantastic!'
Now they're both ready to take the food to the market with Lynn's daughter. More than 5,000 people visit Liverpool's monthly farmers' market. Indian food is very popular, but the question is, will the local people like these Keralan specialties?
At first, things are not easy – people are not sure. It's the first time Lynn has ever cooked outside and she's very nervous. But then things change – people seem to love the food and soon all of it has gone!
'Beautiful!'
'Mmm, tastes lovely!'
'That is excellent – but very hot!'
Since she began this project, Lynn has learnt a lot about cooking Indian food and they have raised lots of money for charity. Lynn's really, really happy! So, what do the British really eat? Keralan food – at least in Liverpool they do!

🔊 PC1–3.1 Progress Check Units 1–3, Exercise 7

1
Ali: I eat really healthily in my new school. The school uploads the food choices in the morning and I read them on my phone with a simple app I have downloaded. I can see what's on the menu, but also the ingredients that go into the dishes. So, I choose something healthy on the app before I even get to lunch. Then I have time to think about what sauces and flavours I can add to make it tasty too!

2
Sonya: We've got really nice school grounds. A group of us like to sit under some trees and eat our packed lunches. We've got a rule: no phones! It's a time when we can talk to each other and hang out before the afternoon lessons start. I think eating in the open air makes you feel hungry and makes the food taste better.

3
Tim: There's a lot of talk about healthy eating these days, but I think it's also important to enjoy your food. The chips are really good at school. They also have a lot of energy, which is important for me because I play a lot of sports. I sometimes have chicken with my chips, and tomato ketchup. I eat some green vegetables too – not because I like them, but because they're good for you.

4
Ian: I get up a bit earlier in the morning and make sandwiches. One of the reasons I do that is because I like to know the ingredients in my food. Another reason is that I can put in both healthy and tasty things, although I have to use what I can find in the kitchen. I think my sandwiches are great and other people seem to agree. I sometimes share them with school friends and they always say they enjoy them!

5
Barbara: Most days I go home for my lunch because I live near the school but the walk makes me hungry. Sometimes Mum or Dad are at home and then they prepare me something. But if they're not there, it's no problem. I just eat something quick and easy instead, like a muesli bar or a piece of fruit. And a packet of nuts! They're so good for you that just a few of them can help to give you everything you need for a good lunch.

UNIT 4

🔊 4.2 Unit 4, 4.1, Exercise 5

1
M = Man W = Woman
M: There's only one thing to do.
W: What's that?
M: Dance!

2
The helicopter is on fire! We have to jump!

3
G = Girl C = Cartoon
G: What are you?
C: Half duck, half cat. I'm a dat – half duck and half cat. Quiaow!

4
Is she a person or a robot? It's so hard to tell in the twenty-second century.

5
I loved you then. I love you now. I'll always love you.

6
It's spring and the birds have returned to the garden.

▶ 20 Wider World, Unit 4, 4.1, Exercise 9

P = Presenter J = Jaycee Jay = Jay
P: What's your favourite TV series?
J: Yeah, I've got a few British TV series that I like. I like the one called *Not Going Out*. It's like a short sitcom. So, there's two people sharing the house together, they're housemates, and they got friends. It's just general life things really. They go to work; they share a house. It's quite funny, so it's nice and relaxing to watch that.

Jay: I've recently been watching *Wolf Hall*. *Wolf Hall* is a TV series that depicts the Tudor era about Henry VIII, starting from Henry VIII and the numerous wives that he had in search for a son. Because, I suppose, because I have studied British history of that period, the Tudor, Tudor time especially.

🔊 21 Wider World, Unit 4, 4.2, Exercise 6

P = Presenter S = Sophie Ja = Jacqui Jo = Jonathan
E = Ellie C = Celia Jay = Jaycee

P: Which is better: the theatre or the cinema?
S: Theatre is better than cinema, in my opinion. The only reason I think that theatre is better than cinema is because it's more of an experience overall.
Ja: Theatre is better than cinema because it's live and it's, you can't com, you know, compete with a live performance.
Jo: Theatre is better than the cinema because you have a much closer experience with the actors involved. Every day you can go see the same show at the theatre and the show will be a bit different.
E: I think the theatre is better than the cinema because it is, you feel like you're there more, you're more involved. I've always personally loved the theatre because I'm very into theatre myself. The cinema, I don't think you get that real feel from it, that real emotion from it, I feel you get that more from the theatre.
P: Which is better: comedies or documentaries?
C: I think documentaries are better than comedies because you can learn something and sometimes they can be a bit funny as well. I like David Attenborough. He's very popular and he does actually say some things that are quite funny inside his documentaries.
Jo: Comedies are better than documentaries because, um, for me I watch TV to kind of distance myself from my real life, to take a break, and comedies, with their jokes and funny scenarios, allow me to relax.
P: Which is better: books or films?
Jay: Well, in books, if you compare it to films, you can actually imagine in your head, but in films you don't have that option because it's already there for to watch, but in books you can already imagine the characters, you can even create their hair colour, their characters and everything. You've got that option with books, so books can be better than films sometimes, actually.

🔊 4.10 Unit 4, 4.5, Exercise 2

P = Presenter B = Bruno

P: Hello. In this series we're hearing about festivals that are special to you and your friends. In the studio today we've got Bruno. Bruno is sixteen and his parents come from Brazil. He was born in the United States and goes to school here. He speaks English at school and Portuguese at home, and he's here to tell us about his favourite festival. Hi, Bruno, and welcome to the show.
B: Hi.

🔊 4.11 Unit 4, 4.5, Exercise 3

P = Presenter B = Bruno

P: So, the Junina Festival takes place every year – in June, of course.
B: Yes, it's a huge family party for me. The festival is at the end of winter in Brazil, but it's summer vacation for me, so I visit the family. It's the perfect chance for a huge family party. We enjoy doing things together, especially my little sister Maria, who loves dress-up. We all do!
P: What fancy-dress costumes do you wear?
B: Well, they're country clothes – the sort of thing people wore when they worked on the land. The boys wear jeans and checked shirts with straw hats that protect your head from the sun. In the past the girls wore party dresses, but now they're also beginning to wear jeans with a shirt; and they paint freckles on their faces.
P: Mhm … Now, I've heard that there are a lot of games.
B: Yes, last year there were some funny races and games. I ran in an egg race – I had to carry an egg in a spoon while I was running! It was very difficult! In one of the traditional games you go fishing with small toy fish. In another game, you send a message to somebody, but you don't say who you are. It's fun.
P: What about the music? Is it like a carnival with dancing in the streets?
B: Not at all. It's traditional music that celebrates life in the country. We do a traditional square dance with partners. Old and young people do it and it's lots of fun.
P: And the food?
B: The food is brilliant. Corn was the food people had at the beginning of winter, so there are a lot of corn dishes. There's popcorn, of course, a corn cake which is nice and sweet, and a type of corn pudding – I think that's the dish I like most.
P: That all sounds delicious! Well, thanks for sharing, Bruno. Now it's …

🔊 4.17 Unit 4, Revision, Exercise 9

I've been to a lot of live music performances. I like listening to music at home too, but it isn't as exciting as seeing a great singer when he or she is performing for a live audience.

🔊 4.18 Unit 4, Set for Life, Exercise 4

L = Layla C = Connor E = Ed T = Tessie

L: Hi, guys. Thanks for coming to the meeting. I've got some good news. Six people have volunteered. I've got a list of names here.
C: That's great!
L: Yes. So now we need to decide the type of event.
E: Well, in the last meeting we talked about a cake sale. I still think that's a good idea. A lot of people like baking cakes, and even more people like eating them. It's an easy event to organise too.
C: I'm not sure. A lot of people these days don't want to eat too much sugar.
T: How about a video games competition? That type of event is always fun.
C: Yeah, I agree. But do people pay to watch events like that?
L: I don't think so. It's probably not the best way to make a lot of money for charity.
E: I love the idea of a fashion show, but it's difficult to organise. Where can we get the clothes from?
L: Let's look at the list of volunteers. Maybe they have some skills that can help.
T: Good thinking.
C: Hey, there's a guy on the list who's in a band. Maybe we can have a music concert!
E: That's a great idea! A music concert on the school field!
T: Cool!
L: OK, let's vote. Who votes for a music concert? Everyone! OK, perfect. Now we need to make a list of all the jobs that we need to do. Let's start with …

🔊 4.19 Unit 4, Set for Life, Exercise 5

L = Layla C = Connor E = Ed T = Tessie

L: … want to do the work. Can you print and sell tickets for the concert, Tessie? You never lose things, so the money will be safe with you!
T: Sure.
L: Thanks, Tessie. And that volunteer, David, can invite bands to the concert. He plays in a band, so he probably knows lots of musicians.
C: Who can we ask to sell food and drink at the event?

E: I think friendly people enjoy that kind of job.
L: Yes. And creative people like you, Connor, can design tickets and prepare the field before the concert.
C: OK, that'll be a fun job. And the volunteer who's good at art, Stanley, can help me. The sports field will look beautiful, I'm sure!
L: Then we need a few strong people to move tables and equipment. How about you, Ed?
E: Yes, I'm quite strong. I'm happy to do that.
T: Thanks. And why don't we ask Lucy to help you set up the field? She's a rugby player, and people who play rugby are usually very strong. We can …

UNIT 5

🔊 5.2 Unit 5, 5.1, Exercise 6

K = Ken S = Sandi

K: OK, so the Olympic Games are taking place soon and here to talk about it is our sports journalist Sandi Awobi. Sandi, which are the most surprising Olympic sports, in your opinion?
S: The one that surprises me the most is skateboarding. I mean, I knew snowboarding was in the winter Olympics, but I didn't know skateboarding was in the summer games.
K: Which sports are not in the Olympics?
S: It changes. For example, baseball was in the Olympics in South Korea in 2008, it wasn't in 2012 or 2016, but now it's back for the next Olympics. Surfing has never been an Olympic sport before, but it's also in the next Olympics. It's the same thing with climbing: it was never an Olympic sport, but now it is. Skating is in the Olympics, but only ice-skating in the winter games; so roller skating is not an Olympic sport – for now, anyway.
K: In Rio in 2016 there was a lot of talk about yoga becoming an Olympic sport, wasn't there?
S: Yes, but it never happened and I'm not surprised. I mean, is yoga really a sport?
K: Maybe not. Which sports have been in every Olympic Games?
S: That's a difficult question. Um … I think athletics, cycling, swimming and gymnastics have been in every summer games, but I'm not one hundred percent sure of that.

▶ 25 Wider World, Unit 5, 5.3, Exercise 6

P = Presenter J = Josie A = Athena M = Monica S = Sunita

P: Would you like to be a volunteer at a sports event?
J: I would like to be a volunteer at a sports event to help others get inside, kind of insight into something that you wouldn't see as a customer and be part of a large scale sports event.
A: I would like to be able to be a volunteer at a sports event because it's good for my CV and I would like to meet some new people that are interested as well in the same area. So, yeah.
M: I would like to volunteer at a sports event because I think that volunteering is important and everyone should volunteer and because sport is fun.
S: I would like to volunteer for a sports event because it's something that I've never done before and I think I'll enjoy it.

▶ 26 Wider World, Unit 5, 5.4, Exercise 6

P = Presenter M = Michael C = Christine F = Francis A = Athena

P: Finish the sentences. If there's a new sports centre in town, …
M: If there is a new sports centre in our city, I will probably go there.
P: If my friends are free this evening, …
M: If my friends are free this evening, I will probably go with them to some park or something like that for throwing a Frisbee or something.
P: If I get some money for my birthday, …
C: If I get some money for my birthday, I will buy a whole meal for my family.
F: If I get some money for my birthday, depending how much I get, I'll look at flights and see where I can book a flight to.
A: If I get some money for my birthday, I will, I will go, like, maybe travel in Africa, basically.

🔊 5.11 Unit 5, 5.5, Exercise 4

P = Presenter C = Callum M = Megan

P: Don't forget, the BBC TV Sports Personality of the Year Award is next Sunday at seven o'clock. You've still got time to vote! What are you waiting for?
C: Who are you going to vote for?
M: Marcus Rashford.
C: Who?
M: Marcus Rashford.
C: Is he an athlete? No, a tennis player.
M: No, he isn't. You know who he is. He's a footballer. He plays for Manchester United and England.
C: Oh, yeah, that's right. Why are you going to vote for him? He's not the best sportsperson in the UK. I mean, he's not even the best footballer in the England team. He's good, but Harry Kane's better.
M: What do you know about Marcus Rashford?
C: Let's see … He was born in 1997, he joined Manchester United when he was only seven years old, he's an attacker, he wears the number ten shirt for his club and number eleven for England. He played his first match for Manchester United when he was eighteen years old and he scored two goals. The English manager, Gareth Southgate, compared him to Cristiano Ronaldo.
M: OK, Callum, very good. Now put your phone down and listen. The award isn't just about who's the best athlete or who's won the most tournaments or who scores the most goals. It's about who has the best personality, who has done the most.
C: OK, so why vote for Marcus Rashford?
M: Because apart from being a great player, he's a great person.
C: Why? What's he done?
M: Well, he started up a charity and people gave that charity over twenty million pounds, and with that money they bought three million meals for four hundred thousand hungry school children. Then he wrote a letter to the government and got them to provide free school meals for children during the summer holidays.
C: That's amazing! I didn't know that.
M: That's not all. He also helps people who have nowhere to live.
C: Wow!
M: He's really kind and he's intelligent, too. He learned sign language so he could judge a poetry competition in a school for deaf children.
C: Awesome!
M: The University of Manchester gave him a special award and his photo was on the cover of Vogue magazine!
C: You're right, Marcus Rashford is great. There's only one problem.
M: Oh yeah? What's that?
C: He's not on the list of candidates.
M: Oh no! Why not?
C: Because they're giving him a special prize for everything he's done.
M: Really? Are they? That's fantastic!

🔊 5.18 Unit 5, Revision, Exercise 8

Everybody listen, please. We're going to warm up first and then we're going to have a football match. We'll decide the teams then. Right … now everybody, jog once around the pitch. One, two, three, go!

▶ 28 BBC Culture, Exercises 5 and 6

The Highland Games, Part 1
The Highland Games are a very old tradition. They were set up as a way of bringing together Scotland's historical families. They capture the cultural life and sports of this magical nation. They include the colours and symbols of a culture that almost disappeared but is now stronger than ever. The Highland Games are a meeting place of strength, speed and celebration. Today on sports grounds, farmers' fields and city parks across this country, they are Scotland's very own Olympics!

This is the village of Ceres. It is home to Scotland's oldest Highland Games. For centuries the whole village has gathered for this annual summer celebration. For the people of Ceres, it's a day as important as Hogmanay – New Year's Eve in Scotland – or Christmas.

▶ 29 BBC Culture, Exercises 7 and 8

The Highland Games, Part 2
The Highland Games are a mixture of fact and fantasy. They are a unique blend of sport and culture. There is highland dancing, bagpipes and drums, and there is a series of sports too. There is usually athletics, sometimes cycling and wrestling but always the 'heavy events'. These include the stone shot, the hammer throw and tossing the caber.

At most games the caber is people's favourite sport. It's the final event and a symbol of the Highland Games. The caber is about six metres long and weighs around fifty-five kilograms. Competitors have to throw it, then flip it over and the caber has to land flat. If it lands absolutely straight, it's a perfect throw.

The Highland Games are now also celebrated outside Scotland, in the USA, Canada, Australia and the Far East. These games are organised by families who emigrated from Scotland. The biggest Highland Games in the world take place here, in the Blue Ridge Mountains in North Carolina. They last over four days and 22,000 people come every year to enjoy this traditional Scottish event of their ancestors.

The Highland Games are the most visible display of Scottish identity that you can imagine. They are about competing, of course, but they are also about community, keeping tradition alive and making time for old friends. If you come, you won't regret it.

UNIT 6

🔊 6.4 Unit 6, 6.1, Exercise 5

1
G = Girl B = Boy
G: Come on, the train station's not far away! You can make it!
B: Yeah, yeah. I'm coming. Why is my backpack so heavy? Why's it so hot in this country? Can't we take a taxi?

2
W = Woman M = Man
W: I've got the map and the guidebook, so we're ready to explore Paris. Let's go!
M: Oh, wait! I haven't got my passport with me. It's in my suitcase!
W: Don't worry. I've got it.
M: Oh, no, I've forgotten my sunglasses!

3
M = Mother S = Son
M: Right, darling. Here we are! Now put on some sun cream and …
S: I've already done it.
M: Have you got your swimsuit on?
S: Yes.
M: Now here's your towel. Oh!
S: What is it?
M: I've forgotten to bring my swimsuit.

4
B1 = Boy 1 B2 = Boy 2
B1: OK, that's the tent up and the sleeping bags are inside.
B2: It's brilliant here. Much better than a campsite. It's so quiet and peaceful.
B1: Yes, it'll be really dark later on. Did you bring a torch?
B2: Yes, it's in my rucksack. I've got spare batteries, too.

▶ 30 Wider World, Unit 6, 6.1, Exercise 7

P = Presenter H = Harry C = Cecile J = Jan T = Tasha
P: What should you take with you on a backpacking holiday with friends?
H: On a backpack, on a backpacking holiday with friends I should take a backpack. I should also take strong walking boots or shoes, obviously, I'll be walking a lot, and I should be taking a tent for staying around wherever I'm staying.
C: When you go backpacking with friends, you, I always remember to bring sunglasses and an umbrella, and suntan lotion, and anti-mosquito products or any other insects. And that's about it.
J: When you are backpacking you have to take medicine and sleeping bag.
P: What should you take on a city break in Ireland?
C: On a city break to Dublin I would take my camera and good shoes to walk around the city and an umbrella, 'cause it's Ireland.
P: What should you take on a cruise around the Mediterranean?
H: My advice for packing for a cruise around the Mediterranean would be to take sun cream and a large brimmed hat so you can keep yourself safe from the sun and not get sunstroke.
J: When you go on a cruise you have to take your bikini, your, a book, a good book, something to write, and maybe sun cream, very important. And maybe your camera, if you want to take some pictures, and I think it's the most important things.
C: For a cruise on the Mediterranean you must take, obviously, your sunglasses, and then bikinis and that's all you need.
T: So, if you're going, like, abroad on a cruise ship or whatever, you must take your passport, get visas, valid cheques, and all your essentials.

▶ 32 Wider World, Unit 6, 6.2, Exercise 6

P = Presenter J = Jamie L = Liam
P: Finish the sentences. When you are on a beach holiday, you should …
J: When you are on a beach holiday, you should remember to bring your swimsuit.
L: You should jump in the water and look at the fish.
P: When I am on holiday with my family, I don't have to …
J: When I am on holiday with my family, I don't have to see them very much if I'm clever about it.
L: I don't have to worry about showing up at work on time.
P: On an activity camp, you have to …
J: On an activity camp, you have to be good at activities.
L: You have to make sure you enjoy the outdoors.

6.11 Unit 6, 6.5, Exercise 2

P = Presenter M = Mike

P: Thanks for coming to talk to us Mike. Now, can you explain what you do?
M: Yes. I organise holidays for teenagers who need help when they're travelling because they can't see.

6.12 Unit 6, 6.5, Exercises 3 and 4

P = Presenter M = Mike

P: Why did you decide to help in this organisation?
M: Well, I've always loved travelling, and once I was on holiday in South America and I met an amazing girl who couldn't see. She was on holiday with her parents and cousins, and they helped her to climb this really high mountain. It made her very happy because she couldn't do it on her own. I decided I wanted to help people to have a good holiday.
P: And what holidays do you offer?
M: Oh, we've got something for everybody – from city breaks and beach holidays to activity camps. On our activity camps we offer sailing, hiking and cycling. We've got special bikes with two seats. They're popular with kids who can't go cycling at home because they don't have the right bikes.
P: It must be difficult to travel to a place when you have problems with your sight.
M: It can be. We plan the journey carefully so that people feel safe. But we also want it to be exciting – the journey is as important as the holiday.
P: Is it easy to find accommodation?
M: Not always. Some hotels don't understand the difficulties our travellers have.
P: What do you mean?
M: Well, it depends, but … for example, a blind person can't read a menu. Eating can be very frustrating too. Also, he or she can't read the number on their key or the door to the room. Hotels have to understand that.
P: What are the most popular holidays?
M: Both winter and summer holidays are popular, but I think our summer activity camps are the most popular because we offer sailing. Everybody loves the sun on their face and the fresh air. It's a very exciting experience.

6.13 Unit 6, 6.5, Exercise 5

Jess is sixteen years old and comes from New Zealand. She's been blind since she was born, but she's always loved adventure. Last year Jess went on a sailing holiday. During the trip, Jess decided that she wanted to do something different. With the help of the organisers she climbed the mast. It was very high, but she knew she could do it. Jess believes that it doesn't matter what disability you've got – you can achieve anything. As long as you get lots of help, you can still have a good time.

6.18 Unit 6, Revision, Exercise 8

I would like to book a double room with a nice view, please. It must be on a high floor because I can't sleep with traffic noise. Can I get information about sightseeing in the local area at reception?

6.19 Unit 6, Set for Life, Exercises 2 and 4

A: I'm going on holiday with my family next week.
B: That's cool, Charlie! Where are you going?
A: Scotland. We're catching a train from London to Edinburgh on Monday.
B: Why are you going by train, not car?
A: We're trying to be eco-friendly. We haven't got an electric car and petrol cars produce a lot of air pollution. The greenhouse gases from cars make the planet hotter, and that's a serious problem.
B: But your car is very small and light. It doesn't use much petrol.
A: It's not as bad for the environment as a big, heavy car, but it still produces a lot of greenhouse gases.
B: Maybe you could rent an electric car. They're better for the environment.
A: You're right, they produce a lot less air pollution than petrol cars, but I think they're expensive. And we don't get all our electricity from eco-friendly things like the sun and wind. Some of it comes from things that produce greenhouse gas. So, at the moment, we could possibly produce more greenhouse gas because of a journey in an electric car than a journey on public transport like trains and coaches.
B: If you're thinking about going by public transport, why don't you fly? Planes are a lot faster than trains and coaches.
A: Yes, but planes are terrible for the environment! Flying from London to Edinburgh and back could produce more greenhouse gas than someone in Uganda produces in a whole year!
B: Really? So, are planes the least eco-friendly choice?
A: Not always. If there's only one passenger in a car, a car can be even worse than a plane. But there are four people in my family, and four passengers in a car is better than flying.
B: What are you going to do when you're in Scotland? Are you going to stay in the city of Edinburgh the whole time?
A: No, we're going to bring our bikes on the train and cycle from town to town.
B: I guess all types of transport without engines are eco-friendly.
A: That's right. Bikes, skateboards, sailing boats – they don't produce any greenhouse gases. Walking doesn't either.
B: Your holiday sounds great. It'll be fun, it'll make you fitter and it'll help the environment too.

PC1–6.1 Progress Check Units 1–6, Exercise 6

My name is Melanie and I would like to be a great tennis player one day. I need lots and lots of practice. I have training three days a week and every weekend. It's the only way I can stay at my best. Of course, I also have to do school work, so I don't have much free time!

Sometimes my coach comes to my training. She's coming tomorrow to help me improve my game. We'll talk about the things I'm worst at and then make a plan to practise them until they get better. At the moment the biggest problem is keeping my balance. It can be hard to hit a difficult ball and stay on your feet. And what happens if a player falls over? Ninety-nine times out of a hundred they lose the point, that's what.

People often ask why I took up playing tennis. I played tennis at school a few times, but I didn't really take it up until something happened on a long bus journey. We were on a school trip and my friend was watching sport videos on his phone. He showed me one with the famous tennis player Serena Williams. I just loved how she played, and I knew I wanted to be a tennis player.

What was it about Serena Williams that made me want to take up tennis seriously? There are a few reasons. It's isn't just her strength and skill. It's also that she never stopped trying to be better. Another thing that …

PC1–6.2 Progress Check Units 1–6, Exercise 7

1
Everyone likes to watch TV in my family. We all enjoy the sports channel. Most people in my family like science fiction films too. But I think thrillers are better.
2
It's a good day to be on the beach. My friend is putting on sun cream. Then he's going to read. It's hot on the sand, but the water might be cold. No problem! I'm going for a swim!

UNIT 7

▶ 35 **Wider World, Unit 7, 7.2, Exercise 6**

P = Presenter R = Rebecca C = Craig Ja = Jamie L = Liam

- **P:** Finish the sentences. If my friend phoned when I was busy …
- **R:** I, oh dear, depending on what was happening, but I guess I would ignore them.
- **C:** Isn't that terrible?
- **R:** Yeah.
- **C:** So terrible.
- **R:** Unless it was you.
- **C:** Geez, you're mean.
- **R:** I know.
- **Ja:** I would send him to voice mail.
- **L:** If my friend phoned when I was busy, I would drop everything to help them.
- **P:** If there was a big wedding in our family …
- **Ja:** I would try to find a very attractive date to go with me to the wedding.
- **C:** I would try to avoid it.
- **R:** Yes. No, I'd be happy to go.
- **L:** I would invite all my friends and go and have a great time.
- **P:** If I was late for a family meal, my parents …
- **Ja:** would start without me. And probably finish without me.
- **C:** would kill me.
- **R:** Yeah, they'd probably kill me too.
- **L:** would understand if I made something up.
- **P:** I'd be very worried if …
- **Ja:** I lost my keys.
- **L:** I didn't hear from my girlfriend late at night.
- **P:** It would be a nightmare for me if …
- **Ja:** I did not get into drama school.
- **C:** I had no money.
- **R:** if I had no friends.
- **L:** I had to stay in one place for the rest of my life.

🔊 **7.10 Unit 7, 7.4, Exercise 2**

P = Presenter H = Hannah

- **P:** Today on the programme we've got Hannah from the group One Way.
- **H:** Hi!
- **P:** Hello there, Hannah. Are you ready to answer the questions?
- **H:** Yes, I think so.
- **P:** OK, Hannah, you've got ten seconds for each answer. Here are 'Ten quick questions to find the real you'!
- **P:** One. OK. Name one thing which you would rescue in a flood.
- **H:** One thing which I'd rescue is my handheld console. It's very important to me.
- **P:** Two: name one person who you always have fun with.
- **H:** Er, um … Ooh, my uncle Joe is the funniest person I know.
- **P:** Three: a place where you like to relax.
- **H:** One place where I like to relax is our youth club. I hang out with my friends there.
- **P:** Four: one food that you often eat as a snack.
- **H:** Well, you won't believe this, but I eat olives any time I feel hungry.
- **P:** Wow! OK, five: the primary school teacher who helped you the most.
- **H:** Definitely, Mr Kipling, who was my first teacher, was the most helpful.
- **P:** Now six: name a place where you want to go in the future.
- **H:** Hmmm … Iceland, where there are loads of volcanoes, is a place I'd love to visit.
- **P:** Seven: a friend who always listens.
- **H:** I think the guy next door, Ben, is a friend who always listens.
- **P:** Eight: a toy that you loved when you were small.
- **H:** Actually, a teddy bear, which my grandmother gave me, used to be my favourite.
- **P:** Nine: a song which you can't stop singing.
- **H:** Easy! *We Will Rock You*, which is my dad's favourite, is in my head.
- **P:** And finally, ten: the time of day when you work best.
- **H:** Er, I'd say the evening is best for me. It's the time when I write new songs.
- **P:** Thank you, Hannah!

🔊 **7.11 Unit 7, 7.5, Exercise 4**

I've got a half-brother, Finn, who is disabled. He was born with cerebral palsy and he finds it difficult to move around and do things for himself. This means he spends most of his life in a wheelchair. Simple everyday activities like getting dressed and getting ready for school can take a long time. When Finn was young, he hated this and often got very stressed. If he didn't want to go to school, he would shout and cry.

Then, three years ago, when he was nine, Finn got an assistance dog and he named her Nala. Since then, his life has changed a lot. Nala is a very intelligent dog who understands Finn and knows how to help with many different activities. For example, Finn hates putting his shoes on, but Nala can get his shoes or slippers and put them near his feet, which makes him smile. Then he will put his shoes on quite happily. If Finn didn't have Nala, he would never be ready for school on time! She's his best friend too.

🔊 **7.12 Unit 7, 7.5, Exercise 6**

A couple of years ago my step-mum started working as a puppy trainer for assistance dogs. Her job was to teach young dogs a range of skills they would need in order to help people with disabilities. When I was little, she explained that when assistance dogs get older, they will help people, usually those who are disabled in some way. Mum told us that it was not like having a pet because the dogs only stay for about a year. It's very difficult to say goodbye when they go to their new owners. I found that really hard and sometimes cried. The good thing is that we often get letters telling us how much the dogs are helping their new owners.

Prince is different. He's my dog and I trained him – with a bit of help from my step-mum. I have a condition called Asperger's, which is not exactly a disability; for me, it means that I find it hard to deal with meeting people. Prince, who is really calm, helps me to be more confident so I can make new friends. I've got a lot better since I had Prince. He doesn't come to school, but he's always waiting when I get home. He's definitely part of our family now!

▶ 36 **Wider World, Unit 7, 7.5, Exercise 9**

P = Presenter C = Corrine

- **P:** Tell me about a time you got a pet.
- **C:** I really wanted a pet dog when I was a little child and I would always ask my parents for one, and finally, when I was ten years old, they got me a pet dog named Jet and he was just a tiny little puppy, he was a little black Fell Terrier. And then when he was about two years old he ran into the road and he got hit by a car and I came home from school that day and I was crying, I was so upset. He had to go to the vet's and finally he came home with a cast on his leg which he had to wear for a long time, and he cost my parents something like 2000 pounds in vet bills.

🔊 **7.18 Unit 7, Revision, Exercise 8**

We have a small flat with a large kitchen. The kitchen is the place where we eat together and talk about things. We all get on well, of course, but the shared meals help that.

▶ 38 BBC Culture, Exercises 5 and 6

Arctic life, Part 1

This is the Arctic. For half of the year, the sea here freezes into ice, and temperatures can be minus 20 degrees. What is life like for the families who live in this extreme landscape?

This is a village in the Canadian Arctic. Seven hundred people live here.

'People say it is a hard life here but it seems normal for me. It's not a hard life. It's a beautiful life.'

Minnie is 63. She has lived in this village all her life. People here still have to get most of their food from the land – and from the sea, under the ice. If they didn't do this, they wouldn't survive. Minnie is teaching her granddaughter Eva how to fish. But tomorrow they are going on a dangerous journey to find another type of food.

Minnie, Eva and Minnie's sister Siassie get up early and travel far across the sea ice. It looks like there is nothing here, but Minnie knows where to find food. The women in her family have collected food like this for generations. Today is Eva's first time.

▶ 39 BBC Culture, Exercise 8

Arctic life, Part 2

The women are now sixteen kilometres from the land, out on the frozen sea. This is the place where they'll look for food. They make a hole. There is no seawater under the ice at this time of the day. It's safe to go into the ice cave – for now.

'Siassie, it's a good cave. Eva, come down.'

But the women have to work very quickly. The ice above them can move at any time. It might fall on them. More importantly, the seawater will return in only half an hour. But Minnie has found the thing that she came for. Shellfish – thousands of them. The family can cook them to make a good winter meal. But they've been down in the cave for twenty minutes now. They can hear the seawater coming back.

'It's coming in fast now.'

'Should we get out?'

It's time to go. But this is the most dangerous moment on the trip. The ice above them is moving again. Will it close the hole that they made in the ice? Will they get out?

'Eva, quickly now, the water's coming.'

They're safe. The cave is now full of water. The women can take the food back to their community.

The family enjoy the meal together, and Eva has learned some important skills from her grandmother. The tradition continues.

'I learn by following you. I like to learn from you. Yes.'

UNIT 8

🔊 8.4 Unit 8, 8.1, Exercise 6

There isn't much crime where I live. It's not like in the movies, where there's a bank robbery or a burglary every five minutes. I once saw someone shoplifting in our local supermarket, and there is some vandalism – you know, silly vandals painting graffiti on walls or kicking the bins in the park, but that's about all. There's more crime in big cities. Once, when my sister was in London, a pickpocket stole her purse from her backpack and a friend of mine saw a thief on a motorbike who took a woman's handbag as she was walking along the pavement.

🔊 8.7 Unit 8, 8.2, Exercise 2

P = Presenter J = Jess

P: In this round of the *Show What You Know* quiz, we have Jess Walker. Welcome to *Show What You Know*, Jess. What's your special subject?

J: Hi. My special subject is Sherlock Holmes.

P: OK, Jess, your five questions are coming up … now. Question one: The Sherlock Holmes detective stories were written a hundred years ago by …
a) Arthur Conan Doyle or b) Agatha Christie?

J: That's a), Arthur Conan Doyle.

P: Correct. Still with the easy questions … number two: Holmes had a famous assistant. What was his name?
a) Doctor Who or b) Doctor Watson ?

J: The answer is b), Doctor Watson. His first name was John.

P: Good. Next: Were the stories first published … a) in a book or b) in a magazine?

J: They were published in a book first. It was a novel called *Study in Scarlet*.

P: No, sorry. That's incorrect. It was a novel, but it wasn't published in a book. It was published in a magazine first. Now, question 4: Sherlock's flat is located at number 221B of a famous London street. Is it … a) Sherlock Street or b) Baker Street?

J: It's Baker Street.

P: Correct. Of course! Now for the last and most difficult question – five: which famous Sherlock Holmes quote is never really used by Sherlock Holmes?
a) 'Elementary, my dear Watson,' or b) 'My mind is like a racing engine'?

J: Oh, I know this. It's a) Holmes never says, 'Elementary, my dear Watson.'

P: Correct. Holmes says, 'Elementary,' and he uses the phrase 'my dear Watson', but he never says these things together. So, well done, Jess. At the end of the round, you have four points!

🔊 8.12 Unit 8, 8.5, Exercise 3

P = Presenter K = Katrina

P: Good morning! In today's podcast we meet teenagers who are helping their communities to fight crime with the help of the internet. First up is Katrina.

K: Well, this happened a couple of months ago. My mum and I went to the shops, but we were only there for about an hour. When we got home and opened the front door, we immediately knew that something was wrong.

🔊 8.13 Unit 8, 8.5, Exercises 4 and 5

The house was really cold. We went through to the kitchen. The window was open. 'Burglars!' said Mum and she sat down. Her face was white. I ran to my room. My laptop was missing. I was really upset because it was a birthday present. I called the police and they came almost immediately. We told them that my laptop, my new smartwatch and Dad's digital camera were all missing. They started looking for clues. They took fingerprints and photos. Then they searched the area behind the house, but they didn't find anything.

Anyway, later that day I told my friend Mia about the burglary. 'I heard some people in the park talking about a watch,' she said. 'They wanted to sell it "quickly" on the internet.'

Mia and I got our phones out and started looking online. We checked the posts of some people we know from the park and we found a comment and a photo about a watch for sale. It was my watch! I pretended I wanted to buy it and got the seller's name and address. Ten minutes later the police were at the guy's house. They arrested him for burglary.

I'm pleased that social media helped to solve a crime and that I got my smartwatch back. But it's a pity they didn't find my laptop or Dad's camera!

🔊 8.14 Unit 8, 8.5, Exercise 6

Thanks, Katrina. Now, on Sky Radio we'd like to help you find your dad's camera and your laptop. If you're listening this morning, perhaps you could call us if you hear anything about it. The items were stolen on the second of October, sometime between three and five o'clock in the afternoon. The make of the digital camera is Nikon D610 – that's D610. The laptop is an HP Omen. If you hear about it, the number to call is 07836 198 477 – that's 07836 198 477. There's a reward of twenty pounds for anybody who finds either of those things. Thanks a lot. And now it's time for the weather …

▶ 41 Wider World, Unit 8, 8.5, Exercise 7

P = Presenter F = Faye M = Melissa Sh = Shaun
Sa = Sarah K = Kenneth

P: What would you do if your phone was stolen?
F: If my phone was stolen, which it has been in the past, I would be upset about it. I would look for it and try to see if I have it on me. But if not, because I'm not attached to technology, I'd probably go another two months without a mobile phone.
M: If my phone were stolen, I'd go straight to the police station.
Sh: If my phone was stolen, I would go to the police station and I would also buy a new phone.
Sa: If I had my cell phone stolen, I would probably go to the nearest police station.
K: I also might see if anyone had returned it anywhere, but except that I'm probably not getting it back so buy a new one.
P: What would you do if you saw someone shoplifting?
F: If I saw someone shoplifting at a store that I worked at, I would, after like, watching them and understanding what they're doing, I would approach them and ask them to put what they'd taken back and if not, I would call someone of authority.
Sa: If I saw someone shoplifting, I'd probably go tell the nearest cashier or worker for the store.
M: If I saw someone shoplifting, I'd probably go to an employee to inform them.
Sh: If I saw someone shoplifting, I would not do anything at all. I would mind my own business. Most likely.
P: What would you do if you saw someone vandalising something?
Sa: If I saw someone vandalising something, I would call the police.
K: Yeah, I'd call the police as well.

🔊 8.20 Unit 8, Revision, Exercise 8

Everybody listen, please. I'm sorry to say that some windows were damaged by vandals at the weekend. We're having new ones installed. The vandals were arrested this morning.

🔊 8.21 Unit 8, Set for Life, Exercise 4

Do you find it hard to make good decisions? There may be a reason for this. Scientists have found that humans younger than the age of twenty-five don't have an adult brain yet. Teenagers are still developing the connections that an adult has between two parts of the brain: the part that looks after facts and the part that looks after how you feel. When adults make decisions, they can use the part of the brain that looks after facts. But teenagers can't do this very well. Instead, they usually use the part of the brain that looks after how they feel. That's why teenagers usually only think about short-term reasons for a decision – 'If I choose this, what will happen in the next minutes, hours or days?' Adults are more likely to think about the long term – 'What will happen in the next weeks, months or years?' But it's often important for teenagers to think about the long term too.

🔊 8.22 Unit 8, Set for Life, Exercise 5

So, what should you do to make good decisions? Here are some suggestions:

First, do some research. You can't make a good decision if you don't know all the facts. For example, if you're deciding when to go on a camping holiday, find out how much rain there is in different months before you decide.

Then make a list of reasons for and against making a particular decision – both long-term reasons and short-term ones. Give each reason a score – from one for 'not at all important' to ten for 'extremely important'. Add up all the scores for and against. Which gets the highest score?

Remember that sometimes two alternatives can be equally good. There isn't always only one right decision. And even if you make a decision the right way, you won't always have the result that you hoped for. But you *can* be sure that you are making the best decision possible with the information that's available.

UNIT 9

🔊 9.5 Unit 9, 9.2, Exercise 2

D = Daisy M = Mum

D: Hey, Mum. Guess what.
M What?
D: Jack told Mrs Walker that we were starting a debating club.
M: Oh, good. What did she say?
D: She said that was a great idea.
M: Excellent!
D: I told everyone I was looking for some good topics to discuss.
M: Perfect!
D: And Tom said we needed to make a poster to advertise it.
M: Of course!

🔊 9.11 Unit 9, 9.5, Exercise 2

1

T = Teacher E = Eva

T: Right. The test will start in two minutes. Your mobile phones should be switched off. Please put them in the box on my table. Then I'd like you all to sit quietly. You can use the dictionaries on your tables. Eva, can you come here, please? I need some help.
E: Yes, Sir.
T: Here are the papers.
E: OK.
T: Eva is going to hand out the papers for you. Oh, be careful, Eva, don't drop them …
E: Oops! Sorry.

2

M = Max T = Teacher

M: Sorry I'm late, Miss. I had a dentist's appointment.
T: Well, Max, the rest of the class have gone on the trip to the Natural History Museum. Did you sign up on the list?
M: Yes, I did, Miss. But then, erm, I forgot all about it …
T: Well, sorry you've missed out on the trip. Your classmates are on the way to the museum. They left five minutes ago on the school bus. I know: you could do a bit of research about the things in the museum that interest you. You need to look up the website online – I'll put the address on the board.

3

T = Teacher I = Ivan

- **T:** So, before you can go on summer camp, we need to have all the correct information for you. I hope your parents filled in the forms and signed them. Can you make sure you hand them to me after the lesson?
- **I:** Sir?
- **T:** Yes, Ivan? What's the problem? Did the dog eat your form like it ate your homework?
- **I:** No, Sir. It … erm … it got wet.
- **T:** Oh. Well, who did that? Did you spill your drink on it? Or drop it in the sink?
- **I:** Nothing like that. Er, I left it in my trouser pocket when I put them in the washing machine.
- **T:** OK, Ivan. I'll get you another form. But don't give it to the dog!

4

T = Teacher M = Magda

- **T:** Class, please can you pay attention, while I'm writing on the board?
- **M:** Sorry, Miss.
- **T:** What were you doing anyway? Were you writing secret messages?
- **M:** No, Miss. Anya and I were just making notes about the homework, the one where we had to work in pairs. It was the last question and we had a good idea.
- **T:** Show me your book then. Oh, OK.

🔊 9.13 Unit 9, 9.5, Exercise 5

1

T = Teacher B = Boy

- **T:** Who's ready to hand in their essay?
- **B:** I've just finished it.
- **T:** Great … but you've only written one paragraph! It's too short.

2

G = Girl T = Teacher

- **G:** Are we going to look over the test results now?
- **T:** Yes, we are. Did you revise for it, Hannah? You got five out of twenty answers!

3

T1 = Teacher 1 T2 = Teacher 2

- **T1:** Did the students get on quietly with their projects?
- **T2:** No, they didn't. There was a fire alarm in the middle of the lesson!

4

B = Boy T = Teacher

- **B:** Here, come here!
- **T:** Can everybody calm down, please?
- **B:** Yes, Miss.
- **T:** Now, what's going on?
- **B:** There's a cat in the classroom, Miss. It came in through the window.

▶ 44 Wider World, Unit 9, 9.5, Exercise 6

P = Presenter Ja = Jacqui AJ = AJ S = Sophie
Jo = Jonathan C = Celia

- **P:** Tell me about your first school and your first teacher.
- **Ja:** My first school was All Saints School, it was a little Church of England school and it was my favourite little primary school ever. And I had lots of wonder, you know, wonderful teachers and I was just very, very happy there. My first teacher was called Mrs Webster and she took us for everything but she, most importantly, she taught me how to sew.
- **AJ:** My first school was a grade school in a small town, so there was really small classes. One of the first teachers I really remember was really great at sitting me down and explaining things in the way that I learned it.
- **S:** My first school was a tiny school. It had about sixty pupils, and it was a very – a very sweet and humble school and everybody knew everybody cos it was a tiny town and you got to really know the teachers as well. And the learning as well was kind of more one on one than bigger schools, which was really good. My first teacher was a lady called Mrs Buchannan. She was really lovely and she worked in the reception class for many, many years, and everybody that went to that school really knew her very well.
- **Jo:** My first school was in Rome, Italy. It was an international school where I learned both English and Italian. My first teacher was called Miss Carlson. She cared a lot about her Liverpool FC football club, and I'm an AC Milan supporter, so whenever the finals were on, we would always argue who was the better team.
- **C:** My first school was in Auckland, which is a city in New Zealand, and it was a small primary school with only a few hundred children and was right by the beach and that's why I liked it. We got to go to the beach sometimes after school. My first teacher was called Mr Norwell and he was a lovely guy in his fifties, and he used to teach us maths using pebbles that we found outside.

🔊 9.18 Unit 9, Revision, Exercise 8

Good morning, class. This is a busy week. The big question is: what do you want to study next year? That's right. It's an important decision and I want to talk to each of you on your own about it.

▶ 46 BBC Culture, Exercises 4 and 5

Learning goals
The school week is the same for most teenagers across the world.

They get up … They go to school … They have lessons … They come home … They have dinner … They go to bed … And they do it day after day after day! But it's different for those teenagers who want to develop their unique talents.

This is Ian. His school routine is a bit different from most other students. It's 6 o'clock on a winter's morning and Ian's getting up. But he isn't going to school today. Ian spends one day a week at the Stoke City Football Academy. It's a school for young players who might play with the football club professionally one day.

'Let's get going.'

It's time to go.

Like other students, he has lessons in the morning – but they're lessons in football and teamwork! Ian's a hard-working student and a talented footballer. After lessons, it's time for some serious football training. Ian's position in the team is centre back. His job is to stop the other team scoring goals.

Around half past three, most students are leaving school – but not Ian. He's still training!

Other teenagers are at home having dinner or doing homework, but Ian has just left the football academy. He's confident enough to take the train home alone. He finally has some time to relax. Ian arrives home at about half past eight in the evening.

'When I get home, I usually have a small meal, not too big and then straight after that I just go to bed.'

Ian doesn't mind his long day at the academy. He knows that you have to work hard if you want to be the best. But when you have a passion and a talent like Ian, you don't mind doing a little bit extra.

🔊 PC1–9.1 Progress Check Units 1–9, Exercises 7 and 8

I'm going to talk about three crimes. The first is shoplifting. It's very easy to steal something that way. Shoplifters can pick up what they need and instead of paying for it, they can just put it in their bag and walk out of the shop without paying. They just need to make sure no one is looking, especially security staff. But there is something that every shop should do: get security cameras put in. Shop owners can watch what customers are doing and they don't even have to be in the shop! Police can also use the recordings to catch thieves later, and we often do.

I want to talk about burglary next. It's terrible to come home and find favourite things missing, and your house might be in a mess. These thieves are the most difficult to catch because they don't leave clues behind. We often don't find any fingerprints because they wear gloves. They are also well prepared. They often know about the house's security and when the owners are going to be out. That's why you should contact the police if you see someone you don't know near your house. It could be a burglar studying it and making plans!

Pickpocketing is something that could happen to any of you. It's very hard to catch a pickpocket unless you see them at the moment of stealing. Then you need to shout to get other people's attention. You should also take a good look at the pickpocket so you can describe them to police later. The good news is that it's easy to stop pickpockets before they steal something. Just be very careful with your personal things: your phone, wallet, purse or bag. Don't leave them anywhere. It's best to keep them where you can see or feel them so you can check them. Be the most careful when there are a lot of people around you.

I hope this information …

Workbook audioscripts

UNIT 0

🔊 0.1 Unit 0, 0.1, Exercises 1 and 2

S = Simon R = Rob

S: Hey Rob, do you want to see my place?
R: Sure. Wow, your kitchen is really big!
S: I know. We all have dinner together here in the evening.
R: There are a lot of photos on your walls.
S: Yes, my dad takes them. He loves taking photos.
R: Cool. And whose room is this?
S: That's my sister's bedroom. Just look at that original lamp!
R: Where?
S: The one on the ceiling.
R: Wow!
S: She always sits in front of the mirror for hours, doing her hair and make-up. But when she listens to music and sings really loudly, I can't stand it!
R: Ha, I know. My sister is always in the bathroom when I want to use it, and there's only one bathroom in our house. I can't stand waiting for it.
S: I know what you mean! This is my bedroom. It's a bit small, but I love it.
R: Nice! Is there a computer in here?
S: Sure. Do you like playing computer games? There are lots in this box on the floor.
R: I love playing computer games! Let's see what you've got here …

🔊 0.2 Unit 0, 0.2, Exercise 5

Hi, I'm Stacey and I'm fifteen. I live in the north of England. I go to a big school in Manchester. On school days I get up at 7 and have a shower. I usually have a small breakfast, then I go to school.

My mum usually takes me to school. She's a nurse and she works in a hospital. She sometimes works at night, so on those days I walk to school so she can sleep. I don't like walking to school. I need to get up really early because I don't want to be late.

When I get home after school, I always do my homework. Then I can relax for the rest of the evening. I often listen to music in my bedroom or watch TV.

At the weekend I always get up late. In the afternoon I usually go out and see my friends. My best friend is Kyra. She goes to the same school as me and we're in the same class. Kyra's a really nice person, I talk to her all the time.

UNIT 1

🔊 1.1 Unit 1, 1.5, Exercise 3

P = Presenter I = Isla

P: Hello and welcome to our show. Today we're asking the question: could you live without technology? With me in the studio are Isla, Ben, Jeremy and Sara. You're doing an experiment at the moment, aren't you?
I: Yes. We're switching off all our technology for a month to see what life is like without it.
P: Wow! That sounds really difficult!

🔊 1.2 Unit 1, 1.5, Exercise 4

P = Presenter I = Isla B = Ben S = Sara J = Jeremy

P: So, how's it going this month without technology? Isla?
I: Well. I usually message my best friend Lucy in the evenings, but of course, now I can't do that. She's doing the challenge too. For me it's OK because I see her at school, but she hates it. The worst thing is trying to do homework. I can't go online to search for information and that's terrible! Books are OK, but it's much slower without the internet.
P: What about you, Ben?
B: Well, I'm really into music and, of course, I can't download any songs at the moment. I'm playing my guitar more, and I'm getting better. But I know my neighbours can't stand it when I practise playing early in the morning!
P: Sara, what are you finding difficult?
S: Well, I usually upload all my photos from my smartphone to my blog, but I can't do that now. At first, it was hard. But now I'm using my dad's old camera and getting the photos printed in a shop in town. I can put the photos on my bedroom walls – it's so cool! So, what's difficult? I follow my favourite singers on social media and now I don't know what's happening. That's hard.
P: And are there any good things, Jeremy?
J: No! I have a blog, and now I can't update it. I have some funny stories to share, but I have to wait until next month! See this notebook? I hate writing by hand, but I'm doing it because I need to remember everything about my digital detox! I can't wait to blog about it.

UNIT 2

🔊 2.1 Unit 2, 2.5, Exercise 4

C = Chloe A = Alex

C: Hi, Alex. How was your holiday?
A: Hi Chloe. Well, it wasn't really a holiday. I was really tired when I got home. But I learned a lot – and I'm a lot fitter now!
C: Really? So what did you learn?
A: Oh, lots of skills for keeping yourself alive if you get lost in the wild.
C: Scary! Did you see any wild animals?
A: No, we didn't see any, but we heard some at night. I loved listening to all the different wildlife.
C: Wow!

🔊 2.2 Unit 2, 2.5, Exercise 5

C = Chloe A = Alex

C: So, what did you do on this survival course?
A: Well, you know we spent five days there. So, on the first day we learned how to discover plants and find food. And that was cool! We found lots of fruit to eat!
C: All right! Did they teach you how to make a fire and cook food over it?
A: They did. I was pretty excited about it. It's usually quite easy to make a fire if it's not raining, but it rained on the first day. So, you know all the wood was wet and we couldn't make it burn. But we got lucky on the second day and cooked some food over the campfire when it was nice and warm at last.
C: Cool. And did you make a shelter?
A: Yeah, we did. We spent the first two nights in a wooden hut in the middle of the forest, but on the third day we learnt how to make a proper shelter. I was worried that we might be cold at night, but in fact our shelter was quite warm.
C: What about water? Did you have enough?
A: That's what my mum was most worried about. We took some water with us, but on the fourth day we also learned how to find it in the forest and how to make it safe to drink.
C: Did you boil it to make it safe?
A: No, we used special tablets that you put in the water to clean it.
C: And did you have a map to help you to find your way?
A: Yes, we did, but they also taught us how to use the sun to find our way.
C: What about at night? Did you use the stars?
A: No. Usually they teach you how to do that, but it was cloudy most of the time. And then on the last day when the weather was fine, everybody was too tired to watch the stars. But not me – I slept outside because it was quite warm – over 15 degrees.

C: Weren't you scared of wild animals?
A: Not at all. I was just next to my shelter so I felt quite safe.
C: Hmm … It sounds like fun. But sleeping on my own in the middle of a forest isn't my cup of tea!

UNIT 3

🔊 3.1 Unit 3, 3.5, Exercise 3

So, I've just finished making my cake, and here it is. My friends think it looks delicious, but they can't eat it because I've made it for a competition at my school. I love sweet things, and I started making cakes when I was ten. I enjoy making cakes in unusual shapes. I wanted to make a cake in the shape of a boat, but that didn't work out. It was too difficult, and I couldn't make it stand up. So in the end I've made one in the shape of a giant phone. I think it's really cool. I chose chocolate flavour for the cake because that's my favourite, and there's a fresh vanilla cream filling in the middle. On the outside, there's red coloured icing over the main part of the cake, and I've used sweets for the buttons on the phone. The best bit is that I've used icing to write a message on the screen. It says: See you later for tea and cake!

🔊 3.2 Unit 3, 3.5, Exercises 4 and 5

Right, before you all go off to your classes, I just need to remind you about our cake competition. This competition takes place on Saturday the twenty-ninth of June – that's the same day as the School Fair. If you're taking part, you need to bring your cake to the school cookery room. All the cakes need to be there by ten o'clock in the morning. The judges can then have plenty of time to look at all the cakes and, of course, they'll taste them all before they make their decision. Mrs Addison will announce the winner at two o'clock.

There are three different categories in the competition: cupcakes – I'm sure you all know what they are; then there are family cakes – those are larger cakes that you can share – and finally, there are novelty cakes – that's cakes in unusual and interesting shapes. I think last year we had a plane and a football field, and the winner was a very tasty cake in the shape of an elephant, which was amazing! It had a rich, creamy chocolate flavour.

If you'd like to enter the competition, you need to pay an entry fee of two pounds per cake, and fill in your entry form by next week. The winner will receive a cookery book and twenty-five pounds. You can get entry forms from Mrs Cussons or you can download them from the school website. Good luck everyone, and happy cake making! Remember, someone's going to win that prize!

UNIT 4

🔊 4.1 Unit 4, 4.5, Exercise 3

Now, if you're looking for something to do next weekend, why not go to the Leeds Film and Theatre Festival? It takes place in Hyde Park from the fifteenth to the eighteenth of July and there are loads of exciting things to do. There are classes every morning about acting, directing, costume design and filming. In the afternoon you can watch live performances, new films or just relax and chat with other festival-goers. If you want to have a go at acting yourself, there are plenty of performances you can take part in, including the Festival Show on the last night on the big open-air stage. OK, on with some more music now, and …

🔊 4.2 Unit 4, 4.5, Exercises 4 and 5

M = Max J = Jess
M: I didn't know you were interested in theatre. What made you go to the festival?
J: Well, my friend Rosie always invites me to go to see unusual live performances with her. She didn't go to this festival, but we've got this new drama teacher at school. We did some acting with him and I loved it. That's why I decided to go to the festival and get some advice on acting.
M: So, what did they teach you?
J: Well, they organised us into small groups and gave us a short drama to prepare. They gave us lots of tips about remembering the words and how to show different feelings like anger or happiness. They said it's better to hide your real feelings and just focus on acting. You don't have to show the emotions very strongly, but you need to make sure your face and your body show the same emotion. Then we had to give a performance to the whole group.
M: Well, I guess you were good at it because you had a big part in the final show.
J: That wasn't planned. There was a really talented girl, and the plan was for her to play the main character. But she fell at lunchtime and hurt her foot. She had to go to hospital, so the teacher asked me to do it.
M: And did the show go well?
J: Hmm, quite well I think. It was a comedy and the audience laughed a lot. It was about a family party that went wrong. The costumes looked great. I wore a big straw hat and a party dress. I loved it. We had to sing a song at one point and the music was a bit too quiet, but it was OK. Everyone remembered what they had to do. The only thing that went wrong was the stage lights – one of the switches broke, so we had to do part of the show in the dark!
M: And what was your favourite part of the day?
J: Oh I enjoyed all of it. The show was brilliant, but it was a bit scary being up on stage, and I was really stressed about singing. But I made lots of new friends – I think that was probably the best bit.

UNIT 5

🔊 5.1 Unit 5, 5.5, Exercise 3

… and news is just coming in about Anna Martin, one of the country's best young tennis players. She's won a lot of matches this year, but she's decided to give up playing competitively and will focus on coaching instead. We'll definitely miss her on the tennis court and so will all her supporters, but of course we wish her lots of luck with her future career!

🔊 5.2 Unit 5, 5.5, Exercises 4 and 5

A = Angela P = Paul
A: Have you heard the news about Anna Martin? I can't believe she's giving up playing – I wasn't expecting it at all. I hope she changes her mind. She's one of my favourite players and she could be a big star in the future!
P: Anna Martin? I've heard of her, but I don't know much about her.
A: She's amazing. She's beaten some of the best players in the world, and she's still only twenty years old. She plays in lots of charity matches and raises a lot of money to help children with disabilities. She believes everyone can do sport. I even watched her play in one of the matches. She's so strong and powerful. And she looked so happy when I saw her play.
P: Maybe she was happy because she was doing something to help other people. The report said she wants to be a coach. That's a great way to help people. Maybe she'll be happier. I mean, there's no point in training all day every day if you don't enjoy it.
A: That's true. I read that as well as practising on the court for three hours every day, she swims four times a week to build up her strength, she runs every morning for fitness and she does yoga twice a week to help with balance. That's quite tough.
P: Exactly. It must be really hard for her to spend time with her family and friends too. And it must be impossible to have any hobbies.
A: Well, her parents always watch her matches, and sometimes her brother was at the court too, but you're right.

She said she wants to take up some new hobbies as well as work as a coach. But really, she'll never become rich if she works as a coach.

P: She might, if she's popular. But money isn't the most important thing. I think she'll be a great coach. She seems such a nice person – kids will love her.

A: Yeah, she's lovely – I'm sure young players will enjoy working with her.

P: And look, it says here that she wants to coach the stars of the future. She's going to make them stars on the tennis court, but she also wants to be a role model for them. She plans to help them to raise money for charity and find other ways to help people. I think that's amazing. I wish more famous people were like that.

A: That's true.

UNIT 6

6.1 Unit 6, 6.5, Exercise 2

I = Interviewer M = Millie

I: Thanks for coming onto the show, Millie. Tell us about your experiences of working holidays.

M: Well, I love them! I always choose working holidays rather than just sitting around on a beach. I think I've been to eight – no, nine different countries now. I wouldn't go on holiday any other way.

6.2 Unit 6, 6.5, Exercise 3

I = Interviewer M = Millie

I: Why did you first choose a working holiday?

M: When I finished school, I wanted to go to South America, but didn't have enough money. Then a friend told me about Woofing – that's working on organic farms. I looked online and it looked amazing. I spent two months in Peru working on a vegetable farm. I loved it!

I: Do you see a lot of the country where you're working?

M: Yes, you get days off, so you can go on excursions or weekend trips. And I always save a bit of money so I can go travelling at the end of the job.

I: What's your favourite kind of working holiday?

M: Well, working on farms is OK, but I prefer activity camps. I've done summer camps in America – they're great – but my real passion is skiing. So I enjoy the winter ski seasons the most.

I: Do you have to be good at sport to work at activity camps?

M: It helps if you're sporty. I teach tennis and horse-riding in the summer and, of course, skiing in the winter. But you don't have to do activities. You can do other jobs, like cooking or working at a reception desk.

I: It can't be easy working with young children.

M: Yes, it can be tiring. That's one of the disadvantages of activity camps. Also, the kids don't always behave well – that's annoying. And you don't earn much money – you get your food for free and a place to sleep, but then just a bit of pocket money, really.

I: But you must enjoy it because you keep going back.

M: Yes. Working holidays are a great way to travel. You see some amazing places, it's a great way to keep fit, and probably the best thing is that you meet other young people from all over the world. I guess it could be difficult as you get older because it's hard work – but luckily, I'm still young!

UNIT 7

7.1 Unit 7, 7.5, Exercise 2

Autism is quite a common condition, so it's important that all teenagers understand it. It isn't a physical or mental disability, but students with autism find it difficult to relate to other people, so they can have problems making friends. We noticed that our students with autism were fine during lessons, when the teacher was there, and before and after school they had support from their families. But it was between lessons – at lunchtime, for example, that they sometimes found it difficult to join in. That's why we started a buddy system here last year. 'Buddy' is an informal word for a friend, and the buddy system is about students helping those who need it. The buddies' role isn't to tell autistic classmates what to do or how to behave. And it isn't necessarily about becoming best friends. It's just to be there to help when they're needed. The system has done very well. Our students with autism definitely don't have as many problems at break times now and actually, the buddies have also got a lot out of it – we didn't expect that, so it was an extra benefit.

7.2 Unit 7, 7.5, Exercises 3 and 4

I first started being a buddy to Matt when I got back to school after the summer holidays. I didn't really know Matt before, although he's in my class, because he was very quiet and I didn't think he had much in common with me and my friends.

I didn't know much about autism before I knew Matt, but he explained that he gets quite stressed if there are people around him the whole time. He's OK chatting to them in small groups, but if there's a big activity going on, like a game of football, he finds it difficult to join in.

Matt felt worried about making friends because he thinks he's different. I've helped him to deal with that problem, I think, and he's now much more relaxed and gets along quite well with others. He even plays football with us sometimes. If he gets a bit better, I think he'll get into the school team!

I get a lot out of the whole experience of being a buddy. Before, I was only into football and computer games, and I thought that anyone who didn't share those interests was just boring. Matt's shown me that we don't all have to be the same – it's fine to just be who you are.

UNIT 8

8.1 Unit 8, 8.5, Exercise 2

M = Man L = Sergeant Linfield

M: So, Sergeant Linfield, can you give us your report?

L: Yes, Sir. We received a call at around 2.30 from Mr and Mrs Jones, of Bridge Street. They wanted to report a burglary at their house. I know the area well, so I went straight to the house. Mr and Mrs Jones were quite upset, so I interviewed them about what had happened. It seems they'd come home and found the door open and some things missing. Some other officers arrived then, and they took fingerprints and looked for clues inside the house. Mrs Jones went out into the back garden to get a bit of fresh air, and that's when she found a mobile phone, under a bush. I looked at the phone and saw that it had a phone number on it labelled 'Home'. I called the number and spoke to a woman, and I asked her where she lived. I then went round to the house and found the burglar. The phone was his, and the woman I'd spoken to was his mum! I arrested the burglar, of course, and found Mr and Mrs Jones's things in his bedroom.

M: Good work, Sergeant!

8.2 Unit 8, 8.5, Exercise 3

The police are asking for information about a robbery that took place last week at the post office on Park Street. The crime took place on the fifteenth of June, at about half past three in the afternoon. This was a serious robbery, and thirty thousand pounds in cash was stolen, along with some other items. The police are looking for three suspects, who were seen near the crime scene that afternoon. They are also interested in information about a dark green car that the suspects were seen driving off in. If you have any information about this crime, please call the police on 0141 557 6231. I'll repeat that number for you: it's 0141 557 6231.

🔊 8.3 Unit 8, 8.5, Exercise 4

1
Thieves broke into a jeweller's shop in the town centre last night. The crime happened at about half past eleven and the criminals stole a diamond necklace and some earrings worth over fifty thousand pounds. Luckily, they couldn't get into the safe, so they didn't get away with any money, and they also didn't find two valuable diamond rings that were in a drawer under the counter.

2   S = Sophie D = Dan
S: Hi, Dan. How are things?
D: Not very good. There's been a burglary at our house.
S: Oh no! When did it happen?
D: Yesterday afternoon.
S: That's awful. Were you at home?
D: No, but my dad was. He was really tired after a business trip, so he was asleep in bed. He didn't hear a thing! I was playing computer games earlier in the day, but then I went out to play football, and that's when it happened.
S: What did they take?
D: My laptop and my mum's tablet – it's a real pain!

3
Hello, I'm PC Emma Robinson and I'm investigating some vandalism at the school last night. You probably know there have been problems in the past with vandalism – broken windows and paint sprayed on the walls, things like that. Well, this time it was the head teacher's car, which was outside the school. Someone damaged it so he couldn't drive home. Did you see anyone near the school last night?

4   W = Will L = Lucy
W: Come on, Lucy. Our train leaves soon.
L: I can't find my purse or my phone. They were definitely in my bag this morning. I think someone's stolen them.
W: Well, there are a lot of pickpockets about.
L: I know and that's why I never keep money in my back pocket – it's too easy to steal it from there.
W: Yeah. Look, there's your phone.
L: Oh! Thanks, Will. But my purse is definitely missing, so someone's taken it. I think I'll have to go to the police.

5   P = Police officer SA = Sales assistant
P: So, can you tell me what happened?
SA: Yes. The shop was quite empty. There were only about four or five people in here. There was a teenage boy, about fifteen years old. He bought a game and left. Then there was a man – he was about fifty, I guess. He wanted to know about computer games for his children. I was talking to him when I saw the woman. She was about twenty-five, with long hair. She just took the game and walked out! I was still serving the man, so I couldn't run after her.

UNIT 9

🔊 9.1 Unit 9, 9.5, Exercise 2

1   T = Teacher B = Boy
T: Have you all finished the first exercise?
B: Not quite, Mr. Cowen. It's difficult.
T: OK, I'll give you a few more minutes.

2   G = Girl B = Boy
G: Did you manage to answer all the questions in the test?
B: No, I didn't. I couldn't do the last two.
G: No, I couldn't either. It was really hard!

3   B = Boy G = Girl
B: Could you lend me a pen, please?
G: Of course. I've got one in my bag. Here you are.
B: Thanks.

4   G = Girl B = Boy
G: How long did you spend on your Maths homework?
B: About an hour. I didn't really understand it.
G: Yeah, I know what you mean. I think we need to ask the teacher to go over it again.

🔊 9.2 Unit 9, 9.5, Exercise 3

1   G = Girl B = Boy
G: Oh it was so embarrassing today!
B: Why?
G: Well, I was in my Geography lesson. We were watching a film about volcanoes, so the lights were out. I was really tired. I think I was hungry because I missed lunch. I didn't even have time to eat a sandwich because I had to finish my Maths homework. Anyway, I didn't understand the film. We were meant to go on the internet before the class to learn a bit about volcanoes, but I didn't have time. And the next thing I remember is Mr Appleby telling me to wake up! I fell asleep at my desk! In future, I'm going to make sure I always have something to eat before class!

2   G = Girl B = Boy
G: Hi, Paul. I thought you wanted some help with your Maths homework yesterday. Why didn't you text me?
B: Well, I tried. I wrote you a text quietly in class yesterday afternoon saying, 'Can you give me the answers to the Maths homework?' But unfortunately, just as I was sending it, someone texted me, so my phone made a noise. And, of course, Mr Smith, the teacher, heard it!
G: Oh dear!
B: Yes, it was 'Oh dear'! He asked me to bring my phone out to show him and there was the text to you. Of course, he wasn't very pleased, and then he called my mum and told her, and she was really angry with me! I've got extra Maths for two weeks now!

3   T = Teacher E = Emma
T: Right, quiet everyone. Today we're talking about …
E: Hello, Ms. Moore. Sorry I'm late.
T: OK, Emma. What happened this morning?
E: I had to go to the doctor's. Remember, I broke my arm a few months ago. Then I had to go back home again after that because I forgot to put my glasses in my bag. But I've got them now.
T: OK, Emma. Sit down and take out your notebook.

4   W = Woman G = George
W: Hi, George. How did your school play go?
G: Well, good and bad, really. It was good because, of course, I'm really pleased that I'm studying Drama and I'm happy the performance is over. But it was a bit embarrassing.
W: Why?
G: Well, part of my costume was a big hat. When I went on stage, the hat fell over my eyes and I couldn't see. Unfortunately, I fell flat on my face! It was really embarrassing! But at least I remembered my lines. One girl couldn't remember what to say. She felt worse than me.

5   T = Teacher L = Lucy
T: Right. Is everyone ready? Lucy? What are you doing?
L: Er, I'm just looking for my French book and my pencil case. I'm sure I put them both in my school bag last night, but now I can't find them.
T: Well, I'm sure you can borrow a pen from someone else.
L: Yes, I know, but … Oh. Here's my pencil case, right at the bottom of my bag.
T: OK. Well, let's get started. Put your bag down now. You can share books with Karen.

EXAM TIME 1

🔊 ET1–3.1 Exam Time 1 Units 1–3, Exercise 1

1 B = Boy G = Girl
- **G:** I didn't see you at the skate park last weekend.
- **B:** No, we went to stay with my cousins in the countryside. It was OK, just a bit boring. I wanted to do some walking because it's a lovely area, but it rained. So I spent the whole weekend in front of the television. There was some skiing on so it wasn't too bad!
- **G:** I saw a bit of that too. OK – see you at the park next weekend then.

2
Amy? Hi! It's Emma. We've just finished moving in and I just *love* the new house. We're very near the shops – which is good, although a bit noisy. But my room is at the back and I can see the garden. It's lovely. Of course, I'd like to live near the beach, like you, but Dad needs to be near his work. Come and stay soon. Call me back later!

3
There's some interesting weather in the UK at the moment. If you're in Scotland, you know it's raining and it's really cold whereas in the London area you've got some fog right now, with cloudy skies later on. In Ireland the winds are getting worse and there are a lot of trees down – dangerous for people on the roads. Today is certainly a different story from yesterday, when we all enjoyed clear blue skies.

4 B = Boy G = Girl
- **B:** My cooking is improving! I cooked dinner for the family last night.
- **G:** Wow! Did you cook chicken and mushroom soup like we did in cookery class on Monday?
- **B:** No, that takes too long. I wanted to do chicken salad, but my sister doesn't eat meat, so I did noodles with cheese.
- **G:** Delicious! But next time you must do some chocolate cupcakes for dessert. Yours were yummy in class!

5 G = Girl M = Mum
- **G:** Mum! I can't find my phone and I'm late for school.
- **M:** Have you looked in your bag? Maybe you put it in last night.
- **G:** I don't think so. I didn't leave it on the train because I used it last night. It was definitely on my desk because I phoned Eliza about homework.
- **M:** I hope you haven't lost it again.
- **G:** Oh, you were right. Here it is. Now I remember. I put it in before I went to bed!

6 G = Girl B = Boy
- **G:** Have you read this article in the magazine? It's all about your sister. There's a cool picture of her with a big plate of yummy food!
- **B:** I'm not surprised. She's got a great job. She wanted to be a chef and she trained for a couple of years. Then she decided that it's a really hard job, so now she just takes pictures of food for restaurants and magazines. She's always liked working with food! She won 'Waitress of the year' when she was a teenager!

🔊 ET1–3.2 Exam Time 1 Units 1–3, Exercise 2

OK everyone, we've now made all the arrangements for our visit to the exhibition at the Science Museum next Thursday. We were planning to go on Wednesday, but unfortunately we couldn't book a coach for that day.

So, the exhibition is called Robot Life and as you can guess, it's about robots! It's a great opportunity to see the latest developments in robotics. There's a waiter robot called 'Jack' and a hotel receptionist robot called 'Maria'. Jack takes orders and brings your food, but Maria can actually talk and reply to visitors' questions. Amazing!

Arrangements for the day are as follows. Firstly, the coach leaves school at 8.30, so I would like everyone to be here by 8.15. Ask your parents to be here at school to meet you from the coach at 5.30 in the afternoon.

The restaurant at the museum is always very busy, so please bring sandwiches and drinks. We can have them in the museum gardens. Also remember to …

🔊 ET1–3.3 Exam Time 1 Units 1–3, Exercise 3

A = Ashlyn J = Jamie
- **A:** So, I've got a great recipe we can cook for dinner tonight. It's chicken with sweet potato and pineapple.
- **J:** That sounds yummy! So how do we cook it?
- **A:** OK, so first, we heat the oven to 180 degrees and we put the chicken breasts in to roast them.
- **J:** OK.
- **A:** Then we can prepare the vegetables.
- **J:** What's first?
- **A:** The sweet potato. First, we peel the skin off, then chop it into small pieces, then put it in boiling water for fifteen minutes.
- **J:** Ah, OK.
- **A:** Next is the pineapple. Now usually people like to fry it, but I think it's better not cooked. We can just chop it into small pieces.
- **J:** OK, what about this garlic?
- **A:** Ah yes. We wait until everything's ready, then chop it and fry it quickly. Then we spread it all over the top.
- **J:** That sounds delicious. What about dessert?
- **A:** Peaches with cream!
- **J:** Oh, they're not those awful tinned peaches, are they?
- **A:** No, I've got some lovely fresh ones. Look.
- **J:** Oh, they look really nice. Right, shall we get started? I'm hungry!
- **A:** Yes, me too!

🔊 ET1–3.4 Exam Time 1 Units 1–3, Exercise 4

The weather forecast today is mixed around the country. In the north, it will be cold with heavy snow. In the south, however, it will be cloudy with some sunshine!

EXAM TIME 2

🔊 ET1–6.1 Exam Time 2 Units 1–6, Exercise 1

1 B = Boy G = Girl
- **B:** You haven't seen the new TV talent show, have you?
- **G:** I saw the first programme, but I didn't really enjoy it. I decided to watch the new cookery programme instead last night.
- **B:** That is so boring!
- **G:** How do you know? You didn't see it.
- **B:** I've seen the reviews and they all said the same thing.
- **G:** Well, I liked it. The reviews said that the wild animal documentary last week was terrible and they were wrong about that too!

2
Yes, hi. My name's Paul Matthews and I'm phoning to see if you've found a silver smartphone. I was at the leisure centre from about two until five o'clock. I asked for some information about tennis lessons at the reception desk as I was leaving, so it's possible I left it on the desk there. I had a sandwich in the café after going swimming and I remember using it there to call a friend, so I'm sure I didn't leave it by the pool. If someone has found it, please phone me on 09876876574. Thanks.

3 G = Girl D = Dad
- **G:** Can you drive me into town tomorrow, Dad?
- **D:** No problem. I've got to go to the bank. Where do you want to go?

260

G: I need to go to the camping shop.
D: Oh no – is there a problem with your new tent? You've only had it a month.
G: It's fine. I just want to check out some new sleeping bags they've advertised. They're only fifty pounds! I've got that money from my birthday to spend.
D: That sounds good value. I'm going at about half past ten. OK?

4 B = Boy G = Girl
G: Where did you go last summer, Gary?
B: I went to the New Forest with my family. It was lovely there. We stayed in the middle of the forest and did loads of activities in the day.
G: Like what?
B: We hired a boat one day and went on a river trip, played football, and I even tried horse-riding!
G: Really? I can't imagine you on a horse!
B: I know! I didn't like it, to be honest. The best thing was in the evening: we cooked over a fire and then my dad told us scary stories.
G: That sounds fun!
B: Yeah, it was. I really liked sleeping in a tent, too. It felt like a real adventure.

5
Hi, my name's Jill Roland and I'm calling about the advert for people to help at the race this weekend. I'd like to help out if possible. I usually take part in the race myself, but at the moment I have an injury, so I can't run. I'm happy to help with anything that you need me to do, like give out water to the runners or just cheer them on! I'm available for the whole day that day. If you need anyone to help, then please contact me on 01297459173. Thanks.

🔊 ET1–6.2 Exam Time 2 Units 1–6, Exercise 2

I = Interviewer S = Suzy
I: Suzy Davies has just got a part in the new Shark Beach movie. Congratulations, Suzy! How are you feeling?
S: Thank you. Well, of course I know it's going to be hard work – very long days and lots of lines to learn. But I can't wait for the filming to start.
I: It sounds quite a scary film! Do you need to be able to swim well for this role?
S: Well, I learned to swim when I was younger and I'm OK, but not really fast, and I look a bit silly in the water. They've got another actor who will be me in the swimming scenes, thank goodness!
I: This isn't your first film role, is it?
S: No. I've known that I wanted to act since I was at primary school. When I was six, a film company was making a film in the area. They asked all the children in my class to be in the crowd scenes in the film. We had to dress up as children from the last century. It was amazing fun! So that was my first role.
I: Did you go to drama school?
S: I wanted to go to drama school and I chose a couple to apply for. However, my parents wanted me to get a degree at university first. Then, while I was studying, I took part in a play. A famous director saw me and asked me to do this film.
I: Are you worried that you haven't done many acting classes?
S: It's good to have training, but you can also learn while you do something. A lot of the other actors are very experienced and I know I'll learn a lot of techniques from them. But the director believes that I can do this and that gives me a lot of confidence!
I: Do you have any plans for later in the year?
S: Well, filming will take at least six months. At some point, I want to do some real training. But this filming is on location in Australia, which is a place I've always wanted to go to! Afterwards it would be great to stay on and tour round for a while. Also, I might be in another film next year. So it might be difficult to do many acting classes before then. We'll see.
I: Well, good luck with everything, Suzy.

🔊 ET1–6.3 Exam Time 2 Units 1–6, Exercise 3

I'm very pleased to tell you that there will be another Music in the Park festival in August. Last year's event on the third and fourth of August was very successful, and the organisers decided to repeat that success. This year, put the ninth and tenth of August in your diaries and make sure you're free!

Like last year, the festival will take place at the north end of King's Park. Parking will once again be in the area at the south entrance to the park. However, please try to leave cars at home as there won't be a lot of space.

You've probably read on social media that Paul Bailey and Free Voice are going to sing at the festival. Unfortunately, Paul Bailey wanted to come, but he will still be on tour in the USA at the time. Free Voice will be on stage on Sunday afternoon, though, to close the event.

A new feature of the event this year will be a dance competition. The competition will take place on the main stage. It will be at lunchtime on both days, and the categories will be hip-hop, salsa and street dance. The judges will be Jack Bennet and Mary Jake from the TV talent show *Time to Dance*. It should be fun! You'll be able to see the winners of the competition in Channel 5's documentary *Young Dancers* in September.

So, remember to get your tickets early. You can book by phone on 07640832511 or you can get a better price by booking online at festivals.com.

See you there, guys!

🔊 ET1–6.4 Exam Time 2 Units 1–6, Exercise 4

When you take up a new sport, it's important to check you're healthy enough to do so. If you try to do too much too soon, you can hurt yourself. So unless you want an injury, take it slowly at first.

EXAM TIME 3

🔊 ET1–9.1 Exam Time 3 Units 1–9, Exercise 1

T = Trish A = Aidan
T: Ah, that's a nice photo, Aidan. When did you take that?
A: Oh, that was a family barbecue we had last year. All the family got together to celebrate my great-grandmother's birthday. She was eighty-five!
T: That's nice. What's her name?
A: Elsie, but everyone calls her GeeGee.
T: And that's Nathan, your dad, right? The man standing behind GeeGee? Who's he with?
A: That's right. He's with Mia.
T: Your mother?
A: No, Mia is his sister. And that's her son, Jack. He's five.
T: Right. He looks like trouble!
A: Jack? Ah no, he's lovely. He's playing with Ryan there, my brother … Jack and Ryan get on really well.
T: That's lovely. You have a great family!

🔊 ET1–9.2 Exam Time 3 Units 1–9, Exercise 2

S = Spencer D = Debbie
S: So, Debbie, how was the school trip to France?
D: I had a great time. I was staying with my French friend, Jeanette. Nearly all of us were in Paris. Jeanette's house was a few miles outside, but we went in every day by train to her school.
S: How was your French?

D: Before I went, I was very worried about understanding everything. French people speak so quickly! And when other people speak to you, they use all sorts of vocabulary and you need to guess a lot of things. But I actually understood quite a lot. I was pleased.

S: And what was the food like?

D: Well, I'm not very adventurous when it comes to unusual food. Jeanette's mum is a good cook, but I couldn't eat everything she cooked. I'm not very keen on fish and we had it nearly every day!

S: Did you go to many galleries or museums?

D: Yes, I went to the Rodin Museum – he was a great sculptor and you can see a lot of his statues in a lovely garden. Luckily, it wasn't raining. We wanted to see a special art exhibition by Monet, but it closed the day before we went. I think it's coming to London soon though.

S: Do you think you'll go back for another visit?

D: Well, first my friend Jeanette will come over to stay with us for two weeks in October – that's only a few months away. And then my parents are planning a trip to France with me in the spring.

S: Are you still thinking about becoming a French teacher?

D: I love French and I think I speak it a lot better now. But I'm not sure I could help other people learn. I think I'd prefer to do some translating – books, reports or even films!

🔊 ET1–9.3 Exam Time 3 Units 1–9, Exercise 3

Dame Agatha Christie was one of the world's most famous writers of detective stories. Born in 1890, she had a very interesting life and lived until she was eighty-five.

Her work includes sixty-six detective novels and fourteen short-story collections. These included her two most famous characters: the detectives Hercule Poirot and Miss Marple. You have probably heard of them as they were made into TV programmes.

She was also a playwright, and her play *The Mousetrap* was the longest ever running play in the world. It first opened at the Ambassador's Theatre in London in 1952 and in over sixty-five years, there were nearly thirty thousand performances!

During both world wars in the twentieth century, she worked at a hospital. She later married an archaeologist, and went with him to work in the Arab World. Both of these experiences taught her many things that she later included in her stories.

Incredibly successful, the *Guinness Book of World Records* describes her as the best-selling author of all time, as her books have sold over a billion copies, both in English and translated into other languages. One of these, her novel *And Then There Were None*, has sold over a hundred million copies alone. Some of her other novels include …

🔊 ET1–9.4 Exam Time 3 Units 1–9, Exercise 4

Three bank robbers were given long prison sentences today. The robbers were caught when their fingerprints were found at the scene. When reading out the sentence, the judge said this was a terrible crime.

Workbook answer key

Starter unit

0.1

Exercise 1
1 bathroom, bedroom, ceiling, floor, kitchen, mirror

Exercise 2
1 c   2 a   3 a   4 c

Exercise 3
1 c   2 a   3 e   4 b   5 d

Exercise 4
1 love   2 can't   3 mind   4 likes   5 stand

Exercise 5
1 bath   2 bed   3 window   4 garden
5 cupboard

Exercise 6
1 There's   2 There are   3 some   4 any
5 isn't   6 Are there

Exercise 7
1 Jack's   2 my parents'   3 your   4 our
5 my brother's

0.2

Exercise 1
A chef   B scientist   C hairdresser
D mechanic   E farmer   F nurse

Exercise 2
1 I usually have lunch at one o'clock.
2 Martha is always late.
3 I sometimes go to school by bus.
4 Sara is often tired.
5 Paul never does his homework.
6 My dad usually cooks dinner for the family.

Exercise 3
1 do you live   2 live   3 works   4 Does
5 does   6 doesn't work   7 take   8 don't

Exercise 4
1 b   2 c   3 a   4 b   5 b   6 c

Exercise 5
1 F   2 F   3 T   4 T   5 F   6 T

0.3

Exercise 1
A jacket   B earrings   C watch
D baseball cap   E jumper   F hoodie

Exercise 2
1 is having
2 am doing
3 Are your sisters visiting
4 aren't wearing
5 isn't playing … Is he watching
6 aren't working … are sitting … are having fun

Exercise 3
1 are you doing … I'm playing … I'm not doing
2 Is he … isn't … watching
3 Are … am … I'm feeling

Exercise 4
1 b   2 a   3 c   4 a   5 c   6 a

0.4

Exercise 1
1 French   2 Portuguese   3 Poland
4 German   5 Italy   6 Turkey   7 Spanish
8 Chinese

Exercise 2
1 b   2 a   3 c   4 c   5 b   6 a

Exercise 3
1 worked   2 cooked   3 liked   4 lived
5 tried   6 enjoyed   7 studied   8 played
9 stopped   10 planned

Exercise 4
1 didn't enjoy   2 lived   3 didn't play
4 studied   5 wanted   6 didn't rain

Exercise 5
1 Did you like your birthday presents?
2 Did your parents help you with your homework?
3 Did she invite all her friends to the party?
4 What did you watch at the cinema?
5 Did you work hard last term?
6 When did you visit New York?

Unit 1

1.1 Vocabulary

Exercise 1
1 charging cable   2 wireless earbuds
3 password app   4 power bank
5 remote control   6 smart speaker
7 wi-fi router

Exercise 2
1 remote control   2 password app
3 wireless earbuds   4 charging cable
5 wi-fi router   6 smart speaker
7 power bank

Exercise 3
1 send   2 take   3 set   4 share
5 connect   6 search   7 upload

Exercise 4
1 router   2 search   3 upload   4 send
5 password   6 screenshot

Exercise 5
1 d   2 f   3 c   4 a   5 g   6 i   7 b
8 e   9 h

Exercise 6
[word search grid]

Exercise 7
1 b   2 a   3 b   4 c   5 b   6 c   7 a
8 c   9 a

Exercise 8
1 earbuds   2 bank   3 search
4 chat   5 selfies   6 social
7 story   8 follow   9 uploads

1.2 Grammar

Exercise 1
1 c   2 f   3 a   4 b   5 e   6 d

Exercise 2
1 know   2 feel   3 don't understand
4 wants   5 don't think

Exercise 3
1 usually post … am/'m not uploading
2 is learning … wants
3 am/'m trying … need

4 usually cycle … is/'s raining … are/'re going
5 am/'m looking … don't know

Exercise 4
1 are you doing … I'm trying … I think
2 Do you like … do … I'm not spending … I'm working
3 are you listening … Do you know

Exercise 5
1 'm staying   2 comes   3 wants   4 know
5 love   6 am/'m downloading
7 are you doing

1.3 Reading and Vocabulary

Exercise 1
1 Yuan   2 Jemima

Exercise 2
Text 1:
1 Jemima   2 young people aged 11–16
3 1/one week.   4 2/two to 4/four.
Text 2:
1 Yuan   2 Maths   3 how to make a password app.   4 Jemima

Exercise 3
1 original   2 clever   3 strange
4 excellent   5 complicated   6 safe
7 boring   8 terrible   9 dangerous
10 cool   11 stupid

1.4 Grammar

Exercise 1
1 I enjoy chatting with friends online.
2 I sometimes forget to do my homework.
3 He's hoping to pass his exams.
4 She misses seeing her cousins.
5 I would love to come to the party.
6 He always avoids cleaning his room.

Exercise 2
1 c   2 f   3 a   4 e   5 d   6 b

Exercise 3
1 to learn   2 doing   3 to buy   4 seeing
5 to do   6 to help

Exercise 4
1 to watch   2 listening   3 to be   4 to pay
5 to take

Exercise 5
1 making   2 to talk   3 to organise
4 to come   5 cooking   6 sending
7 seeing   8 to visit   9 to meet   10 to give

1.5 Listening and Vocabulary

Exercise 1
1 a.m.   2 a minute   3 at   4 once   5 at
6 in

Exercise 2
1 f   2 c   3 d   4 b   5 e   6 a

Exercise 3
b

Exercise 4
1 c   2 b   3 e   4 a   5 d

Exercise 5
1 usually   2 evenings   3 hates
4 information   5 terrible

1.6 Speaking

Exercise 2
1 think … could   2 about … idea
3 Shall … try   4 Let's … can't

Exercise 3
1 Let's   2 could   3 idea   4 weak
5 don't   6 about

263

Exercise 4
1 c   2 a   3 e   4 b   5 d
Exercise 5
1 c   2 d   3 a   4 b   5 e

1.7 Writing
Exercise 1
a 2   b 1   c 3
Exercise 2
1 T   2 T   3 F   4 F
Exercise 3
1 However   2 so   3 as well as   4 too
Exercise 4
1 sister   2 school   3 tennis
4 weekend   5 smartphone   6 online
7 hours   8 friends
Exercise 5
Students' own answers

UNIT 1 Self-check
Exercise 1
1 charging cable   2 take … selfie
3 upload   4 wireless earbuds   5 post
6 link   7 remote   8 follow
9 add … group   10 take … screenshot
Exercise 2
1 b   2 b   3 a   4 a   5 c
Exercise 3
1 twice   2 evening   3 minute   4 day
5 mealtimes
Exercise 4
1 'm/am chatting   2 don't often watch
3 lives   4 don't like   5 isn't/is not raining
6 Does … want   7 Are … doing
Exercise 5
1 being   2 to pay   3 to connect
4 to stay up   5 helping   6 to buy
7 to delete   8 going
Exercise 6
1 Shall   2 could   3 Why   4 not   5 how

Unit 2

2.1 Vocabulary
Exercise 1
1 snowy   2 sun   3 foggy   4 cloud
5 windy   6 ice   7 stormy   8 rain
Exercise 2
1 c   2 c   3 a   4 b   5 c   6 a   7 b   8 b
Exercise 3
1 It's very foggy today.
2 Oh no! It's getting cloudy.
3 The sun is beautiful today.
4 Look, it's snowy/snowing. Let's build a snowman.
5 It's getting a bit stormy now.
Exercise 4
1 hurricane   2 drought   3 flood
4 sunshine   5 gale   6 thunder
Exercise 5
1 thunder … lightning   2 shower
3 breeze   4 hurricanes   5 flood
6 drought
Exercise 6
1 strong   2 minus   3 freezing   4 falling
5 fine   6 climate
Exercise 7
1 b   2 c   3 a   4 c   5 a   6 a

Exercise 8
1 showers   2 falling   3 floods   4 raining
5 shower   6 freezing   7 snow   8 icy
9 mild   10 boiling
Exercise 9
1 hot   2 windy   3 temperatures   4 low
5 drought   6 degrees

2.2 Grammar
Exercise 1
1 c   2 e   3 d   4 b   5 a
Exercise 2
1 wanted   2 didn't stay   3 studied
4 didn't help   5 spotted   6 didn't look
Exercise 3
1 saw … didn't know
2 didn't take … went
3 got … didn't go
4 felt … made
5 met … didn't like
Exercise 4
1 did you save
2 did the hurricane happen
3 did you put
4 Did you take
5 did you move
Exercise 5
1 Did (you) see   2 didn't think   3 became
4 didn't stop   5 didn't sleep   6 felt
7 didn't want   8 visited   9 helped
10 Did (you) watch
Exercise 6
1 saw   2 last   3 ago   4 took   5 in
6 didn't   7 Did

2.3 Reading and Vocabulary
Exercise 1
1 b   2 f   3 a   4 e   5 d   6 c
Exercise 2
Takashi mentions: the weather, skiing, taking photos
Exercise 3
1 c   2 a   3 c   4 a

2.4 Grammar
Exercise 1
1 was visiting   2 weren't listening
3 were you doing   4 were swimming
5 Was it snowing   6 wasn't looking
Exercise 2
1 dropped   2 was watching   3 started
4 were staying   5 appeared   6 came
Exercise 3
1 saw … were looking
2 was shining … arrived
3 was waiting … messaged
4 was crying … found
5 heard … were having
6 arrived … was sitting
Exercise 4
1 Did … have   2 had   3 was shining
4 started   5 were eating   6 didn't stop
7 did (you) do   8 wasn't raining   9 told
10 heard   11 was running   12 fell

2.5 Listening and Vocabulary
Exercise 1
1 cave   2 path   3 waterfall   4 sunset
5 spider   6 leaf   7 bear   8 bat

Exercise 2
1 cave   2 stars   3 wildlife   4 path   5 sky
Exercise 3
1 d   2 c   3 a   4 g   5 b   6 f   7 e
Exercise 4
b
Exercise 5
1 c   2 a   3 e   4 h   5 b

2.6 Speaking
Exercise 2
1 do   2 explain   3 mind   4 all right
5 realise   6 see
Exercise 3
1 Why did you take my laptop?
2 I thought it was mine.
3 What's going on?
4 I didn't mean to hurt you
Exercise 4
1 on … can … thought … see
2 did … to … didn't … Never
3 so … That's
Exercise 5
1 b   2 c   3 a   4 b
Exercise 6
1 Why … thought
2 on … explain … mean … see
3 sorry … right

2.7 Writing
Exercise 1
1 20–25 degrees Celsius
2 May–October
3 bungee jumping, paragliding
Exercise 2
1 where   2 just   3 For   4 activities
5 One   6 find   7 as   8 like
Exercise 3
1 somewhere   2 everybody   3 anything
4 everywhere   5 something   6 anybody
Exercise 4
1 mild   2 snow   3 city   4 See
5 kayaking   6 restaurant

UNIT 2 Self-check
Exercise 1
1 sunny   2 gale   3 foggy   4 mild
5 boiling   6 degrees   7 flood   8 lightning
Exercise 2
1 strange   2 awesome   3 worried
4 absolutely   5 different   6 boring
Exercise 3
1 leaves   2 path   3 make   4 discovered
5 for   6 cave
Exercise 4
1 stayed   2 didn't see   3 took
4 didn't want   5 Did (you) have
Exercise 5
1 saw … was walking
2 were skiing … started
3 watched … were staying
4 was sitting … got
5 were watching … when
Exercise 6
1 Why did you do that … I didn't realise … I thought
2 I didn't mean to … I see

Unit 3

3.1 Vocabulary

Exercise 1
Across:
2 peach 5 olives 6 chillies 8 pear
Down:
1 pepper 3 mushroom 4 vinegar
7 seeds

Exercise 2
1 a 2 b 3 c 4 b 5 c 6 a 7 b
8 c 9 b

Exercise 3
1 pepper 2 peaches 3 sausages
4 onion 5 pineapple 6 chillies

Exercise 4
1 boiled 2 frozen 3 recipe 4 roast
5 fresh 6 fried 7 sauce 8 ingredients
9 flavour

Exercise 5
1 Frozen 2 raw 3 cooked 4 recipe
5 ingredients 6 sauce

Exercise 6
1 chocolate 2 coffee 3 coconut
4 mango 5 melon 6 mint 7 strawberry
8 vanilla

Exercise 7
1 melon … strawberry
2 chocolate … vanilla
3 mint
4 Coconut … coffee

Exercise 8
1 fried 2 fresh 3 Mango 4 tuna
5 nuts 6 chocolate 7 sausages 8 sweet potato
9 pineapple 10 recipes
11 ingredients 12 flavour

Exercise 9
1 fresh … recipe … strawberries … flavour … vanilla
2 tuna … chillies … roasted

3.2 Grammar

Exercise 1
1 've/have invited 2 Have you tried
3 haven't had 4 's/has eaten
5 Has your dad ordered

Exercise 2
1 Have you ever tried making bread?
2 I've never cooked a sweet potato.
3 Molly has just left.
4 We haven't finished eating yet.
5 I've already had lunch.
6 Have you ever eaten food from another country?

Exercise 3
1 Have you ever made dinner for your friends?
2 The film has already started.
3 Your email hasn't arrived yet.
4 Have you made Sara's birthday cake yet?
5 Mike has never cooked a meal.
6 We have just ordered our food.

Exercise 4
1 ever 2 already 3 yet 4 just 5 never
6 yet

Exercise 5
1 Have you finished your homework yet? … haven't … has already done
2 Have you ever tried … have … have just made

Exercise 6
1 've/ have 2 ever 3 yet 4 just
5 never 6 has 7 haven't 8 yet

3.3 Reading and Vocabulary

Exercise 1
1 juicy 2 crunchy 3 salt 4 butter
5 crisps 6 creamy 7 spice
8 healthy 9 fatty 10 tasty

Exercise 2
1 for 2 from 3 of 4 with 5 to

Exercise 3
b

Exercise 4
1 plants and vegetables
2 energy and water
3 chips and potatoes
4 (very) expensive
5 like fish
6 (nut) allergies
7 in your/the garden

3.4 Grammar

Exercise 1
for: five minutes, a couple of hours, a long time, four weeks, ten minutes, two years
since: 1998, five o'clock, I was a child, last weekend, Wednesday, yesterday

Exercise 2
1 for 2 since 3 since 4 for 5 for
6 since

Exercise 3
1 went 2 opened 3 have lived
4 have known 5 Did you see
6 Have you ever been

Exercise 4
1 Have you seen … saw
2 have never tried … tried
3 Have you met … met
4 hasn't done … did

Exercise 5
1 went 2 Have you eaten 3 had 4 was
5 have tried 6 didn't like 7 was
8 has improved 9 ate 10 have never had

Exercise 6
1 Have … have … didn't … since
2 been … haven't … for

3.5 Listening and Vocabulary

Exercise 1
1 sweet 2 hard 3 bitter 4 sour 5 rich
6 dry 7 delicious 8 hot

Exercise 2
1 hard 2 delicious 3 rich 4 sweet
5 dry 6 sour

Exercise 3
1 F 2 T 3 F 4 T 5 F 6 T

Exercise 4
1 29/29th/twenty-nine/twenty-ninth (of)
2 10/ten 3 elephant 4 2/two
5 cookery book 6 school website

Exercise 5
1 taking 2 announce 3 enter 4 fill
5 win

3.6 Speaking

Exercise 2
1 c 2 f 3 g 4 b 5 e 6 a 7 d

Exercise 3
1 Excuse 2 thanks 3 please 4 have
5 any

Exercise 4
1 Take a seat and I'll get you the menu.
2 What would you like to drink?
3 Can I get you something?
4 Not for me, thanks.
5 Excuse me, can I have some water?

Exercise 5
1 b 2 c 3 b 4 a

Exercise 6
1 ready … have … anything … any … Just
2 like … excuse … have … Would … Not

3.7 Writing

Exercise 1
1 chop 2 Fry 3 Slice 4 pour 5 add

Exercise 2
1 are things 2 great to hear 3 can't wait
4 just finished 5 decided to have
6 I was wondering 7 Let me know

Exercise 3
1 First 2 Next 3 After that 4 Then
5 Finally

Exercise 4
1 I'm writing to ask if you'd like to come.
2 See you soon.
3 It was great to hear about your holiday.
4 Thanks for getting in touch.
5 Bye for now.

Exercise 5
1 to email 2 at her new school
3 next Friday 4 I'm making 5 invite her
6 suggest what she

UNIT 3 Self-check

Exercise 1
1 garlic 2 pineapple 3 chillies 4 vinegar
5 ice cream 6 sauce

Exercise 2
1 healthy 2 Crunchy 3 creamy 4 juice
5 for 6 from 7 to 8 with

Exercise 3
1 a 2 b 3 c 4 c 5 a 6 b

Exercise 4
1 haven't ordered yet
2 Have you ever tried
3 have just finished
4 have never seen
5 Has it stopped
6 Have you ever cooked
7 has just won

Exercise 5
1 have visited
2 didn't go
3 enjoyed
4 has just opened
5 wrote … hasn't replied
6 have never had … tried

Exercise 6
1 I'll have 2 something to drink
3 Excuse me 4 your starter 5 you are

Reading Time 1

Exercise 1
A 4 B 1 C 2 D 3

Exercise 2
Students' own answers

Exercise 3
1 doesn't like 2 make 3 doesn't use
4 have an idea

Exercise 4
a 4   b 2   c 6   d 1   e 3   f 5
Exercise 5
1 b   2 b   3 c   4 c   5 a
Exercise 6
1 got up   2 put on   3 Go away
4 talk about   5 take (the tourists) out
Exercise 7
Sharks; adventure story; Freddy and Kristin; shark fin

Unit 4

4.1 Vocabulary
Exercise 1
1 comedy   2 documentary   3 action
4 science fiction   5 musical   6 cartoon
7 drama   8 thriller   9 romance
Exercise 2
1 romance   2 comedy   3 science fiction
4 documentary   5 drama   6 cartoon
7 action   8 musical   9 thriller
Exercise 3
2 actor   3 entertain   4 perform
5 producer   6 review
Exercise 4
1 actor   2 entertainment   3 producer
4 perform   5 reviews
Exercise 5
1 d   2 a   3 f   4 e   5 c   6 b
Exercise 6
1 episode   2 viewers   3 special effects
4 channel   5 hit   6 series
Exercise 7
1 c   2 b   3 c   4 a   5 b   6 c   7 b   8 c
Exercise 8
1 reviewers   2 documentary
3 entertainment   4 episode
5 series   6 hit   7 special   8 actor
9 romance   10 performance
11 character   12 reviews

4.2 Grammar
Exercise 1
1 better   2 funniest   3 more important
4 most uncomfortable   5 more exciting
6 worst
Exercise 2
1 a   2 b   3 a   4 a   5 c
Exercise 3
1 than   2 the funniest   3 than   4 as
5 interesting enough
Exercise 4
1 D   2 S   3 D   4 S   5 D
Exercise 5
1 the best   2 more exciting than
3 as good as   4 too uncomfortable
5 old enough   6 disappointed as

4.3 Reading and Vocabulary
Exercise 1
1 Yuki   2 Javier   3 Karol   4 Cara
Exercise 2
1 b   2 c   3 a   4 b   5 a   6 c
Exercise 3
1 write   2 sing   3 livestreamed   4 playlist
5 recorded   6 going   7 stream
8 lip-synch

4.4 Grammar
Exercise 1
Countable nouns: (a) few … many
Uncountable nouns: (a) little … much
Countable and uncountable nouns: a lot of … any … lots of … some
Exercise 2
1 many   2 much   3 some   4 any   5 any
6 a lot of
Exercise 3
1 c   2 a   3 d   4 b   5 f   6 e
Exercise 4
1 a   2 c   3 c   4 b   5 a   6 a   7 c   8 b
Exercise 5
1 few   2 of   3 some   4 any   5 lot
6 much   7 few

4.5 Listening and Vocabulary
Exercise 1
1 d   2 c   3 e   4 a   5 b
Exercise 2
1 square dance   2 family party   3 summer clothes   4 straw hat   5 country music
Exercise 3
1, 2, 3, 5
Exercise 4
1 c   2 a   3 b   4 c   5 c
Exercise 5
1 performances   2 teacher   3 part
4 comedy   5 lights

4.6 Speaking
Exercise 2
1 What would you rather do on Saturday?
2 I'd prefer to go shopping.
3 This film sounds very funny.
4 Where would you rather go on holiday?
5 What would you prefer to do tonight?
6 I'd rather watch a film at home.
Exercise 3
1 healthier   2 prefer   3 rather   4 sounds
5 rather   6 look
Exercise 4
1 b   2 c   3 a   4 b
Exercise 5
1 d   2 a   3 g   4 b   5 f   6 c

4.7 Writing
Exercise 1
a 3   b 1   c 4   d 2   e 5
Exercise 2
1 brilliantly   2 particularly
3 really   4 extremely   5 absolutely
6 well   7 recently   8 highly
Exercise 3
1 recently   2 particularly   3 brilliantly
4 well   5 absolutely
Exercise 4
1 b   2 d   3 a   4 e   5 c

UNIT 4 Self-check
Exercise 1
1 science fiction   2 cartoon
3 performance   4 character   5 hit
6 audience   7 action   8 episode
Exercise 2
1 stream   2 record   3 lyrics   4 playlist
5 along   6 performance
Exercise 3
1 holiday   2 family   3 dance   4 hat
5 party   6 music
Exercise 4
1 more popular than   2 were too
3 the tallest   4 as expensive as
5 the best play   6 old enough
7 better than   8 older than
Exercise 5
1 many   2 lots of   3 any   4 much
5 a few   6 little   7 some
Exercise 6
1 I'd rather … it sounds
2 would you prefer … I'd prefer … looks better

Unit 5

5.1 Vocabulary
Exercise 1
1 b   2 c   3 f   4 g   5 e   6 j   7 i   8 d
9 h   10 a
Exercise 2
1 snorkel   2 helmet   3 skis   4 mat
5 bat   6 football kit   7 racket   8 flippers
Exercise 3
1 changing   2 courts   3 opponent
4 stadium   5 track   6 scoreboard
Exercise 4
1 stadium   2 scoreboard   3 fans   4 pitch
5 tournament   6 opponent
Exercise 5
1 d   2 c   3 a   4 b   5 f   6 e   7 h   8 g
Exercise 6
1 a   2 b   3 c   4 a   5 c   6 c   7 b
Exercise 7
1 take   2 volunteer   3 won   4 part
5 beat   6 score   7 break
Exercise 8
1 snowboard   2 helmet   3 mat
4 records   5 opponent   6 take   7 fan
8 support

5.2 Grammar
Exercise 1
1 c   2 e   3 a   4 f   5 d   6 b
Exercise 2
1 they'll win   2 starts   3 I'll help
4 I'm going   5 is going to join
6 you're going to fall
Exercise 3
1 b   2 c   3 a   4 b   5 b   6 a
Exercise 4
1 is coming   2 are you going to watch
3 you'll enjoy   4 finishes
5 is going to order   6 I'll bring

5.3 Reading and Vocabulary
Exercise 1
climbing, handball, yoga
Exercise 2
1 James   2 Miles   3 Li   4 James   5 Li
6 Miles   7 Li
Exercise 3
1 up   2 programme   3 coach   4 balance
5 skills   6 strength
Exercise 4
1 work   2 warm   3 stretch   4 practise
5 exercises   6 programme

5.4 Grammar
Exercise 1
1 You'll enjoy … you try
2 have … you'll be
3 won't go … is   4 You'll get … you join
5 won't improve … you practise

Exercise 2
1 unless   2 if   3 unless   4 unless   5 if

Exercise 3
1 will lend   2 ask   3 will hurt   4 fall
5 won't get   6 are   7 is   8 will/'ll wait
9 won't go   10 feel

Exercise 4
1 will go   2 unless it   3 if the weather
4 you don't unless our train

Exercise 5
1 b   2 a   3 b   4 c   5 a

5.5 Listening and Vocabulary
Exercise 1
1 winner   2 attack   3 manager
4 present   5 defend

Exercise 2
1 training   2 practises   3 player   4 race
5 supporters   6 coach   7 scored

Exercise 3
1 T   2 F   3 T

Exercise 4
1 b   2 a   3 b   4 c   5 b

Exercise 5
1 giving   2 changes   3 raises   4 point
5 role

5.6 Speaking
Exercise 2
1 c   2 e   3 f   4 b   5 a   6 d

Exercise 3
1 First   2 After   3 about
4 know   5 What   6 Then

Exercise 4
1 b   2 a   3 c   4 b

Exercise 5
1 any   2 First   3 after   4 about
5 doing   6 Then   7 could   8 great

5.7 Writing
Exercise 1
1 B   2 C   3 A

Exercise 2
1 Claudia   2 Pierre   3 Holly
4 Ahmed and Pierre

Exercise 3
1 a quick note   2 on doing   3 later
4 Would it be   5 you mind buying
6 me know if

Exercise 4
1 for   2 before   3 after   4 to   5 on

UNIT 5 Self-check
Exercise 1
1 b   2 a   3 c   4 a   5 a   6 b   7 c   8 c

Exercise 2
1 warm down   2 coach   3 exercise
4 stretch   5 balance   6 programme

Exercise 3
1 supporters   2 defender   3 practice
4 score   5 player   6 manager

Exercise 4
1 opens   2 'll win   3 's going to score
4 'm going to take up   5 'm meeting
6 'll pay   7 're training

Exercise 5
1 'll get … do
2 don't practise … won't get
3 won't win … run
4 rains … 'll play
5 won't hurt … wear
6 'll arrive … is
7 won't be … go
8 buy … 'll swim

Exercise 6
1 up to … What about … don't know
2 got any plans … First

Unit 6

6.1 Vocabulary
Exercise 1
1 sightseeing holiday   2 city break
3 ocean cruise   4 beach holiday
5 camping trip   6 backpacking holiday
7 activity camp

Exercise 2
1 c   2 a   3 f   4 b   5 d   6 e   7 h   8 g

Exercise 3
1 break   2 flat   3 off   4 abroad
5 train   6 around

Exercise 4
1 swimsuit   2 rucksack/backpack   3 tent
4 suitcase   5 guidebook   6 torch

Exercise 5
1 guidebook   2 map   3 sun cream
4 sleeping bag   5 sunglasses   6 passport

Exercise 6
1 reception   2 reservation
3 single   4 floor   5 view   6 pool
7 guests   8 facilities   9 check out

Exercise 7
1 cruise   2 by   3 facilities   4 on   5 break
6 room   7 out   8 pool   9 views   10 go

6.2 Grammar
Exercise 1
1 You must wear a life jacket.
2 We don't have to pay for parking.
3 You ought to use sun cream.
4 Does your dad have to work all summer?
5 Should we buy a guidebook?
6 You shouldn't lie in the sun for too long.
7 Do I have to bring mosquito spray?
8 You mustn't forget to take your passport.

Exercise 2
1 c   2 d   3 e   4 b   5 a

Exercise 3
1 mustn't worry   2 don't have to pay
3 must go   4 should drink
5 shouldn't spend   6 will have to ask

Exercise 4
1 should look online   2 don't have to buy
3 mustn't play   4 will have to get
5 ought to wear

Exercise 5
1 must   2 should   3 don't   4 ought/have
5 mustn't   6 must

6.3 Reading and Vocabulary
Exercise 1
1 bus stop   2 traffic jam   3 route
4 single … return   5 travel card
6 pedestrians

Exercise 2
1, 2, 3, 4, 6, 10

Exercise 3
1 At tram and bus stops.
2 The price./It's very expensive.
3 They can cycle/ride a bike.

6.4 Grammar
Exercise 1
1 can't   2 must   3 must   4 can't
5 must   6 can't

Exercise 2
1 a   2 b   3 b   4 a   5 a   6 a

Exercise 3
1 b   2 c   3 a   4 b   5 b   6 a

Exercise 4
1 might be   2 can't be   3 must be
4 may be   5 might be   6 could be

6.5 Listening and Vocabulary
Exercise 1
1 c   2 a   3 b   4 b   5 c   6 a

Exercise 2
c

Exercise 3
1 F   2 T   3 F   4 T   5 F   6 T

Exercise 4
1 winter   2 France   3 sport   4 stop
5 best   6 Two years   7 right leg

Exercise 5
1 c   2 e   3 a   4 f   5 b   6 d

Exercise 6
1 organic farm   2 pocket money
3 working holiday
4 reception desk   5 weekend trip
6 ski season

6.6 Speaking
Exercise 2
1 d   2 e   3 a   4 c   5 f   6 b

Exercise 3
1 c a b   2 b c a   3 c b a

Exercise 4
1 b   2 d   3 a   4 c

Exercise 5
1 catch … Could … wanted
2 What … said
3 say … What

6.7 Writing
Exercise 1
1 10 a.m.   2 at a (great) hotel in Warsaw
3 by train

Exercise 2
a 5   b 2   c 1   d 4   e 3

Exercise 3
1 let   2 will/could   3 overnight   4 know
5 could/will   6 later   7 now

Exercise 4
1 d   2 a   3 e   4 b   5 c

Exercise 5
1 when   2 as soon as   3 When   4 before
5 until   6 after   7 when

UNIT 6 Self-check
Exercise 1
1 reservation   2 view   3 campsite
4 cruise   5 double   6 camp   7 sunglasses
8 torch   9 rent   10 facilities

267

Exercise 2
1 travel card 2 return ticket
3 traffic jams 4 single ticket 5 route
Exercise 3
1 trip 2 voyage 3 journeys 4 travel
5 excursion
Exercise 4
1 e 2 g 3 b 4 c 5 d 6 f 7 a
Exercise 5
1 S 2 S 3 D 4 D 5 S 6 S 7 D 8 D
Exercise 6
1 didn't catch … What I asked
2 first part … I said that
3 say that again

Reading Time 2

Exercise 1
A 3 B 4 C 2 D 1
Exercise 2
Students' own answers
Exercise 3
1 sad 2 foot 3 newspapers 4 father
5 spy 6 prison 7 friend 8 train
Exercise 4
1 c 2 b 3 a
Exercise 5
Students' own answers
Exercise 6
Students read the summary to check their ideas.
Exercise 7
The Railway Children; adventure story; Roberta, Peter, Mother, Father, the old man; a letter/a newspaper article

Unit 7

7.1 Vocabulary
Exercise 1
1 b 2 f 3 c 4 e 5 a 6 d
Exercise 2
1 stepbrother 2 great-grandparents
3 half-sister 4 stepmother
5 stepdaughters
Exercise 3
1 get 2 deal 3 hanging 4 with 5 got
6 up 7 away
Exercise 4
1 get along with 2 deal with 3 went out
4 moved away 5 get together
6 hang out with 7 grow up 8 get on
Exercise 5
1 a 2 c 3 a
Exercise 6
1 get 2 time 3 share 4 argument
5 see 6 sense 7 have
Exercise 7
1 get 2 stepmother 3 stepsisters
4 spend 5 share 6 deal 7 get 8 out
9 grow 10 share/have 11 get 12 with

7.2 Grammar
Exercise 1
1 d 2 a 3 e 4 f 5 b 6 c
Exercise 2
1 would be … got
2 would … was
3 had … would take
4 were … wouldn't worry

Exercise 3
1 wouldn't be … didn't have
2 wouldn't get … got
3 would watch … was/were
4 would invite … had
Exercise 4
1 were 2 wouldn't worry 3 would be
4 didn't remember 5 knew
Exercise 5
1 would 2 If 3 wouldn't 4 didn't
5 would 6 were 7 be 8 was/were
9 wouldn't

7.3 Reading and Vocabulary
Exercise 1
1 mates 2 classmates 3 best friends
4 stranger 5 teammates
Exercise 2
1 make 2 have 3 is/'s 4 keep
Exercise 3
1 d 2 c 3 b 4 e 5 a
Exercise 4
1 friends 2 hang out 3 on your side/friendly
4 something in common 5 something new
6 older than 7 answer some questions

7.4 Grammar
Exercise 1
1 e 2 d 3 b 4 a 5 c
Exercise 2
1 who is three years older than me, is
2 , which is the capital of Scotland, is
3 the house where she lived
4 who grows vegetables
5 , where my grandparents live, is
Exercise 3
1 b 2 a 3 c 4 b 5 a 6 a 7 c 8 b
Exercise 4
1 That's the café where we sometimes have lunch.
2 The prize that we won wasn't very exciting.
3 Sophie, who is French, can speak French and English.
4 Their car, which is over twenty years old, still works well.
5 I lent the book to Dan, who loves adventure stories.

7.5 Listening and Vocabulary
Exercise 1
1 arrive 2 become 3 received 4 buy
5 find 6 bring
Exercise 2
1 c 2 b 3 a 4 a
Exercise 3
1 b 2 c 3 b 4 c
Exercise 4
1 got back 2 gets quite stressed
3 get into 4 get a lot out of

7.6 Speaking
Exercise 2
1 f 2 a 3 e 4 b 5 c 6 d
Exercise 3
1 talking 2 back 3 wearing 4 near
5 standing 6 playing 7 one 8 tall
Exercise 4
1 c, a, b, c 2 b, c, a, d 3 a, d, c, b
Exercise 5
1 with 2 Who's 3 Which
4 background 5 wearing 6 standing

7.7 Writing
Exercise 1
1 b 2 a 3 b 4 a 5 b
Exercise 2
1 b 2 a 3 c 4 e 5 d
Exercise 3
1 First 2 Afterwards 3 Just 4 After
Exercise 4
1 C 2 E 3 S 4 E 5 S 6 C

UNIT 7 Self-check
Exercise 1
1 go 2 get 3 half-sister 4 same
5 have 6 common 7 gets 8 spending
9 stepmother
Exercise 2
1 strangers 2 best friend 3 mate
4 teammates 5 classmates
Exercise 3
1 a 2 f 3 e 4 b 5 c 6 d
Exercise 4
1 spent … would/'d get
2 would/'d go … was/were
3 had … would/'d travel
4 would/'d talk … was/were
5 would/'d do … lived
6 enjoyed … would/'d study
7 would/'d learn … had
8 knew … would/'d help
Exercise 5
1 who 2 where 3 who 4 that
5 which 6 who 7 where
Exercise 6
1 that boy 2 one do 3 one with
4 Which one 5 the back

Unit 8

8.1 Vocabulary
Exercise 1
1 thief 2 vandals 3 pickpocket
4 shoplifter 5 burglar 6 robbers
Exercise 2
1 steal 2 break 3 solve 4 commit
5 rob 6 damage 7 break
Exercise 3
1 b 2 c 3 a 4 c 5 b 6 b
Exercise 4
1 burglars 2 vandalism 3 robbers
4 shoplifting 5 pickpocket 6 theft
Exercise 5
1 d 2 a 3 g 4 f 5 b 6 e 7 c 8 h
Exercise 6
1 fingerprint 2 security 3 suspect
4 case 5 detective 6 witness
Exercise 7
1 prison 2 court 3 punishment 4 judge
5 fine 6 reward
Exercise 8
1 b 2 c 3 a 4 a 5 c 6 b 7 c 8 a
9 c 10 c 11 a 12 b

8.2 Grammar
Exercise 1
1 asked (R) 2 built (I) 3 caught (I)
4 chased (R) 5 hid (I) 6 made (I)
7 saw (I) 8 used (R) 9 watched (R)
10 written (I)
Exercise 2
1 were 2 Is 3 Was 4 are 5 aren't

Exercise 3
1 My purse was stolen by a pickpocket.
2 A lot of mobile phones are stolen every year./Every year, a lot of mobile phones are stolen.
3 She was asked questions by the police.
4 Some crimes aren't reported to the police.
5 When was your car stolen?

Exercise 4
1 were hidden in   2 was caught by
3 are watched by   4 the thief sent
5 is stolen from   6 wasn't found

Exercise 5
1 was created   2 were published
3 is helped   4 is known   5 are solved
6 was made   7 are watched

8.3 Reading and Vocabulary
Exercise 1
1 illogical   2 illegal   3 unusual
4 irresponsible   5 unimportant
6 impatient   7 uninteresting

Exercise 2
1 d   2 d   3 a   4 c

8.4 Grammar
Exercise 1
1 I had my bedroom painted last summer.
2 The suspect had her photo taken.
3 You can have the sofa delivered.
4 Where do you get the car cleaned?
5 He had his wallet stolen last week.

Exercise 2
1 get … cleaned   2 having … tested
3 having … taken   4 had … stolen
5 get … repaired   6 gets … cut

Exercise 3
1 get a pizza delivered
2 have my hair cut
3 had her make-up done
4 get that injury checked

Exercise 4
1 having … made   2 getting … put up
3 have … replaced   4 get … installed
5 have … connected   6 get … checked

8.5 Listening and Vocabulary
Exercise 1
1 area   2 clues   3 witnesses
4 fingerprints   5 criminal

Exercise 2
a 2   b 4   c 6   d 5   e 1   f 7   g 3

Exercise 3
1 post office
2 15/fifteen/15th/fifteenth (of) June
3 30,000/thirty thousand
4 3/three
5 dark green
6 0141 557 6231

Exercise 4
1 A   2 B   3 C   4 A   5 C

8.6 Speaking
Exercise 2
1 Come   2 know   3 course   4 mean
5 talk   6 happened

Exercise 3
1 e   2 b   3 a   4 d   5 f   6 c

Exercise 4
1 b   2 a   3 b   4 c   5 b

Exercise 5
1 wrong   2 tell   3 think   4 Personally
5 Really   6 opinion   7 mean   8 Definitely

8.7 Writing
Exercise 1
a 2   b 1   c 4   d 3

Exercise 2
1 F   2 T   3 F   4 T

Exercise 3
1 f   2 a   3 c   4 e   5 d   6 b

UNIT 8 Self-check
Exercise 1
1 shoplifter   2 fine   3 prison   4 vandal
5 theft   6 judge   7 clue   8 witness
9 pickpocketing   10 suspect

Exercise 2
1 uncomfortable   2 impossible   3 unkind
4 unfair   5 irresponsible

Exercise 3
1 fingerprints   2 criminals   3 witness
4 clues   5 area

Exercise 4
1 are used   2 was arrested   3 was found
4 are solved   5 wasn't seen   6 aren't sent
7 are given   8 Was (your sister) interviewed

Exercise 5
1 repaired   2 my hair cut
3 a pizza delivered   4 made   5 cleaned
6 stolen   7 taken

Exercise 6
1 wrong   2 fine   3 tell   4 that   5 see

Unit 9

9.1 Vocabulary
Exercise 1
1 Maths   2 Chemistry   3 Cooking
4 History   5 Music
6 IT/Information Technology

Exercise 2
1 Literature   2 Geography   3 Biology
4 Economics   5 Drama   6 Art
7 Languages   8 D&T/Design and Technology   9 PE/Physical Education
10 Physics

Exercise 3
1 talented   2 confident   3 creative
4 problem   5 general   6 intelligent
7 teamwork   8 hard-working   9 critical

Exercise 4
1 learn   2 study   3 memorise   4 revise
5 practical exam   6 curriculum

Exercise 5
1 b   2 c   3 a   4 c   5 a   6 a

Exercise 6
1 b   2 a   3 c   4 c   5 a   6 a   7 c   8 b
9 a   10 c   11 b   12 b

9.2 Grammar
Exercise 1
1 wanted   2 was   3 did   4 weren't
5 wasn't   6 was

Exercise 2
1 said   2 told   3 said   4 told   5 told
6 told   7 said   8 told

Exercise 3
1 liked   2 was starting   3 gave
4 wasn't raining   5 wasn't revising
6 played

Exercise 4
1 told … was   2 said … was
3 told … did   4 said … needed
5 told … was   6 said … was

Exercise 5
1 Tom said (that) he was writing 3,000 words for his essay.
2 Kate said (that) Amy didn't know the answer.
3 The teacher said (that) Magda worked hard in History lessons.
4 The club president told us (that) the debate started at 4.00.
5 Luke said (that) they were making some new posters.
6 Hannah said (that) Paul wasn't speaking very clearly.

9.3 Reading and Vocabulary
Exercise 1
1 make   2 make   3 make/take   4 make
5 take   6 take

Exercise 2
a 2   b 4   c 1   d 3

Exercise 3
1 b   2 f   3 a   4 e   5 d

9.4 Grammar
Exercise 1
1 Why   2 When   3 Who   4 Where

Exercise 2
1 Are you OK?
2 Where do you live?
3 Did you enjoy the book?
4 Have you met Sam's brother?

Exercise 3
1 told you about the party
2 did Sam give you
3 did Anna phone last night
4 did Tom help you with

Exercise 4
1 Is it raining
2 does Rosie go to school
3 did the film finish
4 teaches them French
5 did she phone

Exercise 5
1 What are you doing
2 Is it OK
3 Who took these photos
4 What subjects did you study
5 Did you enjoy school
6 What were your teachers like
7 Who's that
8 Have you stayed friends

9.5 Listening and Vocabulary
Exercise 1
1 miss out   2 hand in   3 look over
4 Calm down   5 look up   6 get on
7 fill in   8 hand out

Exercise 2
1 b   2 a   3 c   4 a

Exercise 3
1 C   2 A   3 B   4 B   5 A

9.6 Speaking
Exercise 2
1 Where   2 are   3 long   4 do   5 Have
6 Would

269

Exercise 3
1 c 2 a 3 c 4 b 5 b
Exercise 4
1 e 2 c 3 f 4 d 5 a 6 b
Exercise 5
1 been 2 think 3 for 4 from 5 doing
6 like

9.7 Writing
Exercise 1
1 T 2 F 3 F 4 F 5 T
Exercise 2
1 writing 2 mind 3 tell 4 aim
5 forward
Exercise 3
1 d 2 a 3 f 4 c 5 b 6 e

UNIT 9 Self-check
Exercise 1
1 critical 2 revise 3 confident 4 IT
5 general 6 teamwork 7 memorise
8 talented 9 speaking 10 presentation
Exercise 2
1 makes 2 make 3 made 4 take
5 take
Exercise 3
1 in 2 down 3 in 4 up 5 out
Exercise 4
1 was 2 said 3 gives 4 us 5 was
6 was writing 7 started
Exercise 5
1 Did you watch
2 Does he go
3 Have you finished
4 Why was Carrie
5 Who called
6 Who did you see
7 Who does
8 Why are you standing
Exercise 6
1 Where are 2 How long
3 Have you been 4 What are
5 Would you

Reading Time 3
Exercise 1
A 2 B 4 C 1 D 3
Exercise 2
Students' own answers
Exercise 3
1 F 2 T 3 F 4 T 5 F
Exercise 4
a 3 b 4 c 2 d 1 e 5
Exercise 5
1 b 2 c 3 a 4 b 5 c
Exercise 6
1 complete 2 terrible 3 empty 4 sure
5 strange
Exercise 7
1 (her) dad/Dad was very excited that morning
2 the men from the government were coming soon
3 he couldn't remember things like that
Exercise 8
The Professor; crime story; the professor, Miss Green, Inspector Hadley; the (professor's) papers

Exam Time 1 Units 1–3
Exercise 1
1 C 2 B 3 A 4 C 5 B 6 B
Exercise 2
1 next Thursday 2 Robot Life 3 Maria
4 8.30 5 5.30 6 sandwiches and drinks
Exercise 3
1 h 2 a 3 c 4 e 5 g
Exercise 4
The weather forecast today is mixed around the country. In the north, it will be cold with heavy snow. In the south, however, it will be cloudy with some sunshine!
Exercise 5
1 C 2 B 3 A 4 C 5 A 6 C
Exercise 6
1 b 2 b 3 a 4 c 5 a 6 c 7 b
Exercise 7
1 food festival 2 a year 3 live music
4 cherries and nuts 5 Polish community
6 1980
Exercise 8
Students' own answers
Sample answer:
My favourite traditional dish from my country is called Feijoada. It's a dish made from black beans, with different types of meat in it. In my family, we make it with beef. The ingredients vary in different parts of Brazil, but it always has black beans. We eat it with rice and salad.
We usually eat Feijoada on Sundays, for lunch. We eat it slowly and usually watch the football on TV at the same time. I really like it because it's much more than just lunch. It's a time for family to come together and have fun.

Exam Time 2 Units 1–6
Exercise 1
1 c 2 c 3 a 4 c 5 c
Exercise 2
1 b 2 c 3 b 4 c 5 b 6 a
Exercise 3
1 9 and 10/9th and 10th/ninth and tenth (of)
2 (at the) south 3 Free Voice
4 street dance 5 Young Dancers
6 festivals.com
Exercise 4
When you take up a new sport, it's important to check you're healthy enough to do so. If you try to do too much too soon, you can hurt yourself. So unless you want an injury, take it slowly at first.
Exercise 5
1 C 2 J 3 H 4 J 5 C 6 H 7 J
Exercise 6
1 d 2 d 3 b 4 c 5 a
Exercise 7
1 Hounslow
2 £20/20 pounds/twenty pounds
3 yoga
4 once/one
5 (a/the/their) summer party
Exercise 8
Students' own answers

Sample answer:
Hi Fiona,
I'm really excited about your visit too! I can't wait to see you again!
I've got lots of plans. We aren't going to visit anywhere outside the city because I don't think we'll have time. Anyway, there are lots of things to do here. You're right, the shops here are great. My favourite one is a big department store in the centre. We can spend at least a day there!
Can you bring some comics from the US? I love comics, and they'll also help me practise my English, so I'd love to read some.
See you soon,

Exam Time 3 Units 1–9
Exercise 1
1 d 2 e 3 g 4 c 5 f
Exercise 2
1 a 2 b 3 b 4 c 5 a 6 c
Exercise 3
1 1890 2 66/sixty-six 3 *The Mousetrap*
4 hospital 5 Arab World 6 a billion
Exercise 4
Three bank robbers were given long prison sentences today. The robbers were caught when their fingerprints were found at the scene. When reading out the sentence, the judge said this was a terrible crime.
Exercise 5
1 c 2 d 3 f 4 a 5 h
Exercise 6
1 nothing 2 (They were) useful.
3 intermediate and elementary
4 student ID and a telephone number
5 two months
Exercise 7
1 over 160 million
2 (up to) seventy percent/70%
3 go to school
4 (around) thirty/30
5 watch videos
Exercise 8
1 formal justice system 2 a meeting
3 share their experiences
4 make things better 5 pay money
6 improve 7 the same time
Exercise 9
1 an opinion essay
2 the advantages of exams, the disadvantages of exams, your opinion
Sample answer:
Personally, I believe that exams are a good way to assess students. They are an easy way to test if a student has learned a subject. For example, if they need to know how to calculate something in Maths, they can show this during an exam.
On the one hand, people often say that exams are too stressful and that it is better to test students during the school year, through projects and quizzes.
However, while exams are stressful, this can help students take them seriously. And when they pass exams, it will improve their confidence.
In conclusion, I agree with the use of exams to assess what students have learned.

Pearson Education Limited
KAO Two
KAO Park
Hockham Way
Harlow, Essex
CM17 9SR
England
and Associated Companies throughout the world.

pearsonenglish.com/widerworld2e

© Pearson Education Limited 2022

All rights reserved; no part of this publication may be reproduced, stored in a retrieval system, or transmitted in any form or by any means, electronic, mechanical, photocopying, recording, or otherwise without the prior written permission of the Publishers

Photocopying
The Publisher grants permission for the photocopying of those pages marked 'photocopiable' according to the following conditions. Individual purchasers may make copies for their own use or for use by the classes they teach. Institutional purchasers may make copies for use by their staff and students, but this permission does not extend to additional institutions or branches. Under no circumstances may any part of this book be photocopied for resale.

First published 2022

ISBN: 978-1-292-34226-9

Set in Frutiger Next Pro
Printed by CPI, UK

Acknowledgements
The Publishers would like to thank all the teachers and students around the world who contributed to the development of Wider World Second Edition: Milena Aleksić, Tuğba Arslantaş, Gülşah Aslan, Mahgol Baboorian, Katarzyna Beliniak, Burcu Candan, Seri Diri, Hanna Dudich, Sema Karapinar, Nadiia Kasianchuk, Duygu Kayhan, Iryna Kharchenko, Ana Krstić, Ilknur Manav, Fulya Mertoğlu, Ivana Nikolov, Banu Oflas, Duygu Özer, Jagoda Popović, Marija Šanjević, Karmen Irizar Segurola, Elif Sevinç, Ludmila Shengel, Ayşe Sönmez, Anna Standish, Natalia Tkachenko, Pamela Van Bers, Jelena Vračar, Agnieszka Woźnicka, Münevver Yanık.

The Publishers would like to thank the following people who commented on the Wider World Second Edition content: Milena Aleksi, Mahgol Baboorian, Hanna Dudich, Izabela Kołando, Karmen Irizar Segurola, Joanna Srokosz, Anna Zając.

We would also like to thank the authors of the first edition of Wider World whose work has been the basis for creating this adaptation: Kathryn Alevizos, Carolyn Barraclough, Catherine Bright, Sheila Dignen, Lynda Edwards, Rod Fricker, Suzanne Gaynor, Bob Hastings, Jennifer Heath, Liz Kilbey, Stuart McKinlay, Sarah Thorpe, Tasia Vassilatou, Damian Williams, Sandy Zervas.

Photo Acknowledgements
BBC Studios: 6; **Pearson Education Ltd:** Dardanele Studio 6, Jon Barlow 6; **Shutterstock.com:** Pavlo S 3, 4

Student's Book pages:
123RF.com: 41, Adam Borkowski 43, Andrey Safonov 34, Andrii Starunskyi 103, Andriy Popov 12, anyaberkut 100, auremar 78, bowie15 22, bracknell 55, Brent Hofacker 39, Cathy Yeulet 113, czarnybez 36, Dan Grytsku 19, denisfilm 74, dolgachov 143, elenathewise 45, Elizaveta Galitckaia 141, fazon 25, Fokke Baarssen 77, goodluz 137, Ian Allenden 122, 122, ibrester 138, Igor Salnikov 27, Ijupco 71, Iriana Shiyan 7, ismagilov 115, Jozef Polc 98, Katarzyna Białasiewicz 100, M Production 34, Matthew Benoit 41, natthanim 36, nitr 43, Olga Yastremska 36, 36, pixelrobot 100, Pop Nukoonrat 39, serezniy 12, Sergey Novikov 65, subbotina 39, Tatiana Epifanova 34, tatiana Gladskikh 41, Viacheslav Iakobchuk 91, vimart 12, yatomo 39, Yuliya Belenkova 25; **Alamy Stock Photo:** Douglas Lander 1, Matthias Scholz 24, Pacific Press Media Production Corp 51, Steve Speller 50, Universal Images Group North America LLC/DeAgostini 140; **BBC Studios:** 23, 47, 73, 99, 123; **Getty Images:** Â©Hello Lovely/Corbis 60, Barcroft Media 24, bortonia/DigitalVision Vectors 37, Cameron Soencer/Getty Images AsiaPac 72, CasarsaGuru 65, Caspar Benson 34, Corbis/VCG/Corbis 65, fotografixx/E+ 66, Gary S Chapman/Photographer's Choice RF 93, Guerilla 110, Image Source/DigitalVision 62, JohnnyGreig/E+ 74, kali9/E+ 74, Karl Tapales/Moment 43, Michael Putland/Hulton Archive 139, Michael Regan/Getty Images Europe 67, ShutterWorx/E+ 119, Thomas Barwick/Stone 15, Tim Robberts/Stone 53, Westend61 74, 105; **Jubilee Sailing Trust:** 79; **Pearson Education Ltd:** 28, 30, Ian Wedgewood 113, Jon Barlow 6, 8, 9, 10, 11, 16, 18, 38, 42, 54, 56, 64, 68, 76, 80, 90, 94, 104, 106, 116, 118, Studio 8 114; **Sean Ebsworth Barnes:** 57; **Shutterstock.com:** 52, 78, 78, 89, 110, 114, adriaticfoto 138, Aleksandra Duda 100, AlohaHawaii 93, Anton Chernov 43, Arcady 140, Artur Bogacki 25, Billion Photos 92, Bruce Rolff 141, Castleski 139, christianpinillo 26, Cookie Studio 74, daseaford 29, David Prado Perucha 137, Djent 13, Dusan Zidar 36, Erika J Mitchell 60, Fotos593 31, gladcov 13, 13, 13, 13, 13, Gorodenkoff 60, Graphic design 55, Hendrika Koerts 55, I Wei Huang 46, ictor Moussa 102, Image Source Trading Ltd 40, Izf 14, javarman 36, joyfull 98, Kuzma 107, Lukas Gojda 62, makuromi 138, mauricioalvesfotos 55, molekuul_be 138, Moneca 114, NASA 139, North Devon Photography 112, pajtica 63, Paul Prescott 125, Pavlo S 2, 3, Photo Spirit 78, Photo Volcano 33, Picsfive 39, pornpan chaiu-dom 81, Sergey Zaykov 29, Sopotnicki 25, SpeedKingz 100, Stephen Coburn 103, stockphoto-graf 62, theerasakj 78, Timolina 36, Tom Wang 74, UfaBizPhoto 60, vitstudio 141, wavebreakmedia 113, 143, WAYHOME studio 114, Wildlife World 48

Student's Book Illustrations
Gergley Fórizs (Beehive) 77, 88; Maguma AKA Marcos Guardiola Martin (IllustrationX) 35, 61, 85, 111; Dina Ruzha 84; Rupert Van Wyk (Beehive) 17.

All other images © Pearson Education

Cover photo © *Front:* Alamy Stock Photo: Sara Winter

Pearson Education Limited
KAO Two
KAO Park
Hockham Way
Harlow, Essex
CM17 9SR
England
and Associated Companies throughout the world.

pearsonenglish.com/widerworld2e

© Pearson Education Limited 2022

All rights reserved; no part of this publication may be reproduced, stored in a retrieval system, or transmitted in any form or by any means, electronic, mechanical, photocopying, recording, or otherwise without the prior written permission of the Publishers

Photocopying
The Publisher grants permission for the photocopying of those pages marked 'photocopiable' according to the following conditions. Individual purchasers may make copies for their own use or for use by the classes they teach. Institutional purchasers may make copies for use by their staff and students, but this permission does not extend to additional institutions or branches. Under no circumstances may any part of this book be photocopied for resale.

First published 2022
Second impression 2022

ISBN: 978-1-292-34226-9

Set in Frutiger Next Pro
Printed and bound by CPI Group (UK) Ltd, Croydon, CR0 4YY

Acknowledgements
The Publishers would like to thank all the teachers and students around the world who contributed to the development of Wider World Second Edition: Milena Aleksić, Tuğba Arslantaş, Gülşah Aslan, Mahgol Baboorian, Katarzyna Beliniak, Burcu Candan, Seri Diri, Hanna Dudich, Sema Karapinar, Nadiia Kasianchuk, Duygu Kayhan, Iryna Kharchenko, Ana Krstić, Ilknur Manav, Fulya Mertoğlu, Ivana Nikolov, Banu Oflas, Duygu Özer, Jagoda Popović, Marija Šanjević, Karmen Irizar Segurola, Elif Sevinç, Ludmila Shengel, Ayşe Sönmez, Anna Standish, Natalia Tkachenko, Pamela Van Bers, Jelena Vračar, Agnieszka Woźnicka, Münevver Yanık.

The Publishers would like to thank the following people who commented on the Wider World Second Edition content: Milena Aleksi, Mahgol Baboorian, Hanna Dudich, Izabela Kołando, Karmen Irizar Segurola, Joanna Srokosz, Anna Zając.

We would also like to thank the authors of the first edition of Wider World whose work has been the basis for creating this adaptation: Kathryn Alevizos, Carolyn Barraclough, Catherine Bright, Sheila Dignen, Lynda Edwards, Rod Fricker, Suzanne Gaynor, Bob Hastings, Jennifer Heath, Liz Kilbey, Stuart McKinlay, Sarah Thorpe, Tasia Vassilatou, Damian Williams, Sandy Zervas.

Photo Acknowledgements
BBC Studios: 6; **Pearson Education Ltd:** Dardanele Studio 6, Jon Barlow 6; **Shutterstock.com:** Pavlo S 3, 4

Student's Book pages:
123RF.com: 41, Adam Borkowski 43, Andrey Safonov 34, Andrii Starunskyi 103, Andriy Popov 12, anyaberkut 100, auremar 78, bowie15 22, bracknell 55, Brent Hofacker 39, Cathy Yeulet 113, czarnybez 36, Dan Grytsku 19, denisfilm 74, dolgachov 143, elenathewise 45, Elizaveta Galitckaia 141, fazon 25, Fokke Baarssen 77, goodluz 137, Ian Allenden 122, 122, ibrester 138, Igor Salnikov 27, Ijupco 71, Iriana Shiyan 7, ismagilov 115, Jozef Polc 98, Katarzyna Białasiewicz 100, M Production 34, Matthew Benoit 41, natthanim 36, nitr 43, Olga Yastremska 36, 36, pixelrobot 100, Pop Nukoonrat 39, serezniy 12, Sergey Novikov 65, subbotina 39, Tatiana Epifanova 34, tatiana Gladskikh 41, Viacheslav Iakobchuk 91, vimart 12, yatomo 39, Yuliya Belenkova 25; **Alamy Stock Photo:** Douglas Lander 1, Matthias Scholz 24, Pacific Press Media Production Corp 51, Steve Speller 50, Universal Images Group North America LLC/DeAgostini 140; **BBC Studios:** 23, 47, 73, 99, 123; **Getty Images:** ©Hello Lovely/Corbis 60, Barcroft Media 24, bortonia/DigitalVision Vectors 37, Cameron Soencer/Getty Images AsiaPac 72, CasarsaGuru 65, Caspar Benson 34, Corbis/VCG/Corbis 65, fotografixx/E+ 66, Gary S Chapman/Photographer's Choice RF 93, Guerilla 110, Image Source/DigitalVision 62, JohnnyGreig/E+ 74, kali9/E+ 74, Karl Tapales/Moment 43, Michael Putland/Hulton Archive 139, Michael Regan/Getty Images Europe 67, ShutterWorx/E+ 119, Thomas Barwick/Stone 15, Tim Robberts/Stone 53, Westend61 74, 105; **Jubilee Sailing Trust:** 79; **Pearson Education Ltd:** 28, 30, Ian Wedgewood 113, Jon Barlow 6, 8, 9, 10, 11, 16, 18, 38, 42, 54, 56, 64, 68, 76, 80, 90, 94, 104, 106, 116, 118, Studio 8 114; **Sean Ebsworth Barnes:** 57; **Shutterstock.com:** 52, 78, 78, 89, 110, 114, adriaticfoto 138, Aleksandra Duda 100, AlohaHawaii 93, Anton Chernov 43, Arcady 140, Artur Bogacki 25, Billion Photos 92, Bruce Rolff 141, Castleski 139, christianpinillo 26, Cookie Studio 74, daseaford 29, David Prado Perucha 137, Djent 13, Dusan Zidar 36, Erika J Mitchell 60, Fotos593 31, gladcov 13, 13, 13, 13, 13, Gorodenkoff 60, Graphic design 55, Hendrika Koerts 55, I Wei Huang 46, ictor Moussa 102, Image Source Trading Ltd 40, Izf 14, javarman 36, joyfull 98, Kuzma 107, Lukas Gojda 62, makuromi 138, mauricioalvesfotos 55, molekuul_be 138, Moneca 114, NASA 139, North Devon Photography 112, pajtica 63, Paul Prescott 125, Pavlo S 2, 3, Photo Spirit 78, Photo Volcano 33, Picsfive 39, pornpan chaiu-dom 81, Sergey Zaykov 29, Sopotnicki 25, SpeedKingz 100, Stephen Coburn 103, stockphoto-graf 62, theerasakj 78, Timolina 36, Tom Wang 74, UfaBizPhoto 60, vitstudio 141, wavebreakmedia 113, 143, WAYHOME studio 114, Wildlife World 48

Student's Book Illustrations
Gergley Fórizs (Beehive) 77, 88; Maguma AKA Marcos Guardiola Martin (IllustrationX) 35, 61, 85, 111; Dina Ruzha 84; Rupert Van Wyk (Beehive) 17.

All other images © Pearson Education

Cover photo © *Front*: Alamy Stock Photo: Sara Winter